GERMAN RENAISSANCE
ARCHITECTURE

GERMAN RENAISSANCE ARCHITECTURE

Henry-Russell Hitchcock

PRINCETON UNIVERSITY PRESS

PRINCETON, NEW JERSEY

Publication of this book has been aided by a grant from
the Graham Foundation for Advanced Studies
in the Fine Arts

This book has been composed in Linotype Granjon
Clothbound editions of Princeton University Press books
are printed on acid-free paper, and binding materials are
chosen for strength and durability

Printed in the United States of America
by Princeton University Press, Princeton, New Jersey
Plates printed by Meriden Gravure Company,
Meriden, Connecticut

Designed by Zoran Cvetichanin

Library of Congress Cataloging in Publication Data

Hitchcock, Henry-Russell, 1903-
German Renaissance architecture.

Bibliography: p.
Includes index.
1. Architecture, Renaissance—Germany. 2. Architecture—Germany. I. Title.
NA1065.H57   720′.943   80-16399
ISBN   0-691-03959-3

Contents

xiv

Aretin, *Landshut*	K. O. von Aretin, *Landshut* [Landshut, n.d.]
Baedekers *Benelux*	Baedekers Autoreiseführer, *Benelux*, 4th ed., Stuttgart [1967/1968]
Baldass, *Österreich*	P. von Baldass, R. Feuchtmüller, W. Mrazek, *Renaissance in Österreich* [Wien-Hannover, 1966]
Bechstein, *Kilianskirche*	H. D. Bechstein, *Die Kilianskirche zu Heilbronn*, Heilbronn, 1965
Becker, *Schloss Neuhaus*	W. Becker, *Schloss Neuhaus, das ehemaliger Wohngebäude der Paderborner Bischöfe*, Paderborn [1970]
Bernt, *Bürgerbauten*	A. Bernt, *Deutschlands Bürgerbauten*, Tübingen [1968]
Bezold, *Baukunst der Renaissance*	G. von Bezold, *Die Baukunst der Renaissance in Deutschland, Holland, Belgien und Dänemark*, 2nd ed., Leipzig, 1908
Białostocki, *Eastern Europe*	J. Białostocki, *The Art of the Renaissance in Eastern Europe* [London, 1976]
Białostocki, *Spätmittelalter*	J. Białostocki, *Spätmittelalter und beginnende Neuzeit* (Propyläen Kunstgeschichte, Bd. 7), Berlin, 1972
Blunt, *France*	A. Blunt, *Art and Architecture in France 1500 to 1700*, 2nd ed. [Harmondsworth, 1970]
Braun, *Jesuiten*	J. Braun, *Die Kirchenbau der deutschen Jesuiten*, 2 vols., Freiburg-i.-B., 1908-1910
Breuer, *Augsburg*	T. Breuer, *Die Stadt Augsburg* (Bayrische Kunstdenkmale I) Munich [1958]
Büchner-Suchland, *Hieber*	I. Büchner-Suchland, *Hans Hieber* [Munich, 1962]
Christoffel, *Augsburger Rathaus*	O. Christoffel, *Augsburger Rathaus*, Augsburg [1929]
Correll, *Fachwerkbauten*	F. Correll, *Deutsche Fachwerkbauten der Renaissance*, Berlin-New York [n.d.]
DKD, *Baden Württemberg*	Deutsche Kunstdenkmäler, *Baden Württemberg*, 2nd ed. [Munich, 1970]
DKD, *Bayern*	Deutsche Kunstdenkmäler, *Bayern nordlich der Donau* [Munich, 1960]
DKD, *Bremen Niedersachsen*	Deutsche Kunstdenkmäler, *Bremen Niedersachsen* [Munich, 1963]
DKD, *Hessen*	Deutsche Kunstdenkmäler, *Hessen* [Munich, 1964]
DKD, *Mecklenburg*	Deutsche Kunstdenkmäler, *Mecklenburg* [Munich, 1971]

DKD, *Sachsen*	Deutsche Kunstdenkmäler, *Provinz Sachsen Land Anhalt* [Munich, 1968]
DKD, *Thüringen*	Deutsche Kunstdenkmäler, *Thüringen* [Munich, 1968]
Dehio, *Baden Württemberg*	Dehio-Handbuch der Deutschen Kunstdenkmäler, *Baden-Württemberg* [Munich] 1964
Dehio, *Brandenburg*	Dehio-Handbuch der Deutschen Kunstdenkmäler, *Mark Brandenburg und Berlin* [Munich, 1971]
Dehio, *Dresden*	Dehio-Handbuch der Deutschen Kunstdenkmäler, *Die Bezirke Dresden, Karl-Marx-Stadt, Leipzig, Berlin,* 1965
Dehio, *Hamburg*	Dehio-Handbuch der Deutschen Kunstdenkmäler, *Hamburg Schleswig-Holstein* [Munich] 1971
Dehio, *Hessen*	Dehio-Handbuch der Deutschen Kunstdenkmäler, *Hessen* [Munich] 1966
Dehio, *Neubrandenburg*	Dehio-Handbuch der Deutschen Kunstdenkmäler, *Die Bezirke Neubrandenburg, Rostock, Schwerin,* Munich, 1968
Dehio, *Niederösterreich*	Dehio-Handbuch: Die Kunstdenkmäler Österreichs, *Niederösterreich,* 4th ed., Vienna [1962]
Dehio, *Oberbayern*	Dehio-Handbuch der Deutschen Kunstdenkmäler, *Oberbayern,* 3rd ed., Munich, 1960
Dehio, *Oberösterreich*	Dehio-Handbuch: Die Kunstdenkmäler Österreichs, *Oberösterreich,* 4th ed., Vienna [1956]
Dehio, *Östliches Schwaben*	Dehio-Handbuch der Deutschen Kunstdenkmäler, *Östliches Schwaben,* Munich, 1954
Dehio, *Rheinland*	Dehio-Handbuch der Deutschen Kunstdenkmäler, *Rheinland* [Munich] 1967
Dehio, *Steiermark*	Dehio-Handbuch: Die Kunstdenkmäler Österreichs, *Steiermark,* 4th ed., Vienna [1956]
Dehio, *Tirol*	Dehio-Handbuch: Die Kunstdenkmäler Österreichs, *Tirol,* 4th ed., Vienna [1956]
Dehio, *Westfalen*	Dehio-Handbuch der Deutschen Kunstdenkmäler, *Westfalen* [Munich] 1969
Dehio, *Westliches Schwaben*	Dehio-Handbuch der Deutschen Kunstdenkmäler, *Westliches Schwaben,* Munich, 1956
Evans, *Rudolf II*	R.J.W. Evans, *Rudolf II and his World,* Oxford, 1973
Fehr, *Ried*	G. Fehr, *Benedikt Ried, Ein deutscher Baumeister zwischen Gotik und Renaissance in Böhmen,* Munich, 1961
Fleischhauer, *Württemberg*	W. Fleischhauer, *Renaissance im Herzogtum Württemberg,* Stuttgart [? 1971]
Gaul, *Schloss Brake*	O. Gaul, *Schloss Brake und der Baumeister Hermann Wulff,* Lemgo [1967]
Gerson-ter Kuile, *Belgium*	H. Gerson and E. H. ter Kuile, *Art and Architecture in Belgium 1600-1800,* Harmondsworth [1960]
Gerstenberg, *Sondergotik*	K. Gerstenberg, *Deutsche Sondergotik,* Munich, 1913.
Glück, *Renaissance in Deutschland*	G. Glück, *Die Kunst der Renaissance in Deutschland, den Niederlanden, Frankreich etc.,* Berlin [1928]
Goettert, *Kölnische Rathaus*	K. Goettert, *Das kölnische Rathaus,* Mönchen-Gladbach [1959]

Groszmann, *Alsfeld*

Grundmann, *Kirchenbau*

Grundmann-Schadendorf, *Schlesien*

Habich, *Residenz Bückeburg*

Harksen, *Wittenberg*

Harris, *King's Arcadia*

Hartwig, *Cracow*
Hauttmann, *Kirchliche Baukunst*

Hempel, *Geschichte*

Hentschel, *Dresdner Bildhauer*

Hirschfeld, *Schleswig-Holstein*

Hitchcock, *Scrolled Gables*

Horn-Meyer, *Neuburg*

Horst, *Architektur*

JSAH
Jahn, *Deutsche Renaissance*

KDM *Schweiz*

KDÖ, *Kärnten Steiermark*

KDÖ, *Oberösterreich*

KDÖ, *Salzburg*

KDÖ, *Wien*
Karpa, *Wolfenbüttel*
Klapheck, *Schloss Horst*

Knox, *Bohemia*
Knox, *Poland*
Koepf, *Heilbronner*

Kowalczyk, *Kolegiata*
Kratzsch, *Bergstädte*

D. Groszmann, *Alsfeld* [Munich, 1960]

G. Grundmann, *Der evangelische Kirchenbau in Schlesien*, Frankfurt am Main, 1970

G. Grundmann and W. Schadendorf, *Schlesien* [Munich] 1962

J. Habich, *Die künstlerische Gestaltung der Residenz Bückeburg.* . . . Bückeburg, 1969

[S. Harksen] *Die Schlosskirche zu Wittenberg* [Berlin, 1966]

J. Harris, S. Orgel, R. Strong, *The King's Arcadia: Inigo Jones and the Stuart Court* [London] 1973

E. Hartwig, *Cracow*, 2nd ed., Warsaw [n.d.]

M. Hauttmann, *Geschichte der kirchlichen Baukunst in Bayern/Schwaben und Franken 1550-1780*, 2nd ed., Munich, 1923

E. Hempel, *Geschichte der deutschen Baukunst*, 2nd ed., Munich, 1956

W. Hentschel, *Dresdner Bildhauer des 16. und 17. Jahrhunderts*, Weimar, 1966

P. Hirschfeld, *Herrenhäuser und Schlösser in Schleswig-Holstein*, 3rd. revised ed. [Munich] 1964

H. R. Hitchcock, *Netherlandish Scrolled Gables of the 16th and Early 17th Centuries*, New York, 1978

A. Horn and W. Meyer, eds., *Die Kunstdenkmäler von Schwaben, V: Stadt- und Landkreis Neuburg an der Donau*, Munich, 1958

C. Horst, *Die Architektur der deutschen Renaissance*, Berlin [1928]

Journal of the Society of Architectural Historians

J. Jahn, *Deutsche Renaissance: Baukunst, Plastik, Malerei, Graphik, Kunsthandwerk*, Leipzig, 1969

Kunstdenkmäler in der Schweiz, 2 vols. [Munich, 1969, 1970]

Kunstdenkmäler in Österreich, *Kärnten Steiermark* [Munich, 1966]

Kunstdenkmäler in Österreich, *Oberösterreich, Niederösterreich, Burgenland* [Munich, 1967]

Kunstdenkmäler in Österreich, *Salzburg Tirol Voralberg* [Munich, 1965]

Kunstdenkmäler in Österreich, *Wien* [Munich, 1968]

O. Karpa, *Wolfenbüttel*, 2nd ed. [Munich] 1965

R. Klapheck, *Die Meister v. Schloss Horst im Broiche*, Berlin, 1915

B. Knox, *Bohemia and Moravia*, London [1962]

B. Knox, *The Architecture of Poland*, London [1971]

H. Koepf, *Die heilbronner Kilianskirche und ihre Meister*, Heilbronn, 1961

J. Kowalczyk, *Kolegiata w Zamościu*, Warsaw, 1968

K. Kratzsch, *Bergstädte des Erzgebirges: Städtebau und Kunst zur Zeit der Reformation*, Munich [1972]

Krause, *Schlosskapellen* — [H.-J. Krause] *Die Schlosskapellen der Renaissance in Sachsen* [Berlin, 1970]

Kreft-Soenke, *Weserrenaissance* — H. Kreft and J. Soenke, *Die Weserrenaissance*, 3rd ed., Hameln [1964]

Kunstreisboek — *Kunstreisboek voor Nederland*, Amsterdam, 1965

Lauterbach, *Krakau* — A. Lauterbach, *Die Renaissance in Krakau*, Munich, 1911

Lieb, *Fugger* I — N. Lieb, *Die Fugger und die Kunst: Die Zeitalter der Spätgotik und frühen Renaissance*, Munich, 1952

Lieb, *Fugger* II — N. Lieb, *Die Fugger und die Kunst im Zeitalter der hohen Renaissance*, Munich, 1958

Lieb, *München* — N. Lieb, *München; die Geschichte seiner Kunst*, Munich [1971]

Löffler, *Alte Dresden* — F. Löffler, *Das alte Dresden*, Dresden, 1955

Łozinski-Miłobedzki, *Guide* — J. Z. Łozinski and A. Miłobedzki, *Guide to Architecture in Poland*, Warsaw, 1967

Matthaei, *Lüneburg* — J. Matthaei, *Lüneburg*, 2nd ed. [Munich] 1965

Merian, *Schönsten Schlösser* — M. Merian, *Die schönsten Schlösser, Burgen und Gärten* [Oldenburg, 1965]

National Museum, *Kronborg* — National Museum, *Kronborg; the Castle and the Royal Apartments*, 2nd ed. [Copenhagen] 1964.

Neu-Otten, *Landkreis Augsburg* — W. Neu and F. Otten, *Landkreis Augsburg*, Munich [1970]

Neumann, *Jülich* — H. Neumann, *Die Zitadelle Jülich* [Jülich] 1971

Niederlanden — *Kunstdenkmäler in den Niederlanden* [Munich, 1971]

Oechelhaeuser, *Heidelberg Schloss* — A. von Oechelhaeuser, *Das Heidelberg Schloss*, 7th ed., Heidelberg, 1955

Osten-Vey, *Germany* — G. von der Osten and H. Vey, *Painting and Sculpture in Germany and the Netherlands 1500-1600*, Harmondsworth [1969]

Piltz, *D.D.R.* — G. Piltz, *Künstführer durch die D.D.R.*, 4th ed., Leipzig [1973]

Rauch, *Augsburger Baugeschichte* — M. Rauch, *Zwei Jahrtausende in Stein und Farb. Augsburger Baugeschichte im Wandel der Zeit*, Augsburg [1973]

Reclams *Baden-Württemberg* — Reclams Kunstführer, II: *Baden-Württemberg Pfalz Saarland*, 3rd ed., Stuttgart [1960]

Reclams *Bayern* — Reclams Kunstführer, I: *Bayern*, 6th ed., Stuttgart [1966]

Reclams *Niedersachsen* — Reclams Kunstführer, IV: *Niedersachsen Hansestädte Schleswig-Holstein Hessen*, 2nd ed., Stuttgart [1962]

Reclams *Rheinlande und Westfalen* — Reclams Kunstführer, III: *Rheinlande und Westfalen*, 2nd ed., Stuttgart [1961]

Reclams *Schweiz und Liechtenstein* — Reclams Kunstführer: *Schweiz und Liechtenstein*, Stuttgart [1966]

Serlio, *Architettura* — S. Serlio, *Architettura*, 7 vols.

Skovgaard, *Christian IV* — J. A. Skovgaard, *A King's Architecture: Christian IV and his Buildings*, London [1975]

Slothouwer, *Denemarken*

D. F. Slothouwer, *Bouwkunst der Nederlandsche Renaissance in Denemarken*, Amsterdam, 1924

Stange, *Deutsche Baukunst*

A. Stange, *Die deutsche Baukunst der Renaissance*, Munich, 1926

Stein, *Bürgerhaus in Bremen*

R. Stein, *Das Bürgerhaus in Bremen*, Tübingen [1970]

Stelzer, *Braunschweig*

O. Stelzer, *Braunschweig*, 2nd ed. [n.p.] 1965

Stierhof, *Wandmalerei*

H. Stierhof, "Wand- und Deckenmalereien des Neuburger Schlosses im 16. Jahrhundert" in *Neuburger Kollektaneenblatt*, v. 125, 1972

Summerson, *Britain*

J. Summerson, *Architecture in Britain 1530-1830*, paperback ed. [Harmondsworth, 1970]

Th.B.

U. Thieme and F. Becker, *Allgemeines Lexikon der bildenden Künstler*, 37 vols., Leipzig, 1907-1947

Unnerbäck, *Welsche Giebel*

E. Unnerbäck, *Welsche Giebel* [Stockholm, 1971]

Van Gelder, *Dutch Art*

[H. E. van Gelder] *Guide to Dutch Art*, 3rd ed., The Hague, 1961

Zimmer, *Hofkirche und Rathaus*

J. Zimmer, *Hofkirche und Rathaus in Neuburg/ Donau*, Neuburg an der Donau, 1971

Tʜɪs book aims to provide a comprehensive account of architecture in Germany from the early influx of new Italian ideas in 1509 or 1510 to the outbreak of the Thirty Years' War more than a century later. In German nothing so extended has been made newly available since the volume by Carl Horst of 1928 in the Propyläen Kunstgeschichte. In another Propyläen volume, also of 1928, Gustav Glück's *Kunst der Renaissance in Deutschland, den Niederlanden, Frankreich, etc.*, all of northern Europe is included, and German architecture in any case receives less attention than do German painting and sculpture.

Internationally, German Renaissance architecture has long been an even more neglected subject. Sir Nikolaus Pevsner devotes very little space to it even in the latest and more expanded English editions of his *Outline of European Architecture*, although he did deal with it more liberally in the earlier German one; nor did he, as editor, plan for a volume on the German architecture of the sixteenth and early seventeenth centuries in the Pelican History of Art to parallel Summerson's on England and Blunt's on France. Henry Millon includes very few illustrations of German buildings of this period, two of interiors and all very late, in *Key Monuments of the History of Architecture*: the Jesuits' St. Michael in Munich and the Rathaus of the city of Augsburg. Moreover, the church and the Goldener Saal in the latter, of the decorations in which only traces now survive, are represented by prewar photographs. The late Eberhard Hempel in the second, 1956, printing of his history of German architecture in Bruckmann's Deutsche Kunstgeschichte covered the subject in 38 pages—including all of Austria as well as Strasbourg and Gdańsk—while to the Baroque he assigned 176. In the sixteenth-century volume of the new Propyläen Kunstgeschichte Jan Białostocki offers only a dozen or

so illustrations, far fewer than for France much less Italy.

The Heidelberg Schloss (Figs. 23, 27, Pls. 139, 177-179), however, with Renaissance wings of various dates from the 1540s to the 1610s, has never lost its fame, and publications concerning it continued to come out all through the last century, including at least two in French. The more elaborate of these has text by Daniel Ramée, a far cry from his republication of C. N. Ledoux. The peak of the flood was in the 1880s, but articles and even monographs have never ceased to appear, the latter often in several successive editions.

There is a paradox here in the contrast between the relative neglect of the German Renaissance by leading historians such as Pevsner and Hempel and the existence of so prolific a specialized literature. But it is significant that the peak came in the 1880s; for it was in the early decades of the new German empire—what many think of as the Bismarck period rather than the reign of Wilhelm I—that the architecture of the German Renaissance was most admired and most frequently emulated. It was then that the Ottheinrichsbau of the Heidelberg Schloss (Pl. 177), with its profusion of decoration and its northern corruption of Italian Renaissance forms, appealed more than any other surviving sixteenth-century work in Germany to the taste of the day. The visitor to the Heidelberg Schloss today soon realizes that taste survives with vast numbers of tourists: American soldiers from the Schwetzingen barracks are always there in quantity and such crowds of other non-Germans that the guides break them up into groups to be addressed not only in English but in French, in Dutch and so forth. How different is the situation at such Schlösser as the splendid Plassenburg above Kulmbach and many other remarkable monuments, particularly in the East! In them the visitor may easily have the whole place to himself and thus find an opportunity to consider calmly the injustice of the continued rejection of German Renaissance architecture on grounds of taste by many scholars—German and foreign both—who are still influenced by the ambivalent attitudes of the last forty or fifty years.

Though the German Renaissance finds only a very reduced place in present-day general works of architectural history—or none at all—the old Propyläen history of art included more than a generation ago both Glück's book, even if architecture did not receive as much space or as many illustrations as painting or sculpture, and Horst's *Architektur der deutschen Renaissance*. It is not unjust after a half-century to consider these out of date, as also Alfred Stange's *Baukunst der deutschen Renaissance* (Munich, 1926), not to speak of Gustav von Bezold's volume seven (2d ed., Leipzig, 1908) in the Handbuch der Architektur series, a work that includes the Netherlands and even Denmark as well.

Although the Heidelberg Ottheinrichsbau is in some sense the most conspicuous, and certainly the best known, German work of the third quarter of the century, it is fortunately not typical. But then various others among the major productions of the German Renaissance, such as Schloss Hartenfels at Torgau (Pls. 78-80) and the Schöner Hof of the Plassenburg (Pls. 191-193) or the Rathaus in Nürnberg (Pl. 421), are hardly typical either; several of the most interesting monuments, moreover, have been difficult of access for the last thirty years because they are in what is now the D.D.R. (East Germany) or in Poland. These include, most notably, the Fürstenhof at Wismar (Pls. 146-148) and Schloss Güstrow (Pls. 186-189), both in Mecklenburg; the Französischer Bau of the Heldberg Veste above Heldburg in Thuringia; and Schloss Augustusburg (Fig. 36, Pls. 200-202) in Saxony—all in East Germany; and the Piastenschloss at Brieg (Brzég) in Silesia (Pl. 135, 136), southwest Poland now. Still others are so ruined as hardly to be intelligible to the visitor: Schloss Horst in the Ruhr district not far from Essen (Pls. 180-181), for example, or the relevant sections of the Residenzschloss at Dresden, where little but the portal, dated 1555, of the chapel (Pl. 130) survived the bombing of 1945 in recognizable form. Those in Berlin and Kassel are known only from drawings (Pls. 100-101).

Mention of postwar East Germany brings up the question as to what areas of northern Europe should be considered "German" in the Renaissance period. It is too simple just to say "the central German lands,"

while the fantastic extension of Hitler's Third Reich forty years ago is quite beside the point. More realistically, what are in this book considered the central German lands—"Germany" in the sixteenth century—include principally the much more restricted territories of the Weimar Republic of the 1920s and 1930s and, in effect, those of the post-war D.B.R. (West Germany) and D.D.R. (East Germany) today. To these have been added, however, accounts of work in certain provinces that were German in the sixteenth century but have been handed over by the Russians to the Poles and the Czechoslovaks or, in the case of East Prussia, retained by them.

Rough boundaries, though not definable politically or even linguistically in the sixteenth and early seventeenth centuries, can best be suggested by exclusion. To the west, the line of division from German lands can neither be located consistently at the Rhine nor at the Maas; but the southern and northern Netherlands—Belgium and Holland today—were not and are not German. Yet, on the other hand, Strasbourg, on the west bank of the Rhine in Alsace, must be considered to have been a German rather than a French cultural center during the Renaissance. Like Alsace, Schleswig is ambiguous historically, yet somewhere above or below that geographical entity Germany ends and Denmark begins.

To the east, in territories ethnically Slav, neither Czechoslovakia nor Poland as it exists today is German. In the sixteenth century, however, Pomerania and Silesia, both now provinces of Poland, were German and East Prussia was a German exclave; Bohemia—Habsburg territory after 1529—was ambivalent; and it is even more difficult to establish a meaningful line in the sixteenth century within the Habsburgs' older Austrian lands between Magyar Hungary—clearly not German, and for most of the relevant period under Turkish domination—and Bavaria and the Upper Palatinate, equally clearly within the central German lands. It is relevant for German architectural history, moreover, that in the southern Austrian duchies, the Tyrol, Carinthia and Styria, North Italian or Italian-Swiss architects were rather consistently employed for major building operations rather than Germans or local men. That was also true in Salzburg, if not to the same degree of Upper and Lower Austria. There was a somewhat similar situation in Switzerland; therefore Swiss as well as Austrian Renaissance work is discussed in this book only occasionally and, when illustrated, chiefly for contrast and comparison.

All the same, in connection with various topics dealt with recurrently in the central German lands, certain buildings in other northern countries are mentioned and some even illustrated. One of these topics is early Protestant church architecture, so largely confined down to the 1590s to Germany; another is that most characteristic feature of northern secular architecture, the scalloped or scrolled gable. This feature, to which I have already devoted a whole book, was much influenced in its decoration in the second half of the sixteenth century and well into the seventeenth in Germany, as all over northern Europe, by the engravings, issuing from Antwerp, of the southern Netherlander Cornelis Floris and of Jan Vredeman de Fries—"the Frisian"—who was born at Leeuwarden in the north. Moreover, since American and English readers are so much more familiar with sixteenth- and early seventeenth-century architecture in England and even in France, many very well-known works, from the chateaux on the Loire and Henry VIII's screen in King's College Chapel at Cambridge to de Brosse's *Temple* at Charenton and the Banqueting House of Inigo Jones, are mentioned without being illustrated. The work of Jones is particularly relevant, since an attribution to him of the design of the Englischer Bau of the Heidelberg Schloss is proposed and defended.

As regards church architecture, the situation in Germany is especially crucial. The Reformation, the major cultural and even political event of the sixteenth century, rivalling in consequence the early opening of the New World, began in Saxony and was long centered in Germany. The architectural effect of the Reformation, balanced from the 1580s by that of the Counter Reformation, is not as great—at least not as recognizable—as might be supposed. Beginning in the 1520s, older churches were taken over for Lutheran use with no structural change and only some purging of subsidiary altars, and were not affected by the broader iconoclasm common in other regions of the north or the frequent abandonment of chancels in England. In the next decade, the first church designed especially for reformed services was built not in electoral Saxony, as would have been expected, but further to the east and south, in Bohemia. Then, in the 1540s two chapels were built or decorated, one consecrated by Luther himself, the other with Lutheran frescoes; and the construction of several large churches, projected to be Catholic—as was that latter chapel—halted entirely until it was begun again, after a considerable hiatus, more modestly for Lutherans.

The religious situation is not a simple matter of Lutheran *versus* Catholic, however: princes could and did turn first one way and then the other. Moreover, the Elector Palatine at Heidelberg, the Landgrave of Hesse, and the Elector of Brandenburg were Calvinists, if only briefly. But this variety of faith had even less effect on secular architecture than on the design and functional organization of churches and chapels. If the most ambitious builders among the innumerable electors, dukes, prince-bishops, margraves, landgraves and plain gentry who erected "country houses" —so to call their *Schlösser* rather than "castles"— seem to have been in higher proportion Lutherans than Catholics, such a loose statistic is probably not significant. However, when it comes to the cities and towns, large and small, where municipal officers— *Bürgermeister* and councillors belonging to the local *Rat*—were the clients, the Protestant ones may have been more prosperous than those that remained Catholic. Internationally, it should be recalled that with the bottling up of Antwerp's port on the Schelde in the late sixteenth century, the greatest commercial center of the day, ruled by the Spanish Habsburgs, was forced to cede primacy to independent and Protestant Amsterdam.

However, the earliest Renaissance works, dating actually from a decade before the Reformation began, were commissioned by a rich Catholic, the banker Jakob Fugger, who is often noted as a sort of Swabian parallel to the Medici. Economic historians try to explain the rise and fall of great cities and individual fortunes by the hows and whys of inflation; architectural history can only record the results. For example, the prosperity of the dukes of Saxony deriving from silver mining in the late fifteenth and early sixteenth century was not equalled later. The new silver finds in the Schwarzwald were of little profit to the dukes of Württemberg because of the rising influx of the metal from the New World. Finally, there is the curious situation of the Habsburg emperors and archdukes: poorer than many of their subject-princes at the opening of the Renaissance, their later wealth from America did not avail when they went bankrupt in 1547; and even in Antwerp their rule was interrupted for some years in the early eighties.

Neither Charles V, who rarely entered the central German lands, nor his successors as emperor had occasion to build in Germany. But Habsburg building elsewhere, in the southern Netherlands, in Bohemia and in the Austrian homelands cannot be ignored, from Margaret of Austria's Palais de Savoie in Mechelen near Antwerp to the Maximilian Cenotaph in the

Hofkirche in Innsbruck or Schloss Ambras just outside. In the case of the last, there is the irony that the Archduke Ferdinand was able to build so sumptuously only because of the wealth he inherited from his commoner wife Philippine, the daughter of the Augsburg banker Bartholomäus Welser, whose firm handled for the Habsburgs the bullion from the New World.

So much detail has no proper place in a Preface, but it may suggest some of the ramifications in the history of the Renaissance period in Germany and surrounding regions in northern Europe that throw light on, if they do not completely explain, what was erected and where.

Architecture has not been considered purely, or even primarily, in terms of design; much less merely for the infiltration of ideas from Italy followed by their partial acceptance—which came in irregular waves, reaching a peak only at the end of the period covered—or the balancing influx of Northern Mannerist ornament from the Netherlands. These facets of the story receive considerable attention all the same, as they do also in my extended account, *Netherlandish Scrolled Gables of the 16th and Early 17th Centuries* (New York, 1978) that has just been mentioned.

One may well ask, therefore, if this book has a definable thesis. In fact, there are two: one is quite simply that German monuments of the Renaissance deserve the examination, and indeed the appreciation, they have never had outside Germany, and only intermittently—and for decades rather grudgingly—even there. They merit attention for various reasons that have their roots in the general historical situation in the sixteenth and early seventeenth centuries, roots that are at once cultural, religious and even politico-military. For possible appreciation, of course, the illustrations are more important than the facts and the analyses in the text. To equal the body of relevant visual material provided here a very considerable library of postwar books would be required, from such monographs as Norbert Lieb's *Die Fugger und die Kunst*, I and II (Munich, 1952 and 1958), or Kreft and Soenke's *Weserrenaissance,* latest (4th) edition (C. W. Niemeyer, 1975), to the still more detailed accounts of particular areas such as Fritz Loeffler's *Das alte Dresden* (Dresden, 1955) and Werner Fleischhauer's *Renaissance in Herzogtum Württemberg* (Stuttgart, 1971). Not even the Institute of Fine Arts of New York University, where this author is an adjunct professor, now possesses such a library.

A special problem exists as regards Eastern Europe, especially the D.D.R. (East Germany), for nearly half of what are considered here the central German lands, not to speak of Poland and Czechoslovakia, have been in varying degree closed to westerners, whether scholars or tourists, for more than a generation. Moreover, up-to-date illustrations and firsthand descriptions, including references to war damage and to restorations, have not been available. For an architectural guide book comparable to the postwar editions of the Dehio *Handbücher* or Reclams *Kunstführer* for West Germany it was necessary to wait for Georg Piltz's *Kunstführer durch die D.D.R.* (Leipzig, Jena, Berlin, 1969). American and English readers have been better served lately in such countries—in any case more accessible—as Poland and Czechoslovakia by Brian Knox's books: *The Architecture of Poland* (London, 1969) and his earlier *Bohemia and Moravia* (London, 1962). Now a far more ample work covers all of Eastern Europe—Hungary as well as the Slavic lands. This is Jan Białostocki's Wrightsman Lectures, given in the autumn of 1972 for the Institute of Fine Arts of New York University at the Metropolitan Museum, on *The Art of the Renaissance in Eastern Europe.* Four years later the lectures appeared in book form (New York, 1976), profusely illustrated and provided with a very extensive bibliography in which the titles of publications in Hungarian, Czech and Polish are happily given parenthetically in English. Now the Białostocki book largely supersedes earlier publications in English.

As the recurrent brief references to monuments in Eastern Europe were written before the Białostocki book became available, the citations to earlier publications in English have been retained. References to the Białostocki text are usually made only where he is not in agreement with the dating or the attributions given earlier by Knox or by Łozinski and Miłobedzki in their *Guide to Architecture in Poland* (Warsaw, 1967). It has mostly seemed preferable to refer to the earlier works rather than to Białostocki's text. However, because of the wealth of visual material he provides, his illustrations, the captions of which repeat the dates and attributions included in the text, are sometimes cited. Not least valuable to those unfamiliar with the area—which includes most westerners—is the historical background Białostocki recurrently offers in his text.

As has already been suggested in regard to economic history, the intricate politics of the sixteenth century, dynastic and religious, particularly in Germany but hardly less to the east, are beyond the comprehension of anyone but specialists. However, a large number of German contemporaries of monarchs famous for their building activities elsewhere in Europe such as Francis I, Henry VIII and James I are briefly identified, as well as various Polish and Danish rulers. Frequent reference is made in the earlier chapters, moreover, to figures of European stature like the Emperor Charles V and his successors, the reformer Martin Luther and a few others of less consequence, including Jean Calvin outside Germany. There is even a certain amount of genealogy, mostly consigned to footnotes, since the relationships, frequently international, of the north European princes are relevant to the character of their building production. Various ambitious builders were clearly out to rival their brothers-in-law as often as their brothers and their cousins!

The variety of material involved has usually, in the hands of native writers, led to regional subdivision of the German lands in dealing with this period, while modern studies are likely to be confined within the boundaries of present-day states. Although neither geographical contiguities and relative distances, nor yet the availability or the absence of suitable building stones, bricks and timber, are neglected, this account of German Renaissance architecture is organized "nationally"—or so one may put it—in a single chronological sequence. Implicit in this is the recognition of a linked series of stylistic subperiods, in considerable degree individualized, from the quattrocento Italian sort of design reflected (if with considerable modification) in the first quarter of the sixteenth century in southern Germany at Augsburg and Regensburg, to the opposing forces—international both in their sources and their connections—of anti-Italianate late Northern Mannerism and its Academic alternative a century afterward. Without arbitrary shaping—or at least only a little in the terminal chapters—the story pretends to discover, and aims to present, a sort of historical plot, one that comes to an end in the opening decades of the seventeenth century just before the close of the period around 1620. It was then the German Renaissance ended, though the Baroque still lay ahead.

Inevitably in a history not of building but of architecture, certain facets are neglected, or at least unevenly treated. Though *Fachwerk*, timber-framed construction, was in many parts of Germany as consistently used in the Renaissance decades as in England, and much more is extant, it receives only occasional mention. This is because Fachwerk seems in

this period to have had little consistent stylistic development and is related to contemporary currents in the design of masonry architecture only in a belated and even vernacular way.

Men who were primarily specialists at the new sort of fortifications required by advances in weaponry—usually in this period Italians, though Henry VIII thought himself rather good at it—are frequently mentioned, since several of them were capable of up-to-date architectural design that was more than routine; but actual military construction, though often referred to, is not discussed and only incidentally illustrated. At the other extreme from such predominantly utilitarian building, the production of sculptors, when expanded to edicular scale in tombs and such, has usually been briefly described, though for the most part only in terms of the architectural elements, from the Dauhers' altars in the second decade of the sixteenth century to the mausoleums of Nosseni and his associates around and after 1600.

To return to the question of the thesis or theses of this book: implicit, at least, is the claim that, even though there can be no over-all definition of German Renaissance architecture, a series of overlapping stylistic episodes can be recognized that seem to have been to a large extent autochthonous. This is increasingly true down to about 1610, if not much beyond. Particularly in the Weser region in the fifty years from the 1570s to the 1620s, some of these episodes were highly productive, not only quantitatively but in the quality of the finest work. Much more is provincial or even vernacular. Strangely enough, a good deal of quite conspicuous work remains, even to the last, nearly anonymous. Of the many craftsmen involved in building who are mentioned in documents, only a few in any case have definable artistic personalities, any more than do most of the English "architects" before Smythson whose names are known, or the Dutch ones before Lieven de Key. An exception might be Hans Hieber—to whom Dr. Irmgard Büchner-Suchland devoted a monograph (Munich, 1962)—or Elias Holl; the first belongs to the early part of the period, the second to the end. Holl is the subject of a considerable number of studies old and new, the most important listed in a footnote to Chapter IX.

How unfair it is to dismiss German Renaissance architecture, chiefly because of exclusive familiarity with the Heidelberg Ottheinrichsbau, should be evident as soon as the reader turns to the illustrations of things as different as Schloss Hartenfels at Torgau (Fig. 12, Pls. 78-80, 82), the Schöner Hof of the Plassenburg above Kulmbach (Pls. 191-193), and, among churches, the Schlosskapellen at Augustusburg (Pl. 201) and in the Wilhelmsburg above Schmalkalden (Pls. 267-269), not to speak of the Stadtkirche at Bückeburg (Pls. 434-435). A different sort of interest attaches to the modest but historically important chapel—the earliest surviving Protestant ecclesiastical edifice—Luther dedicated at Torgau (Pls. 125, 127) two generations and more before. Above all, the houses at Hameln (Pls. 227, 384, 386, 387, 390, 391) and the nearby Schloss of Hämelschenburg (Pls. 299-305) have an originality and a maturity of design unmatched in Elizabeth I's England or Christian IV's Denmark and, some may feel, even Marie de Médicis's France, if not Paul V's Rome.

Henry-Russell Hitchcock
April 1979

Acknowledgments

In the dozen years, and more, during which this book has been in preparation, William G. Foulks has continually assisted in various ways, from the typing and retyping of the text, beginning with the early drafts of the 1960s, down to the preparation of the index. My indebtedness to him is therefore manifold, and not least for the arduous work he has done in gathering copy for the illustrations.

As the photographs and other material used have been acquired from some eighty photographers and photographic agencies, it is not feasible here to acknowledge them all individually. However, photographic credits are given for all in the List of Illustrations. In addition, I would like to acknowledge specifically here certain sources on which I have been especially dependent: in the East, Klaus Beyer in Weimar and the Deutsche Fotothek Dresden; in the West, Herbert Kreft in Minden and the Bildarchiv Foto Marburg. Two photographers in the West took pictures especially for me: Ursula Pfistermeister and the late Lala Aufsberg, whose negatives are now in the Bildarchiv Foto Marburg.

Among German scholars, I should note with gratitude, Dr. Jürgen Soenke, Kreft's fellow-author of the book *Weserrenaissance*, and Professor Norbert Lieb. Needless to say, the few names mentioned here are but a very small proportion of those who have assisted me in one way or another, not the least the many owners of Schlösser who permitted me to visit them and, in the cases of Frau von Klencke at Hämelschenburg and Frau von Gallen at Assen, who entertained me. Herr von und zur Mühle took me to visit many of his neighbors in Westphalia.

Finally, I should mention my friend, Robert Schmidt, who drove me, over so many years, again and again through West Germany and twice even into East Germany.

GERMAN RENAISSANCE
ARCHITECTURE

One

THE BEGINNINGS
OF THE RENAISSANCE
IN GERMANY, 1510-1525

THE earliest examples of Renaissance architecture in Germany, as has long been recognized, are the Fugger burial chapel at St. Anna in Augsburg in Swabia and the three remodelled houses in the Weinmarkt there of Jakob II Fugger (1459-1525). Elements of Italianate architecture had already appeared in paintings and prints; and priority may be allowed—at least as a work designed by a German for German clients—to the Fontego dei Todeschi (Pl. 1) in Venice.[1] But among executed works of architecture in German lands the Fugger commissions of around 1510 are the first. These came, however, some years after comparable Renaissance design had been introduced in Hungary, in Bohemia and in Poland to the east and in France to the west.[2] The opposing claim of the Rathaus at Überlingen on the Lake of Constance in southern Germany may be disregarded, not because of its early date—1489-1494—but because of the general Late Gothic character of the facade.[3]

It is appropriate that the immediate forerunner of German Renaissance architecture should be in Venice; for the first Renaissance works on German soil are of rather Venetian character[4]—the earlier northern examples in Magyar and Slavic lands have other Italian sources.[5] Yet the designers who worked in Augs-

[1] The Fontego—the Venetian name; *Fondaco dei tedeschi* in Italian—was built in 1505-1507 from a design by Gerolamo Tedesco that was executed by Scarpagnino. John McAndrew's *Venetian Architecture of the Early Renaissance*, Cambridge, 1980, which appeared while the present book was in press, summarizes and supersedes the earlier literature.

[2] As already stated in the Preface, the best account in English of what went on in this period to the east of Germany, with profuse illustration, is the published Wrightsman Lectures of 1972 by Jan Białostocki, *The Art of the Renaissance in Eastern Europe* [London, 1976], henceforth cited as Białostocki, *Eastern Europe*. The most convenient reference for France is Anthony Blunt, *Art and Architecture in France, 1500 to 1700*, 2nd ed. [Harmondsworth, 1970], henceforth cited as Blunt, *France*.

[3] The south front of the Rathaus at Überlingen on the Bodensee was begun shortly before 1494, some say as early as 1489: G. Dehio, Handbuch der Deutschen Kunstdenkmäler, *Baden-Württemberg* [Munich] 1964 (henceforth cited as Dehio, *Baden-Württemberg*), pp. 486-487. This has flat rustication all over of a rather Italianate sort; but the whole is markedly asymmetrical and quite without Renaissance de-

tail. The lintelled windows are not exceptional for the period in Germany, and those in the tower are topped by a drooping curve in a manner quite unknown in Italy, while the entrance arch is actually pointed.

[4] Venetian influence is well documented in Austria: R. K. Donin, *Venedig und die Baukunst von Wien und Niederösterreich*, Wien, 1963, pp. 42-47. Donin's fig. 41 shows a quattrocento lunette carrying the date 1497 over a portal at Lugeck 7 in Vienna. This is very simple, however, compared to the Lombardesque portals carried out nearly a generation later in the 1520s in Vienna and in Wiener Neustadt (Pls. 21, 22). See also Note X 59.

[5] In Hungary and in Poland Italians had been employed very early—already in the 1480s at Buda by King Mátyás Corvinus. From Buda, where he had been brought up in Mátyás's palace, the Jagellon prince who would soon be king of Poland as Zygmunt I brought with him to Kraków (Cracow) in 1502 to work at the Wawel Zamek, the royal residence, Franciscus Florentinus—known to the Poles as Franciszek Florenticzik, or Wloch, and evidently a Florentine—well before his accession in 1506. In Prague, however, it was the native Beneš Rejt (Benedikt Ried, or von Launa, †1534), the greatest Late Gothic architect of central Europe, who introduced Renaissance features in buildings on the Hrad around 1500. His Italian sources are uncertain, but his window-framing suggests Urbino.

The latest account in English of the beginnings of the Renaissance in Eastern Europe, that provided by Jan Białostocki in the Wrightsman Lectures for New York University in the autumn of 1972, has been mentioned in Note 2. See also B. Knox, *The Architecture of Poland*, London [1971] (henceforth cited as Knox, *Poland*), p. 14; A Lauterbach, *Die Renaissance in Krakau*, Munich, 1911 (henceforth cited as Lauterbach, *Krakau*), pp. 9-39; E. Hartwig, *Cracow*, 2nd ed., Warsaw [n.d.] (henceforth cited as Hartwig, *Cracow*), a picture book with minimal text in English.

For Bohemia and Moravia, see Białostocki, *Eastern Europe*; B. Knox, *Bohemia and Moravia*, London [1962] (henceforth

burg seem to have been Germans. No Italian collaborators are recorded, at least, for the work done there for Jakob Fugger. This work immediately followed the completion of the Fontego in Venice, where the Fugger firm henceforth had its quarters in the new commercial *palazzo*.

Considering the important part played by Cosimo de' Medici in Florence during the initiatory decades of the Renaissance in the previous century, it is not surprising that Jakob Fugger, the head of the great Augsburg family of merchant-bankers, who had a primacy comparable to that of the Medici at this later period in international finance, and not some prince or prelate, should have played a rather similar role in Germany. There is no certainty, however, as to who his Brunelleschi was or even his Michelozzo when the family's burial chapel and the remodelling of Jakob's house were commissioned in 1509 and in 1512 respectively.[6]

The contacts of the Augsburg bankers with Italy had long been cultural as well as commercial. Already in 1474, the youthful Georg Fugger (1453-1506), a brother of Jakob, had had his portrait painted in Venice by Giovanni Bellini.[7] After the turn of the century the mature Jakob, known as "der Reiche" (the Rich), became even more active than his contemporary, the Emperor Maximilian, as a patron of the arts, employing many northern artists, medallists and sculptors as well as painters and engravers. Such Germans were already introducing not only Italianate ornamental detail, but full-scale architectural settings in their pictures, their prints and their bronzes whether or not they had actually travelled and studied in Italy. Most of this avant-garde production was associated with Augsburg, Nürnberg and Regensburg in the southern portion of the central German lands.

In the years just before 1508, the elder Hans Holbein, who had been born in Augsburg in the 1460s, set the Angel and the Virgin of the Annunciation of his Sebastianaltar, now in Munich, inside a single Renaissance interior that is seen through two narrow round arches carried on arabesqued columns. In that year 1508, moreover, Albrecht Dürer of Nürnberg provided in his early project for a painting—executed by others only in 1511—of the Adoration of the Trinity, now in Vienna, a rich Renaissance frame with flanking half-columns and a semicircular lunette[8] above a full entablature; the drawing is at Chantilly in the Musée Condé. The lunette is one form of a feature that became common in German Renaissance archi-

cited as Knox, *Bohemia*); and G. Fehr, *Benedikt Ried*, Munich, 1961 (henceforth cited as Fehr, *Ried*). For Rejt's Vladislav Hall on the Hrad, see in particular Białostocki, *Eastern Europe*, ills. 42-58. There are two Renaissance portals dated, respectively, 1502 and 1509 at the Hrad by Rejt and also others of his design which cannot be dated so precisely: E. Samánková, *Architektura ceski Renesance*, Prague, 1961, figs. pp. 5, 6. Knox, *Bohemia*, pp. 25-26, mentions the portal of 1502 and gives the further information that the south range on the Hrad was completed by 1510. Another account is provided by Fehr, *Ried*, pp. 30 ff., who dates the portal which Samánková assigns to 1502 "kurz nach 1500." Especially interesting is the one illustrated with a photograph and a section by Fehr, figs. 23, 24, for this has a Gothic frame on one side and fluted columns carrying an entablature on the other. Again the date is given by Fehr as "kurz nach 1500."

[6] The account, occupying much of this chapter, of the Fugger commissions of 1509-1512 and 1512-1515 depends so heavily on Norbert Lieb's very detailed text in *Die Fugger und die Kunst* [I] *Die Zeitalter der Spätgotik und frühen Renaissance*, Munich, 1952 (henceforth cited as Lieb, *Fugger* I), that no particular references for this and other statements based on his meticulous and extensive research will be given here. It is worth noting specifically, however, that the account of the burial chapel at St. Anna in Augsburg occupies his pp. 135-249 and the account of the houses in the Weinmarkt, today Maximilianstrasse 36-38, pp. 92-119. The latter section is preceded by much general information concerning Jakob, his ancestors and his brothers that is repeated, often without specific credit, here.

N. Lieb, *Die Fugger und die Kunst im Zeitalter der hohen Renaissance*, Munich, 1958 (henceforth cited as Lieb, *Fugger* II), continues the story to the death of Anton Fugger in 1560, with recurrent reference to changes made in the Fuggerhäuser; for work done for Hieronymus Fugger (1499-1538), see pp. 16-18, and for Anton Fugger (1493-1560), pp. 158-196.

Also relevant at this point are his "Nachträger zu Band I," pp. 473-481.

Briefer mention can be found in several current guidebooks: *Reclams Kunstführer I: Bayern*, 6th ed., Stuttgart [1966] (henceforth cited as Reclams *Bayern*), pp. 93-94 and pp. 101-102; G. Dehio, *Handbuch der Deutschen Kunstdenkmäler, Östliches Schwaben*, Munich, 1954 (henceforth cited as Dehio, *Östliches Schwaben*), pp. 8-9 and 19; and T. Breuer, *Die Stadt Augsburg*, Munich [1958] (henceforth cited as Breuer, *Augsburg*), pp. 20-22 and p. 86. M. Rauch, *Zwei Jahrtausende Farb und Stein: Augsburger Baugeschichte im Wandel der Zeit*, Augsburg [1973] (henceforth cited as Rauch, *Augsburger Baugeschichte*) is valuable for its many illustrations, including several plates in color.

Various specific references to I. Büchner-Suchland, *Hans Hieber* [Munich] 1962 (henceforth cited as Büchner-Suchland, *Hieber*) are given in later notes.

[7] The Bellini attribution is queried by some, though not the date or the subject.

[8] What was probably its first appearance in the north at relatively large scale is over one of Beneš Rejt's portals at the Hrad in Prague. That cannot be dated exactly, but is probably of about 1500 (Białostocki, *Eastern Europe*, ill. 46).

tecture from the 1520s and soon spread, especially to the north.

Dürer had been to Italy, and more precisely to Venice, already in 1495. On a second longer trip he spent there the years 1505-1507 during which the Fontego dei Todeschi was in construction. But in 1510 he came to Augsburg to contribute to the Fuggers' burial chapel. That had just been commissioned, if not actually initiated, the previous year by Jakob Fugger and his elder brother Ulrich (1441-1510)— Georg had died in 1506.[9]

At much the same time, Renaissance detail in the form of candelabrum motifs of Lombard rather than Venetian character were being introduced in bronze by Peter Vischer (c.1460-1529) and his sons in Nürnberg on their somewhat hybrid, but predominantly Late Gothic, masterpiece, the Sebaldusgrab in St. Sebald (Pl. 33). That was begun in 1508 and eventually completed, after a hiatus, by 1519.[10] More remarkable at this time because of the total absence of Gothic detail is the bronze slab that was very likely modelled and cast by the Vischers—perhaps more particularly by Hermann II (†1517)—on the front of the tomb of Fryderyk Cardinal Jagellon (†1508), a brother of King Zygmunt I. It survives at the entrance to the chancel in the cathedral of Kraków, which rises beside the Wawel Zamek, Zygmunt's royal residence. On the tomb, however, which carries the precise date MDX, only the superb Roman inscription across the top and the figural composition of the Adoration of the Magi of Bellinesque character show positive Italian influence.[11] However, the incised effigy of Fryderyk on the associated horizontal tomb-slab on top, also of bronze,

is set in an elaborate frame of a distinctly hybrid character almost as much Late Gothic still as Early Renaissance.

A few years after came the carved wall-monument to Uriel von Gemmingen (†1514) in the cathedral of Mainz (Pl. 40). This was presumably commissioned by Gemmingen's successor as archbishop and elector of Mainz, Albrecht (later Cardinal) von Brandenburg. On this the sculptor Hans Backoffen (c.1465-1519) also mixed Late Gothic and Italianate elements of architectural detail. Albrecht's more purely Renaissance commissions at Halle-a.-d.-Saale in Saxony and Aschaffenburg on the Main followed only in the twenties.

Dürer began the enormous woodcut of a Triumphal Arch (Pl. 32) for the Emperor Maximilian in 1515 and completed it two years later. In that he purged the detail of all Late Gothic elements and, in their place, evolved a quite personal sort of Renaissance detailing. The ornament here is wildly elaborate by Lombard—much less Venetian or Florentine— standards of the day, or even in comparison to the framing on the bronze tomb at Kraków, and totally unrelated to the restrained tectonic membering of the High Renaissance, then still at its climax in the Rome of Leo X, the Medici prince who became pope in 1513. Indeed, though the initiation of the German Renaissance in the first quarter of the century coincides in date with the Roman work of Bramante, Raphael and San Gallo, there is little evidence of familiarity with their mature production. Quite exceptional are certain drawings (Pl. 2) by Hermann Vischer. These were made either in this year 1515 in Italy or just after his return and before his death in 1517.

In the Nativity of the Virgin by the Regensburg artist Albrecht Altdorfer (c.1480-1538), now in Munich, the event is set in the aisle of a large church of mixed Gothic, Romanesque and Renaissance design. This has an apse recalling that begun by Antonio Gambello (†c.1480) in San Zaccaria (Pl. 4) in Venice and executed by Mauro Coducci. The painting probably postdates by a good few years the completion in 1512 of the earliest Renaissance church interior in Germany, that of the Fuggerkapelle at St. Anna in Augsburg, if not its consecration in 1518.

In Augsburg the most prominent artist in the opening decades of the century was Hans Burgkmair (1473-1531). Born there, he was taken into the local painters' guild in 1498. Influenced by the elder Holbein, whose Renaissance Annunciation has just been

---

[9] It may well have been the death of Georg that first led Ulrich and Jakob Fugger to project a chapel to hold family tombs. F. Anzelewsky, *Albrecht Dürer: Das malerische Werk*, Berlin, 1971, identifies two drawings (his Nos. W484 and W485) as "preparatory" to Dürer's so-called "model drawings" for Fugger tomb-slabs (his Nos. W486 and W488). The latter carry the date 1510. On the strength of the watermark of "Two crossed Arrows," which is already found on drawings Dürer executed in Italy during his stay in 1506-1507, as contrasted with the "Crowned Snake" watermark of the 1510 drawings, he assigns the "preparatory" drawings to the earlier date, that of Georg's death. Although Anzelewsky associates the preparatory drawings with Rome, it is worth noting that the years 1506-1507 were within the period of construction of the Fontego in Venice, bringing a possible early project for the chapel very close in date to the latter.

[10] Reclams *Bayern*, pp. 628-629. There is, of course, a very considerable body of specialized studies concerning the Sebaldusgrab as well as mention in most general works.

[11] Białostocki, *Eastern Europe*, ills. 156, 158.

mentioned, Burgkmair probably also travelled and studied in Italy, more especially in Venice. Already in 1501 his painting of the Basilica of St. Peter in Rome, now in the Städtische Kunstsammlungen at the Schäzler Haus in Augsburg, shows Renaissance rather than Early Christian arches and pilasters on the front of the church, such as in fact existed at the time. Moreover, the portal on the right side of the facade is topped by a segmental lunette. Like Dürer's semicircular one on the Chantilly drawing, this is a motif soon to become popular in German Renaissance architecture.

The segmental lunette probably made its earliest architectural appearance in the north well ahead of the other form. Two of them cap the Lazarus chapel, dated 1475-1481, in the north transept of La Major in Marseille. Later, just before the Fuggerkapelle was commissioned, on the gatehouse of 1508-1510 at Georges Cardinal d'Amboise's chateau of Gaillon in Normandy looser versions of the Italianate segmental lunette crown many of the windows. A similar one, moreover, tops the throne of Burgkmair's painting of the Madonna of 1509 which is now in Nürnberg.

In 1518, a few years later but very early still in the German story, the Augsburg artist made a woodcut portrait of Maximilian. This shows the emperor, even though on horseback, in a vaulted interior with both arabesqued pilasters and a frieze of Lombardo-Venetian character. And in Burgkmair's "Weisskunig" series of woodcuts the protagonist—who was Maximilian idealized—visits the artist in an interior with a Renaissance doorway and a full entablature carried all around the walls. If this room does not represent his workshop at the time, it must indicate what he wished it to be. Fugger commissions are more relevant here, and with some of these Burgkmair was involved.

That Georg Fugger's portrait was painted in Venice, perhaps by Giovanni Bellini, in 1474 has been mentioned. Jakob Fugger sat to the elder Holbein twice, around or before 1509, for crayon and pen portraits. But a year or so later Burgkmair made a color woodcut of him. That was when Jakob was building the burial chapel at St. Anna and beginning to remodel his house. On these projects Jakob may have had, at least, that artist's advice, though only the employment of others is actually documented. Somewhat later still, in 1518, Jakob was drawn by Dürer, whom he had already employed in 1510 to design the carved slabs for the arched panels on the end wall of the chapel. A painted portrait followed. Dated 1518 also, the year the chapel was consecrated, are two silver

medals of Renaissance character by Hans Schwartz (c.1492-p.1530) with Jakob's portrait on the obverse. These various works of art help to define the range of Fugger taste down at least to the 1520s. The character of the altarpiece of the Madonna with Saints in Santa Maria dell' Anima in Rome that Jakob commissioned from Giulio Romano a bit later, after his brother Marx's death in 1522, is in sharp contrast. That painting is, indeed, a rather extreme manifestation of nascent Italian Mannerism such as one would not have supposed acceptable to the elderly Jakob Fugger.

The counter-charged blue and yellow fleurs-de-lys of the Fugger arms—granted to Jakob II and his brothers, the sons of Jakob I Fugger, by the Emperor Friedrich III in 1473—suggest Florence. Their business and banking interests, however, brought the Fuggers of that generation rather into close contact with Venice. In Rome, moreover, they were transfer agents for the indulgence moneys collected by Johannes Tetzel for Cardinal Brandenburg. It was convenient in this connection that Marx Fugger had a position in the Curia. But Georg and Ulrich spent much of their time at the Fontego in Venice. Not surprisingly, the German artists whom the Fuggers usually employed were those who favored Venetian rather than Florentine models.

Around 1493 the sons of the elder Jakob Fugger built a house near that of the other great Augsburg bankers, the Welsers, at what is now Annastrasse 25 in Augsburg. This Fugger house was primarily, it would seem, for the use of their widowed mother. Situated on the Rindermarkt, the house—or at least the store that replaces it—still extends, as rebuilt since the war, from the present Philippine-Welser-Strasse to the Annastrasse where it is numbered 19. The Fugger house of the 1490s had no Renaissance detailing at all and the two extant portals, like those surviving on the Welser house, are of typically Late Gothic character.

Another property, the Fugger Haus at Schwaz near Innsbruck, from which the Fugger mining interests in the Tyrol were managed, is of uncertain date but probably a decade later. This has arcading in four storeys on the east side of the court. The doubling of the rhythm above the round-arched ground storey faintly recalls the court of the Fontego dei Todeschi even though the smaller arches above are pointed. But the motif is hardly exceptional enough to justify any theory of specific derivation.

Of the housing of the Roman branch of the Fugger firm, which had been founded in the 1470s, nothing survives today in the Via dei Banchi Vecchi. But it is known that special decorations ornamented the structure for the coronation of Julius II in 1503 and again in 1513 for that of Leo X. In the early 1520s Perino del Vaga provided Raphaelesque frescoes in a loggia and in some sort of structure in the court. All the same, this actual Roman patronage had no effect on Ulrich's and Jakob's choice of artists to design and execute the family's burial chapel in Augsburg. It is easy to forget that this was in the climactic years of Julius's papacy while the new St. Peter's was rising in Rome to Bramante's plans.

As indicated above, Jakob II, Georg and Ulrich were sons of Jakob I. In 1441 he had married Barbara, the daughter of a goldsmith who was master of the Augsburg Mint, Franz Basingen. Three other sons died young: Peter, born in 1473, in Nürnberg, and the considerably older Andreas (born 1443) and Hans (born 1445) in Venice, where they were learning the family business in the old Fontego dei Todeschi. Another, Marx (born 1448), was not a member of the firm but university-educated and a secretary in the papal Curia, as has been mentioned, and he died in Rome. The Giulio Romano altarpiece in Santa Maria dell' Anima recalls, in the prominence of St. Mark among the Saints that attend the Madonna, Marx's burial in that church in 1522, but his marble graveslab is lost.

Ulrich Fugger, the eldest son of Jakob I, maintained his headquarters in Venice from 1484. Jointly with Jakob, he was among the first to take premises for the firm in the new Fontego dei Todeschi on its completion in 1508; but of the rich and famous decorations of these interiors nothing now survives. Ulrich may also have been the client for whom Dürer painted in 1506 the so-called Feast of the Rosary. This was intended for San Bartolomeo near the Fontego, the church of the German community in Venice, but has ended up in Prague. Georg had already visited Venice in 1474, as the Bellini portrait indicates. From 1484 to 1500 he was chiefly in Nürnberg, though from 1488 onward quite as often in Augsburg living in the house on the Rindermarkt with his mother.

Jakob II, born in 1459, was the youngest brother but, by surviving the others, he became the richest, as his appellation "der Reiche" indicates. Since he was the patron who carried to completion the first work of Renaissance architecture in Germany, he is of more importance here than Ulrich, though Ulrich was still alive when the chapel in St. Anna was commissioned in late 1509. He died, however, in the following spring. The Fuggers had, by the early sixteenth cen-

tury, connections with several Augsburg churches, but the chapels they had built in 1478-1493 off the right aisle of the great Benedictine church of Sts. Ulrich and Afra were not suitable for family burials. These had long been in St. Moritz, which is much nearer the Rindermarkt house. There Georg was buried in 1506 and even Ulrich in 1510, although their bodies were later removed to the crypt of the chapel at St. Anna.

This church of a Carmelite monastery, though founded in the fourteenth century, was largely rebuilt in 1487-1497. It was the Carmelites at St. Anna who provided a refuge for Martin Luther when he came to Augsburg to answer the Papal legate Cardinal Cajetani in 1518 after the close of the Reichstag that was held at Augsburg at just the same time the Fuggerkapelle was consecrated. Even more significantly, it was the site in 1524, the year before Jakob Fugger's death, of the first Protestant communion service. The following year St. Anna went over to the Lutherans and it is now the principal Protestant church in Augsburg, though the Fuggers and their chapel remained Catholic. Rather surprisingly in a Protestant church, Rococo decoration in stucco of the mid-eighteenth century obscures the original late fifteenth-century design of the nave of St. Anna. This serves to reduce somewhat the contrast between the Gothic body of the church and the new chapel Jakob added at the west end.

Both the two great new movements of the sixteenth century, the Renaissance and the Reformation, were thus, coincidentally, then in their initiatory stage at St. Anna. But even Luther's original revolt in 1517 lay some years ahead when the Fuggers' chapel was being planned, so that one may say correctly that the Renaissance reached Germany before the Reformation began. On April 7, 1509, Prior Johannes "Fortis" (i.e. Starck latinized) of the Carmelites granted to Ulrich and Jakob Fugger permission to erect at the church a chapel for their own burial and that of their relatives and descendants; to decorate it with their arms; and to endow masses to be said in it. This grant was confirmed from Rome by Julius II in a bull of November 19, 1509. The earlier document leaves ambiguous in its Latin tenses the question whether the chapel was, in fact, first projected before Georg Fugger's death in 1506. Moreover, as Ulrich died in the spring of 1510, construction would barely have started within his lifetime. Since he was then the head of the family, however, he probably shared with Jakob responsibility for the early development of the project and may well, after his long residence in Venice, have dictated its Renaissance character. That year 1510 Dürer made preparatory drawings, as has been mentioned, for the *Epitaphien* (tomb-slabs). These were carved by Sebastian Loscher (†1548) though with considerable modification of Dürer's designs. The ones of Georg and Ulrich, occupying the two central positions, were in place by 1512; the outer ones, honoring Jakob, were not executed until the 1520s after the Carmelites of St. Anna had turned Protestant and Jakob was dead.

The chapel was physically complete much earlier, and the date MDXII appears on both of its side walls. As noted, consecration in the names of Corpus Christi (*Fronleichnam*), the Virgin (*Mutter Gottes*) and St. Matthew, did not, however take place until January 17, 1518, the year of Luther's visit to the Carmelites. The previous six years had seen the preparation and the installation of many rich fittings. The earliest to be commissioned was the brass grille intended to shut off the chapel from the body of the church. This Peter Vischer of Nürnberg and his sons began only in 1515, and it was still unfinished in 1525 at the time of Jakob's death and even when Vischer died in 1529.

A rather detailed description in Italian of the Fuggerkapelle by Antonio de Beatis, one of the entourage of Luis Cardinal de Aragona who was in Augsburg May 25-27 in 1517 as the Pope's representative at the Reichstag, indicates how great an impression this chapel made even upon Italians when it was new. De Beatis also gave the cost: 23,000 florins.

Ironically, as has already been suggested, the next important events related to St. Anna had little connection with the design of the Fuggerkapelle. In 1523, Bernhard Rein, the organist of the magnificent organ made in 1515 by Jan Beheim von Dubrow or Dobrau and installed in the chapel by 1518, went over openly to the Lutherans; two years later, the year that Jakob Fugger died, the Carmelite prior, Johann Frosch, Starck's successor, celebrated in St. Anna his own wedding. In 1534, however, the Carmelites were disbanded and the church closed until 1548. Later, in the seventeenth century, it was for some time again Catholic.

This much abbreviated account provides the chronological framework within which the chapel came into existence and received a large part of the fittings Jakob Fugger ordered for it. The Vischer grille never reached Augsburg, however. The Count Palatine Ottheinrich, who ruled in the Upper Palatinate and was a notable patron of the arts, is believed to have sought to acquire it for his Schloss at Neuburg-a.-d.-Donau in the early thirties, that is, soon after Peter Vischer's death in 1529. Eventually the Nürnberg *Rat* (City Council) bought it. After it was finally brought to completion with various changes by Peter's son, Hans, and probably also Pankraz Labenwolf (1492-1563), the Rat had it set up in the Great Hall of the Rathaus between two stone piers. Other features, even though once actually installed in the Fuggerkapelle, were later taken away. These included the handsome choir-stalls, carved in pearwood, of which portions of the figural sculpture survive in museums, chiefly in Berlin, in Vienna and in Boston.

What one sees now in the Fuggerkapelle is the result of the thorough and, on the whole, conscientious restoration initiated after the last war to repair the damage of a bomb-set fire resulting from an air-raid in February 1944. This epoch-making work must here be described, not as it may have been originally, but as it is today after the latest restoration (Pl. 3). The absence of such a notable intended feature, commissioned but never installed, as the grille and of elements now removed like the choir-stalls can only be indicated. Moreover, such elements as the *Epitaphien* that appear to be Loscher's are, in fact, only copies of damaged originals that survive in various museums. In addition, the organ, with its painted wings by Jörg I Breu, was completely destroyed in 1941. The present organ, its casing and its wings are, like the *Epitaphien*, copies.

For the architecture of the chapel these losses and replacements are not so serious. The major portions of the interior, as executed principally in 1510-1512, survive so that the original architectonic characteristics have not been seriously affected by the later vicissitudes. To begin with, the chapel is not an independent entity. In basic form it can be, and was sometimes in the past, identified as a western choir. Such are frequent features of early mediaeval architecture in Germany though uncommon by the sixteenth century. The chapel is, essentially, an extra bay added at the west end of the existing nave and of the same width and height as the contiguous mediaeval bays to the east. But it is not of the same shape, for the earlier ones are oblong transversely and this is a full square (Fig. 1). In association with the round arches that are consistently used, the proportions distinctly enhance the Renaissance character of the space-composition.

Indeed, in what is probably only a coincidence, the proportions and even the dimensions of the Fuggerkapelle are close to those of the bays of the nave of

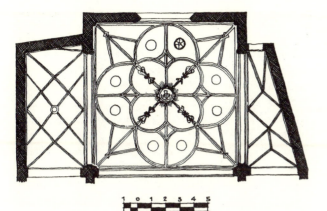

Fig. 1. S. L. (?Sebastian Loscher): Augsburg,
St. Anna, Fuggerkapelle, 1510-12, plan

San Zaccaria in Venice (Pl. 4). That Mauro Coducci had constructed in front of Antonio Gambello's Gothic apse shortly previous to his death in 1504 and thus not long before. The supports of the nave arcades, however, are not columns, as at San Zaccaria, but square piers, as at the Fontego. Marble-faced, these carry panelled pilaster strips topped, not with capitals, but with plain molded imposts that resemble those used in the Fontego (Pl. 1). At the lower level the imposts continue as an abbreviated entablature across the west wall. Higher up a more complete entablature extends from the tops of the upper sections of the eastern piers along the side walls of the aisles. This also runs above the arches opening from the nave into the aisles and across the west wall.

The aisles play little part in the spacial composition. The one to the north, moreover, is reduced in width towards the west almost to a sharp point because of pre-existing construction on the site (Fig. 1). Both are covered with Gothic net-ribbed vaulting, and this is necessarily quite irregular over the nearly triangular bay on the north side. A more conspicuous Gothic feature, in fact the only one likely to be noticed by a casual visitor, is the elaborate decorative pattern of ribbing on the main vault that assists structurally— or perhaps merely "fudges"—the transition from a cross-vault at the base to a flattened domical surface at the crown. Except for this, the architecture of the chapel is consistently quattrocento, i.e. Early Italian Renaissance, in character. It is even rather specifically Venetian, not Lombard or Tuscan, much less related to the contemporary High Renaissance of Bramante and Raphael in Rome.

At the entrance to the chapel, along the edge of the slightly raised floor, runs a balustrade which was, by

1515, intended to be replaced or supplemented by the Vischer grille that never arrived. This consists, like the balustrades of the balconies at the corners of the Fontego (Pl. 1), of ranges of tiny Tuscan columns. At the center of the balustrade rises a rather plain marble altar, now crowned with a sculptured group, which is decorated with an abstract rosette pattern in colored marble intarsia inlaid in the eastern face. Across the further end of the chapel, slightly bowed toward the west at this level, are four arched panels sunk between marble-panelled pilasters that contain the carved *Epitaphien*—or more accurately now, copies of Loscher's original tomb-slabs. Though all of them depend more or less on the drawings Dürer supplied in 1510, the first pair were completed by 1512, while the other two were installed only very much later, after Jakob's death in 1525 as already mentioned.

Above these arches is a shallow gallery with another balustrade like that below at the entrance to the chapel. This bows eastward over the two central arches to carry the minor organ and to provide room for the console and the organist. Higher up there were originally—and perhaps still are, though now invisible—two plain sunken arches framing small doors; from 1518, however, almost the whole of the upper west wall was filled, as now, by the case of the great organ and its open painted wings. This organ case was shaped in a concave curve at the top to accommodate the large round window which was there from the first. Further illumination is provided at clerestorey level by broad arched windows set high on either side. These are divided by plain vertical mullions, almost in the ancient Roman way that Palladio would later revive.

The decoration of the chapel and, perhaps more especially, such furnishings as survive are very rich. But the general impression is still restrained by contemporary Venetian standards, and even more so in contrast to the Lombard or Emilian taste that would soon be influential in Germany, especially to the east and north. The chapel at St. Anna in Augsburg may profitably be compared with the somewhat later Zygmunt Chapel at the cathedral of Kraków in Poland. That was commissioned in 1517 and begun in 1519 by the Florentine Bartolomeo Berrecci (†1537) assisted by other sculptors from Tuscany.[12] These artists were

[12] *Ibid.*, front., pls. III, VII-IX, ills. 102-124.
Polish taste seems to have been ahead of that of the German lands to the west in these years to judge by the court arcades in the Wawel Zamek that Franciscus Florentinus very possibly began to construct before his death in 1516, if not the

hired by the Polish king Zygmunt I—the year before he married his Italian second wife, Bona Sforza from Bari—to succeed the older Italian, Franciscus Florentinus, whom he had brought with him from Buda in 1502, after Franciscus died in 1516. Yet it is the Fuggerkapelle that a little recalls in its relative simplicity the quattrocento burial chapels in Florence, while that at Kraków seems in its decorative elaboration more Lombardo-Venetian. Though it is both larger and plainer, the Fuggerkapelle rather rivals in quality the distinctly Florentine chapel (Pl. 5) that Archbishop Thomas of Bakócz erected at the cathedral of Esztergom in Hungary still earlier in 1506-1510.[13]

In the Augsburg chapel, all the same, considerable coloured marble—blue-grey and two tones of red—was used though it is confined to the panels of the main piers, the pilasters at the rear and the rectangular members of the balustrades. There is no further elaboration on the walls except for the plain disks of the grey marble inset halfway up the shafts of the pilasters. The patterned marble floor is much richer and more varied in design, expanding the theme of the intarsia rosette on the altar. There is also, today, some restored gilding and painted polychromy as well as small focal elements of stained glass in the clerestorey windows and the western rose. These last may well be original, at least in part.

Architectural carved work in the chapel, other than the moldings, consists chiefly of rosettes. Small ones

appear on the intradoses of the eastern arch and those of the arches opening into the aisles, while a much bigger one is at the center of the vault overhead. This frames a polychromed relief of the crowned Madonna with the Christ Child. Still other rosettes in the eight broader compartments of the rib-pattern carry the Fugger lilies. Three-dimensional elaborations of the lily-motif, hanging half free of the vault-surface, also extend diagonally outward from the central rosette.

A great deal of small-scale figural sculpture is closely associated with the architectural features in the chapel. Perhaps the most appealing elements, indeed, in the surviving decoration are the putti on the tops of the balustrade flanking the altar, pudgy children of Germanized descent from Donatello's. Further examples of these, carved in pearwood and coming from the choir-stalls, are now in the Kunsthistorisches Museum in Vienna. Three low reliefs, equally quattrocento in character, of Christ Carrying the Cross, of the Deposition and of the Harrowing of Hell occupy the broad base of the larger three-dimensional group of the dead Christ supported by an angel between the Virgin and St. John on the altar. Finally, there are the four tall arched *Epitaphien* on the west wall.

All this decoration is monochromatic in the Fuggerkapelle; but, over and above the minor painted touches of color mostly overhead, there are the copies of Breu's original panel paintings on the shutters of both the large and the small organ. The latter illustrate the Invention of Music and Pythagoras demonstrating the Relationship between Weight and Tone; the former—much larger but necessarily of rather irregular shape because of the cut-out tops—carry an Ascension of Christ to the left and an Assumption of the Virgin to the right. The modest decorative motifs in the windows, executed in stained glass, consist of pairs of Fugger lilies flanked in each case by four tiny seraphim.

Three artists were responsible for the sculptural and the painted decoration: the elder Jörg Breu (c.1480-1537) for the latter, as has been noted, and for the former Sebastian Loscher (†1548) and Adolf Dauher (1460/1465-1523/1524). Dauher contributed the sculpture on the altar, both that in the round and in relief; Loscher, the putti on the top of the balustrade and both the earlier and the later *Epitaphien*. He, with his workshop, was also responsible for the wooden choir-stalls.

Of these three the most important was Loscher; for there is considerable—and acceptable—evidence that he provided the general architectural design. Pre-

still hybrid decoration in the rooms he had probably already remodelled for Zygmunt I immediately after his accession in 1507: *ibid.*, ills. 60-63.

The tomb of Zygmunt II August was interpolated below that of Zygmunt I in 1571-1575: *ibid.*, ills. 200-202.

[13] *Ibid.*, pls. IV, V, ills. 91-97. See also A. Zador, *The Cathedral of Esztergom*, Budapest, 1970, pp. 21-32, figs. 20-31, a well-illustrated summary in English of the results of the research of J. Balogh, *Az Esztergomi Bakóca Kápolna* [Budapest or Esztergom, 1955]. Balogh's research is also accessible in an Italian version: *La Capella Bakócz di Esztergom*, Budapest, 1956 (*Acta historiae artium*, III, fasc. 1-4).

The white marble altar, contrasting with the red marble of the walls of the chapel, is dated 1519 and by Andrea di Pietro Ferrucci (1465-1520), also known as Andrea di Firenze. As Dr. Zador expressed it, "The uneven outlines of the altar and its unbalanced composition . . . speak of the decline of the mature Renaissance paragons [*sic*]. . . ."

Ferrucci will hardly have been responsible for the design of the chapel as a whole. That is close in character to Giuliano da San Gallo's Capella Barbadori in the sacristy of 1489-1498 at Santo Spirito in Florence and much superior to Ferrucci's work. The chapel was rebuilt in 1823 in association with the completion of the new cathedral by Johann Baptist Pack as designed by Pál Kuhnel in 1820-1821.

served today in the Städtische Kunstsammlungen at the Schäzler Haus in Augsburg is a perspective drawing of the interior of the chapel (Pl. 6). Significantly, it shows no organ or choir-stalls, nor is there any sculpture on top of the altar or in the arched niches of the west wall for which Dürer made drawings in 1510. This is signed with the initials S.L., presumably standing for Sebastian Loscher. It *could* be a not wholly accurate view of the chapel as all but physically complete towards 1511 or 1512; but more probably this is the project approved by Jakob, and even perhaps by Ulrich, in late 1509 or early 1510. That would have been when the work was commissioned and before Dürer was asked to provide designs for the *Epitaphien*.

The inclusion in the drawing of pilaster-strips joined by the eastward-facing archivolt of an arch is, of course, not correct. The earlier vault of the first bay of the nave and the spandrels of the nave arcade below are actually in the same plane as the inner faces of the supports flanking the entrance to the chapel; moreover, the new eastern arch of the chapel fits against the pointed vault of the nave as closely as its half-round shape permits. These inaccuracies are more understandable in a project than in a representation of executed work. However, they are repeated in a late seventeenth-century drawing by Johann Weidner now in the Fuggerschloss at Kirchheim-a.-d.-Mindel, which is certainly of the chapel as executed. This last is valuable since it shows the choir-stalls in place; yet, curiously enough, the Dauher sculpture is absent from the top of the altar—perhaps it had already been removed by the Lutherans. Weidner's drawing also indicates that there were once further rosettes, not replaced in the latest restoration, both over the western rose and flanking the clerestorey windows at the sides. The redundant arches and pilasters on these two drawings are surely to be considered decorative frames for the composition such as were frequently included in sixteenth-century paintings—a relevant example is the elder Holbein's Annunciation of 1508 in Munich.

Further evidence of Loscher's involvement is the presence twice of what must be his initials S.L. on the vaulting ribs. But it may also be assumed that some experienced local builder[14] actually planned the construction required to execute the sculptor Loscher's perspective project. Such a man would probably himself have designed the unrelated aisle-vaults (Fig. 1)

[14] Possibly Hans Hieber.

in order to meet, in a traditional Late Gothic way, the exigencies of the confined site. The exterior is totally devoid of architectural features other than the bare shapes of the windows, but those of the clerestorey do have deeply bevelled intradoses. This plain exterior also suggests the collaboration, as the actual builder, of a mastermason lacking familiarity even at secondhand with quattrocento exteriors in Italy as was probably true of Loscher himself.

It is somewhat surprising, all the same, that this remarkably mature Early Renaissance interior could have been so successfully erected from a project drawn in perspective by a native Augsburger. Of Loscher little is known except that he was apprenticed in 1497 to the local carver Stromair and accepted as a master-sculptor in 1510. One would rather have expected the Fuggers to import a Venetian architect; or, if not a master actually born in Italy, they might well have called on the mysterious Gerolamo Tedesco, who seems to have been the designer of the Fontego. It was in 1508, the year before the chapel was begun, that Ulrich, who had for so long had ties with Venice, took extensive business premises in that just completed structure beside the Rialto and provided them with decoration of an exceptionally elaborate and up-to-date character. However skeptical one may be as to the ability of the German Loscher to provide, without Italian assistance, the design for the chapel, no stylistic evidence supports a hypothetical attribution to any specific Italian and very, very little, for that matter, to Meister Hieronymus, to give Gerolamo Tedesco here his contemporary German name.

The slight resemblance of the chapel to the Fontego results chiefly from the generically Venetian-1500 character of the two buildings, one of which has today no surviving interiors that are original and the other no architecturally developed exterior. All the same, the avoidance in both cases of columns may perhaps be considered significant, and even more the similarity of the balustrades in the Augsburg chapel to those on the balconies of the Fontego (Fig. 1, Pl. 3).

It is not so peculiar, however, that at the opening of the story of the German Renaissance a sculptor should appear as the earliest architectural designer in the new imported manner. A hundred years earlier Brunelleschi, at the beginning of the Renaissance in Florence, had been a sculptor before he became an architect. In collaboration with Masaccio, moreover, he had probably been the expert in the new science of perspective who provided for the fresco of the Trinity in Santa Maria Novella such an advanced architectural setting in paint as would not be created in three-dimensional reality for decades. Other Florentine sculptors and painters, most notably Donatello in his reliefs in the Chiesa del Santo at Padua, also represented at a very early date complete architectural compositions of a mature Renaissance character that were not equalled for some time in executed buildings. In Donatello's case and that of several later men Italian sculptors also contributed rather more than did quattrocento architects to the elaboration of a repertory of Early Renaissance architectural decoration. Often quite original rather than plausibly derived from the Antique, this decoration is not so unlike what Dürer provided on the Triumphal Arch print (Pl. 32) he began in 1515, a few years after the Fuggerkapelle was completed.

Sebastian Loscher's father Antoni was the Augsburger *Stadtbrunnenmeister* (master of fountains) in charge of the city's public water supply, a technician rather than an artist; his uncle Konrad was a highly esteemed master-carpenter employed by the Council. Thus already, while Sebastian was apprenticed to Stromair or perhaps after the latter's death in 1505, he may well have had some direct experience of practical building. As to his artistic formation, more significant than the training under Stromair was doubtless his connection with that leading contemporary painter in Augsburg, Hans Burgkmair. In 1510 he was living in Burgkmair's house; moreover, he continued to live with Hans's father Thomas over the years 1511-1514. That was an especially relevant period for the completion and furnishing of both the Fuggerkapelle and also the next Renaissance work carried out for Jakob Fugger in Augsburg immediately afterward.

That Burgkmair himself was the designer chosen by the Fuggers in 1509 for so architectural a project as their burial chapel is unlikely—it is relevant in this connection that not he but another Augsburg artist, Breu, was later employed by Jakob to paint the shutters of the organs in the chapel. Though Burgkmair was in these years introducing elements of Renaissance architectural decoration into his paintings, they offer no such complete architectural interiors as the elder Holbein's or Altdorfer's works until his 1518 woodcut of Maximilian and that of the "Weisskunig" artist's workshop.

On the other hand, even the church represented by Altdorfer as the *locus* of his Nativity of the Virgin, also of around 1520, resembles the Fuggerkapelle less than the chapel does, at least in its detailing, the

Fontego in Venice. All the same, Altdorfer's setting is more Venetian than Florentine or Roman in character, for it recalls somewhat the chancel and apse of San Zaccaria (Pl. 4). In any case, Altdorfer was a Regensburg artist, not an Augsburger, so that he is a less plausible candidate than Burgkmair. Furthermore, it is Burgkmair who seems, at least metaphorically, to hover in the wings as some sort of associate or even an influential adviser of Loscher, if not of Jakob Fugger. Burgkmair may even have been a relative of Sebastian Loscher, for Sebastian's son Hans was referred to in 1542 as "Loscher, genannt Burgmair."

Loscher's cooperation with the painter on a public commission in these years is recorded, a commission related to his father's official position in the city. In 1510 Sebastian carved the column of the Firch Fountain, for the design of which Burgkmair had received a first payment in 1508. In 1512-1515, after the Fuggerkapelle was physically complete, but while the remodelling of the Fuggerhäuser in the Weinmarkt where Jakob lived was proceeding, Loscher also executed three more marble fountains for the city authorities, one beside the church of Sts. Ulrich and Afra, another at the Weberhaus near St. Moritz and a third by St. Anna. A fourth fountain followed in 1516 which was actually in the Weinmarkt and right in front of the Fuggerhäuser. This replaced an already outdated Late Gothic fountain by Burkhard Engelberg (†1512) on which 300 florins had been spent as late as 1508,[15] the year the Firch fountain was commissioned. That replacement indicates how significant a change of taste there had been in Augsburg in the six years during which Jakob Fugger, probably employing Loscher as designer and possibly with Burgkmair's advice, was having his family chapel erected and his own residence remodelled. Although the chapel was not actually consecrated until 1518, the year the organ was installed, by which time most of the furnishings, except for Peter Vischer's grille, were in place, the first campaign of remodelling and rebuilding at the Fuggerhäuser had already been completed by 1515.

It would seem, then, that the drawing signed S.L. (Pl. 6)—if it is, indeed, a project and not a view of the chapel as completed by 1512 except for the fittings

---

[15] None of these fountains survives. The extant Augustusbrunnen, Merkurbrunnen, Herkulesbrunnen and Georgsbrunnen are all works of the late sixteenth century; only the Neptunbrunnen is earlier, c.1530, and that is not by Loscher: Breuer, *Augsburg*, pp. 97-98; Rauch, *Augsburger Baugeschichte*, pp. 81-86, with illustrations on unnumbered plates.

—should date like Dürer's drawings for the reliefs on the west wall from 1510 or, just possibly, from late 1509 shortly after the Pope's November bull. Later work by Loscher,[16] some of it in renewed or continuing association with Burgkmair as noted, cannot establish how accomplished he may have been at Renaissance design in the relevant years 1509 and 1510. The recumbent figure of St. Alexis, carved in wood at Schloss Erbach near Ulm in Württemberg and signed and dated "M(eister) B(astian?) Loscher, Bildthauer desses Bildwerk, A. 1513" actually recalls more the Late Gothic aspects of Burgkmair's style. Yet there is no Gothic architectural detail on this monument and the handsome inscription, indicating the Rehlingers of Augsburg as the donors, is in Roman capitals: DI. ALEXIO. ROM. SACR. ROECHLINGERI. PATRICII. AUGUSTANI. RESTITVERVNT. The lettering somewhat resembles, even though it does not equal in Classical authority, the inscription of 1510 perhaps by Hermann II Vischer on the bronze tomb-relief of Fryderyk Cardinal Jagellon in Kraków Cathedral.[17]

Then there is Loscher's tomb of Ambrosius Worsing, who died in 1513, in the parish church at Bolzano (Bozen). This suggests, both by its location in what is today the Italian Tyrol and in the Italianate character of its frame of panelled pilasters and correctly proportioned entablature, that by the time it was executed Loscher had already been in the south. A visit to Italy by Loscher might be fitted in, hypothetically, during the years the Fuggerkapelle was in construction but is perhaps less probable before it was designed and begun in 1509/1510. The considerably later Rosary Altar of 1521-1522,[18] in St. Rochus in Nürnberg, on which Loscher is believed to have collaborated again with Adolf Dauher, has similar elements. Compared to their work in the Fuggerkapelle, however, the design of this is less plausibly quattrocento Italian. The fussy elaboration of the Nürnberg altar recalls a little the one Ferrucci executed at Eszter-

gom in 1519 (Pl. 5) and perhaps reflects local taste of the period. Like the Worsing tomb-slab, it displays a somewhat special sort of assimilation and modulation of borrowed Italian elements—notably the fluted lunettes over the outer niches. This taste is even more evident a bit earlier in Dürer's Triumphal Arch print begun in 1515. Shortly after Dürer's print was completed in 1517 detail of this sort is not uncommonly encountered in executed works of architecture elsewhere in the north. The earliest surviving example is probably the sacristy doorway of that date (Pl. 19) in the cathedral of Breslau (Wrocław), well to the east of Augsburg, and Nürnberg in Silesia, which is now part of Poland.

The elaborate architectural framework of the high altar in St. Anna at Annaberg not so far away, in Saxony (Pl. 57), was executed in various colored marbles largely by the Dauhers, Adolf and his son Hans (c.1485-1538), without Loscher's assistance in 1519-1522.[19] This is far more advanced than the portal of the old sacristy there (Pl. 20) of the previous year, 1518, a feature in which Renaissance influence seems first to have appeared in Saxony. All the same, it is less "pure" in style than Adolf's earlier Pietà and its base at Augsburg in the Fuggerkapelle (Pl. 3). The columns, for example, that flank the principal relief of the Tree of Jesse are set diagonally, though beneath quite normal, even if compressed, ressauts. This solecism must be a Gothic survival here rather than an avant-garde novelty reflected from early Mannerist work in Italy: It is surely too early for that. There will be more to say about the altar at St. Anna below.

Jakob Fugger never lived in the house he and his brothers built in 1493 in the Augsburg Rindermarkt. Instead, he stayed on for a while in the one where he had been born "Am Judenberg" at what is Maximilianstrasse 21 today. When the construction of the chapel at St. Anna was well underway, however, he began to acquire the site for a new family "palazzo,"[20]

[16] G. von der Osten and H. Vey, *Painting and Sculpture in Germany and the Netherlands: 1500-1600*, Harmondsworth [1969] (henceforth cited as Osten-Vey, *Germany*), pp. 36-37, 256-258, have much to add about Loscher's work both early and late. In discussing, pp. 36-37, the Fugger chapel they note: "Many hands must have labored in this enormous work. Older Augsburg artists—Muscat, Erhard too perhaps—played their part," mentioning also Adolf Dauher and Leonard Magt. It remains probable, however, that Loscher and Dauher contributed most of the sculpture.

[17] Białostocki, *Eastern Europe*, ill. 16.

[18] Reclams *Bayern*, p. 639.

[19] [G. Dehio] Handbuch der Deutschen Kunstdenkmäler, *Die Bezirke Dresden, Karl-Marx-Stadt, Leipzig*, Berlin, 1965 (henceforth cited as Dehio, *Dresden*), pp. 13-14. K. Kratzsch, *Bergstädte des Erzgebirges*, Munich [1972] (henceforth cited as Kratzsch, *Bergstädte*), pp. 115-120, provides the most detailed account. See also the "Adolf Daucher" article in Thieme-Becker. References to Thieme-Becker, henceforth cited as ThB, are restricted to mention of some of the fuller of the relevant notices, chiefly those signed by respected authorities. There will be more concerning this altar below.

[20] As stated earlier in Note 6, the accounts of the Fugger commissions here lean so continuously on Lieb's research that

as de Beatis would later call it, by purchasing on January 21, 1511, for 3,573 florins paid in gold the house of his mother-in-law, Sibylla Arzt-Saulzer in the Weinmarkt (Fig. 2). There, indeed, he had actually been living most of the time since his marriage in 1498. Then, on September 26, he brought from Thomas Ehinger the neighboring house to the north for 2400 florins. These properties now carry the single number 36 in the Maximilianstrasse. In 1520 he added two contiguous plots to the west in the Pfaffengasse and, in 1523, he paid Georg Kunigsberger and his wife, Regina, the sister of Jakob's own wife, 13,000 florins for the house to the south, now numbered 38 and the present seat of the Fürst Fugger Bank. This house the Kunigsbergers had probably built after they acquired the site in 1507.

Though records are lacking, the presumption is that the transformation of the two houses, ex-Arzt and ex-Ehinger, at Maximilianstrasse 36 began in the autumn of 1511 or, perhaps more probably, the spring of 1512, thus about two years later than the burial chapel but before that was complete. The date 1515 was found by Julius Groeschel in the 1880s in the Damenhof that occupies the site of the former Ehinger house. In early October of that year, moreover, Jakob had obtained from the Emperor Maximilian the right, in return for a large loan, to import copper from Hungary. This was then brought by ship up the Danube to clad the roofs of his own house and those of his friends in place of the tiles previously used in Augsburg. Copper roofs were also installed on Schloss Wellenburg outside the city, just erected for Matthäus Cardinal Lang around 1513 at a cost of 3200 gulden, and on the new church of Heilig-Kreuz within, built 1502-1508 by the Engelbergs: Burkhard, city-architect of Augsburg from 1506 to his death in 1512, and his son Hans.[21]

It seems possible, though hardly supported by convincing internal evidence, that Loscher and perhaps even Burgkmair may have had a part in designing these new, or at least drastically remodelled, houses in the Weinmarkt at Augsburg. The assumption is also plausible that Jakob Zwitzel, a pupil and successor of Burkhard Engelberg, who may already have been employed on the Fuggerkapelle, carried out the work.

He was, perhaps, assisted by Thoman Krebs who was responsible for the Fuggerei, a housing project begun by Jakob Fugger a few years later. Another Augsburg master-builder whom Irmgard Büchner-Suchland would also associate with the Fuggerkapelle, a younger man, Hans Hieber (†1521),[22] is in her estimation even more likely to have been involved, but perhaps only as a mason and stonecarver.

Antonio de Beatis, on his visit to Augsburg in May, 1517, was as impressed by the "palazzo de li Fuccari" as by their burial chapel. For him it was one of the most beautiful houses in Germany, being decked with much marble-work within and having its facade along the Maximilianstrasse painted in gold and colors, with the high roof above all of copper. Many of the interiors, he said, were in German style, but several were "a la italiana bellissimi et assai bene intese."

The original external murals were touched up in 1761 and completely renewed in 1860-1863. In the 1944 destruction, the whole complex was much damaged. Restoration started the following year and is now as complete as it is ever likely to be. Colored decoration has been replaced only in the spandrels of the Damenhof arcade, with nothing but plain, near-monochrome, painted panels on the Weinmarkt facade.

The Weinmarkt, occupying a considerable part of the broad present-day Maximilianstrasse, was in the sixteenth century defined to the south by the free-standing Late Gothic Tanzhaus, or city ballroom, and later to the north by the Siegel Haus of 1605. That stood behind the site of Loscher's fountain, which had already been replaced around 1600 by the existing Herkulesbrunnen designed by Adriaen de Vries (c.1546-1626) and cast by Wolfgang II Neidhart (c.1575-1632). In front of the Fuggerhäuser—the reason for the plural designation should be evident from the account of Jakob's piecemeal acquisition of the property—the Weinmarkt was the actual scene of various great festivals in the relevant period of the Emperor Maximilian, who died in 1519, and of his grandson and successor Charles V.

The long front (Pl. 8) has—and already had, as regards Maximilianstrasse 36, after the completion of the remodelling in 1515—an exceptionally horizontal emphasis for a German facade of the early sixteenth century. Twelve rectangular windows in each of the upper storeys are arranged in regular lines; fourteen more continue across No. 38. Above, the roof, tiled

individual facts are not referenced to his text. Lieb, *Fugger* I, pp. 92-199, deals with the Fuggerhäuser in the Weinmarkt as has already been noted.

[21] W. Neu and F. Otten, *Landkreis Augsburg*, Munich [1970] (henceforth cited as Neu-Otten, *Landkreis Augsburg*), p. 317; Breuer, *Augsburg*, p. 29.

[22] Büchner-Suchland, *Hieber*, pp. 80-84.

today but then all of copper, is moderately high-pitched. It was broken only by tiny penthouse-roofed wooden dormers and a profusion of small square chimneys, now all confined to the ridge, but once less evenly spaced lower on the roof-slope. There were no cross-gables or dormers of masonry. And, as the external murals have not been renewed since the war, the extreme plainness of these facades appears more utilitarian than palatial. They are, in fact, less to be described as Italianate than merely "non-Gothic" or even "modern." The breaks between the ex-Ehinger, the ex-Arzt and the ex-Kunigsberger houses consist principally of a very slight shift of alignment between the ranges of windows. However, there are three extra top-storey windows on the ex-Ehinger house and the tip of the party wall can be seen rising above the roof between the other two houses.

More piquant were certain crowning features that no longer survive any more than does the original treatment of the ground storey. As can be seen in a woodcut of 1566 by Hans Tirol of the Weinmarkt (Pl. 7), as also in that of 1626 by Wolfgang Kilian, which offers a bird's-eye view of Augsburg in the early decades of the seventeenth century, the Fuggerhäuser had above the eaves several small turrets. On No. 36 these were square in the lowest stage, then round, and finally capped with the sort of rounded roofs then known as *welsche Hauben*—i.e., "Italian bonnets."[23] Similarly Maximilianstrasse 38 had two turrets, one at either end of the facade, rising in three stages, first square and then octagonal. The top stages of each of these latter had round-arched openings (or perhaps blind arches) and were capped as seen in the Tirol woodcut by short concave spires. At the base of each of the eight faces of the spires was a small semicircular lunette.

These lunettes over the facade of Maximilianstrasse 38 were presumably posterior to Jakob's purchase of the property in 1523, yet previous to his death two years later, though they might have been added even earlier by Kunigsberger. They must in any case have been very early—not impossibly the earliest—examples of a characteristic German Renaissance motif. That motif became very popular from the mid-twenties, as has already been mentioned. Such features, then called in the vernacular *welsche Gebel* (not *Giebel*)—i.e. Italian gables—would soon be em-

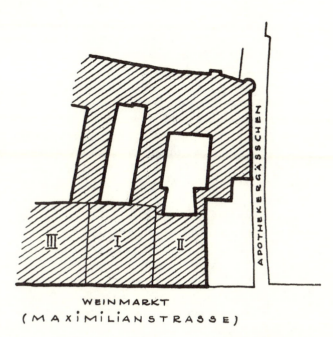

WEINMARKT
(MAXIMILIANSTRASSE)

Fig. 2. Plot plan of Fuggerhäuser site, Maximilian-strasse 36-38, Augsburg

ployed at considerably larger scale to terminate end-gables, cross-gables and large stone-faced dormers. Such were common in German secular architecture well into the following century, and even beyond.[24]

As has been noted, the Fuggerhäuser never had decorated gables or dormers. These features, moreover,

---

[23] Only two can be made out in the Tirol woodcut (Pl. 7), but three are clearly visible in the seventeenth-century print by Kilian.

[24] Unnerbäck, *Welsche Giebel* [Stockholm, 1971] (cited hereafter as Unnerbäck, *Giebel*) is the best general account of the motif but does not mention any examples in Augsburg, doubtless because none seem to survive there. In any case, those of the Fuggerhäuser were very small and on turrets, not on end-gables, cross-gables or stone dormers. Their date, moreover, is uncertain. Uncertain in date also, but probably of the early or mid-twenties, too, are the ones on the Dom at Halle (Pls. 45, 46) that Unnerbäck believes to be the earliest German examples. Jörg Unkair's on the Schloss at Schloss Neuhaus (Pl. 44) have nearly as good a claim to be the first: H. Kreft and J. Soenke, *Die Weserrenaissance*, 3d ed., Hameln, 1964 (henceforth cited as Kreft-Soenke, *Weserrenaissance*), pp. 276-278.

Unnerbäck not only covers many districts of Germany from Schleswig-Holstein in the north to Bavaria and Baden in the south, but also Poland and Bohemia as well as Denmark and Sweden. His maps (Unnerbäck, *Giebel*, pp. 78-79) indicate that the greatest concentration of such gables is in the central German regions of Westphalia, Anhalt-Saxony and Thuringia.

were not much used on houses elsewhere in Augsburg in the sixteenth century, to judge from Tirol's and Kilian's prints.[25] On the other hand, the gable of the north transept of Sts. Ulrich and Afra, rising high at the south end of the Maximilianstrasse, is elaborately decorated and very conspicuous. This must be the work either of Burkhard Engelberg, if before his death in 1512 or, if shortly after 1514, of Hans König, and thus in either case almost contemporary with the remodelling of the Fuggerhäuser. Whoever was responsible, the gable is still entirely Late Gothic in its gridded and traceried design.

Dome-like "bonnets," and even similar lunettes, of earlier date exist in Venice—for example, the slightly more hemispherical one on the campanile of Santa Maria del' Orto (Pl. 9). A similar combination, without the bulge, had also appeared, considerably before that and at much larger scale, over the choir of Santa Maria dei Miracoli as carried out by Pietro Lombardo and his sons in the 1480s.

In contrast to the hybrid turrets on the Fuggerhäuser, so different from the plain raised corner bays of the Fontego dei Todeschi (Pl. 1), were the balconies below the two northernmost top windows of 36 Maximilianstrasse. Like the turrets, these have not survived. Their balustrades of tiny Tuscan columns, however, seem to have been identical with those in the chapel at St. Anna (Pl. 3). Such balustrades, as restored in the *Damenhof* (ladies' court) behind this ex-Ehinger house, and those on the front corners of that house evidently closely resembled, both in their placing and in their design, the ones on the Fontego in Venice (Pls. 1, 7).

An engraving of 1634 by Jakob Custos gives some idea of the character of the original painted decoration on the two facades of Nos. 36 and 38. That offered, it would seem, another significant echo of the Fontego although these German frescoes will hardly have rivalled Giorgione's and Titian's in quality.[26] The quadratura architectural painting on the front of

the ex-Arzt house in the middle incorporated panels with figural compositions in each bay just under the window sills of the main storey. Then came rather larger figural panels the full width of two of the simply mullioned and transomed windows above and below them. Further such panels of smaller size, the width of one window only, appeared on the front of the ex-Ehinger house on the right. The painted pilasters between the windows in this section seem to have been somewhat less closely set than those on the left portion of the front of No. 36.

The Killian woodcut of 1626 is diagrammatically the most interesting because it shows the two courts behind the frontal blocks of No. 36 and also the contiguous properties in the Pfaffengasse that Jakob acquired in 1520. It provides, however, little detail. There is more, but of an even later date, to be seen in Custos's engraving of 1634 as was just indicated. The most attractive of the old views, the Tirol woodcut of 1566 (Pl. 7), shows the facades in too sharp perspective to be very satisfactory as a visual document. It offers, however, excellent evidence concerning the architectural setting the then existing buildings of the Weinmarkt provided for the Fuggerhäuser. It also indicated the way that generous open space was used for recurrent public festivals. Even so, none of the prints really illustrates for our delectation the original character of these facades. Now so dull, they were presumably once as brilliantly colored, as those of the Fontego in Venice. The frescoes of 1508 on that, moreover, must still have been fairly fairly fresh even in the damp air of Venice when the Fuggerhäuser were being decorated six or seven years later, so that the rivalry was surely intentional.

The surviving and restored courts and interiors of the Fuggerhäuser, although distinctly Italianate in a way the facade along the street is not, now that its murals are gone, are also relatively simple in their treatment. This is in sharp contrast to most of the ambitious secular work carried out in later stages of the German Renaissance over the next hundred years. In the ex-Ehinger house to the right (Fig. 3) the entrance is through a solid-walled passage. That leads to a rectangular hall opening on the Damenhof beyond. The hall is vaulted in six square compartments carried on half-columns along the walls, quarter-columns at the corners and two freestanding columns in the center (Fig. 4). This hall is readily accessible to-

[25] Gables were not unknown in Augsburg later. Some survive and others have been restored, but they seem rarely to have been much elaborated there, even around 1600.

[26] Frescoes of this period that have been dated c.1520 survive on the facade of the Weisser Adler, Hauptstrasse 14, in Stein-am-Rhein, which is in Switzerland not far from Schaffhausen: *Kunstdenkmäler in der Schweiz* [Munich, 1969] (henceforth cited as KDM, *Schweiz*), II, p. 388, pl. 79. These, the earliest of their sort that are extant, have been attributed to a local master, Thomas Schmid: Reclams Kunstführer *Schweiz und Liechtenstein*, Stuttgart [1966] (henceforth cited as Reclams *Schweiz*), pp. 686-687. Other external murals that

still exist in this district in Switzerland are much later, around 1600 or after: KDM, *Schweiz*, pls. 246, 278.

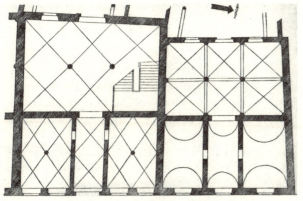

Fig. 3. Augsburg, Fuggerhäuser, Maximilianstrasse 36, 1512-15, Damenhof and Haldenhof, plan of front sections

Fig. 4. Augsburg, Fuggerhäuser, Maximilianstrasse 36, 1512-15, Damenhof, entrance hall

project for decorating the facade of the Haus zum Tanz at Basel. That may be as early as 1515 when he settled there and thus almost precisely contemporary.

Beyond the entrance hall the court of the Damenhof in the Fuggerhäuser, which runs from east to west, is rather irregular in shape as is more apparent in a drawn plan than in actuality (Fig. 5). Moreover,

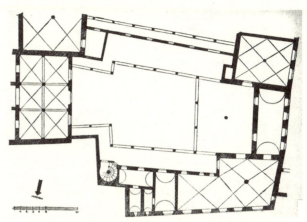

Fig. 5. Augsburg, Fuggerhäuser, Maximilianstrasse 36, 1512-15, Damenhof, plan of court

day, though the floor-space is much broken up and difficult to photograph because of the counters of the bookshop which is the present occupant.

The hall in the ex-Arzt house is somewhat larger but not as handsome, at least as restored. The bays in both of the surviving halls are round-arched and cross-vaulted. The broad transverse and longitudinal ribs in that of the Damenhof seem almost more Romanesque than Gothic or Renaissance in their plain design. Moreover, there are no subsidiary ribs such as contribute a hybrid character to the vaults of the chapel in St. Anna; indeed, there are not even any diagonal ribs at all in that of the Damenhof. The columns are all rather short and sturdy in their proportions. Above fluted collars they are topped with heavy volutes from which the ribs spring. These volutes also look more Romanesque—or even Byzantine—than Gothic or Renaissance (Pl. 10). They can be closely matched, however, in the younger Holbein's

the east end is narrowed in two bays of the arcade that extends all around to meet the facade of the hall. This arcade, the principal surviving feature, is carried on very simple near-Tuscan columns. These are of slimmer, and hence more Italianate, proportions than those in the hall (Pl. 11). The narrow terra cotta intradoses of the arches are barely molded and the sunken red marble disks on the pilaster strips, like the disks in the chapel, are quite unframed and unornamented. This is because the spandrels were decorated with painted motifs. Above, there is a single storey, with one rectangular window divided by a wooden mullion and a transom in each of the bays, four to a side. The court of the ex-Arzt house, called the Haldenhof, beyond the hall is rather longer and narrower since it extends in this case asymmetrically further to the west. The similar detailing of the arcade and of the walls above in this section of the Fuggerhäuser is less regularly disposed than in the Damenhof court.

Where some portions of the ex-Ehinger house rise higher at the east end of the Damenhof there are roof-terraces protected by the balustrades mentioned earlier. Julius Groeschel,[27] when making in the 1880s his

[27] J. Groeschel, "Die ersten Renaissancebauten in Deutschland," *Repertorium für Kunstwissenschaft*, XI, 1888, pp. 240-255.

paper restoration of the court in its original condition, supposed that these terraces and their balustrades had extended across the east end and along both sides, and thus they have been restored. From fragments that still survived in his day—and, one suspects, a good deal of guesswork—Groeschel also prepared perspective views of the court complete with its painted decoration. In these, garlands and wreaths flank and surround the marble disks in the spandrels of the arcade. So they do again since the latest restoration. Then, up to the sill-level of the windows of the upper storey, there came a broad figural frieze. That has not been renewed. Still according to Groeschel, the windows on the east, the north and the south had painted architraves and little cornices serving as imposts for the broad painted arches. Under these arches groups of half-length figures, as if seen above a continuous painted sill, further exaggerated the syncopation of the real and the painted openings.

If Groeschel's reconstruction is approximately correct, the unreality of the quadratura system must have been especially apparent at the eastern corners. There half-arches are shown as meeting at the external angles of the projecting elements of the plan and at the reëntrant angles as well. Since the real windows, not the painted arches between, were centered over the bays of the arcade below, painted pilasters occupied the reëntrant angles and were also introduced between the windows in the eastern wall. There they quite unexpectedly bisect the painted arches in what would seem already a Mannerist way unlikely in the north at this early date, or so it might be supposed. Above, a frieze painted in grisaille ran all around just below the terra cotta cornice.

On the western wall of the Damenhof, at least as restored in these drawings by Groeschel, the treatment over the arcade was quite different since the three windows there were much wider and segmental-arched. Shorter painted pilasters supported an architrave that, Groeschel believed, was bent upward most awkwardly around two large marble disks in order to connect with segmental pediments in the top zone. The top zone elsewhere in the court is occupied by the balustrade of the roof-terraces, but here this was true only over the middle bay.

The fantasy of the organization of the quadratura elements of the painted decoration in the Damenhof court, unless it be largely of Groeschel's imagining, suggests that there was little or no over-all control of the design of the painted decoration by an architectural designer. However such surviving elements as

are truly architectural—the Tuscan columns of marble, the thin terra cotta archivolts and the terra cotta cornice (Pl. 11)—must have been projected and executed by someone who was structurally, rather than decoratively, slanted. The frescoing would, presumably, have been carried out independently by another artist. This artist is not likely to have been Albrecht Altdorfer, as G. F. Wagner once suggested, nor yet the Augsburg painter Jakob Abt (†1518), to whom the monogram IA was thought by Max Friedländer to refer. Perhaps it was Hans Burgkmair, to whom the initials H. B. and H. B. P. (pinxit?), found by Groeschel,[28] might well apply. In the absence of any surviving elements there is little more hope as regards the Damenhof than for the Maximilianstrasse facade of arriving, without documents, at an attribution for the painted decoration based on style alone. The problem is likely to remain unresolved.

In the present context, however, the more important and so far equally insoluble question is: who was responsible for the original architectural design before the painter or painters set to work frescoing the upper walls? Here stylistic comparisons are possible. The first conclusion must be that the resemblances both to the Fontego in Venice and to the Fugger chapel in Augsburg are generic not specific. Granted the basically Venetian rather than Lombard, Tuscan or Roman inspiration, there is really no reason to assign responsibility either to Gerolamo Tedesco or to Sebastian Loscher, even if the latter was actually the "architect" of the burial chapel. Perhaps closest to that in character is the pair of marble door-frames under a broad segmental pediment in the principal storey of the Damenhof between the front room, with its string of six windows toward the Maximilianstrasse, and the rear room, with three windows only that all open on the east end of the court. The flat panelled architraves of red marble around these doors, decorated by inset disks of lighter colored marble, resemble the pilasters in the chapel rather closely despite their smaller dimensions. But the cornice above, and especially the pediment with its inclusion of large twisted shields, are of quite different, more cinquecento Italian, character.

The extensive use of marble and the relatively sophisticated quality of the detail in the Damenhof court might suggest that Italian marble-workers were employed. They would be at Landshut and at Neu-

[28] J. Groeschel, "Der Meister des Fuggerhofes in Augsburg," *Kunstchronik*, June 1891/1892, pp. 513-519.

burg-a.-d.-Donau, but only some twenty years later. Already by this early date, of course, they were active in Hungary and Poland, if not also in Bohemia. Were Italians on the job in Augsburg—a gratuitous assumption since their presence is totally undocumented—they would probably not have had sufficient authority to establish the general design. That Franciscus Florentinus seems to have done some years earlier at Kraków;[29] others would, even more comprehensively, at Landshut in the late 1530s. The marble used for the Augsburg commissions came not from Italy or Hungary but from the Tyrol, where the Fuggers had very considerable mining interests; that province is, of course, contiguous to northern Italy, and Italians and Italian-Swiss were often employed there in the building trades.

Clues as to the identity of the master or masters Jakob Fugger employed at Augsburg for architectural design in 1510-1515 have been sought by comparing specific features of the buildings he sponsored—especially the capitals of the columns and half-columns of the halls of the Fuggerhäuser—with other such work dating from the same second decade of the century and the early years of the next. During the years while the remodelling of the Fuggerhäuser in Augsburg was being planned and executed several church projects in which Renaissance elements make an appearance were also proceeding there and elsewhere. It was, for example, in 1513 that the construction by Hans Schweiner of the Oktagon crowning the west tower of St. Kilian in Heilbronn,[30] above a shank that had been begun just after 1507, got under way; this big and very conspicuous work was not finished until 1529.

Although the Augsburg chapel (Pl. 3) and the Heilbronn Oktagon (Pl. 16) include many, indeed a majority, of Italianate or at least post-mediaeval elements of architectural decoration, there is little specific resemblance between them. Moreover, Schweiner's personal style is not at all close to that of whatever designer or designers may have been responsible for the Damenhof and the Haldenhof. Discussion of this third significant structure, begun at the very opening of the Renaissance in Germany, may better be postponed for a while.

Some time around 1515 or a year or so earlier, con-

struction of the church of St. Martin at Lauingen,[31] on the Danube near Dillingen, started on plans provided by Stephan I Weyrer. He had earlier carried out the vaults of the St. Georgskirche at Nördlingen in Franconia in 1495-1505. St. Martin was completed, at least as regards the walls, by 1518 though not by Weyrer. At first sight it may seem, like St. Georg, to be merely a three-aisled Gothic hall-church of the sort long common in Germany. It is dominated, moreover, by a tall freestanding Romanesque tower that was retained on the south side. The plan does have a notable peculiarity, however. The east end is not flat internally like the west end of the Fugger chapel; three shallow apses, identical in design, are linked at the top on the outside by plain round arches, thus producing a rectangular effect (Pl. 12). This effect is quite different from the prismatic grouping of polygonal elements at the rear of Saxon churches of the period such as the Annenkirche at Annaberg[32] (Fig. 8), which was just reaching completion in 1519. At St. Martin there are only concave Vs in the rear wall and corners that are canted.

The squaring off need not be considered of Italian origin. This and other things do at least suggest, however, that the designer—whether or not Weyrer, if hardly the local Lauingen builder Michel who most probably carried out St. Martin—was not altogether unaware of the innovations introduced shortly before in the Fuggerkapelle. The star-vaults, executed after 1520, are still distinctly Late Gothic; but the rather broad longitudinal ribs of the nave arcades are round-arched, as are all the tall narrow windows except those in the apses (Pl. 13). As restored, the intradoses of these ribs—there are no continuous transverse ribs

[29] Białostocki, *Eastern Europe*, ills. 52-57.

[30] H. D. Bechstein, *Die Kilianskirche zu Heilbronn*, Heilbronn, 1965 (henceforth cited as Bechstein, *Kilianskirche*); H. Koepf, *Die heilbronner Kilianskirche und ihre Meister*, Heilbronn, 1961 (henceforth cited as Koepf, *Heilbronner*).

[31] Dehio, *Östliches Schwaben*, p. 84. Büchner-Suchland, *Hieber*, pp. 76-80, places the initiation of construction between the request to the Nördlingen city council for Weyrer's advice, dated January 8, 1513, and further correspondence in 1516-1517 indicating that Weyrer had by that time actually been on the job in Lauingen. She believes, all the same, that Hieber was really responsible for the design of the church. The vaulting dates from after 1520, but not necessarily after 1522 when Hieber died in Regensburg.

[32] St. Anna at Annaberg, begun in 1500 or shortly thereafter, was consecrated in 1519: Kratzsch, *Bergstädte*, pp. 82-86, 110-115, with bibliography, p. 149, n. 240. The duke of Saxony, Georg der Bärtige, with his brothers Heinrich and Friedrich had ordered on April 25, 1499, the replacement of the existing wooden church on the Schreckenberg, then renamed St. Annaberg, by a new edifice of stone. The builder-architect in charge of the construction was Konrad Pflüger, who was responsible for the Schlosskirche at Wittenberg, with Peter Ulrich and Jakob Heilmann as assistants or collaborators.

—are painted a sort of mottled pink to suggest colored marble as are also the shafts of the two easternmost pairs of slim cylindrical columns. These columns, however, have octagonal capitals consisting only of thin moldings of impost-like character. These are not unlike the ones in such a wholly Late Gothic interior of almost exactly the same date as the choir of St. Michael at Schwäbisch-Hall. The vaulting of that was begun in 1521 and completed only after 1525.[33] The moldings on the capitals there, however, are somewhat bolder than at Lauingen, and their sides are concave to give a prismatic look. However, unlike St. Michael's, the windows at Lauingen, both the pointed and the round-arched ones, all have slightly curving tracery at their heads of a sort that may already be considered Italianate; at least it is no longer Gothic.

In 1516-1517,[34] well before St. Martin at Lauingen was finished in the early 1520's, the church of the Dominican nunnery of St. Katherine in Augsburg (Pl. 14), where one of Jakob Fugger's sisters was a nun, was also being rebuilt in the new mode and much more consistently. This is a two-aisled hall-church with a narrower polygonal apse at one end and, originally, a raised nuns' choir at the other. The square bays of the vaulting have both longitudinal and transverse ribs as in the hall before the Damenhof (Fig. 4). These are plain in the western bays but have sunken intradoses, as in the longitudinal ribs of St. Martin, in those to the east. There is, however, no star-ribbing in between as at Lauingen (Pl. 13), only heavily molded diagonals to the east and none at all to the west. The round columns are very tall and slim like those in St. Martin, not short and sturdy like the ones in the halls of the Fuggerhäuser (Fig. 4). In detail, rosettes decorate the intradoses of the main ribs in the three bays to the east before the apse and also the intersections of the diagonal ribs. The columns throughout are capped with Corinthian capitals of unexpectedly correct design; yet above them the curious semi-Ionic volutes used in the hall at the Damenhof (Pl. 10) are inserted at the bases of the main ribs.

Restoration since the war has made evident the distinctly quattrocento character of several aspects of this interior despite its Germanic two-aisled plan. Unfortunately, however, the later cross-walls, which divide

the interior into nave, choir and apse, were not removed. Moreover, the rebuilt vaulting may have been simplified, if the testimony of contemporary prints is accepted as accurate. But the original quality could always be appreciated in two prints by Daniel Hopfer that present the interior of the church from the east and from the west. The apse that he shows is much more Italianate than what exists since the restoration —presumably based on surviving evidence—so that his view toward the east is not in this respect to be trusted. That toward the west seems to have been more accurately depicted (Pl. 15).

Here at St. Katherine the responsible designer *could* have been Loscher. Before discussing the possibility that it was rather Hans Hieber,[35] it is chronologically more sequential to say something first about a third major building commission of Jakob Fugger's begun in the years while St. Martin at Lauingen and St. Katherine in Augsburg were in construction, as the Heilbronn Oktagon was also, before describing Hieber's two projects. It may here be mentioned that Hieber's major recorded architectural designs—one for the Perlachturm at Augsburg and another for the church Zur schönen Maria at Regensburg, both of which are known in finely executed wooden models that survive (Pls. 23, 25)—date from 1519, though he is already recorded as a *geschworener Werkmann* in Augsburg in the years 1509-1511. By that year 1519 the project known as the Fuggerei was already at least under way.

In the twentieth century, and outside Germany, Jakob Fugger has been best known as a patron of architecture, not for the Early Renaissance elegance of the Fuggerkapelle and his own "palazzo" in the Maximilianstrasse, but for what can be described in modern terms as a "charitable low-cost housing development." That is the Fuggerei.[36] Here the emphasis need not be on the long-recognized social significance of this landmark in the history of such schemes but rather on its physical modernity (Pl. 18) Very notable are the regularity of the layout and the standardization of the houses, as also the provision of public open spaces and even of small individual gar-

[33] Dehio, *Baden-Württemberg*, pp. 438-439.
[34] Breuer, *Augsburg*, p. 54, plan on p. 55.

[35] Büchner-Suchland, *Hieber*, pp. 72-75, attributes the church to Hieber. The vaults, it is worth noting again, are earlier than those at Lauingen by some four years or more.
[36] Lieb, Fugger I, pp. 250-258; Breuer, *Augsburg*, pp. 68-70. There is a current account of the sixteenth-century context of the Fuggerei in M. N. Rosenfeld's text to S. Serlio, *On Domestic Architecture*, New York [1978], 43 ff.

den plots. Nor should the inclusion of a communal infirmary, not to speak of the modest church that was eventually added, be ignored, for most modern housing projects lack one or more of these communal assets.

The programme for the Fuggerei goes back, at least in conception, to the first decade of the century before the deaths of Georg and Ulrich. The execution began, however, only in 1514 when Jakob bought for 900 florins from Anna Streussin, the widow of Alderman Hieronymus Welser, a piece of property in the Jakobsvorstadt outside the Streffiner Gate of the city. On March 10, 1516, he further acquired from the butcher Hans Zoller contiguous property at a cost of 440 florins, and on June 6 obtained the formal approval of the city council. That included a helpful arrangement with the Rat providing for tax-abatement.

That year only two houses were completed; in 1517, however, seventeen houses were built and, by 1523, fifty-two had been added, all within that year. The builder was Thoman Krebs. He had been the master-mason for the Augsburg church of St. Moritz in 1513-1514 and may have assisted Zwitzel on the Fuggerhäuser before that in 1511 or 1512. Considering the vernacular simplicity of the architecture of the Fuggerei, Krebs was presumably also the designer. Yet the houses, if hardly at all affected by Italian Renaissance ideas, cannot be considered very Gothic either. The main entrance arch is segmental (Pl. 18), not pointed, and framed only by bevelled jambs and intradoses like the clerestorey windows of the Fuggerkapelle. The only ornamental carving is the Fugger arms flanking the dedicatory tablet above the gate on the Sparrenlech. But a well-head, crowned by an Italianate statue of Neptune, does occupy the center of the Jakobsplatz.

To turn from the Fuggerei, so much more "modern" than Renaissance, to Schweiner's Oktagon at Heilbronn (Pl. 16) exaggerates the contrast between German secular and religious design in the second decade of the sixteenth century. But the one is exceptionally plain in design, the other exceptionally rich. Heilbronn, which lies on the Neckar not far north of Stuttgart in present-day Baden-Württemberg, was not a center of international commerce and finance like Augsburg; however, it had and still has considerable importance for the regional wine trade and had long been a free city of the Empire. As was often the way in such secondary German towns—and also at Boston and Bristol in England or Abbéville and Vendôme in France, to name a few well-known instances outside Germany—St. Kilian,[37] the parish church, Protestant since the late 1520s, approaches in size and elaboration a cathedral. It is also very prominent like Boston's St. Botolph or Abbéville's St.-Wulfram, rising high in the center of the town across the marketplace from the Rathaus. Built originally in the thirteenth century, its most striking feature internally is the choir of 1426-1480. This eastern portion is capped by net or crisscross ribbed vaulting that has been excellently restored after the bomb damage of the last war. The aisles are also of the mid-fifteenth century.

Although the Heilbronn church already had two towers flanking the west end of the choir, in 1506 a great western tower was planned and begun a year or two later. Square in shape, this has a round and an octagonal stair-turret at the southwest and northwest corners, respectively. Great sunken central panels on each side are flanked by flat buttresses decorated with Late Gothic pinnacle-work. The sunken panels recede in four orders of right-angled and cylindrical members with big openings set one above another in the inner plane. Because of their lace-like curved pelmets inside the archivolts these arches have a transitional air that makes one think a little of Manoeline Portugal. Most notably, they are all half-round; but that shape need not, in the early sixteenth century, be considered Italianate as will later be discussed in relation to one of the portals of the Schloss at Schloss Neuhaus. Rather, by their grand scale, they seem here like a belated echo of the German Romanesque of the thirteenth century. The master-builder or someone associated with the work could well have seen examples of that in the Rhineland or elsewhere.[38] The square portion of the Heilbronn tower terminates in a flat platform. The platform is surrounded by a parapet with panels of pierced Late Gothic tracery, at least as last restored; the prewar balustrade of tiny pointed arches was doubtless the work of nineteenth-century restorers.

The master-builder of the Heilbronn tower, pre-

---

[37] Bechstein, *Kilianskirche*, pp. 23-24; Koepf, *Heilbronner*, pp. 28-33, figs. 1-9.

[38] Bechstein, *Kilianskirche*, pp. 25-34; Koepf, *Heilbronner*, pp. 33-35. In 1513 Schweiner visited Frankfurt, Mainz and other places. The trip may well have included Worms and Speyer, where he could have seen the great Romanesque churches that were the work, in his terms, of "den Alten" (the old ones).

sumably also responsible for the design, was Hans Schweiner (†1534), who came from the small nearby town of Weinsberg. He had become a citizen of Heilbronn as early as 1496 and had been employed on St. Kilian since 1507. After the shank of the tower was completed, he began to work on the crowning feature around 1512-1513. That rises in four octagonal stages to culminate in a statue of a *Landsknecht* (mercenary soldier) carrying a pike with a banner. On the northeast side, beside the tall bottom stage of the octagon, there is a freestanding spiral staircase of stone. This is an example of the sort of *Wendelstein* or *Wendeltreppe* that provides—more usually within walled towers than open as here—vertical circulation in Late Gothic structures. Such continued in use through most of the German Renaissance. One of the largest of the earlier ones, however, that built by Arnold of Westphalia in the 1470s on the court side of the Albrechtsburg at Meissen (Pl. 81), was also open, though not to the same degree.[39] Except for the obvious Late Gothic parentage of this element, which is also topped by a *Landsknecht* with a pike, there are few mediaeval details on any of the four stages of the tower, though the openwork character of the two upper levels does approach that of the Wendelstein.

But the detailing is not very plausibly Italianate either. Like that of the great arches below, it is so hybrid in character as to have a slightly exotic flavor. There are other lanterns of the period, or slightly earlier, that are not dissimilar. The originality, not to say the illiteracy, of Schweiner's ornamental treatment, for example, of this octagonal lantern is a sort of parallel to that of the octagonal crown of the north tower at St. Gatien (Pl. 17), the cathedral of Tours, as built by Bastien and Martin François, 1505-1507. No precise relationship, as of copy to original, is discernible in the details to those of that very early French Renaissance feature, nor was the more compact and solid organization of the French example emulated by Schweiner.

Another prototype sometimes proposed for the Heilbronn Oktagon is the lantern over the crossing of the Certosa di Pavia. That also rises in four octagonal stages and is more open than the tower of St. Gatien; but such a particular connection between an Italian and a German work seems no more likely at this period. The recurrent colonnades of the Cer-

tosa lantern, all carrying complete entablatures, certainly were not repeated by Schweiner. But there is a resemblance, so generic as to be meaningless, between the arched terminal stage at Pavia and the lowest stage at Heilbronn. Yet this stage of Schweiner's Oktagon rises high above the platform atop the tower on a buttressed podium in distinct contrast to the lowest stage at the Certosa, which rides the roofs of the church below. Moreover, the colonnettes that support the Heilbronn arches are not in the least canonical. Rather they are clumsy approximations of the sort of candelabra-motifs used earlier on the facade of the Certosa, begun in 1473, but not on the lantern. This is a common Lombard motif then being introduced in various parts of northern Europe; only very occasionally is it likely to have been specifically of Pavian origin.

Above these arches at Heilbronn the signs of the zodiac filling the spandrels, being carved in rather flat relief, may again seem a sort of echo of the Romanesque, like the great openings in the shank of the tower below. Over this stage a decorated quarter-round molding serves as a cornice, and that is crowned by a balustrade whose precise detailing is hard to read from below. Bold gargoyles project conspicuously at the eight corners, however, and within the arches tall narrow windows are cut through a second plane at the rear.

In the next stage of the lantern of St. Kilian, which is considerably shorter, the candelabra-colonnettes are abbreviated but doubled at the angles. The jambs of the windows between recede in three orders, an even more plastic treatment than in the stage below. These are square-headed and have additional signs of the zodiac carved above them. Then the cornice, the gargoyles and the balustrade of the stage below are repeated at slightly reduced scale.

As noted already, the next two stages of the Heilbronn Oktagon are as open as the attached Wendelstein. In them some, at least, of the detailing is more canonically Italianate. Slim square piers with capitals, for example, serve here as buttresses outside tiny radial arches, somewhat as on Brunelleschi's lantern atop the Florence Duomo of nearly a century before. The big round capital at the top, which is more Late Gothic than Renaissance, crowns a very short shaft and supports the terminal figure of the *Landsknecht*.

It is hard to believe that Schweiner knew the very early Renaissance work of the years 1510-1517 at Augsburg in Germany, or had actually seen Renaissance buildings in Italy or even France, much less in

---

[39] For a description of the most remarkable Renaissance example, that of Schloss Hartenfels at Torgau (Pl. 80), see below.

the east of Europe at Buda, Esztergom, Prague or Kraków. Of course, he might have heard reports of the Certosa di Pavia from prelates or fellow-craftsmen who had visited Italy; but the mixed character of his detail suggests rather a misunderstanding of graphic sources that he could well have known without travelling. The more or less Italianate prints of Dürer, Burgkmair, Hopfer and other Germans were being produced in some quantity by this time, and some of them were presumably accessible to him. Many such single woodcuts and book illustrations appeared during the years down to 1529 while the Heilbronn Oktagon was being carried to completion. The somewhat exotic look of Schweiner's detail, if not the faintly Romanesque flavour, is certainly approached—to mention a major graphic monument of the day—in Dürer's Triumphal Arch woodcut of 1515-1517 (Pl. 32). As regards contemporary three-dimensional work in the north of Europe it is closest to—but less Italianate than—the rich but clumsy sacristy portal of 1517[40] (Pl. 19) in the cathedral of Breslau (Wrocłav) in Silesia far to the east. It is not very similar, on the other hand, to the more elegant and original one of the sacristy in the Annaberg Annenkirche (Pl. 20). Dating from the following year 1518, that is the earliest Renaissance work in Saxony,[41] as has been noted, and is considerably nearer to Heilbronn.

Yet both these newly added features in Silesia and Saxony indicate how much less real was the grasp of the character of quattrocento Italian design that the executants—like their contemporary Schweiner—had than did those whom Rejt employed on his portals

and windows at Prague in the early decades of the century, or the ones who worked with Franciscus Florentinus at Kraków. This is not to speak—rather more relevantly here—of the artists whom Jakob Fugger had employed in Swabia in the years 1510-1515. Moreover, the Palais de Savoie, as extended a few years later at Mechelen (Pl. 41) in the southern Netherlands to the west and, in Austria to the southeast, the portal of the Salvatorkapelle in Vienna (Pl. 21) of the 1520s[42] and that inscribed with the date 1524[43] of the Zeughaus (Arsenal) in Wiener-Neustadt (Pl. 22) should also be mentioned: in their various ways these are all more advanced as northern reflections of the Italian quattrocento than anything of the period outside Augsburg in the central German lands.

Though precisely established by an inscription,[44] the dating of Schweiner's Oktagon at Heilbronn is disconcertingly extended in comparison to the relatively short periods within which the work at the Fuggerhäuser and St. Katherine in Augsburg, or even St. Martin at Lauingen, is confined by recorded evidence. Thus, although it is known that the Oktagon was begun in 1513, it is unlikely that the design was then determined as regards all its multifarious elements of detail.

The story should return now to Augsburg. It is uncertain, however, whether the Heilbronn Oktagon was effectively prior to, or in fact followed, two remarkable projects by the Augsburger Hans Hieber,[45] both of around 1519. One of these is for an independ-

[40] J. Z. Łozinski and A. Miłobedzki, *Guide to Architecture in Poland*, Warsaw, 1967 (henceforth cited as Łozinski-Miłobedzki, *Guide*), p. 268. This portal is not mentioned by Białostocki it might be noted.

[41] Kratzsch, *Bergstädte*, pp. 112-114, sees a model for the sacristy doorway at Annaberg of 1518 (Pl. 20) rather improbably in the south portal—dating several years too late, others believe—of the church of sv. Jiří on the Hrad in Prague (Białostocki, *Eastern Europe*, ill. 51a). However, Kratzsch assumes it was executed, not by some craftsman trained under Rejt in Prague, but by Saxons such as Christoph Walther or Franz Maidburg, both from Dresden, who were already working on the church. The resemblance is not close, for the Prague portal is in the more severe style of Rejt's maturity, even if not of his design. W. Hentschel, *Dresdner Bildhauer des 16. und 17. Jahrhunderts*, Weimar, 1966 (henceforth cited as Hentschel, *Dresdner Bildhauer*), p. 166, does not list the portal among Christoph Walther's works at Annaberg. Maidburg was responsible for the north portal of the Chemnitz Schlosskirche carried out in 1522-1525 (Pl. 50).

[42] *Kunstdenkmäler in Österreich, Wien* [Munich, 1968] (hereafter cited as KDÖ, *Wien*), p. 315.

[43] This portal in Wiener-Neustadt is of low and broad proportions that are quite un-Italian; but the execution of the arch, its spandrels and the flanking pilasters and crowning pediment (Pl. 22) almost suggest it was the work of a North Italian, if not a Lombard, as does the portal in Vienna (Pl. 21). It does not much resemble that, however, and must be by a different hand: P. von Baldass/R. Feuchtmüller /W. Mrazek, *Renaissance in Österreich* [Vienna, 1966] (henceforth cited as Baldass, *Österreich*), pl. 29; Dehio-Handbuch: Die Kunstdenkmäler Österreichs, *Niederösterreich*, 4th ed., Vienna [1962] (henceforth cited as Dehio, *Niederösterreich*), p. 384.

Wiener Neustadt is the Austrian town where the Emperor Maximilian was born and is buried.

[44] Bechstein, *Kilianskirche*, p. 34. It is of coincidental interest that the Reformation was reaching Heilbronn just as the Oktagon was being completed: *ibid.*, pp. 10, 36-41.

[45] The facts, but not the conclusions, concerning Hieber's work derive from Büchner-Suchland, *Hieber*, as recurrently cited below.

ent tower in Augsburg, the other for a whole church at Regensburg on the Danube, and they both survive as models in the City Museums of the two cities. Moreover, the actual construction of the Regensburg church, originally called Zur schönen Maria and later the Neupfarrkirche, for which one of these models was prepared was already underway in the next two years preceding Hieber's death early in 1522—well before the Heilbronn Oktagon was completed, that is, and possibly even before St. Martin at Lauingen received its vaults. These models are Hieber's earliest works. His first as an architectural designer to be recorded was the project commissioned by the city authorities of Augsburg for the Perlachturm in 1519.

The old Romanesque and Gothic Perlachturm rose at the west end of the church of St. Peter, yet this tower was a civic rather than an ecclesiastical structure. Considered still a prime symbol of Augsburg today, it stands beside the Rathaus halfway between the cathedral and the great Benedictine church of Sts. Ulrich and Afra, on the heights to the north and to the south, respectively. Whether or not Hieber was already responsible for the Lauingen church and for St. Katherine at Augsburg in the immediately preceding years, as Dr. Büchner-Suchland believes, when he was asked in 1519 to prepare a project for remodelling and heightening this landmark in the Augsburg *Stadtbild*,[46]—as Elias Holl would actually do a hundred years later—he had probably been working for the city in one capacity or another for a decade.

The model (Pl. 23) shows Hieber intended that the two lowest stages of the tower, long in existence, should remain plain and massive even though refaced, but with tall diagonal buttresses added to reinforce the corners. Except for a modest rose-window high on each side, string-courses at the top and bottom of the stage immediately above the base provide the only relief on the walls of the lower part of the tower. These were possibly to be cladded with stone, but more probably they would have been of surviving mediaeval brickwork only covered over with smooth stucco lined to suggest ashlar. Even the doorway that cuts through the high base of the model below is a simple round arch. But inside the bevelled circles of the roses Hieber proposed to insert simple tracery of smaller tangent circles.

Above the lower shank the tower was evidently to be built anew. The upper stages were to be faced with red and grey marbles such as were used in the Fug-

gerkapelle and the Fuggerhäuser—or, more likely, with stucco marbled in those colors. Cylindrical members rising from the tops of the corner buttresses then frame large rectangular panels on each of the sides. Within these panels there are single round arches that are without imposts or molded archivolts but have raised jambs and spandrels.

This storey on the model is of about the same height as each of those below and only slightly less massive. The next stage is both taller and more open. On this the cylindrical elements at the corners have become real engaged columns with Corinthianesque capitals, though both their bases and their topmost members, which are more like little cornices than proper abacuses, are circular not square. A large rectangular window with a raised frame occupies most of each face. The spaces beside and above these openings were to be filled with red marble. Raised disks of grey marble would be introduced at half their height, much as on the pilasters in the Fuggerkapelle (Pl. 3) and the door-frame in the Damenhof.

The treatment proposed within the frames of the openings in the upper storey of the Perlachturm is more Gothic. Much as in the lower stage of late fifteenth-century date on the southwest tower of the Cathedral of Regensburg—the other city where Hieber was employed at this point in his career—there would be on each face of the tower a grille of vertical mullions, these linked by pointed arches, in front of a large window. The windows, however, were to be round-arched and filled with curved tracery. As indicated, that is similar to the tracery at the top of the windows of the church then still in construction at Lauingen (Pls. 12, 13).

Above the small circles of "cornice" at the corners of the tower little open-arched edicules rise on very slim colonnettes above a continuous balustrade enclosing a flat roof. Between them a somewhat larger terminal feature of octagonal plan rises from the balustrated flat. That modest lantern has cylindrical members without capitals at each angle and plain round-arched openings between. The *welsche Hauben* which cap both the lantern and the corner edicules proposed by Hieber are of more interest. They doubtless had their remote models in the crowns of such Venetian campaniles as those of Santa Maria del' Orto (Pl. 9) and also at San Michele in Isola. The fact should be underlined that these domelets, designed by Hieber in 1519, are several years at least prior to the best-known early sixteenth-century examples that survive in Germany, those added in the mid-

[46] Büchner-Suchland, *Hieber*, pp. 65-76.

twenties atop the west towers of the Frauenkirche in Munich[47] (Pl. 24). The domelets that once crowned the turrets of Maximilianstrasse 36 were, of course, a good deal earlier. Hieber's domelets would have been modest in scale, even if executed, as were those on the Fuggerhäuser. Moreover, they were surely much less striking to contemporaries who could only see them on the model, not yet carried out at monumental scale as they shortly would be in Munich. Posterity is hardly cognizant of them at all, while the tower-tops of the Frauenkirche are an accepted symbol of Munich still.

If one compares the Perlachturm model with St. Martin at Lauingen (Pls. 12, 13) and St. Katherine in Augsburg (Pl. 14), it should be evident that the tower project is more advanced than the former, but less so than the latter. On the one hand, that comparison may support the attribution of St. Martin to Hieber, even though he is mentioned in no Lauingen document; on the other, it seems to make his responsibility for the designing of St. Katherine in 1516 very doubtful, much less the remodelling of the Fuggerhäuser earlier in the decade.[48]

The other and more important surviving wooden model (Pl. 25) of a project by Hieber is for the pilgrimage church *Zur schönen Maria*[49] (Mary the Beautiful) to be erected in Regensburg. The character of this design makes it still more doubtful that he had more than a stone-carver's part in the work carried out in Augsburg for Jakob Fugger between 1509 and 1518. The Regensburg project is as original as Schweiner's Oktogon and, like that, neither predominantly Late Gothic nor Early Renaissance. But Hieber's originality as made evident in this model, even more than in the one for the Perlachturm, is transitional, despite the date, in a way the Fuggerhäuser, much less the Fuggerkapelle, are not. In an effectively contemporary woodcut by Michael Ostendorffer, moreover, the project looks still less advanced than in the wooden model.

The church for which Hieber prepared the model was to be built on the site of Regensburg's synagogue. Under imperial and, from 1322, electoral protection, the Jews of Regensburg had prospered during the Middle Ages. In the fifteenth century, however, the city's business began to decline with the rise of Augsburg, Nürnberg and Vienna, for all three of these cities were more strategically placed along the main trade routes of the day. The Regensburg Jews came once more under imperial protection after 1503, the happy result for them of the local war that followed the death of the territorial ruler, the Wittelsbach Duke Georg known, like Jakob Fugger, as "der Reiche." But their difficulties soon increased in the new century. This resulted in good part from the anti-Semitic sermons of the priest Balthasar Hubmaier, who was brought to Regensburg in 1516 as *Domprediger* (cathedral-preacher). After the death of Maximilian in January 1519, during the brief hiatus in imperial rule before the coronation of Charles V as his successor the next year, the Christian merchants of Regensburg, who had earlier not been unfriendly towards the Jews, took advantage of the situation to throw them out and begin the demolition of the ghetto.

Almost before the Torah and other sacred objects could be removed workmen had already started to raze the synagogue when one of them, a master-mason named Jakob Kern from Nördlingen, fell from a loose beam, hit his head on a block of stone and was taken home to die. When he rapidly recovered, it was considered a miraculous favor of the Virgin. Specifically, it seemed to provide evidence of her approval of Hubmaier's proposal to raise a new chapel dedicated to the *schöne Maria* upon the cleared site. That would expurgate supposed calumnies recurrently uttered by the Jews in their former synagogue.

Not least, the miracle—as soon well publicized by Hubmaier—encouraged contributions toward the construction of the chapel as the goal of a *Wallfahrt*. This pilgrimage, the municipal authorities hoped, would draw great numbers of visitors to the city, much as the provision of facilities for holding conventions and sporting events does for modern cities. With the approval of the Wittelsbach Count Palatine Johannes, who was the diocesan *Administrator* (deputy bishop), the work went forward, many giving their services on the job in lieu of money. The first chapel, erected of wood from the plans of Jakob Kern, was consecrated on March 24, 1519. In front of this a stone statue of the Virgin, carved in 1516 by the master-

---

[47] N. Lieb, *München: Die Geschichte seiner Kunst*, Munich [1971] (henceforth cited as Lieb, *München*), p. 74. In 1522 a committee visited Augsburg and the members would almost certainly have seen Hieber's model for the Perlachturm. It was not long after their return that the decision was made in 1524/1525 to crown the Munich towers with dome-like features, i.e. *welsche Hauben*, rather than with pointed spires. These were carried out by the master-mason Wolf Ringkler and the master-carpenter Ramer.

[48] See Notes 22, 31 and 35, above.

[49] Büchner-Suchland, *Hieber*, especially pp. 15-27, 34-43, but her whole text is relevant in one way or another.

mason of the Cathedral, Erhard Heydenreich (†1524), was set up, and over the altar was placed a panel painting of the Madonna "as St. Luke had painted her": *einer Tafel der Schönen Marie nach der Pildnus als Sy. Lukas der Evangelist gemalt hatte.*

The new *Wallfahrt* to the chapel was an immediate success. The favors received by those who visited the shrine were widely proclaimed by their recipients and by Hubmaier to the great satisfaction of the Regensburgers. Already by Pentecost, 1519, the construction of a more permanent church of stone was being considered, and the Council of the city turned not to Heydenreich but to professionals from elsewhere for plans. Models were sought from Hans I Beheim (†1538), then a leading Nürnberg masterbuilder of whom something more will be heard later, with the assistance on this project of Hans Gamer of Marlbronn, and also from Hans Hieber of Augsburg. It was Hieber's design that was at once accepted by the Council. Since Easter the demolition of the houses in the ghetto had proceeded rapidly. There remained on the site, beside the new wooden chapel, only the house of the surveyor and the *Tanzhaus*, the city's ballroom. By early July, work began on the foundations, including a high podium built from the rubble of the destroyed synagogue. However, the absence of the *Administrator* Johannes in Vienna delayed the laying of the cornerstone until September 9.

There is good reason, therefore, to believe that some model prepared by Hieber—as, indeed, also another by Beheim—existed in 1519, and even from early in the year. But that was not necessarily the one which still exists. The surviving model of Hieber's project must at the latest have been ready by July if it was finally approved by the Council before work began on the foundations. Thus it might represent accurately what was originally accepted or it could, alternatively, be an elaborated later version. In either case the Regensburg model is the oldest surviving German one completely worked out in detail both as regards exterior and interior—that for the Perlachturm naturally has no interior. It seems unlikely, moreover, that the model was still incomplete when Hieber died early in 1522. Yet the still later date 1523, together with Hieber's mason's mark, is clearly visible painted on the east wall of the choir inside the model. Payments to Hieber and to various cabinet-makers that certainly refer to work on some model or models are recorded for 1519/1520. There is also evidence of a further sum which was paid on March 17, 1521, to a "Maister Michel"—who is surely Ostendorffer—for

paintwork on the model. Ostendorffer's woodcut and his payment indicate his familiarity with the surviving model. That must, therefore, have been very nearly complete within a year or two after 1519. It should also be noted that the payment to Hieber in 1519/1520 refers to "zwo Visierung" (two designs) which might well mean that the existing model was preceded by a simpler or less complete one accepted by the Council in the spring or summer of 1519.

The extant model (Pl. 25) for Zur schönen Maria is more a flattering "presentation" of the church as it would look when built than a guide for the masons and other craftsmen who would execute it. So, for that matter, are most twentieth-century architectural models. Today they are primarily intended to please the client and—as was very likely already true in this case—to encourage the contribution of funds. Today these are expected to come from individual donors and foundations; then, it was high ecclesiastics and the pious in general, both rich and poor, from whom financial help was expected.

The completeness of the model makes it a landmark in the development of architectural design in the North in these decades of the sixteenth century. That justifies considering it somewhat independently of the church actually begun by Hieber at this time.[50] The Neupfarrkirche, indeed, was finally finished in its present truncated form only with the construction of the western apse from plans made as late as 1859. Yet various original elements of the church do exist, for it was actually begun in 1519 and some of the fabric was executed either before Hieber's death early in 1522 or in the next few years under Valentin Stopfer. Stopfer, who came from Wessobrunn, had been Hieber's former *Palier* (principal assistant and supervisor of construction). Portions also remain that were carried out somewhat later, probably by others, down to the demolition of the wooden chapel and the consecration of its successor in 1540. There is, therefore, much in the surviving church to compare with Hieber's intentions as known from the model and the Ostendorffer woodcut. Two years after the church was finished on October 15, 1542, the Protestants took it over, and the devotion to the *schöne Maria* ended. However, it was not reopened for Lutheran use as the Neupfarrkirche until 1549.

The plan of the model for Zur schönen Maria is most unusual, not to say unique. The church was to stand—and indeed the executed one still stands—on a

[50] *Ibid.*, pp. 27-33.

high podium (Pls. 25, 28). This provides a narrow terrace all round. The terrace is reached by curved steps rising on either side of the polygonal apse and beside each of the transeptal towers. At the west, moreover, Hieber intended to provide a broader flight bent outward by canted sides and a central bow. This was to lead directly to the principal volume, a hexagonal nave. The nave was to be vaulted from a single central column like a mediaeval English chapter-house, with half-columns at the six angles (Fig. 6). For such a plan the prototype could well have

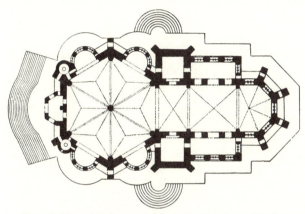

Fig. 6. Hans Hieber: model of Zur schönen Maria, Regensburg, 1519-21, plan

been the mediaeval nave of the Benedictine abbey-church at Ettal in southern Bavaria, though that has not six but twelve sides. There was also the generic tradition of circular churches dedicated to the Virgin.[51] Unlike Ettal, Hieber's nave was to have no aisles. Instead, the space was elaborated internally and the mass externally by semi-circular projections rising in two storeys on each of the two northern and the two southern faces. Recalling a little the lobes of San Vitale at Ravenna, these provide four *Emporen* (tribunes) protected by balustrades that are not unlike those in the Fuggerkapelle and on the Fugger-häuser. However, these balustrades are somewhat coarsened by the problem of reduction in scale that the turner or wood-carver faced who made these elements of the model. The lobes are crowned by half-domes, not by ribbed vaulting, and one has shell-like fluting painted on the inner surface. This decoration of the vault-surface was repeated in the model over

[51] My colleague Richard Krautheimer could provide no precise iconographic meaning for the exceptional hexagonal shape but pointed out the generic tradition.

the main apse at the east end of the choir but not in the Neupfarrkirche as executed. The existing vault there, dating from as late as the 1580s, is divided by ribs into three main compartments. These are flanked by very narrow severies that follow a domical curve at their western edge (Pl. 29).

Corresponding to the external lobes on the model of Zur schönen Maria, there is on the west face of the nave of the model (Pl. 25) a triangular porch. The east side opens through its entire height into the choir. The porch resembles a little the V-shaped mediaeval one on the west front of the Regensburg cathedral. In the model the porch rises two storeys to a hip-roof; below, it is open with free-standing supports in the form of columns. The proportions of the columns are not unclassical but they are capped with even more extravagantly voluted confections than those on the Perlachturm model. These remotely Corinthianesque capitals are quite unlike anything in earlier executed work at Augsburg; they recall rather the crude and illiterate detailing of the sacristy portal of 1517 at Breslau (Pl. 19).

The three sides of the upper storey of the porch, like the lower and upper storeys of the lobes, have broad but short round-arched windows with curving tracery in the heads. This is similar, as on Hieber's Perlachturm model, to that in the much taller and narrower windows at Lauingen (Pl. 13). Below the sills of the upper range of windows a blind balustrade, identical with those in the lobes inside, runs around the whole exterior. This is, however, set a little lower on the western face than at the sides.

The *welsche Hauben* crowning the lobes of the model, are slightly bulbous at the base like the ones on the Munich Frauenkirche (Pl. 24) of a few years later. In this case, however, they curve up reversed to a sharp point at the top rather like those on the turrets of Tudor mansions in England of the following decades that are called "types." These domelets are repeated over the smaller cylinders containing staircases near the northwest and southwest angles. In the woodcut, but not on the model, blind arches supported by engaged columns frame the upper windows of the lobes externally. Ostendorffer also indicated large foliate patterns on the roof, but that is probably artistic license.

Rather more than on Schweiner's Heilbronn Oktagon (Pl. 16) some aspects of Hieber's hexagonal nave must still be considered to be Gothic. Each of the five exposed faces of the nave in the model for Zur schönen Maria has, above the lobes and the porch, a large rose-window filled with tracery. That is thoroughly mediaeval, even to the extension of the molded members beyond their intersections in the manner often seen in the ribs of German Late Gothic vaulting[52] as well as in tracery. On the external angles, moreover, there are radial buttresses ornamented with Gothic pinnacle-work as well as more ambiguous column-like members. The spirit of the radial vault within is also Gothic, though the curvature of the heavily molded ribs is round not pointed (Pl. 26). The central column, as slim as those at Lauingen (Pl. 13), is set on a high cylindrical base and ringed by a heavy molding at the upper-storey level. That detail somewhat resembles the linking member halfway up the double-height columns of the top storey in the court of the Wawel Zamek in Kraków which may be of about the same date.[53]

The semi-columns in the Regensburg model are identical in design and, like the column in the center, they are crowned with very broad polygonal abacuses specially designed to carry the vaulting ribs. Thus the general form of the capitals is more Gothic than Renaissance, but High Gothic rather than Late. Yet, between the expanding molded collar at the top of each shaft in the model and its abacus Hieber inserted cushion-like elements derived from the sides of Ionic capitals. Such were used earlier over the piers in the halls of the Fuggerhäuser, it will be recalled (Pl. 10), and even—though they are much less conspicuous there—on top of the Corinthian capitals in St. Katherine (Pl. 14).

The rosettes indicated in paint on the intradoses of the arches of the lobes in the model of Zur schönen Maria also recall St. Katherine or even the Fuggerkapelle (Pls. 3, 14). The marble panelled pilasters of the latter, ornamented with disks, are also repeated in paint at the choir-arch in the model. These minor echoes of advanced Augsburg buildings of the previous ten years are not surprising in the project of an Augsburger active in the building trade there through

those years. Very likely, indeed, Hieber had worked in a subordinate capacity on several Augsburg jobs for the Fuggers, perhaps carving himself some of the capitals that are the prototypes of the ones in the wooden model.

Behind the hexagonal nave of the model at Regensburg rise two square towers, one on either side of the church. Up to the belfry stage these are nearly identical with the Perlachturm project for Augsburg (Pl. 23); above, all is Late Gothic. The rectangular overlay of pointed tracery outside round-arched openings recalls again the treatment of the west towers on the Regensburg cathedral. But here strange tracery-like elements with pointed arches, inverted above to make a parapet, wreath the top of the belfry stage. These provide a transitional element from the square shaft below to the octagon of the terminal lantern, something quite lacking in the more up-to-date design of the crown of the Perlachturm. A possible Venetian prototype for this would be the treatment of the top of the campanile of San Michele in Isola though Hieber is not likely to have known of it.

In the lanterns of the towers on the model of Zur schönen Maria the tiny windows are round-arched, not pointed. Moreover, the engaged colonnettes set between them at the angles are as approximately Italian as the larger ones that again bind—quite as on the Perlachturm—the corners of the belfry stage. Above the colonnettes on the lantern the tracery-like membering of the belfry stage is repeated at smaller scale. Thus the arches that the colonnettes at the angles of this stage carry are pointed above round-arched windows. This hybrid combination resembles that of the lower screen of Gothic tracery that is set in front of the round-arched openings both here and on the Perlachturm model. Finally, there is a *welsche Haube* like that proposed for the Perlachturm or, for that matter, like the one on the campanile of San Michele in Isola. The domical shape of this is interrupted, however, by a cylindrical member capped in its turn by a tiny *Zwiebel*, i.e. "onion." That at least is the metaphorical term used for later and more developed examples of such characteristic Bavarian tower-terminations. The much larger and more bonnet-like *welsche Hauben* on top of the towers of the Frauenkirche in Munich were added only some years later.

In this extremely hybrid project of Hieber's—hybrid to a degree unequalled in any of the Augsburg work with which he has been hypothetically associated—the most consistently Renaissance portion is

[52] An example of almost precisely this date would be the vault of the sacristy of the Annenkirche at Annaberg, completed in 1519, to which the Renaissance portal of 1518 gives access. See Note 32.

[53] Unless, of course, the exceptionally tall top storey in the court of the Wawel Zamek was planned by Franciscus Florentinus from the first, i.e. around 1507, or this upper gallery only added after the arcades below were completed some time in the mid-1530s (Białostocki, *Eastern Europe*, ills. 52-57). Most probably, however, it was introduced by Berrecci in the 1520s, though it is hard to guess what his Italian model might have been. See Note 12.

the choir as proposed in the model and as later executed. Both as planned and as built (Fig. 6) the choir consists of two square bays covered by round-arched cross-vaulting. The vaults rise high above what appear from the exterior to be side aisles. In the executed church, though not in the model, these are actually quasi-independent. Above the side elements the model indicates that Hieber intended an upper storey to provide tribunes corresponding to those in the lobes of the nave. This storey was never built. The lower storey as executed (Pl. 28) has on each side three round-arched and traceried windows identical in design with those proposed for the nave. Thus it follows closely the model and even more closely the woodcut. Just as projected, these windows are separated by panelled stone pilaster-strips, each with a central carved rosette, above podia that rise up to the sill-level.

Had the storey above been executed, it was to have been even more Italianate, for Hieber proposed to introduce engaged columns carrying blind arches above each of the windows. That sort of elaboration appears also, indeed, on the lobes of the nave in the woodcut, though not on the model. Still higher up in the side walls of the choir, Hieber intended to introduce, in the easternmost bay on each side, a large rose-window. This would have lined up with the ones at the same level in the nave. Like the latter, these were to be filled with tracery more Gothic than Italianate in character. The executed choir, however, only has pairs of arched windows at this level, windows slightly narrower and taller than the ones below and without tracery. Perhaps the rose windows were suggested by the shape of the arched openings of the Emporen that were proposed in the model but omitted in the eventual completion of the church.

Still taller, but set much lower in the wall, are the windows in the three sides of the apse (Pl. 28). Though the late vault inside is quite different from the fluted conch proposed in the model, as was previously noted, externally the apse is close to what was projected though not so tall. Hieber intended, as both the model and the woodcut indicate, an external gallery at the level of the internal tribunes, and he would have set his apse windows well above that line at the base of tall rectangular panels resembling those indicated on the Perlachturm model. The buttresses between, moreover, were executed merely with three plain setbacks; according to the model they were meant to be elaborated with the hybrid pinnacle-work such as tops those at the angles of the projected nave.

It might have been Hieber, but it was more probably Stopfer, who reduced considerably the dimensions and simplified the decoration of the church well before the choir and the apse were finally vaulted. The decision will presumably have been made by 1524 when the authorities began to sell off stone assembled for the completion of the church. It was only the following year, however, that the Regensburg Rat formally gave up their earlier intention of making Zur schönen Maria a great devotional shrine to profit the city by drawing hordes of pilgrims. After that, active construction seems definitely to have been halted.[54] The truncated church was then only very gradually brought more or less to its present state in the course of the 1530s. By the time of the consecration in 1540, for example, the great arch at the western end of the choir had been filled by a plain wall—the existing western apse was built in 1859-1860 from the plans of Ludwig Folz. The towers as first executed, moreover, did not at all resemble what Hieber had planned except for their location at the sides of the west end of the choir. The top stage of that on the north was rebuilt in 1594 after being damaged in a storm, and the south tower was completed to match it only in 1860 (Pl. 28).

Altogether it is surprising, considering its long and chequered history, that the exterior of the Neupfarr-kirche today, at least as seen from the northeast or southeast, does have a sort of consistency in its hybrid Early Renaissance design that is not unworthy of Hieber's intentions. Yet there is little on that exterior to link his work at Regensburg with the Fugger-kapelle (Pl. 3)—which, in effect lacks any exterior—or with the Fuggerhäuser, which have no comparable variety and complexity of external massing (Pl. 8). In the latter, moreover, there is a quite different kind of extensive rectangular fenestration, suitable to a secular structure, quite as the large arched windows at Lauingen and Regensburg are only appropriate for churches. On the other hand, resemblances in the detailing are readily discernible between Hieber's interior—or should one say interiors?—and the buildings of 1510-1517 at Augsburg with which, at the least, he must have been familiar whether or not he actually worked on them.

In the southern side chapel, now the sacristy (Pl. 27), of the Neupfarrkirche the vaulting is probably

[54] Hold-ups in the construction of early sixteenth-century churches were usually occasioned by a change in religion. Here the decision not to proceed preceded by more than fifteen years the local turn to Lutheranism.

as early as 1524 and the character of the detail could well have been determined by Hieber before his death in 1522. The vaulting of the north side chapel, like that of the main volume of the choir, though undertaken only in 1586, is very similar. All these vaults have diagonal ribs, of the sort that are also used in St. Katherine, though such ribs are not indicated in Hieber's model. Moreover, the executed capitals of the half-columns throughout are closer to those of 1516-1517 in St. Katherine (Pl. 14) than to the projected ones. For example, voluted cushions are again inserted below the bottom ends of the ribs just as in Augsburg rather than being crowned merely with a molded collar below and a spreading abacus above, as seen in the model for the order used in the nave (Pl. 26). However, the simpler molded collar used in the nave of the model, but without abacus, does recur in the middle storey of the arcade of the Regensburg structure, which will shortly be described. For that Hieber probably provided the design also in these years just before his death.

As in so much Italian quattrocento work, the Corinthianesque form of the capitals varies throughout the Neupfarrkirche. The capitals approach most closely the sort consistently used at St. Katherine, both in their design and in the quality of the workmanship, over the relatively short columnar elements in the sacristy (Pl. 27). The capital of the one tall engaged column that survives beyond the panelled southern pilaster of the choir arch is somewhat thinner and cruder than the others.. This is inside the western arm built in 1860, but surely not of so late a date. It may, rather, be the earliest of all. It could indicate that Hieber had actually begun the construction of the hexagonal nave, of which it would have occupied one angle, before his terminal illness in late 1521.

Incidentally, the pilasters in the Neupfarrkirche are all of plain stone like the columns, not encrusted with red marble as the model proposed. Moreover, carved rosettes in rondels, quite like those on the pilaster-strips between the lower side windows on the exterior, take the place on the pilasters inside the church of the grey marble disks used on the ones in the Fuggerkapelle and on the Damenhof doorway.

It is perhaps irrelevant to compare the spacial character of the choir and apse of the Neupfarrkirche with the interiors of either St. Katherine or Lauingen (Pls. 13, 14, 29). The *parti*, here effectively single-aisled, is necessarily quite different from that of either a three-aisled or a two-aisled hall-church. There is even less rapport between the proposed hexagon of the nave and the basically rectangular plans of these two earlier churches. The window shapes throughout are also shorter and broader than in either of the latter because of the two-storeyed elevation of the choir at Regensburg.

It is hard to believe that the same man, after designing and executing such an accomplished Early Renaissance church interior as that of St. Katherine, could have been responsible for the Late Gothic and hybrid features of the model for Zur schönen Maria and of the Neupfarrkirche as that was begun within his lifetime. The case for attributing existing work earlier than 1519 to Hieber is somewhat stronger, perhaps, as regards St. Martin at Lauingen—and even, just possibly, the Fuggerhäuser—despite the lack of documents and, at St. Martin, the recorded involvement of Weyrer. Hieber's place as a really important figure at the opening of the Renaissance in Germany is not open to question. He should be considered a characteristic protagonist of "transition after the event" because of the Late Gothic elements included in the two surviving models for which he was certainly responsible.

Other things in and near Regensburg dating from the years around and just after 1520, however, may be attributed not unplausibly to Hieber. The most important, though in sad condition today, and the one closest in style to Hieber's model for Zur schönen Maria is the three-storey loggia in the court of the *Bischofshof* (bishop's palace) that lies to the north side of the Regensburg cathedral. Though walled up today, three storeys of a loggia, each with a range of six arches, can still be made out. Originally these provided a more extensive succession of open galleries, one above another, than in either of the courts of the Fuggerhäuser where the arcading is only at ground-storey level (Pl. 11).

In Freising, north of Munich, however, in the court of the bishop's palace, Stephan Rottaler (†1533) had already built in 1519[55] a two-storeyed arcade (Pl. 30). That has broad archways of segmental shape on two sides cut through the lower wall, with somewhat narrower segmental arches above. The latter are carried on piers of red marble that are carved, in an even cruder and more misunderstood way than on the Heilbronn Oktagon, to resemble candlabra-columns.

[55] [G. Dehio] Handbuch der Deutschen Kunstdenkmäler, *Oberbayern*, 3rd ed., Munich, 1960 (henceforth cited as Dehio, *Oberbayern*), p. 74.

The prelate who commissioned the work, Philipp von der Pfalz, was bishop of Freising, then and for long afterward the metropolitan see of Upper Bavaria. It is surely relevant that the client for the Bischofshof, Johannes, the Regensburg *Administrator*, was Philipp's brother.

The detailing of the Bischofshof arcades supports an attribution to Hieber or his local workshop.[56] The capitals of the columns in the top storey have, as has been noted, voluted cushions above molded collars very like those Hieber proposed for the nave of Zur schönen Maria. In this quite different situation, however, they lack broad abacuses. The squarish proportion of the arches is identical with that of the blind arcades Hieber intended to introduce on the exterior of the tribunes that would flank the choir of Zur schönen Maria as proposed and also—at least according to Ostendorffer's woodcut—on the lobes of the nave. Moreover, they are thus more similar to the arches in the large court of Maximilianstrasse 38[57] in Augsburg than the latter are to the taller and narrower ones in Venetian courts of around 1500 that were, most probably, the prototypes for both. Of course, those arches in Augsburg might, just possibly, have been executed—and even by Hieber himself before his early death—for the Kunigsbergers several years before Jakob Fugger's purchase of the property in 1523.

A most conspicuous feature of the court of the Bischofshof that no longer survives must have been the *Erker* or oriel. Very likely this was the earliest Renaissance example of a feature, carried over from the Late Gothic, that long offered a favourite field in German secular architecture[58] for rich Italianate decoration. Scrolled consoles, their faces panelled and ornamented with rosettes, supported the three bays of the Bischofshof oriel. Just above the consoles, Corinthianesque capitals carried the ressauts of a complete, if miniscule, entablature. Then panelled pilaster-strips framed the carved arms of the diocese and of the *Administrator* Johannes. Between the windows, each with a plain bevelled mullion and a wooden

transom, were additional panelled pilasters. These had capitals like those below. Over them, a second entablature carried a bolder cornice at the edge of a modest hip-roof.

The Regensburg oriel is known today only from a drawing made before its removal in 1830 from the west wall of the Bischofshof. From the drawing it would appear to have been marble-encrusted, like certain mid-sixteenth-century windows that still survive on the south and west sides of the court, but with the heraldic elements brightly polychromed. The whole design, and most notably the carving of the capitals and of the putti that flank the shields, has a delicacy not equalled in the detailing of the Neupfarrkirche. This delicacy is confirmed, up to a point, as regards the execution, by a single surviving Corinthianesque pilaster-capital now set in the wall of the Bischofshof, just above one of the Tuscan columns of the ground-storey arcade on the north side of the court.

Since Johannes died in 1538, the inscription associated with the carved arms: JOAES DEO GRA. ADMINISTRA. ECCLESIAE RATISBONENSIS —ARMA EPISCOPATUS RATIS BONENSIS— COMES PATINUS RHENI DVX BAVARIAE, will have been no later than that. Were comparison of the oriel still possible with the relatively crude execution of the arcade—admittedly now in poor condition—it might be concluded the oriel was not designed and executed by Hieber or his immediate followers in the early 1520s, but rather in the next decade by someone who remains unknown. The issue must remain unsettled.

More surely of the early 1520s is work Johannes von der Pfalz undertook at the Schloss above Wörth,[59] on the Danube not far to the northeast of Regensburg. This he restored and enlarged as his favorite residence. The extremely picturesque pile that survives is mostly of earlier or later date, but the gatehouse has an inscription naming Johannes as the builder and giving the date MDXXV. The portal, flanked by two half-round towers with low-pitched roofs, is framed in a broad rectangular panel. The panel subsumes two arches, one without imposts on the left for horsemen and a narrower doorway for pedestrians on the right. Both are set in sunken rectangles. Similar round arches, but molded, and rectangular windows with molded frames also appear where two earlier portions of the Schloss were joined together, presumably at the same time. Actually the gatehouse must be

[56] Büchner-Suchland, *Hieber*, pp. 68-69.

[57] *Ibid.*, pl. 60.

[58] On the oriel of 1514, once on the rectory of St. Sebald in Nürnberg and since 1898 in the Germanisches Museum there, some minor Italianate touches in the general Late Gothic elaboration of detail are the earliest examples of Renaissance influence in a city where, otherwise, the new alien mode penetrated very belatedly in architecture: Reclams *Bayern*, p. 629.

[59] Büchner-Suchland, *Hieber*, pp. 70-72.

somewhat earlier than the inscription indicates since it can be seen in a watercolor of the Schloss dated 1524 by Albrecht Altdorfer that is now in Dresden.

Whether or not these modest bits and pieces at Wörth should be attributed to Hieber or to his workshop, the date of completion is evidently posterior to his death in 1522. However, work might have been started at the same time as in the Bischofshof court. Of what Hieber had done, according to documents, still earlier for the Trainer family[60] in Regensburg no trace survives.

For the remodelling in this period of the early Romanesque cloister of the Cathedral of Regensburg the responsibility lay with the master-mason of the cathedral, Erhard Heydenreich, who had carved the statue of the Virgin set up in front of the wooden chapel that preceded Hieber's church. That was not the case probably with the Bischofshof, where Johannes lived, much less at Wörth, where he was personally the client. The vaulting of the central passage of the cloister, already broadened in the mid-twelfth century, and of the passages surrounding the eastern and western halves had been carried out by a fifteenth-century predecessor a hundred years before. Heydenreich may, of course, have delegated the work to his younger brother Ulrich (?†1538). In association with Ulrich he was executing at about this time the fantastic vaults of the southern side chapels in the Ingolstadt Münster.[61] Whether the remarkable transitional windows in the central passage of the Regensburg cloister (Fig. 7, Pl. 31), with their jamb-statues of the Apostles, are of Erhard's or of Ulrich's design cannot be determined. However, the extreme ambiguity of their style seems to indicate that they can hardly have been projected or executed by Hieber and his followers. They almost certainly date, all the same, from the early to mid-1520s[62] when Hieber's atelier was active in Regensburg.

As on the tomb in Mainz of Archbishop Uriel von Gemmingen (Pl. 40) executed five or six years earlier or, for that matter, still at the top of Hieber's projected towers of 1519-1521 for Zur schönen Maria (Pl.

Fig. 7. ? Erhard or Ulrich Heydenreich: Regensburg, Dom, cloister windows, early 1520s

25), Late Gothic canopy-work is conspicuous above the jamb statues flanking the Regensburg cloister windows in contrast to the slightly Italianate colonnettes between. But the receding arches, in three orders like Schweiner's on the Heilbronn tower (Pl. 16), are round as at Heilbronn and the openings are also traceried in a rather Italianate way quite like the windows at Lauingen. The colonnettes, on the other hand, are almost as corrupt examples of the candelabrum type as Schweiner's at Heilbronn or even Rottaler's at Freising (Pl. 30). However, in the southern Netherlands at this point, the piers in the court

[60] *Ibid.*, p. 68.

[61] Reclams *Bayern*, p. 373; J. Białostocki, *Spätmittelalter und beginnende Neuzeit*, Berlin, 1972, pl. 378b.

[62] Reclams *Bayern*, p. 721; K. Zahn, *Der Dom zu Regensburg*, Augsburg [1929] has nothing to offer concerning the work in the cloister except pl. 66. The most satisfactory illustration of one of the windows is in Horst, *Die Architektur der deutschen Renaissance*, Berlin 1928 (henceforth cited as Horst, *Architektur*), fig. 16.

of the Palais des princes-évêques at Liège, as begun in 1526 for the local ruler, the Prince-Bishop Erik de la Marck,[63] are still more corrupt in their semi-Italianate design. Like some of Schweiner's detail, these elements in Regensburg have a pseudo-Romanesque flavor. Heavy rings interrupt their shafts, and the detailing can best be described as lumpy. In the other passages of this cloister the round-arched windows, also most probably of the early 1520s, are smaller. These are somewhat more conventionally framed by plain flat pilasters slightly canted toward the traceried openings.

Like Schweiner's Oktagon, the work of the 1520s in the cathedral complex at Regensburg is autochthonous in spirit, representing once again a "transition after the event." Even by the contemporary standards of Loscher, of Hieber or of Rejt, not to speak of the Italian Berrecci, the more elaborate Heydenreich windows in the central passage are considerably less literate in the way they reflect quattrocento design than even the clumsy anonymous portal of 1517 at Breslau (Pl. 19). The evident aspirations of the Regensburg designer, whichever Heydenreich he may have been, were certainly supported by much less informed familiarity with relevant sources than those of their more advanced northern contemporaries. Yet these window-frames offer a distinct foretaste of the bold scale and the free invention to which later German Renaissance builder-architects would eventually return after the mid-century. Then, however, the designers' foreign sources would be in the contemporary Netherlands rather than the earlier Italy of the quattrocento and opening cinquecento from which Germans derived their inspiration at first or second hand in the early decades of the century.

The infiltration of Italian details and forms into the architecture of Regensburg around 1520, though hardly comparable to what had already been long under way in Bohemia and Poland, not to speak of France or Hungary, could not be matched in Nürnberg, the chief commercial city other than Augsburg in this south German region. Her prosperity had not declined, like Regensburg's; yet the Nürnbergers, for all their prestige in the arts and crafts, were very slow to adapt Renaissance forms in architecture. The high reputation of their artistic products had been established in the previous century; a sort of cultural inertia, at least as regards architecture if hardly the other arts, then set in. The lag in Nürnberg is notable not only in comparison to the major trading centers of the day in the south, Augsburg and Regensburg, but to such a more northerly place in Saxony, far to the east on the Neisse, as Görlitz. In that small city, as the third chapter will describe in some detail, houses of Renaissance design began to be built in quantity from the mid-twenties. Even England has more to offer at Layer Marney and at Sutton Place[64] from these years than does Nürnberg, at least in work that has survived the centuries and the destruction of the last war.

The court arcades executed in stone in the Welserhaus at Theresienstrasse 7 in Nürnberg, begun in 1507 three years before the Fuggerkapelle and completed like that in 1512, surely did not owe their broad segmental shape to Italian influence. Two years later, however, the oriel added in 1514 on the north side of the rectory of St. Sebald, though almost totally Late Gothic in its design, included some minor details of Renaissance inspiration. But Nürnberg's executed buildings of this period never approach Dürer's consistently Venetian and truly architectural project of 1508 for the frame of the Adoration of the Trinity or that of this altarpiece as executed by others in 1511. The Nürnberger Dürer had, of course, already twice visited Italy, spending several years principally in Venice the second time, as most of his compatriots had not.

Though Dürer's Triumphal Arch woodcut, of 1515-1517, is not a realistic project for a structure to be erected in Nürnberg or elsewhere, it is the most considerable Renaissance architectural design produced in this decade by a Nürnberger (Pl. 32). The major artistic production actually carried out in Nürnberg in these years was the *Sebaldusgrab* (shrine of St. Sebald) in the like-named church that houses the remains of the chief local saint. Almost of architectural scale and wholly architectural in conception, this edicule is cast in bronze, not carved in alabaster or marble. It was begun in 1508, the same year Dürer designed the frame of the Adoration of the Trinity, and it was completed before 1519[65] when Hieber was pre-

---

[63] Baedekers Autoreiseführer, *Benelux*, 4th ed., Stuttgart, 1967-1968 (henceforth cited as Baedekers *Benelux*), p. 203. Liège was not part of the Habsburgs' Burgundian inheritance and the prince-bishop was an independent ruler. The point is that one would expect anything he commissioned at this point to be in advance of Swabia, as was distinctly not the case.

[64] The dates of Sutton Place cannot be established but are usually assumed to be between the mid-twenties and the late thirties, say c.1525-1535.

[65] G. Glück, *Die Kunst der Renaissance in Deutschland, den Niederlanden, Frankreich, etc.*, Berlin [1928] (henceforth

paring the models for the Perlachturm and Zur schönen Maria. Yet it is still Late Gothic in more than spirit, indeed a masterpiece of the last phase of mediaeval art. All the same, candelabrum elements and other Italianate details make an incidental appearance, especially at the base (Pl. 33). Moreover, the hybrid character of the openwork crown recalls a little Schweiner's Oktagon at Heilbronn (Pl. 16), which must have been almost exactly contemporary in so far as it can be at all precisely dated.

As noted earlier, the Sebaldusgrab is the work of the most famous of Nürnberg craftsmen, Peter I Vischer (c.1460-1529). He had been considered for the commission as early as 1488, when he inherited his father's bronze foundry a score of years before work actually started. Peter was assisted by his sons, Hermann II and Peter II (1487-1528), especially in the late stages, after a hiatus of two years in 1512-1514, just when Schweiner was beginning his Oktagon.

As regards architecture Hermann, born in 1486, is the most interesting. He travelled in Italy in 1515 and brought back with him the next year an album of drawings[66] of buildings he had seen there. These are remarkable in several ways. For example, various ancient Roman monuments are included, but also some of the current work of Bramante and Raphael. Such seem to have been appreciated only rarely by other northern artists who were in Italy in these years. In Hermann's drawings an almost professional competence in architectural delineation underlines the up-to-date choice of subjects. Considering that Hermann was trained as a metal-worker, not a mason or stone-carver, this competence may be explained by his experience as an engraver. Yet Hermann's interest in what he drew was, as would hardly have been expected, distinctly architectonic, not decorative or pictorial. That is very unusual in other illustrations of ancient and modern Roman architecture in drawings and prints by contemporary northern artists and already premonitory of Serlio's publications of a generation later.

With Hermann's drawings of Italian buildings are included, moreover, several projects in a Renaissance style of Albertian purity unmatched, even much later, in executed work of the German Renaissance. The one for the Sebaldusgrab (Pl. 34) is the most surprising since it is totally unrelated to the actual scheme on which he was assisting his father and brother. That for remodelling the Romanesque east end of St. Peter in Bamberg, on the other hand, is naturally somewhat hybrid. Indeed, it is not dissimilar in character to the church interior in Altdorfer's Birth of the Virgin. Other schemes for interior wall elevations were evidently inspired by various monuments of antiquity he had seen and drawn, yet they actually represent original, if quite hypothetical, projects of his own.

Had Hermann lived to build along these lines—he died in 1517—Nürnberg's architecture around 1520 would have been far in advance of Regensburg's or even Augsburg's. As it was, one of the few architectural reflections of his and Dürer's contacts with Italy at this point seems to have been the frieze of dolphins and festoons carved on the galleries in the court of the Heller'sches Haus at Winklerstrasse 1. That dated from 1516, the year of Hermann's return to Nürnberg, but is not likely to have been of his design. Two years after his death, however, there was more considerable evidence of Renaissance influence. In the house dated 1519 next to the fifteenth-century "Nassauer Haus" the supports of the wooden galleries in the courtyard had rather corrupt Composite capitals below friezes decorated with Italianate rosettes.[67] In 1519 also, the local artist Hans Springinklee, perhaps Dürer's closest associate, employed in the mural decorations he executed in the Kaisersaal of the Burg above the city various motifs taken from Dürer's Triumphal Arch print of 1515-1517.

The following year, however, the remodelling of the fourteenth-century Rathaus in Nürnberg by Hans I Beheim, later the losing competitor in the Regensburg competition of 1519, was still entirely Late Gothic in style. It is significant, moreover, that as late as 1521, two years after the Dauhers from Augsburg were called on to supply the high altar of St. Anna at Annaberg (Pl. 57), the Nürnbergers also imported Augsburg artists in order to obtain an up-to-date altar. (It will be recalled that the earliest example of

cited as Glück, *Renaissance in Deutschland*), p. 630, pls. 399-405; Osten-Vey, *Germany*, pp. 22-24.

[66] Glück, *Renaissance in Deutschland*, pp. 69, 70, 631; pls. 407-410. The Hermann Vischer drawings are now in the Louvre: Osten-Vey, *Germany*, p. 22.

[67] None of these Nürnberg houses survives. Such are illustrated, however, by Horst, *Architektur*, pp. 271-274; as also, and in much greater profusion, in collections of plates published in the 1880s and later that were intended primarily to serve as "crib-books." These often include new interiors and pieces of furniture of revived German Renaissance design as well as originals. Though the heliogravure plates are of high quality, the graphic illustrations reflect unflatteringly the bourgeois taste of the Bismarck epoch. Unfavorable comparison with the English "Pont Street Dutch" of the period, so similar in its choice of models, can hardly be avoided.

Renaissance design in Saxony is the sacristy portal of 1518 [Pl. 20].) This altar, located on the south side of the wholly Gothic Rochuskapelle Hans Beheim began in 1520 in the Rochus Friedhof, was probably designed by Loscher. He was more certainly responsible for the carved portions, while the painted wings are by Hans Burgkmair, with whom he had already collaborated in Augsburg. Structurally, however, the altar was the work of the local joiner Thomas Hebendanz.

The first Italian associated with building recorded as active in Nürnberg was not called there until 1538,[68] the year of Beheim's death. Antonio Fazuni from Sicily was a specialist in fortifications. Other Italians were already being employed in the north such as Donato di Buoni Pellizuoli, whom Charles V brought to the southern Netherlands in the 1540s, and Alessandro Pasqualini, who worked in the 1530s on the Breda Kasteel in Holland. Fazuni carried further, over the years to 1545, the construction of the series of great up-to-date defensive bastions around the city that had been started about 1520 doubtless by Beheim. Unlike Buoni Pellizuoli and Pasqualini, this Sicilian seems to have been responsible for no architecturally interesting gates or portals; at least none survive.

Finally, the Tucherhaus of as late as 1533-1544 might be mentioned even though, like the other houses noted above, it no longer survives. The Nürnberg merchant who was the client for this had spent much time in Lyons. It is not surprising that the design of the house reflected, even if faintly, the *style François I*er. That is an influence rarely evident elsewhere in early sixteenth-century German architecture. But compared to the Nürnberg Tucherhaus even such an almost precisely contemporary facade in the northern regional tradition of brick construction as that of the *Haus der Schiffergesellschaft* (shippers' company house) of 1535[69] in Lübeck (Pl. 35), with its consistent use of round-arched panels, segment-topped windows and decorative plastered oculi on a tall stepped gable, hardly appears more mediaeval.

Both fall chronologically beyond the limits of this chapter, yet neither is characteristic of the advanced German Renaissance architecture of the fourth decade of the century with which Chapter II will deal at some length. The stylistic stasis characteristic of Nürnberg architecture through most of the first half

of the sixteenth century is, however, more typical statistically of the German scene than the exceptional monuments to which the most attention has so far been given. That German scene, and also the broader North-European situation, in this earlier half of the sixteenth century, deserves some description at this point.

Despite the importance historically of the earliest instances of Renaissance architectural design in German lands that have already been discussed—both work actually executed and projects known from surviving evidence—their place in the contemporary scene was modest. That can be made clearer by some comment on the profusion of continuing construction in Germany which was still Gothic, or at least Late Gothic. Priority or tardiness in the contemporary importation of Italians and of Italian motifs and forms elsewhere in northern Europe from Poland to England also deserves mention since this is rarely correlated internationally.

In the period covered in this chapter the attention of architectural historians has long focussed on the High Renaissance in Rome and, in current studies, on what followed later in the century in Italy and in France. With the advanced Roman architecture of the first quarter of the sixteenth century German and other northern European work in this period rarely has as much in common as Hermann Vischer's projects (Pl. 34); by the 1530s, however, some northern production was more up-to-date by Italian standards.

Earlier, even in France the architecture of the opening decades of the century does not often show more than an incidental reflection of contemporary Roman work by Bramante, Raphael and San Gallo.[70] On the other hand, the influence of Italian Mannerism came early to France with the arrival of Il Rosso at the court of Francis I in 1530 and, for architecture, Sebastiano Serlio's arrival a decade later was still more consequential. High Renaissance design, rather than advanced Mannerist variations, did reach Bohemia and even Bavaria in the thirties all the same, as also the northern Netherlands.

By exception to the presumed secularism of Renaissance architecture most of the earliest German examples are chapels and churches, it will have been noted, or at least more or less independent items in such. After these, however, the Renaissance had little or no

---

[68] Reclams *Bayern*, p. 624.

[69] [G. Dehio] Handbuch der Deutschen Kunstdenkmäler, *Hamburg Schleswig-Holstein* [Munich] 1971 (hereafter cited as Dehio, *Hamburg*), pp. 388-389.

[70] For that matter, in no surviving work except possibly at Chambord, is there any reflection of the projects of Leonardo despite his presence at Amboise in France in the last years before his death in 1519.

effect on the architecture of German churches for several decades. Yet, as regards secular building in the opening decades of the century, the remodelling of the Fuggerhäuser in Augsburg was begun only after the Fuggers' chapel at St. Anna was structurally complete. Following upon the erection of a nunnery church sponsored by the Fuggers, St. Katherine in Augsburg, in 1517-1518 the next works in Germany emulating Italian models—the arcaded court of the bishop's palace at Freising of 1519 and that of the Regensburg Bischofshof of several years later—though secular, were commissioned by prelates. Some minor monuments of Renaissance design introduced very early in German churches—altars, tombs and pulpits, not to speak of portals—have already been mentioned; others, including several imported from the Netherlands, will be noted later.

The major religious event of the sixteenth century, nearly contemporaneous with the arrival of the Renaissance in Germany, was the beginning of the Reformation. Very soon the Reformation became also a political event, or series of interrelated events, in much of northern Europe. Religious reform, however, though initiated and for some time centered in Germany, was barely under way even there in the early 1520s; the major upheavals lay well ahead. As everyone knows, it was in 1517 that the Augustinian monk Martin Luther[71] nailed his ninety-five theses to the door of the new *Schlosskirche* (court church) at Wittenberg in Saxony. That had been begun for the Elector Friedrich der Weise of the Ernestine line of the Wettins by Konrad Pflüger in 1490, vaulted 1503-1506, and completed by 1509.[72] This Schlosskirche was also, from 1508, the church of the university Friedrich had founded in 1502. It was to Friedrich's new university Luther was called from Erfurt to be professor of theology. Because of its initial and continuing association with Luther, the interior of the Wittenberg Schlosskirche (Pl. 36) had an important influence on early Protestant church-design. Yet no

Lutheran services were held there until 1525, the year after the first such service took place in St. Anna in Augsburg. It was also at this point, relevantly, that the Catholic Elector Friedrich died and was succeeded by a Lutheran son, Johann der Beständige (the Steadfast).

Other things that eventually set the religious revolt into irreversible motion happened only in the third decade of the century: The treatises Luther had published three years after the original theses led directly to his excommunication by Pope Leo X in 1520; but the translation of the Bible into German, on which Luther started work in 1521, was of more ultimate importance. His marriage to a former nun in 1525, however, was no more than a significant incident, although of a sort that would once more become topical in our own day.

Yet hardly before the Diet of Speyer in 1529, if even then, can a separate and organized Lutheran "church" be said to have come into being. The secular power of the Lutheran princes, moreover, was first marshalled in the League of Schmalkalden only in 1531. Henceforth, for some twenty-five years until the Peace of Augsburg in 1555, there was religious and related political turmoil almost everywhere in Germany as well as economic decline in many German towns. Such conditions inhibited the initiation of large-scale church construction whether by Catholics or by Lutherans. There was none elsewhere in Europe either by or for Protestants except one edifice in Bohemia which is no longer extant. The other exception is a much larger Catholic edifice, Unsere liebe Frau, now the Marktkirche, in Halle-a.-d.-Saale (Pl. 37) not far from Wittenberg. That was begun as late as 1529[73] by Albrecht Cardinal Brandenburg. Albrecht, a Hohenzollern, was archbishop and elector of Mainz on the Rhine as well as bishop of Magdeburg in this region and a very early patron of the Renaissance in Germany. The Halle church, however, was not brought to completion until 1554-1555 after a long hiatus, for the city turned Protestant in 1541. More important for the beginnings of German Renaissance architecture was Albrecht's completion earlier in the twenties of the *Dom* (Cathedral) at Halle which he took over from the Dominicans.

Already, before the construction of the Halle Marktkirche was halted, the first Protestant church had been built in a region where memories of the mediaeval reformer Jan Hus still survived. The local ruler, more-

---

[71] R. Friedenthal, *Luther: His Life & Times*, New York [1970]. This English translation of a standard German work is currently the best available source. It seems unnecessary to provide specific references since the whole is, in varying degree, relevant to this chapter and the next.

[72] G. Piltz, *Kunstführer durch die D.D.R.*, 4th ed., Leipzig [1973] (henceforth cited as Piltz, *D.D.R.*), p. 252; [S. Harksen] *Die Schlosskirche zu Wittenberg* [Berlin, 1966] (henceforth cited as Harksen, *Wittenberg*), p. 4. Ironically, the church was particularly erected to house Friedrich der Weise's collection of religious relics, a devotion increasingly scorned and attacked by Luther.

[73] Piltz, *D.D.R.*, pp. 234-235.

over, the Catholic king of Bohemia, who was Charles V's brother Ferdinand, was fairly tolerant despite his Spanish upbringing. This church was at Joachimstal (Jachymóv), which is on the southern side of the Erzgebirge and today in Czechoslovakia. There a rich silver find had been made considerably earlier[74] and, in 1517, Count Schlik struck at Joachimstal the first silver dollar (Joachims-"Taler"). On June 1, 1534, a modest edifice, of which the plan will be described in a later chapter, was begun by Johannes Matthesius (1504-1565).[75] A follower and later a biographer of Luther, he had been since 1528 at the University of Wittenberg. Thence he was called by his friend Burkhard Weidlich to be the schoolmaster at Joachimstal; eventually, in 1545, he became the pastor also.

Following a few years after this church at Jachymóv was completed in 1540, the next ecclesiastical settings decorated or erected specifically for Protestant use were chapels incorporated in the Schlösser of two princes. Construction of the one at Neuburg on the Danube in the Upper Palatinate, well to the west and south, was started by the Count Palatine Ottheinrich in the late thirties for Catholic use, but it was only completed for the same client, who turned Lutheran in 1542, with the frescoing of the vault the next year. The other is on the Elbe in electoral Saxony, to the north and east, begun at Torgau in that year 1543 for the Elector Johann Friedrich, another of the Lutheran sons of Friedrich der Weise who succeeded Johann der Beständige, and consecrated by Luther himself the next. Description of these may also be postponed because of their relatively late date.

In recognizing the Renaissance in Germany as a pregnant new movement that began there in the first quarter of the sixteenth century, one must not forget that during those same years an extremely vigorous, even if terminal, florescence of mediaeval church-building continued. This is illustrated in more than a few examples of what is usually called *Sondergotik* ("Special" Gothic), examples that rival all but the grandest German churches of the fourteenth and fifteenth centuries.[76] St. Georg at Nördlingen in Fran-

conia, with characteristic star-ribbed vaulting by Weyrer of 1495-1505, has already been mentioned. Even more notable are certain churches in ducal Saxony, which was ruled not by Friedrich der Weise but by his cousin, belonging to the Albertine line of the Wettins. Among these, Pflüger's Annenkirche (Fig. 8, Pl. 38) at Annaberg is the most splendid; the Wolfgangskirche (Pl. 109) at Schneeberg is much less impressive, in part because of the damage done in the last war. Albrecht von Brandenburg's prominent

Fig. 8. Annaberg, St. Anna, begun 1499, cons. 1519, plan

Marktkirche at Halle, farther north, has already been illustrated (Pl. 37). Quite as imposing as the Annaberg church, moreover, are those at Pirna and at Zwickau,[77] both also in southern Saxony. Of almost equal scale was the extension and completion of such churches to the west and south of Saxony as the Stiftskirche at Altötting in the Upper Palatinate[78] and, in Swabia, Heilig-Kreuz at Schwäbisch-Gmünd and St. Michael at Schwäbisch-Hall,[79] as also the paired southern aisles of the *Münster* (Minster) at Ulm[80] on the Danube in Württemberg.

By 1512, the Fuggerkapelle was structurally com-

---

[74] Kratzsch, *Bergstädte*, pp. 38-43. He calls the town St. Joachimstal, but nineteenth-century guide-books omit the "St." Today it is known as Jachymóv as indicated in the text.

[75] [K. Siegl] *Die Joachimsthaler Chronik von 1516-17* [Berlin] 1923. Siegl's introduction provides a biography of Matthesius, who only became pastor at Joachimstal in 1545 well after the church was completed.

[76] Horst, *Architektur*, pp. 19-35, relates the churches mentioned here with the earlier phase of *Sondergotik*. K. Gerstenberg, *Deutsche Sondergotik*, Munich [1913] (henceforth cited

as Gerstenberg, *Sondergotik*) [1913]. E. Hempel, *Geschichte der deutschen Baukunst*, 2d ed., Munich [1956] (henceforth cited as Hempel, *Geschichte*) devotes twice as many pages, pp. 209-281, to the *Sondergotik* as to the Renaissance, pp. 282-320.

[77] Dehio, *Dresden*, pp. 324-326, 445-449.

[78] Reclams *Bayern*, pp. 29-31.

[79] Dehio, *Baden-Württemberg*, pp. 432-434, 438-439; Reclams Kunstführer II, *Baden-Württemberg Pfalz Saarland*, 3rd ed., Stuttgart [1960] (henceforth cited as Reclams *Baden-Württemberg*), pp. 493-494.

[80] Dehio, *Baden-Württemberg*, pp. 488-491; Reclams *Baden-Württemberg*, pp. 572-579.

plete and work on Schweiner's Oktagon that tops the tower of the Kilianskirche at Heilbronn was starting. Among the monuments listed above only the Altötting Stiftskirche, the least interesting of the group of new churches begun just before 1500, had been finished, actually the previous year. The latest campaign of construction at St. Nikolaus in Überlingen[81] on the Bodensee in present-day Baden-Württemberg, and also the completion by Beneš Rejt of sv. Barbóra at Kuttenberg (Kutná Hora) in Bohemia,[82] his culminating work as a major Late Gothic architect, began in both cases in that year. A little later is the church, dated 1518-27,[83] even further from the central German lands at Kötschach in Carinthia, with vaults still more idiosyncratic and "un-Gothic"—though hardly more Italianate—than Rejt's in their decorative ribbing executed in terra cotta. Elaborately ribbed vaulting of around 1520 resembling his more closely is also found in the churches at Königswiesen in Upper Austria and at Weistrach in Lower Austria,[84] both rather nearer to Bohemia.

In Saxony the building of the nave and aisles of the Nikolaikirche in Leipzig began in 1513 and of the nave of the Schlosskirche at Chemnitz (Karl-Marx-Stadt) in 1514.[85] To the south of Saxony, in Swabia, moreover, the modest two-aisled hall-church of the Dominicans in Augsburg, St. Magdalena, was erected in 1513-15,[86] the same years work was proceeding on the Fuggerhäuser. The church at Schneeberg was not started until 1515[87] and, as mentioned earlier, the Halle Marktkirche only in 1529.

More relevant here are the dates of completion of several of the new German churches under way ten years or so before the Fuggerkapelle. That at Annaberg, begun at the opening of the century, was consecrated in 1519, as noted already, though work continued into the mid-twenties.[88] Moreover, Renaissance

design had just made a rather tentative appearance in Saxony in the portal dated 1518 of the old sacristy there (Pl. 20). The Marienkirche in Zwickau, also in Saxony, begun in 1499, was not vaulted until 1535-1537. The work at both Schwäbisch-Gmünd and Schwäbisch-Hall, though initiated earlier than the Saxon churches—the one in 1491 and the other in 1494—was concluded in 1521, and at Leipzig and Chemnitz in 1526. The southern aisles of the Münster at Ulm, in effect a goodsized two-aisled hall-church, received their vaulting only in 1529. The Marienkirche at Pirna, an especially fine example of Saxon *Sondergotik* begun in 1502, did not reach completion until 1546, and sv. Barbóra at Kuttenberg only in 1548, long after Rejt's death, but before the Halle Marktkirche in 1555. At Überlingen, not one of the more interesting of these churches, the work dragged on until 1563; it would doubtless have come to a halt earlier had the town not remained Catholic. The exceptionally tall and elaborate high altar (Pl. 427), the most notable feature of this church, is much later.

Marienberg in Saxony, like nearby Annaberg and Schneeberg—not to speak of Joachimstal and Kuttenberg—is a silver-mining town, in this case founded as late as 1521,[89] which was laid out on a regular plan with a central square. The Lutheran Marienkirche there was not begun until 1558,[90] almost a quarter century after the earliest of all Protestant churches at Joachimstal across the mountains in Bohemia. First finished with a wooden ceiling in 1564, the Marienberg church was only vaulted late in the next century. It now has visually little or no sixteenth-century character despite the retention of the original plan and the exterior walls.

Electoral Saxony, of course, was the region in which Luther had started his campaign of reform and where he received his earliest and strongest support. Had any churches been built in Wittenberg or elsewhere in the second quarter of the century under the Electors Johann and Johann Friedrich, both Lutherans, after the death of the very tolerant and humanistic, but still Catholic, Friedrich der Weise in 1525, they would surely have been Lutheran. Actually no edifices specifically intended for Protestant worship were provided in Saxony, any more than elsewhere in Northern Europe, except for that at Joachimstal, before the 1540s.

[81] Dehio, *Baden-Württemberg*, pp. 483-484; Reclams *Baden-Württemberg*, pp. 564-567.

[82] Knox, *Bohemia*, p. 71; Z. Wirth, *Kuttenberg in Böhmen*, Prague, 1912, pls. 4-16; J. Białostocki, *Spätmittelalter*, pl. 428.

[83] Kunstdenkmäler in Österreich, *Kärnten Steiermark* [Munich, 1966] (henceforth cited as KDÖ, *Kärnten Steiermark*), p. 344.

[84] Dehio-Handbuch: Die Kunstdenkmäler Österreichs, *Oberösterreich*, 4th ed., Vienna [1956] (henceforth cited as Dehio, *Oberösterreich*), p. 135; Dehio, *Niederösterreich*, p. 375.

[85] Dehio, *Dresden,* pp. 182-185, 225-227.

[86] Breuer, *Augsburg*, pp. 56-58.

[87] Kratzsch, *Bergstädte*, pp. 86-88, 123.

[88] *Ibid.*, pp. 82-86, 110-113, 115-122.

[89] *Ibid.*, pp. 43-44, 67.

[90] *Ibid.*, pp. 91-92.

It may be recalled at this point that the building of Zur schönen Maria at Regensberg came to a halt in the mid-twenties. In the thirties, however, construction proceeded again at a very slow pace, still under Catholic auspices, though the projected hexagonal nave had by that time been abandoned. Consecrated in 1540, two years before the Lutherans took over and terminated devotion to the Virgin Mary, the church was finally completed only in the 1860s. At Augsburg construction of the choir of Sts. Ulrich and Afra, begun in 1500,[91] halted in 1526 though the church remained Catholic. The work was not even finished by 1560 and the vaulting was completed as late as 1603. The execution of the three tall altars (Pl. 428), the most conspicuous features of the interior, followed immediately after that.

The designing and the construction of the half-dozen initiatory works of the first quarter of the century at Augsburg, at Heilbronn, at Freising and at Regensburg as already described—despite their signal importance at the opening of the Renaissance in German lands—were thus exceptional and isolated events. They contrast sharply with a background of continued Late Gothic activity, extending through the 1520s and even several decades beyond, which was still remarkable both for its profusion and for its quality. Already by the third decade of the century, however, this activity was drawing to a close. The reasons were, as in England in this period, largely religio-political, though in Germany also economic; for the great prosperity so many German towns had enjoyed in the late fifteenth century was by this time declining.

The marked changes in European trade routes that the opening of the New World induced had their effect even in Germany. Mounting interference in the cities and towns from neighbouring princes—Protestant and Catholic alike—related to their struggles with each other and with the Emperor Charles V, also took its toll. Only in 1555 did the Diet of Augsburg bring a religious peace, one that would last until 1618. Earlier, the exploitation of the silver mines in the Erzgebirge in southern Saxony and western Bohemia explains the wealth of the new towns in those districts around 1500.[92] Schneeberg was founded in 1471; Annaberg was laid out in 1494; and, as has been noted, the first silver *Taler* (dollar) was struck in 1517 at Joachimstal; while Marienberg was

planned as late as 1521. Later in the century, however, the prosperity of these towns was peculiarly vulnerable to the influx of silver from beyond the Atlantic.[93] Moreover, the resultant inflation had its effect everywhere.

The mention of Charles V (1519-1556) brings into the picture Luther's major opponent in Germany. He is the other single personage whose importance in the second quarter of the century balances the reformer's historically, not only as regards Germany but the whole Western world. Even more than his Habsburg grandfather the Emperor Maximilian I, Charles[94] was an international figure. His father, Philip the Fair, was already ruler of the Netherlands as regent for Maximilian down to his early death in 1506. Charles, born at Gent in northern Flanders, was brought up by his aunt, Margaret of Austria,[95] at Mechelen in southern Brabant—like Flanders a province of Belgium since 1830—and much of his later life was spent in Spain, the country of his mother Joanna the Mad,[96] who was at least nominally the ruler of Castille. There he died in retirement a year after his abdication in 1555. In Spain his son Philip II became, after Charles's abdication, king of Aragon and eventually also of Castille, as well as ruler of the Netherlands. It was Philip's uncle Ferdinand, the favorite of his Aragonese grandfather for whom he was named, already since 1529 the elected King of Bohemia, who succeeded as emperor.

In his whole life Charles paid only nine visits to German lands and he never learned to speak German, preferring to use his native French or, later, Spanish. He had no direct effect on architectural development in Germany and little even indirectly. Though his palace at Granada in Spain is a major Renaissance work of the late 1520s which can be matched at that

[93] The bullion from the New World was largely handled for the Habsburgs by Augsburg bankers—not the Fuggers, but the Welsers.

[94] Habsburg, Otto von, *Charles V*, New York, 1929. E. Crankshaw, *The Habsburgs*, New York, 1971, pp. 57-77, is more objective, not being a descendant of the subject.

[95] Maximilian's daughter, Margaret of Austria—more properly known as Marguerite de Savoie—was made regent of the Netherlands after the death of her brother, Philip the Fair, in 1506. She had been the widow first of the heir to the Spanish thrones, Carlos, and then of Philibert the Fair, duke of Savoy.

[96] Juana la Loca, as she is known in Spanish, was a sister both of Margaret of Austria's husband Carlos and of Katherine of Aragon, Henry VIII's first wife.

[91] Breuer, *Augsburg*, pp. 42-44.
[92] Kratzsch, *Bergstädte*, pp. 12-54.

date only in Italy, what was built for him in the Netherlands in these decades was markedly retarda-taire.

More should be said, however, of the general situation, architectural and even political, in northern, western and eastern Europe in the early years of the century before Charles was elected emperor after the death of Maximilian in 1519, and most particularly as regards the Netherlands. Maximilian, emperor since 1493, was an art patron of some consequence though he was never rich enough to build much. He did, however, begin the Maison du roi (Broodhuis) in Brussels in 1514 or 1515,[97] employing Anthonis I Keldermans. Keldermans came from Mechelen and worked in the Brabantine Late Gothic vein, chiefly north of the Schelde in what are now the Dutch provinces of Zeeland and Noord-Brabant. This builder-architect was the father of Rombout II Keldermans, historically a more important figure. As regards Renaissance architecture, Maximilian was content to have Dürer provide him in 1515-1517[98] with the Triumphal Arch in the form of a vast woodcut, mentioned earlier, which consists of 192 blocks and is 11.5 by 9.75 feet when assembled! The profusion of ornamental detail on this arch (Pl. 32), mostly of generically Lombardo-Venetian character, was provided by Dürer, in a very personal style; but it is all but lost in a cumbersome framework organized by Jörg Kolderer (†1540)[99] of Innsbruck.

Characteristic of German Humanism is the dominance of the written word on this architectural elevation—for that is what the total woodcut of the arch amounts to. The result, however, is like an enormous billboard, many storeys high, covered with panels inscribed with political maxims chosen and arranged by the learned Johannes Statius. It is certainly not a plausible project for even so purely representative a work of architecture as a constructed triumphal arch. An arch of that sort a Holy Roman Emperor of the

Renaissance as expansive as Maximilian might well have aspired to erect. He had been extraordinarily effective in extending the territorial holdings of his family, though chiefly through his own and his children's marriages rather than by armed conquest.

Maximilian had first brought to the house of Habsburg the prosperous lands of his Burgundian wife Mary, the heiress of Charles the Bold, including Franche-Comté and even more notably the Netherlands, where his grandson Charles was actually born. Moreover, he had arranged for his son Philip, Charles's father, to wed Joanna, heiress to the two Spanish thrones of her parents, Ferdinand and Isabella. This followed after the death of Joanna's brother Carlos, to whom Maximilian had married his daughter Margaret. An earlier alliance with the French Dauphin, initiated when both were mere children, had fallen through. Thus the new Habsburg interests in the early sixteenth century reached southward from the Netherlands as far as Franche-Comté, in what is today eastern France, and more significantly, westward and southwestward to the North Sea, to the Mediterranean and even the Atlantic; indeed, for Charles, because of the Spanish colonization of the Americas in this period, beyond the Atlantic.

Above all, Antwerp was Maximilian's. Early in the sixteenth century that city on the lower Schelde had become the greatest port and the richest commercial and financial center of Europe. So it would remain through most of Charles's life, down at least to the Habsburg bankruptcy of 1547; upon recovery from that, Antwerp flourished once more, despite the burning of the city in 1576 by the Spanish troops, especially in the next eight years when it was free of foreign rule. Eventually, however, the closing of the Schelde by the Dutch led to the rise of Amsterdam to commercial primacy by the end of the century. Thus the Habsburg holdings were extended by Maximilian from their Austrian core far outside the central German lands and beyond the old borders of the Holy Roman Empire. As a result the dynasty's center of gravity moved to the west and south as first Charles and then his son Philip II became more Spanish than Austrian.

The situation was quite different to the east. Extension of Habsburg rule in that direction came only after Maximilian's death. It was in 1529 that his second son Ferdinand was elected King of Bohemia, as noted earlier, having already married Anna Jagellon, sister of the previous King Ludvik II. In Hungary, however, invasions followed by Turkish rule began

[97] As with the palace in Granada, this no longer extant royal residence in Brussels is not illustrated or discussed here. That will be true for much work outside the central German lands which is only mentioned in passing. If surviving, these things are for the most part well-known and illustrated in currently standard works such as the volumes of the Pelican History of Art on architecture in France and in England by Blunt and by Summerson, respectively, though less thoroughly by ter Kuile for the Low Countries north and south.

[98] Osten-Vey, *Germany*, p. 81. Much of the work was based on designs by others, particularly Wolf Traut (†1520), Hans Springinklee, Erhard Schön and Albrecht Altdorfer (†1538).

[99] *Ibid.*, pp. 121-122.

already in the second quarter of the century, long halting Habsburg expansion in that direction. It had been to the east—well before Charles's time and thanks mostly to Jagellon, not Habsburg, patronage—that Renaissance influence from Italy first reached northern Europe.[100]

The distant royal residences begun in the 1480s at Buda and at Visegrád in Hungary for King Mátyás Corvinus and, from 1502, at Kraków in Poland for the Jagellon prince who became king as Zygmunt I, not to speak of Beneš Rejt's Vladislav Hall on the Hrad at Prague in Bohemia, started as early as 1493 for Vladislav II and continued after 1500 for his son Ludvik, provided no models for the designers of the Fuggerkapelle and the Kilianskirche—if, indeed, Loscher and Schweiner knew of them or of the newly built burial chapel of Archbishop Bakócz in Hungary at Esztergom (Pl. 5).

What is of special interest here is that the designers of these things in Hungary and in Poland—though not, it would appear, in Bohemia, where Rejt's assistants probably came from Buda[101]—were Italians. That was rarely the case in the first quarter of the sixteenth century in Germany. Unless Jakob Fugger did, in fact, import an architect or architects from Venice whose names, and even whose presence in Augsburg, are undocumented, indeed, one could say "never." The character of the Fuggerkapelle and the Fuggerhäuser, whether or not the designer of either was Italian, certainly implies some knowledge of Venetian buildings of around 1500 rather than emulation of earlier or contemporary work in eastern Europe: Ulrich and Jakob Fugger had such knowledge, if not perhaps Loscher.

Though they should not be considered German, certain of the earliest Renaissance monuments in Hungary and in Bohemia—of which one has already

been illustrated (Pl. 5) for comparison with contemporary work in Swabia—should be at least briefly described. The Bakócz chapel in the cathedral of Esztergom had been begun in 1507 on a Greek-cross plan but in these years it was still in construction.[102] Though close in purpose to the Fuggerkapelle, the chapel is more Florentine than Venetian in character and of a quality unrivalled by the one in Augsburg. Moreover, Esztergom is about as far from Augsburg as Venice, with which such Augsburg magnates as the Fuggers had close commercial and financial connections.

The royal burial chapel (Pl. 39) that Zygmunt I commissioned beside the cathedral of Kraków postdates the chapel in Augsburg by nearly a decade. His architect Bartolomeo Berrecci (c.1480-1537), a Tuscan born at Val di Sieve near Lombroso and trained in Florence, was called to Poland by Zygmunt after the death in 1516 of Franciscus Florentinus—evidently a Florentine—whom Zygmunt had brought with him from Hungary. That was in 1517, the year before his marriage in 1518 to his Italian second wife Bona. A Sforza, she had been living in Bari, but was in touch at least with Milan and other cultural centers in Italy. Berrecci came to Wilna and prepared plans for the Kraków chapel the following year. The cornerstone was laid May 17, 1519, and it was completed in 1528, though not consecrated until 1533.[103]

The profuse arabesque ornament[104] on the pilaster shafts and elsewhere in Zygmunt's chapel was executed by another Tuscan, Giovanni Cini (†1565) from Siena. The Renaissance arcades, surrounding

[100] Already in the mid-fifteenth century almost a full repertory of quattrocento architectural forms and details had appeared in the miniatures of Jean Fouquet in France. Nothing followed from this, however, even in France before the French invasion of Italy in the 1490s. My colleague Charles Sterling reminded me of this curious fact.
As Jan Białostocki made clear in his Wrightsman Lectures (Note 2), by the eighties Italian craftsmen were working in Moscow and in Buda well before they were called to France: Białostocki, *Eastern Europe*, pp. 3-9, 13-15. The Hungarian King Mátyás Corvinus had an Italian wife, Beatrice di Aragona.
[101] Rejt's craftsmen were probably, indeed, actually Hungarians, though trained by the Italians who were working at Buda and elsewhere in Hungary in the eighties: Białostocki, *Eastern Europe*, ills. 91-97.

[102] See Note 13.
[103] See Note 12 and, more particularly, J. Z. Łozinski, *Grobowe kaplice kopułowe w Polsce 1520-1620* [Warsaw, 1973], pp. 25-44, pls. 1-4. As his title indicates, Łozinski deals also with many later chapels that follow the Kraków model.
[104] Such ornament had first been used in Kraków by Franciscus Florentinus on the frame of the niche, dated 1502-1505, in which the tomb of King Jan Olbracht is set in the cathedral on the Wawel: Białostocki, *Eastern Europe*, ill. 15. The red marble figure of the deceased in that, however, carved in 1501 probably by Stanislav Stosz or Jörg Huber, is still completely Gothic in character. The great sculptor Veit Stoss (Wit Stosz, †1533) after twenty years in Poland had returned to Nürnberg in 1496, but his workshop to which these men belonged still continued active in Kraków.
There are many other tombs of quattrocento character in the cathedral by the Italians Bartolomeo Berrecci, Giovanni Cini and Santi Gucci, not to speak of the more hybrid bronze slabs that form the tomb of Fryderyk Cardinal Jagellon which have been mentioned earlier: Łozinski-Miłobedzki, *Guide*, pp. 115-116; Lauterbach, *Krakau*, pp. 70-85; Białostocki, *Eastern Europe*, chap. IV.

three sides of the great court of the Wawel Zamek, front to the west what had been a section of Casimir IV's late fifteenth-century castle. The rebuilding of that was underway from designs by Franciscus in 1502-1507, even before Zygmunt's accession in 1507, to house Queen Elizabeth, the widow of Jan Olbracht the Polish ruler who died in 1502.[105] The much-extended arcading on three sides of the court, moreover, had presumably been at least projected in 1507 or a little later, but before Franciscus's death in 1516, though the arcades were not completed by others until the 1530s.

Though the artists Zygmunt and others employed in the early sixteenth century for important tombs in Kraków were mostly from Florence and Siena except for that of Cardinal Jagellon, the princely taste to which they catered may seem Lombard rather than Tuscan, not impossibly thanks to Bona's influence. In Florence, however, arabesque detailing of the sort used already at Kraków in 1502-1505 by Franciscus on the tomb of Jan Olbracht in the cathedral had long been common on quattrocento monuments, especially tombs, and appears in many paintings as well. Relative geographical propinquity to northern Italy and the French military incursions there, beginning with Charles VIII's in the 1490s, followed by an occupation of Milan of some duration and a shorter one of Genoa, explain why emulation of North Italian detail began earlier in France and was more common than in German and Slavic lands. Moreover, the importation of craftsmen from Milan and Genoa, as well as such a major Florentine artist with Milanese connections as Leonardo da Vinci, is documented through several decades at the opening of the century. In the Netherlands, however, the Italians who arrived in these decades came from Bologna, at least the two who were most productive in Holland as regards architecture: Pasqualini and Vincidor. Pasqualini's major work came later at Jülich in Germany, which lies to the north of Aachen. Other southern artists are recorded as visitors to Margaret of Austria's court at Mechelen, where Charles V was brought up, and unrecorded Italians were responsible for two Renaissance tombs of the 1530s in Onze lieve Vrouwenkerk at Breda[106] commissioned by Hendrick (III) of Nassau-Breda.

Considering the supposèd this-worldly character of Renaissance art, it is perhaps curious that tombs and burial chapels should in Germany and elsewhere in northern and eastern Europe in the early sixteenth century so frequently represent the first manifestations of Italian influence in architecture. But such were small in size compared to churches, castles or civic buildings, and their clients were individuals. Even when these individuals were high ecclesiastics like Cardinal Brandenburg in Germany, the Cardinaux d'Amboise in France or Archbishop Bakócz in Hungary, it was not the hierarchy as such but these princes of the church, *en rapport* with Rome and often familiar with Italy, whose cosmopolitan taste determined the advanced character of the commissions.[107]

Clients who were not prelates, moreover, were usually either secular princes or merchants like the Fugger, all men distinctly international in their activities and interests who had travelled widely in their youth.[108] A series of tombs, some hybrid, others more thoroughly Renaissance in design, were commissioned in Germany in the second decade of the century and by the mid-twenties there were examples in several widely separated districts. But Renaissance tombs had been begun well before that not only in Poland, as has been noted, but also in France under Louis XII and from the first years of Henry VIII's reign in England. There another cardinal, Wolsey, as well as the king was an early employer of imported Italians.

It is not inappropriate at least to recall here what was going on in France[109] at this point, since French work of the period is so much better known than such things as the Jan Olbracht tomb-niche in Poland. The tomb of François II of Brittany, whose daughter was married to Charles VIII after the latter's child-marriage to Margaret of Austria was annulled, was begun at Nantes in 1502, in the same year Franciscus Florentinus was designing the tomb-niche in Kraków with its arabesque decorations. The Nantes tomb is in part by Girolamo da Fiesole—very evidently not a Lombard but, like Franciscus, a Tuscan. He provided the quattrocento decorative elements in association with the French sculptor Michel Colombe (c.1430-

---

[105] Białostocki, *Eastern Europe*, ills. 52, 53, 55.

[106] *Grote Kerk at Breda* [Breda], n.d., pp. 7-11.

[107] Moreover, the commissioning of tomb-sculpture from foreigners of international repute was by no means uncommon in the later Middle Ages throughout Europe.

[108] For the travels of one prince, Ottheinrich von der Pfalz, see pp. 70-75. Other Germans who built actively often had acquired the wherewithal by military employment abroad.

[109] Illustrations of the sixteenth-century English and French works mentioned in this chapter can be most readily found in the current editions of the relevant volumes of the Pelican History of Art by John Summerson and by Anthony Blunt.

1512) who was responsible for the *gisants*, these last much more advanced in style than the one in Kraków which is, of course, earlier and not by Franciscus.

Much of what once existed at Cardinal Georges d'Amboise's demolished chateau de Gaillon as built 1501-1508—to judge from drawings and prints, if not from the various fragments surviving in the court of the Ecole des Beaux Arts in Paris—was somewhat retardataire compared to the west wing of the Wawel Zamek carried out in almost exactly the same years 1502-1507 by Franciscus Florentinus or the door and window-frames Beneš Rejt was designing at this time for the Vladislav Hall in Prague. All the same, it seems to have been the work of Guido Mazzoni[110] and other Italians. More plausibly quattrocento is another French tomb, that of the dukes of Orleans in the abbey church of St.-Denis, which was begun in 1502; but this is by a different Italian, Girolamo Viscardi, who probably came from Genoa, and his assistants. Still more advanced by international standards is that of Louis XII, also at St.-Denis. This Francis I commissioned in 1516, shortly after his succession in 1515, probably from Mazzoni, though it was not completed by Antoine and Jean Juste until 1531. The rich tomb of the two Cardinaux d'Amboise in Rouen cathedral, however, which was begun by the younger cardinal as late as 1520, is considerably more hybrid stylistically than either of the tombs at St.-Denis, not to speak of the one in Kraków. Doubtless that is because no Italian seems to have been involved.

In England the tombs at Westminster of the Lady Margaret Beaufort, mother of Henry VII, and that of Henry VII himself and his wife, were commissioned in 1511 and in 1512 though not completed, respectively, until 1513 and 1518. As intended by Henry VII, these provided the *raison d'être* for that late masterpiece of the English Perpendicular, Henry VII's chapel,[111] which was designed and built by English master-masons beginning in 1502. The tombs, however, were executed by a Renaissance sculptor from Florence, Pietro Torrigiani (*anglice*, "Petir Torryzany," 1472-1528) who is much better known than Viscardi if not Mazzoni. Torrigiani, who returned to Florence in 1519 and then, after another short visit to London, proceeded to Spain where he died, probably worked only on tombs and had nothing to do with large-scale architectural design. He was, early and briefly, also in Mechelen. Torrigiani's finest extant work in England is the Yonge tomb-niche of 1516 in the Museum of the Rolls in London. That hardly rivals in quality Franciscus Florentinus's tomb-niche in Kraków, completed ten years earlier, but it is all the same distinctly more advanced in style—cinquecento, one could say, rather than quattrocento. Of the work of other Italians employed in England in Henry VIII's time nothing is surely identifiable except the terra cotta rondels with heads of the Caesars by Giovanni da Majano on Wolsey's Hampton Court Palace; these must date from before 1525[112] when Wolsey ceded the palace to Henry.

The earliest individual tomb in Germany that reflects Renaissance ideas in its decoration—those of the Fugger in St. Anna being integral elements in the architecture—is generally recognized as that of Archbishop Uriel von Gemmingen (†1514) in the Dom at Mainz[113] (Pl. 40). Commissioned by one of his successors, Albrecht von Brandenburg, this is first of all a splendid work of sculpture, in this case by the established Mainz artist Hans Backoffen (c.1465-1519). Backoffen had earlier provided Gothic tombs in the Mainz Dom for Archbishop Berthold von Henneberg (†1504) and for his successor Jakob von Liebenstein (†1508), the predecessor of Uriel von Gemmingen.

The Gemmingen tomb is still transitional as regards its architectural enframement as was earlier noted, retaining Late Gothic canopy-work above supporting elements at the sides that are also quite Gothic except for their vaguely Corinthianesque capitals. Thus it is more premonitory of the windows (Fig. 7, Pl. 31) of some six or seven years later in the cloister of Regensburg Cathedral than related either to the Fuggerkapelle, where only the ribbing of the

---

[110] Guido Mazzoni had been too long in France for his Italian hand to be easily recognizable. He came originally from Modena, but Charles VIII met him in Naples in 1495 and brought him back to France. He worked later, from about 1508, for Cardinal d'Amboise on his chateau at Gaillon.

[111] The chapel at Westminster was Henry VIII's responsibility in execution of Henry VII's will after his accession in 1509. An earlier design for the royal tomb of less elaborate character had been obtained from Mazzoni.

King's College Chapel in Cambridge and St. George's Chapel at Windsor were both also completed by Henry VIII early in his reign. Another of his benefactions was the Renaissance screen of the thirties in the Cambridge chapel.

[112] It seems worthwhile listing here a few of the Italians active very early in Poland, in France and in England to underline the apparent absence of such foreigners in Germany in the opening decades of the sixteenth century.

[113] Reclams Kunstführer, III: *Rheinlande und Westfalen*, 2nd ed., Stuttgart, 1961 (hereafter cited as Reclams *Rheinlande und Westfalen*), pp. 419-420.

vault overhead can still be considered Late Gothic, or to Schweiner's rather consistently "non-Gothic"—if not very Italianate—Oktagon at Heilbronn. The tomb has, however, considerable sophistication and even elegance in contrast to the clumsy, still almost Romanesque, detailing of the windows at Regensburg with their ringed colonnettes. It is thus more comparable in quality to the Fuggerkapelle than to the Heilbronn Oktagon. Backoffen's slightly later tomb of Canon Peter Lutern (†1515) in the Stiftskirche at Oberwesel[114] is even less advanced, although after 1520 his pupils produced many tombs in the Mainz electorate that were quite Italianate. But these are all works of sculpture with little relevance to architectural design.

The canonical handling of the order that supports the canopy of the somewhat later tomb of Louis XII at St.-Denis—as a whole an exemplary work of cinquecento architecture whether thanks to Mazzoni or to the Justes—cannot be matched in German work of the second or third decade of the century any more than the earlier French examples. In Poland, however, the canopy erected over the Gothic tomb of King Władislaw Jagellon, though richer in its use of colored marble for the column shafts and the high-relief carving on the spandrels, rivals the tomb of Louis XII in the High Renaissance character of the column-supported canopy. The dates are 1519-1524 and the responsible artists Berrecci and Cini.[115]

On the other hand, so far as French church-work at fully architectural scale is concerned, there seems to be little extant—except for the crowns of the towers of St.-Gatien at Tours (Pl. 17), earlier than the chevet of St.-Pierre at Caen, which was begun in 1528—that can match Schweiner's Oktagon, much less Hieber's project for Zur schönen Maria. The earliest surviving secular work in France of consistently Renaissance design is the elder Cardinal Georges d'Amboise's gatehouse at Gaillon. That is dated 1508-1510, after the transitional main portions of the chateau were completed, yet well before Francis's accession to the throne in 1515. The hand of Mazzoni might perhaps be recognized there even in the regular organization of the facades as well as in the detailing.[116]

The story sketched in this initiatory chapter in terms of well-known monuments outside German lands has inevitably strayed far from the Habsburgs

and from the lands they controlled in order to cite some examples of Italian influence dating from the first two decades of the sixteenth century. The more familiar ones were in the realms of Charles's unsuccessful rivals in 1519 for the imperial crown, Francis I and Henry VIII, various others being in those of their contemporaries in Hungary, Bohemia and Poland. Since the Netherlands, south and north, were not only contiguous but under Habsburg rule, what was going on there around 1520 is more parallel to German work than to Henry VIII's activities across the North Sea and Francis I's along the Loire or, for that matter, the borrowings from Italy in Prague, in Kraków and in Esztergom to the east that remain still little known. However, the situation in the first quarter of the century in what are today Belgium and Holland, deserves some special comment here even though that provided the principal subject of another book of mine, lately published by the New York University Press as a College Art Association monograph, on *Netherlandish Scrolled Gables of the 16th and Early 17th Centuries*,[117] to which attention may appropriately be called at this point.

What may be considered despite its miniscule dimensions as the first Netherlandish example of consistent Renaissance architectural design is the *Epitaph*, dated 1518,[118] of Jakob von Croy (†1516), bishop of

[114] *Ibid.*, p. 517.
[115] Białostocki, *Eastern Europe*, ill. 145.
[116] See Note 110.

[117] New York, 1978 (henceforth cited as Hitchcock, *Scrolled Gables*). That book includes illustrations of the monuments extant in Holland and Belgium which are mentioned in this chapter. Such illustrations are generally less accessible elsewhere than the French and English ones in the volumes of the Pelican History of Art. They will not be referenced individually in these Notes, but illustrations of all of them may be found there.
[118] The Netherlandish authorship of the *Epitaph* of Jacques de Croy (Jakob von Croy) is not surprising since Croy, though a canon of Cologne, was a member of a Netherlandish family and bishop of Cambrai when he died in 1516: [G. Dehio] Handbuch der Deutschen Kunstdenkmäler, *Rheinland* [Munich] 1967 (hereafter cited as Dehio, *Rheinland*), p. 322. Osten-Vey, *Germany*, pp. 57, 58, suggest that the gilded bronze edicule was cast, very likely at Louvain (Leuven), by Hieronymus Veldener but from a design by someone else. The consistently Renaissance character of this small monument makes it one of the earliest Netherlandish examples of such design, for it is almost precisely contemporary with the extension of the Palais de Savoie in Mechelen (Note 110). After the Croy tomb, the screen in St. Maria-im-Kapitol in Cologne, commissioned in 1523 by the Hackeney family and executed in 1524 most probably by Jan van Roome (Jean de Bruxelle), seems to be the earliest example of Renaissance work imported from the Netherlands that survives in Germany: Dehio, *Rheinland*, pp. 358-359. Horst,

Cambrai, in the Treasure of the Cathedral of Cologne, of which he had been a canon. The work was executed not in Cologne but in Brabant, possibly indeed in Mechelen. The *Epitaph* takes the form of a sculptural relief set in an edicular frame, the whole executed in gilded bronze. Despite the architectural *parti*, the over-all arabesque decoration makes this a characteristic example of goldsmith's work, not a model for a full-scale edifice.

Already, however, a far more considerable structure at full architectural scale was under way at Mechelen in Brabant.[119] This is the northern portion of the Palais de Savoie as (Pl. 41) extended over the years following 1517 down probably to 1526 by Rombout Keldermans for Margaret of Austria whom her father the Emperor Maximilian had made viceroy of the Netherlands in 1507.[120] The new work is on the north side of the court of the earlier mansion that Rombout's father or his brother had built, beginning in 1507, just after Margaret's arrival in Mechelen. Despite the rather loose dating within these critical years in northern Europe—though a decade or more was not excessive for a building campaign in the sixteenth century—and uncertainty as to the responsibility for its Renaissance design, this is of special historical importance. It was here that the scrolled gable, later the most typical feature of the new post-mediaeval architecture not only in the Netherlands but in most of Germany and even Scandinavia, if not so much in England, made its first appearance.

That Keldermans was the executant builder-archi-

Architektur, p. 158, places the commissioning five years earlier, in 1517, and gives 1523 as the date of completion.

[119] Mechelen remains even today the seat of the primate of Belgium as arranged with Rome by Philip II in 1559 for Cardinal Granvella.

[120] As first built, beginning in 1507 shortly after Margaret's arrival in Mechelen, presumably by Anthonis I or Anthonis II Keldermans, Rombout's father and brother, the Mechelen city architects, the palace was a rather simple, though quite large, Late Gothic domestic structure of stone-trimmed brick surrounding three sides of a court. The much more interesting north and northwest wings of the palace were begun in 1517 and carried to completion within ten years, still for Margaret, who continued as Stadholder down to her death in 1530. But see Hitchcock, *Scrolled Gables*, pp. 23-28.

The contrast on the Palais de Savoie between the stepped gables of the earlier portions—the inherited mediaeval sort that would continue in general use in the Netherlands through the century and into the next—and the scrolled gables of the later wings emphasizes the innovative originality of the latter. For more detail concerning the Palais de Savoie, see Hitchcock, *Scrolled Gables*.

tect when construction began in 1517 is generally accepted, but nothing in his earlier or even his later work suggests he had any capacity for Renaissance design. Another man, Guyot de Beaugrant, seems to have had full artistic command here, with Keldermans serving only as "master of the work." It is evident, however, whence-ever Guyot may have come, that his immediate models were not Italian but French, notably the chateaux Francis I was then building along the Loire. The stone dormers, for example, have a distinctly *François Ier* look. With its flanking pilasters, concave-scrolled sides and pediment termination, the dormer on the exterior is, indeed, not dissimilar in design to the ones on the court side of Francis's new wing at Blois, built over the years 1515-1520, and even more to those on the late wing at Amboise, which must be of about the same date.

The boldest and, for later architecture in German lands and eventually in Denmark, the most premonitory elements here are the scrolls that enliven the silhouette of the larger gables against the sky. The S-curved ones flanking the second stage above the main line of the eaves actually seem anachronistic in their exuberance, if not the plainer ones on the next stage, just below the simple segmental pediment which crowns the whole. That pediment does not much resemble, however, the sort of lunettes on the German gables known as *welsche Gebel*. These would make their first significant appearance on the Dom at Halle a.-d.-Saale (Pls. 45, 46) and on the Schloss at Schloss Neuhaus near Paderborn (Pl. 44) in the early or midtwenties—that was, of course, when the Palais de Savoie was being brought to completion. To be noted also are the urns, and more especially the stone balls, punctuating the outline, much as on innumerable German gables from the mid-1520s to after 1600.

A good deal of attention has been given here to a monument that is not German and which may not have been reflected—though it was certainly often paralleled—in later German Renaissance architecture. That is true, at least, until well after the initiatory period 1500-1525 was past. Nor were the Mechelen gables influential in these early decades even in the Netherlands.

Though there was throughout Europe a notable increase in Italian influence between the mid-1520s, by which time the Palais de Savoie must have been complete, and the mid-1530s, this influence came largely from work of the quattrocento and very early cinquecento in Lombardy, Emilia and the Veneto, and hardly at all from the advanced monuments of the

High Renaissance in papal Rome. The earliest exception to this was Pedro Machuca's palace at Granada, begun for Charles V in 1526-1527; the most internationally significant artistic event of the thirties, however, is generally considered to have been the arrival in Fontainebleau of the Florentine Francesco Primaticcio (1504-1570) coming from Mantua, where he had worked in the Palazzo del Te. His arrival, however, and the initiation of the decorations in the Galerie François Ier there followed after that of Il Rosso at the opening of the decade.

All the same, the architecture and decoration of this period—Francis I's reign, 1515-1547—in France has long been better and more widely known than that in the northern countries. It should therefore help to round out the picture of the architectural scene throughout Europe in the first half of the sixteenth century further to recall certain, at least, of the more famous events associated with the introduction of Renaissance architecture outside Italy, that followed the very earliest examples of work by Italians or under Italian influence in the first two decades of the century contemporary with the German monuments described earlier in this chapter. Without question, moreover, a national Renaissance style was firmly established in France at an early date, more firmly than in contemporary England, Germany or in the Netherlands, much less Scandinavia, though it seems to have had very little influence in Germany. In this local development both builders and craftsmen, French master-masons and Italian stone carvers, participated jointly, and even to some extent indistinguishably, to a far greater degree than in the Netherlands or in the central German lands.[121]

In 1519, some four years after the wings at Blois and Amboise, Francis I's wholly new chateau at Chambord was begun, just when Nottaler was executing the Freising arcades and Hieber designing his projects for Augsburg and Regensburg. For this, preparatory drawings by an Italian (probably Domenico Bernabei da Cortona, called Le Boccador, a pupil of Giuliano da San Gallo) survive; equally notable, however, are the drastic modifications made there later. Because of these changes, the work is exemplary of an even more autochthonous sort of *style François Ier* than Blois or Amboise, especially as regards the

very elaborate dormers. There is no persuasive evidence, however, that the Loire chateaux had early imitators in Germany—except, rather doubtfully, Conrad Krebs at Torgau. This question concerning his great outside staircase on Schloss Hartenfels there will be discussed in the next chapter.

In French church architecture, activity that was essentially Late Gothic—that is, Flamboyant—continued into the third decade of the century and even beyond, quite as did the late *Sondergotik* in Germany. There is little as notable in the way of Early Renaissance or hybrid design as the French king's chateaux before the erection of the chevet of St.-Pierre of Caen which began in 1528. The chief exception would be the already mentioned tops on the towers of the cathedral of Tours (Pl. 17), the earlier one of 1505-1507 preceding and even rivaling the Heilbronn Oktagon. At Caen the master-builder Hector Sohier carried on, well into the thirties, hybrid work that is more comparable, as is also the tower at Tours, to Schweiner's Oktagon, completed in 1529, than to Hieber's projects of ten years before. Sohier's east end of St.-Pierre is profusely decorated externally with quattrocento arabesques despite a Gothic plan and Gothic rib-vaulting within. But the ribs of this vaulting are enriched with fantastic pendants covered with decoration presumably here of Lombard inspiration. These vaults rival those in the Heydenreichs' Late Gothic chapels at Ingolstadt, of roughly a decade earlier, which Sohier will hardly have known. The traceried round-arched windows, however, are of the sort Hieber proposed for Zur schönen Maria in 1519 (Pl. 25) and those already used a year or so before on the sides of St. Martin at Lauingen.

St.-Eustache in Paris, of which the transepts were begun in 1532, provides a quite different example of hybrid church architecture in Francis I's realm. It recalls a little the setting, inside a vast church, that Altdorfer provided in his painting of around 1520 of the Birth of the Virgin but it does not at all resemble anything actually carried out in sixteenth-century Germany, nor is any cross influence likely either way.

Something has been said earlier concerning architecture of the early decades of the century in the southern Netherlands, particularly that of Rombout Keldermans and Guyot de Beaugrant (Pl. 41), despite its lack of connection with contemporary production in Germany. The considerably more literate Renaissance design that appeared in the northern Netherlands in the thirties, with the actual employment of Italians, now deserves comment. This new influence

[121] Because the dates of the relevant French monuments to be mentioned shortly are well-established, it has seemed unnecessary to provide footnote references. In English, the most up-to-date account of French Renaissance architecture is still that of Blunt as noted already.

is not yet very notable, except for the portals on the outworks of the Breda Kasteel as begun in 1532[122] by an Italian who later worked in Germany. However, if these portals seem unexpectedly "correct" today, that is in part the result of later emendation. The original pediments over the entrance through the outworks, supported though they were—and still are—by well-proportioned compound orders, were rather sharply pointed, as can be seen in early views.[123] Moreover, the open gallery which once existed above the outer one was curiously roofed with a range of tiny cross-gables decorated with scrolling dolphins. Quite different is the church tower at IJsselstein just southwest of Utrecht, begun at about this time and completed by 1535.[124] It is hardly exaggerated to call that "Bramantesque."

Both the outworks of the Kasteel and this tower are by Alessandro Pasqualini (1485-1559), who had been brought to the northern Netherlands by the Lord of Breda, Count Hendrick (III) of Nassau-Breda. The latter was Charles V's deputy there and his wife, Claude de Chalon-Arlay, was the heiress of the principality of Orange in France. Pasqualini came from Bologna and was active at first, like so many Italians employed abroad in the mid-sixteenth century, as an adviser on the design of fortifications. In this case these protected Amsterdam, s'Hertogenbosch and Middelburg and were, of course, of the new sort now rising everywhere in the north in these sixteenth-century decades. That explains the particular location of his work in Breda at the Kasteel.

At IJsselstein Pasqualini had a different client. Most probably this was the Count of Buren, Floris van Egmond,[125] for whom he was building around 1540 at the no longer extant castle at Buren. Later, in 1548, he entered the service of Duke Wilhelm V of Jülich-Berg-Kleve. Wilhelm may be considered a German prince since most of his duchies of Berg and Kleve, if not Jülich, lay east of the Rhine. Pasqualini carried out his most extensive work, which will be discussed at length in Chapter IV, at Jülich (Fig. 24, Pls. 142-145) down to his death in 1559. Because of this later

activity in Germany, Pasqualini made his major contribution there rather than in the Netherlands, but it is appropriate to describe his earlier work at this point.

The IJsselstein tower rises in three rather broad stages and two slightly telescoped octagonal ones. The three lower storeys are divided into bays on each side by panelled pilasters executed in stone in proper sequence of Doric, Ionic and Corinthian. The central arch at the base on the west has a molded stone archivolt and stone imposts of which the moldings are carried all around the tower. In the upper storeys there are three arches on each face, a tall open one in the center and lower ones framing shell-topped niches on either side. The pilaster-imposts and the archivolts are banded in brick and stone, the only Netherlandish note in the whole composition.

Niches and open arches alternate on the sides of the octagonal stages of the IJsselstein tower and the bent pilaster strips at the corners are stone-banded, as are the frames of the windows and niches, to match those below. Actually the upper octagonal stage, which is simpler than the other, is not by Pasqualini but dates from a hundred years later, having been rebuilt after a fire in 1633-1635. The delicate terminal lantern is of the twentieth century and by Michel de Klerk. The cinquecento design of the tower is equalled in Germany in the thirties only by the Stadtresidenz at Landshut as that was designed and carried out, later in that decade and after 1540, by Italians brought to Bavaria from Mantua (Pl. 117). In Czechoslovakia the Letohradek or Belvedere pavilion on the Hrad in Prague is also comparable. That was begun by the Italian, Paolo della Stella, in 1538 and completed by the Swiss Bonifaz Wohlmut in 1563,[126] so it is also later even in conception.

At Breda Pasqualini was succeeded by another Italian Tomaso di Andrea Vincidor (†1536), also from Bologna, who was responsible for the design of the main quadrangular structure of the Kasteel as built for Hendrick in 1536-38.[127] Vincidor, a painter, had been sent to the Netherlands in 1520 by Leo X to supervise the weaving of the Raphael tapestries for the Sistine Chapel. By the mid-thirties he had been in the north, chiefly in Antwerp and in Mechelen, long enough to be somewhat influenced—not to say corrupted—by local ideas of architectural design. Yet the

---

[122] *Kunstreisboek voor Nederland*, Amsterdam, 1965 (henceforth cited as *Kunstreisboek*), pp. 542-543; M. D. Ozinga, "Die strenge Renaissancestÿl in de Nederlanden naar de Stand van onze tegenwoordige Kennis," *Bull. van de Kon. Ned. Oudheitsbond*, 6th series, XV, pp. 10-34. The Dutch situation is described and illustrated in Hitchcock, *Scrolled Gables*, as regards the 1530s.

[123] *Ibid.*, Fig. 20.

[124] *Kunstreisboek*, p. 288; Hitchcock, *Scrolled Gables*, p. 30.

[125] *Kunstreisboek*, pp. 199-200.

[126] Białostocki, *Eastern Europe*, ills. 279-282.

[127] *Kunstreisboek*, pp. 542-543. Hendrick died in 1538, two years after Vincidor. Whether René, and to what extent, continued the work at Breda is not clear.

relative "correctness" of the membering on the Kasteel by sixteenth-century Italian standards is somewhat unexpected. All the same, Vincidor capped the court facades with tiny scrolled gables very like those over the outworks, and also introduced staged gables ornamented with sculpture that rivalled contemporary German examples in elaboration.

To conclude these disparate references to advanced architecture outside of Germany in the early decades of the century one more Dutch work partially of the late thirties or early forties, the Kasteel at Buren, ought to be briefly described here.[128] This is because its lone gable is so parallel to those Knotz introduced on the north wing of the Schloss at Neuburg (Pl. 90), on the Danube in the upper Palatinate, in the years 1534-1538 which will later be discussed in some detail. Unfortunately the Kasteel in Buren in Gelderland was demolished in 1804.

Surviving graphic documents give some idea of what the Buren Kasteel was like. As in the thirties at Breda, a mediaeval castle surrounded by a moat was regularized in plan and largely, if not completely, rebuilt for the Lord of Buren, Floris van Egmond, the probable client for the IJsselstein tower. Like that at Breda, the Kasteel at Buren was quadrangular. As far as is known, it had little of the relatively advanced character of Vincidor's contemporary work otherwise. However, above the projecting centerpiece of the main facade on the court there rose a conspicuous gable. That was, in all probability, the earliest example of such a feature in the north derived from a specific Italian source.

The dates are tight; for Pasqualini's work at Buren terminated in 1545 on the death of Floris—his daughter and heiress Anna, married to William of Orange, apparently did not continue the work. It was in that year, 1545, the *Segundo libro* of Sebastiano Serlio appeared with the well-known plate of a *scena tragica*, or stage-setting for tragedy (Fig. 19). At the rear of the scene is a gateway with bold S-scrolls on the sides and a pediment above. This is in the tradition of Renaissance church-facade design, descending from that of Santa Maria Novella in Florence, which was in fairly common use in Italy by the 1490s.

Pasqualini introduced a composition that was almost identical with Serlio's gateway to top the projection above the main entrance from the court; perhaps, however, this was not modelled on Serlio's plate but only parallel to it. Pasqualini's may well be a reduced version of a contemporary Roman church-facade such as that on Antonio da San Gallo's Santo Spirito in Sassia of these very years 1537-1545. In any case, he elaborated the one at Buren, in a way that recalls his gablets on the gallery of the outworks at Breda, by adding scrolling dolphins on the slopes of the pediment.

It is easy to exaggerate the morphological importance of Pasqualini's long-lost gable in the story of the international development of the scrolled gable. On the Schloss at Neuburg-a.-d.-Donau, Hans Knotz's gables (Pl. 75)—very likely as much as a decade earlier in date—had no similarly Serlian flavor. In the over-all north-European historical pattern, however, Knotz's are already more advanced in the multiplicity of their stages and the variety of the combinations of curved elements in the outline than Pasqualini's at Buren or Vincidor's at Breda. For all the probable priority of the Mechelen gables (Pl. 41), moreover, the further modulation of the scrolled gable is at least as much a German as a Netherlandish development, if not more so—something that later chapters should make very evident.

---

[128] See Note 124 and Hitchcock, *Scrolled Gables*, pp. 38-39. Pasqualini's work at Buren began in the 1530s, according to some as late as 1539 but probably earlier.

Two

THE GERMAN
EARLY RENAISSANCE,
1525-1550

In the latter part of the initial chapter a broad historical background was sketched encompassing much of northern Europe in the early decades of the sixteenth century. The focus now should once more be on the situation in Germany, specifically in the 1520s. In the third decade of the century neither Charles V—who first came to Germany in 1520, the year of his election as emperor—nor anyone else, international banker or cosmopolitan prelate, evinced such an interest in the new Renaissance idiom as had Thomas of Bakócz in initiating his chapel at Esztergom (Pl. 5) in Hungary in 1506 or Zygmunt I that of St. Sigismund at Kraków (Pl. 39) in Poland some ten years later. Moreover, the presence of skilled Italians of the sort those eastern magnates employed is not recorded so early in German lands nor, as far as is known, did they appear there before the mid-thirties. That was shortly after they first began to make an early contribution, as previously noted, in the northern Netherlands.

However, Renaissance design, often somewhat hybrid still, was coming to be used more and more in German churches for tombs, portals, pulpits and other fittings. In addition to the Gemmingen tomb (Pl. 40) of c.1515 at Mainz and the sacristy doorways, of 1517 and 1518, respectively, in the Cathedral of Wrocław (Pl. 19) and the Annenkirche at Annaberg (Pl. 20), the Croy *Epitaph* in Cologne imported from the Netherlands in 1518 should be recalled. Moreover, in the mid-1520s a prelate who was also a secular ruler, Prince-Bishop of Paderborn Erich of Brunswick-Grubenhagen (†1532), began the first *Schloss* (castle or, later, "country house," plural *Schlösser*) in which Renaissance, or at least near-Renaissance, features were introduced. For this he employed Jörg Unkair (†1553), a stone-mason trained in Württemberg. As a whole, however, Unkair's Schloss at Schloss Neuhaus[1]

(Pls. 44, 49), which is in Westphalia just north of Paderborn, was far less advanced than the Fuggerhäuser as rebuilt some ten years or more earlier.

Modest the novel features at Schloss Neuhaus certainly are, and most of Unkair's detailing there as afterward elsewhere remained Late Gothic. Yet that favorite architectural device of the German sixteenth century, the so-called *welsche Gebel* (vernacular: Italian gable), made what seems to have been its first appearance here in secular work. However, those that a more important prince of the church, Albrecht Cardinal Brandenburg, the archbishop-elector of Mainz and bishop of Magdeburg, added above the side aisles and over the two ends of the Dom (Pl. 45) at Halle, well to the east on the Saale in Saxony, may be as much as four or five years earlier.[2] A significant variant of the plain *welsche Gebel* on the sides and rear at Halle, moreover, is the stepped gable over the west front (Pl. 46). Each of its five steps is capped by a lunette and the panels are all decorated with round-arched blind tracery. The very modest lunettes which once capped the turrets above the ends of the facade of the house at Maximilianstrasse 38 in Augsburg (Pl. 7) that Jakob Fugger acquired in 1523 might have preceded, if not the ones at Halle, those at Schloss Neuhaus by a year or two, were they added by Jakob before his death in 1525. These were hardly comparable, however; for the *welsche Gebel* at Halle

---

[1] W. Becker, *Schloss Neuhaus, das ehemalige Wohnge-* *bäude der Paderborner Bischöfe*, Paderborn [1970] (henceforth cited as Becker, *Schloss Neuhaus*), pp. 18-26; F. Wurm, *Schloss Neuhaus*, enl. ed., Paderborn [1957] pp. 29-31; Kreft-Soenke, *Weserrenaissance*, pp. 276-278. References to Soenke's earlier articles in which he first put together the career of Jörg Unkair will be found there. The term "Weser-Renaissance" was already used by Horst, *Architektur*, pp. 76-82, in 1928.

[2] Unnerbäck, *Giebel*, pp. 9-12, assigns priority to the Halle examples. Whether those or the ones at Schloss Neuhaus are earlier, such features first appeared in Germany around or shortly before 1525.

are bigger even than Unkair's and the ones on the sides and rear of the church are very conspicuous, though the multiple gable over the west end is difficult both to see and to photograph.

As regards the dating of the Halle gables, it is relevant that Albrecht had taken over the unfinished church from the Dominicans as early as 1520. It was then he set up in Halle a new Catholic Institute to combat the heresies Luther and his associates were propagating so effectively at the University of Wittenberg, not far to the northeast of Halle, which the Elector Friedrich der Weise of Saxony had founded in 1504. Albrecht may have had these gables built before 1523, the year the church was consecrated, or perhaps a little later when the south portal (Pl. 47) and the sacristy entrance were added.[3]

The Halle portals are somewhat more sophisticated than the ones at Wrocłav and Annaberg of 1517 and 1518 (Pls. 19, 20) in their Lombardesque detailing, but not dissimilar to that—presumably of the mid-twenties—on the Salvatorkapelle in Vienna (Pl. 21). They are less conventionally quattrocento, however, than the one carrying the date 1524 at Wiener Neustadt (Pl. 22). Since the Halle doorways are dated 1525 and the Renaissance pulpit there, 1526, those years, when Unkair's work at Schloss Neuhaus was being initiated, are possible also for the addition of the Halle gables. Three of the just-mentioned portals, the one in Vienna and those in Halle, are capped with lunettes like the earlier ones at Breslau and Annaberg (Pls. 19, 20), thus resembling *welsche Gebel* in outline.

Five tall stone dormers on the south front of the Schloss at Schloss Neuhaus and two around the corner on the west (Pl. 44), where construction started probably a year or two before 1526, are still extant. Those on the south, however, have lost their idiosyncratic character by being trimmed at the edges.[4] On them only the paired windows are original. But in an engraving of 1723 these gables can be seen as they once were and still are on the west, each with a first broad stage above the eaves of the main roof, next

a narrower stage—again with two windows, though smaller ones—and then the *welsche Gebel*, decorated here only with small stone balls on the extrados.

Very similar gables, though a storey taller, are to be seen on a wing of Schloss Schelenburg, also in Westphalia but nearer Osnabrück than Paderborn, which was begun by the same architect—if one may so call Unkair—a year or two before 1530.[5] The broader main gable (Pl. 48) there has sloping elements at the base, however, conforming to the pitch of the roof.[6] From this time on *welsche Gebel* became very common through the next twenty or thirty years, and they survived as a common motif even longer in out-of-the-way places (Pls. 96, 97).

Before suggesting how such gables probably derived from Italian models via northern intermediaries in paintings and prints as was touched on in the previous chapter, there should be some comment on the ground plan[7] of Schloss Neuhaus (Fig. 9) and also

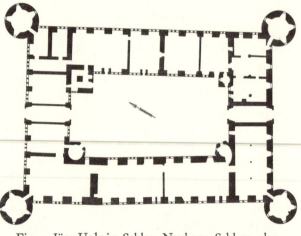

Fig. 9. Jörg Unkair: Schloss Neuhaus, Schloss, plan

on the type of windows used throughout as well as the several sorts of enframement of the portals (Pls. 44, 49). Today Schloss Neuhaus has rather a French air because of its round corner towers capped by

---

[3] The Halle Dom was completed by Albrecht over the years following 1520; Piltz, *D.D.R.*, pp. 236-237, E. Neuss and W. Piechocki, *Halle an der Saale*, Dresden, 1955, pp. 33-38. The gables were originally plastered and painted, not as now of exposed brickwork, so that they resembled somewhat more the contemporary portals with figural or armorial carving in their lunettes (Pls. 45-47).

[4] Kreft-Soenke, *Weserrenaissance*, p. 276; Becker, *Schloss Neuhaus*, pls. 109-110, provides an isometric reconstruction with the original gables included.

[5] Kreft-Soenke, *Weserrenaissance*, p. 276.

[6] This variant, though much larger and without the lower curves at the sides, would be almost precisely contemporary with the trilobe dormers in Saxony mentioned below in Note 13 (Fig. 10).

[7] F. Bernstein, *Der deutsche Schlossbau der Renaissance (1530-1618), Typen und Entwickelung seiner Grundrissanlage*, Strasbourg, 1933, summarizes the development of secular planning, but does not illustrate the plan of Schloss Neuhaus or any other before Schloss Hartenfels of 1533-1536 except for some mediaeval Schlösser not relevant here.

plain conical roofs and the vertical linking of the windows on these towers by panelled pilaster-strips. It recalls not Blois, however, where the *aile François Iᵉʳ* had probably been nearly completed before Francis in 1524 was captured by Charles V at the battle of Pavia, but rather Bury, a chateau begun as early as 1511 and finished by 1524, just as Unkair was probably starting to work at Schloss Neuhaus. But the external towers at Schloss Neuhaus were not part of his original design; these were only added around 1590 by a later prince-bishop of Paderborn, Dietrich von Fürstenberg, whose architect was most probably Hermann Baumhauer.

The quadrangular layout of Schloss Neuhaus, though less regular than at Sutton Place in this period in England, distinctly resembles that of Bury, though such a plan was probably not of any stylistic significance. Late Gothic builders had no antipathy to such schemes where large new structures were to occupy open sites, though many—perhaps most—of the early Renaissance Schlösser in Germany of necessity continued to be irregular in plan (Figs. 11, 12, 23, 33). As elsewhere in northern Europe, what survives today usually represents the result of recurrent rebuildings and additions of the sixteenth century and later. These increments are closely associated with, and often constricted by, older mediaeval elements of which the arrangement had been determined chiefly by the needs of defense. Nor could such needs be ignored in the turbulent sixteenth century when, in answer to new weapons of offense, a new Italian type of fortification was reaching the north parallel with the importation of the new decorative features.

It is possible, all the same, that the plan at Schloss Neuhaus was modelled on the much larger quadrangular court of the Schloss at Tübingen, on the Neckar in Swabia, as rebuilt for Duke Ulrich of Württemberg beginning in 1507.[8] That Schloss Unkair would certainly have known; indeed, he may actually have worked on it in his youth as a mason. But the ground at Schloss Neuhaus was flat, quite unlike the high site of the Swabian Burg; moreover, of the existing fourteenth-century castle of the bishops of Paderborn Unkair was able, without seriously compromising the regularity of the new work, to incorporate the lower portion of the residential tower while razing the rest. The stair-towers in the inner

corners of the court, unlike the later round towers on the outer corners, do not match. Those in the southwest and northwest corners are hexagonal and effectively identical whether or not the second is actually by Unkair and of the twenties; the other two are square, and one of them, which is certainly not by Unkair but perhaps by Baumhauer, is considerably lower and larger than the other three.

Unkair's windows, distinctly "modern" in their simplicity, are paired in the upper storey and single below, as also in the gables (Pl. 44). But they are all of plain rectangular shape, and those that are single are only slightly smaller than the double ones. The more usual sixteenth-century German window, inherited from the Late Gothic but still in common use for several decades, was the so-called "curtain-topped" sort of which the arch or lintel is scalloped inward in a purely decorative and quite anti-structural way. Among many others, characteristic examples exist on the Rathaus at Wittenberg (Pl. 247), begun in 1522, and the Johann-Friedrichsbau of Schloss Hartenfels at Torgau of the 1530s (Pl. 78). They even appear as late as 1579 on the Rathaus in Marktbreit (Pl. 249). The molded stone trim of the much plainer openings at Schloss Neuhaus is flush with the stucco covering of the brick walls. It consists of rounded fillets, with sunken channels between, that intersect at the upper corners, a Late Gothic type of framing which lasted well into the 1590s in some districts. The moldings begin, in a manner still true of many later window-frames, a quarter to a third up the sides from the sills, though Renaissance architraves would have continued to the bottoms of the openings as on the contemporary Palais de Savoie at Mechelen (Pl. 41).

The five dormers over the south front at Schloss Neuhaus (Pl. 44) are symmetrically arranged as are also the two windows in each of them. The paired windows of the main storey below, however, are quite unevenly disposed both in relation to the gables above and to the main entrance in the ground storey. In its present form this last is an eighteenth-century intrusion like the one on the garden side. Because of the regularity of the fenestration on the later east and north sides, with triple windows lined up under the recurrent gables and also in the bays between, not to speak of the dominance of the towers now flanking the original southern front, this casual distribution of Unkair's windows is not especially noticeable. Nor is it by any means unknown in later stages of the German Renaissance, even though many early sixteenth-century civic buildings such as *Rathäuser*

---

[8] W. Fleischhauer, *Renaissance im Herzogtum Württemberg*, Stuttgart [1971?] (henceforth cited as Fleischhauer, *Württemberg*), figs. 1, 2.

(town halls) have their Late Gothic windows evenly spaced. The large one (Pl. 247) at Wittenberg that was just mentioned is an especially striking example a few years earlier than Schloss Neuhaus in date.

At Schloss Neuhaus two of the doorways that lead to the spiral staircases in the towers at the front corners of the court are inscribed with early sixteenth-century dates. The one of 1526 (Pl. 49) has a broader version of the characteristic enframement of the windows. But this is here elaborated, like the border of Dürer's woodcut of the Betrothal of the Virgin of 1504-1505, by a semicircular inner arch around which the fillets spring off from, and intersect, the verticals and horizontals. Since this is wholly Late Gothic in spirit the introduction of the round arch here need not be considered evidence even of secondhand Renaissance influence whether or not the portal was in fact modelled on Dürer's woodcut.

As elsewhere in northern Europe in this period, four-centered, semi-elliptical—that is, three-centered—segmental and even half-round shapes had more and more been accepted as decorative and, indeed, also as structural alternatives to sharp-pointed Gothic forms. In German secular work, however, "curtain-top" windows were perhaps most common in the second quarter of the sixteenth century when Unkair was active though he himself rarely used them. This avoidance of pointed arches is even evident in the cross-section of such a church interior as that of Unsere liebe Frau, now the Marktkirche, in Halle (Pl. 37) begun by Albrecht of Brandenburg in 1529, and even in the earlier vault of St. Moritz there which is dated 1511. Moreover, the great round-arched openings at the top of the tower below the Oktagon at Heilbronn (Pl. 16) were carried out in 1508-1512 before Schweiner began the Oktagon. Many of these special types of arch, moreover, most particularly the segmental or truncated semicircular, long persisted in common use.

A second doorway at Schloss Neuhaus, inscribed 1528, is equally pre-Renaissance in character. Rectangular in shape, this differs from the window-frames in the provision of Late Gothic bases at the bottoms of the fillets and the addition of a rustic molding with broken-off branches. That molding curves round the upper corners like a very depressed pointed arch and flips up at the center in a sharp peak. At Chemnitz (Karl-Marx-Stadt), on the north portal of the Schloss-kirche (Pl. 50), Hans Witten and Franz Maidburg combined in 1522-1525 the Düreresque design of the first-mentioned doorway at Schloss Neuhaus (Pl. 49) with the rustic work of the second in an elaborate decorative composition rising high against the side wall of the church.[9]

At Schloss Schelenberg, in the wing that Unkair added around or just before 1530, several stone doorways in the interior, though somewhat different from the one at Schloss Neuhaus, are equally Late Gothic; while the main entrance from the court, dated 1532, repeats exactly the 1526 portal at Schloss Neuhaus. The window-frames, moreover, where of this period (Pl. 48), follow those at Schloss Neuhaus. Still later, on the Schloss at Stadthagen near Hanover, under an armorial achievement carrying the date 1541,[10] Unkair repeated once more the round-arched door-frame of Schloss Neuhaus. In another portal there, dated 1536, he had used a flattened variant with curved upper corners and a raised peak, somewhat like his 1528 doorway at Schloss Neuhaus, but without a rustic member. There is no such decoration at Stadthagen, however, around an interior doorway dated 1537 that has a segmental arch at the top. Another doorway in the interior there, if indeed of these years, is more advanced. Its rectangular sides and top are framed with a very corrupt and misunderstood Renaissance candelabrum-motif; but this may well not be of Unkair's design any more than are the three late sixteenth-century chimneypieces that survive in this Schloss.

However that may be, Unkair used the arched door-frame of 1526 without change much later at the base of the stair-tower in the court of Schloss Petershagen in Westphalia, a seat of the bishops of Minden northeast of that city, where it carries the date 1546.[11] The window-frames on this tower (Pl. 51), moreover, are identical with those at Schloss Neuhaus of twenty years earlier: coupled and—as in all of Unkair's earlier stair-towers beginning with those at Schloss Neuhaus—slanted at top and bottom to match the rising spiral within. Equally common in Unkair's work, even the latest, are the rounded elements at the angles of the Petershagen tower, cut off quite abruptly shortly below the eaves. These do not derive from such Renaissance column-shafts as Hieber proposed for the corners of the Perlachturm in 1519 but are rather, it would seem, of Gothic descent—the ancestry of the *welscher Gebel* is somewhat clearer and ultimately Italian.

[9] Piltz, *D.D.R.*, p. 456. Begun by Witten as early as 1502-1505 and completed twenty years later by Maidburg; restored in 1897 and undamaged in the last war.
[10] Kreft-Soenke, *Weserrenaissance*, pp. 279-281.
[11] *Ibid.*, pp. 270-271.

Lunettes above lintels or, more usually, full entablatures were a common quattrocento motif still in general use in northern Italy well into the sixteenth century. Two types exist: the half-round—there is an open one of that shape over the main entrance to the Fontego dei Todeschi from the Grand Canal—and the segmental. In the former the lunette, if solid, often contains a sculptural group; in the latter there may be radial fluting, not unknown in semicircular ones. The enframement in both types varies a great deal in the degree of elaboration. The curved top may have richly carved bands, but more often it is merely molded like an ordinary archivolt. On the outside, at the base, there are usually akroters of rosette form, sometimes provided with upward-spraying half-palmettes; over the crown, doubled rosettes, palmettes or even figural sculpture may further enrich the outline.

Such lunettes had already made a rather early appearance outside of Italy if not in Germany. The Lazarus chapel in the transept of La Major at Marseilles, built 1475-1481, for example, has two of the segmental sort. These stand well forward from the wall at the transept's north end and are flanked and topped by small statues. A laurel band on the exterior frames a dished and fluted field that suggests a shell. Twenty years or so later in Prague, over one of the several Renaissance portals at the Hrad—framed in this case by curiously un-Italian spirally twisted pilasters—Rejt set a plain half-round lunette with a simple, but very correct, molded archivolt and no akroters. Still later, over the sacristy portal (Pl. 19) of 1517 in the cathedral of Wrocław in Silesia that was mentioned earlier, the somewhat narrower half-round lunette encloses a high relief of the Decollation of St. John the Baptist. This is flanked, not by rosettes, but by torch-bearing angels perched on plain stone spheres, while above the crown is a seated figure holding a bishop's miter. The style of the figural sculpture is somewhat less illiterate in Italian terms than the architectural detailing it may be noted.

A decade before that, Dürer had designed lunettes differing significantly from those eastern European ones in Bohemia and Silesia. His are not indicated as set against solid walls but are rather free-standing, so as to provide a bold terminal silhouette. As mentioned in the first chapter, such a lunette appears in his drawing in the Musée Condé at Chantilly of the Adoration of the Trinity, dated 1508, which includes the design of the proposed frame. The motif was repeated, with some changes in detail, above the paint-

ing as executed by another hand three years later. Moreover, atop the throne of a Burgkmair Madonna, dated 1509, now in the Germanisches Museum in Nürnberg, there is a solid half-circular lunette with scrolled dolphins on the extrados rather resembling those on Pasqualini's and Vincidor's gables (Pl. 43) in Holland of the 1530s. Then, on his woodcut of a Triumphal Arch made for the Emperor Maximilian in 1515-1517 (Pl. 32), Dürer introduced another form over the sections at the sides. These lunettes are nearly full circles linked at their base to lamp-like elements by soft concave curves, a type not often—or, indeed, perhaps ever—imitated in executed architecture.

Lunettes rising above portals in solid walls must be considered generically quattrocento Italian, but silhouetted half-round forms, as the particular character of Dürer's frame of the Chantilly drawing makes particularly evident, are rather specifically Venetian. Their ultimate source is the front of St. Mark's on which the extradoses of the old Byzantine vaults of the narthex were elaborated in the fifteenth century with rich Late Gothic cresting. But the most striking use of decorated lunettes against the sky in Italy is over the facade of the Scuola di San Marco in Venice (Pl. 52), largely built by Pietro Lombardo and Giovanni Buon in 1488-1490, but completed only toward 1500 by Mauro Coducci. There, moreover, the intended reference to the front of St. Mark's is obvious.

The range of three identical lunettes over the right half of the facade of the Scuola in Venice is distinctly premonitory of the long line of welsche Gebel over the aisles and the apse of the Dom at Halle as modified for Cardinal Brandenburg in the 1520s (Pl. 45). The group of three over the left half, however, with that in the center taller than those flanking it, approaches the five-part gable (Pl. 46) atop the west front at Halle.[12] The elaborate treatment of these Venetian lunettes includes archivolt-like frames, flanking pilasters and even, below the taller ones, colonnettes—as on Dürer's design of 1508 for a frame—not to speak of much carving and marble incrustation over-all. Such decorative elaboration would be rivalled on gables in the north only much later in the sixteenth century. By that time, Northern Mannerist models of architectural ornament, initiated in the Netherlands and carried all over Europe by published engravings in books had largely superseded those of Renaissance Italy.

[12] Unnerbäck, *Giebel*, p. 6, fig. 6.

It seems fairly clear that most, if not all, half-round *welsche Gebel* in Germany of the first half of the sixteenth century were at least indirectly Venetian in ancestry. Flat decoration, as at Halle, may once have echoed, moreover, the marble incrustation of the Venetian models but has now largely disappeared. Hybrid gables of the twenties and thirties, however, often have raised tracery that is still Gothic (Pls. 53, 55, 56).

Segmental lunettes also appear on the facade of the Scuola di San Marco in Venice over two of the windows of the first storey and over the righthand entrance, though a hooded relief of semicircular shape caps the main entrance (Pl. 52). Similar lunettes, with akroters at their ends as on the Scuola, crown also the entrance portals below the two largest Venetian examples of what may conveniently be called, even there, *welsche Gebel*, those of Santa Maria dei Miracoli and of San Zaccaria. Moreover, the facade of the former, built by Pietro Lombardo in 1481-1489, terminates in a half-round gable the full width of the two storeys below. Framed by a vigorously modillioned "archivolt" and filled with an arrangement of large circular windows and equally circular marble-incrusted motifs of rather Byzantine character, this gable has rosette akroters on each side at the base and again paired at the top, all supporting small figures silhouetted against the sky. As was earlier noted, other half-round gables, somewhat smaller and much plainer, rise over the sides of the choir below the dome. These are much like the still smaller ones at the tops of Venetian campanili (Pl. 9) that may have influenced the capping of the turrets of Maximilianstrasse 38 (Pl. 7) whatever their date.

At San Zaccaria the main portal is set in the lower part of the facade for which Antonio Gambello, who began the church as early as 1458, was probably responsible, but is certainly much later. The feature crowning the central portion of the facade that fronts the nave is hood-like in its projection and rises over pairs of freestanding colonnettes at either side. But like the somewhat flatter front "gable" of Santa Maria dei Miracoli this has rosette-akroters at the sides and top that carry angels with symbols of the Passion. Two more angels stand on the rosettes at the base of the quadrants crowning the fronts of the lower side-aisles. The silhouette against the sky is, therefore, a tall half-circle flanked by quarter-circles. The contemporary facade of San Michele in Isola in Venice, built over the period 1468-1479, is similarly topped. Very simplified and much reduced in size, these might

have been models for the dormers on the side of the Gewandhaus (Fig. 10) at Zwickau in southern Saxony and the Rathaus in Dresden-Neustadt of 1525 and 1527-1528 respectively, both illustrated by Unnerbäck.[13] To judge from the well-known medal by

Fig. 10. Friedrich Schultheiss: Zwickau, Gewandhaus, side elevation with dormers of 1525

Matteo de Pasti, Alberti had already intended such a treatment for the upper storey of the front of the Temple Malatestiano in Rimini in the 1450s as Unnerbäck has also noted.[14]

The upper portion of the front of San Zaccaria was

[13] *Ibid.*, pp. 12-20. For the modest dormers along the sides of the Gewandhaus in Zwickau (Fig. 10) Friedrich Schultheiss seems to have provided the design himself. Actually those dormers, though trilobed, may have the best claim to be the first *welsche Gebel*, for H.-J. Krause, "Das erste Auftrete italienischer Renaissancemotive in der Architektur Mitteldeutschlands," *Acta Historiae Artium*, XIII, Budapest, 1967, pp. 1-3, 99, gives documentary evidence for dating Schultheiss's design for them to February, 1525. Probably of some two years later were the trilobe gables of the dormers at either end of the front of the demolished Rathaus in Dresden-Neustadt; these can be seen in a painting by Bernardo Bellotto in the National Museum in Stockholm (Unnerbäck, *Giebel*, Fig. 20). A variant, with two quadrants on each side, was introduced on the dormers of Schloss Vorderglauchau (*ibid.*, Fig. 11) at Glauchau, which is on the Mulde between Wittenberg and Leipzig. That was begun by E. von Schönburg in 1527 and carried to completion under the direction of Andreas Günther in 1534 (Dehio, *Dresden*, p. 127). There are doubtless other early examples of all these types, but the dated ones noted by Unnerbäck are quite sufficient to establish their fairly common use, at least in Saxony, from the mid-twenties.
[14] Unnerbäck (*Giebel*, pp. 6-7, Fig. 7) calls attention also to more modest and obscure Italian examples at Sedrina near Bergamo and Motta di Livenza northeast of Venice.

carried out by Coducci after 1500 and perhaps not completed before 1515 even though he died in 1504. Thus, although the Italian models for *welsche Gebel* go back at least to the 1480s and, as regards portals, considerably earlier, such were still being used in Venice up to a decade or so before the presumptive date of their introduction at Halle and by Unkair at Schloss Neuhaus. The possible, even likely, Venetian prototypes of the much smaller lunettes on the turrets at Maximilianstrasse 38 in Augsburg, which may also date from the mid-twenties, have just been recalled.

The *welsche Gebel* theme was soon elaborated, and there are certain very early German variants that should be mentioned here. Only one of them certainly antedates Schloss Neuhaus, if that was under way by 1525, or those at Halle. At Zwickau the *Gewandhaus* (guild house), begun in 1522[15] by Friedrich Schultheiss, probably from a design by Jakob Heilmann, has a very remarkable front gable (Pl. 55) which may well be earlier than the dormers on the side by a year or two. This gable caps a conventional two-storeyed Late Gothic facade with a central pointed entrance arch and regularly spaced windows in pairs—these last very like Unkair's at Schloss Neuhaus though somewhat taller and narrower. The gable, rising in five additional storeys or stages, is subdivided by vertical elements with S-curved members between them embracing small paired windows that are framed like those below. In the blank outer compartments at the third level the S-curved members interlace, while in the terminal double compartment there are circular elements in relief.

A rather similar treatment, without even the faintest Renaissance flavor, is very conspicuous on the tall gable of the north transept of Sts. Ulrich and Afra at Augsburg. This was built either by Burkhard Engelberg (†1512) or rather more probably by Hans König and could well be earlier than that at Zwickau; in any case construction halted at Sts. Ulrich and Afra in 1526.[16] Even more premonitory of the one at Zwickau, however, is the gable of the Unterkirche of the Franciscans, now a concert hall, at Frankfurt-a.-d.-Oder

(Pl. 54). Originally consecrated in 1301, the exterior of this was remodelled in 1516-25 by A. Lange.[17]

The general impression made by the facade of the Zwickau Gewandhaus is mediaeval despite the clock turret, added in 1745, which rides the peak of the gable over the front. However, outside the slanting lines of the gable's sides a series of curved bows is silhouetted against the sky. Those flanking the topmost stage actually join to form a half-circle, though the effect of this as a crowning lunette is compromised by the central vertical element that rises from below. Each bow carries on its extrados three small spheres like those on Unkair's *welsche Gebel*. The more advanced trilobe gables on the dormers above the side of the Gewandhaus (Fig. 10), designed in 1525, have already been mentioned.

Tracery of an even more consistently Late Gothic character than that on the front of the Zwickau Gewandhaus decorates the many gabled dormers—six along the side toward the market-place, two at each end—on the Rathaus at Naumburg-a.-d.-Saale, a town southwest of Leipzig, which was completed in 1528.[18] This was very possibly built by Andreas Günther who was working also at Glauchau, between Chemnitz and Gera, on Schloss Vorderglauchau in these years. The motif appears at smaller scale a few years later at Pössneck, which lies to the east of Saalfeld in Thuringia (Pl. 53) not far from Zwickau. The mediaeval Rathaus there, built 1478-1486,[19] presents like that at Naumburg its side rather than one of its stepped and crenellated gables to the main square. In front of this there was added in 1530-1531[20] a double stair before the main portal over which a series of eight lunettes rise in echelon, six on the front and one on each end. These are framed by relatively strong moldings suggesting Italian archivolts. Yet, ex-

---

[15] Piltz, *D.D.R.*, p. 485. This sort of tracery on the face of a gable is clearly the prototype of the blind arches on that over the west front at Halle (Pl. 46). The many surviving examples with patterns of Late Gothic character are not very relevant though some—indeed perhaps most—are of early sixteenth-century date.

[16] Breuer, *Augsburg*, p. 42; M. Rauch, *Augsburger Baugeschichte*, p. [61] is a plate illustrating the transept gable on Sts. Ulrich and Afra.

[17] Piltz, *D.D.R.*, p. 152; Horst, *Architektur*, figs. 146-147 illustrating relevant examples of Late Gothic gables in Brandenburg (Kurfürstenhaus)—no longer surviving—and Torgau (Leipziger Strasse 28). He gives no dates, however. Dehio, *Dresden*, p. 402, mentions the gable in Torgau and implies an early date for it. Piltz, *D.D.R.*, p. 438, merely places it "nach 1482," the date when much of the town was demolished in a great fire.

[18] Unnerbäck, *Giebel*, pp. 14-15, figs. 13-14; *Bau- und Kunstdenkmäler der Provinz Sachsen* (24), p. 282; Piltz, *D.D.R.*, p. 281. Unnerbäck, *Giebel*, pp. 15-26, figs. 15-26, cites and illustrates many more early Saxon examples of varying types several of which are described in Note 13 above.

[19] Deutsche Kunstdenkmäler, *Thüringen* [Munich, 1968] (henceforth cited as DKD, *Thüringen*), p. 393.

[20] Piltz, *D.D.R.*, p. 152. Restored 1969.

cept for the lobe in the center, which has a flat inner frame and carries two shields, their fields are filled with simple Late Gothic elements in relief. This treatment is similar to the more elaborate tracery that occupies the panels of the slanting parapets of the staircase.

Much the same sort of tracery, executed in brick and more like that in the third stage of the Zwickau Gewandhaus gable (Pl. 55), appears on the *welsche Gebel* of the *Torbau* (gatehouse) of Schloss Gifhorn near Wolfsburg (Pl. 56). That was built for the Welf dukes of Brunswick-Lüneburg—at the start, either for Ernst der Bekenner (the Confessor), who ruled there until 1539, or for his younger brother Franz, who then succeeded him at Gifhorn.[21] It is the resemblance to the Zwickau Gewandhaus and also to the Naumburg Rathaus that suggests mention of the Gifhorn Torbau at this point though there is considerable uncertainty as to its date. Here two broad *welsche Gebel*, with regularly spaced windows in their upper stages, flank a stubby polygonal stair-tower—probably of later date—on the court side; while a third, at a right angle to the one on the right, crowns the narrow entrance front. On the other front of the Gifhorn Torbau a taller tower, rising beside a fourth gable, has a segmental lunette over each of its eight sides, somewhat as on the Fuggerhäuser turrets (Pl. 7), below the roof of S-curved profile, a variant of a *welsche Haube*.

Construction of this portion of the Schloss at Gifhorn, where further building continued under Franz down to his death in 1549—the Kavalierhaus in the town is dated 1540; the chapel in the Schloss 1547—probably started in the thirties. Some believe Ernst began the work as early as 1533;[22] others attribute the whole Schloss to Franz, employing Michael Clare, from 1539, when he began to rule alone, into the forties. In any case, it either paralleled or followed close upon the initiation of the rebuilding by Ernst, whose rule at Celle ran from 1527 down to his death

in 1546, of the big Schloss (Pl. 98) of the Welf dukes there in 1533.[23] The similarity of the windows—in both cases mostly segment-topped within a rectangular frame of intersecting fillets—and also the handling of the tops of the towers, suggest that both Schlösser were designed by the same master-builder, but the Gifhorn Torbau looks earlier than anything at Celle. In any case construction continued at Celle under Ernst's son Franz Otto into the fifties, with Clare in charge from 1553 in succession to Frederic Soltesburg who seems to have begun the work.

In relation to Unkair's gables at Schloss Neuhaus and Schelenburg (Pls. 44, 48) those on the *perron* of the Pössneck Rathaus inscribed 1531 and the undated ones on the Gifhorn Torbau (Pls. 53, 56), with their raised Late Gothic banding, represent in both cases the sort of "transition after the fact" that is a frequent phenomenon of stylistic modulation in the history of architecture. Other later portions of the Gifhorn Schloss complex may better be discussed in the next chapter and the Celle Schloss further on in this one. A possible link with Unkair at Celle will then be mentioned: the fact that Ernst's presumed architect Soltesburg came there from Stadthagen in 1533 or soon afterward.

Unkair lived until 1553 and, as late as 1548, initiated the drastic remodelling of the Schloss of the counts of Lippe at Detmold in Westphalia. But before discussing his late works, from Stadthagen—where Soltesburg might have assisted him—begun for the counts of Schaumburg before 1535, to Detmold, and also the Schloss further to the north and east at Celle which seems to be related to Unkair's work, probably for the reason just noted, something more should be said concerning the general situation as regards ecclesiastical architecture in extension of what was recounted in the first chapter. Moreover, certain modest town-houses and several grander princely seats dating from the late twenties through the mid-thirties in Saxony and in the Upper Palatinate should now be described.

From the mid-twenties to the mid-thirties there was in Germany little change of consequence in church architecture, in large part because so few new building projects were then initiated. As has already been indicated, however, subsidiary Renaissance features were introduced in increasing quantity in existing churches in several different regions not closely

[21] Kreft-Soenke, *Weserrenaissance*, p. 245. Merian, *Die Schönsten Schlösser, Burgen und Gärten* [Oldenburg, 1965] (henceforth cited as Merian, *Schönsten Schlösser*), pl. opp. p. 32, shows the Gifhorn Schloss as considerably extended by Duke Wilhelm of Brunswick-Lüneburg in 1575-1576; Merian, *op. cit.*, p. 32, gives the date 1525 in a quoted seventeenth-century text for the initiation of the work by Duke Franz, but that seems rather too early.

[22] Reclams Kunstführer IV: *Niedersachsen Hansestädte Schleswig-Holstein Hessen*, 2nd ed., Stuttgart [1962] (henceforth cited as Reclams *Niedersachsen*), pp. 258-259.

[23] Kreft-Soenke, *Weserrenaissance*, p. 239.

related to one another. In particular, the Italianate sacristy door in the cathedral at Wrocław of 1517 (Pl. 19) in Silesia and that introduced in 1518 in the Annenkirche at Annaberg (Pl. 20) in southern Saxony, by that time structurally complete, have been mentioned, as also the portals of 1525 (Pl. 47) at the Halle Dom further north and those, both probably also of the mid-twenties, way to the southeast in Austria (Pls. 21-22). Following so soon after the completion of the Fuggerkapelle and St. Katherine in Augsburg, the portals in Saxony and Silesia—both far from Augsburg—were certainly among the first such in German lands. Earlier, of course, and hybrid still was Backoffen's Gemmingen tomb at Mainz on the Rhine of c.1515 (Pl. 40). Moreover, before his death in 1523 or 1524, Adolf Dauher of Augsburg, assisted by his abler son Hans (c.1486-1538), provided the elaborate high altar (Pl. 57) in the Annaberg church. On this the carved limestone relief is flanked by carefully designed Renaissance columns and pilasters of colored marbles. No trace of the Gothic remains other than the basic concept of the carved stone triptych and, perhaps, the diagonal setting of the columns. Completed on March 12, 1522, the altar cost the large sum of 2,551 gulden of which 1,200 were provided by Duke Georg der Bärtige (the Bearded) of Saxony who had commissioned it from Dauher in 1519.[24] The local *Rat* (Council) paid the rest, which went for the large expense of transporting the finished altar from Augsburg.

Just after this, in 1522-1524, the first choir-stalls of consistently Renaissance design north of the Alps —capped, incidentally, with half-round lunettes—were executed in wood for the cathedral of Bern in Switzerland.[25] These were also carved by northern craftsmen, in this case Jakob Ruess and Heini Seewagen, though they are far more up-to-date in their almost undiluted Italianism than the elaborate screen (Pl. 58), commissioned from Jan van Roome probably in 1523 by the Hackeney family and executed the next year, in St.

Maria-im-Kapitol.[26] Carved in black Tournai marble and alabaster, that was an exceptional importation from the Netherlands at this date though preceded by the Croy *Epitaph* of 1518. The still distinctly hybrid character of the screen illustrates by contrast how much more advanced Renaissance taste was in centers to the south and east from Switzerland to Poland— and, indeed, in German lands also—than in the southern Netherlands, even while the Palais de Savoie was in construction there.

As reinstalled now at the west end of St. Maria-im-Kapitol the Hackeney screen has four piers running across the nave and two more at each side against the walls. These piers are stylistically ambiguous, for each consists of a bundle of black marble shafts, still a Gothic element, bound by bands of alabaster at the base and at half-height elaborated with Italianate moldings. Moreover, the more-or-less Corinthian alabaster capitals of these piers are designed as if to top compound pilasters rather than clustered colonnettes. The heavy marble lintels over the intercolumniations are horizontal, but their architrave-like moldings curve down at each end to meet the capitals of the piers. The resultant semicircular elements frame the bottom half of complete rondels of alabaster. These are deep-sunk and filled with armorial carving.

Next comes the main body of the screen (Pl. 58), a series of statue-filled niches separated by marble supports that echo, in flattened form and at less than half-scale, the clustered piers below. These also are bound by alabaster bands and capped with Corinthianesque pilaster capitals. The lines of statues, of which there are twenty, ten above the transverse lintels and five on either side, are interrupted over the rondels by figural reliefs set in shallow niches within a duplex frame. The statues stand on projecting podia of trilobe section and are each flanked, within the niche behind them, by candelabrum elements. These support hoods that project outward above the statues in a double three-dimensional curve that is almost Flamboyant. Under the hoods are shell motifs and above them pairs of putti are included in the arabesque decoration carved on members which bow well forward in the zone of the pilaster capitals. On top of all this turgidity a continuous entablature with an architrave of black marble breaks slightly outward

[24] Glück, *Renaissance in Deutschland*, pp. 72, 633; his Pl. 432 includes the top of the altar missing in Pl. 57 here. Kratzsch, *Bergstädte*, pp. 115-120, notes that Georg der Bärtige knew Augsburg well from visits to Jakob Fugger. That doubtless explains the choice of an artist who had worked in the Fuggerkapelle rather than one of the Dresdeners, Christoph Walther or Franz Maidburg, who were already employed at Annaberg. For the two Dauhers, Osten-Vey, *Germany*, pp. 37, 256-257, supersedes the article by H. Vollmer in ThB.

[25] KDM, *Schweiz*, II, p. 365.

[26] Dehio, *Rheinland*, pp. 358-359. An earlier example exists in the Treasure of the Cologne Cathedral, the already-mentioned gilded bronze *Epitaph* of Jacques de Croy (Jakob von Croy, †1516), bishop of Cambrai, cast in Brabant in 1518.

above the reliefs over the main piers. The architrave in turn carries an alabaster frieze ornamented with scrolls below a dentil course, also of alabaster, and is crowned with a modest molded cornice of marble.

Although the decorative carving on the Hackeney screen is predominantly, if not exclusively, of Renaissance character, the spirit is still Brabantine Late Gothic. The general effect is therefore closer to that of Hans van Roome's earlier tombs in the church at Brou than, for example, to the portals executed in these years of the mid-twenties in Vienna and Wiener Neustadt or even the ones in Wrocław and Halle (Pls. 19, 21, 22). This imported feature remains as exceptional in Germany at this point for its luxurious elaboration as was the Croy *Epitaph* in the previous decade. It can be matched only in the paintings of the contemporary Antwerp Mannerists. Netherlandish influence became significant again in Cologne in the 1550s and sixties but with no comparably magnificent, if rather retardataire, result.

By 1525-1526 Albrecht of Brandenburg, who had commissioned the Gemmingen tomb at Mainz some ten years before, was introducing at Halle not only the earlier-mentioned portals carved in stone (Pl. 47) but also the considerably less advanced wooden choirstalls, not to speak of a richly decorated pulpit of Renaissance design. More literally Italianate is the bronze baldacchin (Pl. 59) he commissioned a decade later from the Vischers, presumably as part of a never-completed tomb, that survives in the Stiftskirche at Aschaffenburg. Still almost as remote from Italian standards on the other hand, whether quattrocento or cinquecento, and recalling in its use of tubular members both for supports and to enframe arches the Heydenreichs' windows of c.1520 in the cathedral cloister at Regensburg (Fig. 7), was the south porch, also dating as late as 1536, of St. Georg in Cologne.[27] Of this, since the war, only a few fragments survive in the Schnüttgen Museum in Cologne; their character, which is distinctly retardataire, provides no reason to suppose the craftsmen involved were Netherlanders like Jan van Roome.

From this time onward and for most of the rest of the century the German Renaissance would develop its regional characteristics not in features added to existing churches but primarily in secular construction, even though more and more Renaissance tombs, some carved in stone and others in the form of slabs cast in bronze by the Nürnberg foundry of the Vischers and of others elsewhere, found their way into existing Gothic churches, and often pulpits and altars as well. These represent more the cosmopolitan taste of the particular clients who commissioned them, it may be supposed, than that of the local civic or ecclesiastical authorities responsible for the few wholly new churches. There are, for example, the decorative elements in bronze from the Vischer foundry dating from 1525, 1530 and 1536[28] commissioned by Albrecht of Brandenburg that survive in the Stiftskirche at Aschaffenburg of which the latest, the baldacchin, has just been mentioned. In 1527 Albrecht also commissioned the Renaissance Marktbrunnen at Mainz beside the Dom.[29] This was very likely carved in stone by some pupil of Backoffen, though it is often loosely attributed to Peter Flötner (c.1485-1546) of Nürnberg in the way so much ornamental work of these decades has been by German writers.

As much for the subject and the location as for the design, the bronze tomb-slab (Pl. 60)—which is dated 1527[30] and by Peter II Vischer—of the Elector Friedrich der Weise of Saxony, closely resembling Albrecht's at Aschaffenburg of two years before, should be mentioned. This was commissioned by Friedrich's Lutheran successor Johann der Beständige and is in the Wittenberg Schlosskirche that Friedrich had built in the 1490s, the church on whose door Luther a decade before had nailed the 95 theses that initiated the Reformation. Friedrich himself, though a tolerant humanist, never left the Catholic church even though he was much influenced by Philipp Melancthon, the leading Protestant intellectual who had found refuge, like Luther, in Wittenberg. The Wittenberg milieu, more considerably "reformed" and at least as cultivated as Henry VIII's England, was clearly not averse to mild Italianism in a tomb—or even to the Classical nudities of the court-painter Lucas Cranach (1472-1553). It was Cranach who provided the drawing on which the Vischer tomb-slab was based.

It does not seem possible, even in the chapels in

---

[27] Dehio, *Rheinland*, p. 334.

[28] Reclams *Bayern*, p. 68.

[29] Reclams *Rheinlande und Westfalen*, p. 428. Reputedly the earliest Renaissance well-head in Germany.

[30] [S. Harksen] *Die Schlosskirche zu Wittenberg* [Berlin, 1966] (henceforth cited as Harksen, *Wittenberg*), pp. 27-29; Piltz, *D.D.R.*, p. 252. Luther's tomb-slab by the Erfurt bronzecaster Heinrich Ziegler was installed in St. Michael in Jena in 1571 and brought to Wittenberg only in 1892: Harksen, *op. cit.*, p. 31.

various Schlösser that were built or remodelled from the 1540s to the end of the century, to distinguish unmistakably Protestant architectural characteristics in any of the religious edifices in Germany for which Lutherans were responsible. The situation changed in the next century, especially after the Thirty Years' War came to an end in 1648. In Holland, however, where church-building revived much later than in Germany and under Calvinist rather than Lutheran auspices,[31] no Catholic churches at all were erected in the mid- and later sixteenth century any more than in England, and the earliest Protestant ones of around 1600 have idiosyncratic plans unrelated to German examples, either of that period or earlier. Not so surprisingly, there are no differences in Germany between what Catholics and what Lutherans built to live in and to house their public activities. Catholic churches both old and new, moreover, were usually taken over for Protestant use with a minimum of modification of their ritual arrangements other than the removal of subsidiary altars. On the other hand, very considerable delay in completing churches still in construction when the change of religion came locally was common.

Although the prince-bishop of Paderborn who began Schloss Neuhaus in the mid-twenties was naturally a Catholic, Sweder von Schele, who was soon employing Unkair at Schloss Schelenburg, had a son Kaspar, who became a pupil of Melancthon in 1543-1546 and was a table-companion of Luther at Wittenberg in the latter's last years. The new religion had reached Heilbronn already by 1520, which doubtless explains the very delayed completion of the Oktagon there until almost a decade later. Augsburg accepted Lutherans within the next few years; indeed, as has been noted in the first chapter, St. Anna in Augsburg was turned over to them very early by the Carmelite prior himself and the first Lutheran communion service was held there in 1524; work on Sts. Ulrich and Afra in Augsburg halted from 1526 to 1560, even though that remained Catholic as it is still today. It will also be recalled that Protestants had taken over Hieber's Neupfarrkirche in Regensburg by 1542. That was the year after the Catholic Cardinal Brandenburg left Halle with his church of Unsere liebe Frau, henceforth called the Marktkirche by the Protestants, which he had begun in 1529 still far from completion.

There is, thus, little correlation either positive or negative between the new religion and the new architecture, nor even such differences between the north and the south as would appear later in Germany. The vaulted gallery of Frederik I of Denmark at Schloss Gottorf in remote Schleswig is, indeed, perhaps a decade earlier[32] than the arcades at Schloss Binsfeld in the Rhineland (Pl. 77) that it somewhat resembles in its hybrid Late Gothic character; yet Halle, lying to the northwest of electoral Saxony, was much more advanced than Freiburg-in-Breisgau in southern Baden, across the Rhine from Alsace, to judge from the Kaufhaus there of 1525-1532.[33] That was because of the patronage of the ruling prelate Albrecht Cardinal Brandenburg. Yet, in so far as Augsburg and Heilbronn, Nürnberg and Regensburg are considerably nearer the Alps than the Baltic, it can be said more generally that in the first quarter of the century the Renaissance in architecture reached first the southern portions of the German lands before it did Saxony. The reason is not the relative propinquity to Lombardy and the Veneto but, in the case of Augsburg and Nürnberg particularly, rather the close commercial and cultural relations that had long existed with Venice. What is surprising is that this connection had in Nürnberg so little effect on architecture as contrasted with the other arts.

The architectural commissions of the 1520s in Westphalia, beginning with that for the Schloss at Schloss Neuhaus, and Albrecht of Brandenburg's activities at Mainz on the Rhine and at Aschaffenburg on the Main, paralleling that well to the east at Halle, have no particular geographical significance. Prelates such as the prince-bishop of Paderborn and the elector-archbishop of Mainz—in Albrecht's case also a cardinal—naturally had connections with Italy of a sort that Lutherans did not, although in fact Luther and others travelled there occasionally. In France, in England, and eventually in the Spanish Netherlands, cardinals also led the way in varying degree: the two Georges d'Amboise, Wolsey and Granvella.[34]

---

[31] J. T. McNeill, *The History and Character of Calvinism*, New York, 1954, Chapter XVI.

[32] Frederik I succeeded in 1523, which suggests a probable date for this gallery in the mid-twenties: E. Schlee, *Das Schloss Gottorf in Schleswig*, Flensburg [1965], pp. 13-14, pls. 25-26; P. Hirschfeld, *Herrenhäuser und Schlösser in Schleswig-Holstein*, 3rd ed. [Munich, 1964], pp. 25-26.

[33] Deutsche Kunstdenkmäler, *Baden-Württemberg*, 2nd ed. [Munich 1970] (henceforth cited as DKD, *Baden-Württemberg*), p. 387; Dehio, *Baden-Württemberg*, pp. 145-146, gives the date as "gegen 1520," however.

[34] The elder Georges d'Amboise built the chateau of Gaillon

The remarkably early, if rather naïve, acceptance of Italian design in Görlitz on the Neisse, where Saxony and Silesia meet, is to be explained rather differently. The reason was, undoubtedly, that the latter district was contiguous to Bohemia on the south and to Poland on the east where, as already stressed, Italian influence and, in the latter case, even Italian craftsmen had appeared shortly before and just after 1500. The clumsy illiteracy rather than "hybridity," so to put it, of the sacristy portal of 1517 (Pl. 19) in the Cathedral of Wrocłav in Silesia has been mentioned; but the tomb of Margarethe Irmisch (†1518)[35] in St. Maria Magdalena there, though only a modest arched slab largely occupied with a relief of Christ appearing to the Three Maries, already shows somewhat more sophistication in its design and execution as a result, doubtless, of influence from Kraków in Poland to the southeast.

Saxon priority in the 1520s as regards a certain sort of rudely acclimated Italianate design in architecture is most strikingly illustrated at Görlitz. Görlitz had long been a prosperous town thanks to its location on the Neisse—a river better known now than then since it has become the border between East Germany and Poland—where the east-west traffic between Thuringia and Silesia crossed the north-south traffic between Bohemia, Pomerania and the Baltic. In the fifteenth and sixteenth centuries it was a center for textile manufacture. There existed since the high middle ages a type of house in Görlitz, influenced by the cloth trade, that had its side rather than its gable-end toward the street and a vaulted stair-hall, which was usually related to a small open court, halfway to the rear. Despite a fire in 1525, the Görlitz Untermarkt retains quite a few such Gothic houses, mostly with arcades at the base of their street fronts; some of them, however, are dated considerably later than the earliest Renaissance facade associated with a similar plan, that at Untermarkt 3, which is as late as 1535.

The many early Renaissance buildings in Görlitz[36] erected after the 1525 fire are largely the work of three members of the Rosskopf family, Wendel I (†1549), Wendel II and Jonas. Wendel I was appointed *Stadtbaumeister* (city-architect) in 1518; fifty years later, in 1568, Wendel II became the *Werkmeister* (chief of the building department) of the city and continued the work on the Rathaus his father had begun remodelling and enlarging in 1534. The elder Rosskopf was certainly first employed as a master-mason rather than as a designer of buildings. For example, the Gothic Nikolaikirche in Görlitz, begun in 1452, was completed by him over the years 1515-1520. Even in this church, and more notably in the great hall in the eastern wing, dated 1522-1524, of the ruined castle of Gröditzburg (Grodziec)[37] and the town hall at Lwówek Ślazki,[38] both in Silesia, which are plausibly attributed to Rosskopf, there seems to be a relationship to Beneš Rejt. Although it is not very likely that Rosskopf had been Rejt's pupil,[39] some knowledge of the Renaissance work for Mátyás Corvinus of the 1480s in Hungary, when Corvinus was protector of the town, such as Rejt himself evidently had, is not to be discounted. All the same, the ground-storey hall (Pl. 61) at Lwówek Ślazki, of the years 1522-1524 like that at Gröditzburg, with its low vaulting and twisting ribs over walls cut by rectangular doors and windows all framed by Renaissance moldings, does look to be a copy at much smaller scale of Rejt's great Vladislav Hall at the Hrad in Prague as completed some dozen years before. For all the profusion of Renaissance pilasters and entablatures Rosskopf employed here for the first time in his career around the windows on the exterior, he did not approach the sophisticated elegance of Rejt's detailing of such things. His originality is that of an ill-informed provincial not, like Rejt's, of a man always a great and independent designer whether his work was Late Gothic or Renaissance. That Rosskopf was assisted here by a certain Meister T.L., a local mason,[40]

over the years 1502-1510; Wolsey was erecting Hampton Court in 1515-1525; Granvella's palace in Brussels was later, toward 1550. In this connection the tomb of Fryderyk Cardinal Jagellon in Kraków Cathedral of 1508 should be recalled.

[35] G. Grundmann and W. Schadendorf, *Schlesien* [Munich], 1962 (henceforth cited as Grundmann-Schadendorf, *Schlesien*), p. 117, pl. 92.

[36] Piltz, *D.D.R.*, pp. 556-558; Dehio, *Dresden*, pp. 131-143, especially pp. 138-141.

[37] Grundmann-Schadendorf, *Schlesien*, p. 58; Knox, *Poland*, pp. 63-64. Reconstruction of the castle except for the east wing was the work of "obscure Silesians," to quote Knox, dating from 1473-1488. The architect Bodo Ebhardt partially rebuilt the ruin in 1906-1908.

[38] Grundmann-Schadendorf, *Schlesien*, p. 58; Łozinski-Miłobedzki, *Guide*, p. 146.

[39] Rosskopf is not mentioned at all by Fehr in his monograph on Ried.

[40] Knox, *Poland*, p. 53, states that it was a fire in 1518 which led to the rebuilding of the Rathaus here and that Hans Richter assisted Rosskopf. He does not mention Meister T.L. It is not certain all of the window-frames on the exterior are of the same very early date.

doubtless without relevant experience, may explain in part the inferiority of the execution, but most of his mature work continued later to be almost as provincial in character.

The mature production consists chiefly of a series of houses in Görlitz ranging in date from 1526 to 1547, but also includes work on the Rathaus there of greater refinement which was carried out in the mid-1530s and later. Rosskopf's son and others, moreover, continued the local tradition well into the third quarter of the century as the remarkably rich, even if distinctly retardataire, Early Renaissance facade (Pl. 62) of Neissestrasse 29, dated as late as 1570, indicates. Whether Rosskopf's ideas of Renaissance design came from Rejt in Prague, from Hungary or possibly from Wrocław is uncertain; certainly he had no firsthand knowledge of Italy. But he displayed already—if the house called the Schönhof is of his design, as is generally believed—a rather personal style in the facade dated 1526 of that house which stands on the corner of the Untermarkt at Brüderstrasse 8 (Pl. 63). Another house at Untermarkt 2 of the previous year 1525, also of Renaissance design, is clearly not by him, but both are well in advance of Unkair's work at Schloss Neuhaus that is probably of these years (Pl. 44).

Because of a jog in the street at the southwest entrance to the Untermarkt the Schönhof is L-shaped, with a vaulted passage under the projecting arm of which the round arches continue externally the Gothic arcade of the houses to the left along the marketplace. Two features deserve particular comment: the two-storeyed oriel, set diagonally across the projecting corner, and the apparatus of pilasters and entablatures, much like those on the exterior at Lwówek Ślazki, which link not only the windows of the oriel but all those in the upper storeys. What is missing among the more characteristic features of Early Renaissance design in Germany is gables and a portal of the twenties; the existing portal is much later. But the absence of gables is generally true of Görlitz houses except for that dated 1536 at Untermarkt 23 (Pl. 64).

Something very like the Renaissance portal (Pl. 67) at Peterstrasse 8, with the date 1528, is probably what Rosskopf originally provided on the Schönhof. A peculiar treatment, repeated by Rosskopf on the portal of the Rathaus in 1537 (Pl. 69), as also at Peterstrasse 7 in 1544 and Brüderstrasse 11 in 1547, is the setting of the pilasters on the jambs edgewise to the facade. Above the imposts of the arch of the doorway, which cut across these pilasters, the shafts are carved with rather delicate arabesques, while over the skimpy entablature there is a fluted segmental lunette with rosette-akroters at its ends. That is a familiar quattrocento motive in Italy, as has been noted earlier in this chapter, and one that does not recur over the doorways of the forties and later here. Those are of a special character (Pl. 62) matched in Saxon towns by many examples, some of which date well into the next century.

Except for the later portal, the detailing of the facade of the Schönhof is consistent with Rosskopf's other work of the twenties and thirties. It lacks the suavity of that on his addition of 1534 at the back of the court of the Rathaus (Pl. 65) but this house belongs to a considerably earlier stage in his career. The facade may well be his first attempt at coherent Renaissance design; certainly it is well in advance of his work at Lwówek Ślazki of only a few years before. There the novel door and window frames look almost like interpolations and, indeed, may actually be emendations of later date.

The two windows to the left of the portal and the three in each of the storeys above at the Schönhof are flanked by pilasters and crowned with cornices quite as are those at Lwówek Ślazki. Despite the incorrectness of the orders—the use of only two deep flutes on the pilaster shafts is a characteristic Rosskopf abbreviation—the treatment here is once more best explained as a provincial echo of Rejt's windows on the exterior of the Vladislav Hall. The execution, however, is as amateurish as at Lwówek Ślazki and far from the Urbino-like proportions and finish of the ones on the exterior of the Vladislav Hall in Prague even though Rejt's may have been designed as early as 1493.

On the oriel and the two contiguous sides of the projecting wing of the Schönhof in Görlitz the coupled windows are connected all the way around by an entablature of sorts—at least there is a carved frieze as well as a cornice—and joined together vertically by curious elements in the form of even stubbier pilasters than those between the windows. These last are crowned by flat scrolled brackets supporting the podia of the order above. Despite the relatively bold scale and the simplification of the elements this treatment slightly suggests the *style François Ier*, but French influence on the banks of the Neisse at this point is as unlikely as it would be further east in Silesia or Poland. A generation later Henri d'Anjou was elected king of Poland in 1573 though he played little part there because of his accession at home as Henri III.

Surprising for the date is the fashion in which the entablature of the top-storey windows of the Schönhof becomes in effect the architrave below the heavy terminal cornice. More immediately premonitory of mid-sixteenth-century secular architecture in Germany, however, is the diagonally-set oriel at the corner, with its richly molded supports and its big lozenge-shaped panels, below the first-storey windows. Corner oriels, both angular ones and round or polygonal ones, are markedly picturesque elements that recur in Germany well down into the seventeenth century despite the impropriety of their projection on Renaissance facades. Those on the electoral Schloss at Mainz, for example, flank a wing that was begun as late as 1627,[41] when the Baroque was already reaching Germany.

The most successful of the elder Rosskopf's works in Görlitz is in the court of the Rathaus.[42] There he built in 1534 a wing to house the town's archives. Thoroughly competent in design, if still distinctly quattrocento in character, this has also a very personal flavour yet little of the crudity of the Schönhof. Like so many of the houses along the Untermarkt in front of the Rathaus and in the nearby streets, the archive wing rides on an arcade of two relatively low arches whose molded archivolts describe broad segments above sturdily capped imposts. From the frontal elements of these supports rise stone strips that are simpler and more elegant versions of those on the apron of the Schönhof oriel. Their upper members, panelled and with large convex disk ornaments in the middle, are repeated above the centers of the arches over small scrolled keystones; in the spandrels are larger stone disks surrounded by concave moldings. Despite the modest size of the archive wing and the finesse of many of the moldings, all this is rather bold in scale for so small a facade.

In the storey above on the archive wing of the Görlitz Rathaus, where four large windows—two to each of the arches below—are separated by small pilasters, the scale is not so great nor is the effect so clumsy as on the Schönhof. Broad molded architraves frame these windows between pilasters with delicate Corinthianesque capitals, high fluted podia and panelled shafts. The shaft of the central pilaster has daintier carved decoration, including a mask below and a shell at the top; the others carry guilloche patterns, broken in those at the ends by raised circles much like

the ones on the vertical elements below the heavily molded sill. This sill and the architrave of the entablature above have slight ressauts corresponding to the pilasters. In the frieze, which reverts to the larger scale of the ground storey, raised disks above the pilasters divide the whole into four identical sections below the continuous cornice. This is scaled to the total height, somewhat as on the Schönhof, not to the order of the upper storey. In each section raised lozenges alternate with triple fluting. It is not clear whether either of the two types of metal window-grilles is original, but the very simple "eyebrow"-dormer in the low-pitched roof appears to be a later emendation.

The oriel in the court of the Görlitz Rathaus (Pl. 66) is not cantilevered but carried up to first-storey level on a pair of stubby octagonal columns with Ionic capitals. Though this feature carries the date 1564, fifteen years after Wendel I Rosskopf's death, the detailing is closer to that on the Schönhof oriel than to the upper storey of his archive wing. Three windows on the face are separated by Ionic pilasters with only two flutes and the pairs of close-set windows on each side are framed only by molded architraves. One might well have presumed on stylistic grounds that it was actually earlier than the archive wing. Evidently the tradition the elder Rosskopf had established was maintained locally for a generation and more. To the 1560's also belong, for example, the wooden ceilings and wainscoting by the joiner Hans Marquiert in the *Kleine Ratssitzungsaal* (small council room) and the archive (formerly *Praetorium*) of 1564-1566 and 1568, respectively, but this decoration accords with the local work of the thirties not with what was going on elsewhere by these later dates.

The house at Untermarkt 4 of 1536 has a facade somewhat like that of the archive wing but the arches—probably already in existence—are pointed. The two storeys above, with paired windows in each of the four bays, are handled more as on the later Rathaus oriel and also linked together vertically as on the Schönhof. Again there are paired flutes on the pilaster shafts and capitals barely recognizable as Ionic. Also similar, except for the absence of an open arcade below and the presence of the exceptional scrolled gable above, is the house at Untermarkt 23 mentioned earlier (Pl. 64), also of 1536; while that at Brüderstrasse 11 of 1547 has a window treatment close to that on the Rathaus. If this is, indeed, by the elder Rosskopf and not by his son or some other imitator, it would suggest that his style developed no further

[41] Reclams *Rheinlande und Westfalen*, p. 426.
[42] Dehio, *Dresden*, pp. 137-138; Piltz, *D.D.R.*, p. 556.

after the mid-thirties. Thenceforth what might be called the "Görlitz Renaissance" represents a sort of stylistic backwater, despite the remarkably high quality of the facade of Neissestrasse 29 (Pl. 62) of 1570.

Rosskopf's portal on the Rathaus (Pl. 69), across the street from the Schönhof, is no more than an honorific entrance. But it includes an open stair, a sort of rostrum or outdoor "pulpit" on which the date 1537 is inscribed and an arched doorway with a pair of windows above. Not surprisingly, this is Rosskopf's most ambitious work. The stair curves down away from the corner, connecting at half-level with a surviving Late Gothic doorway some twenty years earlier in date. Over that is a high relief, dated 1488, of the arms of Mátyás Corvinus, king of Hungary, as protector of the town, but that is evidently not by one of the Italians he had by then been sponsoring in Buda for a decade or more. To the left the rostrum, though set against the wall, is carried like the oriel in the court on a pair of very stubby columns, here not octagonal but round and rather swollen, and capped by a cantilevered cornice with ornamentally carved moldings. The four panels of the parapet are separated by pilaster-like members with arabesque decoration above and, below, disks like those on the archive wing. These deep-sunk panels, framed with foliate moldings, are carved with mermaids in high relief—replaced by copies in 1951—and the whole is topped by a bold cyma.

In the actual doorway of the Görlitz Rathaus, and also at the sides of the paired windows above it, the pilasters are set in Rosskopf's frequent way, not in the plane of the wall, but at an angle to it, as earlier in the doorway at Peterstrasse 8 of 1528 (Pl. 67). Above the guilloche-decorated archivolt of the doorway bold scrolled brackets with fluted ends support the shelf-like sill of the windows above. The lower pilasters, across which the molding that tops the imposts of the arch is carried as at Peterstrasse 8, are decorated with framed disks and sunken fluting. The pilasters that flank, and the one that separates, the windows above have arabesques in rather high relief interrupted by inset disks of dark marble or slate. The sill and the cornice over the windows, both brought forward to the wall-plane, and also the angular ressauts above the pilasters at the sides are crowned with paired scrolls. These are somewhat like those over the lower windows on the facade of the Certosa di Pavia but much simpler. Rosskopf was evidently drawing, with considerably more facility than before, on whatever were the intermediate sources for Italian design he

could have easily found by this time in books, in prints and even perhaps small imported *objets*. The result, however, is hardly as happy as his earlier and more original archive wing. It should be noted that the tall candelabra at the foot of the stairs dated 1591 is not by one of the Rosskopfs. The statue of Justice on its top may be by the son-in-law of Wendel I, Hans Cromer, or less probably by Andreas II Walther. Both were from Dresden.

Architecturally another town hall, that at Saalfeld in Thuringia (Pl. 70), is in several respects more interesting and almost certainly earlier than Rosskopf's portal on the one at Görlitz. This includes several features of great significance for later German Renaissance architecture—two external oriels and several gables of varied outline—which are among the first of their sort on a civic structure to approach in some degree Renaissance forms. On this town hall, begun like the Schönhof at Görlitz in 1526[43] though not completed until 1537, there is at the lefthand outer corner a tall polygonal oriel echoing in plan the distinctly Gothic stair-tower rising at the middle of the front and, like that, wholly Gothic in design. To the right, however, a two-storeyed rectangular oriel of thoroughly Renaissance character carries engaged columns—these rather more correctly detailed than Rosskopf's pilasters—which frame paired rectangular windows. This oriel may well be, not of the twenties, but of the mid-thirties. Each of its storeys, however, closely resembles the pilastered oriel, dating from the early to mid-twenties, once on the Bischofshof at Regensburg, so that Vollmer's attribution of this feature to Nickel Gromann and a date as late as 1580 seems unlikely.[44]

Even more prominent on the Saalfeld Rathaus are the gables at the two ends of the main rectangular block and, on the front, those of the almost equally large stone dormers at the level of the sharp-pointed roof—"steeple," so to call it—of the stair-tower. All these gables are, like the transitional one of the twenties on the front of the Zwickau Gewandhaus (Pl. 55), tightly reticulated by vertical strips and horizontal string-courses. Below, moreover, the paired rectangular windows of the main storeys are nearly identical with Unkair's at Schloss Neuhaus (Pl. 44), also of the twenties, though here regularly if not symmetrically arranged. These windows float in the broad surface of the stuccoed wall much as on the Rathaus

[43] DKD, *Thüringen*, p. 397.
[44] H. Vollmer, article "Nickel Gromann" in ThB.

begun in 1522 at Wittenberg (Pl. 247) and on many others that are both earlier and later. What is more significant are the lunettes crowning the central panels of all the gables. These are considerably smaller than Unkair's *welsche Gebel* at Schloss Neuhaus, but quite comparable in size to such Saxon examples as the one at the peak of the gable of the Zwickau Gewandhaus (Pl. 55) of 1522-1525 and those over the outer stair dated 1531 at Pössneck (Pl. 53). However, the treatment of the vertical elements as simplified pilaster-strips, if not unique, is rather novel at this date, even if the date be sometime in the thirties. It should also be noted that the two steps on each of the dormers over the front and the six on the gable at the right-hand end here are S-curved like those on the gable of the house of 1536 at Untermarkt 23 (Pl. 64) in Görlitz though somewhat more boldly detailed. This is distinctly premonitory of the later elaboration of the outline of German Renaissance gables.

Unlike the richly decorated oriel on the right, these scalloped gables at Saalfeld may date from the mid to late twenties and are certainly no later than the mid-thirties. If of the twenties, they are prior even to the most notable very early examples of this German feature, henceforth so characteristic, which once crowned the ends of the west wing begun by Knotz in 1530-1531 at Neuburg-a.-d.-Donau (Pl. 75). Those at Neuburg will shortly be described at some length. Yet in their simplicity and verticality the Saalfeld gables seem quite unrelated to those on the Palais de Savoie[45] (Pl. 41) as completed in 1526, the most obvious examples in northern Europe that are certainly earlier in date, since the S-curves at the edges are not scrolled and there is no other post-mediaeval detail except the very plain pilaster-strips. Netherlandish influence was not yet a factor in the development of a German sort of Renaissance architecture despite the early imports that have been described in Cologne (Pl. 58).

Before leaving the 1520s and proceeding to the much more considerable roster of secular buildings definitely begun, like Rosskopf's later work at Görlitz, in the thirties another structure dated 1526 should be mentioned. In many parts of Germany as, of course, also throughout much of England and even France the use of masonry for buildings other than churches was still rare. Many whole towns, when rebuilt like Görlitz after the recurrent fires, continued through the sixteenth century and even down to 1800 to be almost entirely of *Fachwerk* (timber-framed construction).[46] Exceptions, however, were the few churches and quite often the town halls, not to speak of new-built fortifications and associated castles, if there were any such. For these last, in any case, the clients were more likely to have been local lords than the burghers of the town Council.

Such a town is Goslar near Brunswick—which, incidentally, became Protestant rather early, in 1528. The house called the Brusttuch there was built of stone as regards its lower storey in 1521 in a wholly Late Gothic manner.[47] Five years later the owner, Magister Johannes Thilling, added an upper storey of Fachwerk beneath a very tall and steep slated roof and had the structural members carved with amusing mythological scenes, fables and ornament in a Renaissance vein. Not surprisingly at so early a date, this decoration is distinctly provincial, not to say rustic, in character. The carver may well have been Simon Stappen from Brunswick. He had been working in Brunswick since 1517 at this sort of ornamental carving on external timber-framing, but previously in a more mediaeval mode.

Except for the carved decoration the Brusttuch at Goslar has nothing to do with the new developments of the period in stone architecture; but here at Goslar other similar houses soon followed, as also in many other German towns. Particular mention should be made of the famous Knockenhaueramtshaus of 1529

---

[45] So specific a source for German Renaissance gables as those on the Palais de Savoie has, I think, rarely been suggested; but carelessness as regards chronology has allowed the more general theory of a Dutch or "Flemish," i.e. Brabantine, origin for German gable-design to be widely accepted. As regards these decades before the mid-century, it is worth noting that continental influence in the England of Henry VIII flowed, not from the Netherlands, but from Italy and France: J. N. Summerson, *Architecture in Britain 1530-1830*, paperback ed. [Harmondsworth, 1970] (hereafter cited as Summerson, *Britain*), Chapters I and II. What are called "Dutch" or "Holborn" gables in England date from the time of James I after 1600 and will be discussed at some length in the last chapter.

[46] F. Correll, *Deutsche Fachwerkbauten der Renaissance*, Berlin/New York, n.d. (henceforth cited as Correll, *Fachwerkbauten*) provides 60 fine heliogravure plates of timber-framed houses. Most of them are relatively late, however, some even of eighteenth-century date. A. Bernt, *Deutschlands Burgerbauten*, Tübingen [1968] (henceforth cited as Bernt, *Burgerbauten*) is also relevant for its profusion of illustrations.

[47] Reclams *Niedersachsen*, p. 277.

(Pl. 72) in the Marktplatz in Hildesheim,[48] even though that was destroyed in 1945, and of those decorated in the thirties, almost certainly by Stappen, at Brunswick,[49] Osterwieck and Celle (Pls. 102-103). There are even more dating from the forties and fifties at Einbeck[50] and street after street of them—mostly rather late in date—at Hannoversch-Münden,[51] two towns in which innumerable extant examples create still remarkably consistent urban entities.

Around and shortly after 1530, however, a more significant if less ubiquitous development began in which princes, rather than town councils, as at Zwickau, Saalfeld and Pössneck, or prosperous individual citizens, as at Görlitz and in the Fachwerk towns, led the way. By the time—probably in the early thirties—that Unkair started building the big new Schloss at Stadthagen near Hannover for Adolf XI, Count of Schaumburg, mentioned earlier in this chapter, several other major Schlösser were in process of enlargement or replacement, especially for clients who had lately, or would soon, become Protestants. The three most important of these clients, at least as it seems to posterity, were the Count Palatine Ottheinrich, a Wittelsbach, who began at this point to rebuild the Schloss at Neuburg on the Danube in the Upper Palatinate; Friedrich der Weise's successor, Elector of Saxony Johann Friedrich, who did the same at Torgau on the Elbe; and another Wettin, his cousin Duke Georg der Bärtige of Saxony, at Dresden. Then there were the Welf dukes of Brunswick-Lüneburg, whose Schlösser at Celle and Gifhorn have already been mentioned; and the Brabants who ruled in Hesse, where the modest Neues Schloss at Giessen was erected by the Landgrave Philipp der Grossmütige (the magnanimous). A few more such magnates should also be added. Count Philipp III of Nassau-Weilburg—not a close relative of the Dutch Hendrick of Nassau-Breda—was building early in the thirties at Weilburg on the Lahn. Charles V's and Ottheinrich's cousin, another Wittelsbach, Duke Ludwig X of Bavaria erected somewhat later, in 1537-1543, the Stadtresidenz at Landshut on the Isar, the most advanced example of Renaissance design of the period in Germany; for that reason it will not be described here but in the next chapter. Then, almost contem-

porary with Ludwig's commission, there was that of the Hohenzollern Elector of Brandenburg Joachim II for the Joachimsbau of the Berlin Schloss to be discussed toward the end of this chapter.

In none of the Schlösser that these men started to remodel or rebuild in the thirties, and that their successors so often extended later, is it possible to pin down with assurance the dates of construction for all of the various portions. The work could continue, as noted for Gifhorn and Celle, through a decade or more, and most were still further modified in the terminal decades of the century or after 1600. In a good many others additional changes were made in the later seventeenth century when the Thirty Years' War was finally over, more especially because they required drastic repair of the damage caused by recurrent bombardment or occupation by roving German and Swedish soldiery. Moreover, even where names of master-builders are recorded as at Gifhorn and Celle, their artistic personalities are rarely as distinguishable as Hieber's, Unkair's or Rosskopf's so that stylistic attribution is precarious and, as regards dating, may seem to conflict with actual documentary evidence.

The account can begin—somewhat arbitrarily perhaps—with a discussion of Ottheinrich's big Schloss at Neuburg even though, because of overlaps, the chronological sequences of construction there are not easy to establish at all precisely.[52] Already in 1527 a presumably defensive "runder Bau" had been added to the mediaeval castle from which Ottheinrich, at first together with his brother Philipp, ruled intermittently in the Upper Palatinate from the time he came of age in 1544 until he moved to Heidelberg in 1556[53] upon succeeding his uncle Friedrich II as Elector Palatine. Possibly something of this structure still survives

---

[48] *Ibid.*, p. 391.

[49] O. Stelzer, *Braunschweig*, 2nd ed. [n.p.] 1965 (henceforth cited as Stelzer, *Braunschweig*), p. 19, pls. 62-69.

[50] Reclams *Niedersachsen*, pp. 146-150.

[51] *Ibid.*, p. 355.

[52] Volume V in the series *Die Kunstdenkmäler von Schwaben, Stadt- und Landkreis Neuburg an der Donau*, Munich, 1958 (henceforth cited as Horn-Meyer, *Neuburg*), for the preparation of which A. Horn and W. Meyer were responsible, provides on pp. 58-266 the most complete account of the Neuburg Schloss, very superior to the modest booklet of J. Heider, *Neuburg an der Donau . . .* , 7th ed., Neuburg, 1967. Both accounts were prepared before restoration began in the late 1960s. More current is H. Stierhof, *Wand- und Deckenmalereien des Neuburger Schlosses im 16. Jahrhundert*, Munich, 1972 (henceforth cited as Stierhof, *Wandmalerei*), but that is limited in subject to the painted decorations.

[53] Horn-Meyer, *Neuburg*, pp. 160-166, gives information concerning Ottheinrich's rule and some account of his predecessors and successors.

within the tall tower that flanks on the left the bare but impressive east wing, of late seventeenth-century date, that rises above the Danube and the lower town. The following year Ottheinrich took into his service the master-builder Hans Knotz from Nürnberg. Down to 1538 Knotz would direct the operations at Neuburg with the notable assistance of various other artists and craftsmen both Germans and, later, some Italians. Beginning in 1532, for example, Paulus Beheim (†1561), also from Nürnberg, the son of Hans I Beheim who was mentioned earlier, even though primarily concerned with fortifications rather than being a builder-architect in general practice like his father, gave advice from time to time as regards painters and such who might be employed. It was at his suggestion, reputedly, that Ottheinrich vainly attempted to obtain for Neuburg from the Vischer firm the grille begun for the Augsburg Fuggerkapelle.

In 1530 a complete replacement of the mediaeval Schloss at Neuburg (Fig. 11) was initiated.[54] First came the cellars of a new west wing, largely built, it would appear, in that year and the next. The construction of the upper storeys proceeded more slowly and was finally completed as regards the interiors only toward the middle of the next decade. In the same years of the early thirties Knotz was also responsible for the modest Alter Bau ("Old Build") at Schloss Grünau,[55] nearby to the north, a hunting lodge (Pl. 124) that Ottheinrich erected to please his wife Susanna.

In 1532-1533 the south wing at Neuburg, where the kitchens were located, rose more rapidly and is detailed much like the west wing; then came the north wing, begun in 1534 and completed by 1538. Important changes were made even after that date, most notably in the chapel (Pls. 121-123) which occupies the north end of the west wing. That received its vault- and wall-paintings only in 1543. Of the decorative work in other interiors of the west wing, originally of 1538 and later, the greater part has been destroyed or dispersed.

At this point only the architecture of the wings as built in the thirties will be described.[56] Moreover, the description will be broken off before discussing the north wing in order to deal with the still more important Schloss Hartenfels at Torgau of Johann Friedrich of Saxony. There a major campaign of reconstruction started in 1533 and was largely completed by 1536, a year or two before the Neuburg north wing. At Torgau another wing, including a new chapel, followed in the early forties. The work of the thirties at Neuburg, alas, has been subjected to recurrent degradation over the centuries[57] so that many questions as to its original character must remain unanswered. Happily, the Schloss has in the last years been appropriately restored and is now well maintained by the Bavarian state.

Schloss Neuburg is undoubtedly impressive when seen from across the river or from the town below, but this is chiefly because of the scale of Duke Philipp Wilhelm's plain but grand tower-flanked range of 1665-1668. The north wing of 1534-1538—or at least its crowning gables—is visually effective too from this side and also from the upper town to the west (Pl. 91). But the exterior of the west wing lost much of its original character with the replacement of the top storey in 1824. The remodelling of that date entailed the loss of the gables on the ends and also of the *Riesensaal* (hall of giants) within that once occupied the whole of the third storey. The spiral staircase and the two-storeyed chapel (Pls. 121-122) inside survive, but very little else, except for the panelled wooden ceilings of the principal apartments (Pl. 105), those on the main storey in which Ottheinrich actually lived.

The Schloss ceased to be used as a princely residence when Philipp Wilhelm succeeded as elector Palatine and settled in Heidelberg in 1685. In 1828 the Bavarian military authorities adapted the interior to house a regiment. Indeed, until lately, the military continued to use the east wing and parts of the north wing. The west and south wings were less damagingly occupied by the Bavarian State Archives.

What most conspicuously survives externally of Knotz's earliest wing[58] at Schloss Neuburg is a shallow two-storeyed projection (Pl. 73) housing the main entrance from the upper town. The ground storey of this presents a very attenuated triumphal-arch composition with a central segment-headed opening and four slim Corinthianesque columns ris-

---

[54] *Ibid.*, pp. 116-183.

[55] *Ibid.*, pp. 476-494.

[56] It is here assumed that the west wing, though finally brought to completion only after 1538, when additional work on the interiors was undertaken once the north wing had been finished, was designed by Knotz at least no later than the more securely dated south wing of 1532-1533, and hence several years before the north wing was begun in 1534.

[57] Horn-Meyer, *Neuburg*, pp. 183-191, gives the later history of the Schloss.

[58] *Ibid.*, pp. 191-208, provides a very detailed and thoroughly illustrated description of the west wing at Neuburg before the current restoration.

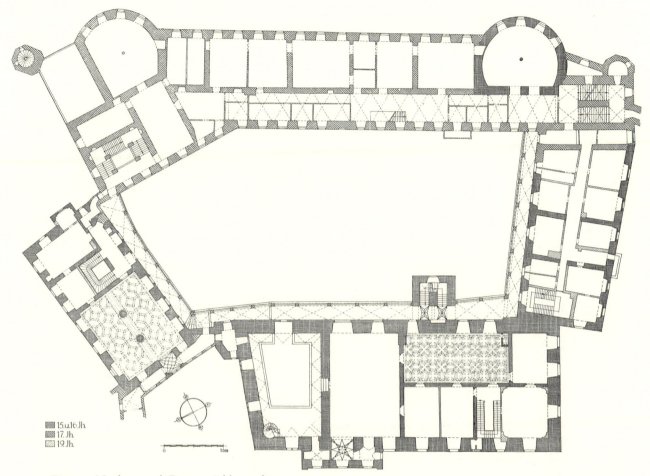

Fig. 11. Neuburg-a.-d.-Donau, Schloss, plan

ing from round podia. Though not spirally fluted, these recall in their slim proportions the ones on the sacristy portal of 1518 at Annaberg (Pl. 20). The motif is larger and more pretentious than the portals of Rosskopf's contemporary houses at Görlitz (Pls. 63, 64) if not so coherent as the design of his archive wing of 1534 (Pl. 65) in the Rathaus court there. However, there is none of the plausibly Italian quattrocento quality of the work at Augsburg and Regensburg of the 1510s and early twenties described in the first chapter, much less of what existed by this time in Prague, in Esztergom and in Kraków (Pls. 5, 39). The columns and, indeed, all the carved trim are of red Tyrolean marble as at Augsburg and Freising, providing a somewhat Italianate note of color.

The storey above the entrance has three good-sized segment-headed windows, with those at the sides not centered over the intercolumniations below. Similar windows, rather widely spaced, continue along the wall to the right. The three windows over the portal itself are also linked at top and bottom by thin string-courses that are rather more Gothic in character than Rosskopf's and also flanked by narrow pilaster-strips. These are doubled at the corners. Their shafts are panelled and further ornamented with plain round disks at half-height, somewhat in the way of those in the Fuggerkapelle and the ones proposed in Hieber's projects (Pls. 23, 25, 26), not to speak of Rosskopf's on the archive wing of the Görlitz Rathaus (Pl. 65) which may be a year or two later since that is dated 1534. As on the Schönhof (Pl. 63) and the wing of the Rathaus, moreover, similar strips also run downward to the entablature—complete here, but rather pinched—of the order below. Originally the top storey had widely spaced windows with curtain-tops.

To the left, close against the vertical buttress that frames the projecting entrance feature on that side of the west front of Schloss Neuburg, there is in the first storey a window of different shape. This is tall, narrow and round-arched, with a simple traceried head like the ones at Lauingen and those of the Neupfarrkirche in Regensburg (Pl. 28). This lights the west end of the chapel and is probably of the same date in the late thirties and early forties. Below it to-day is a plain segment-headed doorway leading directly into the chapel from the street. This doorway does not appear, however, in the drawing by a Swiss artist, Georg Ludwig Vogel (1788-1879), of about 1824 that provides such important evidence concerning the original character of the upper storeys of this wing.

The remodelling in 1824 of the second storey of the west wing at Neuburg had a more serious consequence than the disappearance of the range of curtain-topped windows. The replacement of Knotz's very high roof by a much lower one entailed the demolition of the original gables at the ends, gables far more elaborately decorated than any known German ones provably of earlier date.[59] These gables rose in five stages above the line of the eaves (Pl. 75), rather than the three of Unkair's at Schloss Neuhaus (Pl. 44), to a height nearly half again that of the three storeys below. At the northwest and southwest corners there were also small blind gablets. Vogel fortunately made watercolor drawings not only of both the north and the south ends and the left portion of the west front but also of the heads in medallions that provided the principal figural decoration. These and the pilaster orders and pedimented edicules with which the surface of the gables was articulated were not of red marble like the architectural elements around and above the entrance but of terra cotta as is much of the detail inside another Schloss Neuburg, further to the east on the Inn, where some of the interiors of much the same date still survive (Pl. 106).[60]

The profuse decoration of Knotz's gables on the west wing at Neuburg (Pl. 75) would hardly be rivalled before the 1560s. They certainly do not resemble at all Unkair's simple *welsche Gebel* at Schloss

Neuhaus or those on the Dom at Halle (Pls. 44, 45). Moreover, if there be any relation at all between them and those at Saalfeld (Pl. 70)—well to the east in Thuringia—it is that the treatment of the latter *might* be an extreme simplification of Knotz's if they are, indeed, as late in date as 1536 or 37. Quite probably, therefore, the treatment of the former was original with Knotz or some other designer employed here whose name has been lost. The way the large circular window in the center of the lowest stage not only required the omission of the middle pilaster but extended downward into the podium zone of the order might, in fact, suggest that the decorative elaboration of the Neuburg gables was, in part at least, the work of an intervening hand. As so often, Peter Flötner has been proposed as the designer of the medallions or else one of the Dauhers, all three artists known for their skill as medallists, but this attribution is no more plausible than elsewhere at least as regards Flötner. Such artists, in any case, are not likely to have been responsible for the architectural design of the gables as a whole.

Each of the four stages of the Neuburg gables (Pl. 75) carried a pilaster order with the number of bays diminished by two in each stage until there was only one, capped by a basket-like stork's nest, at the top. In the lowest stage each of the bays, except for the double one at the center enclosing the big round window, contained a blind arch. In the next two stages the central bays, four in the second and two in the third, contained edicules of which the pediments slightly overlapped the architraves above. It is probable that the arches within these edicules also capped windows. However, the flanking bays in these two stages and all three in the top two stages have blind arches and these were, rather surprisingly, pointed not round. To achieve a slanting outline following the pitch of the roof each stage was flanked by two rather flat C-scrolls separated at mid-height by an arch-supported horizontal member corresponding, at least apparently, to the imposts of the pointed arches. Each break in the outline was punctuated by a small projecting sphere like the stone balls on Unkair's gables.

At the base of the Neuburg gables an extra bay on the end toward the front of the lowest stage connected with the gablets around the corner that faced west. The lowest stage of each of the latter contained a tiny edicule under an arch and this complicated motif was repeated in simplified form in the terminal stage where it is both flanked and topped by flattened scrolling. These minor features, that on the left rising

[59] Even if, as is admittedly possible, these gables were posterior by a year or two to those on Schloss Hartenfels dated 1533-1536, the ones at Neuburg were quite unlike the convex one that alone survives on top of the stair-tower there (Pl. 78). So also the gables on the Georgenbau in Dresden (Pls. 83, 84), probably completed only by 1534/35, are more likely to have been a year or two later rather than earlier than the ones at Neuburg.
[60] Reclams *Bayern*, p. 594.

almost directly above the entrance, were quite uncoordinated in scale and proportion, as well as in the
materials probably used, with the marble trim of the
lower portion of the west facade. Yet the round spots
that Vogel's drawing indicates in the spandrels of the
blind arches on the gablets, as also those of the
pointed arches of the main gables and above the
round windows, may have been an intentional echo
of the disks on the marble ressauts and pilasters below, whatever their material.

Clearly the rather repetitious treatment of the Neuburg gables has little relation to other German gables
of approximately the same date. Except for the concentration of most of the decoration above the roof-
line, they are not lineal descendants either of the
welsche Gebel of the 20s at Schloss Neuhaus and
Halle (Pls. 44-46) or of such a half-Gothic one as that
on the front of the Zwickau Gewandhaus (Pl. 55);
even less are they related to the still earlier ones, those
in the Netherlands on the Palais de Savoie at Mechelen, of the previous decade (Pl. 41). The character of
the architectural detail suggests—though quite remotely it must be admitted—inspiration from Lombardy or Emilia rather than from the Veneto as at
Augsburg. Furthermore, the portrait heads in the
medallions with their Classical gear indicate some
awareness of the Antique, at least as certain aspects of
Roman art could by then be known to a northern
craftsman from coins, medals or prints. An Italian
such as Giovanni da Majano, who supplied around
1520-1525 the wreathed terra cotta busts of the Caesars
at Hampton Court for Cardinal Wolsey, would have
known such models at first hand before leaving home.
As in Henry VIII's England, moreover, no one man,
the master-mason Knotz or a hypothetical collaborator on the decoration, need be supposed to have
controlled the design as a whole or executed all its
various features.

The principal feature of the court side of the west
wing at Neuburg is an arcade (Pl. 74) at ground-
storey level over which runs the second gallery of
seventeenth-century date, which is of very plain design. The ground-storey gallery has elaborately ribbed
Late Gothic vaulting and, above the variously treated
pillars, a series of arches of broad segmental shape like
the one at the entrance. Such arches existed already in
the arcade at Freising of 1519 (Pl. 30) and were being
used by Rosskopf under his archive wing at Görlitz in
1534 (Pl. 65), to mention two early German examples
both of more distinctly Renaissance character. In designing the pillars that support the arcade Knotz

made no attempt to provide Italianate detail even to
the degree that Rottaler had done at Freising. They
are, however, mostly cylindrical like the tall piers in
early sixteenth-century German churches both Late
Gothic and Early Renaissance (Pls. 13, 15, 47). The
simply molded capitals, for example, carry little
shields to mask their awkward juxtaposition with the
moldings of the intradoses above, a distinctly Gothic
device.

To the right of the entrance passage one solid bay
of the arcade houses the low rectangular apse of the
chapel. The three round-arched windows, one in each
wall, with cusped tracery like that in the west window are probably also of 1538 or a little later, not of
the early or mid-thirties when the wing was in
construction.

There are difficult problems of historical interpreta-
tion in considering the evidence of what survives at
Neuburg. The most noticeable elements of the whole
today are the black and white sgraffito murals that
have lately been restored. These resemble much enlarged engravings or woodcuts and cover most of the
court walls of the west and south wings. Although
still most probably of the mid-sixteenth-century, these
must date from well after the period of Knotz's original construction even if not actually after Ottheinrich's removal to Heidelberg in 1556[61] as seems very
unlikely. However, similar murals may well have existed here from the first; their one-time presence on
the west front of the wing might explain the sparsity
of the architectural features surrounding and sur-
mounting the entrance. Even later—seventeenth-century—are the large unframed arches of the windows
in the second storey above the upper gallery, which is
also of that time.

The surviving frescoes of the Legend of Tobias on
the interior walls of the stair-tower of this west wing

[61] Stierhof, *Wandmaleri*, pp. 43-62, pls. [3-5] proposes
c.1555 as the date, just before Ottheinrich left for Heidelberg.

Similar grisaille murals, more architecturally organized,
cover the four walls of the court of Schloss Ambras outside
Innsbruck (Pl. 347). These were executed for the Archduke
Ferdinand II by his court-painter Heinrich Teufel, following
prints by Virgil Solis (1514-1562), in 1566-1567: Dehio, *Die
Kunstdenkmäler Österreich, Tirol*, 4th ed., Vienna [1956]
(henceforth cited as Dehio, *Tirol*), p. 77. Extensively restored,
the effect they make today is artistically more persuasive than
at Neuburg and makes evident how much is lost where similar decoration has disappeared as is generally the case. Equally
notable is the restored mural decoration on the so-called
Sgraffitohaus in the main square of Retz in Lower Austria
which is dated 1576: Baldass, *Österreich*, pl. 31.

at Neuburg date from the mid-fifties.[62] The interiors once had various handsome earlier fittings of which, as has been noted, little but the wooden ceilings survive *in situ*.[63] Several marble door-frames from Neuburg were removed and installed at Berchtesgaden by Crown Prince Rupprecht of Bavaria in the 1920s. One, dated 1538 and attributed to Loy Hering,[64] will be described later; others that are now also in the Schlossmuseum there are some twenty years posterior and have been attributed to Bernhard Dauher.[65] These must have come from the north wing.

Earlier frescoes, definitely by Breu and dated 1537, survive in the Alter Bau at Grünau that Knotz was building in the same years 1530-1531 the construction of the west wing of the Neuburg Schloss began.[66] The simple rectangular block at Grünau, standing a little to the right and rear of Ottheinrich's larger Neuer Bau of 1550-1555 and dominated by a tall square tower (Pl. 124), bears little resemblance to the work at Neuburg which is probably several years later. The plain stepped gables at the ends, varied only by tiny pediments over the arches in the crowning steps, are quite unlike those that once must have been so conspicuous a feature of the Neuburg Schloss. Stepped gables were the sort most commonly used in the Netherlands in the sixteenth century—as for instance the earlier portions of the Palais de Savoie—and long afterward; but the form is so simple and obvious it is not even as likely to have been derived here from a Netherlandish source as in the contemporary England of Henry VIII.

The arcading on the court side of the west wing at Neuburg was continued across the base of the north wing built in 1534-1538 (Pl. 74). As regards their un-Italian character, these arcades with their columns of very varied section—some plain round, some octagonal and others reeded (Pl. 76)—may be compared with a far more striking and elegant two-storeyed example, dated 1533, which survives in the Rhineland. This arcade at Schloss Binsfeld,[67] lying between Cologne and Aachen near Düren and built by no magnate like Ottheinrich but by a minor local lord, is all of red sandstone though it runs across the court facade of a rectangular block of plain red brick. The brick is here exposed, moreover, in the Nether-

landish way, not stuccoed like the brick walls of Neuburg and Grünau as was by this time common practice in Bavaria and the Upper Palatinate. The high roof of this block, broken only by tiny slated dormers, ends in stepped gables of brick, but to the left of the arcades an octagonal stair-tower projects. The tower is banded with stone like some of the elements on Pasqualini's tower at IJsselstein in Holland, which is of almost precisely the same date, but there is no suggestion at all of the Renaissance.

The detailing of the Binsfeld arcades, on the other hand, is transitional (Pl. 77). All the arches are round, not segmental, and framed by broad flat archivolts; the supports are square, and panelled in the lower range though octagonal above. The arches have internal Gothic scalloping below, like Schweiner's below the top of the west tower of St. Kilian at Heilbronn (Pl. 16), but only molded intradoses in the upper storey. A frieze over that, right under the molded eave of the main roof, repeats at small scale the Gothic tracery patterns of the balustrate below, and simple Gothic cusping decorates not only the spandrels throughout but also the panels on the lower piers. Yet, for all the fact that the minor details are mostly Gothic, the particular proportions of the arches and the recurrent horizontals present a far more "modern," not to say Renaissance, effect than does Knotz's court arcade at Neuburg (Pl. 74). This effect is enhanced by the particular character of the moldings, for these are quite as Italianate in section as Rosskopf's at Görlitz.

It is unlikely that the large rectangular windows under the arcade at Binsfeld with their distinctly Academic eared architraves are original; but the entrance doorway, which has deep-sunk jambs, a broad plain frame and calligraphic ribbon ornament on the lintel, may well be. Like the arcades, the portal has a rather "modern" flavor in contrast to the Gothic vaulting overhead which is less elaborate than at Neuburg but still heavily ribbed. Comparison with Rosskopf's work is more instructive. The evident differences support a contention that the new style was entering Germany in the late twenties and thirties from the east for the most part, not from the west. The advanced character of Pasqualini's work of the early thirties at Breda and IJsselstein for Dutch clients found as yet no imitators east of the Rhine nor was he himself employed in Germany before the late forties.

Returning to the Neuburg situation, where work was continuing well after Binsfeld must have been

[62] Stierhof, *Wandmalerei*, pp. 35-43.
[63] Horn-Meyer, *Neuburg*, pp. 227-239.
[64] *Ibid.*, figs. 175-176.
[65] *Ibid.*, figs. 177-180.
[66] *Ibid.*, pp. 477-494.
[67] Dehio, *Rheinland*, pp. 64-65.

completed, there should be some account of the client, Ottheinrich von der Pfalz,[68] since he was one of the most ambitious German builders, not only there but later at Heidelberg. He is usually considered Knotz's sole employer, but in fact he ruled jointly with his brother Philipp until their lands in the Upper Palatinate were divided in 1535, somewhat as was the case with the Welf dukes Ernst and Franz of Brunswick-Lüneburg in these years. By 1535 all three wings of the Schloss were under way; yet, as a result of Ottheinrich's voyages in western Europe in 1519-1520, when he was seventeen, and the following year in North Italy and the Near East, it is likely he took from the first the greater interest in the project and made the controlling decisions. Certainly it was he for whom the north wing was completed in 1537-1538 and the chapel in 1543, the year after he became a Lutheran. In 1544, however, Ottheinrich went bankrupt with debts amounting to 300,000 gulden. From 1545 he was in exile at Heidelberg and the next year Charles V besieged and captured Neuburg. Ottheinrich regained control of his duchy only in 1552 with the Treaty of Passau, for that brought to a conclusion the emperor's war against the Lutheran princes with whom Ottheinrich had been associated in the League of Schmalkalden. Four years later he again left for Heidelberg on succeeding as Elector Palatine and died there in 1559 after beginning the construction of his best-known work, the Ottheinrichsbau of the Heidelberg Schloss.

In 1546 the Neuburg Schloss had been plundered by the imperial troops. This was only the first of a series of disasters that befell what Knotz was responsible for at Neuburg. But that is to get far ahead of the story in the 1530s when first the south wing and then the north wing were added at the two ends of the court behind the west wing. The short south wing,[69] built 1532-1533, is of little intrinsic interest. It has almost exactly the same sort of window-trim and so forth as on the west wing that has already been described, but it is in general simpler as is appropriate to kitchen quarters. The north wing is of considerably greater elaboration externally and even retains some interior fittings of the forties and fifties. Unlike most of those in the west wing, these are in good condition today since the latest restoration.

But before Knotz built the third wing at Neuburg

68 See Note 53.
69 Horn-Meyer, *Neuburg*, pp. 239-243. A storey was added on this wing in the seventeenth century.

at the north end of the court, starting in 1534, Johann Friedrich of Saxony, who succeeded as elector on the death of Johann der Beständige in 1532, had begun the extension of Schloss Hartenfels at Torgau, which lies to the southeast of Wittenberg. The mediaeval Schloss here, rising beside the Elbe east of the town—somewhat as Neuburg does above the Danube but not so high—had burned in 1482 together with the whole town. Luther's protector, Friedrich der Weise, ruler of electoral Saxony since 1486, began the total reconstruction of both, though some earlier portions of the Schloss complex survive. On the southwest side of the roughly triangular court (Fig. 12), for example, is the Albrechtsbau (Pl. 79). That was begun around

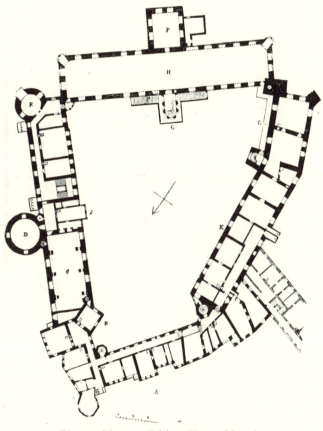

Fig. 12. Torgau, Schloss Hartenfels, plan

1470, probably by Arnold von Westfalen (†1481), for the Elector Albrecht. Later it was extended for Friedrich der Weise by Konrad Pflüger, later the architect of his church at Wittenberg that stands beside the Schloss there and of the Annenkirche at Annaberg. The other wings are predominantly of Johann Friedrich's time. However, the northwest range where the entrance is, running between the Albrechtsbau and the Schlosskirche wing, was not built until 1616-1623.

The Johann-Friedrichs-Bau, built over the years 1533-1536[70] by Konrad Krebs (1492-1540), a master-builder who came originally from Büdingen near Hanau on the Main, dominates the whole complex. This is a rectangular block with a big square projection toward the Elbe at the center of its very considerable length. In line with that on the court front (Pl. 78) an open stair-tower of horseshoe plan rises high above a square base. That *perron*, so to call it, is approached by long flights of steps at either side. Also on the court side to the right, at the junction with the Albrechtsbau, is the Wächterturm, a very tall slim watch-tower.

This court facade at Torgau, the first monumental production of the German Renaissance, was rarely exceeded in grandeur of scale and regularity of design before the next century. Rising originally three storeys high on the court side—the present attic storey was added around 1800 when the roof was modified—and even higher at the rear, where the ground by the river was considerably lower, this portion of Schloss Hartenfels has unhappily lost, like the west wing at Neuburg, all its original big gables except one. Of the original cross-gables or big gabled dormers, which must have been as tall as the main roof or nearly so, there survives only the exceptional one of convex plan at the center of the court side crowning the stair-tower, though four quite small stone dormers are still in place at the top of the tower to the right. The rather simple design of the cross-gables on the Elbe side is evident in a print by Lucas II Cranach and those on the court side were presumably identical.

The absence of the cross-gables and the low pitch of the present roof of the Johann-Friedrichs-Bau undoubtedly enhance the sweeping horizontality of the court facade of which the thirteen nearly identical bays are broken only by the vertical stair-tower at the center (Pl. 78). But equally effective in this connection is the long parapeted balcony that runs the whole length of the court front at the base of the second and principal storey. This leads to the superposed open galleries that surround—at this level and on this side only—the Wächterturm (Pl. 82).

Very "modern," if one may again so express it, is the size and the profusion of the windows of the Johann-Friedrichsbau at Torgau, even though their spacing is not quite as regular as on the Fuggerhäuser (Pl. 8) or the Wittenberg Rathaus (Pl. 247). It is a little surprising, therefore, to note that the window-heads are not rectangular but have—as did those in the top storey of the contemporary west wing at Neuburg originally—simplified versions of the curtain-top. A comparison of these flattened examples of the 1530s with the narrower and sharper ones of two generations earlier on the Albrechtsbau, or with the much larger and more fantastic ones Arnold von Westfalen used on the Albrechtsburg at Meissen (Pl. 81), also in the 1470s, is instructive. It provides evidence of a gradual change in German taste even as regards motifs that were still Late Gothic, a change which had long been underway by the 1530s.

A quarter-circular oriel links the facade of the Johann-Friedrichs-Bau of Schloss Hartenfels, in the first and second storeys on the left, with the contiguous north wing of the early forties. The oriel, which is more probably of the 30's than of the forties, has curtain-topped windows bound vertically and horizontally in a stone grid, with Renaissance detailing only in the panels below the tall narrow lights. On the rear corners of this wing towards the Elbe (Pl. 79) other circular oriels, certainly of the thirties, resemble rather more that on the corner of the Saalfeld Rathaus (Pl. 70) than the one in the court here. These rise through the top three storeys and are crowned by domical roofs terminating in sharp spirelets. The latter, though technically *welsche Hauben*, are more Late Gothic in spirit than Italianate compared with the terminal feature of the west tower of St. Elisabeth at Wrocłav in Silesia, also of about 1530-1535,[71] which has a crown of eight lunettes surrounding the base of its domed roof. This crown is much closer to such a Venetian model as the top of the campanile of Santa del' Orto or to the capping of the turrets on Maximilianstrasse 38 in Augsburg (Pls. 7, 9) than the Torgau spirelets.

The Wächterturm at the right end of the court front of Schloss Hartenfels offers in its delicately arcaded double gallery, dated 1535, at first and at second-storey level the most plausibly Italianate feature of Krebs's work here (Pl. 82). This tower is otherwise little elaborated below the roof level, though very

---

[70] Dehio, *Dresden*, pp. 403-405; DKD, *Provinz Sachsen*, pp. 402-403; Piltz, *D.D.R.*, pp. 436-437.

[71] Knox, *Poland*, p. 46, states that the spire of the Late Gothic tower of St. Elisabeth in Breslau fell in 1529. It may be presumed that reconstruction in the present form shortly followed; Łozinski-Miłobedski, *Guide*, p. 270, gives the date as 1535. The best available view of the tower is in T. Broniewski, *Wrocław*, Warsaw [1968] pl. 23.

heavy stone brackets carry an open balcony for the use of the watch all around the top storey well above the roofs of the wings on either side. But the crown with its four dormers, tiny arched lantern, and spiky termination—so like those over the oriels on the rear —is a hybrid version of such a Late Gothic "steeple" as tops the tower on the front of the Saalfeld Rathaus (Pl. 70) which presumably dates, like the corner oriel on the left there, from the late twenties. On the other hand, the dormers with their scrolls at the sides and pediments on top are as early as any of this particular character surviving in Germany, though probably not actually the first. Some secondary relationship to the gables on the Palais de Savoie of the previous decade is not impossible, though hardly very likely in the absence of known intermediate versions either in the Netherlands or in Germany dating from the late twenties. Of course, however, such may once have existed. Pasqualini's "Serlian" gable at Büren (Pl. 43) is probably later by several years if not more.

More relevant at Schloss Hartenfels than these tiny gabled dormers is the much bigger and quite differently organized gable over the stair-tower (Pl. 80). That must have repeated, in a bent or convex version, the design of the four or more cross-gables that once rose above the court facade—if those were, as one must suppose, like the ones on the rear. Despite its shape in plan, this extant gable is also rather similar to the end gables and the gabled dormers at Saalfeld (Pl. 70) which may well be of about this date rather than of the late twenties. Certainly it is not at all like those of the Palais de Savoie (Pl. 41), on the one hand, nor does it much resemble those of the west wing at Schloss Neuburg (Pl. 75), on the other, which must be contemporary or perhaps a year or so earlier.

The pattern of the Torgau gable can best be described as a grid resulting from the subdivision of the surface vertically by pilaster-strips and horizontally by modest cornices. This produces four rectangular panels in the lower stage and two in the one above, the whole flanked and crowned by S-curved members. These members are not scrolled at the ends any more than those at Saalfeld, but the outline of the whole is punctuated here by balls of stone above the ressauts that top the pilaster-strips. These balls are somewhat like the ones, presumably of the 20's, on Unkair's *welsche Gebel* at Schloss Neuhaus (Pl. 44) and elsewhere or—to mention an example nearby in Saxony a decade earlier in date—the front gable on the Zwickau Gewandhaus (Pl. 55) of 1522-1525.

A surviving link with the Late Gothic, however, is evident in the similarity of the treatment of the top storey of the gable crowning the stair-tower of Schloss Hartenfels to that of the oriels on this wing (Pl. 78). However, on the gable the coupled windows of the standard curtain-topped sort are separated by arabesqued pilaster-strips and the panels below them are also carved with arabesques. This elaboration of the gable continues, though at diminished scale, the grandeur and more Italianate handling of the open cage of the staircase as it rises through the first, second and third storeys. It repeats also the motif of the panelled parapet carved with delicate arabesques of the second-storey gallery (Pl. 82), not to speak of the more boldly sculptured one that surrounds the *perron* at first-storey level.

Krebs's major achievement, and one of the most striking features in the sixteenth-century architecture of northern Europe, is the tall cage that encloses, yet reveals, a Wendelstein within. Whether or not this reflects Francis I's staircase of some ten years earlier at Blois, it certainly rivals that famous work in monumentality and in elegance of execution. Though it does not at all resemble the Roman High Renaissance in its elements it has, all the same, a good deal of the grandeur of scale of Bramante's Cortile di Belvedere at the Vatican and somewhat recalls his earlier work in Lombardy also. Yet the immediate prototype was almost certainly German and even Saxon: the open polygonal stair-tower on the court side of the Albrechtsburg at Meissen (Pl. 81). Rising through five storeys, with a wide pointed opening on each of the external faces, this earlier Wendelstein was part of the Meissen Schloss as begun in 1471 for Albrecht of Saxony by Arnold von Westfalen.[72] Krebs's treatment, Renaissance in spirit and in detail if without over-all Italian precedent, naturally differs a great deal from Arnold's—particularly, it is curious to note, in its much more vertical emphasis.

In the verticality of the Torgau stair-tower and in the character of the decorative carving on the slanting parapets of the stairs between the piers—here curved, however, rather than straight in plan—the resemblance is closer to the one at Blois. But the whole conception is more unified, less articulated, and actually nearer to Italian work of the quattrocento in the delicacy and coherence of the detailing than what Francis's architect produced. The three principal openings toward the court are crowned by plain semicircular

[72] U. Czeczot, *Die Albrechtsburg Meissen* [Meissen, 1969].

arches with molded archivolts that continue, rather in the Late Gothic way, the moldings of the jambs. On each side, at right angles to the main facade, three similar arches rise one above another in correspondence with the first, second and third storeys of the block behind. These are of more Italianate proportions, even though the ones at second-storey level are awkwardly adjusted to the long gallery and its parapets—the gallery was perhaps an afterthought to provide horizontal communication as later at Langenburg (Pl. 356).

There is no attempt to suggest, by introducing terminal pilaster capitals as at Blois, that the piers enframing the stair at Torgau are elements of an order. However, except for the moldings that run across above and below what may be called the "podia" of the upper range, the clustered pilaster-strips have continuous panelled shafts, and the panels are carved with exceptionally refined arabesques not unlike those on the horizontal panels of the gallery (Pl. 82). Thus these echo in their delicate scale the detailing both of that feature and of the arcades on the tower to the right. The carving of the armorial panels on the parapet cantilevered out from the square *perron* below is much bolder and less Italianate; but such heraldic decoration generally retained a Gothic flavor for decades after this time (Pl. 179).

Like the Neuburg Schloss, Schloss Hartenfels has suffered much damage over the centuries. Happily, this major masterpiece of the German Renaissance, unrivalled before the rebuilding of the Plassenburg above Kulmbach (Pls. 191-193) in the 1560s, was not affected as regards the exterior and the remarkable spiral staircase—one of those feats of sixteenth-century masonry construction that continued the Late Gothic tradition of technical virtuosity—by later degradation as much as might have been feared when, in the eighteenth century, the Schloss became a prison and, after 1815, military barracks. In the late 1920s a complete remodelling of the interior accompanied a restoration of the exterior and of the chapel; a second restoration followed the last war beginning in 1952. The brick walls are stuccoed as at Neuburg and the present rendering is, of course, quite new. If there ever were external wall-paintings, no trace of them survives. The stone trim of Elbe sandstone, the work originally of masons from Dresden, was much renewed in the earlier restoration. Moreover, the statues of Johann Friedrich and his brother Johann Ernst, at the base of the stairs that lead up to the *perron*, were replaced in 1928 by copies.

Krebs's own portrait, with the date 1536, on the front keystone of the elaborate ribbed vaulting that tops the spiral staircase above the third-storey level remains *in situ*. Moreover he is buried, appropriately enough, under a slab carved by Georg Diener which is in the north corner of the Hartenfels court. Of interiors earlier than the chapel of 1543-1544, which will be described in the next chapter, nothing survives. The principal loss is presumably that of the decorations in the great hall. That occupies the center of the front range on the court as well as the whole of the wing that projects behind toward the Elbe and is entered through a carved portal leading from the main staircase. With the decorations Lucas I Cranach (1472-1553) was probably much concerned since he had been the principal artist attached to the electoral court since his appointment as *Hofmaler* by Friedrich der Weise in 1505. Except for the chapel, access to the interiors and even the stair is now forbidden[73] so that the present condition of the great hall is uncertain and even the portal cannot be seen from the court below.

Krebs was a German Renaissance designer who had not been approached in architectural talent, up to this time, by any other except Loscher in the Fuggerkapelle—or should one add Hans Hieber on the strength of his projects? In this decade Krebs was rivalled only by the obscure master-mason who directed the Mantuan craftsmen working from 1537 for Duke Ludwig of Bavaria at Landshut. Happily, a modicum of information has been recovered concerning Krebs's previous experience,[74] although it does not reveal much about his training or his development as an architect. Born at Büdingen in Hesse in 1492, Krebs was a mature forty when called to work at Torgau. Identifiable in documents as a stone-mason in Saxony from early in the century, his mark is found in various churches of the years 1506-1531. There is little or no evidence, however, as to his architectural responsibilities, if any, in those years. When still young, he was employed on the Annenkirche at Annaberg in 1507-1509—a decade, i.e., before the Renaissance sacristy portal there was designed and executed. Surely this was only in a subordinate capacity under, first, Konrad Pflüger and then Peter Ulrich. In 1532, however, the year before he began to work on Schloss Hartenfels, Johann Friedrich appointed him *Kur-*

[73] Some of the restored portions of the Schloss serve as local government offices; the Johann-Friedrichs-Bau is apparently empty.

[74] See H. Vollmer, article "Konrad Krebs" in ThB.

fürstlicher Baumeister (electoral architect). It may therefore be presumed that he designed as well as built the church at Langendorf near Zeitz, begun the previous year, if not so probably the choir of the earlier one at Burgstädt near Chemnitz which is dated 1522.[75] His responsibility for the rebuilding of the fifteenth-century nave of St. Moritz, now the Evangelical Parish Church of Coburg, also in the twenties, is generally accepted;[76] but his church-work of that decade and the early thirties incorporates no Renaissance elements in the way of Rosskopf's secular buildings of the period to the east in Görlitz.

As at Neuburg, conjecture has suggested the possible involvement of Peter Flötner (1490/1495-1546), a Nürnberg designer and sculptor who was never a builder.[77] That has been thought to explain the sophisticated character of the arcades on the tall watch-tower at Schloss Hartenfels and the elegance of the arabesques the stone-masons executed on the stair-tower, the oriel in the court and the gallery parapet (Pl. 82). The presence of an Italian or Italians, however, as documented at the Landshut Stadtresidenz just after Krebs's work at Torgau came to a conclusion is a more plausible assumption. It is difficult, all the same, to believe any Italian can have been responsible in the mid-1530s for the major architectural decisions that controlled at Schloss Hartenfels in the way Berrecci had been in Kraków in the twenties or even Franciscus Florentinus there well before him. Krebs's personal reputation with contemporaries as a designer, moreover, once this great work at Torgau was completed, is confirmed by his call in 1538 to Berlin by the Elector of Brandenburg Joachim II to advise the Saxon architect Kaspar Theiss (†1550) on the Joachimsbau of the Schloss in Berlin. He seems, however, to have spent only five weeks there. Krebs also provided in the same year a project for the Zeughaus at Coburg which was not carried out. Earlier, in 1534 while he was busy at Torgau, he executed a wellhead there which is no longer extant.

As with Schweiner, Hieber, Rosskopf or Knotz, one must accept, in considering Krebs's status as a Renaissance "architect," that German master-builders experienced in Late Gothic design could in the early sixteenth century blend into their work to excellent effect some, at least, of the alien ideas of the Italian quattrocento. Certainly they were already able to practice with some distinction by the 1520s and 1530s in a manner that may be called "German Early Renaissance," whether or not they employed as aides decorative craftsmen who were Italians or, perhaps, merely Germans who were more familiar with the new idiom than they. Thus Rejt had presumably used his Hungarian assistants, a good deal earlier, in Prague.[78] The success of such work, moreover, is largely independent of the degree of any particular master-builder's acceptance of Renaissance design as the total architectural discipline it had become in Italy by this time. Such acceptance was still beyond all these men, though it had not been in the case of Loscher well before this—if he was really the artist responsible for the design of the Fuggerkapelle—nor, less surprisingly, for the two Bolognese, Pasqualini and Vincidor, in Holland.

As regards intrinsic quality, indeed, Schloss Hartenfels has its equals in northern Europe in the mid-1530s only in Pasqualini's more consistently Renaissance IJsselstein tower or the less advanced, but more elaborate, screen in King's College Chapel at Cambridge, presumably the work of an Italian or French sculptor. The buildings of Rosskopf or Knotz at Görlitz and Neuburg are not in the same class, even though Rosskopf incorporated in his work a much higher proportion of imported elements than Krebs. Italianate charm he provided successfully in the archive wing (Pl. 65) of the Görlitz Rathaus in these years, but of such architectonic grandeur as Krebs achieved at Schloss Hartenfels he was incapable. The same is true of the other architect-builders who were then active elsewhere in Saxony.

At Dresden the early mediaeval Schloss of the margraves of Meissen received, beginning in 1471, a west wing that was designed, like the contemporary Albrechtsburg at Meissen and probably the Albrechts-bau at Torgau, by Arnold von Westfalen. Around 1530 or, it has here been assumed, two or three years

---

[75] Neither Dehio, *Dresden*, pp. 45-46, nor Piltz, *D.D.R.*, p. 460, mentions Krebs in connection with the Burgstädt church.

[76] Reclams *Bayern*, pp. 193-195.

[77] Osten-Vey, *Germany*, pp. 267-268, 285-286, makes no mention of any building operations with which Flötner was concerned except the decoration of the Hirschvogelsaal of 1534 in Nürnberg (Pl. 107); Glück, *Renaissance in Deutschland*, p. 631, calls Flötner, among other things, an architect but mentions his employment as such only for the Hirschvogelsaal.

[78] On Rejt's works, as on Krebs's, no Italian collaborators are documented so that the situation in Bohemia and in Germany was apparently rather different from that at Kraków or at Esztergom. By the mid-thirties, however, Italians were being employed in Prague and somewhat later in Moravia.

later,[79] Friedrich der Weise's cousin Georg der Bärtige, Duke of Saxony since 1500, began construction of a new gatehouse between the old Residenzschloss and the *Elbtor* (Elbe gate) of the city.

For the work Georg employed a master-builder named Bastian Kramer (†p.1553) who had come to Dresden in 1527. No earlier work of Kramer's is known to survive and, indeed, almost nothing is left today of the Georgenbau itself. As at Neuburg and Torgau, conjecture has long associated Peter Flötner with this work since it is known that Georg was one of his clients. A more plausible guess, which would explain the special elegance of much of the carved detail on the portals here, is that an Italian was involved.[80] But, as at Torgau, the general responsibility for the quite un-Italian, if hardly still Gothic, design of the gate-tower as it rose to completion in 1534-1535 must have been the local master-builder's, not any foreigner's.

In 1701 the Georgenbau burned; over the years 1889-1901, perhaps even more disastrously, the whole Schloss was "restored," not to say rebuilt, by the architects Dunzel & Fröhlich. There was, still later, a very great deal of further damage from bombs and fire during the notorious air-raid of 1945. Fortunately, seventeenth-century prints give a good idea of the two main facades of the Georgenbau, one toward the Elbe (Pl. 83) and the other toward the court (Pl. 84). Moreover, one portal was left largely untouched in the nineteenth-century restoration and another partially so.

Various fragments of the Dance of Death frieze from the Elbe side are known today also, thanks to old photographs preserved at the Deutsche Fotothek Dresden. This frieze was carved by Christoph I Walther (†1546), a Dresden sculptor, the first of a very productive artistic dynasty, whose work has lately been exhaustively studied by Walter Hentschel.[81] Walther's frieze ran across the facade just below the crowning gable and was interrupted only by a small covered balcony that stood on top of an oriel in the second storey. The oriel was on the axis of the elaborate portal below, the one that survived the 1701 fire, not on that of the gable, so that the facade was strongly asymmetrical.

The gable on the front facing the Elbe had four stages of diminishing height (Pl. 83). In the first stage, in front of which the covered balcony was set, there were also three architrave-framed windows. Shorter than those in the storeys below, these were linked to the top of the second storey by low-placed double-S-scrolls beyond the flanking pilaster-strips. These last were continued above the base of the next storey to carry small statues. Except for the cyma roof of the balcony, the following stage was symmetrical and cut only by two small square windows. An extra pair of pilaster-strips here led up to the outer ones on the third stage. As below, each of these stages and also the tiny crowning stage had S-scrolls at the edges and statues set above the tops of the pilaster-strips. Between the inner strips on the face of the third stage there were two small oculi; while on the terminal stage a globe, flanked by more scrolls, supported another small statue.

For all its elaboration with statuary and with carving on the scrolls, this Georgenbau gable is not dissimilar to the one on the right end of the Saalfeld Rathaus (Pl. 70). That civic example might even be a modest prototype; more probably, however, it represents a contemporary or later simplification of the Dresden model: a princely client might well have welcomed innovation in design sooner than an urban council. This would be especially true for such a patron of the arts as Georg der Bärtige, who had commissioned the Renaissance altar of the Annenkirche in Annaberg as early as 1518 from the Dauhers of Augsburg and was acquiring Renaissance objects in precious metals by Peter Flötner[82] of Nürnberg.

The relationship of the gable to those (Pl. 41) of the Palais de Savoie was remote, if indeed there was any Brabantine influence in German lands in this decade such as there had been, at least thanks to imports, in Cologne rather earlier than this. The innovative sort of design that resulted from the attempt in Dresden to Italianize the decorated gable, an inherited northern feature, seems to have been original. The result was parallel to, rather than derivative from, the *welsche Gebel* of the twenties at Halle and Schloss Neuhaus, just as were the ones by Knotz on the west

[79] F. Löffler, *Das alte Dresden*, Dresden, 1955 (henceforth cited as Löffler, *Alte Dresden*), p. 348.

[80] Löffler, *Alte Dresden*, believes Kramer worked from designs provided by Flötner; and Hentschel, *Dresdner Bildhauer*, pp. 22, 27, does not deny the possibility, noting that Georg der Bärtige admired the work of Flötner as a goldsmith and even acquired some examples of it. However, resemblances to Flötner may only be due to borrowing by Kramer. For Bastian Kramer, see the article in ThB.

[81] Hentschel, *Dresdner Bildhauer*, pp. 27-36.

[82] Flötner was probably born in Switzerland. First recorded in Augsburg, he came to Nürnberg from Ansbach in 1522 and that seems henceforth to have been his headquarters: see Note 77.

wing at Neuburg (Pl. 75). Those last, indeed, may actually have been no earlier despite the sequence that is suggested by their successive presentation here. Working in Saxony, however, Kramer or whoever was responsible here may, all the same, have known the gables at nearby Halle, Zwickau and Glauchau, if not so probably Unkair's in Westphalia (Pls. 44, 48) or Knotz's at Neuburg on the Danube. For that matter, the Rathaus in Dresden-Neustadt, attributed by Unnerbäck to Melchior Trost and the years 1527-1528,[83] had two trilobe-gabled dormers on the front.

The richly decorated portal on the outer side of the Dresden Georgenbau is more difficult to appreciate in the seventeenth-century engraving (Pl. 83) than the gable. That shows an edicule flanked by S-curves above the entrance, much as over the north entrance to the Palais de Savoie (Pl. 41). Again no influence from Mechelen need be assumed. The source for both might well have been such a Lombard feature as the Rodaris used in the 1480s atop the entablature of the earlier-mentioned Porta della Rana (Pl. 85) on the cathedral of Como. Furthermore, the resemblance of the rest of this portal to such an Italian example of half a century earlier was rather closer in actuality (Pl. 86) than appears in the engraving. This was most particularly true of the candelabra-elements set against the pilaster clusters that flank the entrance arch and the canting of the jambs and the archivolt. However, other northern portals of the mid-1520s flanked by candelabra-elements at Halle and in Vienna have already been illustrated (Pls. 21, 47).

As with the Palais de Savoie, however, one may wonder whether the nineteeenth-century restorers of the Dresden Residenzschloss may not have "corrected" the design of these elements to make them more Italianate. Dunzel & Fröhlich took out the inscribed panel originally in the center of the frieze and placed it over the cornice of the entablature. The flanking horizontal S-scrolls at this level were certainly then newly designed and carved to imitate, more or less accurately, the ones over the windows on the facade of the Certosa di Pavia. Even so, there is plenty of other internal evidence in the similarities of various decorative elements of this portal to details of that at Como to support the assumption that an Italian worked here, and very likely one from Como, even though Hentschel has found no documentary trace of such an alien craftsman this early. Many Italians who worked in Germany in the following

centuries, however, actually came from the Como district.

At the top of the first storey on the outer side of the Dresden Georgenbau and at the bottom of the second, as also over the second, there are carved friezes. The lowest, decorated with a continuous foliate scroll, might well have been designed, if not executed, by an Italian. The second frieze, however, had a series of heraldic shields set under squat arches carried on stubby engaged colonnettes. This is more likely to have been designed, like the facade as a whole, by a German—presumably Kramer or perhaps Christoph Walther—and executed by German assistants as was Walther's frieze above of the Dance of Death.

The inner facade of the Georgenbau (Pl. 84), opening on the old court of the Dresden Residenzschloss, was much richer than that toward the Elbe. It was, moreover, almost entirely symmetrical except for the placing of the two archways at the base. Of the larger portal, that of the passage running through the gatehouse, nothing apparently survived the fire of 1701. As can be seen in the print, this was very similar to the one toward the Elbe, for it was flanked by candelabra-elements and crowned by an edicule containing, in this case, a relief of the Crucifixion. The relief was framed at the sides by scrolls outlining irregular fluted quadrants. Happily the other archway to the left, which had already been filled in by the seventeenth century when the print was made, was largely extant until the fire of 1945, though the tall inscribed attic above seems already to have gone. The lettering on the frieze gave the date ANNO DOMINI MDXXXV between the two horizontal S-scrolls. The question arises, however, whether this represents the completion of the whole Georgenbau, including the gables, as seems most likely,[84] or merely that of the particular feature.

The execution of this inner portal of the Georgenbau (Pl. 87), with its canted jambs covered with arabesques and the variously beaded moldings of the chamfered archivolt, not to speak of the medal-like portrait reliefs set in circular frames in the spandrels, was of exceptional delicacy and refinement for Germany in these years. Comparison with the portal on the Elbe side supports the suggestion that the carving on the latter may have been largely recut and even in part actually designed by the restorers at the end of the last century.

---

[83] Unnerbäck, *Giebel*, pp. 18-19, fig. 20.

[84] A sandstone medallion with a portrait bust of Georg der Bärtige by Christoph I Walther also carries the date ANNO D MDXXXV: Löffler, *Alte Dresden*, fig. 30.

The five windows of the first and second storeys on the court side of the Georgenbau (Pl. 84) are flanked by pilasters. These were repeated between the storeys to provide continuous vertical lines across the blank wall. In principle this is very like the treatment of the oriel and the side walls of the Schönhof at Görlitz (Pl. 63), but the work was much more elaborately and carefully executed here. The strips at the sides, moreover, were carried down in two stages to the ground, with the lower stage corresponding to the pilaster order on the larger portal, and also up to the top of the third storey. On either side of the central windows the pilasters were doubled and the narrow panels between each pair filled with interlaced foliate decoration. This was possibly painted rather than carved, as also its extensions above and below. The panel with the image of the Madonna between the upper and lower windows in the central bay may also have been either painted, like the figures in the outer corners of the third storey, or carved as was the scrolled frieze over the lower windows.

Above the median level on the court side of the Georgenbau the intertwined foliage continued upward in a tapered central strip across the third storey and the fourth, which last was also the lowest of the three stages of the gable. The gable was considerably shallower than the third storey below and flanked by scrolled sea-monsters. The monsters were evidently not unlike the ones on the large southwest gable of the Breda Kasteel which must, however, be at least a year or two later in date. There were also small *Landsknechte* with raised banners standing on the podia that rise over the terminal pilasters of the third storey. Similar motifs flanked the still shallower second and terminal stages, though the second stage had plain S-scrolls enclosing roughly triangular fluted fields. These were similar to the ones at the sides of the edicule on top of the broader portal below. The second stage, like the corresponding third stage on the Elbe side, had two small square windows in contrast to the four large paired windows, joined by fluted panels, in the third.

The second and third stages of the inner Georgenbau gable had paintings of religious subjects divided by additional very short arabesqued pilaster-strips. The crowning feature was a winged nude figure with a long pike, perhaps a classicized Archangel Michael rather than, as one might have expected, Georg der Bärtige's name-saint. As on the Elbe side, where the gable is not quite so tall and steep, this was presum-

ably of Kramer's devising, but with much of the decorative work designed and executed by Italians. The *Landsknechte*, however, were by Walther or one of his assistants.

The portals on both sides, being placed asymmetrically, do not seem integral to the facade compositions as a whole and hence may well not have been the work either of Knotz or of Walther, but of another hand though it need not have been an Italian one. The wealth that the dukes of the Albertine line of the Wettins who ruled ducal Saxony from Dresden were obtaining from silver-mining in the Erzgebirge helps to explain the exceptional elaboration of these facades on the Georgenbau as it does the grand Saxon churches begun a generation earlier. To judge from the engravings of the complete facades (Pls. 83, 84), rather than from the prewar photograph of the portal at the left on the court side (Pl. 87), the general effect must have been rather *nouveau riche* compared to the simpler design and more monumental organization of Elector Johann Friedrich's extension of Schloss Hartenfels (Pl. 78). That is, of course, almost precisely contemporary, having been completed in 1536.

Georg der Bärtige died in 1539. Only after Moritz, who succeeded Georg's brother Heinrich der Fromme as duke in 1541, became elector of Saxony in 1547 was the rebuilding of the Dresden Residenzschloss carried further. It was in that year Moritz, having assisted Charles V in defeating the Lutheran princes' League of Schmalkalden[85] and more particularly his cousin, Elector Johann Friedrich, was rewarded with the Saxon electorship. That had been held since the death of Friedrich II in 1484 by the Ernestine line of the Wettins who ruled from Wittenberg. All the same, the influence of Johann Friedrich's north wing of the mid-thirties at Schloss Hartenfels, where the later Schlosskirche wing was completed in 1544, is evident in Moritz's rebuilding of the north and west wings around the larger court of the Dresden Schloss. This will be discussed in the next chapter. It is another Wettin Schloss which should at least be mentioned at this point.

---

[85] Georg der Bärtige remained a Catholic and an enemy of Lutheranism; it was his brother and successor Heinrich who changed his religion. Later, however, Heinrich's successor Moritz was ready for political reasons to join in the emperor's struggle with the Protestant League of Schmalkalden on the Catholic side. Yet, as was noted earlier, Moritz's sister Anna married William of Orange as his second wife, surely an anti-Catholic alliance.

The unknown architect-builder—not impossibly Kramer—of the new *Mittelbau* (central section) of the Schloss at Dippoldiswalde (Pl. 88), south of Dresden—originally a modest mediaeval fortress first erected around 1200 and destined to be more largely reconstructed much later after the Thirty Years' War—echoed the pilastered treatment of the first and second storeys of the inner side of the Georgenbau in a somewhat more literate Italian way. The slightly projecting pilaster orders that articulate the walls are the full height of the storeys, and the rectangular windows, though unframed, are cut into the wall-bays between. The relief of the orders, at least, is premonitory of ensuing developments in facade design a generation later. The date is assumed to be in the mid- to late thirties and the client, therefore, still Georg rather than Heinrich or Moritz.[86]

The burial chapel that Georg built some time in the mid-thirties,[87] on the south side of the fifteenth-century Fürstenkapelle at the west end of the cathedral of Meissen, was redecorated in 1677 with *stucchi* by Caspar von Klengel, but Georg's inner portal survives (Pl. 89). Although of consistently Renaissance design, the heavy-handed treatment, particularly of the entablatures above the two pairs of flanking columns, contrasts with the delicate framing of the Dresden portals and even with the rather bolder detailing of the Dippoldiswalde Mittelbau (Pl. 88) probably of a few years later. Moreover, the capitals of both the lower and the upper pair of columns, very free modulations of the Composite, are set diagonally as on the Dauhers' high altar (Pl. 57) commissioned by Georg and completed more than a decade earlier at Annaberg. The Pietà relief, carved in marble, occupying the panel above the actual doorway is of higher quality and suggests an Italian hand. The dainty ornament on the inner frame of this is very different from the strongly molded cornices and the deeply fluted segmental lunette that crowns the whole.

It is the Georgenbau, not the work at Meissen and Dippoldiswalde, that best illustrates at an early date even for Saxony three of the most characteristic features of German Renaissance secular architecture:

staged and scroll-flanked gables; elaborately Italianate portals; and regularly disposed rectangular windows, often framed by architraves. What is not present in Saxony before Moritiz's time is arcading, such as Knotz provided in this decade at Neuburg in a hybrid style and some anonymous builder on Schloss Binsfeld. Less prominent here at Dresden than at Torgau or in Görlitz was the decorated oriel which appeared, though in rather modest guise, only on the Elbe front. The story now returns to Neuburg.

It was in 1534-1537 that Knotz added the north wing to Ottheinrich's Schloss at Neuburg.[88] On that, extremely significant elements survive which are missing today from the earlier work on the west wing here and on the Dresden Georgenbau, as effectively also at Schloss Hartenfels: the big gables at the ends of the rectangular block and the smaller ones of the dormers on the sides. These vigorously shaped features are among the first examples of a new sort of decorated gable. Once they had been standardized in succeeding decades, gables of this sort eventually superseded all but totally the simpler *welsche Gebel* of the Halle Dom and Unkair's Schlösser. Yet they do not have much resemblance to the earlier sort, once crowning the west wing at Neuburg (Pl. 75), that were so significant earlier in the decade both for their multi-staged articulation and for the S-curved elements at their edges.

The end gables of the north wing at Neuburg rise, not in five stages as on the west wing, but in four (Pl. 90). Strongly molded string-courses separate the stages, but there are no vertical elements as at Saalfeld and Torgau (Pls. 70, 80) or on the exceptional gabled house of this date in Görlitz (Pl. 64). The first stage, of full storey-height, is flanked by a short straight member with an in-curving scroll below and a simpler out-curving one above. The next stage is edged with plain quadrants followed by straight verticals, while the final stage carries two broken S-scrolls below a tiny terminal lunette. Because of all these curved elements, the resultant outline may more accurately be called scalloped, or even scrolled,[89] than that

[86] Dehio, *Dresden*, p. 53. Most probably this followed, however, after the completion of the Georgenbau.

[87] *Ibid.*, p. 264. The work on the chapel probably followed the completion of the Dresden Georgenbau but could have been contemporary. The date 1534 of the death of Georg's wife is at least suggestive; he lived until 1539 as was noted earlier.

[88] Horn-Meyer, *Neuburg*, pp. 244-254. This was known as the Kneiselbau. The earliest definite date, inscribed under a medallion of Ottheinrich carved on a pilaster, is actually XXXVII, i.e. [15]37: *ibid.*, fig. 199.

[89] There is, apparently, no old German equivalent for the term "scalloped" in distinction to the common use of *welsche Gebel* for the simpler rounded sort introduced in the 1520s. The term "scrolled" is better reserved for gables with bold

of any of the just-mentioned gables in Saxony. In addition, stone balls on the edges of both the lower stages and the crowning lunette provide visual punctuation, much as on various earlier and contemporary *welsche Gebel* in Westphalia and elsewhere described previously in this chapter. It should once more be noted that Pasqualini's gable at Buren was probably several years later than these; in any case the Dutch gable was quite Serlian in character and much more restrained in its detailing except for the scrolling dolphins atop the pediment (Pl. 43).

Two windows in the lowest stage of the end gables on the north wing at Neuburg and one each in the second and third stages are of squarish shape and flanked by little pilasters carrying minimal cornices. Such windows are used consistently on the court side of the wing also, though there they are more oblong and divided by stone mullions and transoms. A large round window in the lowest stage of the gables, not dissimilar to those on the gables of the west wing but surrounded by rusticated voussoirs in stucco, is echoed by two smaller oculi at the sides of the next stage. The rustication is possibly, but not necessarily, a later emendation (Pl. 91).

The four storeys of the wall below the gables at Neuburg have a profusion of plain rectangular windows that are almost, but not quite, regularly disposed. Even more probably than the rusticated voussoirs these must, for the most part, have been introduced later; but the two windows not axially placed, one in each of the upper storeys, have the same segment-heads within pilaster-flanked rectangles as the windows above the entrance on the outer side of the west wing (Pl. 73) and are probably original.

On the court side of the wings at Neuburg (Pl. 74) the windows are also nearly regularly disposed, but their placing is not coordinated on the north either with the bays of the arcades below or with the two big dormers above. The latter are simplified versions of the end-gables though their scalloped outline is somewhat differently treated. S-scrolls flank the base of the first stage; then concave curves reduce the width of the shallow second stage; while the crown consists of a circle flanked by short convex quadrants and even shorter verticals, thus recalling a little the peculiar lunettes on the top of Dürer's Triumphal Arch (Pl. 32). Each dormer has one standard window in the lowest stage and a small oculus in the next.

No external murals survive on this north wing though there are some fragments inside on the walls of the Rittersaal.[90] The restorers have, however, painted the stucco of the court facade a rich Venetian red to contrast with the cream-colored stone that had already been substituted on the south wing for the Tyrolean marble of the west wing's trim.

The gables on the north wing were probably Knotz's last contributions to the Schloss since his employment at Neuburg ended in 1538. They already seem Northern Mannerist rather than Early Renaissance in character and are thus distinctly more advanced than the gables of the Georgenbau at Dresden on which so much of the detailing, however Italianate, is still of early, that is quattrocento, character (Pls. 83, 84).

At the very large but relatively simple Schloss where Unkair was working about this time, further to the north and west at Stadthagen in Westphalia,[91] for the counts of Schaumburg—lesser lords than Ottheinrich or the two rival Saxon rulers of the day at Wittenberg and Dresden—the rectangular windows, as earlier at Schloss Neuhaus, are still rather irregularly disposed and do not have architrave-like frames (Pl. 92). Relatively elaborate oriels are present (Pl. 93), but they are not as conspicuous as at Schloss Hartenfels (Pl. 78) or on the Schönhof in Görlitz (Pl. 63) and may well be much later than the thirties in any case. Over the outer portal below the oriel are, indeed, the arms of Otto IV with the date 1544. At Stadthagen, however, this particular motif of the German Renaissance did eventually play a somewhat more important part than at Dresden, for there are no other decorative features below the level of the innumerable gables except for the modest doorways in the court. Those, as usual with Unkair, are not at all Italianate.

The plan of the big Stadthagen Schloss is nearly quadrangular (Fig. 13) though the northeast corner, to the left of the entrance passage, is open. The south front is exceptionally long—52 m.—and the east wing is 10 meters longer, rivalling Schloss Hartenfels in extent. The dates 1535, 1536, 1537 and 1541 have been found in various parts of the building together with Unkair's initials J. V. or his master-mason's mark so

---

scrolling. The oldest surviving examples in Germany seem to be these on the north wing at Neuburg; the ones on the Palais de Savoie at Mechelen in Brabant are more than a decade earlier. See Note I 120.

[90] Probably by Jörg II Breu and executed in 1539-1540. Stierhof, *Wandmalerei*, pp. 15-20, pl. opp. 72.

[91] Kreft-Soenke, *Weserrenaissance*, pp. 279-281.

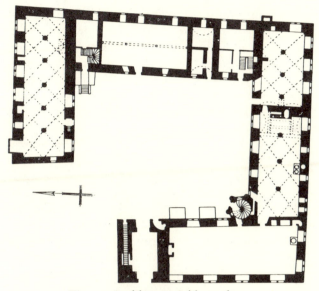

Fig. 13. Stadthagen, Schloss, plan

that the main period of construction will have been the mid-thirties as for the north wing at Neuburg. Since Frederic Soltesburg is recorded as in Stadthagen through 1533 he may well have worked briefly under Unkair on the Schloss before his employment by Ernst der Bekenner at Celle.

The particular Schaumburg who was Unkair's first client for the Stadthagen Schloss was Count Adolf X, later Archbishop of Cologne. At this time he held an ecclesiastical appointment in Paderborn and that may not be irrelevant; it will be recalled that it was for a prince-bishop of Paderborn that Unkair had begun Schloss Neuhaus ten years earlier. Inside the Stadthagen Schloss three handsome fireplaces survive, but these were not commissioned by Adolf or designed by Unkair. Two were executed for Count Otto IV some time before his death in 1596 and the third is dated 1604. The freestanding Kavalierhaus, before the entrance, although very similar to the main structure, is also of Otto IV's time.

Along the south front and the east wing at Stadthagen (Pl. 92) as earlier at Schloss Neuhaus the recurrent dormers are topped by simple *welsche Gebel*. At the ends of the west block, however, larger gables rise in three steps, each step capped by a lunette, a motif Soltesburg may have carried to Celle (Pl. 98). The same contrast, moreover, exists between the broad end-gables and the narrower gables of the dormers on the north wing. Here Cardinal Brandenburg's architect at Halle, it will be recalled, had preceded Unkair in providing over the west front of the

Dom a group of stepped lunettes (Pl. 46), though five rather than three. All the walls at Stadthagen are cut by innumerable rather narrow rectangular windows, some paired as at Schloss Neuhaus, but mostly single and spaced with as little attempt at regularity as Unkair's earlier ones except on the south end of the west wing. Many of these windows, like the nineteenth-century porch of iron on the other end of the south front, may well be of much later date since their framing lacks Unkair's characteristic fillets.

Of the several oriels on the Schloss at Stadthagen, the most conspicuous is the one over the plain and still pointed entrance arch (Pl. 93). As already noted, this opens under Otto IV's arms and carries the date 1544, but the basic structure, to judge from the arch, may well be five years or more earlier. All of the oriels, whatever may be their precise date, have triple lunettes at the top decorated with petal-like convex fluting—a motif that was by this time very popular for carved decoration on timber-framed structures (Pls. 102, 103)—and, above heavy scrolled brackets, square panels below filled with the sort of flat strapwork which is usually thought to derive from the publications of Vredeman de Fries—the first of consequence, Antwerp, 1563, it will be recalled. It is this ornament in the panels, though not so much that on the lunettes, which suggests the oriels might be wholly or partially of the date of the Kavalierhaus, that is, some time in the forties or, even more probably, much later in the lifetime of Otto IV. The long survival of lunette-topped gables, for example, is illustrated here at Stadthagen by those on the ends and front of the Rathaus (Pl. 341) as remodelled and extended in 1595-1597. A still later example (Pl. 94) exists at Meppen, halfway across Westphalia toward the Dutch border: the modest and rather Dutch-looking town hall there, executed in brick with some stone trim, is dated 1601-1605.

An example of a related sort of gable, roughly contemporary with those on the Schloss at Stadthagen, but much closer to the plain stepped type of their ultimate northern, as distinguished from their Italian, ancestry crowns the front of the Weinhaus (Pl. 95) at Alsfeld.[92] Built in 1538, this has six short steps to each

[92] [G. Dehio] Handbuch der Deutschen Kunstdenkmäler, *Hessen* [Munich] 1966 (henceforth cited as Dehio, *Hessen*), p. 9; D. Groszmann, *Alsfeld* [Munich, 1960] (henceforth cited as Groszmann, *Alsfeld*), col. front, pp. 25-26. Technically, the Weinhaus gable at Alsfeld, illustrated as it was originally by Groszmann on p. 27, is close to the west gable at Halle (Pl. 46). In the modest scale of the lunettes, how-

side and one at the top, all capped with tiny fluted and ball-tipped lunettes like those over the oriels on the Stadthagen Schloss. Less securely dated to the thirties is the rather larger but very similar one on the gatehouse—which is incidentally built of brick, not stone, like the so much later town hall in Meppen— of Schloss Bradenhorst at Bochum. The Alsfeld façade originally had curtain-topped windows in its four lower storeys. These were blocked up in a nineteenth-century restoration, but the frames are now exposed. The latter are somewhat more elaborate, and also more Late Gothic in flavor, than those on the Johann-Friedrichs-Bau at Torgau (Pl. 78). At Schloss Bradenhorst the windows in the upper storey are paired and transomed in stone, with single ones above in the four stages of the gable.

The town of Alsfeld is in Hesse, on the Autobahn southwest of Bad Hersfeld, and consists almost entirely of Fachwerk buildings, including the Rathaus, at a right angle to the Weinhaus, which had been built in 1512; Schloss Bradenhorst in Bochum is at the southwestern edge of Westphalia in what is now the industrial Ruhrgebiet. The *welsche Gebel* motif, though first introduced at Halle or near Paderborn, was by no means restricted even in the twenties and thirties to eastern Westphalia and to Saxony and Thuringia. Indeed, the next two large Schlösser to be described that are crowned with such gables are the one of Duke Ernst der Bekenner of Brunswick-Lüneburg at Celle and that of the counts of Nassau-Weilburg at Weilburg, the former to the north and east of Hannover, the latter on the Lahn above Limburg, far to the west and south.

The Late Gothic chapel of the Schloss at Celle[93] was built in the 1480s. Located in the big southeast tower that survived the Renaissance remodelling of the front or east wing and the Baroque reconstruction of the other three sides of the quadrangle—carried out in 1660-1680 by the Venetian architect Lorenzo Bedogni—this chapel was eventually most elaborately redecorated and furnished, specifically for Lutheran use, in the 1560s and seventies (Pl. 207). The client

was Ernst's third son Wilhelm though Ernst himself had actually changed his religion some forty years earlier in 1526. Among the conspicuous new features Wilhelm added before his death in 1592 is a triptych by the Netherlander Maerten de Vos (1532-1603) or his school set over the altar. The wings of this show on one side the east front of the Celle Schloss and, on the other, the Gifhorn Schloss (Pls. 96, 97). Except for two portals dated as late as 1839 and the heavy octagonal tower on the right added by Bedogni, these views make clear that the east front of the Celle Schloss is still effectively in its sixteenth-century condition today and that much of the one at Gifhorn is original. This is true even of the light ochre color of the present painted rendering at Celle. At least for the 1560s and later, however, the white and orange-red used externally by the restorers on the Gifhorn Schloss is evidently not correct.

We are now concerned, however, not with Gifhorn, about which there will be more to say later, but with the rebuilding of the east front of the more important Celle Schloss. This was begun for Ernst der Bekenner in 1533, or a few years later,[94] and ultimately completed for Wilhelm after his succession in 1559. It is not possible to distinguish at all surely between the work done for Ernst, which is of the thirties and probably by Frederic Soltesburg, who arrived at that time from Stadthagen, and what was carried out by Ernst's successor Franz Otto in the forties or still later after Michael Clare took over from Soltesburg as master-builder in 1553.

The east front at Celle is long and three storeys tall (Pl. 98). The many segment-topped windows are not as Italianate as those at Neuburg of the 1530s (Pls. 73, 90) but more like the ones on the Gifhorn gatehouse (Pl. 56) that were attributed, earlier in this chapter, to the same period. These are very irregularly disposed all through the first storey, on the tall left-hand tower, and on the smaller one in the middle, as well as on the cross-gable above that and on all the dormers. The second-storey windows, however, are plain rectangles with simple flat frames, perhaps as a result of seventeenth- or nineteenth-century remodelling.

As at Stadthagen, with which the early stage of the

---

ever, it is more like the broader of the gables at Stadthagen (Pl. 92).

Unnerbäck, *Giebel*, pp. 17, 18, 27, calls attention to others of this sort in Saxony: a demolished house in Meissen dated 1535 (his fig. 17); the Gemeinde Kirche in Brockwitz nearby (his fig. 18); and even one in Bavaria, a house in the marketplace at Weiden, northeast of Amberg (his fig. 30).

[93] Reclams *Niedersachsen*, pp. 110-112; also *Kunstdenkmäler der Provinz Hannover*, III, pp. 5, 89 ff., pls. 33-35, 38.

[94] See previous Note. Unnerbäck, *Giebel*, pp. 45-46, on the contrary, the latest to discuss the gables at Celle, inclines towards the years after Clare took charge in 1553. As at Gifhorn, a considerably earlier date seems stylistically more acceptable, and attribution to Soltesburg is more plausible than to Clare.

construction here must have been nearly contemporary, the principal interest of the east front of the Celle Schloss is above the eaves. There are no end-gables; but that on the tallest dormer resembles the five-stepped ones at the ends of the wings at Stadthagen, doubtless because of Soltesburg's earlier employment there. The smaller gables of the other dormers, set very much closer together than any of Unkair's, each have two large segment-headed windows of the sort that are standard here. Flanked by thin side-strips, these are then capped by pairs of lunettes and a third lunette rises above a single tiny window at the top. Since such dormers were repeated —and very probably by Soltesburg—here at Celle on the Rathaus (Pl. 230) in the early sixties, quite as the ones on the Stadthagen Schloss would be so much later on the Rathaus there, these may well date from the early fifties, but still before Clare took over in 1553. In character, all the same, they are quite consonant with the earlier work of the thirties here and with the undated Gifhorn Torbau (Pl. 56).

Each face of these towers at Celle, as on the similar ones at Gifhorn and the tall single tower of St. Elisabeth in Wrocław as completed in the thirties—or, for that matter, the probably much earlier Fuggerhäuser turrets (Pl. 7)—is topped by a lunette. On the bigger one to the left there are short, but otherwise standard, windows and, below a string-course, pairs of human heads carved in high relief that suggest by their circular framing coins or medals in the frequent Early Renaissance way.

Such were once the chief ornaments of the earlier gables on the west wing at Neuburg (Pl. 75) as decorated about the time the rebuilding of this side of the Celle Schloss got under way or a year or two earlier, and at Dresden, or, the Georgenbau portals of 1535 also. Below this carved decoration and above the surviving Gothic windows of the chapel, shallow two-storey oriels project on three of the exposed sides of the corner tower. These oriels are linked by panelled bands between the storeys and capped by plain pediments above a second such band. The top stage of the smaller tower and the corresponding lowest stage of the gable of the dormer not only have vertical strips closely framing the segment-topped windows but also another horizontal band to serve as the frieze of a flattened and compressed entablature.

The special sort of invention on the east front of the Celle Schloss—which may doubtless be credited to Soltesburg—and the almost total absence of plausibly Italianate detail other than the portrait disks relate

this facade more closely to Unkair's work in Westphalia, whether or not Soltesburg had actually worked with or under him at Stadthagen, than to that of Knotz at Neuburg, Krebs at Torgau or Kramer at Dresden. The last had, however, its often modest echoes in many places from this time forward. The Schloss at Dornburg of around 1539, just north of Jena in the Elbe Valley—better known than most of its small size because Goethe once lived there— though actually in Thuringia, is quite typical of the period in Saxony also.[95]

At Gifhorn the Kavalierhaus (Pl. 99) was built for Duke Ernst's brother Franz in 1540, presumably under the direction, if not from the design, of Michael Clare. Well away from the Schloss, on the main street of the town, this repeats the segment-topped and fillet-framed windows used on the Torbau there that are also seen on the Celle Schloss[96] (Pl. 56). The gable, however, is elaborated in a manner alien to the district, at least in the thirties, with convex and concave quadrants, respectively, in the first and second stages as well as more Unkair-like lunettes over the third and fifth stages. The designer seems to have sought to approach the scalloped sort of gable of the Neuburg or Dresden Schlösser (Pls. 75, 86, 87) without relinquishing in favor of scrolls the lunettes that had first been introduced some fifteen years before. This he accomplished by adding below them the quarter-circle elements Saxon architects had already employed occasionally in association with lunettes (Fig. 10) in the 20s.[97] Broad lunettes also crown the two-storeyed oriels in the lower storeys. The north wing of the Schloss itself may be either of this date or later in the forties, for Clare continued to work here down to Franz's death in 1549, if not until he himself moved to Celle in 1553. The chapel, dated 1547, will be described in the next chapter.

The culmination of secular building in the 1530s was not such a relatively minor work as the Gifhorn Kavalierhaus of the end of the decade but the slightly earlier Joachimsbau in Berlin of the Hohenzollern electors of Brandenburg. Of this nothing has survived, yet enough is known of its character to make a

---

[95] DKD, *Thüringen*, p. 360.

[96] This is, at best, a very dubious argument for attributing the work on the Schloss at Celle to Clare since he did not take over until so much later.

[97] The earliest examples were those mentioned earlier on the side of the Zwickau Gewandhaus, designed in 1525 (Fig. 10), and the ones on the Altes Rathaus in Dresden-Neustadt dated 1527-1528: Unnerbäck, *Giebel*, pp. 13-14, 18-19.

fairly full description possible. On the site of the fifteenth-century castle of the Elector Friedrich II, Joachim II began in 1538 a new electoral seat.[98] The new range to the east along the edge of the Spree was very irregular in organization because it incorporated earlier elements, or at least made use of their foundations. This rambling pile, parts of which survived into the twentieth century, originally terminated to the north in a small octagonal turret capped with an S-curved roof like the one at Gifhorn. But the dominant feature was a tall square tower, the *Burgfrit* (keep), toward the Spree. From that a rounded apse protruded below and to the side of it a lower round tower clung. The massive Burgfrit, though a survival of the mediaeval castle as regards its shank, was capped like the slimmer watchtower at Torgau (Pl. 80) with four gables. Above these rose both a larger and a smaller lantern, providing a rather unexpected asymmetrical termination. To the left came the seven regular bays of the end of the southern block, and a richly decorated cylindrical oriel on the southeast corner balanced the octagonal turret at the northern extremity.

Toward the south, the long main facade of this large block—known specifically as the Joachimsbau—must have represented much better than the eastern front along the Spree the aspirations of the elector and his Saxon architect Caspar Theiss, for that extended unbroken for thirteen bays between the oriels on the eastern and western corners (Pl. 100). The three storeys of paired windows on this front, with curtain-tops rather simpler than those at Torgau (Pl. 78), would have produced a composition almost as monotonous as the facades of the Fuggerhäuser were it not for various subsidiary features: the oriels on the corners; a complicated two-storey porch at the center; and a row of tall cross-gables and smaller dormers set against the high roof. Arabesque decoration in relief was confined to the oriels and the porch. That on the oriels here was evidently very similar to the decoration on the one at the lefthand end of the Johann-Friedrichs-Bau at Torgau whence Krebs was called to advise briefly on the design of this larger and more sumptuous Schloss in Berlin.

The porch of the Joachimsbau has no analogue at

[98] Horst, *Architektur*, pp. 74-76; E. Hempel, *Geschichte der deutschen Baukunst*, 2nd ed., Munich [1956] (hereafter cited as Hempel, *Geschichte*), p. 289, gives the dates of construction as 1537-1540. His authority was A. Geyer, *Geschichte des Schlosses zu Berlin*, I. Bd., 1936, it would appear from his bibliography.

Torgau. It was perhaps suggested rather by the more modest central feature on the outer side of the Georgenbau at Dresden (Pl. 83). The plan was rectangular in the ground storey and there were two arches—probably semi-elliptical rather than round and carried on freestanding columns—that fronted coffered barrel-vaults. The first storey was elaborated by a central bow and at that level five columns, one of them in the middle of the bow, carried segmental arches. The complex shape of this storey was repeated in the plan of the terminal parapet which was panelled and carved with arabesques like the corner oriels.

Five cross-gables topped the south facade of the Joachimsbau. These were all identical except for the ones at the ends which were, apparently, partially overlapped by the corner oriels. The final open stages of these edicules, rather like the ones Hieber had proposed for the corners of the Perlachturm (Pl. 23), were capped with *welsche Hauben*. Quite as complex was the treatment of the cross-gables, of which there were two more on the eastern end—as doubtless also on the western end—one up against the southeast corner oriel and the outer side of the Burgfrit. In the lower stage of each, two windows, smaller than those on the facade below, were framed both by blind arches and by a pilaster order. The elaboration of the design recalls a little that of Knotz's gables over the west wing at Neuburg (Pl. 75). The upper three stages, however, were more like those on the gables completed a year or so before this on the north wing at Neuburg (Pls. 90, 91). The vertical lines of the pilasters were carried upward through the second stage and further pilasters, though differently aligned, flanked the third stage. The most striking novelty here must have been the boldness of the scrolls—S's in the second and in the terminal stage—that outlined the edges of the gables. Nothing like these had been seen since the Palais de Savoie either in Germany or in the Netherlands.

Between the big cross-gables on the Joachimsbau there were also gabled dormers (Pl. 100). Each of these had very small windows in a lower stage and, above, a second stage that repeated the top one on the cross-gables even to the obelisk-like finial. The somewhat broader gables on top of the keep copied the upper three stages of the cross-gables, not the simpler design of those on the dormers.

Since the cross-gables no longer survive on the Johann-Friedrichsbau of Schloss Hartenfels except over the staircase, the outer facade of the Joachimsbau, as known from existing visual evidence, does not now seem to have much resembled Krebs's along the court at Torgau, and he may have had little if any part in designing it. However, the relation of the court front (Pl. 101) here to that of the Johann-Friedrichs-Bau (Pl. 78) must have been a good deal closer. Just as at Torgau, a cantilevered gallery ran all along the facade below the standard windows of the second storey, though the parapet was evidently open not solidly panelled. This horizontal feature was interrupted at the center by a great open staircase, polygonal in plan, above a rectangular *perron* at first-storey level very much like that at the base of the staircase of Schloss Hartenfels (Pl. 80). Up to the cantilevered and parapeted platform on top of this led flights of stairs running parallel to the main wall, just as at Torgau. Evidently, however, there was a considerable difference —doubtless considered by Joachim, if not by Krebs and Theiss, to be an improvement—in the treatment of the top of the stone cage of the great spiral stair. This was not assimilated in design to the cross-gables here as Krebs had done on the Johann-Friedrichs-Bau. Instead, the terminal stage rose two storeys above the eaves—though still not quite as high as the cross-gables that were repeated from the south front —and ended in a strong horizontal cornice. This was not unlike the one over the open stair at Blois.

In regularity of fenestration, variety of outline and boldness of feature, as well as in mere extent, the Joachimsbau rivalled any of the German Schlösser being built in its day or, indeed, Henry VIII's Nonsuch Palace if not Francis I's Chambord elsewhere in Europe. Its distinctly northern characteristics suggest that any Italians who may have been employed worked only as carvers of the arabesque decoration and had no such responsibility for the general design as Boccador seems to have had at Chambord. That responsibility must have been Theiss's here, even though with significant advice from Krebs and some intervention, doubtless, by the client.[99] Such a presumption sets the Berlin Schloss quite apart from the other major work in progress in the late thirties, the

Stadtresidenz at Landshut as designed by Italians, which will be discussed early in the next chapter. The Berlin Schloss brought the German Early Renaissance to a splendid conclusion; the Stadtresidenz (Pls. 114-120) opened a new phase. For the immediate future of secular architecture in Germany, however, the Joachimsbau is more significant.

Unless it be accepted, as some scholars have believed, that a quadratura apparatus of pilaster orders in each storey (Pl. 100) was painted on its exterior walls,[100] the Joachimsbau seems, moreover, to have had rather fewer Italianate features even than the Johann-Friedrichs-Bau (Pl. 78). But this might not have been the original impression if the hypothetical wall-painting or, indeed, even the carved decoration had survived, both presumably the work of Italians. Well into the seventeenth century, however, secular work of the later Renaissance in much of the north of Europe would remain closer to the almost hybrid sort of Schloss design which first reached maturity here in Berlin than influenced by the new and more conceptual Italianism that had, in Germany, both its beginning and its early climax at Landshut. Not least relevant for that sort of design, from the mid-century onward, was the new illustrated architectural literature. This literature will be briefly discussed in later chapters as also the publications carrying counter-currents from Antwerp.

In Berlin it is, of course, not alone the Schloss which does not survive. In any case, that was very largely rebuilt by Andreas Schlüter and J. F. Eosander von Goethe just before and after 1700; it was totally demolished only after the last war by the Communists to extend the Marx-Engels-Platz (the former Lustgarten). Nothing remains from the sixteenth century in Berlin today. But, even before the war, Berlin was for the most part a relatively modern city. The more conspicuous buildings and all those districts which gave it so handsome a metropolitan texture were built in the two hundred years between 1730 and 1930 for the electors of Brandenburg and their royal successors, the kings of Prussia and emperors of Germany.

Celle never developed into a metropolis, and the House of Welf that ruled there came to an imperial throne not, like the Hohenzollerns of Berlin, in Germany, but in England—or, more accurately, in India.

---

[99] As in sixteenth-century England, one must allow for the fact that basic architectural decisions were probably most often made by the *Bauherr* (the client) himself and that the various *Baumeister* (builders) of whom there are records were far from having the autonomy and the authority of later architects. The situation at the Heidelberg Ottheinrichs-bau will be discussed below. Since this matter is in most cases largely hypothetical it is unnecessary to bring it up with each commission, much less to support guesswork with specific citations in the Notes.

[100] It was mentioned above that such an all-over treatment in grisaille can be seen as restored in the court of Schloss Ambras outside Innsbruck (Pl. 347) though that is some twenty-five years later in date.

Yet, specifically, as regards the preservation of consistent architectural character, the modest seat of the dukes of Brunswick-Lüneburg is still today far more exemplary than the city of those prolific later builders, Frederick the Great, Frederick William IV and Wilhelm II. Doubtless that was because it never became a center of any such considerable political power as the Berlin of the Prussian monarchy. Celle has, moreover, even for the sixteenth and early seventeenth centuries, a somewhat special character, owing to the profusion of extant timber-framed construction. This contrasts with various other old towns in northern Europe, where extensive areas are still filled with surviving buildings of some antiquity in stone or brick.

Except for the stuccoed brick Schloss and Rathaus (Pls. 98, 230), Celle was built up for the most part with Fachwerk houses dating from 1500 to 1800. In this decade of the 1530s the Hoppener Haus (Pl. 102) is, in fact, more securely dated by an inscription to 1532[101] than the work at the Schloss which began probably about a year later and continued for decades. The elaborate and rather hybrid carving on this house at Postrasse 8, often attributed to Simon Stappen from Brunswick, is even less Italianate in character than that on the Brusttuch at Goslar (Pl. 71) of six years earlier. The squares and streets of Celle are lined with comparable houses, all in excellent condition, quite as in certain other towns, especially in the present-day state of Lower Saxony, such as Einbeck or Wolfenbüttel, that are better known for their profusion of Fachwerk.

The Hoppener Haus easily rivals the more famous Huneborstelsches Haus in Brunswick of 1536,[102] in the richness of its carved decoration, if not the height of the Knockenhaueramtshaus of 1529[103] in Hildesheim (Pl. 72) that once dominated the marketplace there. But, as was said of the Brusttuch in Goslar, this decoration is better considered—whether or not also by Stappen—as a sort of "folk art" than either Late Gothic or Renaissance. A simpler and more abstract treatment, such as was henceforth in increasingly common use for several decades, appears on the house (Pl. 103), dated 1536 by an inscription, at Langegasse 9 in Brunswick.[104] On that all the windows have

curtain-tops, a motif that may well have originated in wooden construction. Still more characteristically, where diagonal chunks of wood brace the intersections of vertical and horizontal members at the base of each storey, fluted lunettes are carved, sometimes with figural masks or busts at their centers. This fanlike motif, usually much simplified, soon became ubiquitous on timber-framed facades. Despite their "Bauer-Renaissance" decoration German houses of Fachwerk, with their overhanging storeys and tall gables, remained essentially mediaeval in design even longer than did wooden houses in North America.

All the same, however, masonry houses more up to date in their styling must have contrasted in many towns with the vernacular Fachwerk that continued so long in favour with only slight modification. A remarkably elegant early example of such a house, dated 1538,[105] is the so-called "Haus zur hohen Lilie" (Pl. 104) which has lately been restored in Erfurt. Whether or not historically correct, the carefully differentiated polychrome paintwork on the detail now emphasizes the Italianate delicacy of the panelled pilasters flanking the windows. These are single in the ground, first and third storeys, but coupled in the second. The scrolled decoration flanking the inscription above the broad arched portal and that over the entablatures of the windows in the ground and first storeys is of exceptional refinement, moreover, in contrast to the familiar fluted segmental lunettes used here over the paired windows of the second storey. The frame of the portal has niches set diagonally at the sides as on Rosskopf's doorways in Görlitz (Pl. 69) and on many later examples in Saxony. But the rather restrained treatment of these gives full value to the finesse of the coin-like portrait medallions carved in the spandrels.

The design of the gable of the Erfurt house is much coarser. In the first stage the molded edges merely follow the steep slope of the roof as at Schloss Schelenburg (Pl. 48), but the next stage has stiff vertical S-scrolls at the sides and the topmost carries a half-round lunette above an entablature. Perhaps the present form of this gable is largely the result of cautious restoration that eschewed all renewed decoration. Certainly the membering does not accord even in scale

[101] Reclams *Niedersachen*, p. 116.

[102] *Ibid.*, p. 59.

[103] Horst, *Architektur*, p. 189.

[104] [G. Dehio] Handbuch der Deutschen Kunstdenkmäler, V, *Nordwestdeutschland*, Berlin, 1912, pp. 68-69, lists a considerable number of similar sixteenth-century houses in Brunswick of which a great many were destroyed in the last war. For those that survive, see Stelzer, *Braunschweig*, pls. 62-69.

[105] Piltz, *D.D.R.*, p. 305.

with the dainty richness of the detail around the openings below; yet neither does it much resemble the scallopped gables of the north wing at Neuburg (Pls. 90, 91), which date from the years just before this.

Before moving on to consider in the next chapter the following stage of the German Renaissance, a stage that lasted through the mid-century and in many districts even later, something should be said of the interiors of the Schlösser of the late twenties and early thirties. Alas, later remodelling and often serious degradation has left very little of consequence of the same period as the exteriors, except for certain spiral staircases. The most remarkable of these, moreover, the one at Schloss Hartenfels, is even more an exterior than an interior feature. Happily, however, at Landshut, at Neuburg, at Torgau and at Gifhorn, chapels dating from the forties survive which will shortly be discussed. From the twenties and thirties, moreover, some fragments of mural painting are extant, as most notably at Grünau. But in this respect also a new cycle started around 1540 at Landshut and in the chapel at Neuburg, dated 1543 as regards the frescoes.

In Ottheinrich's own apartments in the west wing of the Neuburg Schloss not much of the original decoration remains.[106] However, the large room known as the "Grosses Flez" still retains its panelled ceiling carried out in two sorts of wood. The pattern already combines crosses and elongated hexagons as seen in a wood engraving offered by Sebastiano Serlio in his published works. That presumptive source would suggest a date in the 1540s for the ceiling. There is no carved or painted ornament. The presumably rather earlier red marble door-frame, flanked by panelled Corinthian pilasters and crowned by a sunken lunette, which is now in the Schloss Museum at Berchtesgaden, did not come from this room. That portal, executed by Loy Hering (c.1485-1554) and carrying the date 1538, has Ottheinrich's arms carved in the lunette above, and the panels on the inset door are decorated with perspective compositions in intarsia of Roman ruins. These are surrounded by arabesque decoration. It is generally believed that this doorway was originally in the principal apartment of the north wing, the Rittersaal on the first storey where the mural paintings were destroyed in 1546.[107] The sur-

viving panelled wooden ceiling of that hall (Pl. 105) is carried by two massive twelve-sided pillars, one plain and the other with a pattern of small diagonal facets on the surface. The carved wainscoting by Hans Phel around the walls was installed only after Ottheinrich's day in the 1560s or even the seventies though it is still of Early Renaissance character. The largely extant stucco-work and frescoes of the Neuburg chapel (Pls. 121, 122) which date from the early forties, will be described in the next chapter.

The Schloss complex at another Neuburg, that on the Inn south of Passau, includes many elements of various dates both early and late.[108] But the sixteenth-century interiors, executed for a Graf von Salm who acquired the property in 1528, are all that is relevant here. These were completed two or three years later, very likely before any decorative work had begun inside Ottheinrich's Schloss. The Weisser Saal and the Rotmarmor Zimmer on the ground storey of the south wing beyond the chapel retain net-ribbed vaulting, though the severies in the latter carry painted acanthus decoration of 1705 between the decorated terra cotta ribs. The walls of the first room were once cladded with white marble. In the second room the elaborate terra cotta door-frames and other trim were reconstructed in this century in a drastic programme of restoration that leaves uncertain which parts are original and which are new (Pl. 106). The general character of this decoration is more Lombardesque than anything extant from Ottheinrich's rooms at Neuburg-a.-d.-Donau.

As already at Augsburg in the case of Jakob Fugger, rich burghers in the principal commercial cities rivalled princes and nobles as patrons of architecture and interior decoration by the mid-1530s; Jakob's heir Anton was, however, not active as a patron until somewhat later. Even in Nürnberg, where southern ideas penetrated very slowly in architecture, there were notable interiors of which one, at least, survives in part. Though very heavily restored and much reduced in its present postwar setting in the court of the Fembohaus, the decorations in the Hirschvogel-saal in Nürnberg (Pl. 107) offer a rather consistently Italianate example of an elaborate German interior of this period still today more complete than any at Neuburg-a.-d.-Donau.

Dated 1534,[109] this exceptional room in Nürnberg

106 Horn-Meyer, *Neuburg*, pp. 227-239.
107 Stierhof, *Wandmalerei*, pp. 15-20.

108 Reclams *Bayern*, pp. 593-594.
109 *Ibid.*, p. 642. Glück, *Renaissance in Deutschland*, pl. 492,

was originally installed in a garden pavilion. Arabesqued pilasters raised on podia, varied with freestanding columns flanking the arched doorways, support a full entablature with a very broad scrolled frieze just above the tops of the arches. All the rest of the decoration that occupied the upper walls is now gone and known only from old photographs. The designer responsible for the Hirschvogelsaal was Peter Flötner (c.1490-1546), to whom one scholar or another has attributed so much decorative work on buildings of the early 16th century in Germany, at least as a collaborating decorative artist-craftsman, from the Fuggerkapelle—begun when he would have been only about twenty, or even younger, and probably still in Italy—to the Gläserner Saalbau at Heidelberg, completed in 1549, where work had perhaps not even started by the time of his death in 1546.

Flötner, however, may well have been concerned with another example of advanced Renaissance design of this date in Nürnberg: the wooden galleries, surviving no longer, in the court of Tucherstrasse 23. These were once replete with three Classical orders, one above another.[110] Moreover, Flötner almost certainly provided the design for the remarkably Classical Apollbrunnen, dated 1532,[111] the well with a statue of Apollo, which once stood in the court of the Nürnberg Rathaus and is now in that of the former Pellerhaus (Pl. 396), today the *Stadtbücherei* (city lending library) of Nürnberg. This was cast by the local coppersmith, Pankraz Labenwolf, who was helping the younger Vischers to complete the grille, originally commissioned by Jakob Fugger for his chapel in Augsburg, that Ottheinrich tried to acquire.

On a more modest economic scale, as befitted a scholar and university professor, are the interiors in the house dated 1536[112] of the famous Humanist and Reformer Philipp Melancthon in Wittenberg. His carefully restored study (Pl. 108), however, has a door framed with a coarsely molded round arch, just as the gable on the exterior is crowned by five rather crudely

executed *welsche Gebel* arranged in a stepped pattern. Mention of Melancthon, so important a figure intellectually in the early stages of the Reformation, leads back appropriately to a topic of great historical interest, even though one that had as yet little connection with the advance of the Renaissance in Germany: the beginnings of Protestant church architecture.[113]

It should first be reiterated that any church-building, whether Catholic or Lutheran, in Germany in the decades with which this chapter has dealt remained Late Gothic in essentials. The inclusion in Catholic churches of Italianate furnishings and even occasional external emendations—most conspicuously the *welsche Gebel* Albrecht added on the Halle Dom (Pls. 45, 46)—was still exceptional. But the new Catholic edifice (Pl. 37), then dedicated to the Virgin (*Unsere liebe Frau*), that the same ambitious prelate began beside the Halle marketplace in 1529[114] does already show certain changes. These were pregnant for the future, especially the future of Protestant architecture, though they do not yet reflect, even faintly, Italian Renaissance church-design whether Early or High.

A background should be provided for these changes at the expense of some recapitulation. The curious east end of St. Martin at Lauingen (Pl. 12), erected earlier in the decade it will be recalled, was provided with three identical apses squared off, so to say. The Wolfgangskirche at Schneeberg was begun by Hans von Torgau at much the same time, 1515, and vaulted by 1526, though not completed until 1540[115] by Fabian Lobwasser. That also has a somewhat flattened east end (Fig. 14). But at Schneeberg the shape is differ-

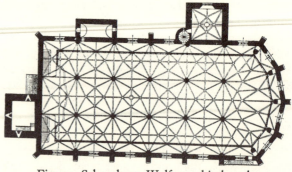

Fig. 14. Schneeberg, Wolfgangskirche, plan

---

illustrates the Hirschvogelsaal before the last war. It is evident that all the decoration on the upper half of the walls was destroyed and no attempt made by the restorers to recreate it.

[110] Horst, *Architektur*, pp. 272-274, fig. 192. The parapets, however, were decorated with rather coarse Late Gothic blind tracery.

[111] Osten-Vey, *Germany*, pl. 244.

[112] DKD, *Provinz Sachsen*, p. 394; Piltz, *D.D.R.*, pp. 250-251.

[113] K.E.O. Fritsch, *Der Kirchenbau des Protestantismus*, Berlin, 1893, provides an early summary of the subject.

[114] DKD, *Provinz Sachsen*, p. 367.

[115] Kratzsch, *Burgstädte*, pp. 86-88.

ent, best described as a segmental curve broken into four straight sections, with the outer sections terminating the side aisles and the middle pair the nave. Like many earlier churches in Germany, and most particularly the Schlosskirche at Wittenberg (Pl. 36) as largely built in the 1490s, the Schneeberg church has Emporen running along the outer sides of the aisles below the windows, that are continued behind the altar in all four bays of the flattened east end to connect with the Emporen of the side aisles and provide a continuous gallery (Pl. 109). This gallery was carried out by Wolff Riedinger in 1536-1537.

Although at Halle the galleries in Albrecht's church in the Marktplatz were not added by Nickel Hoffman (†c.1589) until 1554-1555 under Lutheran auspices, the east end is quite flat as had long been common in English churches. Moreover, the broad segmental arch supporting the gallery at the east end enframes the altar, with its triptych of the Cranach school, and also carries the organ (Pl. 37). This segmental arch, whether dating from the thirties or the fifties, is an evident echo of the half-round, rather than pointed, curvature of the net-vault overhead. Indeed, as has been noted, a vault of the same curvature, though with star rather than net ribbing, had already been built at Halle in 1511 to complete the fourteenth-century Moritzkirche.

The builder of the Marktkirche must have been influenced by the decision to retain beyond the altar end of the new church the towers of the thirteenth-century Marienkirche, which had occupied the eastern portion of the site, like those of the earlier Gertrudenkirche that still face the market-place before the west end. Yet the result, though doubtless only by coincidence, is quite similar to the Fuggerkapelle if that be considered as a second "east end," so to say, rather than a westernmost bay added to the nave of St. Anna in Augsburg (Pl. 3).

When, five years later in 1534, the earliest Protestant church of all was begun at Joachimstal in Bohemia, one might have expected the model to have been the Wolfgangskirche at Schneeberg (Pl. 109) across the Erzgebirge mountains in southern Saxony—in construction by that time for two decades but not yet completed as regards the Emporen—or perhaps even the much grander Annenkirche at Annaberg (Fig. 8, Pl. 38) in the same region, even though the Annenkirche did not become Lutheran until 1539. Neither of these, in fact, influenced the Joachimstal church. Nor was the rather confused and makeshift reorgani-

zation of the mediaeval church at Emden,[116] considered the *Moederkerk* (mother-church) of the Reformed communities of Holland and northeastern Germany, echoed at Joachimstal. The church of 1534-1540 there was demolished in 1873 but the plan is known (Fig. 15) and photographs of the exterior survive.[117] It was evidently a single broad rectangle with a very shallow three-sided projection in the middle of the east end through which a slim tower rose to a sharp steeple considerably taller than the double-pitched main roof. It hardly provided an attractive model for emulation and, indeed, seems not to have been at all influential.

Fig. 15. Jachymóv, Protestant church, plan

The authority of Friedrich der Weise's Schlosskirche at Wittenberg (Pl. 36), so especially associated with Luther, and the fact that the next edifice to be built for Lutheran use was a chapel in a Saxon Schloss, the one at Torgau that Luther consecrated in 1544, thenceforth encouraged German Protestants to follow more imposing Saxon models such as the one at Schneeberg and the Halle Marktkirche (Pls. 37, 109). Both of these, moreover, had been taken over from the Catholics by the early forties. However, the next cycle of Lutheran church-building opened—at least as regards edifices in towns—only in 1558 after the peace of 1555 with the beginning of the Marienkirche at Marienberg, also in the Erzgebirge but nearer to Schneeberg than to Joachimstal.

[116] Largely destroyed in the last war: Reclams *Niedersachsen*, pp. 154-155.
[117] Kratzsch, *Burgstädte*, pp. 38-39, 89-91, 125-127, fig. 10. Twentieth-century guidebooks such as K. Baedeker, *Österreich*, 27th ed., Leipzig, 1907, p. 297, do not even mention the one-time existence of the church. That uranium ore had already been found nearby, however, was noted, information more interesting today than then!

In the five years between the initiation by a Catholic archbishop of the large, handsome church in the considerable city of Halle and that of the modest but historically important Protestant one in Joachimstal—a town so small that in the early twentieth century it had less than 8,000 inhabitants, though it was doubtless much larger in the early sixteenth century—the vitality seems to have drained out of the late *Sondergotik*. That was equally true of English Perpendicular by the thirties, if not perhaps as yet of French Flamboyant. Nevertheless, German churches even more than French ones—most in both cases begun considerably earlier—were still being carried to completion according to the original intentions so long as the towns in which they rose remained Catholic. At the same time local master-masons were more and more forced, in the way of the Heydenreichs in Regensburg, to come to some sort of terms with their clients' increasing demand for Italianate features and fittings. Often, however, such were obtained from outside artists and these were not necessarily of foreign birth now that some Germans were becoming competent to work in the new vein.

At least down to 1540, despite the debts they both owed to the Humanism of 1500, the Renaissance and the Reformation in Germany were pursuing independent paths as regards architecture, if not to the same degree painting and sculpture. This was true despite the fact that certain princes, as individuals, were much involved with both. As was noted earlier, the Saxon Elector Johann der Beständiger, father of the builder of Schloss Hartenfels and its chapel, by this time a Protestant and Luther's political sponsor in these crucial decades, commissioned from Peter II Vischer (1487-1528) a tomb-slab of Renaissance design (Pl. 60) in 1527 for his Catholic elder brother Friedrich der Weise, with whom he had shared local rule as co-regent. The latter had died in 1525 at about the time when one of the leading—if later wavering—opponents of Luther, Cardinal Brandenburg, was introducing more conspicuous Renaissance features in the Halle Dom and soon also, far to the west on the Main, in the Aschaffenburg Stiftskirche (Pls. 45, 46, 59). A Catholic prince who turned Protestant only in 1542 when his Schlosskapelle at Neuburg-a.-d.-Donau must have been all but completed—Ottheinrich von der Pfalz—first introduced a concerted programme of Renaissance painted decoration (Pls. 121, 122) in an edifice under Lutheran control.[118] The churches discussed in the preceding paragraphs were unrelated to the general evolution of Early Renaissance architecture in Germany. In the patronage of the arts by Henry VIII in the England of the twenties and thirties the link was closer, if only slightly so, both before and after his break with Rome. The masterpiece of Early Renaissance church-furnishing in northern Europe, outranking in quality anything ecclesiastical in Germany after the Fuggerkapelle and up to this time, except perhaps the imported Hackeney screen in Cologne (Pl. 58), is the one Henry had erected in 1533-1535 in King's College Chapel at Cambridge. The breakdown of cultural communication with Catholic Italy and France that followed the not very drastic religious change in England was only partial. That change was in any case reversed by Queen Mary in the mid-century and only finally confirmed, on her accession in 1558, by Elizabeth I.

On the other hand, the work of a leading Early Renaissance painter much employed at Wittenberg in these years, Lucas I Cranach,[119] *Hofmaler* (court painter) to Friedrich der Weise and his Protestant successors, deserves brief mention in this connection. Cranach not only provided—though only for Johann Friedrich in the 40's—the altar-piece in the Stadtkirche, where Luther preached as often as in the Schlosskirche down to his death in 1546, but was also responsible earlier for some secular decoration, including most probably that in Johann Friedrich's Festsaal in Schloss Hartenfels. Portraits of Luther and other Protestant figures affirm Cranach's close personal ties with the leading early Reformers. As a result of his own early conversion, moreover, after the Madonna of 1516 now in Dessau he painted no more religious pictures with specifically Catholic subjects. He is, of course, chiefly famous for his semi-Classical nudes, some in the guise of Bathsheba but even more in that of Venus. These provide evidence of his Humanist rather than his Lutheran connections, and also of the breadth of princely taste in Wittenberg. All the same, the taste of Friedrich der Weise's successors did not affect architecture in electoral Saxony before Krebs's work of the mid-thirties at Torgau (Pls. 78-80, 82).

[118] Stierhof, *Wandmalerei*, pp. 21-34.
[119] Osten-Vey, *Germany*, pp. 132-135, 205-209.

Three

GERMAN
ARCHITECTURE OF THE
MID-CENTURY

T HE next stage of the German Renaissance in architecture opened only toward 1540. Yet even as the emulation of Italian forms and ideas spread more widely and became more coherent, many builders in the mid-century—and indeed considerably later—continued to repeat and even to develop such motifs of distinctly Northern character as tall decorated gables. Thus there existed by this time an independent Renaissance tradition in German architecture, but that tradition was soon being modified by reflections of more up-to-date Italian design. On the other hand, from the sixties, that later Italian influence was more than balanced by a current that originated in the north, or at least had been strengthened and elaborated there. The principal source for what is called "Northern Mannerism" was in the Netherlands, most particularly the books of engraved plates published in Antwerp and widely circulated all over Europe. The southern Netherlands was by that time firmly under Spanish rule, yet hardly at all affected by the austere taste of Philip II, Charles's son, who succeeded on his abdication in 1556. (There is no reflection of the Escorial in the Netherlands.) A secondary source, especially for Denmark and for Danzig (Gdańsk), was rebellious Holland. A third influence, though much less important for Germany, was that of the France of the Valois kings.

In the later decades of the century, Northern Mannerism would have a broad and cosmopolitan field. That field extended not only throughout both Germany and the Netherlands, but to Britain and Scandinavia as well, if not Bohemia and Poland—except for Danzig—to the east, where Italians continued to be more frequently employed than in Germany. For the new developments of the sixties and after, which will be discussed in the next chapter, no significant foundations had yet been laid in Germany in the third or most of the fourth decade of the century,

with which the previous chapter was concerned; by the late forties, however, the situation was at least beginning to change. The change was in large part the result of the increasing availability of new printed and graphic material then being published in some profusion not only in Italy but also in the North.

The album of drawings of ancient and modern buildings in Italy made by Hermann Vischer in 1515-1516 still represented a method of transmitting elements of architectural design that went back, at the least, to Villard de Honnecourt in the thirteenth century. But the development of effective means of multiplying graphic images in engravings and woodcuts, parallel with the invention of printing, was already by Vischer's time providing far more effective media, somewhat as photostats and Xerox have done in our day.

Such drawings as Hermann Vischer's were primarily of use to the artist who made them, although in his case they were doubtless also accessible to his associates in the family bronze-foundry. But Dürer's and Burgkmair's prints and those of various other Germans[1] were soon very widely available, and by no means in Germany alone. These prints, however, when not primarily pictorial or figural, offered for the most part samples of ornamentation rather than total architectural images. Yet Hopfer's prints of the "Darstellung" (Pl. 15), at least, did provide rather accurate views of one very early German Renaissance church interior; all the same, that interior was, in fact, very rarely, if ever, emulated.

The middle third of the century saw in the north the accumulation of a body of architectural literature henceforth of the greatest formative and normative importance throughout the western world. Such a literature in print had begun to appear in Italy in the

[1] A. Lichtwark, *Der Ornamentstich der deutschen Frührenaissance*, Berlin, 1888, covers the subject exhaustively.

late fifteenth century with the publication of Alberti's *De re aedificatoria* in 1485 and the first printed edition of Vitruvius, probably the next year. Of Alberti's treatise a Latin edition was published in 1512 at Lyons; but this was of little significance for northern Europe generally, and Jean Martin's French translation did not appear until 1553. Altogether, however, some dozen editions of Vitruvius, mostly in Latin or Italian, came out in the sixteenth century. Among these the first in the north was that issued in Strasbourg in 1543 in Latin, but the German translation by Walter Riff (Rivius), with the imprint: Nürnberg, 1548, is the one relevant here.

Far more important for the transmission of the essential elements of High Renaissance architectural design, as these had been crystallized in the first quarter of the century and then modulated by various Italians, were the books of Sebastiano Serlio (1475-1551). Serlio brought out a work on the five orders—according to his ambitious publishing plans, the *Quarto libro* (Book IV)—and also his *Terzo libro* (Book III), illustrating major works of the ancient Romans and some modern buildings in Rome by Bramante and Raphael, in Venice in 1537 and 1540, respectively. A year before the *Terzo libro* appeared, Pieter Coecke (1502-1550) had published in Antwerp a Dutch translation of the *Quarto libro* making the Serlian canon of the orders considerably more accessible to Northerners. A German translation, also published in Antwerp, followed in 1547, the same year as Riff's German Vitruvius.

Book III was dedicated to Francis I, and about the time of its appearance the French monarch invited Serlio to Fontainebleau, where the Italians Il Rosso (1494-1540), Francesco Primaticcio (1504-1570) and Giacomo Barozzi da Vignola (1509-1573) were already settled. More of Serlio's Books came out in France in 1545, 1547 and 1551, though Book VI was never published until the present century. One manuscript version dedicated to Francis, and hence dating from before his death in 1546, has in our day been identified in New York and another later version dedicated to his successor Henri II is in Munich.[2] Book VII was prepared for publication by the Milanese antiquary Jacopo Strada long after Serlio's death and appeared in Frankfurt-am-Main in 1575 though Strada was himself then living in Vienna.

The first German, or German-language, author other than Riff to compete with Serlio was Hans Blum. He published his *Quinque columnarum* in Zürich in 1550 in Latin, but a German edition followed from Nürnberg in 1554 with the title *Grundtlicher Bericht von den fünff Saulen*. In France the first architectural engravings of any consequence other than Serlio's plates were those of Jacques Androuet du Cerceau (c.1515-1585), founder of a long-dominant clan of builder-architects. He started issuing them in the mid-century, but he did not produce a major printed work, the first edition of his *Livre d'architecture*, until 1559. Next, the *Nouvelles inventions* of another French architect, Philibert de l'Orme (†1570), appeared in Paris in 1567. These two books were too late to be influential in Germany in the period with which this chapter deals. Incidentally, in England John Shute (†1563) led the way with his *First and Chief Groundes of Architecture* in 1563, early in Elizabeth I's reign, although he had actually visited Italy some ten years before.

More important for northern Europe than the French works of the fifties and sixties, perhaps, was Pieter Coecke's rather special publication, *Le Triumphe d'Anvers faict 1550 en la susception du Prince Philips, Prince d'Espaigne*. This illustrated the arches and other gala features erected by Cornelis Floris (1514-1575) for the ceremonial entry of Charles V and his son Philip into Antwerp the previous year. As the first book to illustrate a new Netherlandish sort of architectural ornament (Fig. 16) destined to be widely popular henceforth in the north—and not least in Germany—this deserves special emphasis.[3] The most influential Antwerp publications of such ornament came somewhat later, beginning with the *Veelderleij niuwe inventien van Antychsche* of Floris (Pl. 110), issued by Hieronymous Cock (c.1510-1570) in 1556-1557, and above all the principal works of Jan Vredeman de Fries, the first of which appeared in 1563. Before mention is made of even the earliest reflections of this sort of design in Germany, however, there is much to recount of the architectural situation, around 1540, ten years and more earlier.

In the middle third of the century, as before, the central European regions to the east of Germany were still in advance of those to the west, except for Hungary which was by this time mostly under Turkish

[2] Modern facsimiles of both the manuscript in the Bayrische Staatliche Bibliothek and the one in the Avery Library of Columbia University now exist. Strada brought this manuscript to Munich.

[3] Some attribute the designs for the *Triumphe* to Coecke rather than Floris, and he may well have been responsible for the title page.

Fig. 16. Cornelis Floris: Antwerp, reviewing stand
(*échaffaulx*) for imperial entrée on the
Coepoortbrugge, 1549

occupation. Around 1540 it is not in the southern
Netherlands, of which Charles V's sister, Mary of
Hungary, followed his aunt Margaret as the viceroy,
that the first echoes of the Italian High Renaissance
are recognizable. There was nothing comparable to
the palace Pedro Machuca began for Charles in
Spain in 1526-1527 at Granada or to Pasqualini's
IJsselstein tower (Pl. 42) in Holland of some five
years or so later. What is probably the earliest echo at
least in works that are extant is not in the Netherlands but in Bohemia. Even though Bohemia should
not be considered truly German then any more than
the Netherlands but—at least ethnically—half Slav, it

was all the same under the immediate control of a
Habsburg, Mary's uncle and Charles's brother, Ferdinand. He had been elected king of Bohemia in 1529
after marrying Anna, the sister of the last Jagellon
ruler, Ludvik II. The *Letohradek*, a large pavilion
generally known as the Belvedere, was begun in the
next decade by Ferdinand in the gardens north of the
Hrad above Prague for that wife. After Pasqualini's
tower, this edifice (Pl. 111) has a strong claim to be
considered the first authentically cinquecento structure north of the Alps: it is more up to date by a
good deal than Zygmunt I's arcaded court in the
Wawel Zamek—which was being brought to comple-

tion in the 1530s whenever it may have been begun—and considerably more correct than Vincidor's almost precisely contemporary Kasteel at Breda of 1536-1538. In 1534, the year the Belvedere was first projected,[4] the great local architect Beneš Rejt died and the work was undertaken the next year by Italians. The most identifiable of these is Paolo della Stella (†1552), a pupil of Andrea Sansovino (c.1460-1529). He was, of course, primarily a sculptor like so many of the Italians who worked in the north both earlier and later in the century.

The model Paolo and his associates followed in Prague, at least up to a point, was the mediaeval Palazzo della Ragione at Padua; however, the loggia surrounding the Belvedere is not at all Gothic or even hybrid, but of mid-sixteenth-century Venetian character. Moreover, the distinctly Academic frames of the doors and windows might even suggest that the designer or designers had early access to Serlio's *Quarto libro* that appeared in Venice in 1537, if not to his *Terzo libro* of 1540. In 1541, indeed, a great fire held up construction and the building was not completed until 1563. In charge by then was Bonifaz Wolmut (†c.1579), who came originally from Überlingen on the Bodensee but had been trained in Vienna. He had taken charge of the construction in 1558 as *Kaiserlicher Baumeister* (imperial architect) after Ferdinand succeeded as emperor in 1556. The upper storey is by Wolmut as is also the S-curved roof of copper which gives a somewhat inappropriately northern flavor to the skyline.

Less advanced in its reflection of North Italian sixteenth-century architecture in this period is the Salamanca Schloss (Pl. 112)—more usually known as Schloss Porcia from a later owner—at Spittal-a.-d.-Drau, south of the Alps in Carinthia. Ferdinand was also ruler there as archduke, but both Carinthia and neighboring Styria are as far from the central German lands as Bohemia, rather farther indeed. This Schloss was begun for Ferdinand's Spanish chancellor, Gabriel de Salamanca (†1539), whom he created Graf von Ortenberg,[5] at almost the same time as the Belvedere, shortly after Salamanca's second marriage to Elisabeth von Baden in 1533.[6] His architect, whose name has not survived, was Italian, a Lombard from the region of Lake Como, and this architect provided a model. By recourse to that, later builders were able

in completing the Schloss with its arcaded quadrangular court to continue the design as originally projected. Though much of it was only carried out in the forties and fifties—a pillar of the ground storey arcade carries the date 1542 and a doorway in that storey is dated 1551—the Schloss may be considered to represent, as regards both the outer facades and the court, what was intended in the thirties. The outer walls, indeed, were largely constructed for Salamanca even before his death in 1539 (Pl. 113).

Nothing of so early a date in German lands to the north and west compares with either the ranges of arcades in the court or the treatment of the arched and coupled windows in the exterior walls of the Salamanca Schloss. But Spittal is, after all, close to the present Italian border, and the detailing of the windows and balconies on the outside was actually the work of a second architect from northern Italy who was called to Spittal in 1549 by Gabriel de Salamanca's son. The Salamanca Schloss is hardly to be considered, even to the same ambiguous degree as the Prague Belvedere, a German Renaissance monument, but rather as a measure by contrast of the relative retardation of Italianate architecture in German territory to the west and north in these decades.

Certainly the bordering lands to the east and the southeast, from Poland to the Tyrol—if no longer Hungary under Turkish rule—were in these years still ahead of those in the west, except for Holland, in the acceptance of up-to-date Italian ideas and in the actual employment of Italians. The lag, however, was no longer measured in decades as at the opening of the century. A Wittelsbach, one who had been a rival of Ferdinand for the Bohemian kingship in 1529, almost at once successfully rivalled, at Landshut on the Isar, what his Habsburg cousin was building in Prague not to speak of Salamanca's still quattrocento work at Spittal.

This town in Lower Bavaria had been in the fifteenth century the seat of the "rich dukes" of Bavaria-Landshut but, after the last of the line died in 1503, it was taken over by the Munich branch of the Wittelsbachs, despite the claims of Ottheinrich and Philipp of the Palatine branch as grandsons through their mother of the last "rich duke." From 1516 to his death in 1545 Duke Ludwig X, whose own mother had been a sister of Emperor Maximilian, ruled Lower Bavaria from Landshut and Straubing jointly with his brother Wilhelm IV in Munich. His inherited seat was mediaeval Burg Trausnitz, high above Landshut to the southeast, hardly a proper setting for

[4] Knox, *Bohemia*, pp. 26, 66.
[5] R. Wagner-Riege, *Das Schloss zu Spittal an der Drau in Kärnten*, Vienna [1962], pp. 10-31.
[6] *Ibid.*, pp. 38-44; plans, figs. 1-4, section, fig. 5.

a mid-sixteenth-century prince; it was brought up to date only in the 1570s by a later Wittelsbach, Wilhelm V.

Long surrounded at his court by Humanists, Ludwig in 1536 went on a trip to Italy and paid a visit to Mantua. There he saw the Palazzo del Te, which had been begun for the Gonzagas by Giulio Romano (1499-1546) some ten years earlier and just brought to completion with Giulio's frescoes and the *stucchi* of Primaticcio and Briziano.[7] This especially delighted him as it did most contemporaries. Now that the major building project in Mantua was at an end, it was easy for Ludwig to recruit there a full team of Italian craftsmen, quite as Francis I successfully tempted Primaticcio to settle in Fontainebleau at this point.

Even before his visit to Italy the duke had planned to build what is now called the Deutscher Bau of the Stadtresidenz on the main street of the Altstadt of Landshut.[8] The original front of this, as executed in the immediately following years, had a small tower over a projection in the middle and a richly sculptured portal below, with painted figures of giants above and other Renaissance decoration on the frieze under the terminal cornice. This was all lost when the facade was drastically refaced in 1780 by the Elector Karl Theodor in the cold and flat Academic manner of the *Zopfstil*. Beyond the front wing, however, the other three sides of the square court—the Italienischer Bau —were untouched externally in the eighteenth century although there was some modest redecoration within.

The master-builders responsible for the Deutscher Bau were Bernhard Zwitzel and Niklas Überreiter. Zwitzel was the *Stadtwerkmeister* of Augsburg, a stone-mason employed by the city authorities and also, as has been mentioned, by Jakob Fugger on the Fugerhäuser. He was not long at Landshut,[9] but kept on working at Augsburg and elsewhere for Anton Fug-

ger down to the sixties. Überreiter also came from Augsburg and it was he, rather than Zwitzel, who must have supervised the Italienischer Bau, though he can hardly have designed it. Northerners also executed most of the fresco-painting in the interiors of that despite the up-to-date Italian idiom used throughout.

In the loggia at the rear of the court, for example, the small Old Testament scenes in the panels of the stuccoed vault are by Ludwig Refinger (c.1510-c.1548) from Munich (Pl. 114). In the principal room above, the Italienischer Saal (Pl. 115), the frieze of putti, if not the heads of ancient heroes and such on the vaulted ceiling, are by Hans I Bocksberger from Salzburg who worked here in 1542-1543.[10] He also painted the mythological subjects on the ceilings of the succeeding rooms that are named for Venus, Apollo, the Planets, etc. A third painter, Hermann Postumus, whose background is unknown, was perhaps the most competent of the three. He provided the altarpiece of the Adoration of the Magi in the chapel (Pl. 120) and much of the frescoing on the vaults throughout (Pl. 116).

Such Humanists at Ludwig's court as Dietrich von Pleningen, who published a translation of the works of Sallust in Landshut in 1515, had prepared the way for the Classical iconography in the decoration of the Stadtresidenz, but the inspiration for the architecture was not at all local. Ludwig wrote from Mantua of the Palazzo del Te at Easter, 1536, before the cornerstone of the Deutscher Bau was even laid: "Der gleichen glaube ich dass kein sollicher gesehen worden" (The like, I believe, has never been seen).

By January 1537 he had arranged for a certain Meister Sigismund (? Sigismondo) and his assistant Anthoni (? Antonio) to come from Mantua to Landshut and soon afterward Bernhard Walch (? Bernardo the Italian) arrived, bringing with him twelve more Italian workmen, some of whom must have been *stuccatori* (plasterers) though all were called *Maurer* (masons). Whether either Sigismund or Bernhard Walch should be considered Ludwig's "architect" is, as always in the sixteenth century, a question of terminology, but certainly neither Zwitzel nor Überreiter was responsible, except as regards the Deutscher Bau, for the architectural design of the Stadtresidenz.[11] Of the three wings surrounding the

_____

[7] It was not Ludwig but Albrecht V of Bavaria who sent Jacopo Strada to Mantua in the 1560s to make drawings of the Palazzo del Te. These provide the best evidence of what it was like originally: K. F. Forster and R. J. Tuttle, "The Palazzo del Te," *JSAH*, December 1971, pp. 267-293. Strada also designed for Albrecht the Antiquarium in Munich.

[8] H. Thoma and H. Brunner, *Stadtresidenz Landshut*, 2nd ed., Munich, 1956; K. O. von Aretin, *Landshut* [Landshut, n.d.] (henceforth cited as Aretin, *Landshut*), pp. 19-22, pls. 100-110.

[9] On Zwitzel's work for Anton Fugger in the late thirties and early forties at Donauwörth and Babenhausen, see Chapter V.

[10] Osten-Vey, *Germany*, pp. 310-311.

[11] The Mantuan, Meister Sigismund, probably the real designer, was accompanied by his apprentice Antonelli or Antoni. They arrived in January 1537. With them were asso-

court (Fig. 17, Pl. 117) that were erected over the next five or six years—the consecration of the chapel in 1543 provides a rough terminal date—every visitor still exclaims: "But this is not German, it is wholly Italian!" in one form of words or another. Moreover, it is not merely generically Italian like the Prague Belvedere or the Salamanca Schloss, rather is it so close to the work of Giulio Romano that one must describe it either as "High Renaissance" or perhaps—in the current northern context rather more ambiguously—as "Mannerist." It is certainly not at all like the Northern Mannerism of later generations.

The entrance hall in the Deutscher Bau of the Landshut Stadtresidenz, through which one passes to reach the court, has six bays of cross-vaulting carried on two sturdy columns of red Tyrolean marble and corresponding half and quarter columns along the walls. The vaguely Corinthian capitals are shaped in an almost Romanesque way to carry on their broad abacuses the ribs of the vaulting. In comparison with the similar ground-storey halls (Fig. 4) in the Fuggerhäuser of twenty years earlier this still appears transitional, though the flat panelling in diamond shapes on the severies of the vault seems more proto-Borrominian—so to put it anachronistically—than at all Gothic like the molded ribs of stone that divide the bays and provide the diagonals. This must be the work of the Augsburgers, probably with no assistance at all from the Mantuans, and may well date from before Zwitzel's departure and Walch's arrival.[12]

Through the low central arch of the doorway leading into the court of the Stadtresidenz and the paired windows in the bays at either side of that one seems to look straight into Italy. On each of the three sides of the court ahead correctly proportioned Roman Doric columns—of red marble in the rear range, of marbled stucco at the sides—carry in the ground storey the arches of the open loggias. These arcades do not much resemble the delicate near-Venetian ones of 1512-1515 in the Damenhof court of the Fuggerhäuser (Pl. 11), much less the hybrid ones at Neuburg and Binsfeld (Pls. 76, 77) that date from the early thirties.

Even in comparison to the contemporary arcading around the Prague Belvedere (Pl. 111) and in the court of the Salamanca Schloss (Pl. 112) the result here is more Roman by far despite the extremely bold treatment immediately over the arches. At each end of the three walls are narrower bays containing small unframed niches. The arches of the loggias also have only plain intradoses beneath their heavily rusticated voussoirs with similar raised blocks filling out the spandrels. Only this rustication recalls directly Giulio Romano's work in Mantua; however, the rustication on the Palazzo del Te itself was eventually made much more aggressive when the stucco coating was renewed in the eighteenth century.[13]

Above this sturdy base there rises in the court of the Landshut Stadtresidenz a giant order of Corinthian pilasters between the large vertical windows in the main storey and the rather short horizontal ones above them. Alternating pointed and segmental pediments over the bigger windows echo the vigorous scale of the arches below and the full entablature above. The line of the podia under the order is continued as a string-course at the sill-level of the main-storey windows. Projecting forward from the tops of the "aprons" under the windows, the string-course is in the advanced plane of the podia except within the bays lacking windows at the corners. In those bays, moreover, at the level of the attic windows elsewhere plain sunken panels are substituted above a flat string. This string continues the line of the window cornices in the five main bays.

Except for the columns of the rear loggia, the court of the Stadtresidenz is all executed in brick, which was the normal building material at Landshut and in much of Lower Bavaria. Even before this it had often been covered with stucco—and henceforth was nearly always. That, of course, was rarely the case in the north of Germany along the North Sea and the Baltic or toward the Dutch border in the west. In those regions architectural influence had long come from the Netherlands and not usually, even by this time, from Italy.[14]

---

ciated a Meister Bartlmee, a Meister Francesco and a Meister Benedikt—all three presumably Italians despite the names by which two of them were known—as well as twenty-seven Italian workmen, masons and stucco-workers. Soon after came Bernhard Walch with twelve more Italian masons: Aretin, *Landshut*, p. 21. In 1538, it will be recalled, other such masons were brought to Neuburg to work for Otteinrich von der Pfalz.

[12] By 1537 Zwitzel seems to have been working at Donauwörth.

[13] Current investigation has revealed that the original rustication of the Palazzo del Te as seen in Strada's elevations was much coarsened in later repairs, probably of the eighteenth century. See Note 7.

[14] Actually the brick tradition in the Baltic lands was very old and in the Middle Ages largely autochthonous; increasingly in the later sixteenth century, however, influences from both the southern and northern Netherlands are reflected in the local brick architecture, especially in Danzig.

On the exterior of the Stadtresidenz, however, of which the principal facade is now that at the rear toward the Isar (Pl. 118), only the rusticated ground storey retains some of its stucco coating, here given a rather rough texture. This treatment recalls local Late Gothic practice in civil building, yet the actual design strongly suggests, especially in the over-sized keystones of the rectangular openings, the particular sort of early Mannerism of the Palazzo del Te. Above, a giant order of pilasters—Doric rather than Corinthian as in the court—creates a rhythmic pattern as complex as that of the entrance front in Mantua but more regular. At the corners and on either side of the three central bays the pilasters are coupled so that the heavy pediments of the windows in the main storey, alternately pointed and segmental as in the court and carried here on boldly scrolled brackets, are phrased 2-3-2.

Above these windows on the rear of the Stadtresidenz the tall wall-plane, corresponding to the vault of the Italienischer Saal within, is broken only by slightly sunken square panels except for the elaborate armorial achievement, inscribed LVD. VTR. BAV. DUX., that rises up to the bottom of the entablature in the central bay. The attic windows are grouped 2-3-2 in the frieze below the heavy terminal cornice like the windows below. The somewhat freer disposition of the many windows, large and small, in the bays of the south facade is even more Mannerist in character in good part because of the recurrent introduction of flat strings and blank panels in the bays between the pilasters.

Inside the court of the Landshut Stadtresidenz on the west side, opposite the entrance through the Deutscher Bau, the loggia is deepened to provide a generous vaulted *sala terrena* (Pl. 114), to call it by the Italian name it deserves. This has a quite positive spatial character owing to its absidal terminations. These are capped by half-domes of elliptical section with diamond coffering. But the coffering of the main barrel vault, also semi-elliptical, consists of a run of five large rectangles—those filled with the Old Testament frescoes of Refinger—that are separated by small squares and flanked by cross-shaped panels between the bays. Delicate *stucchi*, presumably executed by Italians, ornament the raised framework between the frescoed panels.

The Italienischer Saal (Pl. 115), the principal room of the *palazzo*, as one may not improperly call it, occupies the five central bays toward the west. The severe *Zopfstil* decoration of the side walls dates, like

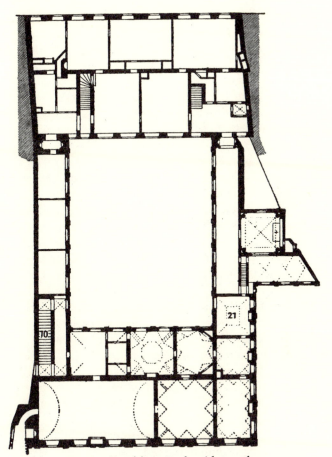

Fig. 17. Landshut, Stadtresidenz, plan

the busts in the niches of the *sala terrena* and the present street front of the Deutscher Bau, from the time of the Karl Theodor. After two hundred years and more of only intermittent use, the Stadtresidenz was then occupied from 1781 to 1800 by his cousin, Duke Wilhelm of Birkenfeld. The heavy marble doorframes, however, with cornices carried on vigorous scrolled brackets, and the even heavier marble chimneypiece in the Italienischer Saal are characteristic details of High Renaissance design moving toward Mannerism.

Overhead in the Italienischer Saal of the Stadtresidenz the principal panels—for this vault can hardly be described as coffered—are arranged in three lines from north to south. The panels are square but the frescoes within them are in slightly dished octagons. In these the busts of the Ancients, probably painted by Postumus, are arranged in groups, each identified by an inscription. More attractive, though somewhat underscaled, are Bocksberger's frieze of putti at the top of the wall and the similarly delicate bands, painted in grisaille, that flank the square panels along the crown of the vault. The stucco-work here is extremely rich and varied, introducing a type of ceiling decoration which, though Italian in origin, would have a brilliant future in Germany, beginning somewhat later in the sixteenth century, but reaching its apogee in the Rococo interiors of the eighteenth century. The delicate polychromy of the stucco-work, including a good deal of gilding, has lately been restored.

Among other interiors with frescoed ceilings of Humanist content Ludwig's bedroom—the Venuszimmer (Pl. 116)—is especially notable. Overhead the hedonistic inscription: *Balnea vina venus corrumpunt corpora nostra, restaurant corpus balnea vina venus* . . . runs continuously round the central octagon overhead, while appropriate Classical figures occupy the narrow panels on the walls below together with arabesques that Postumus painted in 1541. The Planetenzimmer is historically even more interesting. On its vault appears the whole sky of the northern hemisphere as plotted by the learned Peter Apian, one of the scholars at Ludwig's court, who still supported Ptolemaic astronomy against Copernicus.

Important as these particular interiors were as leading toward the ultimate culmination of palace-decoration, and eventually also of church-decoration, in Germany—even including in the Planetenzimmer for the first time that *di sotto in su* sort of aerial perspective which would be integral in Rococo vault-painting of the eighteenth century—others were more pregnant for the later sixteenth century. On the one hand there is the chapel, consecrated in 1542, and on the other the panelled wooden ceiling (Pl. 119)—if by Zwitzel quite a few years earlier in date—which is all that survives of the decoration of the Festsaal in the upper storey of the Deutscher Bau.

The chapel in the Stadtresidenz is approached by a corridor along the south side of the court in the first storey. On the walls of that corridor large imaginary portraits of early Wittelsbachs, framed by painted columns, alternate on one side with windows and on the other with landscapes. The jambs of the windows carry very delicate painted arabesques. At the west end there are no windows or landscapes but instead an illusionistic niche with a nude statue under a painted arch carried on coupled Doric pilasters—for the period an exceptionally persuasive example of quadratura painting. Overhead in this corridor the wooden ceiling has very deep plain coffers framed by heavy molded beams that are coordinated with the painted order on the walls.

The chapel itself at Landshut (Pl. 120) is rather different, equally Italianate but reflecting a purer pre-Mannerist taste. This small square compartment is covered by a cross-vault carried on sturdy marble columns at the corners. The columns are flanked by pilasters of the same Composite order which are narrowed to provide vertical slots of space. Postumus's altarpiece, set against the south wall, is framed by fluted Corinthian columns rising from podia painted in grisaille. The lower walls throughout are plain, but the frieze of the continuous entablature is decorated with a running scroll interspersed with putti, while angels in low relief flank the oculus above the altar. The correctly molded archivolts of the four arches and the guilloche patterns on the flat rib-like members that outline the arrises and subdivide the severies of the vault are doubtless original. The painted interlace-and-rosette pattern on the vault surface, however, may well be a later, presumably eighteenth-century, emendation. Certainly never again until the late eighteenth century was such an abstract sort of centralized space composition essayed in German architecture except for the Schaumburg mausoleum at Stadthagen (Pl. 442) as designed by the Italian-Swiss G. M. Nosseni in 1608-1609.

On the other hand, the wooden ceiling of the Festsaal (Pl. 119), much flatter than that in the chapel corridor and divided into squares by wider bands, belongs already to a type that would be very important in the Schlösser of the last decades of the century.[15] Intarsia decoration in various woods, combined with more or less carving—and sometimes with painted polychromy and gilding also—eventually produced toward 1600 several of the masterpieces of German Renaissance decoration at Heilingenberg, Kirchheim, Ortenburg and Weikersheim (Pls. 349-353). Hung from the trusses of the main roof overhead rather than beamed or supported on piers, these ceilings, as already here though rarely so early elsewhere, are often of remarkable dimensions compared to Ottheinrich's at Neuburg (Pl. 105). Their employment provided a Germanic rival to the Italianate stuccoed and painted vault-decoration first used here at Landshut in the principal rooms of the Italienischer

[15] There were many ceilings of this sort, some presumably by Zwitzel and of the late 1530s or forties, in the Fugger Haus at Donauwörth (Pl. 173) and in Schloss Babenhausen.

Bau. That was only rarely employed elsewhere before the 1570s to judge by surviving and accessible interiors.

Ludwig, in his patronage both of scholars and of the arts, was the *beau idéal* of a Renaissance prince, but unfortunately the glory of Landshut departed with his death in 1545. A generation later, however, there was a revival when Wilhelm V, before his accession as duke of Bavaria and consequent move to Munich in 1579, again employed foreign artists in 1573-1578 to redecorate Burg Trausnitz above the town.

Though the Count Palatine Ottheinrich and his brother had lost Lower Bavaria to the Munich branch of the Wittelsbachs early in the century, the territories Ottheinrich retained in the Upper Palatinate were contiguous to Ludwig's and there was a sort of cultural—and, after Ottheinrich's conversion to Lutheranism in 1542, confessional—rivalry between the cousins. In architecture it was Ludwig who was in the lead in the late thirties as a comparison of the Stadtresidenz with the Knotz's north wing for Ottheinrich at Neuburg (Pls. 90, 91), completed in 1538, makes strikingly evident. Ottheinrich did not, so to say, catch up with Ludwig even later. Indeed, he never provided any landmark comparable in import to the Landshut Stadtresidenz in the development of German Renaissance architecture until he moved to Heidelberg for good in 1556 and began the Ottheinrichsbau there. However, the chapel[16] for which he was responsible at Neuburg outranked in size and richness of decoration, if hardly in distinction of High Renaissance design, that at Landshut. It was, moreover, completed in 1543 for Lutheran use, as a result of Ottheinrich's change of religion the previous year, while the Landshut chapel was Catholic and has so remained. Happily the return of the later Neuburg ruler Philipp Wilhelm to the old faith, the year before his accession in 1614, did not lead to any changes in Ottheinrich's chapel.

The date of initiation of work on the Neuburg chapel is somewhat uncertain though it must fall within the years the Mantuans were busy at Landshut. It occupies a rhomboidal space beyond the entrance passage in the two lower storeys within the north end of Knotz's earlier west wing (Fig. 11) and is covered by a big main vault with intersecting arched severies around the edges. As in most chapels in Schlösser—but not that at Landshut which is all on

16 Horn-Meyer, *Neuburg,* pp. 209-227.

the first storey—an upper gallery connects with the principal apartments of the Schloss. This explains what, from the lower level, appears the excessively high location of the gallery reserved for the use of Ottheinrich, his wife Susanna and his guests (Pl. 121). Below, the public had direct access through the plain segmental-arched doorway to the left of the main entrance on the front of the Schloss—perhaps already in existence, since it is not quite on the axis of the chapel—or another door, carrying the date 1538, near the outer end of the entrance passage.

The west end of the Neuburg chapel, however, is set off by three arches carried on well-proportioned columns of the same red Tyrolean marble that was used for the external trim in the early thirties and on the loggia at the rear of the court in Landshut. These are capped by correct Corinthian capitals and provided with slim molded archivolts of the same marble. Above them is the parapet of the gallery. This has marble stiles and rails between which stucco panels carry bold foliate decoration in relief, except for the central one that bears Ottheinrich's arms. Along the sides of the chapel and flanking the chancel at the east end the continuation of the gallery with its similarly panelled parapet is carried on very heavy marble brackets. These consist of three inverted steps, each terminating in a scrolled or lobed section.

At the east end (Pl. 122) the chancel is necessarily very narrow since it occupies, as was previously noted, only one closed bay of the court arcade (Pl. 74). The coffered barrel vault of this rises awkwardly from an impost halfway up the flanking marble brackets to a crown that is rather lower than the parapets at either side. Above, a plainer parapet confines a second spacial projection. This is identical in plan with the chancel below and capped with a segmental barrel vault. Unexpectedly, that vault is not coaxial with the half-round wall-arch of the middle severy of the cross-vault above it. This feature, like the western door whose shape it recalls, might be a survival from the early or mid-thirties. The awkward bracketing below the chancel arch, however, perhaps results from the uncertainty of modern restorers concerning the original treatment at this point.

As mentioned earlier, the windows in the chancel of the Neuburg chapel, those at the center of the west end, and the ones on the north side at gallery level are round-arched but subdivided by simple cusped tracery. That still remains more Late Gothic in character than at Lauingen or Regensburg twenty years before (Pls. 13, 29). In front of the east window an arched Renaissance frame standing on the altar contains a crucifix with figures of the Virgin and St. John below at either side. Dated 1542, this is by the sculptor Martin Hering, who came from Eichstätt, not Kaufbeuren like Loy Hering, whom Ottheinrich also employed. That date suggests the chapel was largely complete as regards its structural elements at least by the time the Landshut chapel was consecrated in the same year, perhaps even before Ottheinrich's contemporary change of religion.

But the most remarkable aspect of the decoration of the Neuburg chapel, both stylistically and iconographically, is provided by the frescoes, dated 1543, on the upper walls and the vault overhead. These are by Bocksberger and follow closely in style his ceilings at Landshut. In subject matter, however, they provide the earliest large-scale programme of Lutheran church-decoration, thus contrasting with the humanistic Classicism of the secular interiors at Landshut. Since Ottheinrich had left the old faith the previous year, the programme was presumably developed or revised by his Lutheran advisor, the Nürnberg theologian Andreas Ossiander.[17] The vast square panel occupying the center of the vault is devoted to the Ascension, as was suitable either for Lutherans or for Catholics. But four round medallions, two at each end, illustrate twice the Sacraments of Baptism and Communion since those were the only two recognized by Luther and many other reformers. The frescoes in the lunettes round the walls, moreover, illustrate scenes from the Old Testament only. These were presumably chosen to support various aspects of the new doctrine as based on Luther's translated Bible.[18]

Unlike the decorative treatment overhead in the rooms at Landshut (Pls. 115-116), no stucco is used in the Neuburg chapel except on the panels of the balcony. Only illusionistic painted moldings flank the bands that articulate the surface of the vault, while arabesques surround the four circular frescoes of the Sacraments and also occupy the vaulting conoids.[19] Though the painter and the sculptor were northerners, it does not follow that whoever was in general charge—after 1538 no longer Knotz—may not have been a southerner. In any case the four medallions

seem to indicate that the original designer expected all four Catholic sacraments to be illustrated when the decoration of the vault was planned.

For the actual date of initiation of the work here at Neuburg there are clues in the rooms adjoining the chapel at gallery level and also in the entrance passage, though the stucco-work on its vault carries the date 1545. In the first room to the south few original features are extant *in situ* although, as noted earlier, a doorway dated 1538 survives in the Schloss Museum at Berchtesgaden. Of the following rooms, the ones most used by Ottheinrich, the big ante-room called the "Grosser Flez" still retains a marble floor, several simple marble door-frames and the coffered wooden ceiling. This last was mentioned in the previous chapter with the implication that these rooms were decorated—or perhaps redecorated—some years after the wing was first built in the early and mid-thirties. The remodelling of the west wing, including the insertion of the chapel as we know it, may well have begun in 1538, the date that is inscribed on the door-frame at the entrance to the chapel from the passage as well as on the doorway now at Berchtesgaden—that is just after the north wing had been brought to structural completion but was still undecorated inside. Indeed, 1538 is the year in which the arrival of *welsche Maurer* (Italian masons) is recorded, though the doorway at Berchtesgaden is by the northerner Loy Hering.

Later, a continuing campaign of remodelling and redecoration followed in the years just after the chapel was completed and before Ottheinrich's bankruptcy. Then were added the frescoes, attributed to Jörg II Breu, in the stair-tower of the west wing. Also of these years is the coffered barrel-vault, carrying the date 1545, in the entrance passage, with its inset medallions of Ottheinrich and various Roman Caesars. This stucco-work was more probably executed by Mantuans from Landshut, brought to Neuburg after the Stadtresidenz there was completed in 1543, than by the Italians Ottheinrich had hired in 1538.

After his return from exile in the early fifties and before leaving again for Heidelberg in 1556 on his accession as elector Palatine, Ottheinrich undoubtedly carried out further decoration, but of that very little survives. The coffered wooden ceiling of the Rittersaal in the first storey of the north wing (Pl. 105), if not the two sturdy piers of stone in the center—which would more probably be of 1534-1537—may date from the early fifties.

Definitely of the early fifties is Ottheinrich's Neuer

---

[17] *Ibid.*, p. 213. An opponent of Melancthon, Ossiander was vigorously attacked by Calvin.

[18] Stierhof, *Wandmalerei*, pp. 28-29, discusses the iconography, identifying the themes employed.

[19] *Ibid.*, pp. 21-28, describes the decoration in considerable detail.

Bau at Grünau[20] a structure of countrified simplicity (Pl. 124). On this, round towers flank a long low facade with a central projection crowned by a surprisingly plain and steep cross-gable. The main gables at the ends, however, are outlined by small rippling S-curves, common elsewhere by this date, though decorated also here with tiny brick arches that have an anomalous Lombard-Romanesque character.

Almost precisely contemporary with Ottheinrich's chapel at Neuburg is another of greater historical importance. On October 5, 1544, Martin Luther himself consecrated the Schlosskirche in the new northeast wing, begun in 1540, of Schloss Hartenfels at Torgau.[21] This wing extends between the mediaeval keep on the left, which survives, past the old Martinikapelle on the right, which was demolished then or later, to connect with the left end of the Johann-Friedrichs-Bau (Fig. 12). The Hartenfels chapel is generally considered to be the earliest surviving example of Protestant ecclesiastical architecture, not only in Germany but in all Europe. When construction started in 1543 it was certainly the first, anywhere, except for the long-lost one begun in 1534 at Joachimstal in Bohemia (Fig. 15) to be planned specifically for Lutheran use. However, though begun before Ottheinrich's change of religion in 1542, the chapel at Schloss Neuburg was actually completed with the execution of its "Lutheran" frescoes by Bocksberger in that year. Thus the Neuburg chapel was the first newly-built edifice in Germany now extant to be made, not only available, but especially suitable for Lutheran services. Such had been held since the mid-twenties either in secular settings or in existing churches intended for the Roman ritual of the Mass ever since the first Reformed communion was offered in 1524 in St. Anna in Augsburg.

If the Torgau church (Pl. 125) has historical priority as regards its function, at first sight it seems quite retardataire stylistically compared to the chapels at Landshut and at Neuburg. It certainly is not "advanced," if "advance" be measured in terms of the employment of Renaissance forms and details. Typologically, however, in the particular line of development of sixteenth-century German church architecture, it should more properly be considered *more* advanced than they. The simple rectangular plan of the Neuburg chapel, with cantilevered gallery and small square sanctuary, had no immediate future in German church design; much less the one-storeyed central plan of the Landshut chapel. But the two-storeyed rectangular interior with piers at the sides carrying vaulting overhead, as introduced in the Torgau Schlosskirche, would be the favored type—and not by any means only for princely chapels and other Lutheran edifices—when church-building revived in the later decades of the century.

Krebs had died in 1540 and is buried, as has been mentioned, in the Hartenfels court. It was Nickel Gromann who built, and had presumably designed, the church, if not so probably the entire wing which was begun in the year Krebs died. This church interior seems to have been Gromann's first independent work though earlier, in 1537, he had supervised the construction of Schloss Osterburg near Riesa in the Elbe valley between Torgau and Meissen. Here at Schloss Hartenfels the three-storeyed facade of the new wing toward the court, for which Gromann was Krebs's *Palier* (deputy in charge), follows in the main the design of the older man's southeast wing of 1533-1536, with regular rows of double windows in each storey of the same curtain-topped sort.

The principal feature of the court facade (Pl. 126), however, is the so-called *Schöner Erker* (beautiful oriel) which carries the inscribed date 1544, four years after Krebs's death. This rises from a single stubby support of baluster-like character and is provided on its two storeys with slim candelabra-colonnettes set against arabesque-panelled pilasters. The Schöner Erker was probably not designed by Gromann but entirely the work of the experienced sculptor, Stephan Hermsdorf, who had become a citizen of Leipzig as early as 1516. Because of the profusion of foliate and figural carving, this oriel contrasts, somewhat as does Krebs's great staircase on the southeast wing, with the relative severity of the rest of the structure outside and in.

The pulpit by Simon I Schröter (†1568) at the middle of the north side of the church (Pl. 127) is, however, an almost equally rich, if less elegant, example of Renaissance carving, and polychromed into the bargain. Moreover, young angels carrying symbols of Christ's Passion decorate the jambs of Schröter's por-

---

[20] Horn-Meyer, *Neuburg*, pp. 493-494.
[21] Dehio, *Dresden*, p. 405; [H.-J. Krause] *Die Schlosskapellen der Renaissance in Sachsen* [Berlin, 1970] (henceforth cited as Krause, *Schlosskapellen*), pp. 2-15. R. Friedenthal, *Luther*, New York [1967], p. 460, gives the mistaken impression there was no altar. Perhaps he considers what was there first—and is still there today—to be rather a "communion table" as in so many later Protestant churches. A more elaborate altarpiece was brought here from the chapel of the Dresden Residenzschloss in the seventeenth century. See Note IV 19.

tal (Pl. 128) on the court below a relief of the Deposition which is probably by Hermsdorf. Four more of Schröter's angels carry the plain mensa of the altar. One further decorative feature of this otherwise severely plain church is the superb bronze dedicatory tablet, cast in Freiberg by Wolfgang I and Oswald II Hilliger (1511-1576; 1518-1546) in 1545. This includes portrait medallions of Johann Friedrich at the top, his two sons at the sides, and Luther below, while an inscription in fine Roman letters fills the main field.

If one compares the Hartenfels chapel, or such a similar early Lutheran one as that in the Schloss at Schwerin built nearly twenty years later, not with those at Landshut and Neuburg but with the Wolfgangskirche at Schneeberg (Pl. 109), begun in 1515 and completed in 1540, or the Marktkirche at Halle (Pl. 37), begun in 1529, on which construction had come to a halt in 1541, the post-mediaeval character of their hybrid design becomes apparent, though that at Schwerin is naturally somewhat more advanced in its details. The particular model at Torgau, however, must have been Friedrich der Weise's Schlosskirche at Wittenberg (Pl. 36), built by Konrad Pflüger in the 1490's, as has been noted, and completed in 1508.[22] That was the church Luther had made world-famous in 1517 by posting his 95 Theses on the door, and one where he preached on occasion throughout the rest of his life.

The heavily molded archivolts of the broad segmental arches in both storeys of the chapel at Schloss Hartenfels, sinking into the diagonally chamfered inner ends of the wall-piers in both the upper and the lower storeys, recall the arches below the side galleries at Wittenberg and are even closer to the more nearly contemporary ones under the tribunes along the aisles and across the east end at Schneeberg (Pl. 109). Yet because these are not partially masked, as at Schneeberg, by tall ranges of pillars flanking the nave, they resemble rather in their visual effect certain earlier secular examples, especially the upper range of arches in the court arcades of 1519 at Freising (Pl. 30) or those, dated 1534, under Rosskopf's archive-wing at Görlitz (Pl. 65). The most probable models, however, also secular, are the three-storey *loggie* cutting diagonally across the western corners in the court of the Schloss at Wittenberg that are immediately contiguous to the Schlosskirche. Those arches had been built for Friedrich der Weise by Konrad Pflüger, beginning like his work on the church in the 1490s and

continuing intermittently down to Friedrich's death in 1525.[23]

In contradistinction to most Saxon churches of the early sixteenth century built for Catholic use and even to the first Lutheran town-church to be erected in Saxony—the Marienkirche at Marienberg as begun in 1558—the Torgau chapel, like the Wittenberg Schlosskirche, is not a hall-church. Moreover, there is no prismatic shaping of the east end such as was common elsewhere at the time. Of course, this was also true of the square-ended Marktkirche at Halle (Pl. 37) as begun for Cardinal Brandenburg in 1529 and of other early examples mentioned in the previous chapter, notably St. Martin in Lauingen (Pl. 12) and even, in a special sense, the Fuggerkapelle (Pl. 3), all three built also for Catholics. The modest altar at the east end at Schloss Hartenfels stands in front of two half-arches. These are carried in the middle by a single short fluted column with a very simple molded capital more Tuscan than Doric in character. In harmony with these half-arches the side arcades in both storeys terminate similarly at the east. Exigencies of existing mediaeval remains—especially the keep—required a diagonal wall at the southwest, but this was not matched on the northeast; there, however, the sacristy door, with its plain bevelled round arch, is placed off-center well to the right behind the altar.

The plain panels of the parapets of the upper galleries at Torgau, though not very different in size and shape from the traceried ones over the arches of 1536-1537 carrying the Emporen at Schneeberg (Pl. 109), have heavily molded frames. Though undecorated, the parapets seem closer in their un-Gothic look to those in the Neuburg chapel than to the ones Nickel Hoffmann introduced a decade later in completing the Halle Marktkirche in 1554-1555. Those have simple baluster-elements of faintly Italianate character on the stiles in awkward juxtaposition to the Gothic tracery filling their fields. The pattern of the ribs overhead at Schloss Hartenfels, however, despite the actual rounded section of the vault, though a good deal simpler, is hardly more "un-Gothic," so to put it, than in the Halle church. There the close netting of the ribs emphasizes the unpointed section of what is the equivalent of a continuous half-round barrel vault (Pl. 37).

The clean white plaster of the Torgau interior as restored is, except for the polychromed pulpit, varied only by the moldings and ribs of grey stone. Thus it

[22] Harksen, *Wittenberg*, pp. 4-5.

[23] *Ibid.*

seems to Anglo-Saxon eyes to have a distinctly Protestant, not to say Puritan, air. But this may be largely a result of the present empty and stripped condition of the church since its postwar restoration by the East German Communists. There are now no accessories except the plainest of white altar-cloths and a dark metal cross between two simple candlesticks; but this Marxist asceticism need not reflect the original intention of either Johann Friedrich or Gromann. Rather than being the initial example of what Anthony Garvan,[24] writing of the next century in England and America, called the "Protestant Plain Style," the Hartenfels Schlosskirche is very much still a church, even if a modest one, not a "meeting-house."

Schröter's carved reliefs of the Child Jesus in the Temple, of Christ and the Woman taken in Adultery and of Christ driving the Money-changers from the Temple on the Torgau pulpit (Pl. 127) are as unthinkable in a Calvinist "Kirk," such as the oldest surviving in Scotland, at Burntisland in Fifeshire begun in 1592, or a Puritan house of worship of the next century in the American colonies as in a Muhammadan mosque, not to speak of the Italianate angels that flank the portal and support the altar (Pls. 125, 128). Whether the particular choice of subjects is, as in the case of the Neuburg frescoes, specifically Lutheran is not altogether clear, though the Expulsion of the Money-changers may be a reference to Luther's continuing campaign against the sale of indulgences.

The even more modest Schlosskapelle at Gifhorn (Pl. 129), the construction of which for Duke Franz of Brunswick-Lüneburg followed in 1547, three years after the consecration of the Hartenfels Schlosskirche, is of little interest except for the inscribed date. A tiny squarish chamber with a polygonal apse and two galleries one above the other across the west end, this is still almost totally Gothic. The arches below the balconies are segmental, however, and much flatter than at Torgau. Curious ninepin-like batons, perhaps intended to imitate Italian balusters, separate the panels of the parapets of the galleries as on Hoffmann's balconies of 1554-1555 in the Halle Marktkirche; but the panels themselves, as at Schneeberg and later at Halle also, are filled with varied Gothic tracery. The round columns carrying the balconies with their molded capitals approach the Tuscan norm more nearly than the one at Torgau; but the rectangular door-frames have

typically Late Gothic fillets of rounded section intersecting at the corners just like the trim of the windows of the Torbau here at Gifhorn (Pl. 56) for which a date some ten years or more earlier was suggested in the previous chapter.

Before the war the altar in the Hartenfels Schlosskirche was backed by an elaborate carved altarpiece of 1554-1555 transferred from the chapel in the Residenzschloss at Dresden.[25] Of that chapel of the mid-century, already being remodelled in 1662 when the altarpiece was sent to Torgau, there survives only the portal (Pl. 130), now set up in the Judenhof. This was probably designed, and certainly in part executed, in the mid-fifties by an Italian known only as Johann Maria: in the niches at the sides there are statues by him of the two St. Johns, St. Peter and Moses. There is also a large figural relief in the attic and, above that, a crowning statue of Christ flanked by two—originally four—figures of angels again carrying symbols of the Passion. These last, however, were carved not by Maria but by Hans II Walther (1526-1585). Hans II was the son of the Christoph Walther who worked on the Georgenbau; and either he, or perhaps more probably Hans Kramer (†1577), the son of Bastian, will have been the actual builder of the portal, though not of the chapel to which it led. Walther was responsible for such sculptures as Maria did not execute himself.

The Dresden portal comes as close as anything surviving in Germany other than the Landshut Stadtresidenz to being an example of High Renaissance design. It certainly somewhat resembles, if not current Italian work, at least such French buildings of the reign of Henri II by Pierre Lescot (c.1510-1578), Jean Bullant and Philibert de l'Orme as the nearly contemporary chateau of Anet or that at Ecouen. The same was not true of the interior, which was begun earlier in 1549 probably by Melchior Trost (†1599), for Elector Moritz, though the work on the chapel was only completed in 1555 for his brother and successor August.[26] That was evidently an enlarged ver-

[24] Anthony N. B. Garvan, *Architecture and Town-Planning in Colonial Connecticut*, New Haven, 1951.

[25] Löffler, *Alte Dresden*, pp. 18-19, pl. 45; Hentschel, *Dresdner Bildhauer*, pp. 115-117, pls. 17b, 21. The altarpiece taken to Torgau in 1562, destroyed in the last war, is illustrated by Hentschel's pl. 19. A curiously confused work, at least as it appeared after re-erection in the chapel at Schloss Hartenfels, it would seem to owe more to Walther than to Maria.

[26] The chapel must have been largely completed structurally before Moritz's death in 1553, but the altarpiece and the portal may only have been commissioned by August: Krause, *Schlosskapellen*, pp. 15-20; Hentschel, *Dresdner Bildhauer*, pp. 115-117. Löffler, *Alte Dresden*, p. 409, dates the

sion of the Torgau chapel. As known from a print of 1676 by David Conrad, it would appear that this Dresden chapel lacked the appealing simplicity of that earlier example; but this view shows the result of the elaborate remodelling carried out, as has been noted, in the 1660s by W. C. von Klengel (1630-1691), not the original form which was doubtless plainer and with a much less Italianate treatment of the flanking arcades. The Catholic Hofkirche at Innsbruck, planned as early as 1553 but largely of the sixties and later, will be described in the next chapter.

The date MDLV on the Dresden Schlosskirche portal is two years after Moritz's death in 1553. In the preceding decade he had begun other considerable additions to the Residenzschloss to which Georg der Bärtige attached his Georgenbau in the 1530s (Fig. 18). Though Moritz had succeeded as duke in 1541, two years after Georg's death, his building activities seem to have started in earnest only around 1547. That was when he became elector after his defection to the emperor's side in the so-called War of Schmalkalden. The wings of the Moritzbau, completed eventually for Elector August in 1556, enclosed the Grosser Hof (big court).[27] There were polygonal stair-towers in the corners and a central *Altan* or frontispiece consisting of a superposed series of projecting loggias, all of five arched bays but topped by a trabeated gallery. That gallery rose a full storey above the eaves on the north side of the court below the tall octagonal Hausmannsturm (Pl. 133). The core of that tower was the mediaeval keep, but the ultimate form was the result of a remodelling and extension upward undertaken in 1674-1678, doubtless by Klengel, long after Moritz's and August's time. Flanking the uppermost loggia were two large three-stage dormers or cross-gables; while at the same level the stair-towers, much-reduced versions of Krebs's on Schloss Hartenfels, were crowned with slighter cylindrical turrets capped with domical roofs, i.e. *welsche Hauben*, and sharp spirelets like those over the oriels at Torgau on the side of Schloss Hartenfels toward the Elbe (Pl. 79).

All of this portion of the Dresden Residenzschloss was drastically restored in the 1890s. Copies were inserted in place of the original sculptural decoration by Maria and Walther, and a continuous gallery at second-storey level was added along the north side to provide horizontal communication. Most of the Moritzbau, however, was demolished in the disastrous air-raid of 1945. Prints and an elaborate wooden model give a good idea of the original design (Fig. 18, Pl. 132). This model, on which the work was based, had reputedly been provided by Caspar Voigt von Wiegerand. Rather than an architect, Voigt was a German expert on fortifications—a field Italians were gradually taking over elsewhere in the north—who worked under the direction of Hans von Dehn-Rothfelser (1500-1561) over the years 1546-1555 on the fortifications of Dresden. Dehn-Rothfelser was even less an architect than Voigt, but as Moritz's *Intendant* (Works officer) he held the office of *Oberbaumeister* from 1547 and was ennobled by Moritz in 1549.

Prewar photographs show the court as actually executed, partly by Bastian Kramer, who had worked on the Georgentor in the thirties and continued in Moritz's service, and partly—it is most probable—by his son Hans, who did not move to Danzig until the early sixties, but with various modifications that resulted from the "restoration" at the end of the last century. Prints, moreover, show that the walls above the ground storey were covered with sgraffito decoration (Pl. 133). Carried out in 1551-1555, this was the work of the North Italians Francesco Ricchino, Benedetto da Thola (†1572) and the latter's brother Gabriele (†1569). It was not replaced by the nineteenth-century restorers.

On the loggias of the Altan (Pl. 133) the Classical orders succeeded one another correctly; but at all the levels the arches were not quite semicircular and their archivolts were sliced at the base by plain vertical elements rising across the spandrels up to the entablature above. The podia under the columns, moreover, were circular not square. Yet the first-storey parapet was carved with Roman battle scenes of truly Renaissance character executed by Hans II Walther from Maria's designs. Similar was the profuse carving on the stair-towers. This evidently recalled, but apparently did not equal in quality, that of ten or fifteen years earlier on the stair-tower of Schloss Hartenfels; however, much of it was replaced in the 1890s with copies of the original work.

In the walls of the upper storeys of the court of the Moritzbau, as also on the gables, paired rectangular windows were quite regularly disposed. Over the tops of those in the first storey and below the sills of the ones above a continuous sgraffito frieze was carried across. There were also figural groups on the wall-spaces between, while a sgraffito inscription above the

chapel "nach 1548" and its portal 1552, however, before Moritz's death. In any case, the portal carries the inscribed date, presumably of completion, MDLV.

[27] Löffler, *Alte Dresden*, pp. 20-25, 349, pls. 36-43.

Fig. 18. Dresden, Residenzschloss,
plan

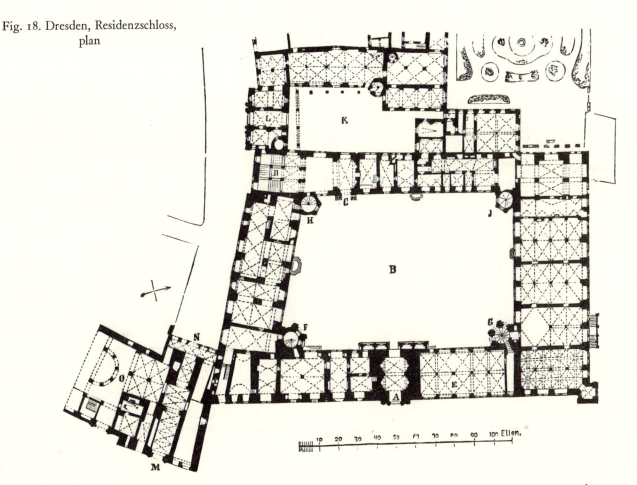

upper range of windows provided a frieze-like terminal band.

On the gables facing the Grosser Hof (Pl. 131), and
indeed on those above the outer side of the Moritzbau
as well, the diminishing stages were flanked by S- and
C-scrolls set, at least in the lowest stage, outside pilasters, and thus similar to the principal stage of Pasqualini's somewhat earlier gable at Buren (Pl. 43).
The terminal stage also carried a crowning pediment,
though a tiny one, and this was henceforth a frequent
element atop such gables in Germany as an alternative to *welsche Gebel*. Thanks to their strong horizontals, these gables were, indeed, rather closer in
character to those of the Palais de Savoie (Pl. 41) and
the one on the Buren Kasteel, both in the Netherlands, than to Knotz's of the mid-thirties over the
north wing of Schloss Neuburg (Pl. 91) in Germany.
However, even by this mid-century decade little actual influence from the Low Countries seems yet to
have reached Germany in architectural design. Such
imports as the Croy tomb in Cologne Cathedral and
even the Hackeney screen by Jan van Roome there in

St. Maria-im-Kapitol (Pl. 58) are more sculpture
than architecture.

The shapes of these gables are more likely to have
been a purely German development from those of
Kramer on the Georgenbau than a derivation from
Pasqualini's at Buren; indeed, they may well have
been designed by that experienced master-builder or
his son rather than by Voigt von Wiegerand, whose
real specialty was fortifications. On the other hand,
they could—and not at all improbably—be direct reflections of Serlio's design for the gateway which
closes the rear of the stage-set he published in his
Segundo libro in France in 1545 (Fig. 19) or the one
for a church which is in the *Quinto libro* of 1547,[28]
though that would be rather early for Serlian influence in Germany.

Moritz's work on the Residenzschloss in Dresden
is all but entirely lost. Moreover, the existing large
structure of the Moritzburg on an island in a lake

[28] Serlio, *Architectura*, II, 1545; V, 1547, last plate, unnumbered.

Fig. 19. Sebastiano Serlio: *scena tragica*, 1545

just to the north of the city has little relation beyond its symmetrical plan to the original rather modest *Jagdschloss* (hunting lodge) he built in 1542-1546[29] probably before work began on the Grosser Hof. The existing big round towers at the corners of the Moritzburg with their *welsche Hauben* do recall, however, those of the older enceinte, and the main block doubtless incorporates Moritz's modest rectangular *corps de logis* of 30 x 15 m. Later modifications and enlargement included scalloped gables added in 1582-1584 by Paul Büchner (1531-1607) and a chapel by Klengel of 1661-1672 in the middle of the left side. More evident today is the almost total recasting of the much-enlarged Schloss for Elector August der Starke over the years 1723-1736 for which his trio of architects, M. D. Pöppelmann, Zacharias Longuelune and Jean de Bodt, were in varying degree responsible. Happily a model of around 1600 (Pl. 134) makes the original character of the Moritzburg very clear. Reputedly Dehn-Rothfelser rather than Voigt von Wiegerand or one of the Kramers was himself responsible for the design. It certainly looks in the model to have been a bureaucratic production of the ducal "Office of Works."

The low round towers of the original Moritzburg at the corners of the enceinte—reflecting new ideas of defensive architecture by this time two generations old in Italy—were capped, as they would not have been in Italy, with slated *welsche Hauben*. Otherwise the exterior was very plain indeed, with the facades broken only by triple rows of fair-sized squarish win-

dows. The residence block occupied most of the court, and also had rows of windows that were regularly spaced but rather widely separated. The steep roof not only ended in gables but also carried, eventually, Büchner's gabled dormers near the ends both on the front and on the back. Generous S-scrolls flanked the first and second stages of these added features of the 1580s, and they were crowned with modest pediments much like those on the Moritzbau gables of forty years before (Pl. 131).

Only one further comment need be made concerning this Saxon hunting lodge: as earlier at Schloss Neuhaus, the site made possible a regular plan, in fact an even greater symmetry here than there on both of the axes. This recalls the Italian symmetry of the Landshut Stadtresidenz but, as was noted before concerning the Schloss at Schloss Neuhaus, is not necessarily evidence of Italian influence. Despite the reflection of the new defensive architecture at the Moritzburg, in Moritz's building operations Italian influence was largely limited to subsidiary employment of a few imported sculptors and painters on the Residenzschloss in Dresden. Moritz's architecture may properly be considered predominantly autochthonous, therefore, whoever was responsible for the designs and the execution: Voigt von Wiegerand, Trost, one of the Kramers or, as most probably for the Moritzburg, Dehn-Rothfelser. The multiplicity of recorded names confuses rather than clarifies the picture, and no individual talent comparable to Krebs's or Gromann's is recognizable.

If there was in Saxony little evidence of architectural influence from Italy in the mid-century except in the sculpture of Johann Maria and in the design of fortifications, further south the modest Schloss of the Counts of Ortenburg in northern Bavaria, some distance west of Passau and below the Danube, largely rebuilt through the sixteenth century, includes in the court a rusticated doorway, dated 1547, that is much more clearly dependent on Serlio's publications or some such Italian source than the Moritzbau gables. This portal contrasts both with the baluster-like colonnettes capped by almost Romanesquoid versions of Ionic capitals used for the arcades at the south end of the court—presumably a decade or more previously—and also with the painted quadratura enframement of the windows above, which may well be as late as 1600. Ortenburg is, indeed, most notable for the very rich wooden ceiling of the original Festsaal, also of around 1600, which served later as a Lutheran chapel (Pl. 352).

[29] Löffler, *Alte Dresden*, pp. 59, 355.

As earlier in the century, Italian influence often arrived first much further to the east. The Renaissance transformation of the Schloss at Brzég (Brieg), lying above Wrocłav on the Oder in Silesia, had reputedly been begun by the local ruler, Duke Friedrich II of the Silesian branch of the Piasts, in 1536 but was much extended by his successor, Georg II, who succeeded in 1547.[30] The earliest Renaissance work (Fig. 20) here resembles somewhat in its clumsy proportions and crude carving the sacristy portal of 1517 in Wrocłav (Pl. 19) and dates most probably from Friedrich's time. The very handsome arcade in the court

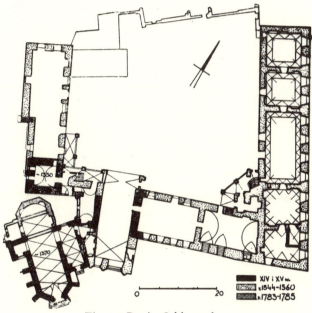

Fig. 20. Brzég, Schloss, plan

(Pl. 135), however, though now much damaged, must once have rivalled the contemporary ones in the Salamanca Schloss (Pl. 112). Carried on sturdy but finely detailed Ionic columns, with portrait medallions in the spandrels of the broad segmental arches and fluted vertical members between, this is more likely to have been the earliest contribution of the Milanese Jakob—i.e. Giacomo or, as it is more usually given, Jacobo Parr or Pahr (†1575). He was first called here to work for Georg upon the latter's acces-

sion in 1547, just when the Moritzbau was probably begun in Dresden.

Parr's masterpiece, and the masterpiece of the Silesian Early Renaissance, is the *Portalbau* (gatehouse) of 1552-1553 on this Schloss at Brzég (Pl. 136). Happily, that survives intact. As a belated example of a North-Italian sort of quattrocento decoration it is exceptional for the *horror vacui* that led Parr to fill all the flat surfaces with ornament and, in each of the upper storeys, to cover both a large and also a smaller pilaster order with arabesques or foliate carving. Also notable for their quality as sculpture are the full-round figures of the duke and his wife, still retaining much of the original polychromy, that stand above the portal, if hardly the two rows of busts of their ancestors running across the facade. These last occupy the frieze of the first-storey entablature and appear again between the podia of the order in the top storey.

As in the case of many other German Renaissance gate-house structures on Schlösser of both earlier and later date, the ground storey of the Brzég Portalbau is not symmetrical because of the disparity between the large arch on the right for mounted visitors and the smaller one on the left for pedestrians. In the triple bays above there are other disparities. All these relative irregularities suggest that Parr at this point in his career was only responsible for the carved detail and that some German, as at Dresden, may well have had general charge.[31] Moreover, other northerners could have supplied a part at least of the figural sculpture, for example, the rather crude ancestor-busts, so inferior to the portrait statues of the ducal couple.

If the Portalbau at Brzég, far to the east in Silesia, is still for the most part "Early Renaissance" of a distinctly North Italian character, in the west of the central German lands a more autochthonous mode continued in common use as in Saxony in the mid-century. At Weilburg, for example, the south and west wings, probably of the forties, still resemble in general the older one of the previous decade that rises high above the Lahn, and their gables all carry similar *welsche Gebel* of trilobe outline (Fig. 21). On

[30] Łozinski-Miłobedski, *Guide*, p. 52; Knox, *Poland*, p. 55; M. Szypowska, *Brzég*, Warsaw [n.d.] pls. 17-29. Horst, *Architektur*, fig. 82, offers a not very persuasive restored perspective of the Schloss showing a staged lantern on top of the Portalbau and four elaborate dormers over the main block.

[31] Three artists with German names are mentioned in documents: Andreas II Walther (†1583), Kaspar Kühne and Jakob Werter; for that matter Parr's name, however spelt, sounds more German than Milanese: Hentschel, *Dresdner Bildhauer*, p. 126. Hentschel identifies only the pulpit, dated 1570, in the chapel of the Brzég Schloss as the work of a Dresden sculptor, not one of the Walthers but Michael Kramer. Several of the younger Parrs including Franz, the best known, may also have worked here early in their careers.

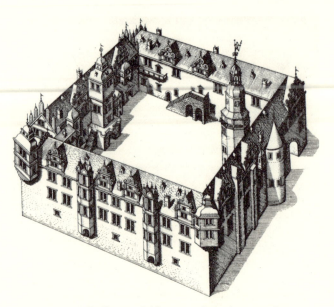

Fig. 21. Weilburg, Schloss, south and west wings,
c.1545

these, moreover, the bounding moldings of the lower
and upper curves overshoot their intersection in a way
that is still distinctly Late Gothic. As at Celle, the
client here, Count Philipp III of Nassau-Weilburg,
remained the same which doubtless explains the absence of significant change. But there are many other
examples of such stylistic stasis.

At Detmold it was the elderly Jörg Unkair whom
Count Bernhard VIII of Lippe called on in 1548[32] to
rebuild his Schloss, and the work continued until Unkair's death here at Detmold five years later. Then
Cord Tönnis from Hameln took over and probably
continued to work here until 1557. This, his first job
for which any record survives, initiated a career that
lasted down into the eighties. Though some external
irregularities at the Detmold Schloss resulted from
the retention of the great round tower of 1470 at the
southeast corner and a few other mediaeval fragments, Unkair provided here, as earlier at Schloss
Neuhaus and at Stadthagen, a quadrangular structure
with four stair-towers at the corners of the internal
court (Fig. 22). The tower beside the entrance at the
northeast is polygonal, the others square, but all have
his usual slanted windows and his quite un-columnar

cylindrical members on the angles, halting abruptly
here a full storey below the roofs.

Unkair's doorways on the Schloss at Detmold, two
of them dated 1550 and 1551, remain Late Gothic like
his of twenty-five years or so earlier at Schloss Neuhaus. Late Gothic also is the window-framing
throughout, with fillets crossing at the corners, as
around the doors in the Gifhorn chapel of 1547 (Pl.
129). But the many *welsche Gebel* at Detmold show
considerable variation (Pl. 137). The simplest are the
two to the right on the east front, miniature versions
of that over the end of the main block at Schelenburg which dates from around 1530 (Pl. 48). The
broadest gable here is not dissimilar, but this is
flanked by two small lunettes as is the corresponding
one over the center of the east side of the court. However, the one to the right of that and another at the
far left of the east front have flanking S-scrolls descending from masks. Radial fluting appears also on
these, not only in the terminal lunettes as on the
Stadthagen oriels, but also at the sides under the
S-scrolls. These more elaborate gables are presumably
of Tönnis's design, at any rate certainly not Unkair's,
as is also the four-storeyed oriel at the far left of the
east front beside the great tower.

But the early work of Tönnis at Detmold is more
than rivalled in quality by that of a third master.
The cantilevered gallery at first-storey level (Pl. 138),
which runs between the eastern stair-towers across
that side of the court, carries on the Late Gothic
ribbed vaulting the initials I.R.[33] and the date 1557
which is that of the completion of the remodelling
of the Schloss in the sixteenth century. Externally
the gallery is supported by powerful curved brackets
projecting above panelled pilaster-strips in the flat
wall below. On the face of the gallery very delicate
panelled pilasters without arabesque decoration separate the ten round-arched windows; armorial carving,
somewhat bolder in scale than the architectural elements, occupies the ten panels below the windows.
The dome-like *welsche Haube* atop the tall fifteenth-
century tower, the most conspicuous feature of the
Schloss when seen from a distance, is by none of the
three sixteenth-century master-builders but was added
around 1600.

At Heidelberg (Fig. 23), a new wing (Pls. 139,

[32] Kreft-Soenke, *Weserrenaissance*, pp. 240-242; O. Gaul,
Bau- und Kunstdenkmäler von Westfalen, vol. 48/I, Münster,
1968, pp. 124-199; [G. Dehio] Handbuch der Deutschen Kunstdenkmäler, *Westfalen* [Munich] 1969 (henceforth cited as
Dehio, *Westfalen*), pp. 118-120.

[33] These might be the initials of Johann Robin, but the date
seems too early for him. The same initials I.R. are signed
on the elaborate well-head of 1552 from Stadthagen that is
now at Bückeburg: Kreft-Soenke, *Weserrenaissance*, pp. 238,
241, pl. 43.

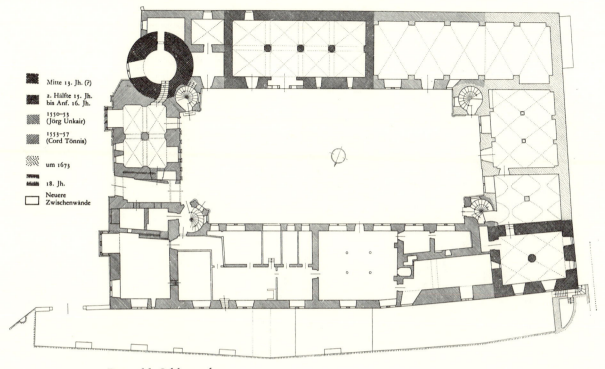

Mitte 13. Jh. (?)

2. Hälfte 15. Jh.
bis Anf. 16. Jh.

1550–53
(Jörg Unkair)

1553–57
(Cord Tönnis)

um 1673

18. Jh.

Neuere
Zwischenwände

Fig. 22. Detmold, Schloss, plan

140) was completed in 1549[34] just when Unkair's work was getting underway at Detmold. The Elector Palatine Ludwig V (1508-1544) had concerned himself chiefly with strengthening the fortifications of the mediaeval castle high above the Neckar, especially on the north and the west. He was also responsible, however, for the wing known as the Ludwigsbau at the southeast corner of the court and made considerable changes as well in the Ruprechtsbau, the Bibliothekbau and the Frauenzimmerbau on the west side. His successor, Friedrich II, who lived until 1556, built the modest block at the northeast corner of the court, known as the Gläserner Saalbau, which offers a sort of epitome of German Renaissance architecture in its secular form up to 1550. Of this, the right half is now masked by the later Ottheinrichsbau to the southeast, while the north and east fronts are overpowered by the tall octagonal bell-tower that Ludwig first erected and Friedrich heightened. This rises from the massive round mediaeval bastion at the outer corner of the

Schloss. The upper section that Friedrich added is now unroofed and ruinous.

With its original *welsche Haube*, the great bell-tower long dominated the view of the Schloss from the city below, somewhat as the southeast tower still does the view of the Detmold Schloss (Pl. 137) on its flat and open site in the center of that town. However, this northeast tower at Heidelberg was accompanied by broader, if lower and less elaborately capped, ones to the south and the west on the periphery of the fortified area. These still provide a notably picturesque and mediaeval silhouette. The two higher stages of the bell-tower, however, built by Friedrich in the later forties, retain his Renaissance cornices and, within round-arched openings, simple pointed tracery. The tracery is rather like that in the chapel windows at Neuburg of a few years earlier but here without cusping. Similar tracery presumably once existed in the heads of the smaller round-arched windows on the north or outer side of the Gläserner Saalbau.

Though this portion of the front of the Heidelberg Schloss rises four storeys above the broad terrace to the north, the east side (Pl. 139) seems even taller since there is no terrace here but only the bare earlier wall of the fortifications below. That end of the Gläserner Saalbau has lost the original outline of its

---

[34] A. von Oechelhaeuser, *Das Heidelberger Schloss*, 7th ed., Heidelberg, 1955 (henceforth cited as Oechelhaeuser, *Heidelberger Schloss*), pp. 48-53. The top storey of this wing of the 1540s was occupied by the so-called *Gläserner Saal* (Hall of Mirrors). This was decorated with many mirrors originally but no trace survives of what must have been a most exceptional interior for the period.

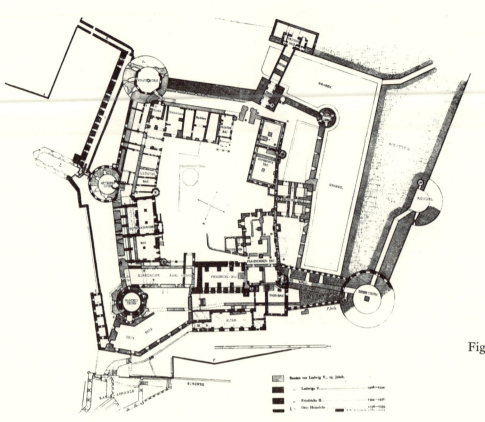

Fig. 23. Heidelberg, Schloss, plan

crowning gable which, presumably, was once very similar to that of the cross-gable toward the court. It does, however, preserve at second-storey level a small oriel, though this is very plain and modest in design compared to the Schöner Erker (Pl. 126) of 1544 at Schloss Hartenfels. After Ottheinrich succeeded as Elector Palatine on Friedrich's death in 1556, Heidelberg's architecture would not again show such restraint until Friedrich V built the Englischer Bau (Pl. 410) at the west end of the north wing for his wife Elizabeth, the daughter of James I, in 1613-1615.

Who designed Friedrich II's new wing and tower and in what year? A chimneypiece of advanced Italianate design in the earlier Rittersaal of the fifteenth-century Ruprechtsbau on the west side of the court carries the date 1546 and the initials C.F. The same initials and the date 1549 appear on the armorial carving on the ground storey of the court side of the Gläserner Saalbau. The initials are thought to be those of Conrad Forster, an Amberg stone-mason, who very likely executed in 1544-1545 the oriel (Pl. 161) on the *Kanzlei* (Chancery) there. That also carries the arms of Friedrich and of his wife, Dorothea of Denmark— it will be described later in this chapter. Forster was doubtless primarily a sculptor, but he may well have designed these buildings for Friedrich both at Amberg and at Heidelberg.

Whoever may have been the designer, description of the surviving south facade (Pl. 140) of the Gläserner Saalbau—which must date from the mid- or late forties—should indicate how neatly its principal features: the arcades, the decorated gable on the left, and the portal in the ground storey, can be fitted into the general sequence of development of the German Renaissance up to the mid-century. The arcades, for example, show as yet none of that response to advanced Italian design of those in the courts of the Landshut Stadtresidenz in Bavaria (Pl. 117) or the Salamanca Schloss in Carinthia (Pl. 112); yet for all the stubby proportions of the orders, their form here does represent a considerable advance beyond those of some twenty-five years earlier at Freising and at Regensburg, not to speak of the hybrid examples of the previous decade at Neuburg and Binsfeld (Pls. 76, 77). The entrance portal is relatively small and inconspicuous because it is shadowed by the arcade; but its carved decoration and asymmetrical placing is typical.

More exceptional is the treatment of the gable. This can hardly be described as scalloped, much less scrolled, for the shape is sharply defined by diagonals at the sides corresponding to the pitch of the roof. Such a clean triangular shape was common in contemporary England and not unknown in the Netherlands but rare, if not unique, in Germany on buildings of any architectural pretension. Outside these diagonals the step-like alternation of arch-topped crenellations, if one may so call them, with small-scale scrolled elements made up of sea-creatures is still predominantly Late Gothic in flavor. There is, all the same, more resemblance in the carved decoration to the edging of the gables of the Georgenbau in Dresden of the early to mid-thirties or to the Breda gables in Holland of the end of the decade than to the plain stepped gables that were in most common use throughout the century in the Netherlands both north and south.

Most of the building projects of the 1540s in the central German lands thus far discussed, those of the Wettins, the Welfs, the Lippes and the Wittelsbachs —all Lutherans by this time except Ludwig of Bavaria—were relatively unambitious, for they involved only the partial reconstruction or the enlargement of existing complexes. None rivals in size and elaboration the Hohenzollerns'[35] slightly earlier Joachimsbau in Berlin (Pl. 100). However, at Jülich on the Rur, in the Rhineland north of Aachen, where the whole town had burned in 1547, a rising Protestant potentate, Duke Wilhelm V of Kleve—called, like Jakob Fugger, "der Reiche"—the brother of Henry VIII's fourth wife, Anne of Cleves,[36] shortly started to rebuild the whole town as well as the citadel and the very large quadrangular ducal residence (Fig. 24) inside it. Work continued there through the fifties and beyond.[37] In 1548, to direct the project and, most particularly, to design the fortifications, he brought over from Dutch Gelderland, of which he was the ruler, Alessandro Pasqualini, whose employment at Buren probably terminated in 1545. Pasqualini worked henceforth at Jülich continuously, or at least recur-

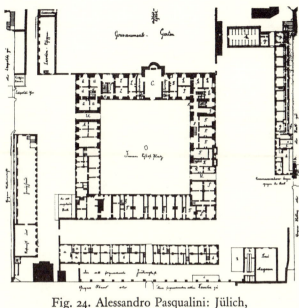

Fig. 24. Alessandro Pasqualini: Jülich, Zitadelle, plan drawn in 1792

rently, from 1549 until his death ten years later, and also at Düsseldorf where Wilhelm also ruled as duke of Berg. In Düsseldorf only one tower of the Schloss now partially survives, and little or nothing by him is extant at Kleve, though he is known to have worked for Wilhelm there in 1554. Elsewhere, in the contiguous regions along the Rhine or to the northeast in Westphalia, only the Vorburg at Rheydt to the west of Düsseldorf—if that was, indeed, begun within Pasqualini's lifetime—may be of his design.

Pasqualini's earliest work at Jülich, the east wing of the residence, was completed by 1555. This was followed by the construction of the north wing and the laying out of the adjacent town to the south and east of the citadel. After Alessandro died in 1558 his son Maximilian (1534-1572) took charge of the erection and extension of the fortifications and, by the time of Maximilian's death, he with his brother Johann I (†1580) had carried the residence to completion, adding finally the Zeughaus beside it in 1571, the year before Maximilian died.

Such was the damage done by bombing at Jülich in the last war that almost nothing survives in the town except one city gate, the Rurtor. Known as the *Hexenturm* (Witches Tower), this is a fourteenth-century structure that was remodelled in the seventeenth century. The vast rectangle of moated and brick-faced earthwork at the northwest corner of the town that forms the *Zitadelle* (citadel) is more largely intact. As a result of the restoration of the late 1960s, more-

[35] Schloss Hohenzollern, the seat of the Catholic branch of the family in the south, was entirely rebuilt for King Friedrich Wilhelm IV, after it came into the possession of the Prussian branch in 1850, by F. A. Stüler (1800-1865) and von Prittwitz: Dehio, *Baden-Württemberg*, p. 225. Apparently, however, there never was work of the sixteenth century of any consequence there.

[36] Wilhelm's wife Maria was a Habsburg, reputedly the only one who ever turned Protestant, though Emperor Maximilian II came near to it; she was a niece of Charles V and a daughter of Ferdinand I.

[37] H. Neumann, *Die Zitadelle Jülich* [Jülich, 1971] (henceforth cited as Neumann, *Jülich*).

over, it is no longer obscured from the outside by a thick growth of trees all around and on top. Very considerable ruins of the ducal residence within the brick-walled enceinte also survive. Archaeological investigation and the stabilization of extensive portions of the ruinous east wing in the last few years, including particularly the nave and apse of the Schlosskirche, have helped to clarify the long sequence of recurrent construction and partial destruction that extended from the late 1540s to the mid-1940s. Rather unfortunately, however, the greater part of the foundations below the north, south and west wings of the residence have now been used for a new school building that impinges on the surviving remains of the east wing.

Certain things are fairly evident in the extant portions to the northeast, the east and the southeast: most obviously, the Italian hands of the Pasqualinis and also Dutch influences from contiguous Gelderland on the west, of which Wilhelm had been duke since 1538[38] and where Pasqualini had been working. The brick is not the clumsy dark red-brown material common in the district but relatively neat pinkish units. Though probably not imported together with Dutch bricklayers—as is often done still in this district—the material distinctly recalls contemporary Dutch brickwork in color and scale. The great quadrangle must, indeed, have resembled rather closely the Kasteel at Breda where the elder Pasqualini had also worked in the early 1530s, and perhaps longer, for Hendrick of Nassau. Moreover, the quality of the work even approaches that of the tower he built, probably for Floris van Egmond, at IJsselstein (Pl. 42) in 1532-1535. There is, however, little resemblance to the Kasteel at Buren, which is nearer both in date and in its location in Gelderland.

The stairs at Jülich in the east wing at the south and north ends, with their parallel straight flights between walls and their restrained detailing of High Renaissance character, are almost a copy of Vincidor's at Breda and totally unlike the usual spiral staircases of the German Renaissance. Indeed, the detailing in stone throughout, around the northeast entrance, between the storeys, and both inside and outside on the apse of the church, is exceptional in its "correctness." The continuation of the work through most of the

third quarter of the sixteenth century, however, followed by much damage in the wars of the seventeenth century and, after that, low-grade restoration during the centuries the residence served as barracks, made a sort of architectural palimpsest of the ruins even before the last war.

The church at Jülich, Protestant from the first, is dated 1552-1553, though the sophisticated execution and even more the Bramantesque elaboration of the surviving east end makes this difficult to believe. For that date it certainly represents a phenomenal achievement on Alessandro's part,[39] yet one quite without influence in Germany in the following decades. Moreover, the Jülich chapel contrasts almost as sharply with the more elaborate but much less sophisticated portal of the Dresden Schlosskirche of the mid-fifties (Pl. 130) as with the hybrid design of Gromann's chapel at Schloss Hartenfels of 1543-1544 (Pl. 125). In the northern Europe of the 1550s it is unique and rivalled only in surviving work by de l'Orme's very different chapel at Anet. Possibly, however, the Italian Chiaramella's chapel at Wolfenbüttel may have been comparable in some respects (Fig. 26).

The external entablature of the lower order of the east end (Pl. 143) of the Jülich chapel—Doric, crossed by quarry-faced stone bands that also stripe the brick wall between—continues all along the exterior of the east wing and the contiguous portion of the north wing that still survives. The detailing of the panelled Ionic order of the next storey on the rear of the church, as also that of the niches flanking the apse, is very close indeed to the handling of similar elements on the first storey of the IJsselstein tower (Pl. 42) as built by Pasqualini twenty years before. The terminal pediment and the attic, with its underscaled Corinthian half-columns, is in its present form an eighteenth-century addition. The original pediment was broader, the full width of the rear of the chapel. However, the Ionic half-columns of the upper storey inside above the blank lower walls are original (Pl. 145).

Even more remarkable than the exterior of the surviving east end must have been the character of the

[38] Wilhelm's importance in the Europe of his day lay in his acquisition of the duchy of Gelderland on the extinction of an earlier line of dukes in 1538. It was after his successful challenge to Charles V over Gelderland that he married the emperor's niece as mentioned in Note 36.

[39] Neumann, *Jülich*, pp. 56-59. Neumann quotes statements published in the 1950s and 1960s by Franz Graf Wolff Metternich that underline a specific resemblance to Bramante's Palazzo di S. Biagio and also stress that Wilhelm intended the chapel for Protestant use. Indeed it was, as Wolff Metternich saw it, already a sort of *Predigtkirche* (preaching church), if hardly a forerunner of the "meeting houses" of the Calvinists the first of which, that in Lyon, was not begun for another ten years.

interior of the Jülich church as that has lately been deduced from excavation of the foundations. The organization seems to have been quite unlike that of any other sixteenth-century church in the north, even the one at Wolfenbüttel, some five years later in date. The plan was an irregular Greek cross covered, as regards the "crossing" and "transepts," by a broad longitudinal barrel-vault.[40] The nave was narrowed by loges on either side at first-storey level, it is now presumed, and covered by a barrel vault corresponding in its lesser width to the surviving half-dome of the apse.[41] How such an interior was utilized for services is not altogether clear. The altar must have been in the apse; but where was the pulpit, certainly of equal importance in an edifice built for use by Protestants? Leaving conjecture aside, certainly the interior view to the east (Pl. 145) is still most striking with its plain lower walls and the elegant order of paired Ionic half-columns, mentioned above, that flank the apse and are repeated on the upper walls of the transepts.

Unhappily the arcade around the court at Jülich was demolished in the seventeenth century. The only conspicuous surviving feature with which the orders and their employment on the church might be compared is the entrance portal (Pl. 144), on the outer side of the north wing, and that could well be later than the fifties. It is certainly Vignolan[42] rather than Bramantesque in scale and in spirit; but Vignolan influence on architects as sophisticated as the Pasqualinis is by no means unthinkable. The superimposed arcades of the court of Schloss Bedburg, not far from Jülich to the northeast, which are sometimes attributed to Pasqualini—of uncertain date but surely of

around this time[43]—may be mentioned here, for they approach rather closely the mature High Renaissance character of the Jülich church, and avoid the solecisms of Vincidor's orders at Breda.

The one round tower of the Schloss beside the Rhine at Düsseldorf,[44] the principal town in Wilhelm's duchy of Berg between Jülich and Kleve, which still survives—the rest burned in 1872—is a mediaeval relic, now covered with stucco, for which Pasqualini provided new windows in the 1550s. The arcaded octagon in two storeys at the top, however, which is today the only notable architectural feature of the tower, was added in 1845 by Rudolf Wiegmann (1804-1865) as was probably the portal also. Nothing else connected with Alessandro Pasqualini seems to be extant and his sons' work is not even as well identified.

Two more princely residences of the 1550s built for Lutheran rulers, neither of them so far mentioned, one way to the north at Wismar on the Baltic, the other in the south at Stuttgart in Württemberg, have happily survived far more completely than Pasqualini's work at Jülich. At the Fürstenhof in Wismar the later portion was built in 1553-1555[45] for Duke Johann Albrecht I of Mecklenburg. It provides the most remarkable example of Renaissance decoration in terra cotta in Germany. The removal in 1574 of the gables and dormers that once gave the facades a somewhat more Northern look left a three-storeyed structure of the richest Lombard or Emilian Early Renaissance character.[46]

The Wismar Fürstenhof[47] is thus quite unlike Vincidor's and Pasqualini's work at Breda and Jülich,

---

[40] Thus the space is directional, not centralized like that of de l'Orme's Anet chapel. The cruciform Zamek chapel at Siedlisko in Silesia (Pl. 444) is considerably later, after 1600.

One wonders if the pulpit could have been in the apse, above and behind the altar or communion table, as at Lyon. Such a placing of the pulpit is not found elsewhere in Germany, in any extant church at least, before the Schmalkalden chapel (Pl. 267) as furnished forty years after this.

[41] Dr. Eberhardt, the architect in charge of the excavations, has very kindly permitted me to see his hypothetical reconstruction of the interior of the church based on the foundations that survive below the nave of the church. He properly reserves the right to publish his restored plan and his perspective of the interior looking west.

[42] Neumann, *Jülich*, p. 46, again quotes Wolff Metternich who saw the portal of the Palazzetto Spada "beinahe als Vorbild des Jülicher Nordportals. . . ." The Palazzetto Spada has been attributed both to Peruzzi and to Vignola.

[43] Dehio, *Rheinland*, pp. 48-49, suggests a date "um 1550." The infilling of terra cotta of the 1920s is very unfortunate, distracting attention from Renaissance arcades which have actually recalled to some German writers those in the court of the palace at Urbino!

[44] *Ibid.*, p. 132. Work on the Schloss at Jülich was continued after Alessandro Pasqualini's death by his son Maximilian.

[45] Deutsche Kunstdenkmäler, *Mecklenburg* [Munich, 1971] (henceforth cited as DKD, *Mecklenburg*), pp. 410-411; Piltz, *D.D.R.*, p. 51.

[46] [G. Dehio] Handbuch der Deutschen Kunstdenkmäler, *Die Bezirke Neubrandenburg, Rostock, Schwerin*, Munich, 1968 (henceforth cited as Dehio, *Neubrandenburg*), p. 70. Altdorfer, possibly the initiator of the Fürstenhof, came from Regensburg but had been at Mecklenburg since 1512, suggesting that he would have been elderly by the 1550s.

[47] Except for the loss of the gables, the Fürstenhof has survived intact externally beside the gaunt red-brick towers and transepts of the two nearby mediaeval churches. The interior has not been restored.

which reflects a distinctly later and less regional sort of Italian Renaissance architecture, despite the fact that both men had come north from Bologna in Emilia relatively early in the century. But the Neue Hof is quite similar to Parr's Portalbau at Brzég (Pl. 136), at least in spirit, a work of precisely the same date though discussed earlier in this chapter. The Baltic lands, like the Low Countries and the contiguous territories between the Maas and the Rhine, had long built chiefly in brick. But at Wismar the walls of the Fürstenhof were from the first stuccoed, thus reversing, thanks to the warm color of the terra cotta decoration, the chord of red-brick walling and light-colored stone trim of the Breda Kasteel and the Jülich Zitadelle.

The builders most responsible for the Wismar Fürstenhof, Gabriel von Aken and Valentin von Lyra, both came from Lübeck, a larger Baltic port, not far to the west. The original design may, however, have been by the elderly Erhart Altdorfer and, in any case, Aken soon returned to Lübeck after he began to have difficulties with Lyra. Lyra was presumably also elderly like Altdorfer, for he had been appointed *Ratsbaumeister* (Council architect) of Lübeck as early as 1485, a post he continued to hold until 1555; he also worked again for the Mecklenburg dukes at Schwerin as late as 1557. If Michael Clare was, indeed, employed at Wismar as some believe, it can only have been at the start, since he was in Celle by 1553. There is certainly nothing at the Schloss there (Pl. 98) recalling the Fürstenhof to support this assumption.

Considering certain differences in the design of the two facades of the Fürstenhof, however, though both have basically similar terra cotta trim executed and probably designed by the brickmaker and sculptor Statius von Düren—by this time long settled in Lübeck, though Netherlandish in origin—it may be that the court side is by Aken (Pl. 146) and the outer front by Lyra (Pl. 147). The division of the court facade into seven bays by pilasters, here arabesque-panelled, in all three storeys recalls the considerably earlier and more modest Mittelbau of the Schloss (Pl. 88) at Dippoldiswalde in Saxony. However, the Wismar pilasters are flatter and quite without tectonic character, more like those on the Georgenbau (Pls. 83, 84) in Dresden. In each bay of all three storeys there is a triple-arched window with extremely delicate arabesque decoration on the pilaster-mullions, foliate ornament on the archivolts and rosettes in the spandrels below a crisp cornice all executed in terra cotta.

The frieze of the ground-storey order of the court

facade of the Wismar Fürstenhof—which serves also as the podium of the order above—is, however, of limestone obtained in 1552 from the quarries at Kull by Aken. Its subject is the story of the Prodigal Son. The upper frieze of portrait medallions in terra cotta by Statius or from his workshop, which operated in Lübeck from 1550 to at least 1566, recalls that dated 1508 on the Palazzo Roverella in Ferrara. The two narrow terra cotta doorways (Pl. 148) at the inner angle of the court have slim half-colonnettes set against wide pilasters, the whole covered with arabesques. Above, there are half-circular lunettes of the Italian sort that originally inspired the *welsche Gebel*. The terra cotta decoration, and particularly these doorways, suffered from insensitive restoration in 1877/1878. Happily, the latest restoration of 1951-1952—after very serious war-damage but not, as has been mistakenly reported, total destruction!—replaced the plain stucco covering the walls more plausibly.

The outer facade (Pl. 147) of the Fürstenhof at Wismar repeats the triple windows and the friezes—the subject of the lower one being here the Trojan War—but there are no pilasters. Instead the arched windows in the two lower storeys are capped with pediments containing heads set in circular niches and flanked by scrolling foliage. Furthermore, the groups of windows in all three storeys on this side are flanked by herm-pilasters that are not at all Emilian quattrocento in character but seem rather to depend ultimately on those on the title-page of Serlio's *Quarto libro* of 1537. One might therefore ask whether the street front was not executed several years after that towards the court; however, the limestone portal on the court side seems at least as up to date internationally as that on the outside. This portal in the court is, moreover, superior in the quality of the figural sculpture in the round—David and Goliath, curiously paired with Judith and Holofernes—on top of the cornice over the broad round arch.

This residence of Duke Johann Albrecht of Mecklenburg, so retardataire in its reflection of a Ferraran palace of nearly a half-century earlier, was paralleled as regards its Emilian Early Renaissance aspect in these years 1553-1555 in the east wing of the same prince's Schloss at Schwerin.[48] Clare may also have worked there; but what is original is now overshadowed by the vast extension and elaboration of the Schloss[49] in the years 1843-1857 mentioned earlier.

[48] DKD, *Mecklenburg*, pp. 395-397, plan, p. 396.
[49] The Schloss, now occupied by a training institute for kindergarten teachers, is only accessible externally.

Well to the south and west of Schwerin, halfway to Berlin and today outside Mecklenburg in Land Brandenburg, is Freyenstein. The Altes Schloss there, which followed in 1556,[50] though but a ruined fragment (Pl. 149) is finer than any original portion of the Schloss in Schwerin. The design is also more striking than that of the Wismar Fürstenhof because of the tiers of shallow oriels flanking the one surviving facade below a tall and elaborately decorated gable. The rich terra cotta cladding on the gable and on the oriels was again provided by Statius von Düren's Lübeck kiln. Still later is the better preserved Schloss at Gadebusch, which lies between Lübeck and Schwerin in Mecklenburg. That belongs to this period in style but not in date, and the detailing is less interesting as is also the over-all composition.

The Gadebusch Schloss was built in 1570-1571[51] for Duke Christoph of Mecklenburg by Christoph Haubitz. On the two surviving facades (Pl. 150) pilaster-strips with repeated ornamental blocks replace the more Ferraran pilasters of the Wismar Fürstenhof. The rectangular windows—perhaps dating only from a restoration of 1903—are much more simply framed than the windows there or at Freyenstein. But the friezes of portrait medallions, two on the main block and three on the broad stair-tower, are apparently from the same moulds, still in use at the Lübeck tile-kiln, as the similar detail employed earlier. Such friezes were also introduced on various house-fronts in Lübeck (Pl. 153), but these houses were mostly destroyed in the last war.

What is notably different from the Wismar Fürstenhof at Gadebusch is the survival of the gables. That above the stair-tower is crowned with three very richly ornamented lunettes, and there are four more on the one at the left end of the main block. The portals, moreover, are at once a little earlier in style—surprisingly, considering the date—and also in better condition than the restored ones they so closely resemble on the court front at Wismar (Pl. 148). Such detailing as is original on the Schwerin Schloss is more similar to that at Gadebusch than to the contemporary decoration on the Wismar Fürstenhof. It is, however, much more elaborate than either, especially as regards the treatment of the top storey and the dormers.

Since it is evident that the Wismar Fürstenhof and the Schwerin, Freyenstein and Gadebusch Schlösser were the work of Lübeck designers, it is appropriate to note here some of the steps in the infiltration of Renaissance forms at Lübeck and certain other far northern towns. In them brick had long been almost exclusively used for building because, as in Holland, neither stone nor timber was locally available, and terra cotta provided the most available material for ornamental detail. The Haus der Schiffergesellschaft in Lübeck, dated 1535 (Pl. 35), has already been mentioned. On its tall gabled facade the pointed arches of the inherited regional Gothic mode had already given way to round and segmental ones; while the stuccoed circular niches, though empty, offered at least a suggestion of Renaissance medallions. With this rather plain early example can be contrasted the so-called Kerkhofhaus in Rostock at Hinter dem Rathaus 8[52] into whose fifteenth-century banded brick facade a profusion of Renaissance ornament in colored terra cotta was inserted, most probably in the third quarter of the sixteenth century but possibly in the forties.

The house dated 1548[53] at Am Sande 1 in Lüneburg (Pl. 151), an important town to the southeast of Hamburg, is predominantly segmental-arched, but it still has blind Gothic tracery in the outermost bays of the shallow stages of its tall stepped gable. On the other hand, in the spandrels of the first and second storey, as in those of the round-arched portal, the wreathed disks contain portrait medallions. Very similar is the house at Lünertorstrasse 5, originally a brewery, with both its segmental arched windows and its Renaissance medallions framed by heavy rope moldings of terra cotta (Pl. 152). The pointed arch of the entrance and the cusped Gothic tracery, located as on that at Am Sande 1 in the outermost bays of the steps of the gable, suggest a date in the 1550s, but Gadebusch indicates that the house could be much later.

Of much the same, if uncertain, period must also be the houses at Mengstrasse 27 and Kohlmarkt 13 in Lübeck. Both have, above the ground storey, friezes of wreathed medallions that came from Statius's local workshop and both have round-arched doorways. In the upper storeys of Mengstrasse 27 the windows are segmental-arched but at Kohlmarkt 13 (Pl. 153) they are round-arched and have molded imposts. The gen-

---

[50] [G. Dehio] Handbuch der Deutschen Kunstdenkmäler, *Mark Brandenburg und Berlin* [Munich, 1971] (henceforth cited as Dehio, *Brandenburg*), p. 381.

[51] DKD, *Mecklenburg*, p. 364; Dehio, *Neubrandenburg*, pp. 92-93.

[52] *Ibid.*, p. 334.

[53] J. Matthaei, *Lüneburg*, 2nd ed. [Munich] 1965, pp. 24-25. The book illustrates dozens of other Lüneburg gabled housefronts, including many of this period.

eral effect of the latter is even more different, because it has a sort of order of coupled colonnettes that are rope-molded like the window-frames of the Lüneburg houses. This motif is used on all four upper storeys, two of which are in the gable. The present bold and simple outline of the gable, quite ignoring the stepped pattern suggested by the arrangement of the windows, is presumably a seventeenth-century or later emendation. The most elaborately decorated house in Lübeck, with three friezes of medallions and caryatid herms instead of an order in all the upper storeys, was at Braunstrasse 4. This did not survive the war. One may again hazard a date somewhere between the mid-fifties and the early seventies.

Much of this northern house-architecture of brick, however, despite the frequent inclusion of Statius's portrait medallions, long remained hybrid. Certainly there was no such pretention to over-all Italianate composition as had already made an appearance nearby at Wismar by the early fifties. Moreover, the stuccoed wall-surfaces, contrasting with the tawny terra cotta trim at Wismar and Gadebusch, and once doubtless at Schwerin and Freyenstein also, are missing on these all-brick town-house facades.

In quite another part of Germany, where brick was also the usual building material, the mid-century saw a very different sort of Renaissance design than in Lübeck and Mecklenburg. The Drostenhof at Wolbeck (Pl. 155), to the southeast of Münster in Westphalia, which was built in 1554-1557[54] for Dirk von Merveldt, has an almost English look because of the diamond patterns of blue-burned headers in the red brick wall and the squarish windows. These are subdivided by very plain stone mullions and transoms and have Gothic cusping at the head of each light as was usual in Tudor England down into Elizabeth's reign. On the other hand, the steps of the tall gables here are crowned in the familiar Westphalian way with fluted lunettes, while the windows in the gable are organized quite exceptionally in a checkerboard pattern between plain panelled pilaster-strips. Dating from as late as 1588,[55] the facade (Pl. 156) of the Krameramtshaus (guildhall) in Münster has at the top an elaborated version of the same scheme, with the alternate flutes in the crowning lunettes of the

gable pierced and half-columns set against the pilasters below. The windows here are still mullioned and transomed in stone, but the Gothic tracery at the heads of the lights was by this time omitted.

In this same district, but somewhat further from Münster, is the modest *Herrenhaus* (manor) of Byink near Ascheberg (Pl. 154). This was built for Heinrich von Ascheberg in 1558[56] and has also a rather larger gatehouse dated 1561. On these two contiguous structures the gables are lower and simpler, but lunettes rise high at the crown on each of them and also flank the sloping sides at the base. The symmetrical garden facade of the main house, with rounded wings projecting at either end, has rather the air of a Norman *manoir*, while the stone-framed window lights again suggest contemporary England. What must be their nearer relatives, however, can best be seen in Holland.

These modest Westphalian works of the fifties are further evidence that, except where Alessandro Pasqualini worked at Jülich—and perhaps at Bedburg—as also probably on certain buildings by him elsewhere that are no longer extant, advanced architectural design was not yet entering Germany overland from the Netherlands, southern or northern. In Cologne, however, projects for the Doxal on the Rathaus were obtained from a Netherlander as early as 1557 as the Hackeney screen had been a generation earlier.

It was in quite a different region that the building activities of the Saxon electors and the Mecklenburg dukes were more than rivalled in scale, if not in richness of decoration, in the mid-century. In 1534, after fifteen years during which Stuttgart, his capital, was occupied by imperial troops, Duke Ulrich of Württemberg returned to his lands, bringing back with him the reformed religion. His son Christoph, who succeeded in 1550, began in 1553[57] the remodelling and extensive enlargement of what is now called the Altes Schloss, employing as his architect Alberlin Tretsch (†c.1577), who had been in the ducal service since 1537. Tretsch's assistants here and elsewhere were Blasius and Martin Berwart.[58]

Of the mediaeval castle on the site in Stuttgart only the Dürnitz at the southwest corner of the Altes Schloss (Fig. 25) survives, and even this was topped by Tretsch with a flat Renaissance terrace. Externally,

---

[54] Dehio, *Westfalen*, pp. 605-606. The associated *Torhaus* (gatehouse) of the Drostenhof carries the date 1545.

[55] W. Hager, *Münster in Westfalen*, 2nd ed. [Munich] 1966, pp. 28, 40. The gable of the Krameramtshaus was restored in 1898, but on the basis of adequate evidence for its original form.

[56] Dehio, *Westfalen*, p. 25. Haus Byink is in the country 3.5 km. N.W. of Ascheberg, more or less in the direction of Lüdinghausen.

[57] Fleischhauer, *Württemberg*, pp. 33-38.

[58] *Ibid.*, pp. 45-50.

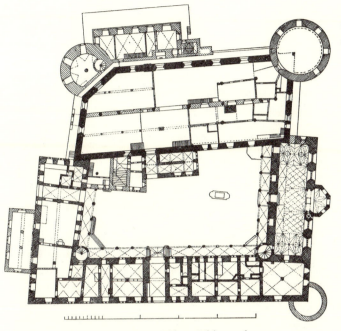

Fig. 25. Stuttgart, Altes Schloss, plan

all the same, the Schloss still has the air of a fortified Burg, thanks particularly to the great round towers flanking the southeast and southwest sides. The main northwest front is less mediaeval-looking but equally severe. It rises through three tall storeys except above the entrance, where the top storey is omitted, and has five very simple hip-roofed dormers that break the low-pitched main roof, also hipped and without gables.

Upon entering the court of the Altes Schloss, however, though the elements lying immediately ahead —mostly parts of the Dürnitz—are plain in design and confused in massing, one receives an entirely different impression. Except inside the entrance, where the top level is missing in two bays as on the exterior, three storeys of arcading[59] surround the court on the southeast, the northeast and the northwest (Pl. 158). Except for the work by Italians in the Salamanca Schloss at Spittal-a.-d.-Drau (Pl. 112) and the Wawel Zamek at Kraków, nothing approaching the court of the Altes Schloss had been seen in any Schloss in northern Europe before this. However, the tall arcaded loggias added by the Italian Giovanni Battista di Quadro on the front of the Rathaus at Poznań

(Posen) in Pomerania (Pl. 241), a civic building, in this same decade should also be mentioned in this connection.[60] Like the Carinthian and Polish examples, these Poznań loggias are much more correctly Italianate in their proportions and their detailing than Tretsch's, but they do not surround a court. Even at Breda and at Jülich in the west, where the architects were also Italians, arcades had been introduced only at ground-storey level. At Binsfeld in the thirties the arcades, though Late Gothic in their detailing like Pflüger's of a generation earlier on the Schloss at Wittenberg, are multiple, as also the Early Renaissance ones on the Gläserner Saalbau at Heidelberg of the later forties. In none of them, however, do these arcades occupy more than one side of a court.[61]

Although the conception of the court in the Altes Schloss is so Italianate, even to the low-pitched hip-roofs, and there are no gables at all, neither welsche Gebel nor scrolled ones, Tretsch's detailing is distinctly Germanic. It has neither the Emilian delicacy and elegance of that by Statius nor the more Roman restraint of Pasqualini's, much less the rich Venetian character of Quadro's. Only the simple cross-ribbed vaulting of the galleries and the cylinders enclosing the spiral staircases in the east and west corners—the latter noticeable chiefly because their low conical roofs project out of the main roof-slopes—are really still mediaeval in spirit. All the same, because of the consistent use of segmental arches and the lack of any elements of the orders other than the innumerable columns and their capitals, the general look of the work—unlike the arcaded courts further east in Kraków and Spittal, not to speak of many larger and rather later ones, also to the east in Moravia[62]—is

[59] It is probable that only wooden galleries, as in the Alte Hofhaltung at Bamberg, were originally intended when the reconstruction of the Stuttgart Altes Schloss began. It is not possible to determine when the arcades of masonry were planned, but they seem to have been executed c.1557-1560.

[60] Łozinski-Miłobedski, Guide, p. 192.
[61] Much earlier, the arcading in the Freising Bischofshof of 1519 and that of the Regensburg Bischofshof, which is a few years later, was multistoreyed and at Freising occupied two contiguous sides of the court (Pl. 30).
[62] Knox, Bohemia, p. 121, fig. 51a. Especially large and impressive is the court of the castle at Bucovice of 1566-1587. That was designed by Pietro Ferabosco (1512-1596). He came originally from Como, grew up in Vienna and, like so many other Italians, worked first in the north only on fortifications. But he was employed as architect by the Archduke Maximilian, later the emperor Maximilian II, at the Hofburg in Vienna on the Stallburg of 1559-1565 and the Amalienburg of 1575-1583: Baldass, Österreich, pp. 21-23, pl. 6. The earlier Schweizertor, carried out in 1552-1553 for Ferdinand I shortly before he became emperor, may already be of Ferabosco's design. It is the only one of these elements of the Hofburg that belongs to the period covered in this chapter: KDKÖ, Wien, p. 300.

quite un-Italian despite its general resemblance to the courts in Italian palaces. The latter in any case are rarely of such large dimensions as this—much less the one at Kraków and those in Moravia.

There is no sequence of orders, but the capitals, whether Corinthian or Composite, are fairly correctly, if not very elegantly, designed and executed (Pl. 158). The proportions of the fluted shafts, however, appear almost as stubby as those of the arcades of the Gläserner Saalbau (Pl. 140) since, as at Dresden (Pl. 133), circular podia at the level of the parapets continue the shafts downward and reduce in effect their length. These podia, moreover, are spiral-fluted in the upper ranges, though plain below, in contrast to the upper portions of the shafts that have normal fluting. Under the podia in the upper storeys roughly hemispherical brackets are set. These must be considered purely decorative since the plane of the column-shafts is actually in advance of that of the spandrels. The parapets have a rather coarse openwork pattern; though evidently derived from the guilloche, this appears hybrid rather than Italianate.

Despite his various solecisms in detail, Tretsch gave the whole northwestern side of the court of the Altes Schloss (Pl. 158) an architectonic character that is really neither mediaeval, except structurally, nor at all persuasively Italian like the various examples further to the east. This character is, moreover, of a volumetric interest rarely approached hitherto in Renaissance architecture in Germany or elsewhere in the north. One should note, for example, the curious fashion in which the round stair-towers take the place of corner columns on the north and west, an arrangement that distinctly emphasizes their plastic interest. So also the way the house-like hipped dormers suggesting pavilions rise above the two topmost bays flanking the lower and wider bays at the entrance produces a novel compositional effect of solid over void seen nowhere else in the period.

The extensive remodelling and enlargement of the Altes Schloss at Stuttgart proceeded slowly though the rest of Duke Christoph's life-time and into that of his successor Duke Ludwig. In the Dürnitz a spiral staircase carries the date 1558, and the chapel, occupying the whole of the two lower storeys of the southwest wing, was built in 1560-1562. Externally this last is signalized by a half-octagonal apse which rises almost like a tower above the main roof of the Schloss. This is topped, not with a plain *welsche Haube*, but with an S-curved roof (Pl. 157). A range of seven tall, narrow and deep-sunk windows, round-arched

on the three sides of the projecting apse though segment-topped on the flat wall-surfaces to left and right, also indicates the existence of a tall interior along this side. The paired and transomed rectangular lights in the top storey over the arched windows and the small hipped dormers above link the design of this wing with that of the main front to the northeast beyond the eastern tower.

Internally the chapel in the Altes Schloss was so elaborately "restored" in 1864 that only the plan (Fig. 25), and probably the vaulting, are original. But this chapel introduces a distinct variation in organization from that of earlier Lutheran churches. As remote from Gromann's still near-Gothic chapel of 1543-1544 at Schloss Hartenfels or the Marienberg Hallenkirche, begun in 1558, as from the Bramantesque High Renaissance of Pasqualini's unique Schlosskirche of 1552-1553 at Jülich, the interior (Pl. 159) suggests a conscious avoidance of arrangements associated with the Roman ritual. The small polygonal apse, as modest as the one at Joachimstal (Fig. 15), is set in the middle of the southeast side, as is evident on the exterior, and the nave extends symmetrically two bays to left and two bays to right. Along the whole southwest side runs a narrow gallery, and wider extensions of this fill each of the end bays. The vault is very much depressed in a shallow ellipsoid curve and has a pattern of net-ribbing, somewhat simplified in comparison to that in the Halle Marktkirche (Pl. 37), such as would long continue to be used in German church architecture, particularly by Catholics. Whether or not original, this ribbing is at least authentic in character in contrast to the cloying mixture of imitated Brabantine Late Gothic and nineteenth-century *style troubadour* of the arcades supporting the gallery, the parapets above and the panelled decoration of the choir-arch and the pulpit.

Except for the capitals of the columns carrying the arcades in the court there is surprisingly little carved decoration on the Stuttgart Altes Schloss. Above the plain round-arched entrance placed asymmetrically in the northeast front appear the arms of Christoph and his wife Anna Maria of Ansbach carved in 1570 by Simon Schlör (c.1530-1597/1598); but there are no Lombardesque portals such as Christoph's father had commissioned for the Schloss at Tübingen—the earliest is dated 1538 but was much restored in 1902. In contrast to the work of the quarter century following 1550 in Mecklenburg, still predominantly quattrocento, or to the Roman sort of High Renaissance of Pasqualini's contemporary Jülich Schloss, one may say that the court of the Altes Schloss represents a special Germanic sort of "High Renaissance." This is in some respects parallel—but hardly very similar—to the French "High Renaissance" of the wing Pierre Lescot and Jean Goujon (†1565) began for Francis I at the Louvre in 1546 at the end of his life and carried out for Henri II, or to Francis's tomb at St. Denis that Henri commissioned from Philibert de l'Orme the following year, not to speak of de l'Orme's chapel at Anet.

Not only are Italianate carved portals of quattrocento character missing on the Altes Schloss at Stuttgart but, as has earlier been noted, even gables of polylobed or scalloped outline, so common a feature of German Renaissance secular architecture since the mid-1520s, are absent. The old mediaeval Schloss of the archbishops of Magdeburg at Plötzkau (Pl. 160), on the Saale halfway between Halle and Magdeburg, as remodelled and enlarged over much the same years, 1556-1569,[63] is actually more typical for the period despite a certain incoherence in its largely inherited massing. Against its tall roofs more than half-a-dozen irregularly spaced cross-gables or dormers are set. These, and even the four that crown the tall keeplike tower rising in the rear, have—somewhat like the gables on the north wing of 1534-1538 at Neuburg—first concave and then convex curves in their upper stages and tiny crowning lunettes at their tops. The windows throughout are rectangular; but only those in the gables are regularly disposed. These gables are evidently additions on top of lower storeys, of which the foundations at least and probably much of the outer walls had survived the devastations of the *Bauernkrieg* earlier in the century. The random picturesqueness of the total composition, rising romantically from a high and easily defensible site, contrasts markedly with the stolid Stuttgart Altes Schloss in its flat urban setting. Though once protected by a water-filled moat as well as by its corner towers, the latter is essentially regular in plan and even nearly symmetrical on its principal external sides to the southeast and the northeast (Pl. 157).

The main building activities of ruling princes concerned the replacement or enlargement of the mediaeval Schlösser they had inherited. As has been earlier noted, however, Ottheinrich at Grünau and Moritz of Saxony in the Moritzburg also erected more modest

hunting lodges, and in Württemberg some ten minor Schlösser were built or enlarged by Tretsch or others in the fifties and sixties for Duke Christoph, his relatives and members of his court circle.[64] In the west, moreover, minor *Herren* were erecting small unfortified manor-houses, of which a few have been described already (Pl. 154), in the way similar English land-owners had long been doing. But great princes with extensive territories also required administrative offices, and to provide for them *Kanzleigebäuden* (chancery buildings) began to be erected in the 1540s, though most that survive are considerably later in date.

The one at Amberg (Pl. 161) which the Count Palatine Friedrich II erected in 1544-1546,[65] does not much resemble Friedrich's contemporary Gläserner Saalbau at Heidelberg even though it is probably the work of the same stone-mason Conrad Forster. Except for the Gothic tracery over the windows at the top of the oriel on the front, however, it is equally postmediaeval. Worth remarking, to begin with, are the deep-sunk rectangular windows, framed by broad cyma mouldings and quite regularly, though not symmetrically, disposed. The very heavy egg-and-dart carving on the cornice that projects above a plain fluted frieze is even more Italianate; but the principal architectural feature here is the two-storeyed oriel, a thoroughly Germanic motif in origin despite increasing use of Renaissance decoration, though the decoration here is actually not very advanced for the date.

The oriel on the Amberg Kanzlei is supported on two Ionic columns flanking the round-arched portal. In its first storey, arabesqued pilasters divide the windows, as in earlier examples at Regensburg, Görlitz and Torgau (Pls. 31, 63, 126), with armorial carvings in the panel below. In the second storey the pilasters are Corinthian and fluted. Also, at this level, portrait medallions framed by wreaths are set between fluted stiles below the sill of the windows. Ignoring the line of the main cornice, the upper entablature of the oriel is crowned by a triple lunette. The lunette has small S-scrolls at the base and is subdivided by three more Corinthian pilasters of unequal height. Thus the gable as a whole is as clumsy a feature as the cluster of heavy superposed moldings that provide a plastic sort of transition between the tops of the two columns at the portal, set close against the wall, and the boldly projecting oriel above. In the court a flatter and better

[63] DKD, *Provinz Sachsen*, pp. 382-383. Piltz, *D.D.R.*, p. 257, notes the survival in the Fürstensaal at Plötzkau of some remains of decoration dated 1567.

[64] Fleischhauer, *Württemberg*, pp. 40-43.
[65] Reclams *Bayern*, pp. 38-39.

organized oriel carries the date of completion, 1546, above a pair of pediments that intersect. The polygonal stair-turret was added only in 1801.

From this early example of a princely administrative building one may well turn to the civil structures that many independent towns and cities were erecting or enlarging around the mid-century.[66] Not surprisingly, the Rathaus in such a small Saxon town as Plauen, on the Weisser Elster southwest of Karl-Marx-Stadt, though considerably larger is even less sophisticated in its faint reflection of the new Renaissance forms than Friedrich's Kanzlei at Amberg. Moreover, the two-storeyed main body of the building dates from 1508[67] and retains its original irregularly sized and spaced curtain-topped windows, while the outside stairs and porch were added only in 1912.

Only the five-stage gable at Plauen is of the period of the Amberg Kanzlei, having been rebuilt after a fire in 1548 (Pl. 162). S-curves in each stage of the gable produce a wavy outline, as earlier on the Saalfeld Rathaus (Pl. 70), and the whole surface is reticulated by plain panelled pilaster-strips and string-courses. In the middle, above a big sundial, is a panel rising through two stages and decorated with the arms of the town and associated figural and animal sculpture. Small squarish windows flank the sundial in the lowest stage and stone balls accent the meandering outline of the gable against the sky.

A great Saxon city such as Leipzig naturally required a larger town hall and expected a handsomer and more up-to-date one. The Altes Rathaus there more than rivals the Schlösser of contemporary princes in size, in regularity and in the number and character of its architectural features. In 1556[68] two existing late fifteenth-century structures were joined together by bridging over an intervening alley. That produced a very long rectangular facade against which a tall clock tower rises near the middle (Pl. 163). The tower is square in plan in the lower storeys but octagonal where it stands free above the main cornice. Even more striking than this enlarged version of such a Rathaus tower as the one at Saalfeld is the range of tall three-stage gables at Leipzig, two to the left and four to the right of the tower, not to speak of the even taller five-stage gables terminating the main roof. In spite of all these vertical accents, the general

effect of the facade Hieronymus Lotter (c.1497-1580) —eventually Mayor of Leipzig from 1568—designed and the master-masons Paul Wiedemann and Sittich Pfretzschner erected in 1556-1564 is strongly horizontal. Thus it bears little resemblance to the conservative architecture then current in Lotter's native Nürnberg. But Lotter had already become a citizen of Leipzig by 1533 and, in 1546, taken charge of renewing the city's fortifications. Of these only some portions of the Moritzbastei of 1551-1553 now survive. His first architectural work, as distinguished from his activity as a military engineer, was probably the *Alter Waga* (old weigh-house) of 1555 which is no longer extant.

The present stone arcade at the base of the Leipzig Rathaus, replacing earlier wooden shops, was added in a drastic restoration carried out in 1906-1909. But the arched portal at the bottom of the tower, flanked by pairs of Doric columns, is original while the wooden gallery above dates from 1564. Original also, though restored, are the large rectangular windows, mostly paired, in the first storey which light the Grosser Saal that occupies two-thirds of the whole length of the building. But the crowning frieze with its prominent inscription is of 1672, and the roof and lantern at the top of the tower are modern recreations of features that dated from 1744. After very serious damage from bombing in 1943, the Altes Rathaus was thoroughly restored, not to say largely rebuilt, in 1948-1950. Nothing inside is old, indeed, except the main fireplace of 1610.

The cross-gables on the Leipzig Rathaus have each four closely-set rectangular windows in the lowest stage and two in the second. In both cases these are framed at the outer edge by pilaster-strips that continue upward to carry urn-like finials above string-courses. The second stage is flanked by S-scrolls and the third, which is pierced by tiny paired oculi, has C-scrolls while a small pediment crowns the top. The design is evidently derived from such advanced Saxon gables of this period as the ones over the Moritzbau in Dresden (Pl. 131), completed just when the Leipzig Rathaus was begun; they have little in common with the earlier gables in Saxony at Schloss Hartenfels, at Saalfeld and at Plauen. The end gables at Leipzig are similar, with single pairs of windows in the first, second and third stages, scrolls at the sides of the second through fifth stages, and tiny pediments at the top.

Pegau, a much smaller town south of Leipzig on the Elster, has a Rathaus which was begun also on

[66] A. Grisebach, *Das deutsche Rathaus der Renaissance*, Berlin, 1907, summarizes the story but is too drastically out of date to be worth specific referencing for individual works.

[67] Dehio, *Dresden*, p. 331; Piltz, *D.D.R.*, p. 495.

[68] Dehio, *Dresden*, pp. 231-232; Piltz, *D.D.R.*, p. 418.

plans provided by Lotter in 1559.[69] As carried out, again by Wiedemann, this is a simplified version of the one in Leipzig. The original scalloped gables at the ends were replaced by plain ones, probably when repairs were made just after 1670; from that time may date also the brick frieze and cornice crowning the long front. This front is much more regular in its fenestration than that of the Leipzig Rathaus. At the base of the tower, octagonal in plan above the cornice line like that at Leipzig, the main portal is double with two arches that do not quite match flanked by fluted Doric columns set on high podia. Above, a pedimented edicule with the town's arms accords awkwardly with the slanting windows below which light, in the usual way, the spiral stair rising inside the tower.

If one recalls the arcades around the court of the Salamanca Schloss (Pl. 112) at Spittal-a.-d.-Drau in Carinthia, it will not seem surprising that certain administrative buildings far to the southeast in that province and in Styria should also have had such Italianate features by the mid-century decades even though, as far as is known, none did in the central German lands. The modest Rathaus at St. Veit-a.-d.-Glau, north of Klagenfurt in Carinthia, was originally built in 1468. Behind its stuccoed Rococo frontal block, rebuilt in 1754, the court has three rows of arcading carried on Tuscan columns. These arcades are thought to date from the middle decades of the century.[70] As lately restored, the spandrels of the arches carry simple symbolic decorations and, in the upper storeys, ranges of balustrading below the columns, all executed in sgraffito.

Compared to this still distinctly quattrocento design, the court of the *Landhaus* (provincial administrative building) of Styria at Graz, with its three ranges of the Roman arch orders, seems a thoroughly High Renaissance work. These were executed over the years 1557-1565[71] and then further extended in the 1580s. Even at that late date such a court, though possibly first planned for Kraków in Poland quite early in the century, can hardly be matched, except in Moravia,[72] in districts more remote from Italy. The original architect—it is almost needless to say—

was a southerner, the Italian-Swiss Domenico dell'-Allio (†1563) from Lugano. The exterior of the Landhaus, however, with its coupled windows is earlier in character, more like that of the Salamanca Schloss (Pl. 113). It is not impossible that dell'Allio worked there also, earlier or at this time.

Town halls were not the only civic buildings of the Renaissance period in Germany that rival in interest those in Styria and Carinthia to the southeast. Somewhat after the time when the Saxon ones that have just been described were being built, *Hochzeitshäuser*, where weddings and other official and semi-official festivities could take place, were often of considerable size and very elaborate design. Several of various periods will be discussed later. Even in quite small towns, moreover, eating and drinking facilities for the use of the members of the Rat were often provided in town halls or else nearby, as at Alsfeld in 1538. At Dettelbach, just east of Würzburg, the Late Gothic Rathaus includes a handsome *Ratstrinkstube* (Council's bar) that is probably of mid-sixteenth century date.[73] This has, above the windows, deep-sunk segmental arches carried on short piers (Pl. 164). The piers are carved rather crudely both with portrait medallions and with other ornaments that approach Renaissance pilaster capitals.

Far more elegant in its Early Renaissance detailing is the surprisingly large Ratstrinkstube (Pl. 165) across from the great church of St. Georg in Dinkelsbühl. For this no precise date is certain either though it must also be of the years shortly following the mid-century. It is now known, however, as the Gustav-Adolf-Haus since the invading Swedish king occupied it during the Thirty Years' War. The righthand end is crowned with a stepped gable of three double steps, each step carrying a tiny decorated lunette. String-courses and flat pilaster-strips panel the surface around a large clock that was interpolated later. The lefthand gable, in contrast, is outlined only with continuous wavy scalloping much as at Plauen (Pl. 162). The paired windows in the first storey are framed by broad architraves decorated with both rosettes and fluting, but what is most notable are the mullions in the form of slender North Italian candelabra-colonnettes. The two decorated portals, set side by side, have nearly

[69] Dehio, *Dresden*, pp. 321-322; Piltz, *D.D.R.*, p. 444.

[70] KDÖ, *Kärnten Steiermark*, p. 356.

[71] W. von Semetkowski, *Graz, ein Führer durch die Stadt*, 7th ed. [Graz, 1971], pp. 19-20.

[72] The next in sequence is also in Austria, the Stallburg of the Hofburg in Vienna, begun two years later by Ferabosco. See Note 62.

[73] Reclams *Bayern*, p. 211, does not attempt to date this interior. A somewhat similar one, dated 1549-1550 and destroyed in 1945, with freestanding supports of candelabra-like design between the windows was in the upper storey of the Collegium Maius at Erfurt: Horst, *Architektur*, p. 206, fig. 207.

identical panelled pilaster-clusters at the sides; but only the smaller and lower is crowned with a segmental lunette—here, as so often, filled with shell-like fluting—of which the curvature matches that of the opening below. Private houses were rarely yet as large and handsome as this municipal building, at least few such have survived.

At Augsburg, where Jakob Fugger had first introduced Renaissance secular design in Germany in the remodelled Fuggerhäuser, one would expect to find comparable big houses of the mid-sixteenth century, but in fact none are extant. Of Fugger commissions elsewhere something will shortly be said, particularly as regards interior design. The Welser, headed by Bartholomäus VI, were the other great local banking family. He handled the gold and silver from Charles V's American colonies and even married his beautiful daughter Philippine to a nephew of the emperor, the Archduke Ferdinand II, later Statthalter of the Tyrol. The Welsers' house in the Annastrasse, in any case probably of the late fifteenth century, was largely destroyed in the last war. Happily, however, a very fine house at Philippine-Welser-Strasse 24 (Pl. 166), now occupied by the Maximilian Museum, survives in excellent condition. This was built for the *Zunftbürgermeister* (civic guildmaster) Jakob Herbrot in 1544-1546.[74] It stands sidewise to the street, like the Fuggerhäuser and most of the early houses in Görlitz (Pls. 63-69), so that the gables with their rippled edges, like the one on the left end of the Dinkelsbühl Ratstrinkstube (Pl. 165), are not conspicuous except where that on the left bends around on to the front, somewhat as on the west wing at Neuburg (Pl. 75); nor is the portal with its low three-centered arch a principal ornamental feature.

The carved decoration on the Herbrot house is reserved for the oriels. Of these there are two here, one double and one single. Except for the scrolled cresting over the broader oriel and the relief carving that fills the panels below the second-storey windows in both, the detailing of these features is of an almost "High Renaissance" severity in contrast to other examples of this date and earlier at Torgau, Saalfeld and Amberg (Pls. 70, 126, 161). The plain panelled pilasters are without decoration, but there are coin-like medallion portraits between them. Moreover, a superb Roman inscription, flanked by putti, is carved on a panel of which the edges are just beginning to roll outward

in the way of later strapwork cartouches. The model emulated here was evidently Italian, not Netherlandish, at this early date, though hardly taken from Serlio's publications of this decade which had been appearing since 1537 first in Venice and then in France.

The ground-storey windows of the Herbrot house, squarish and with iron grilles, have an even more Italianate sort of restraint; in the upper storeys the close-set openings are quite unframed in the stuccoed wall. Inside, a vaulted entrance hall, opening on the court at the rear and subdivided by columns, follows Augsburg examples first provided in the Fuggerhäuser a generation earlier (Fig. 4).

At Lorch, on the Rhine opposite Bacharach, the Hilchenhaus (Pl. 167), begun by Fieldmarshal Johann Hilchen von Lorch in 1546-1548[75] but completed only in 1573, dominates the modest town. This is, indeed, as much a Schloss as a town house. The decoration of the four stages of the single broad gable combines very small fluted lunettes, quite like those on the gable over the right end of the Dinkelsbühl Ratstrinkhaus, with tight S-scrolls. As usual, the surface of this gable is panelled by string-courses and pilaster-strips; and the windows, all subdivided by central mullions and crossed by transoms, are for the most part regularly, if not quite symmetrically, disposed. The entrance feature is very far off center and the facade is slightly extended to the left for balance below the gable. Not at the entrance but to its right, two very sturdy freestanding Doric columns support a balcony that has a parapet carved with arms and other ornament. The balcony also extends to the left over the portal, while above the projecting portion a two-storey oriel rises to a curved roof of slate similar to the one over the oriel on the front of the Amberg Kanzlei (Pl. 161).

A few other houses in towns are of comparable interest and rival in elaboration, if not in size, local Schlösser. At Weimar in Thuringia Gromann, who had built the Schlosskirche at Schloss Hartenfels for the Elector Johann Friedrich in 1543-1544, added to the Schloss for him a gatehouse—not previously mentioned, which is known as the Bastille—in 1545.[76] This gatehouse has a carved portal with delicate arabesque decoration on the bevelled archivolt and S-curved side-panels flanking the Wettin arms above.

[74] Breuer, *Augsburg*, pp. 91-92.

[75] Reclams *Rheinlande und Westfalen*, p. 406.
[76] DKD, *Thüringen*, p. 405; Piltz, *D.D.R.*, p. 314.

Otherwise it is of little interest. The single modest gable seems distinctly retardataire, it might be noted, recalling those of the thirties.

Much richer is the house Gromann (Pl. 168) built in Weimar nearby for Johann Friedrich's chancellor, Dr. Christian Bick, in 1549.[77] Bick was a son-in-law of Lucas Cranach, and the painter himself lived in the house in 1552-1553. Across the ground storey of this runs a continuous arcade carried on candelabra-colonnettes. In the arcade the four broader arches are very similar to that on the outside of the Bastille; two lower and narrower ones containing the doorways are centered on the two halves of the upper storeys of the facade. The windows in those storeys, some paired but mostly single, are almost but not quite precisely symmetrical in their placing. The gables above, however, are in each case over the left portion of the two halves of the facade below. These gables, like that on the Bastille, are rather plain and clumsy in the way of those on the Saalfeld Rathaus; they may well date from a remodelling of 1586 despite their early character.

Of uncertain date, but not improbably also of the mid-century decades, was the handsome house (Pl. 169) at Egidienstrasse 11 in Münster, far to the west of Thuringia in Westphalia and not distant from the Dutch border. In that—not surprisingly—influence from the Netherlands, absent in Weimar, was very apparent. Although much less richly decorated, this followed the model set in the 1530s by such Brabantine facades as that of the Zalmhuis in Mechelen and the entire gable, never modified like the one at Mechelen, survived until the war. Engaged columns of more-or-less Doric character, though of slender proportions that vary in the successive storeys, subdivided the two main storeys and the three stages of the gable. All five bays of the main storeys had wide unframed openings; then there were three windows in the middle bays of the first stage of the gable above and finally, just one in the second. Very Venetian-looking lunettes with deep shell-like fluting capped the outer bays of the second stage. The lower stage and the topmost have near-pediments, however, that are similarly fluted. A very refined detail is the sinking of the plain panels in the solid bays. In general, moreover, the execution was of excellent quality, though hardly as correct as the almost Academic parti might lead one to expect.

In consideration of the date of the Krameramtshaus, also in Münster (Pl. 156), 1588-1589, which still has lunettes over the steps of the gable, the house in the Egidienstrasse may be decades later than the mid-century, but the plain character of the order, as also the mullioned windows, suggest a relatively early date. Although the gables are not at all alike, the use of successive orders recalls such Dutch facades as that of the so-called Kardinalshuis of 1559 at Groningen in Friesland or the demolished Burgerweeshuis of the following year in Amsterdam rather than Cornelis Floris's grandiose Stadhuis in Antwerp of 1561-1564 (Pl. 175) with its more Academic use of the orders. The Dutch analogues suggest a date around the mid-century, before influence from the southern Netherlands began to flow eastward and within the period of the Italian Pasqualini's activity not far away to the east at Kleve and to the south in Düsseldorf. The northern designer's command of the Classical vocabulary, however, was certainly inferior to his. Yet it is perhaps not exaggerated to describe such work as "Dutch High Renaissance," not only in Groningen but also in Münster, and the designer may actually have been Dutch not German in Münster.

On the other hand, where wood was plentiful and good building stone hard to come by, the mid-century decades saw continued use of Fachwerk in many parts of Germany. Much of this carried carved decoration of vaguely Renaissance character such as had appeared so early in Goslar. Near the Brusttuch of 1526 (Pl. 71), there stands the rather larger Bäckergildehaus (Bakers' guildhall). Here, above a lower storey of stone built in 1501,[78] a projecting upper storey in timber-framing was added in 1557. In that, curtain-topped windows of Late Gothic character are set above panels carved with fluted lunettes such as provided the most popular vernacular ornament everywhere in Germany for sixteenth-century timber-framed houses. The market-place at Einbeck,[79] for example, and above all the Tiedexerstrasse there (Pl. 170) are lined with facades of Fachwerk, many of them of the forties and fifties, which are even more profusely carved in this way. The Einbeck houses are the more striking because there, and often elsewhere, the polychromatic painting

---

[77] DKD, *Thüringen*, p. 407; Piltz, *D.D.R.*, p. 314. The Cranach house has lately been restored externally. The polychromy, predominantly pink and green, does not seem very plausible, but the restorers may have found clues in old descriptions or even *in situ*.

[78] Reclams *Niedersachsen*, p. 276.
[79] *Ibid.*, p. 149.

is recurrently restored. Hannoversch-Münden,[80] a larger town than Einbeck, where rebuilding began after a disastrous fire in 1561, preserves even more timber-framed houses. Here there is considerably less carved and painted decoration but more emphasis on recurrent overhangs, X-braced panels, and broad gabled dormers facing the street.

Some of the finest examples of Fachwerk, however, are not in such towns as Celle, Wolfenbüttel[81] or the ones just named, but rather those standing alone among houses which are, today at least, stucco-covered whatever their underlying construction may be. Thus at Dinkelsbühl, across the street from St. Georg, the Deutsches Haus (Pl. 171)—more than possibly as late in any case as 1600[82]—seems to belong to a different country, or at least a different century, from the contiguous Ratstrinkstube (Pl. 165) of around 1560 with its elegant quattrocento detail carved in stone. The semi-structural patterns of the cross-bracing on the Deutsches Haus may still be considered Late Gothic; the way the windows extend the full width of the broad bays in the first and second storeys, however, subdivided only by light wooden mullions and transoms, seems to twentieth-century eyes very "modern." It can be matched, though, by many stone and brick facades of the period in the Netherlands. Even at Hannoversch-Münden such extensive fenestration was rarely equalled either earlier or later moreover. To mention at this point such a work as the Deutsches Haus at Dinkelsbühl is to emphasize how little the design of timber-framed buildings changed as the century proceeded toward its end.

In contrast to this stylistic stasis, in what continued to be a sort of urban vernacular, were the changes—in terms of the acceptance of Italianate design the "advances"—in the decoration of secular interiors in the mid-century decades beginning with the work of the Mantuans at Landshut (Pls. 114-116). By no means as much survives as of exteriors from this period, but a few examples have already been described. The finest work, not surprisingly, seems to have been done for Anton Fugger (b. 1493) who with his elder brother Raymund (b. 1489), as nephews of Jakob der Reiche, had succeeded as heads of the banking house on Jakob's death in 1525. Ten years later Raymund died, but Anton survived until 1560. Nor-

bert Lieb, as noted in Chapter I, deals in his second volume *Die Fugger und die Kunst im Zeitalter der Hohen Renaissance*[83] in the greatest detail with the lives and works of these two, including changes made in the Augsburg Fuggerhäuser and other structures of the earlier decades of the century in Augsburg. But Anton's, if not Raymund's, architectural projects were widespread.

Out of a dozen or more, the most interesting things that survive are the Fugger Haus in Donauwörth, on the Danube north of Augsburg, which was built 1537-1543,[84] and Schloss Babenhausen on the Günz north of Memmingen of 1541-1543.[85] Neither is impressive externally or particularly up to date in design —the gables are steep and stepped; the windows and even the portals unframed. Within, however, both have a profusion of panelled wooden ceilings, some with intarsia inlay, and several interiors have elaborate architectural wainscoting, especially the "Stübchen" from Donauwörth—probably of the 1550s— which is now in the Bayerisches Nationalmuseum in Munich (Pls. 172-174). That more than rivals the Hirschvogelsaal of the thirties (Pl. 107) in elegance and is in much better condition today.

The Fugger Haus in Donauwörth was most probably the work of Bernhard Zwitzel and Hans Breithart. The vaulted entrance hall resembles that under the Deutscher Bau in the Landshut Stadtresidenz of which Zwitzel was, almost certainly, at least one of the designers. The ground-storey hall at Babenhausen is similar but larger.

Whoever was responsible for the design of the Stübchen, however, it can hardly have been Zwitzel; presumably the artist was an Italian. If a Northerner, he certainly had had a more thorough training in Italy than any of the native artists whose work in Germany of these years is recognizable. The exterior is rather severe, but the handling of the elements almost suggests Michelangelo's vagaries. The depressed segmental pediment is carried by scrolled brackets above a door-frame that is not a conventional architrave but merely a flat band with fillets on both edges. The "orders" consist of plain pilasters —panelled only on the side elevations and in the attic—and these have molded capitals that are continued as compressed entablatures below the blind

[80] *Ibid.*, p. 355.
[81] O. Karpa, *Wolfenbüttel*, 2nd ed. [Munich] 1965 (hereafter cited as Karpa, *Wolfenbüttel*).
[82] Reclams *Bayern*, p. 224.

[83] Lieb, *Fugger*, II, pp. 23-313, 332-463.
[84] *Ibid.*, pp. 223-240, pls. 166-198; Reclams *Bayern*, p. 232.
[85] Lieb, *Fugger*, II, pp. 246-258, pls. 202-214; Dehio, *Östliches Schwaben*, p. 110.

lunette over the door and again at the top of the attic.

The interior membering consists also of a storey and an attic. Bold broken pediments carried on ressauts in a Doric entablature are the most conspicuous features, and these extend nearly the full width of each wall. Below, the lower wainscoting consists, above a panelled dado, of shallow shell-topped niches between plain panelled pilasters. The next stage has round oculi filled with simulated ashlar in intarsia and scrolled brackets carved with acanthus under the ressauts of the entablature which support the broken pediments. Additional ressauts at the corners carry fluted Corinthian columns in the attic. But the attic walls have only the four columns, being largely occupied by the rectangular elements behind and above the broken pediments. These are crowned by modillion cornices and topped by scrolled elements of distinctly Serlian character, an influence not otherwise apparent here.

Above, the entablature of the attic, decorated on the underside with rosettes, is a broad flat band carved with a large guilloche pattern. Next comes a sort of wooden cloister-vault with shallow coffering also ornamented by rosettes. The corners are not mitered but have square blocks brought down to the plane of the guilloche band, each with a concave circle in the center. The flat of the ceiling has more square panels with central rosettes arranged in a cross.

The above description of this unique interior may well conclude this chapter. It is unequalled in richness by any work commissioned by a Fugger before Hans in 1569 called Frederik Sustris to Augsburg to decorate—in a wholly different vein, with a profusion of modelled *stucchi* and frescoes—his apartments in the Fuggerhäuser at Maximilianstrasse 38. But those belong in a later chapter. Sustris, though born in Amsterdam, had had all his training in Italy and brought to Augsburg not only the Florentine interior style of the third quarter of the century, but also a team of Italian painters and sculptors later employed in Bavaria. Other imported artists might have designed the Stübchen in the previous decade.[86] None such has been identified, however, even from the times—probably too late by some ten or twenty years—that are dealt with in the following two chapters.

[86] Lieb, *Fugger*, II, pp. 235-236. The date 1546, on another room in the Munich museum from the Donauwörth Fuggerhaus, may also be approximately that of the Stübchen, or so Dr. Himmelheber of the museum staff believes. However, a date some ten years later, as suggested here, seems more probable Professor Lieb tells me. According to Himmelheber the museum has no attribution for the design or the execution of either interior.

Four

PRINCELY SCHLÖSSER,
1560-1580

THE years around 1560 saw a real revival of church-building in Germany, and a few Lutheran edifices of that time have already been mentioned. Differing distinctly from one another, these make evident no standard type had yet evolved. One is a town-church which was later much modified, the Marienkirche at Marienberg in southern Saxony, of 1558-1564.[1] When first built that closely followed the new Catholic churches in the region, by then mostly adapted for Protestant use, with no apparent influence from the Lutheran one at Joachimstal. The exceptional centrally planned chapel of the Schloss at Wolfenbüttel, long lost, is at least to be seen in the distance in an engraving dated 1653 by Merian (Fig. 26). This was also begun in 1558.[2] The surviving chapel of 1560-1562 in the Altes Schloss at Stuttgart (Pl. 159) is

less dissimilar to the church at Joachimstal than either that at Marienberg or the chapel at Wolfenbüttel. It has already been described despite its relatively late date in the early sixties—not to speak of drastic nineteenth-century remodelling—because it occupies one wing of Alberlin Tretsch's Schloss, of which the construction began nearly a decade before.

Another extant chapel of the period is the one in the north wing of the Schloss at Schwerin. This was erected by Johann Baptista Parr, one of Giacomo Parr's five sons, for Duke Johann Albrecht I of Mecklenburg towards the end of his rule in the early sixties.[3] It is quite different from both the Marienberg church and the Stuttgart chapel, but it somewhat resembles in its detailing the work of a decade earlier on the east wing of the Schwerin Schloss, at least in the use of terra cotta elements, presumably from the Lübeck kiln of Statius von Düren, for the ribs of the vault, and probably elsewhere as it was first built.

The Schwerin chapel, now disused and inaccessible, seems to have been no more characteristic of the period than the one in Stuttgart, but it also underwent very considerable modification in the last century. Neither G. A. Demmler nor F. A. Stüler, who were then remodelling and enlarging the rest of the Schloss with the advice of Gottfried Semper, was in charge; rather it was E. F. Zwirner, the architect largely responsible for completing Cologne Cathedral, who was called on to add a deep Neo-Gothic chancel in 1855. At that time the wall-paintings were executed by C. G. Pfannschmidt.

The three bays of the original nave of the Schwerin chapel were still organized much as in the Schlosskapelle at Torgau (Pl. 125) of some twenty years

---

[1] P. Roitzsch, *Die Marienkirche zu Marienberg* [Berlin, 1969] plan inside cover; bibl. p. [32]; Piltz, *D.D.R.*, p. 465.

[2] Karpa, *Wolfenbüttel*, p. 15; article "Chiaramella de Gandino" in ThB. Of this remarkable *Schlosskapelle* by Francesco Chiaramella—who came from Gandino near Bergamo in Lombardy—recalling Milanese projects of half a century earlier, almost nothing survives except a few wall and vault-fragments dated 1570. These must be remains of later construction by Paul Francke, not the work of Chiaramella who had first been employed on the fortifications here. Later, over the years 1562-1578, Chiaramella was in the service of the Brandenburg Hohenzollerns. For the Elector Joachim II, by whom he was knighted in 1569, he carried forward the Zitadelle in Berlin-Spandau. The work was eventually completed over the years 1578-1594 by Rochus von Lynar from Dresden.

The engraving in Merian, *Schönsten Schlösser*, opp. p. 24, shows the Schloss dominated, as it is today, by the Hausmannsturm across from the Zeughaus, and also by Chiaramella's vast chapel to the rear, with its domical roof and corner turrets linked by galleries, which was demolished in 1795. The chapel must have been a most remarkable ecclesiastical structure for the 1550s, all but unique then in Germany for its central plan and even more so as regards the complex massing at the top above the plain square block below. That block seems to have been the equivalent of some six storeys in height, almost as tall as the tower.

[3] Dehio, *Neubrandenburg*, pp. 360-361; Piltz, *D.D.R.*, p. 70. According to Knox, *Poland*, p. 56, J. B. Parr also worked at Borgholm, Kalmar and at the fortess of Kexholm (Priozersk) on Lake Ladoga.

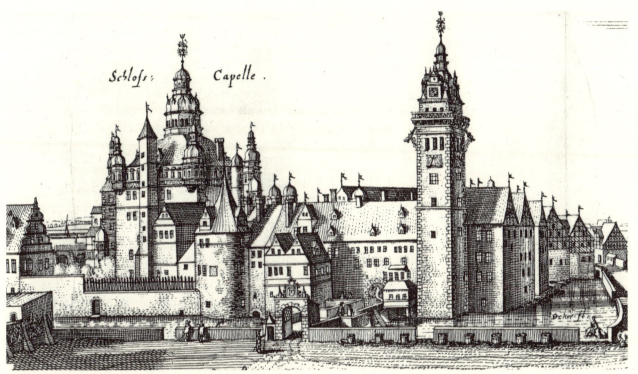

Fig. 26. F. Chiaramella, P. Francke: Wolfenbüttel,
Schloss, with chapel begun in 1558

before. Moreover, though the architect was J. B. Parr from Silesia, the carved furnishings were by Saxon craftsmen from Torgau. In 1562, for example, Georg Schröter (c.1535-1586) provided the altar, now in the Staatliches Museum in Schwerin, and his brother Simon (†1568) the round pulpit. This pulpit is set against one of the middle piers on the north side, as is the one Simon had provided at Torgau, and follows closely that model. The three marble reliefs are of the same subjects, but there are six additional alabaster reliefs by various hands, some Saxon, some Netherlandish, among them possibly Cornelis Floris or a follower, Philipp Brandin (†1594) and Willem van den Broeck. The portal of 1561 leading in from the court is by Hans II Walther (1526-1586) from Dresden, Johann Maria's collaborator earlier on that of the Dresden Schlosskapelle. Though six or seven years later in date, this is less advanced in style, presumably because Maria was not involved.

On account of the reflections of the Torgau chapel, both in the general scheme of the interior and in the fittings, the Schwerin chapel was evidently rather retardataire for the early sixties, except perhaps for the round columns of Pirnaer sandstone. These support the star-vaulting with its ribs of terra cotta. Yet

plain cylindrical columns capped by moldings had been used in St. Martin at Lauingen (Pl. 13) before 1520 and one similar column was introduced by Gromann behind the altar of the Torgau chapel (Pl. 125). Moreover, the piers in the Dresden Schlosskapelle must originally have been of this same near-Tuscan sort. It was probably first illustrated in Germany in some of Dürer's woodcuts of around 1510 though not currently used in executed structures so early. Here in the Schwerin chapel, however, the capitals have hybrid foliate carving rather than simple moldings as elsewhere and thus appear less advanced.

The Mecklenburg dukes were, as the models chosen for Johann Albrecht's chapel and its furnishings indicate, Lutherans. Indeed, new church-building in the decades following the mid-century in Germany was rarely carried out under Catholic auspices. Further to the east and southeast, on the other hand, no Protestant church apparently survives older than the Münster of the 1580s at Klagenfurt in Carinthia. But the Austrian ruler, Charles V's brother Ferdinand, though established since 1529 at Prague as king of Bohemia, had begun even before he succeeded as emperor in 1556 the *Hofkirche* (court-church) at Innsbruck, the Habsburgs' hereditary Tyrolean seat, as a cenotaph and memorial to their grandfather Maximilian. This project was carried on through the sixties and even beyond.

For his Innsbruck church Ferdinand obtained at the start plans from an Italian, Andrea Crivelli. Crivelli came from Trento across the Alps and had been active there from the late 1520s until called to Innsbruck in 1549. Planned by Crivelli in 1553[4] and built by Nikolaus I Türing (or Düring) it was continued, after his death in 1558, by Marco della Bolla—the latter evidently Italian and possibly from Como. If considered as a Renaissance work, the Innsbruck Hofkirche is hardly in advance of St. Katherine in Augsburg (Pl. 14) even though that was erected more than a generation earlier. As at Lauingen (Pl. 13) slim round pillars, here of Tyrolean red marble, divide the nave into three aisles of equal height in the way of a mediaeval hall-church. These have Corinthian capitals not unlike the ones in St. Katherine; but above them there is a Late Gothic vault as at Schwerin. The ribbing, however, is now masked by stucco decoration of the late seventeenth and early eighteenth centuries, and the present capitals may also be of that period.

The interior of the Innsbruck Hofkirche is crowded, around the large cenotaph of Maximilian in the center, by twenty-eight more than life-size bronze statues of Habsburg ancestors standing between the pillars on either side. The arrangement was first planned in 1502-1508 at the instance of Maximilian himself by Gilg Sesselschreiber (c.1460/1465-p. 1520) for the Georgenkapelle at Wiener Neustadt, Maximilian's birthplace, where he is actually buried. The scheme was then elaborated after 1517 by Stefan Godl (†1534). Indeed, not twenty-eight but forty statues were once intended. Among those executed the most famous are the ones of King Arthur and of Theodoric, both cast in 1513 from designs by Dürer at Peter Vischer's foundry in Nürnberg. The one of Count Albrecht IV of Habsburg was modelled just after that, following another design of Dürer's, by Hans Leinberger and cast by Jörg Kölderer (†1540). Seventeen more date from 1518-1533; these were modelled for Godl by Leonard Magt in Innsbruck; while for the latest, that of King Chlodwig, Christoph Amberger provided a design that Veit Arnberger carried out in 1550 in Gregor Löffler's Innsbruck workshop.

The twenty-three statuettes of patron saints of the Habsburgs, modelled after designs of Kölderer by Magt and cast by Godl, were also completed in 1528,

long before construction of the church in Innsbruck began. But the existing cenotaph in the center was only planned in 1561 and not completed, indeed, until 1583. It was then that the statues of the Cardinal Virtues by the Netherlandish sculptor Alexander Colin (c.1528-1612) from Mechelen, whose earlier work at Heidelberg will shortly be discussed, were installed. There are also marble reliefs on the sides of the cenotaph executed by Colin from Florian Abel's designs and, around it, a splendid iron grille, wrought by Georg Schmiedhammer in 1573.

With all this major sculptural interest in the foreground, from the bronze statues after Dürer to the grille, in production through nearly three-quarters of a century the architectural setting as designed by Crivelli and executed by Türing and della Bolla makes little impression. It was always retardataire by Italian and even by German standards; as it has come down to us, moreover, with the alterations of around 1700 —particularly as regards the decoration overhead—it is no characteristic architectural interior of the 1550s and sixties. Now, moreover, the effect of the postwar restoration of 1955, conscientious though that seems to have been, must also be taken into account. The Innsbruck Hofkirche offers a notable ensemble of Northern Renaissance art, but one in which the original architectural elements of the sixteenth century play only a minor role. Thus, despite its functional similarity as a funerary chapel, it is quite different from the Fuggerkapelle (Pl. 3). There the architectural setting, though modest in scale, is certainly at least as important an example of Early Renaissance design as the figural decoration by Loscher, Dauher and Breu.

There do survive, however, other examples of church architecture of this period in Germany, though rather modest ones. The five-sided choir of the small church at Jever, far to the north and west near Bremen, was begun probably by 1556,[5] the date inscribed on the north portal. It was built as a burial chapel by the local ruler who was a Lutheran, but like the Catholic Hofkirche in Innsbruck, the interior is almost completely filled by the enormous tomb (Pl. 203) of Edo II Wiemken, who had died a Catholic long before in 1511. The tomb was erected by Edo's daughter and successor in 1561-1564 and will be described later in this chapter. The simple Late Gothic design of the choir with its small pointed windows is unimpressive compared to what it contains.

[4] Dehio, *Tirol*, pp. 60-64; Baldass, *Österreich*, p. 11.

[5] B. Schönbohm, *Stadtkirche Jever* [Munich, 1968], p. 4.

The only extant town-church of this period in Germany, the Marienkirche at Marienberg in southern Saxony, begun in 1558, was from the first Protestant despite its name. However, so much happened to it later that, despite relative historical priority, the church is of little interest today as a monument of the mid-century.

Both the Marienberg church and the choir at Jever make evident that in the design of Lutheran churches there was no more advance as regards increased acceptance of Renaissance norms of planning and structure during the fifties and sixties than in the Catholic Hofkirche—no more but, on the whole, no less. Real change is hardly evident before the end of the sixties when, as earlier, a Schlosskapelle led the way. Discussion of this chapel in the Schloss at Augustusburg, lying to the south of Chemnitz, which was built in 1568-1572 for the Elector August of Saxony, may be postponed for a while, as well as any description of the somewhat earlier Wiemken tomb at Jever. That is, in any case, more important as a monument of sculpture than of architecture.

In the late 1550s, however, while the Innsbruck Hofkirche was in construction and by the time the Marienberg church had been begun, work had started on a remarkable group of ambitious Schlösser in various parts of Germany, from Heidelberg in the Palatinate, near the Rhine, in the west to Güstrow in Mecklenburg in the north, not distant from the Baltic and the Oder. These truly initiated a new phase of German Renaissance architecture.

Though most of them provide evidence of a limited knowledge of Italian architcure of the immediately preceding decades—knowledge that must have been acquired largely from such illustrated architectural publications as were listed in the previous chapter—none can properly be considered, even to the degree of the Dresden chapel portal of 1554-1555, "High Renaissance" in the way of the Landshut Stadtresidenz as completed twenty years earlier, or at best only "German High Renaissance." Vignola's *Regole* was not published in Italy until 1562 nor Palladio's *Quattro libri* until 1570, so that there could not be in the late fifties any reflection of their respective canons for architecture.

The taste of those who commissioned the major Schlösser of the sixties and the stylistic development of those who designed them seem to have overshot already the High Renaissance, in any case long past in Italy. Rather consistently, moreover, the command of the current Italianate idiom, though admittedly

somewhat better informed than had been common earlier, was combined with—one might almost say contaminated by—new ideas of over-all composition, and more particularly of ornamentation, deriving in part from France but to a much greater degree from the Netherlands. Alien ideas probably reached the Germans for the most part from the west *via* the newly published books of the 1550s and 1560s; but in some cases they were brought in by imported foreigners. Certain of these newcomers were from northern Italy, notably the Parrs who were employed to the north and east in Mecklenburg—in the case of Giacomo Parr long active already further east in Silesia. Another was a Dutchman, Arndt Johannssen, the city-architect of Arnhem, who was in charge at Schloss Horst in the Ruhrgebiet in the west. Alexander Colin, who worked first at Heidelberg for Ottheinrich von der Pfalz and later for Emperor Ferdinand at Innsbruck, was from Mechelen in Brabant. More exceptionally there was the Frenchman, Joist de la Cour, who worked for many years at Horst and may have been employed elsewhere.[6] As in England under Elizabeth I, Protestant craftsmen fleeing from the Inquisition in the Spanish Netherlands also arrived in these decades. That may apply in the specific case of Hendrick Hagart, who almost certainly was the sculptor of the Wiemken tomb at Jever.[7]

Because of the resultant eclecticism, at once an eclecticism of taste, so to say, and a parallel eclecticism of style resulting from the mixture of influences from several disparate sources, there is little unity in the architectural production of these years. Each of the principal monuments has a nearly unique character as a whole despite distinct similarities in individual features to one or more of the others. Moreover, the stylistic amalgam rarely remained constant even in successively built portions of a single edifice when construction, as so often, continued through a decade or more and under changing artistic direction.

The earlier repertory of German Renaissance secular architecture, epitomized at Heidelberg in the late 1540s in the Gläserner Saalbau (Pls. 139, 140), had consisted of a certain range of characteristic elements: more or less elaborately decorated gables; court façades often partially arcaded; fairly regularly spaced

---

[6] R. Klapheck, *Die Meister von Schloss Horst im Broiche*, Berlin, 1915 (henceforth cited as Klapheck, *Schloss Horst*), pp. 205-232.

[7] Considering the date of Colin's departure from Mechelen, 1558, which was three years after Philip II's accession, he may well have been one of these Protestant refugees.

windows, consistently rectangular and most often paired; and richly Italianate portals, in most cases not on axis.[8] This repertory was still current in the late fifties and sixties and even into the seventies; yet some significant changes were rather common. Gables were still ubiquitous; indeed, they would become more prominent and more boldly scrolled in later decades just before and after 1600. For supports in arcades the isolated columns of the quattrocento sort, as introduced early in the century in the Fuggerhäuser courts, now gave way—not infrequently at least—to compound piers of the Roman arch-order.[9] Windows, now less likely to be paired, approached more closely the Italian norm in their oblong vertical shape, their greater size and the regularity and even symmetry of their spacing. Finally, principal portals were also somewhat more likely to be centered as the discipline of symmetry became more generally accepted in external design, if not as yet in plans.

Equally important—indeed, as regards the organization of whole facades, more important—was the way architectural elements such as the orders or the window enframements were now being handled. In many cases these no longer were merely embellishments or individual features in low relief set in or on a flat wall-plane, but provided rather a means of modelling plastically the whole wall-surface. Earlier, and down through the Fürstenhof at Wismar (Pl. 146) and the Schloss at Brzég (Pl. 136) in the early and mid-fifties, pilasters on facades had been little more than flat decoration. Though usually elaborated with arabesque carving or modelling of quattrocento delicacy, these phrased the plane of the wall primarily as linear pattern. The edges of window openings, moreover, were likely to be molded inward rather than outward. Now, in varying degree, walls were conceived not as continuous surfaces abruptly cut by such openings but

as articulated pseudo-structures. For that Dippoldiswalde (Pl. 88) had already been premonitory.

Such a change and the related increase in scale, as well as in degree of relief, of the elements of which the pseudo-structure was made up represented at least a partial adoption—belated by a generation and more—of the High Renaissance system of design as adumbrated in early sixteenth-century Rome. Of course this had been even truer of the Stadtresidenz at Landshut twenty years earlier; but the Italienischer Bau there was then altogether an exception in the current German scene. Even at the Plassenburg (Pls. 191-193) above Kulmbach in the sixties, in many respects still of distinctly Early Renaissance character, it should be noted how much heavier in its membering the arcading has become, while the arabesque decoration is so bold it can be called coarse though it is never crude.

Many writers have called the new sub-style initiated in the mid-century "Northern Mannerist," and surely the term may be plausibly applied to the new Netherlandish mode of ornamentation increasingly dominant in German decorative design through the next two generations. But it is also possible to consider some of the more prominent works of the decades after the mid-century as examples of a "German High Renaissance." This was, indeed, suggested earlier as regards the court of the Altes Schloss at Stuttgart as well as the portal of the Dresden Schlosskapelle. All the same it should be recognized also, as was noted in the last chapter, that similar architectural modulations in other parts of Europe paralleled this German sub-style— thus one may speak of a "French High Renaissance," a "Dutch High Renaissance"; even, indeed, of a rather fragmentary "English High Renaissance." Generally, however, these modes appeared elsewhere somewhat earlier than in Germany in succession to local Early Renaissance style-phases.

As regards England, for example, the term can be applied, at least metaphorically, to such work done under the Protector Somerset in the reign of Edward VI as Somerset House in London, dated 1547-1552, and—so far as what was executed can be hypothesized today—the first building campaign at Longleat in Wiltshire which was initiated in 1553. At Longleat, the term is not inappropriate even for the much enlarged house, mostly of the 1570s, that survives. Just before 1556, when Ottheinrich von der Pfalz began his new wing at Heidelberg, the first version of Burghley House near Stamford in Northamptonshire,

---

[8] This German architectural repertory of the mid-century, except for increasing regularity in the placing of windows, is quite different from that of secular buildings erected during the reign of Francis I in France or in the England of Henry VIII, though Chiaramella's chapel at Wolfenbüttel (Fig. 26) must have had something of the fantasy of Francis's Chambord and Henry's Nonsuch Palace. It was as extraordinary a production for a specialist in fortifications as Pasqualini's chapel of the early fifties at Jülich (Pls. 143, 145) though it did not much resemble that except for its centralized plan.

[9] Early examples of compound piers have already been noted, it will be recalled, far to the south and east at Klagenfurt in Carinthia and at Graz in Styria, regions where Italian influence was considerably more direct.

as proposed at that point by Robert Cecil, seems to have leaned more on French models than had Somerset House. Certainly that is true of the surviving house of the seventies and eighties.

In the Netherlands in this period there were the temporary, but not unimpressive, triumphal arches and the reviewing stand (Fig. 16) designed and erected by Cornelis Floris at Antwerp for the ceremonial entry of Charles V and his son Philip in 1549 and published by Coecke the next year. Because of Floris's idiosyncratic Mannerist decoration of the cresting, however, these can only be loosely called "High Renaissance." Cardinal Granvella's palace in Brussels, also of this period though not precisely datable, seems from the little known about it to have been more truly of that character, if not quite in the specific Roman sense. In the northern Netherlands, well after Pasqualini's and Vincidor's advanced work of the thirties at IJsselstein, Breda and Buren, many prominent buildings of the mid-century decades still reflected much earlier Italian models. Little is extant, but an especially good example is the superbly executed and almost purely quattrocento *Mundpoort* (gate of the mint) in Dordrecht of 1555.[10] That more than rivals in Emilian elegance Statius von Düren's terra cotta decorations of the fifties in Lübeck and Mecklenburg (Pl. 146-149), but the elements cutting across the archivolt would doubtless be considered Mannerist in Italy.

Not Holland but Antwerp, however, was the center from which the sort of ornament usually called "Northern Mannerist" spread over much of Europe in the third quarter of the century. That Cornelis Floris's particular sort of elaborated strapwork had already made a mature appearance there by the late forties is evident from Coecke's book (Fig. 16); the inexhaustible fountain of the Dutch-born Jan Vredeman's decorative invention only began flowing more than a decade later in his *Architectura* of 1563, also published in Antwerp (Pl. 176). However, his development of Floris's kind of ornament was doubtless already known to some of his fellow craftsmen.

The grandest new structure of the mid-century in the Netherlands north or south is the Antwerp *Stadhuis* (town hall). The broad almost unbroken facade of this (Pl. 175), occupying all of the west side of the Groote Markt, differs notably from the narrow guild-houses fronting on the other sides of the great

square. Rather exaggeratedly, this is often considered to have been the particular monument that initiated major Brabantine architectural influence in northern Europe in the later sixteenth century. The enormous Stadhuis, begun in 1561,[11] symbol of the commercial importance of the great port on the Schelde, was designed in part—if not indeed wholly—by Floris.[12] However, the heavily rusticated ground floor and the continuous ranges of sturdy Tuscan pilasters separating the large mullioned and transomed windows in the two main storeys—though not the open eaves-gallery below the boldly modillioned cornice—illustrate better the High Renaissance elements of what is sometimes called the "Floris Style" than its Northern Mannerist aspect. The handling of the detail of the eaves-gallery on the other hand, with short square piers cut at mid-height by the rail of the balustrade and capped with paired scroll-brackets below the lintels, is surely not Bramantesque or even Serlian.

The central pavilion of the Antwerp Stadhuis rises through three stages of full-storey height. The repeated great arches flanked by pairs of engaged columns on the first and second storeys of this, though certainly High Renaissance in spirit, do not much resemble anything rising in Rome at this date: the *parti* is more similar to that of Jean Bullant's frontispiece at Ecouen in France. Moreover, the central bays of the next two stages of the frontispiece, rising past the somewhat Mannerist eaves-gallery, also suggest the "French High Renaissance" of the mid-century. Finally, the horizontal entablatures above the orders of engaged columns counteract in these upper levels the verticalism of the tall obelisks at the sides, as does also the small but heavy triangular pediment that concludes the whole composition.

This pediment crowning the Antwerp Stadhuis is a feature much used later in Germany but hardly, it would seem, in emulation of the one in Antwerp, for such had appeared on the gables of the Moritzbau in Dresden (Pl. 131) nearly two decades before. Not

---

[10] *Kunstreisboek*, p. 400.

[11] H. Gerson and E. H. ter Kuile, *Art and Architecture in Belgium, 1600-1800*, Harmondsworth [1960] (henceforth cited as Gerson-ter Kuile, *Belgium*), p. 13.

[12] Cornelis Floris, of course, was no more a German architect than Alessandro Pasqualini. But he was often employed by Germans both as a sculptor and as an architect before and after the construction of the Antwerp Stadhuis. Most notably, in the immediately succeeding years, he supplied the design of the Hanseaten Huis here in Antwerp, the headquarters in the southern Netherlands of the German merchants.

improbably the design of the Dresden gables was borrowed straight from Serlio, whether or not Pasqualini's on the Kasteel at Buren had already been derived from that source even earlier.

Northern exuberance finds expression on the Antwerp Stadhuis only in the outline of the sculptural groups that flank the two middle stages of the central gable and load the terminal one. In the international morphology of northern Renaissance gable-design this Antwerp example remains closer, except for its great size and the boldly plastic handling of the elements, to Beaugrant's of forty years before on the Palais de Savoie at Mechelen (Pl. 41) than to the advanced German examples of the late fifties and sixties—to be discussed and illustrated later in this chapter and the next—that have been thought by some scholars to show its influence. A predominantly German line of descent from the gables Knotz built for Ottheinrich von der Pfalz at Neuburg in the thirties (Pls. 75, 90) seems more likely than emulation either of the Antwerp Stadhuis[13] as completed in the mid-sixties or, for that matter, of contemporary Dutch models.

The mention of Ottheinrich brings the story back to his last and most ambitious commission, that of five years before the Antwerp Stadhuis was begun, for the east wing of the Schloss at Heidelberg.[14] Even a superficial comparison of the Heidelberg Ottheinrichsbau (Pl. 177) with the Antwerp Stadhuis (Pl. 175) reveals by contrast how "proto-Academic"[15] the latter is. Such a comparison also underlines how original, even if somewhat provincial, is the Ottheinrichsbau. But the relative priority of the plastically articulated facade at Heidelberg in the north European architectural scene should not be ignored either.

Some remarks are now in order, beyond what was provided earlier in connection with Ottheinrich's Neuburg Schloss, concerning the elderly prince who was the client at Heidelberg. He was, to begin with, very much an individual and an authoritarian one,

in contrast to the corporate anonymity of the Antwerp Council that commissioned the Stadhuis. The squat and heavily bearded figure of Ottheinrich in his Heidelberg years that Joachim Deschler from Nürnberg provides in a marble bust now in the Louvre[16] hardly conforms, in the way of the dapper statue of the young Charles V in the Vrij in Brugge, to the ideal image of a Renaissance prince. Yet Ottheinrich was, as regards his patronage of the arts, exemplary in the Germany of his day.[17] A collector in many fields, he had commissioned new works of art from various sculptors and painters, beginning in his earliest days at Neuburg, and even established there a workshop to produce tapestries. More relevantly, before returning in 1556 to Heidelberg—where he had earlier passed the years of his exile in the forties—he had been actively building and decorating his Schlösser at Neuburg and Grünau for nearly thirty years, except during those of his exile.

Though none too fortunate in his original choice of the Nürnberger Knotz as the architect of the Neuburg Schloss, Ottheinrich had later shown his appreciation of the sort of work his cousin Ludwig had been commissioning at Landshut by hiring, in 1543, Hans Bocksberger to fresco his chapel (Pls. 121, 122). In 1545, moreover, several of Ludwig's Mantuan *stuccatori* were employed to decorate the vault (Pl. 123) of the entrance passage beside the chapel.[18] Much earlier, as was noted, Ottheinrich had attempted to acquire the grille that Jakob Fugger had commissioned from Peter Vischer for the Fuggerkapelle in Augsburg; failing that, he eventually obtained through Hans Beheim a more modest one attributed to another Nürnberg bronze-caster, Sebastian Hinder. For his secular frescoes, first at Grünau in 1537 and again—probably—at Neuburg in 1545, he called on the younger Jörg Breu from Augsburg. This Breu was the son of one of Jakob Fugger's artists and a better painter than Bocksberger. For sculpture and for decorative work at Neuburg he employed Martin Hering, and also Loy Hering as was mentioned earlier.

The Neues Haus at Grünau (Pl. 124), begun in 1537 but mostly built in the years between Ottheinrich's return from exile in Heidelberg and his final move there as elector,[19] is extremely conservative in

[13] For an illustration see Glück, *Renaissance in Deutschland*, pl. XXXII.

[14] Oechelhäuser, *Heidelberger Schloss*, provides the best organized and most succinct account of the history of the building of the Heidelberg Schloss. Despite the various controversial issues involved and a vast bibliography of earlier publications, references are confined here to that one book. It should, moreover, be noted that almost all general works dealing with this period give some attention to the Ottheinrichsbau but they need not be cited in detail.

[15] The term as applied to the Antwerp Stadhuis is an exaggeration but emphasizes how little in its design is characteristically Northern Mannerist.

[16] *Münchner Jahrbuch* IX, 1914-1915, pp. 68-86, pls. I-IV.

[17] Horn-Meyer, *Neuburg*, pp. 160-163 and *passim*.

[18] The work of the Italians hired earlier to work at Neuburg in 1538 cannot be identified.

[19] Horn-Meyer, *Neuburg*, pp. 478-482.

style and of an almost rustic simplicity as befits a hunting lodge. However, various books that were in his library indicated that Ottheinrich eventually developed considerable interest both in Classical and in modern architecture in Italy. Among these were the Cesariano edition of Vitruvius, several editions of books by Serlio, including the Coecke translation, dated 1539, of the *Quarto libro* in two copies, and the northerner Blum's early work on the five orders of some fifteen years later.

Some have believed, therefore, that Ottheinrich could, effectively, have been his own architect at Heidelberg rather than either of the master-masons, Caspar Vischer or Jakob Heider, who are mentioned—but only as witnesses—in a contract of 1558.[20] Two Netherlanders, a Meister Anthoni, perhaps Antonis Pauwert from Ypres, and Alexander Colÿns (c.1528-1612) from Mechelen, were responsible for the sculpture. Colin—to use, as hitherto, his Germanized name—whose contract dated 1558 is the one Vischer and Heider witnessed, evidently arrived too late to have been, even hypothetically, the original designer of the facade, though in March of that year the ground storey is mentioned in a document as still incomplete. This is a question of authorship that must probably remain even more unsettled than for the Fugger works at Augsburg of a generation earlier or the Gläserner Saalbau here.

Successive disasters have left the Ottheinrichsbau a hollow shell (Pl. 177). First, it suffered with the rest of the Schloss both from shelling and from military occupation in the Thirty Years' War; re-roofed and restored in 1648, it was again much damaged by the French in a later seventeenth-century war, the one that came to an end only in 1697. Once more re-roofed in 1700, it suffered from a serious fire in 1764. Considered merely as an architectural design, however—an executed elevation, so to say—the court facade is remarkably complete except for the all but total loss of the cross-gables. This loss is unfortunate; for their character, now known only from the seventeenth-century prints, may have been as novel as that of the three extant storeys below.

The absence of gables on the Ottheinrichsbau today, in contrast to the dominance of the tall central one on the Antwerp Stadhuis, increases the strong horizontal emphasis. This emphasis results from the successive entablatures that link the seven double bays of the facade between the octagonal stair-towers at

the two ends. The tower at the right, actually part of the Ludwigsbau, was erected by Ludwig V in 1524[21] before any reflections of consequence from Renaissance Italy had reached Heidelberg; but that which matches it on the left is equally devoid of Renaissance character. So also is the rear facade of the new wing that faces toward the east.

Rising straight and bare on top of the mediaeval wall between the big round *Apothekerturm* (apothecary's tower) on the south, basically of fifteenth-century date, and the outer end of the Gläserner Saalbau on the north, the rear of the Ottheinrichsbau (Pl. 139) is remarkable rather for its distinctly "modern" look. With its three close-set ranges of eleven windows, each with a central mullion and—in the taller ones of the ground storey—a transom as well, this side recalls more the utilitarian severity of the Weinmarkt facade of the Fuggerhäuser (Pl. 8) than the north front of the Gläserner Saalbau around the corner with its arched and traceried openings (Pl. 140). But the plain featureless wall never had such wall-paintings as once gave a Venetian richness to the front of the Fuggerhäuser, for it is all of red standstone like the earlier portions of the Schloss complex.

Overshadowed on the right by the clock tower as heightened by Friedrich II in the 1540s and, on the left, by the Apothekerturm—which was raised three storeys by Friedrich IV after 1600—this rear facade of the Ottheinrichsbau was doubtless designed as well as built by the masons charged with executing the work as a whole, whoever may have been the "architect" responsible for the front on the court. It certainly had even less architectural pretension than the contiguous Gläserner Saalbau with its oriel on the east end, its relatively large round-arched windows on the north side and the decorated gable that once capped the south facade toward the court.

The court facade of the Ottheinrichsbau (Pl. 177), by contrast to the rear (Pl. 139), is a work to which the term "pretentious" applies even in its perjorative sense. It pretends already to the sort of proto-Academic grandeur that the designer, whether Floris or some other, of the Antwerp Stadhuis would soon achieve; yet it also belies that particular sort of pretension in the almost barbaric profusion of the carved decoration and the various solecisms, according to international High Renaissance standards, that are evident in various of its architectural elements. Above all, there is a disturbing lack of consonance between

---

[20] Oechelhaeuser, *Heidelberger Schloss*, pp. 14, 53-63.

[21] *Ibid.*, pp. 45-47.

the harmonic reduction in height of the two upper storeys, dependent doubtless on Serlio, and the retention throughout all three of the same vertical dimension for the niches. So also the windows (Pl. 178), for all the retardataire luxuriance of their Italianate framing, are yet subdivided like those on the east side by mullions. Here, however, the mullions are disguised as herms in accordance with more up-to-date decorative ideas. The excessively tall windows in the ground storey, lighting the vaulted hall within, also have transoms at half their height like the ones on the rear, in this case awkwardly treated as cornices of a non-existent sub-order.

One should not consider these vagaries on the façade of the Ottheinrichsbau as exclusively Mannerist in origin; some represent rather the retention of earlier transitional forms—for example, the steep-pointed pediments above the ground-storey windows—not echoes of current Italian or Brabantine modulations of High Renaissance detail. The general effect of excessive elaboration, moreover, is not due merely to the actual profusion of the carved ornament, both architectural and figural—the latter the more conspicuous since Colin's statues in the niches are of yellow rather than of red stone. Even more it results from the conflict of scale between three and, if one counts the central portal, four major compositional elements: In the first place there are the wide bays of the main orders united by the horizontal entablatures; then there is the doubled rhythm of the windows, themselves top-heavy thanks to the slimness of the flanking pilasters beneath their broad carved lintels, all of this executed in relatively bold relief; third, there are the semi-cylindrical niches, jammed in between the windows as if they were—as, indeed, they may well have been—an afterthought, to provide adequate settings for Colin's sculptural figures.[22] One may even suspect, from the presence of supporting brackets beneath the entablatures where the capitals would have been, that in the original design, doubtless of 1556 or 1557, additional pilasters and columns were intended where the deep-sunk niches were eventually introduced in 1558. The result would have been equally congested, on account of the excessive prominence of the window-edicules, but the continuous range of single bays would have provided a more even rhythm comparable to that of the orders on the Antwerp Stadhuis.

[22] *Ibid.*, p. 55, provides the identification of the subjects—some Biblical, more Classical and others allegorical—of the sixteen statues; four more serve as caryatids at the portal.

Both the irregular terrain in the court of the Heidelberg Schloss, sloping down from right to left, and the desire to continue the level of the lowest storey of the Ludwigsbau in the ground storey of the new wing which superseded its northern half made necessary an extremely high basement for the Ottheinrichsbau, awkwardly high, indeed, in relation to the three storeys above (Pl. 177). To the left of the central *perron* the wall of the basement was appropriately finished with large squarish blocks rather flatly rusticated, but not on the right. There a wall of rubble belonging to the Ludwigsbau or some even earlier structure on the site still survives.

On top of the basement of the Ottheinrichsbau there is a continuous podium. This consists of blocks of two shapes, square and oblong, decorated with diamond rustication inside plain flat frames. These blocks are so grouped that they indicate four, rather than two, bays on either side of the central one. That grouping offers some confirmation of the probability that four more pilasters were originally intended, one in the middle of each of the two double bays at the sides. Instead, every other square block supports, not a pilaster, but the base of one of Colin's statues, all set in the rather plain but deep niches.

On the façade of the Ottheinrichsbau much is consonant with Serlio's distinctly eclectic prescriptions and hence probably derived from his plates; to those in the earlier books, at least, Ottheinrich and his associates certainly had access if not to the latest. Yet the lowest order of pilasters, which is in relatively shallow relief compared to the cornices and pediments of the windows between, is Ionic, not Doric as would have been more Serlian, though the frieze carries Doric metopes and triglyphs. Such a mixture, however, was by this time common enough outside Italy. On the other hand, the rustication of the shafts is by no means unconventional by mid-sixteenth-century Italian standards.

The pilasters on the next storey, however, are much too short both for their Corinthian capitals and in relation to the Ionic order below; moreover, their shafts are not fluted but panelled and carved with arabesques in the quattrocento way (Pl. 177). Thus they are not unlike the ones on the slightly earlier buildings in Mecklenburg (Pls. 146-149) described in the previous chapter and, of course, innumerable older Renaissance works all over northern Europe. Such are hardly characteristic of Serlio even though he does illustrate some arabesqued pilasters. Then, unexpectedly, the introduction of half-columns in the order of

the top storey, as on the central portion of the Antwerp Stadhuis, recalls the more advanced cinquecento
style of the ground-storey pilaster order, though not
its tall proportions, because of the correct Composite
capitals employed here atop fluted shafts of appropriate dimension.

As to what existed originally above the terminal
cornice of this third order on the Ottheinrichsbau it
is impossible to be certain. Merian's prints of 1620
(Fig. 27) show not a longitudinal gabled roof but two
transverse roofs that were fronted, both above this
facade and over the one on the east, by a pair of
gables that occupied the full length of the wing. In
the view of the Schloss complex as seen from the north
these gables appear to be joined together in their lowest stage; and that joint stage, as well as the separated
second stages of both, appears to have been flanked by
S-scrolls. The topmost stage of each is shown as a
welscher Gebel surmounted by a spike, somewhat like
those crowning the tall watchtower and the corner
oriels on the river side of Schloss Hartenfels at Torgau (Pl. 79).

If this view of the Ottheinrichsbau was accurate
and not the result of draftsman's license, the real novelty in these gables was the coupling of the two lowest stages. This unusual—not to say, at this date,
unique[23]—treatment must have diminished the vertical emphasis resulting from the height of the gables
and their general shape. It would, therefore, have ac-
corded somewhat with the horizontality of the main
facade below, itself a more basic novelty for Germany
than the profuse decoration which had been approached a score of years before on the Dresden
Georgenbau (Pls. 83, 84).

The cross-gables on top of the Ottheinrichsbau that
are visible in a later print of 1685 would have belonged
to a new longitudinal roofing scheme introduced in
the restoration after the Thirty Years' War. Of
these mid-seventeenth-century cross-gables—intended,
doubtless, to echo those of 1601-1607 over the Friedrichsbau (Pl. 366) on the north side of the court—
or perhaps of still later ones from the time of the re-
roofing in 1700—a few traces remain *in situ*. Evidently
niches occupied the centers of the lower stage of these
with Colin's statues of Sol and of Jupiter, which still
survive, set in them. These statues line up with those
in the niches in the double bays flanking the central

bay below (Pl. 178). At the side of the niches in the
gables multiple bases indicate each had a range of
ten pilasters of about the same size as the ones framing the windows of the facade and that these were
doubled at the ends.

If the present Italianate horizontality of the ruin
of the Ottheinrichsbau at the top belies the original
more Germanic silhouette—the major break in the
syncopated rhythm of the facade—the portal which
fills the full width of the central double bay and rises
up through the entablature of the ground-storey order has survived intact (Pl. 179). Concerning this
there need be no serious problem of attribution. It
bespeaks, in general, the Brabantine taste of the mid-
century associated with Cornelis Floris, and it must
have been designed as well as executed by Colin after
he arrived in Heidelberg from Mechelen in 1558. The
composition is quite architectural in organization, but
the sculptor-architect substituted caryatids for pilasters
or columns both at the level of the main arch and in
the attic above. These recall a little the ones on the
street front of the Fürstenhof at Wismar (Pl. 147)
as completed earlier in the decade. They are, however,
rather more sophisticated in execution and closer to
those Serlio had illustrated on the title-page of the
Quarto libro of 1537.

The existing horizontals of the podium and the
ground-storey entablature of the Ottheinrichsbau were
continued across the portal. As a result there is less
awkwardness in the relation to the main order at
this level than that of the windows in the upper
storeys—the ground-storey windows, for example,
utilize the top of the podium as a sill. However, the
surface decoration on the portal is both elaborated at
the base and simplified above. The socles of the lower
caryatids and the oblong blocks between are carved
with trophies of arms while the ressauts of the entablature over the upper caryatids are plain. On the
frieze in between a central tablet, flanked by scrolling, is substituted for the Doric metopes and triglyphs associated with the lower pilaster order. The
Ionic volutes of that order are repeated, however, over
the heads of all the caryatids; and above them, on top
of the lower order of the portal, blocks decorated with
rosettes are set just below the ressauts in the cornice.

There is no continuous frieze at this level on the
portal of the Ottheinrichsbau, for the extrados of the
entrance arch and the carved Victories in its spandrels
fill the whole space between the blocks over the heads
of the caryatids. The next horizontal layer should perhaps be interpreted as a frieze, therefore, rather than

---

[23] After 1600 the lowest stages of pairs of cross-gables that
rise side by side are sometimes joined as on the Danzig
Arsenal and the Hannoversch-Münden Rathaus (Pl. 383), but
not so early as this.

Fig. 27. Heidelberg, Schloss from north, c.1620

as a podium for the attic and the "cornice" under it as an architrave. Musical instruments decorate the faces of the ressauts, and small openings at either side correspond to the narrow vertical lights between the pairs of caryatids below.

The central panel in this upper level of the Heidelberg portal carries Ottheinrich's name and his titles carved in a sort of *Fraktur* (black-letter, that is) in marked contrast to the superbly Classical character of the inscriptions on tomb-slabs executed long before by such German artists of an older generation as Hermann Vischer[24] and Sebastian Loscher. Was this very un-Italian lettering an early symptom of the curious backflow of northern influence that reached its climax in the *Nachgotik* churches of 1590-1620? In any case a similarly Northern feeling also pervades the tight-packed armorial panel that fills the central field of the attic.

Around several Herculean episodes, carved by Colin on panels to left and right on the portal of the Otthein-

richsbau, the three-dimensional scrolled bandwork framing them speaks a different language: the new Brabantine dialect, so to call it, initiated by Cornelis Floris in the forties after his return to Antwerp from Italy. This style of ornament—which is not, of course, without its Italian and French roots, particularly at Fontainebleau—Floris had already adumbrated well before he designed in 1549 the decorations illustrated in Coecke's book of 1550 (Fig. 16). It was only just before this in 1556 and 1557, however, that Floris's decorative style became more available for emulation abroad with the publication in Antwerp of his Weeldeley *niewe Inventien van Antÿksche*.

Even more striking than the frames around the Hercules reliefs on the Ottheinrichsbau is the three-dimensional scrolled strapwork Colin introduced above the main entablature around the medallion portrait of Ottheinrich. The flute-playing putti flanking this, on the other hand, are still almost quattrocento in spirit as, indeed, are the arabesques on the jambs of the main arch. These last are literally overshadowed by the big figures in the round that project on either side; but their delicacy all the same contrasts with

[24] Osten-Vey, *Germany*, pl. 5, provides an example: the tombs of Elisabeth and Hermann VIII von Henneberg dating from after 1507.

the coarser treatment of those on the first storey order that were presumably not executed by Colin.

It is not difficult to accept, therefore, that the Heidelberg portal was an interpolation by that Brabantine sculptor in a facade designed earlier, probably by a German or Germans, which had already by 1558 been carried above the ground and first storeys by the same craftsmen or by others. There can be, however, no equally plausible conclusion as regards who those craftsmen were. It is mere novel-writing to suggest that Ottheinrich himself may have proposed originally a *parti* with four narrow bays on either side of a double central bay. It is even more fanciful to suppose this was meant by him to be carried out with a close approach to Serlian standards. Such, in fact, is the character of the detailing of the existing pilasters of the lowest order and also of the half-columns on the second storey; this character could well have been drastically varied elsewhere on the facade as construction proceeded by craftsmen who were either inexperienced or unsympathetic. That, at least, is the most plausible explanation of the stylistic dichotomy so evident here, as also elsewhere, in these years.

The order of the first storey of the Ottheinrichsbau —if not to the same degree the gawky window-enframements—certainly resembles the terra cotta trim from the Lübeck workshop of Statius von Düren used in this decade and later in Mecklenburg. The coarser scale of the detailing here might have been an echo of that of the orders above and below or the result of carving the architectural elements in sandstone instead of using the molded and baked clay that was employed in Mecklenburg in the mid-century. This coarseness may, however, be explained most simply by the presumptive execution of most of the facade, except for Colin's figural sculpture and perhaps the whole portal, by local masons untrained in Renaissance design. Very likely such craftsmen were trying their poor best to emulate what they had seen either in books or in existing northern structures and succeeded, at least relatively, in so doing only with the orders of the ground and top storeys.

Not only should the steep un-Italian pitch of the pediments of the ground-storey window-frames of the Ottheinrichsbau be noted in this connection—so different from the flatter ones over the windows on the Wismar Fürstenhof (Pls. 146-147)—but also the spiral fluting of the small half-columns flanking them. That recalls the columns on the sacristy portal of 1518 at Annaberg (Pl. 20) and even a still earlier example by Rejt in Prague. Yet the members below the tran-

soms of these windows were rusticated, if rather sloppily, doubtless as an echo of the underscaled but more correct rustication of the main order at this level based on Serlio's or other published plates. Then there are the other small pilasters, each with only two flutes like Rosskopf's at Görlitz (Pls. 63, 67) of the 1520s and thirties, that frame the windows of the second storey, by this date almost a vernacular note. So also the decoration above the entablatures of the windows in both of the upper storeys still recalls the Como-like crowning of the portals of the thirties on the Dresden Georgenbau (Pls. 86-87) at the same time that the herm-mullions already reflect new models of the mid-century, whether Italian, French or Brabantine.

Compared to this profusion of miscellaneous carved details on the facade of the Ottheinrichsbau, all so fussy and uncertain in relative scale, the shell-topped niches that hold Colin's conspicuous allegorical figures of yellow stone seem, like the pilaster order of the ground storey, clear and even, one could say, Classical in a Florentine or Roman way. It is hardly credible, therefore, that the sculptor from Mechelen or any other well-trained Netherlander of his generation should either have designed or carved these window-frames. Their character will most probably have been determined, at least for the ground storey, before Colin arrived in 1558. What particular part others, including the master-masons Vischer and Heider, may have played in executing the detail other than that on the portal is impossible to determine. The presence of the sculptor Anthoni, who may have been a Walloon from Ypres in southern Flanders, has been noted. Hans Engelhard (†1573) could also have been involved: employed at the Schloss since 1533, he is one of the several near-unknowns who might have been responsible in the forties, at least for the carved work if not the general design, of the Gläserner Saalbau (Pls. 139-140) rather than—or perhaps in association with—Conrad Forster. As in Elizabethan England, the recovery of craftsmen's names from surviving documents is little help in supporting attributions for over-all design since architectural responsibility was still so diffuse.

In the interiors of the Ottheinrichsbau, often burnt out, various elaborately carved stone door-frames of the early 1560s survive below the scant remains of the vaulting but no complete decorative schemes. Yet even though the Ottheinrichsbau is only a romantic ruin today, the extent to which the facade, at least, has resisted successive disasters is testimony to the solidity of its construction. Up through the crowning cornice the design as executed in 1556-1559 is still complete today and amazingly well preserved. Like the Gläserner Saalbau and other elements of the Heidelberg complex, moreover, the court facade was planned as an independent unit, not as part of a concerted scheme of total reconstruction. Ottheinrich as client must have intended to erect a self-sufficient architectural entity whoever was actually responsible for the design. Earlier, at Neuburg, his north wing was also only very loosely related to the west and south wings that preceded it. Though the Ottheinrichsbau at Heidelberg should not be considered typical of German Renaissance architectural production in the way it has often been so presented in the past, the ruin is, all the same, a very notable survival from the 1550s. Far less is extant of many other major Schlösser of the period, though their original character can often be deduced from what survives physically or from documents. A case in point is the Schloss at Horst concerning which the documents have been published.[25]

At Horst near Essen the erection of a large new Schloss for Rüttger von der Horst, not a prince li'^a Ottheinrich or those responsible for the Torgau, Dresden and Berlin Schlösser but a functionary of the Cologne electorate, began in 1558. The work was directed by a northern Netherlander, Arndt Johanssen,[26] from Arnhem on the Lower Rhine where he had been the city architect, with the assistance of Laurenz von Brachum[27] from Wesel, also on the Rhine near Xanten. That, of course, was the same year the design of the Ottheinrichsbau probably reached final form with the modifications then introduced by the newly arrived southern Netherlander Alexander Colin.

The situation at Horst was, and is, very different from that at Heidelberg. Only a considerable portion of the north wing, the first to be begun, and the basement of the somewhat later east wing now survive of an originally extensive quadrangular layout (Fig.

28) with big square pavilions at the corners.[28] On the outer side to the north the extant portion still includes six bays of what became in the mid-1560s the entrance front, and there are also some surviving interiors at basement level under the modern east wing. A tall oriel, begun in 1564 it would appear, occupies the second bay from the left on the exterior of the north wing (Pl. 184) and a few modest elements of the main portal are extant at the right end. The portal was always asymmetrically disposed between the northeast and the northwest corner pavilions. These pavilions, which perhaps dated from the early sixties but not improbably were somewhat later, are now gone. The work of 1558-1560 should, however, be described first.

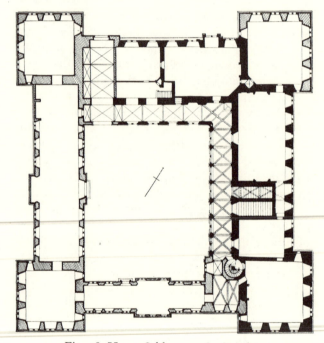

Fig. 28. Horst, Schloss, 1558-c.80, plan

On the court side of the north wing at Horst four bays still stand or, in terms of the continuous arcading of the topmost gallery, thirteen one-third bays (Pl. 180). A doorway in an asymmetrical position occupies the second full bay from the right. The inner end of the entrance passage once opened onto the court in the bay at the other end where the rebuilt western corner of the block now rises in plain brickwork. Since this inner facade carries the date 1559,

[25] Klapheck, *Schloss Horst*. Specific references follow in later Notes.

[26] *Ibid.*, pp. 66-78. Some have seen a resemblance in the small-scale articulation of the north and east court facades at Horst to the Duivelshuis of the previous decade at Arnhem which Johanssen would have known well and may have worked on. Certainly the treatment of these portions of the Schloss at Horst is closer to the Duivelshuis than to the more plastic articulation, with orders in relief, on the Ottheinrichsbau. Another possible borrowing from Holland at Horst will be discussed below.

[27] Klapheck, *Schloss Horst*, pp. 81-85.

[28] *Ibid.*, pp. 44-59.

the year Heinrich Vernukken,[29] a sculptor from Kalkar near Kleve on the west side of the Rhine, joined Johannssen's team at Horst, it is the particular portion of the whole project most comparable in date, as also in scale, and pretension to the Ottheinrichsbau.

Happily, detailed drawings were made of Horst in the nineteenth century before the galleried facade (Fig. 29) above the basement on the court side of the other wing on the east was demolished so that also can at least be described. This eastern front on the court was evidently ten bays long and had an elaborately ornamented gable rising high over the three bays that projected slightly at the southern end. Just how early were the galleries on this side—known to have been in construction by 1560 under the direction of Brachum, but presumably following a design by Johannssen—is uncertain though quite probably they date from that same year. The remarkable gable, however, might have been two or three years later and will be separately discussed below.

Originally the eastern galleries masked an earlier *Herrenhaus* (manor house). Some elements of that still seem to exist in the basement with various carved features, probably no older than the late fifties, under crude brick vaulting that could be in part mediaeval. To this Herrenhaus at least the inner portion of the north wing had been attached as an ell when it was initiated in 1558. The ell was then intended to provide for services rather than to be the entrance block it became in the mid-sixties after the outer facade was erected or, perhaps, only elaborated. The outer side of the east wing (Pl. 181), housing the principal residential apartments as the old Herrenhaus had previously done, was added after 1560, though how long after is a difficult question that will be considered later.

The profusion of surviving documents published by Klapheck provides considerable information as to the artists employed by Rüttger at Horst, including the length of their employment. But the dates when several crucial elements of the Schloss, such as the big gable decorated with raised bands in the southeast corner of the court and the corner pavilions—the earliest presumably those that flanked the eastern front— were first proposed, if not begun, cannot be precisely determined. Since both are recurrent themes in later German secular architecture, this is frustrating for the historian.

[29] *Ibid.*, pp. 84-85.

The general stylistic picture at Horst, indeed, is disappointingly ambiguous even as regards what survives. But that was only a small segment of the Schloss Rüttger gradually erected over some twenty years. The work, however, was carried out mostly in the early years of the prolonged campaign. The galleried facades along the north and the east side of the court (Fig. 29, Pl. 180), the one largely extant, the other at least recorded in drawings, must still be considered predominantly Early Renaissance, even quattrocento, in character; on the other hand various novel features which seem to have been borrowed here for the first time in Germany—some perhaps from the Netherlands and one certainly from France— are not. They can hardly, all the same, be called "High Renaissance" either in any Italian sense of that term.

Just the same, the over-all pseudo-structural articulation even of the surviving north side of the court at Horst (Pl. 180), which carries the date 1559, with broad piers rising between paired windows and statue-filled niches—the latter very like those Colin was providing at almost exactly the same time on the facade of the Ottheinrichsbau—should be considered at least as significant as the very small strapwork cartouches which are almost invisible in photographs. Other similar ornament, more or less of the still very new Northern Mannerist sort, occupies the panels at the heads of the piers below the niches. The demolished galleries on the east side of the court (Fig. 29) were even more retardataire, at least in the extreme delicacy of their detailing. Yet that detailing, for all its tiny scale, was more consistently infiltrated with strapwork elements. These appeared on the shafts of the columns and pilasters, on the transoms and even in the lunettes of the upper windows.

If not to the same degree as the Ottheinrichsbau, these court facades at Horst thus offered a certain amount of novel decoration, novel that is for northern Europe around 1560; but that decoration was subordinated to a general organization which was "early" in character. In that respect it was not unlike most of the identifiable work of the time that survives in Holland whence the architect came here. The same is hardly true of the Heidelberg facade despite its comparable stylistic ambiguity. Of the two, the Ottheinrichsbau is today much the more impressive; but the plan of Horst as given by Klapheck (Fig. 28) makes evident that this was not so before the greater part of the Schloss was demolished in the nineteenth century. The relatively obscure Rüttger seems, indeed, to

140

Fig. 29. Arndt Johannssen and Laurenz von
Brachum: Horst, Schloss, east side of
court, begun 1560

have been a considerably more ambitious builder than
Ottheinrich in his old age at Heidelberg. He certainly
lived long enough to carry out most, at least, of his
project.[30]

However and whenever the architectural direction
changed at Horst, as it certainly did in the early to
mid-sixties, the contract of 1564 with the sculptor Wilhelm Vernukken from Kalkar, whose father Heinrich
had been employed at Horst since 1559, establishes
that the decorative carving on the exterior of the north
wing was only begun at that date, some five years
later than the inner court facade on the north, while
the outer east front will hardly have been designed
more than one or two years before. Thus, if one considers only what was probably under way at Horst
in the years immediately following 1558, that is, those
portions corresponding most closely in date with the

Ottheinrichsbau—the inner side of the north wing
(Pl. 180), by coincidence still largely extant, and
the court side of the east wing as known from drawings (Fig. 29)—the disparity in scale between what the
Elector Palatine, a great prince whose earlier building projects had bankrupted him in the previous decade, undertook in the late 1550s, and Schloss Horst as
initially planned, the seat of a mere official of the
electoral archdiocese of Cologne, need not seem so
great. But to say a "mere" official is to underrate his
relative importance.

Rüttger von der Horst[31] was marshal through several decades to successive archbishops of Cologne. As
electors, these prelates were rulers of a territory at
least as large as and probably considerably more prosperous than the Palatinate, then as now. Thus Rüttger
not only had great influence and power as *Stadthalter*

[30] *Ibid.*, p. 85.

[31] *Ibid.*, pp. 44-51.

tectural ambitions also increased. This must have been particularly evident as regards the east front, not to speak of various elaborately sculptured chimney-pieces[32] in the interior.

Despite the very detailed study made by Klapheck[33] of the original elements of decoration still to be seen at Horst or elsewhere, it is not easy, even with the remarkably complete paper restorations and the many photographs of interior features he published, to envisage what Schloss Horst was like when Rüttger's continuing campaigns of construction and decoration finally came to an end. That seems to have been soon after the death in 1577 of the Archbishop-Elector Salentin von Isenburg in whose service, from 1567 on, Rüttger enjoyed his greatest prosperity. He maintained his position under Isenburg's successor Gebhard Truchsess, dying only in 1581; but after some twenty very productive years his building days were already over.

But now a return to the early 1560s and a consideration of certain other Schlösser that are closely related to Horst is in order.[34] Because the more precise dating of such throws a little light on the uncertain sequence of the work carried out at Horst in those years, the account of Rüttger's Schloss may well be broken off at this point; it will be continued later.

In 1560 Rüttger's daughter Margarete married Bertram von Loë and, as a marriage gift, her father lent Laurenz von Brachum to design the house Bertram's father was to build for them at Geist,[35] just northwest of Beckum in western Westphalia. Of this Schloss, which must have been at least begun very little later, almost nothing remains though the general layout has been established from the excavated foundations. Much like Johannssen's work of 1558-1560 at Horst, Brachum's at Geist consisted of two wings arranged —here not quite at right angles—in an L-shape. The entrance front, as at Horst, was asymmetrical and, according to the evidence of an old painting, this was flanked by large round towers crowned with dome-shaped *welsche Hauben* rather than by the square pavilions that would soon flank the east front at Horst. The walls were decorated with raised bands of brickwork like those on the remarkable gable on the court

Fig. 30. ? Arndt Johannssen and Laurenz von Brachum: Horst, Schloss, gable of c.1562 (early 19th-century drawing)

---

[32] *Ibid.*, pp. 86-105.
[33] *Ibid.*, pp. 142-171.
[34] *Ibid.*, pp. 247-308, covers all the various Schlösser discussed in the next section of Chapter V; individual references follow in the Notes.
[35] *Ibid.*, pp. 247-250.

—lay deputy of the archbishop-elector—but exceptional opportunities to accumulate an ever-increasing fortune which he seems to have spent largely on his Schloss. Not surprisingly, as he grew richer his archi-

side of the slightly later east wing at Horst (Fig. 30) and, more simply, on the external east front there (Pl. 181), of both of which detailed descriptions will shortly follow. There is no strong reason to suppose, however, that this sort of ornament was first developed by Brachum, even though it was he who was executing in the same years that portion of the Schloss at Horst over which the decorated gable rose, if not so probably the east front also.

Brachum still continued to work with Johannssen in the early and mid-sixties at Horst while construction of the Schloss at Geist went forward; but he was soon busy also elsewhere in Westphalia at Hovestadt and most probably on Schloss Assen as well. In 1560 the then archbishop-elector of Cologne, Gebhard von Mansfeld, for whom Rüttger von der Horst was the secular deputy, renewed the lease of the Hovestadt[36] estate to Dietrich von Keteler. This lay to the north of Soest and west of Lippstadt along the eastern edge of the Cologne territories where they touched those under the control of the prince-bishop of Münster. Keteler then commissioned the "Murer and Bawmeister" Laurenz von Brachum in 1563 to build the Schloss, providing him with an annual retainer or "Jaergeltz" as is recorded in an extant document.

Of the Hovestadt Schloss far more remains than at Horst, not to speak of Geist, and there is little question that the two-storeyed north facade was flanked by three-storeyed pavilions capped by octagonal "domes" (Fig. 31). The roofing of the surviving pavilion, now without its domelets, must be a later replacement. Though about half survives of Brachum's quadrangular Schloss only the one corner pavilion on the northeast is extant (Pl. 185). Almost the whole of the east wing is original, however, except for the modern termination where the southeast pavilion once stood. Moreover, the outer front of the north wing is also all but complete, minus the northwest pavilion; that on the court, however, seems to have been considerably modified.

The two wings at Hovestadt both rise on battered basements out of the broad moat. On the north the ground storey is relatively simple, with the eight tall rectangular windows separated by broad pilaster-like piers of brick heavily banded with stone. At the bases of these piers panels decorated with heavy lozenges —apparently of stuccoed brick rather than stone— rise well above sill-level.

[36] Ibid., pp. 269-279.

The treatment of Schloss Hovstadt on the east is different and considerably more plastic (Pl. 185). The pairs of narrow pilaster-strips between the windows are even more boldly banded with stone than the piers on the north side and carry arches of brick reaching up to the sills of the first-storey windows. Heavy strapwork of varying design fills the tympana of the arches and simple geometrical ornament in relief ties together the projecting lintels of the lower windows and covers also the joint podia of the paired pilaster-strips.

The decorative treatment of the upper storey at Hovestadt also differs on the two outer fronts. Most conspicuous on the north (Fig. 31) is a broad band of brick striped vertically with stone members that are rather flatly carved with small-scale strapwork designs. This band occupies the space between the heads of the ground-storey windows and the sills of those above. In the second storey, over high brick podia carrying plain raised circles, paired pilasters recur somewhat as on the lower storey of the east side. The shafts of these pilasters, however, are banded with stone only in their lower halves and have marked entasis above. Over the windows, in the zone of the pilaster capitals, there are segmental bearing arches of brick with alternate voussoirs of stone.

On the second storey of the east front at Hovestadt (Pl. 185) the rather similar pilasters are single and the windows are framed by plain projecting architraves. Above them, in the capital zone, the horizontal members over the windows project rather further; while the capitals—here of vaguely Ionic design— project still more over the plain rounded brackets at the tops of the pilaster shafts. Just above the basement and in the frieze of the terminal entablature raised patterns in brick complete the all-over plastic treatment of the walls of both wings. These patterns are more closely related than the pilaster-orders to the large-scale raised decoration on the corner pavilion. On that, however, half-round bearing arches of brickwork, double in the lower storey, single in the first storey, and segmental, with alternate voussoirs projecting, in the second, do accord to some degree with the arches on the walls of the two wings. Nonetheless the most striking ornament on the pavilion consists of raised bands forming smaller linked arches, lozenges and squares.

Such patterns were used all over the outer walls and the round towers at Schloss Geist and they appear again on work at Schloss Assen initiated in 1564, the

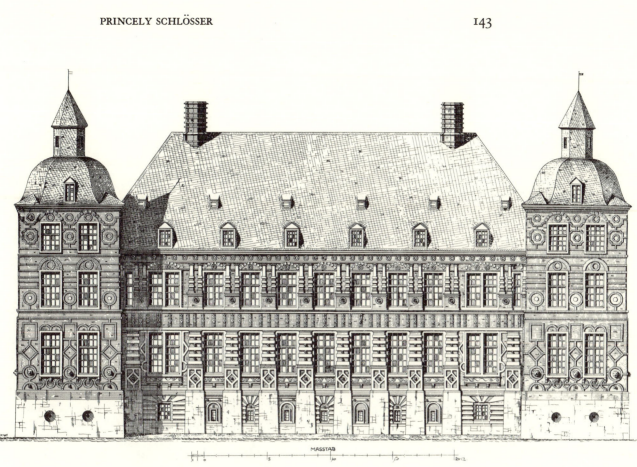

Fig. 31. Laurenz von Brachum: Hovestadt, Schloss,
north front, begun 1563

year after that at Hovestadt. Yet it seems probable
that the earliest German use of this sort of coarse
geometrical ornament, though considerably more varied and elaborate in its patterns, would have been,
not at Geist or Hovestadt, but in the decoration on
the gable in the court at Horst (Fig. 30), difficult
though that is to date precisely. At least such is the
most plausible assumption as to what may, in fact,
have been a rapid sequence of parallel construction
at Horst and the other Westphalian Schlösser of the
early sixties. Brachum's model for the surface treatment at Geist and Hovestadt could well have been
a portion of Johannssen's designs for Horst that
Brachum himself had carried out. In any case, some
relation to contemporary Dutch work may be assumed
because of Johannssen's connection with Arnhem.

The idea for the corner pavilions at Hovestadt,
on the other hand, must surely be French in ultimate
origin, and one quite likely brought to Horst by the
French sculptor Joist de la Cour in the year 1563
when Hovestadt was begun and Geist well under
way. That could have been either just before or just

after the court gable at Horst was designed though
the particular succession of the descriptions here does
imply the former; despite their different sources, these
disparate features at Horst could well have been exactly contemporary though the work of different designers.

Over and above the corner pavilion, the general
impression made by Hovestadt is also rather French,
if somewhat anachronistically so. The mixture of
brick and stone in the walls resembles not so much
French architecture of the period of Henri II as that
of Henri IV and Louis XIII around and well after
1600. In the 1560s, however, the articulation in relief
of the walls of Hovestadt is actually related to the
international modulation of facade-design in this period, just getting under way in Germany. That modulation was substituting more and more for plain flat
walls in which windows were isolated holes, with or
without framing, pseudo-structural grids of orders
modelling the wall plane. Of this treatment the earliest
mid-century German example is the court facade of
the Ottheinrichsbau, though that was preceded twenty

years before by the treatment of the walls of the Landshut Stadtresidenz. But Johannssen had already been moving in this direction in the design of the gallery fronts of 1559 and 1560 on the north and east sides of the court at Horst (Fig. 29, Pl. 180).

Further similarity to Horst, most particularly to the north side of the court there, is evident at Hovestadt on the inside fronts of the east and north wings. The treatment of those facades is generally much simpler, however, even though the upper storey on the east side does carry the same sort of pilasters, banded below and with marked entasis above, as are used on the outer side of that wing. The very plain loggia at the base of the inner front of the north wing is more probably a late addition of the eighteenth or nineteenth centuries.

The greatest difference at Hovestadt from the two gallery facades on the court at Horst is the change in the scale of the detail. Of Johannssen's still rather Early Renaissance sort of delicacy nothing remains. Instead Brachum seems, without much knowledge, to have sought to emulate the new High Renaissance architectural grammar, as was earlier at least attempted on the Ottheinrichsbau.

Variations on the themes of Hovestadt are conspicuous not far away both on the entrance front and in the court (Pl. 183) of Schloss Assen[37] at Lippborg, which is between Lippstadt and Hamm. This was remodelled or rebuilt, most probably by Brachum, from 1564 onward for another von Keteler, Gorwin von Keteler-Neu-Assen, starting the year after Dietrich von Keteler began the work at Hovestadt. Curiously enough, however, the detailing of the entrance portals, both that on the exterior and the one in the court, retains much more of the delicacy of the eastern gallery in the court at Horst (Fig. 29). Though the new strapwork ornament has, at Schloss Assen, almost totally replaced the earlier North Italian sort, the scale of the decoration remains miniscule and the particular combination of small pilasters and tiny arches, especially above the portal on the court side, is still essentially quattrocento in character. Very likely the availability at Lippborg of stone suitable for fine carving, such as was evidently not to be had at Hovestadt, explains the disparity. That will soon be difficult to realize because of the deterioration of the stone, now exposed to the pollution created by the vast chemical plants of Marl-Hüls to the west.

This difference in character at Schloss Assen might

[37] *Ibid.*, pp. 250-267.

also suggest that it was Johannssen rather than Brachum who was here the responsible designer. In any case, Johannssen did not leave Germany and return to his native Holland until 1567 when the city authorities of Arnhem demanded his presence. There are, for example, no corner pavilions at Schloss Assen. Instead, mediaeval round towers, resembling those at Geist, were retained at the southwest and northeast corners. The new wings, however, were here set at a precise right angle to one another, despite the exiguous moated site of the old Assen *Wasserburg*, as was not done at Geist.

The portal in the court of Schloss Assen follows rather closely the design of the galleries at Horst on the north side of the court. Moreover, the handling of one section of the fenestration of the upper storey in the court on the right distinctly recalls the coupled arches of the eastern galleries at Horst even though straight-sided triangles here cap the heads of the windows. However, the windows of the storey below these have the central mullions, transoms at half height and small pediments of the ones on the outer side of the east wing at Horst (Pl. 181) which will shortly be described. The decoration of the walls by raised bands of brick at Assen and earlier at Geist also seems, as at Hovestadt, to derive from Horst, more particularly from the surface treatment of the big gable at the southeast corner of the court there (Fig. 30). Such similarities establish the close kinship of these two Westphalian Schlösser, one definitely by Brachum, the other quite possibly by him, to the work of the early sixties at Horst where he was associated with Johannssen.

The most advanced section of Rüttger's Schloss externally was evidently the east front even though it may well have been designed, if hardly completed, relatively early. A drawing of 1835 by H. J. von Freyser (Pl. 181) makes plain that this long outer facade of the east wing was totally different in character from the shorter galleried fronts (Pl. 180) on the north and east sides of the court, dated 1559 and 1560, and quite as unlike the outer side of the north wing as remodelled or rebuilt on the Vernukken contract of 1564 (Pl. 184) which dates from the very years when the east front, even if designed a year or two earlier, was presumably still in construction.

Above a basement, the nine two-storeyed bays of the east front of Schloss Horst were arranged in a syncopated rhythm between two corner pavilions undoubtedly of French inspiration. These prominent flanking pavilions resembling the one that survives at

Hovestadt (Fig. 31, Pl. 185) were, it must be supposed, the first of their sort in Germany. Each was three bays wide, three storeys tall, and capped by two differing versions of more or less domical roofs. These last were of a French type rather than the *welsche Hauben* hitherto usual in Germany, and they rose nearly, but not quite, as high as the main roof. The regularity and balance of the treatment of this front contrasted even more with the elaboration of the galleried facades on the court, not to speak of the ornate but asymmetrical entrance front, than did the so much simpler and more architecturally scaled decoration.

The standard windows throughout the east front at Horst were capped with plain low-pitched pediments in contrast to the sharp-pointed ones on the Ottheinrichsbau (Pls. 177-178). All the windows, however, except the narrower ones that varied the rhythm in the central portion, were divided by stone mullions and also by transoms at half their height, like the extant ones at Assen (Pl. 183). That treatment may well be considered distinctly Dutch when carried out, as here, in brick and stone and most probably with the approval, at least, of a Dutch architect. Many string-courses, continuing the lines of the sills, transoms and lintels of the windows, striated the facade horizontally, and rather bolder moldings were evidently introduced at the sill-level of the first-storey windows as well as a heavy modillioned cornice that crowned the whole. Between these horizontal string-courses—which were perhaps stone fillets but equally possibly could have been projecting courses of brick-work—square blocks, single in the lower storey but arranged in quincunxes above, provided the only additional decoration. The blocks may also have been either of brickwork or of stone; but in any case they contrasted in their simple geometrical abstraction with the profusion of carved stone ornamentation on other portions of the exterior of the Schloss by the Vernukkens and on interior features by Joist de la Cour such as the elaborate chimneypieces.

Despite the Dutch character of the windows, this eastern facade of Schloss Horst was evidently designed by some other hand than Johannssen's and such a change of authorship is at least suggested in documents that survive. When Johannssen had to return to his official position in Arnhem in 1567 it was the Frenchman, Joist de la Cour, who took general charge of the continuing campaign of construction that went on into the seventies.

Though Joist was hired by Rüttger von der Horst in 1563 primarily to execute elaborately carved chim-neypieces and other show-pieces in the interiors at Horst, it is not unlikely he had already had some influence—even a potent influence—well before Johannssen's departure in 1567 on the architectural design of portions of the Schloss then under way. His professional prestige with contemporaries such as Rüttger must at least have equalled that of the Dutch architect.

Certainly Joist de la Cour was the only artistic figure of any consequence added to Rüttger's team beside the Vernukkens. A pupil of Jean Martin, who had translated Vitruvius into French, as well as reputedly of Jean Goujon—who worked on Francis I's court facade at the Louvre in the forties—he was certainly not unfamiliar with architecture, though he was hired like the Vernukkens as a sculptor. More particularly, he will doubtless have been familiar with —may even in the fifties have worked at—the chateau of Anet for Diane de Poitiers in association with Philibert de l'Orme. Certainly it is French work of the period of Henri II that his sculptured chimney-pieces, executed over the next ten or fifteen years, most resemble. Some of these—or at least reassembled portions of them—were installed in Schloss Hugen-poet, near Kettwig on the Ruhr, in the nineteenth century and may still be seen there.

That it was Joist who proposed the construction of large square pavilions at the corners of the exterior at Horst some years before Johannssen left in 1567 is by no means impossible. He could have known at first hand various French chateaux already designed or in construction that had such features after their first introduction by Serlio at Ancy-le-Franc in the mid-forties, the project for which he illustrated in his *Segundo libro* of 1545. Moreover, he might even have brought with him—and called Rüttger's and Johannssen's attention to—other plates showing such chateaux as published by J. A. du Cerceau in his *Livre d'architecture* of 1559 and his *Second livre d'architecture* of 1561. Plates of this ilk must, in any case, be the immediate and effective source of the corner pavilions at Horst, whoever proposed them and prepared the actual design for their execution.

There may also be French influence in the decoration of the oriel on the entrance facade (Pl. 184), executed so elaborately by Wilhelm Vernukken on his contract of 1564, but it is of a less sophisticated character. Despite the considerable difference in scale, this oriel is more to be associated with the still almost quattrocento character of the galleried facades toward the court (Fig. 29, Pl. 180) and with such surviving carved work of the same years in the interiors as is not by Joist de la Cour—this is, indeed, probably by the elder Vernukken assisted by Wilhelm—than with the relative simplicity of the detailing of the east front.

The novel character of the east front at Horst (Pl. 181) did not primarily result from the character of the detail, however, but rather from the bold external massing provided by the prominent square pavilions at the two corners. Other such pavilions, moreover, once rose also at the west end of the north wing and the southwest corner of the quadrangle. The visual effect of these pavilions may best be appreciated today at Hovestadt (Fig. 31, Pl. 185) since nothing relevant is extant at Horst. However, reconstructions on paper make clear the relation of the pavilions both to the north and east wings and to the wings on the west and the south which Rüttger never raised to the height of the other two. Corner pavilions, all the same, did not soon become standard components of German Schlösser. That at Hovestadt is the only early one which survives and most of them date from after 1600.

There are several possibilities as regards the initiation in Germany of the sort of all-over surface decoration once seen on the east front at Horst that is carried out chiefly with bosses and bands of brickwork in relief. Since this sort of decoration is still more elaborate and conspicuous on the surviving corner pavilion at Brachum's Hovestadt and on both fronts of the south or entrance wing at Assen, it might well have been he who initiated it. Yet, in the case of the similar but undated decoration on the gable in the court at Horst the design may more plausibly be attributed to Johannssen rather than to even such a principal assistant as Brachum seems to have been by this time. It was Brachum who was directly commissioned by Rüttger in 1560 to take charge of the decoration of the galleries below and to the left along this east side of the court. Certainly the gable is not likely to have been designed by either of the two men from Kalkar, Heinrich Vernukken or his son Wilhelm, who had already in 1559 been hired by Rüttger to work as stone-carvers at Horst. Moreover, Wilhelm's sculptural decoration of the mid-sixties surviving on the outer side of the north wing (Pl. 184) has an entirely different character, somewhat resembling the coarser work on the Ottheinrichsbau for which Colin was presumably not responsible (Pls. 177-178). That decoration by the Vernukkens, moreover, probably postdates both the gable in the court

and the initiation of the east front by a year or two.

The tall gable in the southeast corner of the court at Horst (Fig. 30), epoch-making for Germany and, indeed, for all northern Europe in its surface treatment, must have been built in succession to the galleries below and to the left, which are dated 1560, but only perhaps after several years, which would make it at least as late as the east front. That another one, also undated, which will shortly be discussed, survives at Frens in the Rhineland (Pl. 182) does not clarify the problem. Both of these resemble most closely gables that are still extant in the northeastern Netherlands, whence came Johannssen, and in the northern coastal region of Germany and in Denmark, both districts in which Netherlanders were often employed as architects in the late sixteenth and early seventeenth centuries. But those Dutch, German and Danish examples are mostly much later in date, around 1600 or beyond. To judge from what survives in Holland, Dutch architects active at home in the mid-century only very rarely designed similar ones either as regards the great size and verticality of the Horst and Frens gables or the raised bandwork on their surfaces.

Descent from earlier German gables seems rather more likely for the outline of the Horst gable, if not so probably for the bandwork with which it was decorated. The spirit of the large-scale bandwork on these German gables of the sixties, presumably designed by the Dutch Johannssen, and of the rather similar sort of wall-decoration used by Brachum—evident in the old painting of Geist and still surviving at Hovestadt and at Assen (Pls. 185, 183)—seems distinctly Netherlandish and, for all the presumptive date, already more like what Vredeman offered in his *Architectura* of 1563 (Pl. 176) than that in the plates Cornelis Floris published in the fifties (Pl. 110). Still it must be said that no surviving gable in Holland earlier than that of Huis Betlehem of 1566 at Gorinchem or, in the southern Netherlands, before that of the Wenemaerhospital on the Sint-Verle-Plein in Gent, also of the mid-sixties, approaches the one at Horst and the other undated German example that is extant. Earlier, the timid scrolling on the edges of some Dutch gables of the forties and fifties is of a rather different character.[38]

[38] Conspicuous in mid-century Amsterdam were the gabled facades of the *Bushuis* (Arsenal) of 1551-1556 in the Oude Hoogstraat and the Paalhuis of 1560 by the Nieuwebrug on the Damrak. In Edam the Weeshuis had a scrolled front gable of 1558: Hitchcock, *Scrolled Gables*, figs. 37, 40, 44.

At Schloss Frens, which is to the west of the Rhine at Horrem between Cologne and Jülich, the big gable at the north end of the front (Pl. 182) may well be of the mid-1560s.[39] That mediaeval *Wasserburg* was then being enlarged for Adolf Raitz von Frentz, who had inherited the property some years earlier in 1557. This surviving gable, with its elaborate surface-patterning of raised flat bands, certainly resembles rather closely the long-lost one in the court at Horst as known from Freyser's drawing (Fig. 30) more than it does anything at Hovestadt or Schloss Assen (Fig. 31, Pl. 183). In the late seventeenth century this feature was repeated at the other end of the front, while the one over the entrance in the center, as also the segmental-headed windows throughout, date from a drastic "restoration" undertaken in 1838-1850. It is perhaps worth noting that there are no square corner pavilions at Frens, the other significant innovation of the sixties at Horst and at Hovestadt.

To conclude this discussion of gable design in the mid-century decades one may hazard the statement that the German development was still autochthonous in the sixties as regards scrolled outlines, but that the elaboration of the surface with raised bands of strapwork may well owe something to the Netherlands, though probably more to engraved plates than to emulation of executed gables in Holland or south of the Schelde. As noted above, Vredeman's *Architectura* appeared in Antwerp only in 1563, but some of the plates carry an earlier date and may well have been available before that as his less relevant *Compartimenta*, published in Antwerp as early as 1556, certainly was. The possibility remains, however, that direct prototypes of the Horst and Frens gables once existed in the Netherlands, or that some even survive which are not accurately datable or even recognized today as of possible international significance by scholars in Holland or in Belgium.

In 1558, just when Rüttger began to rebuild Horst and Ottheinrich called Alexander Colin to Heidelberg, Franz Parr, a son of Giacomo Parr—who was perhaps also born in Milan like his father rather than in Silesia—began construction[40] of the big quadrangular Schloss at Güstrow for Duke Ulrich III of Mecklenburg-Güstrow (Fig. 32). By 1564 his assistant Hans Stroe had largely completed the very considerable

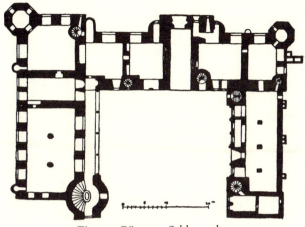

Fig. 32. Güstrow, Schloss, plan

south and west wings that are still extant; the more modest surviving portion of the north wing was built after a fire by Philipp Brandin—he had been working in Wismar over the years 1563-1574 after executing, in Schwerin in the early sixties, one of the alabaster reliefs on the pulpit of the Schlosskapelle there. That late wing at Güstrow dates largely from 1587-1588, but was only finished by Brandin's pupil Claus Midow (†1602); the north gable carries the still later date 1599. Brandin and Midow both came originally from the Netherlands.

The window-ordonnance is somewhat irregular and the organization of the elements at the southwest corner markedly asymmetrical; yet far more than the Schloss at Horst, that at Güstrow recalls a French chateau of the mid-sixteenth century. Indeed, despite the absence of pavilions except in the center of the west front this massively articulated pile of stuccoed brick (Pls. 188-189) even suggests French work of the seventeenth century by its great height, its stony detailing and its generous fenestration. In fact, however, there is not much here that is specifically French in origin; far more of the elements of Parr's very personal vocabulary are generically Italian, even Italian Mannerist; and at least one prominent feature, the gable at the right hand end that is overlapped by the octagonal southwest corner turret, is distinctly Germanic, not to speak of the turret itself.

Above all, Parr's work at Güstrow, lately very thoroughly restored both outside and in, has a spectacular character because of its great height over-all—four-and-a-half-storeys on the exterior, though only three in the court—as well as the broad pavilion rising high above the tall main roof on the front. Moreover, two

---

[39] Klapheck, *Schloss Horst*, pp. 233-240.

[40] DKD, *Mecklenburg*, pp. 370-371; Piltz, *D.D.R.*, pp. 83-84. Knox, *Poland*, p. 56, states that Franz—or, as he calls him, Francesco—Parr worked for King John III of Sweden in Uppsala and Stockholm but gives no details.

good-sized towers punctuate the southwest and north-west corners on the exterior and two more stand at the eastern ends of both the southern and the northern wings in the court. Even more exceptional is the bold-ly plastic detailing of the varied sorts of rustication in stucco that covers all the wall-surfaces. Finally, an accumulation of fantastic chimneys—these with an especially French look, though *François Ier* rather than *Henri II*—breaks through the slopes of the main roofs. Even the single gable at the south end of the west front, moreover, is rather spectacular by the modest standards of previous decades and, in its own way, as premonitory of those still to come in the later years of the century as the ones at Horst and at Frens, which must be almost precisely contemporary.

With a monument of the size and complexity of Schloss Güstrow it is hard to know with what aspect a more detailed description should begin. In terms of style, and presumably of actual construction, there can be little question that the earliest portion of the Schloss is the lower two storeys of the arcaded loggias of four bays (Pl. 186)—doubled in the somewhat later trabeated range at the top—that occupy the western half of the south wing on the court side. These could almost equally well have been built twenty years or so earlier and, indeed, the arcade in the court of the Schloss at Brzég (Pl. 135) must have been rather similar. The construction of the corresponding section of the exterior on the south probably came next, or else that of the top storey here and the great round stair-tower that rises to the left in the court. That tower must have been intended as the central feature of this side. No trace of any loggias survives beyond it to the east, however, nor were they probably ever built even though excavation has revealed surviving foundations. This second campaign presumably followed a bit—perhaps even a good bit—after the completion of the lower loggias, for both the outer facade and the tower display a wholly different and far more advanced approach to design. The former may be described first though there is no actual evidence construction here preceded that of the tower.

On the exterior of the south wing of Schloss Güstrow (Pl. 188) six bays, somewhat irregularly spaced, range between two very narrow semicircular projections rising the full four-and-a-half-storey height to a heavily bracketed cornice. The special sort of fenestration introduced in this area was continued with only slight modifications around the southwest face of the round tower on the court side and the inner facade of the west wing also, though in the court there are

only three storeys. On the outer side facing south, below the level of the court and of the bridge leading to the main west portal, there is, first, a relatively tall plain base capped by very heavy moldings and then what amounts to a storey and a half of extremely bold rustication, each molded block of which has at its center a projecting horizontal batten. Cutting irregularly across the rusticated blocks are small rectangular windows, some of them coupled vertically. Within molded frames in high relief, these windows have both jambs and lintels decorated with miniscule cushion-like rustication quite out of scale with the rustication of the rest of the wall-surface.

At the bottom of the next storey on the south front at Güstrow a heavy band of spherical bosses, set in a chain-like succession of molded and linked squares and much better related in scale to the treatment of the wall below, reaches to the sill-level of what must here be considered the ground-storey windows. These, again, are set within molded rectangular frames, but the actual openings have jambs of much larger rounded rustication carrying not lintels but segmental arches. The voussoirs of these arches are edged on the south side of the Schloss with flat projecting fillets and on the west side with clusters of moldings. The strips of wall between, narrow on the south, much broader on the west where the windows are more widely spaced, are occupied by shallow sunken panels. These are rather plainly framed on the south, but have heavier moldings around them on the west.

Again there follows, between the cornice over the ground storey of the exterior of Schloss Güstrow and the continuous sill of the first-storey windows, a frieze-like band filled with a flat pattern resembling a horizontally stretched Greek fret. This accords in scale with the flat rustication of the whole wall at this level, not the bolder treatments of wall-surface and window-frames on the storey below. The windows again have segmental-arched tops with voussoirs that are here part of the all-over rustication, and there are also narrow ringed roll-moldings outlining each opening. The irregularity of the window-spacing on the south front reflects the internal subdivision of the ground storey (Pl. 188) behind the loggias. A large hall occupies the four evenly spaced western bays with a smaller room, lighted by the narrow paired windows, to the left side of the semicircular projection framing the major portion of this front.

In the second storey at Güstrow the segmental-topped windows have the same small roll-moldings, but the surface of the wall is not rusticated. Instead, narrow rectangular panels of varying width rise from aprons below the continuous sill to the architrave at the base of the entablature. Into that their molded frames are in this case mitered. Within these panels are very shallow arch-topped niches. Unlike the deeper ones at Heidelberg and Horst, however, these provide no perches for statues.

It may be supposed that the extraordinarily rich and plastic vocabulary of the wall and its openings on the Güstrow Schloss was first proposed in a preliminary project and then gradually modified, as the work proceeded through the early and mid-sixties, first on the south and then to the west. One minor motif already present on the south front, though still in rudimentary form, is a very modest order of Tuscan half-columns at the top of the semicircular projections. This is rather awkwardly related both to the panelling on the rest of the top storey and to the very heavy modillioned cornice above. Such an order is repeated more appropriately at each angle of the octagonal towers on the southwest corner. Similar freestanding colonnettes, here carrying segmental arches, are also introduced at this level at the head of the round turret occupying the reëntrant angle on the west front and beside the gabled projection at the right hand end (Pl. 189) as well as on the other two turrets which flank the central entrance pavilion.

The corner towers, the southwest gable and the central pavilion of the Güstrow Schloss all include a second order over the Tuscan one, in this instance Corinthian and with curious clusters of bosses at the base of the shafts. This rather Netherlandish note might indicate another hand than Parr's, very likely Brandin's. On the attic above the main cornice colonnettes are clustered: in threes at the angles of the southwest tower; in pairs on the northwest one; in threes and fours, alternating with single ones, on the lowest stage of the gable; and in pairs, with one additional threesome, over the wide wall-section of the central pavilion. Topping this rather fussy and underscaled terminal order, however, the broad entablature is much more "correct" in its detailing than the main cornice below. Was this also added, one wonders, by Brandin or even Midow?

However that may be, the attic stage at Güstrow is flanked by coarse and muddled scrollwork that is unworthy of Parr yet not at all consonant with the nearby entablature. Above it the pavilion carries a hip-roof broken by a big clock—probably later—and is capped finally with a blind lantern. The top stages of the gable, already perhaps echoing Floris's *Inven-tien* of 1556-1557, are confusedly elaborated with empty niches, panelled pilasters, bits of strapwork, scrolls, balls and rusticated obelisks. As a result the gable is even more out of character with the dignity of Parr's very personal treatment of the lower walls than the ranges of Corinthian colonnettes just below. The north gable with the date 1599 is much more Academic in its organization with regularly superposed orders.

The most original vertical element at the Güstrow Schloss, and not improbably the next portion after the loggias and the south front to be built, is the round tower at the left end of the south facade in the court (Pl. 186). Had the loggias been repeated to the left, this strong focal element would, as has been noted, have been at the center of the facade. Its three storeys, two of them double, are treated like the corresponding ones on the outer facades. Above is a fourth that stands largely free of the high roof of the block behind. The effectiveness of Parr's textured walls is the greater here thanks to the restriction of the openings to one line at the center in the lower double storey and the substitution of circles for rectangular side openings in the lower half of the second double storey.

Unique for this period, moreover, is the boldly plastic treatment of the top storey of the tower, already suggesting the mature Baroque of two generations or more later. On this pairs of Doric columns in the outer wall-plane alternate with half-cylinders on which a sub-order carries blind arches. Above is a circular entablature slightly broken by ressauts. The latter closely resemble the plain uncarved triglyphs, three to a bay, with which they alternate in the frieze, and all these slight projections are here repeated on the under side of the terminal cornice.

Some have seen in this round tower at Güstrow, within which rises an exceptionally generous spiral stair, a reflection of Blois quite as others have at Torgau a generation earlier. However, the elaboration of the top stage below a conical roof carrying a plain blind lantern recalls rather Chambord. That had only been completed a few years before this, though it was begun in the 1520s. Rather than assuming any influence from either of the Loire chateaux of Francis I, Parr's real inventiveness should be recognized here in shifting from the plastic surface treatment of the lower storeys—the more telling on the tower because of its convexity—to articulation of the mass itself in the terminal stage (Pl. 186).

The entrance pavilion on the outside of the Güstrow Schloss facing towards the west is much less successful in its complex plastic organization. As in the composition of the western front as a whole (Pl. 189), the asymmetrically paired entrance arches are more markedly at odds with the basic *parti* than any feature of the south front. Moreover, the minor modifications of the wall-patterning earlier used on the south front are surely no improvement. In the ground storey of the entrance pavilion the very large, flat, rusticated blocks emphasize the disparity between the two openings, one wide, one narrow, yet they do not accord any better with the more nearly standard treatment of the wall-surface in the next two storeys. Further, either the narrow porch-like bays that frame the rather plain center or the flanking round turrets seem redundant.

It is hard, moreover, to associate with the designer of the very severe first storey of the Güstrow Schloss—still Parr?—who presumably determined the generous size and wide spacing of the windows in that and the one above, the amateurish eclecticism of the elements grouped on top of the main cornice, which must be due to Brandin or perhaps Midow. There only the plain hip-roof, rising above the clutter of colonnettes, scrolls and conelets, repeats once more the suggestion, not of contemporary but of seventeenth-century France, in contrast to the equally anachronistic suggestion of Baroque Italy in the top stage of the round tower in the court (Pl. 186).

Even more than in Krebs's Johann-Friedrichs-Bau at Schloss Hartenfels in Torgau, one must recognize Parr's independence at Güstrow—if not so much that of his associates and successors—of most current German architectural trends. It is hard, all the same, to see any relation to such Milanese work of the early or mid-sixteenth century as he might have known in his youth. The architectural quality of Schloss Güstrow should not be measured in terms of hypothetical influences from here or from there but rather by the remarkable vigor of the original designer's personal expression. Yet here, as at Torgau though perhaps less fully, that personal achievement does still accord in a general way with some important aspects of contemporary stylistic modulation in Germany, indeed in Europe, as that was briefly described earlier in this chapter. Where there are apparent disparities here, these might be interpolations by a brother of Franz,[41]

who is known to have assisted in the interiors by executing the *stucchi* on ceilings or possibly, as already suggested, much later emendations of the years 1587-1599 when the north wing was rebuilt and the east wing completed by Brandin and Midow.

The next extant Schloss of consequence, the Heldberg[42] above Heldburg, a seat of the Wettin dukes of the Ernestine line, was considerably more modest in extent and far less original than the Güstrow Schloss. In Saxony, all the same, where the new work at Heldburg—lying to the west of Coburg, though today in the D.D.R. (East Germany) and inaccessible—rose in 1560-1564, a longer tradition of Renaissance design existed than in Mecklenburg. Nickel Gromann, the architect employed by Duke Johann Wilhelm, already had behind him a more considerable *oeuvre* than Franz Parr, at least as the latter's career is distinguishable from that of his more productive father Giacomo Parr. Instead of the brick construction of the north, with all detail carried out either, as at Wismar, in terra cotta or, as at Güstrow, in stucco, freestone was readily available at Heldburg for carved decoration including figural reliefs. The result, therefore, is rather more consonant with the Ottheinrichsbau than with anything of this date or earlier to the north. The local material used, however, does not resemble the red sandstone of Heidelberg but is of a lighter and more neutral tone.

The existing group of structures of the Heldberg, on a fortified hilltop rising over the town of Heldburg, owes its extremely picturesque silhouette more to restorations and additions made in 1875-1876 and 1897-1898 than to its mediaeval and late seventeenth-century elements. But the most considerable surviving portion, extending along the greater part of the long southeast side of the court is still, even as it was restored in the last quarter of the nineteenth century, one of the most coherent facades of the early 1560s (Pl. 190). Though the work of Gromann, a German, this palatial wing, supplementing the addition of more

---

[41] More probably Christoph Parr than Johann Baptista. It was the latter, however, who built the Schwerin *Schlosskapelle* where Brandin was employed as a sculptor in the early 1560s. Knox, *loc. cit.*, notes that Cristoforo (Kristoph)

was, like his brother Franz, employed in Sweden, in his case at Nyköping.

[F. Schwarzer] *Renaissanceschloss Güstrow*, Staatliches Museum, Schwerin [1974] is a useful monograph, especially thanks to its many illustrations of the stucco-work on the ceilings. Thanks to a nearly completed restoration Güstrow is in pristine condition today and houses a Museum of the Hunt. See also O. Gehrig, *Güstrow*, Berlin, 1928, pp. 24-30, pls. 22-26 (plan on p. 23).

[42] DKD, *Thüringen*, pp. 337-338. It is impossible to visit Heldburg today because it is in a "gespehrt" (forbidden) area used by Russian forces.

modern living quarters already made to the mediaeval castle in the early sixteenth century, is known as the "Französischer Bau." In contrast to the uncertainties concerning French architectural influence at Horst, this nomenclature makes evident such influence was recognized here from the first. Much as Ottheinrich had done at Heidelberg a few years earlier, Duke Johann Wilhelm—who was Ottheinrich's brother-in-law—evidently was seeking to break with the tradition of the earlier and more authochthonous German Renaissance of Johann Friedrich's time by introducing a new sort of architectural design as yet little understood in the north. Such an aim might perhaps have been more associated by Germans with France than with Italy at this point; indeed, Serlio's later volumes had been appearing in France not Italy in the forties and fifties.

Gromann had, by the sixties, evidently been studying to considerable profit new architectural books arriving in Germany from France as well as from Italy and the Netherlands. Despite the name, moreover, it is Netherlandish influence that is most evident in the design of the Französischer Bau. For the profuse ornament, though carved, it is believed, by a local Heldburg craftsman, Lorentz Scharaff, the sources seem to have been the published engravings of Floris and Vredeman. More notable than the carved ornament is the regularity and symmetry of Gromann's facade toward the court. The two projecting oriels with arched portals in the ground storey are nearly identical and the coupled windows between are evenly spaced in both the first and second storeys. All the windows are similarly pedimented though the pediments over those on the oriels are flatter. The pedimental theme is bolder in the capping of the oriel and recurs again on the end gable. There the coupled windows of the storeys below are repeated in the first and second stages below a broader terminal window and all have pediments.

In addition to the pedimented windows, the oriels on the court facade are articulated by pilasters and entablatures, Ionic in the first storey, Corinthian in the second, that are exceptionally correctly proportioned and detailed for the period. The octagonal turret at the left end with its helmet-like roof introduces, however, a more Northern note. For all the variety in the carved decoration—figural, for example, in the spandrels of the lefthand portal; foliate in those of the one on the right; delicately figural or scrolled in the friezes; but of strapwork that is almost coarse in the panel below the upper-storey windows on the

oriels—the general scheme may be seen as proto-Academic.

In 1564,[43] when the Französischer Bau was approaching completion, the Grünes (Green) or Französisches Schloss was also begun for the duke by Gromann at Weimar. This was remodelled to serve as the Landesbibliothek in 1761-1766 and enlarged twice in the nineteenth century as well. As first completed in 1569 it was, as the alternative name suggests, very similar originally to the Französischer Bau at Heldburg, but of Gromann's work little is now evident. Some of his other late work may be at least noted: the Rathaus at Altenburg (Pl. 234), to be discussed in the next chapter, was built from his designs in these years though without his supervision. The Rathaus of 1573-1576 at Gera (Pl. 248) is attributed to him, but not very plausibly, on the basis of a generic resemblance to that at Altenburg, and so also is the north portal of the one at Gotha. As noted earlier, some alterations of as late as 1580 on the Saalfeld Rathaus (Pl. 70), which was largely built in 1526-1537 it will be recalled, may be of his design but this is not very likely.

No earlier sixteenth-century German had so long and so productive—or, at least, so well recorded—a building career as Gromann.[44] Yet it is very difficult to recognize any consistent line of development from the early work at Torgau and Weimar in the forties to the late work of the sixties and seventies. Historically important as is the Torgau chapel, since that was the first such edifice in Germany to be built specifically for Lutheran worship, the Französischer Bau at Heldburg and the Altenburg Rathaus are his major and most personal works. It is with the period of their construction that he is most significantly associated.

Although the Ottheinrichsbau is, in some sense, the most conspicuous and certainly the best known German work of the third quarter of the century, it is fortunately not typical. But then others among the major productions of its period such as the Schöner Hof of the Plassenburg, to be described shortly, are not typical either. Moreover, several of the most interesting have been difficult of access for the last thirty years because they are in the D.D.R. or even Poland. These include the Fürstenhof at Wismar (Pls. 146-148) and Schloss Güstrow (Pls. 186, 189) in Mecklenburg; the Französischer Bau of the Heldberg

[43] Ibid., p. 407.
[44] Article "Nikolaus Gromann" by H. Vollmer in ThB.

(Pl. 190), the so-called Cranach house at Weimar in Thuringia and Schloss Augustusburg in Saxony—all in East Germany—and the Piastenschloss at Brzég in Silesia, i.e. southwest Poland today. Still others are now so ruined as hardly to be intelligible to the visitor: Schloss Horst in the Ruhr district, for example, or the relevant sections of the Residenzschloss at Dresden.

It is inevitable that the Plassenburg should be compared with the Ottheinrichsbau, even though it resembles the latter very slightly and is far superior to it in quality. More relevant are comparisons to other Schlösser of the same period, particularly several in the D.D.R. that few Westerners, Germans or others, have been able to visit since the 1930s and which, even before that, were not in the repertory of major German monuments well known, at least by reputation, to foreigners. Two of these, Schloss Güstrow and the Französischer Bau of the Heldberg, have just been described.

The Heldberg Veste as a whole is modest in size and the Französischer Bau but a part of the largely mediaeval and nineteenth-century complex. At the Hoher Burg of the Plassenburg, the scale of the new construction carried out in the sixties was altogether grander, as grand indeed as at Güstrow. Despite the elegance of the rather retardataire Early Renaissance loggias at Schloss Güstrow and the originality of the round stair-tower adjacent to them with its plastically modelled top storey, it is not the court there—now incomplete since the demolition of the rear wing as well as half of the northern wing, and always lacking the eastern portion of the south wing beyond the tower—that is most impressive but the exterior, especially as seen from the southwest (Pl. 188) rising above the trees on an open and somewhat declivitous site.

At the Plassenburg the case is the opposite. The massive ranges remain, even with all their modification in the sixteenth century, of a mediaeval sternness externally. This sternness is hardly relieved by the long regular lines of plain two-light windows in the upper storeys of several of the new blocks and the modest scrolling at the edges of some of the gables that terminate the rather low roofs. On the other hand the court, always called the Schöner Hof (Pl. 192), provides an example of Renaissance architecture that is hardly rivalled for consistency of monumental scale in this mid-century period or, indeed, the entire sixteenth century in northern Europe.

The new construction at the Hoher Burg of the Plassenburg extended over a quarter century from the beginning of the rebuilding under the Amberg master-builder Georg Beck in 1559[45] to the renewal of the Hohe Bastei in 1585. But it was in the mid-sixties that the Schöner Hof received the richly carved arcading that, even more than its generous dimensions and its corner towers of varying height, creates for northern Europe an almost unique effect of Renaissance splendor very different from anything sixteenth-century Italy had to offer. After Beck, who initiated the rebuilding, it was Caspar Vischer (†1580)[46] who became the responsible builder-architect late in 1561 —his contract is dated 6 February 1562. Then, in 1563, the stone-carver Daniel Engelhardt, who executed the carving on the piers, spandrels and parapets of the arcading, began his work.

By the time the southern wing was being designed Alberlin Tretsch and his associate, the elder Blasius Berwart, had among others been called on for advice. They had both been busy on the reconstruction and extension of the Altes Schloss at Stuttgart as described earlier and that at nearby Göppingen through the previous ten years, and were also completing at this point the smaller Jagdschloss at Pfullingen[47] outside Reutlingen, all for Duke Christoph of Württemberg. It may well have been these newcomers who proposed surrounding the court with superposed arcades as in the Stuttgart Schloss (Pl. 158). What resulted, however, is much, much handsomer thanks to the carved decoration Engelhardt carried out over the next six or seven years during which the work proceeded (Pls. 191-193). The rectangular piers in the Schöner Hof with their carved arabesques are very different

[45] E. Bachmann, *Plassenburg ob Kulmbach*, Munich, 1967; Reclams *Bayern*, pp. 429-431; Hempel, *Geschichte*, p. 302 (Hempel does not illustrate the Plassenburg at all); A. Stange, *Die deutsche Baukunst der Renaissance*, Munich, 1926 (hereafter cited as Stange, *Deutsche Baukunst*), pp. 113-114.
Georg Beck may have been the "Georg von Amberg" who designed and built in 1532-1533 the east gate of the Schloss at Liegnitz (Legnica) in Silesia: Knox, *Poland*, p. 55, pl. 75; Łozinski-Miłobedski, *Guide*, p. 136, ill. 158.
[46] Caspar Vischer is first heard of at Heidelberg as a witness to the contract dated July 3, 1558, with Alexander Colin, the sculptor from Mechelen who worked on the Ottheinrichsbau. It is possible, but far from certain, that Vischer also worked there; his employment at Heidelberg would doubtless have terminated at the latest by 1561, for Ottheinrich had died in 1559 and his successor Friedrich III was more concerned, because of his proselyting Calvinism, with making Heidelberg a "German Geneva" than with building activities.
[47] Fleischhauer, *Württemberg*, pp. 33-38; 40-42. Göppingen may have been entirely Berwart's work.

from the stubby Corinthian columns used throughout at Stuttgart where, as has been noted, there is hardly any carved decoration at all except for the capitals.

Leaving aside the fortifications and subsidiary buildings[48] at a lower level to the east, some notably earlier and more later, the Hoher Burg of the Plassenburg —the surviving Schloss as distinguished from the preceding mediaeval castle—is the product of successive building campaigns, the first in the 1550s followed by the more important one in the 1560s. The oldest element visible today in effectively unchanged condition, the eastern half of the north side of the court, is still entirely Gothic in style, though it may not be earlier than 1500 in date. The most considerable enlargement carried out before the Hoher Burg was burned by Nürnberg troops in 1554 had been undertaken by the Margrave Albrecht Alcibiades. This included the surviving eastern half of the north wing and the contiguous northern half of the east wing, now masked by the later arcading (Pl. 192). Even more of Albrecht's new construction undertaken in these years was strictly defensive in character, especially that on the slope below his new east wing of the Hoher Burg. He was evidently emulating there the towers and bastions his opponents had had designed and built at Nürnberg in 1538-1545 by the Sicilian Antonio Fuzano. But before the new fortifications could be completed there came the fall of the fortress to the Nürnbergers and its partial destruction by fire.

Despite his name, Albrecht Alcibiades was no more a Humanist than his father Albrecht Achilles. Georg Friedrich, however, who succeeded him in 1557, known to his Lutheran allies as "der Fromme" (the Devout), was very different from Albrecht, who has been described as a sort of German *condottiere*. From the triumphant enemies of his house, which had long claimed to rule them, the Free City of Nürnberg and the prince-bishops of Würzburg and Bamberg, Georg Friedrich somehow obtained damages of 175,000 gulden and a further 82,000 from the new emperor, Ferdinand I, who had just succeeded his brother Charles V in 1555 on the latter's abdication. With these resources he could undertake the transformation of the Hoher Burg into a Renaissance Schloss of which the decoration would reflect his humanistic and astrological interests, if not so much his Lutheran piety[49]

or his preoccupation with alchemy. In general charge of the reconstruction he placed Vischer, who may have worked at the Plassenburg earlier for Albrecht Alcibiades.

In addition to Tretsch and Berwart, who were mentioned above, client and builder had other advisors and associates. These included, from 1562, the Italian specialist in fortifications, Francesco Chiaramella, who had been working at Wolfenbüttel. He may have been one of the "welsche Bauleute" known to have been employed earlier by Albrecht Alcibiades. That could apply also to the master-builder Jörg Stern (†1565) from Bavaria, who was probably Italian by birth since he was sometimes referred to as Stella. In addition, the second son of Alessandro Pasqualini, Johann I (?1535-1580), from Jülich in the west,[50] may have been involved—Alessandro himself had just died in 1559.

Tretsch and Berwart would have supported—if, indeed, they did not propose—the idea of surrounding the court with arcades. However, the form the arcading took and, above all, the profusion of carved decoration had no precedent in their Württemberg work of the fifties and early sixties. Engelhardt, who designed and largely executed the decorative work, had the advantage of some training in Italy, or so it is believed, but he was probably much aided by the local Kulmbach sculptor and painter Wolff Kelner. It was the latter, indeed, who provided the project for the altar in the chapel of the Schloss.

When the new building campaign directed by Vischer got underway in the early sixties the first major enlargement of the existing Hoher Burg was the doubling of the court toward the south after the level of the higher mediaeval court had been cut down to that of the new Schöner Hof. Eventually many different elements were included in the wings surrounding it (Fig. 33). Already, in 1561-1562, the northeast clock-tower was erected to provide an entrance to the rooms built for Albrecht Alcibiades in the east wing some ten years before. Next came the construction

_____

[48] These include Vischer's Zeughaus and Kanzlei, both of 1563.

[49] Georg Friedrich did, however, rebuild in 1559-1568 the fourteenth-century parish church after its destruction by the Nürnbergers in 1553 even though he was laggard in com-

pleting the chapel in the Hoher Burg: Reclams *Bayern*, p. 431.

[50] If Johann inherited anything of his father's command of High Renaissance architectural design, as his brother Maximilian seems rather notably to have done, there is no evidence of it here. Neumann, *Jülich*, pp. 28-29, has little to offer concerning Johann: ". . . wird Leiter des gesamten Bauwesens in den vereinigten Herzogtümer am Niederrhein," —that is, at Kleve und Düsseldorf as well as at Jülich— with no mention of his hypothetical presence at the Plassenburg which may well have been very brief.

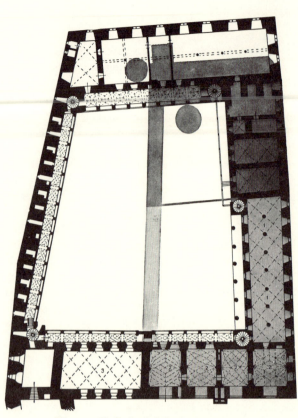

Fig. 33. Kulmbach, Plassenburg, plan

of the wholly new south wing, which is little more than a high screen-wall with open arcaded galleries on the court side (Pl. 192), and the plain southeast corner tower, all this probably in 1563-1564. After that, the east wing was also extended to meet the new south wing at the corner tower and, by 1567-1568, faced with arcaded galleries. Inside that section, the chapel was also completed in the rough by 1568 though it did not receive its Gothic net-vault until 1575. Still later came the west wing, but by 1569 or 1570 the court and its towers must have been effectively finished. All the same, after several years' pause, Vischer undertook before his death in 1580 various subsidiary buildings around the lower court, below to the east, that are unrelated to the Hoher Burg and the Schöner Hof: His *Zeughaus* (arsenal) and *Kanzlei* (chancery), both of 1563, may be mentioned; other work went on considerably later, so that by 1590 Georg Friedrich had spent altogether 237,000 gulden.

As has been indicated, the north side of the court already existed as it is today when Vischer began to work on the Hoher Burg in the early sixties. The left half is quite as plain an example of Late Gothic secular building as is the outside of this portion of the

Schloss. Although the other half is provided in the top storey with identical unframed two-light windows that continue the line of those to the west, there is below a remarkable open arcade, two storeys tall, that survived the war damage of the mid-fifties (Pls. 192-193). Certainly few monuments in northern Europe of sixteenth-century date are comparable to this arcade in grandeur of scale and simplicity of design. Six giant circular piers terminate in heavily molded rectangular imposts into which the top courses of the piers penetrate. These imposts carry arches, only slightly less than semicircular, that are molded back from the wall-plane in a way at once quite straightforward and extremely subtle. The total effect is neither Late Gothic nor Renaissance; it recalls certain round-pillared Romanesque interiors—in Norman England or such an early French church as Tournus, for example—more than anything in Germany.

The giant scale was not maintained further in the Hoher Burg, but a similar early Romanesque simplicity marks the broad unmolded arches of the ground storeys of the south side and the left half of the east side of the court (Pl. 192). The south wing is no deeper than these great barrel-vaulted niches and, as is evident from the almost blank external wall and the very low roof, there are no real interiors at all here, only two open vaulted galleries, one above the other. Still all Gothic internally, these have very heavily molded ribs rising from rather thick crockets to create small net-vaults. The crockets are attached to the wall on the outer side, but on the court side they issue from the square imposts of stubby piers. The curved inner sides of these supports and the plain brackets at the corners of their imposts recall the exceptional detailing of the tops of the much taller piers across the court to the north.

The court front of the arcading that continues across the south wing is treated entirely differently from the earlier arches on the north. The spirit is here quattrocento but the scale is not (Pl. 193). This bolder scale suited carving in freestone in contrast to the delicacy of Statius von Düren's detail modelled in terra cotta on the Fürstenhof at Wismar (Pls. 146-147) and elsewhere of the previous decade. But first one should note the proportions of the arches of the upper arcades, for they are even lower and broader than the plain ones below. This results from the way the rectangular fronts of the supports are handled so that they seem to rise, not from the various floor-levels, but from the tops of the parapets that run along the base of each of the upper storeys. This rather resembles the way the shafts of the columns in the court of the Altes Schloss in Stuttgart, as executed by Tretsch and Berwart, are cut by the railing of the parapets between them. The parapets of the Schöner Hof have no open-work decoration as at Stuttgart; instead, there are ranges of squarish panels boldly carved with more or less Classical heads.[51] The heads, which are framed in the quattrocento way with foliate wreaths and tangled ribands, alternate with rectangular podia and with panels of the same shape that subdivide each bay. These are carved either with mythological figures or with foliate scrollwork.

The panels of the short shafts of the supports in the arcades of the Schöner Hof are hardly taller than the podia below. These shafts and the similar vertical elements rising over them between the spandrels have the same variety of theme, combining or alternating figural and foliate work. The exiguous spandrels are fully occupied by armorial shields and heraldic beasts, and this decorative work is not separated by moldings from the carvings on the intradoses. These, however, are bevelled inward like the molded ones of the earlier arches across the way. The terminal cornice at the top of the second storey is nearly identical with the molded sills and imposts of the ones below.

Engelhardt, or his assistants, must have drawn on a great variety of graphic sources as models for the figural and foliate carving. Yet there is an over-all consistency of character in the depth of the relief and the scale of the otherwise quite unconsonant elements. The strong framework provided by the three ranges of exceptionally broad and low arches is unified by the continuous horizontals of the parapets; moreover, their basic pattern of alternating circular wreaths and rectangular podia is almost as vigorous as that of the arches above. In contrast to this repeated horizontal emphasis the podia, together with the shafts over them and their continuations, provide an equally clear and insistent range of verticals. Thus the two upper storeys with their rich over-all decoration are tightly bound

together visually above the plain ashlar of the ground storey. The interplay between plain and enriched surfaces recalls Spanish architecture of the early sixteenth century more than anything in the north, though the great Elizabethan and Jacobean houses of the later sixteenth century and early seventeenth century in England often have ornate portals, oriels and even arcades set against plain wall-surfaces of brick or stone.

The rebuilding of the Schöner Hof as continued in the mid-sixties around the southeast corner and the surviving series of rooms built for Albrecht Alcibiades in the fifties necessitated some modifications of the basic *parti*. The five bays to the left are almost identical in treatment with those of 1563-1564 on the south side of the court; but the arches, especially the plain ones at the base, are taller (Pl. 192). Moreover, the ground-storey arches are lined up on this side, bay for bay, with those of the arcading, not widely spaced and without such alignment as on the south. The more vertical proportions result from the use of somewhat taller shafts than on the south, just as the jambs of the lower arches also rise a little higher here.

The revised proportions were maintained in the right half of the east side of the court beyond a broad plain strip of ashlar walling like that of the ground storey in the left half of this wing. But in the ground storey here there is an elaborate carved portal, arched and with a sharply pointed pediment. This portal is set almost, but not quite, under the "order" above at the left edge of this section. Several plain windows, rectangular below and arched above, serve the rooms behind. Finally, right against the plain corner of the stair tower that joins this wing to the one on the south, there is a single tall arch. This arch is consonant with the one at right angles to it in the ground storey of the south wing.

On the west side of the court the longest and latest of the new blocks was completed in 1569-1570. On the outer facade of this three regular lines of paired rectangular windows and the unusually broad and low-pitched north gable, striated with horizontal stringcourses, have a rather definitely "modern"—or at least utilitarian—air recalling the facades of the Fuggerhäuser in Augsburg (Pl. 8) as remodelled in 1512-1515. Though this facade is the main entrance front, only the portal near the southern end opening onto a high round bastion has carved ornamentation. On the court side of the west wing, however, eight bays of arcading run unbroken across the upper storeys be-

---

[51] This motif had, of course, appeared very early in the north; Giovanni da Majano's heads of the Caesars in terra cotta on Cardinal Wolsey's Hampton Court Palace are before 1525 and in Germany they were introduced on the gables of the west wing of Ottheinrich's Schloss at Neuburg-a.-d.-Donau (Horn-Meyer, *Neuburg*, fig. 106) less than a decade later. The motif continued long in use, reaching a belated peak of virtuoso profusion on the facade of the so-called Kaiserhaus in Hildesheim of 1586-1589 (Pl. 319) which was unfortunately destroyed in the last war.

tween the two corner towers. The shafts of these towers are of plain ashlar in exceptionally large and nearly regular blocks; thus they frame the arcades firmly at either end. The shafts continue upward the plain walling of the ground storey much as does the vertical area of plain masonry at the center of the ground storey of the east wing.

The western towers are not identical. The tower at the south corner has, like the ones at the southeast and northeast corners of the court, a quite unbroken shaft; but it is topped by an octagonal lantern under a *welsche Haube*. The shaft of the tower on the right —that is at the northwest corner—has somewhat less regular ashlar and is cut by slanted windows quite unlike those of Unkair's stair-towers (Pl. 51) to light the spiral stair inside. These windows are rather crudely framed flush with the wall. Probably the lowest portion of the tower was erected much earlier as part of the north wing. Eventually, however, it was carried up two storeys higher than the other three. The upper storeys of the towers are all of a more regular ashlar and separated by bold string-courses. On each face, moreover, the two rectangular windows are surrounded by vigorous but simple architraves in contrast to the flush trim below. Finally, above a heavily molded cornice, comes a big slate-covered "onion." The "onion" here would be the boldest example of this favorite German feature to be erected up to that time if, indeed, the capping and the rather Academic crowning storeys immediately below were carried out in the late 1560s. More probably they are considerably later in date, nearer the time when Georg Friedrich was having Gideon Bacher heighten the west tower of St. Gumbert at Ansbach in the nineties, or even toward the end of his long life when he was completing the fortifications at Wülzburg.

Though the roof of the west wing of the Schöner Hof is not high-pitched, as has already been noted, the depth of the block is such that its crown rises to the level of the top of the shafts of the flanking towers. In response, perhaps, to the resultant change in the proportions of the court facade on this side, the upper arcade here was slightly heightened by prolonging the shafts of the supports between the parapets and the imposts. The lower arcade, however, is identical in its dimensions, as also in the character of its decoration, to those on the south wing as erected—though not necessarily carved—by 1564. One may assume, therefore, though without documentary support, that the construction of the west wing began soon after

the completion of the earliest arcades on the south side. The carving throughout, however, may well have advanced at a somewhat different pace, perhaps with less of a lag than the building dates indicate.

The ground storey of the west wing facing on the court, though largely of plain ashlar, is somewhat cut up by existing openings and by traces of earlier ones. The dominating feature, however, as at the east end of the court across the way, is a richly decorated portal. Like the other one, this is placed quite without regard to the rhythm of the arcades above, opening where the passage comes through from the main external portal. The arch of this portal is very similar to those of the arcades above, with the same broad and low proportions; but here fluted half-colonnettes, of a crudity surprising for the late date, rise over the imposts, while figural sculpture flanks the armorial panel above. On top of that a semi-hexagonal cartouche, with cut and rolled edges already in the new Northern Mannerist taste, overlaps one podium and one rectangular panel of the parapet above, a casual juxtaposition that recalls German work of as much as fifty years earlier.

The relative unimportance of the gables and even of the portals here at the Plassenburg on the one hand and, on the other, the consistent employment of arcading set this remarkable monument apart from most German Renaissance work both of earlier and of later date. The use throughout of ornament not only mostly of North Italian quattrocento character but applied in a quattrocento way and the absence, except as a minor detail of the portals, of orders either in columnar or pilaster form might lead one to consider the Schöner Hof retardataire. Yet the large scale —not only in the relief of the carving but in the dimensions of the structural elements—is more consonant with the new aspirations of the third quarter of the century as they were finding varied expression in the Ottheinrichsbau, at Güstrow and on the Heldberg than with anything of earlier date. Comparison of the Schöner Hof with the two fronts of the surviving wing at Horst, moreover, make evident that it is with the outer facade there, on which the carved work (Pl. 184) was undertaken by Wilhelm Vernukken (†1607) on a contract of 1564, and not the inner ones toward the court carrying the dates 1559 and 1560 (Fig. 29, Pl. 180) that the Plassenburg belongs. Despite great differences in detail, the bold scale also recalls Schloss Hovestadt (Fig. 31, Pl. 185) which was begun in the same year—1563—as the south wing. But it is as a unique work, quite outside the general line of development of the German Renaissance, that the Hoher Burg of the Plassenburg should be appreciated, deserving at the least the renown long enjoyed by Ottheinrich's work of the previous decade at Heidelberg.

The years during which Erich II of Brunswick-Calenberg re-erected the Schloss in Hannoversch-Münden after the fire of 1561,[52] which destroyed that timber-built town at the head of the Weser, corresponded almost exactly with Georg Friedrich's construction of the Schöner Hof of the Plassenburg. Erich had spent much of his earlier life in the southern Netherlands in Antwerp and at the viceroy's court in Brussels. He also possessed estates in the Netherlands himself and had travelled widely in France, in Italy and even in Spain. This extensive foreign experience might lead one to expect his new Schloss would be at least as cosmopolitan in character as the project on which a Dutch architect and a French sculptor were both working for Rüttger von der Horst in these years of the early and mid-sixties, if no rival in grandeur to Georg Friedrich's Plassenburg.

From a letter written in May 1562 from Woerden, his castle in southern Holland, it is known that Erich was sending Netherlandish, presumably Dutch, builders to Uslar.[53] That lies well to the north of Münden toward Hotten, where a Schloss was also being built for him. On this he was employing a Spanish architect recommended by the viceroy of the Netherlands, Philibert of Savoy. The combination of alien architect for one project and alien workmen for another suggests that Uslar must have been exceptional in the Germany of around 1560, as exceptional as Horst, but even less survives. In the scant remains of the Uslar Schloss there can still be seen, however, a pedimented window-head with a pulvinated frieze (Pl. 194) and a niche-head in the form of a shell above a tablet with the date 1559. All of this is of exemplary High Renaissance character, with no trace of the new Brabantine ornament just becoming available for emulation in published engravings.[54]

Some of Erich's Netherlandish workmen went on

from Uslar to Münden as well as forty German masons. It may be assumed that construction proceeded rapidly there in the years down to 1566. As late as 1572, however, Erich was still sending craftsmen of various sorts, including painters and stone-carvers, to work on the Münden Schloss. The dates on two chimneypieces. 1562 and 1574, seem to bracket the building campaign. The frescoes in the interior of Old Testament and Antique heroes in a painted architectural framework probably date from the early seventies, some ten years after reconstruction began.

The results of Erich's activities at Münden, it must be admitted, are disappointing today because of the remodelling of the east wing of the Schloss in 1788 and the destruction of the southern wing by fire in 1849. The extant north wing (Pl. 195) rises high above the bank of the Werra, just before it joins the Fulda to form the Weser, with four predominantly regular ranges of eighteen tall rectangular windows set close together. These are unframed but subdivided by stone mullions and transoms in a manner originally perhaps more Dutch or French than German, though by no means uncommon in Germany by this date. But their similarity to English windows of Elizabeth I's time must be coincidental.

Only the portals at the base of the stair-tower of the Münden Schloss on the court side and the two pairs of windows above them retain their enframements. Though the detailing of these openings is more up to date in character by international standards and somewhat better proportioned than that of most German work of the sixties, neither the rather squat arches nor their jambs and archivolts, banded by alternately plain and diamond-bossed blocks, suggest definite French or Dutch influence, much less that of the ornament of Floris and Vredeman.

As so often in sixteenth-century Germany most of the architectural interest of the Münden Schloss is above the line of the eaves; there is little attempt to provide the newer sort of plastic interest on the surface of the lower walls except for the framing of the windows over the portal. The west gable of the north wing is the principal feature (Pl. 195), yet even this is asymmetrically fenestrated. Moreover, it reflects the advanced design of the surviving fragments at Uslar (Pl. 194) only in the architraves and pediments of the side windows in the lowest stage. That stage is framed, however, with concave and convex C-scrolls linked by short vertical members. In the next stage, above a rather heavily molded string-course, oculi flank a plain central window similar to that in the

---

[52] Kreft-Soenke, *Weserrenaissance*, pp. 251-253.

[53] *Ibid.*, pp. 284-285.

[54] However, a new decorative treatment for carved stonework known in German as *Kerbschnitt-Bossensteine*, extremely popular both in Germany and in the Netherlands from the 1570s onward, was used here, it would seem, for the first time: Kreft-Soenke, *op. cit.*, pp. 291-302. The term may be rendered in English as "chip-carved blocks" or just "chip-carving."

lowest stage and to the ones in the walls below. To frame the second stage only the short vertical elements and the concave C-scrolls are repeated at the edges of the gable. The tiny top stage concludes with a plain pediment on which stands a human figure, and other such figures flank the base of the second stage. Beside them urn-like finials punctuate the outline of all three stages. There is some over-all resemblance to Dutch gables of the 1550s, but even in the Münden context that is hardly convincing evidence of actual Netherlandish influence. These fit much better into the autochthonous line of development of the scrolled gable in Germany.

There are no large cross-gables at Münden, only a range of stone dormers. Their relatively small size might be a belated reflection of those of Francis I's time on the Loire chateaux; they are hardly to be considered Netherlandish though such are to be seen on Huis Twickel, at Delden in Overijsel, dating probably from 1551. On them the lower rectangular stages each contain one window lined up with every third window in the lower wall; then, above a sort of attic, the terminal stages are flanked by scrolls and capped by small pediments alternately pointed and semi-circular.[55]

In size and elaboration a much more important Schloss than that at Münden is the one remodelled and extended from 1558[56] onwards at Neuenstein in Hohenlohe which lies between Heilbronn and Schwäbish-Hall. The work was undertaken by Balthasar Wolff (†1564), then the city-architect of Heilbronn, for Count Ludwig Casimir of Hohenlohe-Neuenstein, though what survives is by no means all of this period. Indeed, extensive and conspicuous later work has made it difficult to judge what is really of Wolff's design. Ludwig Casimir's son Philipp toward 1600 employed Heinrich Schickhardt from Stuttgart here and probably others as well. Then, in modern times, a first restoration was begun around 1870 and a more drastic one, including a good deal of new construction in sixteenth-century style, was undertaken by Bodo Ebhardt in 1906. The most striking features of the exterior—the court is very small and still mostly mediaeval—are the many boldly scalloped gables, big and little, and the open gazebo-like edicules on the

tops of the mediaeval round towers that flank the entrance, a motif probably unique in Germany. All these would be the work of Schickhardt rather than Wolff, though probably not untouched by Ebhardt. On the other hand, the grand vaulted kitchen dates back to the early fifteenth century.

That Wolff's work, all the same, was very considerable the recorded figure of 80,000 gulden spent by 1564 sufficiently indicates. The Neuenstein Schloss as a whole, incorporating as it does various earlier and later elements, is irregularly quadrangular in plan (Fig. 34). Four round towers on the northwest, south-

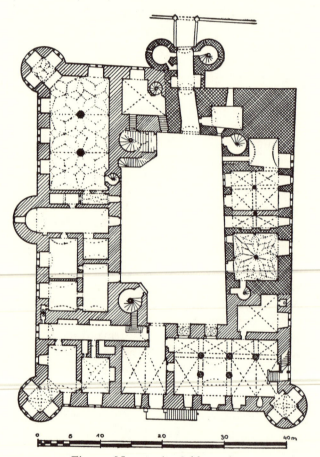

Fig. 34. Neuenstein, Schloss, plan

west and southeast corners echo the Romanesque pair by the entrance at the north end and another rises halfway along the western side (Pl. 197). The present windows, mostly paired rectangular lights as plain as those on the outer sides of the Plassenburg, would appear to be of this present century or the last. However, they doubtless follow Wolff's in their design, if not in their present profusion and relative regu-

[55] The chip-carving introduced at Uslar is used in the Münden Schloss to band the chimney where it protrudes above the main roof: Kreft-Soenke, *op. cit.*, fig. 243. Dated 1565, this is still a very early example.

[56] Dehio, *Baden-Württemberg*, pp. 343-344; Reclams *Baden-Württemberg*, pp. 373-374.

larity of spacing. Atop the second storey of the main body of the Schloss come Schickhardt's gables. However, there is a rather different sort of gable on a lower subsidiary block to the southeast (Pl. 196). Capped with a terminal lunette and outlined by convex scalloping in six steps on either side, this may indicate how Wolff's gables on the Schloss itself were originally treated. Yet the gable in question actually looks to be still earlier. It may perhaps be a part of the work undertaken before the mid-century by Count Albrecht III (†1551) who continued the enlargement of the mediaeval castle his father Kraft VI had begun.

Horst, as carried forward by Joist de la Cour in the late sixties and seventies; Güstrow, when Parr's work there came to an end in 1564; the contemporary enlargement of Neuenstein by Wolff in much the same years and, above all, the Plassenburg as rebuilt and decorated by Vischer and Engelhardt in 1561-1569 were all very large projects, undertaken for great princes or, in the case of Horst, a rich and powerful functionary. Even Hovestadt and Hannoversch-Münden were originally of rather considerable size, not to speak of Assen. Far more modest, but distinctly more advanced than any of these, is Schloss Rheydt as rebuilt for Otto von Byland, a neighbor of Duke Wilhelm V of Kleve in whose circle at Jülich he had an influential position. Construction of the *Vorburg*, the outer works, probably began in the 1550s,[57] contemporary with the building of Albrecht Alcibiades's fortifications at Kulmbach, but on this flat moated site they are quite different. This rather plain and in part poorly preserved Vorburg may have been by Alessandro Pasqualini or, if it dates from after his death in 1558, by one of his sons as was suggested earlier.

Schloss Rheydt is located on the west side of the Rhine, in the present-day state of North Rhine-Westphalia, just outside Mönchen-Gladbach to the southwest of Düsseldorf. Though it is perhaps rather less important historically than several of the Schlösser of the late fifties and sixties already discussed, all the same, thanks to excellent maintenance as a museum by the city of Rheydt, it is considerably more attractive than the grimy ruin at Horst or ill-kept and half-demolished Hovestadt.

The builder-architects responsible for the various parts of the Schloss complex at Rheydt are less certainly known than they are at Horst or Neuenstein. None of the work at all resembles anything known to be by Joist de la Cour though the outer fortifications were—one must believe mistakenly—long ago attributed to him by the Dutch chronicler Arnoldus Buchelius. Joist was certainly not responsible, as Buchelius also states, for the Zitadelle at Jülich. But the residential portions of Schloss Rheydt, forming a roughly T-shaped block set sidewise, are considerably later. It does not seem too presumptuous, considering the resemblance of certain features here to the north and east wings at Jülich and recalling Byland's connections there, to suppose—as hypothetically for the earlier Vorburg—that the designer of the outer front, which carries on its windows the dates 1567 and 1569, may have been one of the Pasqualinis. This could have been Alessandro's elder son Maximilian (1534-1572) or possibly his other son Johann (†1580/1581), the one who is recorded as being employed at the Plassenburg in this decade. The court front, with its open arcade, is dated much later by surviving accounts for the years 1580 and 1581 and may for the moment be ignored.

The rather irregular rectangle of the transverse wing at Rheydt, with a half-round tower near its center and an arched entrance passage cutting through at the right end, was a survival. All this is mostly of fifteenth-century construction, as are also the heavy non-parallel walls and the half-round tower of the end block on the left and its extension to the rear (Fig. 35). But the windows in the stretch on the right of the front (Pl. 198), despite the unevenness of their size and spacing, have the same trim as those of the projection on the left which was presumably built new in the late 1560s. The treatment of this projection provides a most remarkable architectural composition of a sort that had so far been paralleled in Germany only in the work of the Italians from Mantua at Landshut and that of the Pasqualinis at Jülich. Yet the impression it makes today is more French than Italian because of the relatively high hip-roof and the single stone mullions and transoms of the windows similar to those in the tall unframed openings at Münden.

A plain base rises out of the moat at Rheydt on the lefthand wing up to ground-storey level. This base supports an order of engaged columns standing on panelled podia. The order, which flanks the three windows on the front and also the two on each side, is conventionally Doric as regards the capitals and the entablature; what is remarkable is the very elabo-

---

[57] F. Graf Wolff Metternich, *Schloss Rheydt*, Rheydt, 1952; D. Herkenrath, "Schloss Rheydt," *Rheydter Jahrbuch für Geschichte, Kunst und Heimatkunde* (4) 1961.

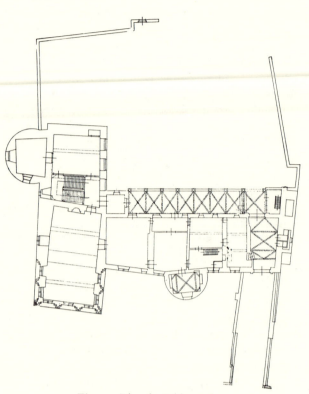

Fig. 35. Rheydt, Schloss, plan

rate treatment of the shafts of the columns, recalling De l'Orme's "French order" on the Tuileries. Ressauts treated as triglyphs break the line of the entablature over the columns and carry small carved figures set against the plain wall of the upper storey. These features, however, only provide a portion of the articulation on the surface of this block. Even more characteristic of advanced taste in this decade in Germany and elsewhere in the North, but rarely so much elaborated, are various other elements. Rectangular members—actually panelled half-pilasters—supported by their own half-podia flank the engaged columns and serve also, with Mannerist ambiguity, as frames at the sides of the windows of the lower storey. Each of these windows is capped, as are also those in the upper storey and along the wing on the right, by a low but boldly projecting pediment carried on scrolled brackets. These pediments are far more correctly proportioned than those of a few years earlier on the Französischer Bau at Heldburg (Pl. 190). Carved heads in the round occupy the fields of all the pediments. Further brackets, set quite closely, provide support for the architrave of the incomplete entablature; this last has a plain frieze but no cornice other than the eave of the hip-roof above.

There is considerable disparity between the plastic articulation of the ground storey of the left-hand wing at Schloss Rheydt and the broad surfaces of plain wall between the quite unmolded frames of the upper windows and those in both storeys to the right (Pl. 198). Moreover, the exceptional density of the composition of the lower storey, equalled up to this point only at Hovestadt (Fig. 31, Pl. 185), is enhanced by the color contrast between the plain stucco of the unarticulated wall areas and the darker tone of the stone trim, not to speak of the special treatment of the shafts of the engaged columns, best described as a sort of imbrication. This bichromy at Rheydt is further evidence of a response to advanced international taste.

So also what can be considered the Classicism of the heads in the pediments and even more of the bucrania flanked by triglyphs in each of the sections of the frieze above at Rheydt, combined with the contrasting fussiness of the decoration that surrounds the panels on the podia and below the window-sills in between, produce an up-to-date amalgam that, without being really at all Netherlandish, yet seems akin to the more restrained and architectonic aspects of Floris's work. All the same, the general effect remains even more hauntingly French than at Hovestadt—and French of this third quarter of the century. That surely explains in part the recurrent attribution to the Frenchman Joist de la Cour, presumably fully occupied still at Horst, on the feeble evidence of Buchelius's statement which does not even refer to this portion of the work at Rheydt. It may or may not be relevant that the Horst client was Catholic while Otto von Byland was Protestant—as Joist de la Cour may well have been also for that matter.

The other side of Schloss Rheydt (Pl. 199), dating from the early eighties, makes quite a different impression. This is to be explained less by the later date than by the presumption that it had a different designer. In 1570 Wilhelm of Kleve returned to the Catholic faith and there ensued a marked change in Otto von Byland's relations with Jülich. Quite possibly it was now a local builder, leaning on published sources, who carried out this rear facade; in any case Maximilian Pasqualini and probably Johann as well were by this time dead.

The range of round arches of the ground-storey loggia on the court side of Schloss Rheydt are varied at the left by a single semi-elliptical one where the entrance passage comes through from the other side. These arches are carried on columns much slimmer than those engaged in the lefthand wing of the front. Thus the arcade has so distinctly an earlier—rather than a later—air that one might almost wonder if it were not really a work of the fifties, a decade before rather than more than a decade after the wing at the front. Even in the upper storey above the arcade, where the mullioned and transomed windows are not only unframed as on the front but unpedimented, the pilasters—though fluted—barely break the plane of the wall and have podia rising above the line of the window-sills between. As a result there is in their very slight relief nothing of the new sort of surface articulation which is so evident here in the work of the sixties. The curious range of hipped cross-gables, moreover, each broken by a dormer, quite lacks the French flavor of the plain hip-roof over the other front.

Finally, on the court side of Schloss Rheydt most of the accessory decoration lies flat on the wall-plane. Even the heads in wreathed medallions, though as boldly three-dimensional as those in the pediments of the windows on the other front, still recall the same quattrocento models as Giovanni da Majano's at Hampton Court which date from some sixty years earlier. Only the rectangular tablets with their strap-work frames are really up-to-date for the years around 1580. Such detailing could have been copied here by local craftsmen from considerably earlier Antwerp publications: By this time such publications had been distributing models for Northern Mannerist ornament over most of Europe for some twenty-five years as has been recurrently noted in this chapter.

Despite the not uninteresting fact that almost all those who built important new Schlösser or rebuilt, wholly or partially, mediaeval ones in Renaissance guise in the late fifties and sixties were Protestants, there are no surviving chapels that were newly built for Lutheran or Calvinist services in any of them that are of much architectural interest; more often chapels are, indeed, entirely lacking or else mediaeval ones were retained. In some cases nearby Gothic parish churches were adapted for Protestant use and served princes as well as the populace.

That the devout Georg Friedrich included a small rectangular chapel in the extension of the east wing of the Plassenburg in the sixties and seventies has been mentioned. In 1559,[58] however, he had already undertaken the restoration of the fifteenth-century parish church, ruined by the Nürnbergers in 1553, when he was only beginning his work at the Plassenberg.

In this modest three-aisled hall-church with a two-bay polygonal choir, all specifically sixteenth-century character was lost in a drastic restoration of 1877-1878. At Hämelschenburg the Schlosskirche (Pl. 299) of 1563[59] is not included in the Schloss but survives as a modest free-standing structure, without aisles but ending in a three-sided apse, across the road near the farm buildings on that side. Thus it seems a quasi-independent village church, not unlike in its location such English ones as stand next to manor-houses. At Neuenstein the somewhat larger church, also separate from but very near the Schloss, was not built until 1611 after work at the Schloss had been completed.

Quite exceptional for this period is the situation at Augustusburg, located just east of Karl-Marx-Stadt, in the vast Schloss that Moritz of Saxony's brother, the succeeding Elector August, built in 1567-1573.[60] There the chapel, begun in 1569 and consecrated early in 1572,[61] which projects in the middle of the east side, is the largest and grandest of the innumerable interiors (Pl. 201). A church rather than a chapel in size, this is not merely the first edifice intended for Protestant use that is consistently of Italianate design —the Neuburg chapel (Pls. 121, 122), though very advanced in style, is Lutheran chiefly because of the iconography of the frescoes, while by contrast that at Torgau (Pl. 125) is hardly affected by the Renaissance except in its furnishings—but may be considered the first church in northern Europe, whether Protestant or Catholic, other than Pasqualini's very special one at Jülich (Pls. 143, 145) and possibly Chiaramella's chapel at Wolfenbüttel (Fig. 26), to approach at all closely the High Renaissance of Italy.[62]

[58] Reclams Bayern, p. 431.

[59] Reclams Niedersachsen, p. 332. The small interior of the Hämelschenburg Schlosskirche is much cluttered with later north and west galleries; the altar stands in front of the polygonal east end. The elaborate stone font carved with caryatids beside it is dated 1610.

[60] Dehio, Dresden, p. 21; Piltz, D.D.R., p. 475.

[61] Krause, Schlosskapellen, pp. 24-31, plan, p. 25. Van der Meer prepared the plans in 1568 and from these a model was made. The cornerstone was laid in the spring of 1569 and the chapel was consecrated on 30 January, 1572.

[62] As stated earlier the term "High Renaissance" is used occasionally in this book in a rather loose or metaphorical way and usually qualified as "Dutch High Renaissance," "French High Renaissance," and so forth. What Pasqualini built at Jülich (Pls. 143, 145), however, is actually quite close to Bramante despite the late date in the 1550s. The Augustusburg chapel (Pl. 201) is hardly so plausibly "Roman" but more parallel to the interior of Bishop Gardner's chantry in Winchester Cathedral. That presumably dates also from the

The same can hardly be said of the Augustusburg Schloss as a whole, except for its almost totally regular and symmetrical quadrangular plan (Fig. 36). On the one hand, the extreme plainness of the exterior (Pl. 200) sets the Augustusburg well apart from the Ottheinrichsbau, Hovestadt or Rheydt (Fig. 31, Pls. 185, 198, 199) with their plastically articulated walls as well as from the decorative profusion of the Plassenburg arcades (Pl. 193) and the more abstractly

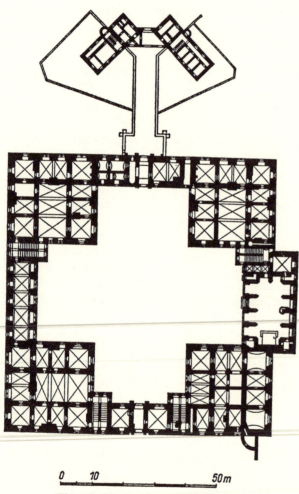

architectonic surface treatment at Schloss Güstrow (Pls. 186, 189). On the other hand, the generous rectangular windows on the outer walls—now, at least, undivided by mullions or transoms—and the almost Roman sobriety of the portals, not to speak of the

0   10   50m

Fig. 36. Augustusburg, Schloss, plan

bold scale of the continuous modillioned cornice, evidence the acceptance of a basic discipline all but unknown up to this point in northern Europe. In hindsight, the massively simple regularity of the Augustusburg exteriors, approaching the plainer sort of Elizabethan architecture of Robert Smythson and his contemporaries, seems more related to the subsequent turn toward the Academic that German architecture would take in the early seventeenth century than a continuation of the almost utilitarian "modernism" of the much earlier facade of the Augsburg Fuggerhäuser (Pl. 8) or that of the outside of the west wing of the Plassenburg, which last must be almost precisely contemporary with the Saxon Schloss.

In making plans for the erection of the Augustusburg Schloss in 1568 on the open flat site of the twelfth-century Schnellenburg—which had burned in 1528 and again in 1547—the original architect of the Augustusburg Schloss, Hieronymus Lotter (1497/1498-1580), mayor of Leipzig in that year, was considerably freer than he had been earlier when designing civic structures (Pl. 163). He could, for example, provide here a wholly regular layout of much greater extent (Fig. 36) than Brachum at moated Hovestadt. Parr may have intended as much at Güstrow (Fig. 32), but lords such as Ludwig Casimir von Hohenlohe who were then rebuilding older Schlösser piecemeal evidently did not have comparable ambitions, except perhaps for Rüttger von der Horst.[63]

[63] Another commission of August's that is of proto-Academic character is Schloss Rottwernsdorf, near Pirna, which he had built as a surprise for his minister Demian von Sebottendorf: *Schlösser und Herrensitze in Sachsen*, Frankfurt, 1957, pp. 17-18; Horst, *Architektur*, pp. 124-125, fig. 93. Dehio, *Dresden*, p. 327, gives little information other than the dimensions, 26 x 10 m., and no authority provides dates, which might be as early as the late fifties, shortly after August's accession in 1556, or as late as the mid-seventies not long before Demian's death in 1579.

A *Herrenhaus* or *Schlösschen* rather than a Schloss in size as the dimensions indicate, the oblong plan of Rottwernsdorf, though irregularly subdivided internally, is all but perfectly symmetrical on all four sides, except that the polygonal stair-tower is not in the middle of the rear: Horst, *Architektur*, fig. 91. Most exceptional are the four identical short wings that project diagonally at the corners recalling a little the diagonal oriel on Rosskopf's Schönhof (Pl. 63). Less exceptional, and something of which the historical significance must depend on the presumptive dating, are the Doric pilaster orders on both storeys of the long fronts; these are repeated, but with fluted shafts, at a higher level on the lowest stages of the gables of the wings and on the elements that link the wings across the ends. At the skyline the character of the architecture changes; the stair-tower is capped with a high

early fifties since he died in 1555. Gardner was a Catholic, which may well account for his relatively "Roman" taste. It was he who married Queen Mary to Philip II.

Lotter had provided the design for the Leipzig Rathaus and also for that at Pegau, respectively in 1556 and in 1559 it will be recalled, but he had not been responsible for their actual construction. Here at the Augustusburg he was assisted from the first by Erhard van der Meer. Van der Meer continued on the job, moreover, under the supervision of Count Rochus von Lynar (1525-1596) after August's dismissal of Lotter in 1572 and was solely responsible for designing the chapel several years before that. Lynar, though of German not Italian parentage, had been born in Tuscany and trained in Italy and France. Like most other Italians—if one may consider him such—who were working in the north at this period, he was employed chiefly on fortifications after arriving from Italy at the court of Francis I in 1542 at the early age of seventeen. As late as 1561-1564 he was engaged in modernizing the fortifications of Metz. Called to Dresden by August in 1569, he continued active in Saxony until 1578 after which he was in Berlin. Unfortunately little or nothing is known concerning van der Meer,[64] though his name suggests he was from the Netherlands.

Several others beside van der Meer and Lynar evidently also played some part in carrying out, and also doubtless in modifying, Lotter's plan for the Schloss, if not the chapel, at Augustusburg. These included Paul Wiedermann, the executant of Lotter's earlier plans at Leipzig and Pegau, and Nickel Hoffmann, an architect active in Halle in the fifties and sixties, who was responsible also in these years around 1570 for the Schweinfurt Rathaus (Pl. 244). Possibly, even,

Gromann who had built the Heldburg Französischer Bau earlier in the sixties and was just completing the Grünes Schloss at Weimar was involved also. To what extent these men made any real contribution except as advisors is, as so often in this period, quite unclear. The executed work certainly has little or no resemblance to their documented production elsewhere.

Whoever may have been the designer or designers in supplement to Lotter, the Augustusburg Schloss is impressive as a whole because of its size and its regularity despite the paucity of intrinsically interesting elements other than the chapel. Indeed the faintly High Renaissance character of the Schloss results more from the absence of both earlier and later features such as quattrocento arcades or Northern Mannerist gables than to proto-Academic elements such as the severe portals and the heavy cornice (Pl. 200). Quite different, however, is the impression made by van der Meer's chapel. Even from the outside the ranges of glazed round arches of the chapel along one side of the court (Pl. 202) provide a generous amount of fenestration that contrasts with the modest and rather widely-spaced rectangular windows used elsewhere. In both storeys lunettes with molded archivolts cap pairs of mullioned lights, while the sunken porch at the entrance, with an arch slightly wider and taller than those of the windows, reveals within a doorway of great simplicity and dignity which is even more Roman than the main portals of the Schloss. That prepares the visitor a little for the special character of the architectonic elaboration inside.

In the interior of the Augustusburg chapel (Pl. 201) double ranges of half-columns, Doric below and Ionic above, are set against the piers supporting the arches on both sides and at the outer end to produce two levels of the Roman arch-order. Though the Doric triglyphs are sparse—one in each ressaut over the columns and one in the middle of each bay—and the lower entablature was considerably heightened to provide a parapet for the tribunes, the general effect is thoroughly cinquecento. Along each side there are four identical bays and two more across the "west" end—the chapel is counter-orientated. At the "east" end, however, an unbroken rectangular space occupies the full width. This is nearly as deep as the regular bays are wide and is covered by a plain semi-elliptical barrel-vault. The vault here is supported at the sides by the Doric entablature of the lower nave arcade which extends all around the interior.

The scale and the simplicity of the squared-off chancel of the Augustusburg chapel prepares one for

welsche Haube that is only slightly Italianate and the gables over the wings at the corners are exceptionally slim and tall, with vertical S-scrolls on two of their six stages.

If Rottwerndorf or Rottwernsdorf—Horst omits the "s"—dates from the late fifties, contemporary with the Ottheinrichsbau, its extreme regularity would be rather precocious; it is much less exceptional if it dates from the years around 1570 when the Augustusburg was in construction. Quite possibly the Italian-trained Count Rochus von Lynar, though chiefly concerned with fortifications, had a good deal to do with the design if not the execution, with no contribution other than, perhaps, the detailing of the gables from Lotter. Lynar entered August's employ in 1569 and did not leave for Berlin until 1579, so that he could have been available to provide Augustus with a design for this Schlösschen in the seventies.

[64] Van der Meer had worked earlier in 1557-1560 at Arnstadt in Thuringia on Schloss Neideck. Of that only the ruins of the east wing and a slim tower 65 m. tall capped by a welsche Haube survived demolition in 1779: DKD, Thüringen, p. 356; Piltz, D.D.R., p. 353.

the roofing of the nave. This is provided by a continuous barrel-vault of semicircular section undivided by transverse ribs. But the surface of this vault carries, rather unexpectedly, a bold geometrical pattern of flat decorative bands totally unlike the inherited Gothic ribbing used hitherto in most sixteenth-century German churches and chapels—exceptions to this, of course, are the chapels at Landshut, at Neuburg and at Jülich where Italian influence was especially strong and, at least at Landshut and Jülich, direct. However, the effect of the banding on the vault here is not Northern Mannerist but in some degree Roman, as if the pattern was meant to represent a kind of coffering. Included in the design on the curved surface of the vault are four open oculi at the haunches on each side. These add slightly to the light that is otherwise so generously provided by the two ranges of windows in the side spaces of the lower storey and in the Emporen; such openings also provide sharp accents in the otherwise regular treatment overhead.

At the two ends of the Augustusburg chapel the infilling of the lunettes under the vault is less consistently Roman than the arcades below. To the "west" two plain low arches are separated by a stubby pilaster and topped with a compressed entablature. This cuts awkwardly at either side into the patterned surface of the vault; with that, the three plain oculi set higher up are more consonant. At the "east" end an open gallery carries the organ of 1758, with two original round-arched windows set in shallow unframed niches in the lunette behind (Pl. 201).

The furnishings in the Augustusburg chapel are of rather different character from the architectural setting. The frame of the large altarpiece at the front of the rectangular chancel, carved in 1571 by Wolfgang Schreckenfuchs (†1603) from Salzburg, is flanked at either side by pairs of attenuated colonnettes with enriched shafts. These carry an extremely ornate entablature above which elaborate armorial carvings flank a tabernacle-like arch that is now empty. The large painting occupying the main frame is by Lucas II Cranach. He also provided the panels on the pulpit, which is dated 1573, This feature interrupts the shaft of the Doric column at the middle of the lefthand side of the nave much as earlier at Torgau (Pl. 125) and again at Schwerin. All the carved work on the altar and the pulpit is polychromed and gilded in contrast to the severe white and grey bichromy of the architectural setting.

The Augustusburg chapel, not surprisingly, follows closely in its ritual organization the one that Luther had consecrated at Schloss Hartenfels some twenty-five years earlier. But here the inherited model was translated by van der Meer into High Renaissance terms to such a degree that the more decorative altar and pulpit, both still in a German Renaissance tradition established as early as the twenties at Annaberg and Halle (Pls. 20, 47), appear quite alien and distinctly retardataire. On the other hand, there is hardly any reflection here of the new current of Northern Mannerism flowing from the southern Netherlands. Rather there is some slight resemblance in the pattern on the vault to the raised decoration used earlier in the sixties by the northern Netherlander Arndt Johannssen and Laurenz von Brachum far to the west (Fig. 30, Pl. 182), but more probably borrowed here from Serlio.

No other wholly new churches, Protestant or Catholic, seem to survive in Germany in original condition from this period. Indeed, except for the chapel at Schmalkalden (Pls. 267, 268), begun in 1586, no Schlosskapelle in northern Europe rivals that at Augustusburg before the one in Slot Frederiksborg at Hillerød in Denmark which was built early in the next century. However, several decorative entities of architectural scale dating from the sixties in German churches already exemplify quite conspicuously the influences from the Netherlands that would be of increasing importance in northern Europe from this time on and well into the next century. In Philip II's time these were likely to be the work of Protestant artists fleeing from the Inquisition in the southern Netherlands.

As noted earlier, it was in 1556 that Maria Wiemken, the *Herrin* (lady) of Jever in succession to her father Edo II who had died in 1511, began to rebuild in this small town, to the northwest of present-day Wilhelmshaven near the North Sea, the local parish church that had burned in 1532. This is an example of the re-erection of an existing independent edifice rather than the inclusion of a new chapel within a Schloss. The simple two-bay choir ending in a five-sided apse survives and is now attached to the striking new church built after a fire in 1959. Inside this choir Maria erected in 1561-1564[65] an extraordinary open edicule that occupies almost the total area in plan and rises in three stages nearly to the wooden vaulting above (Pl. 203). Within the edicule is the tomb of her father. This tomb, as also the setting, was executed it is presumed by the Netherlander

---

[65] B. Schönbohm, *Stadtkirche Jever*, p. 4.

Hendrick Hagart whose initials H H it carries. Hagart, who had been a pupil of Cornelis Floris in Antwerp—or possibly some other northerner of similar training—created here an architectural and sculptural composition more than rivalling in size and complexity, if hardly in quality, the High Renaissance edicules erected by sixteenth-century French kings at St.-Denis as the tombs of their predecessors. Only the cenotaph of the Emperor Maximilian, which his grandson, the Emperor Ferdinand, had been elaborating with attendant sculptures in the Innsbruck Hofkirche since 1553, exceeds the Wiemken monument in the multiplicity of its constituent elements. Floris's own tombs of the previous decade in Germany were of no such size and complexity it should be noted.

Architecturally what is significant about this edicule at Jever is the profuse employment of caryatids as supports in the lower storey and the amount and the relatively large scale of the carved ornamentation. Caryatids also support the tomb-slab and additional ones are set against plain piers to help carry the inner ends of eight wooden beams, detailed as entablatures, that radiate from the freestanding tomb in the center of the choir. The outer ends of these beams, however, are supported by fluted Corinthian columns. The panelled barrel-vaults resting on the beams are of semicircular section over the caryatids but broadened out funnel-wise to a semi-elliptical section over the columns.

Except for the beams of wood, the lower portion of the edicule at Jever is constructed partly of limestone but mostly of black Tournai and white marble, materials that had been popular for Renaissance fixtures in western Germany from as early as the twenties when the Hackeney screen in St. Maria-im-Kapitol at Cologne (Pl. 58) was imported. More significantly—because of the influence such decoration had henceforth—most of the panels of the barrel-vaults, all different, are filled with low relief carving of a new sort of ornament. This resembles that already being transmitted abroad by Floris's engraved plates published in Antwerp, as well as more directly by such pupils and emulators as Hagart, even before the designs in Vredeman's *Architectura* came out there in 1563. There is, indeed, more of this ornament here than on the tombs Floris himself executed elsewhere in northern Europe.

The next stage of the edicule at Jever is a smaller octagon with Classical gods and goddesses, all identified by inscriptions, serving as caryatids below a heavy modillioned cornice. Inside is a very complicated rib-vault made of wood gilded and polychromed. Above the cornice the third and terminal stage of the edicule consists of four freestanding tabernacle-like features elaborated with figural reliefs and much miscellaneous decoration.

This fantastic and belated monument of filial piety at Jever had no influence as a whole. The various motifs from the Antwerp repertory, here profusely exploited for the first time in Germany, were more usually elsewhere the work of Germans dependent on published plates of ornament. All the same, Floris himself had by this time been working off and on in Germany for some fifteen years and Vredeman was a recurrent visitor. In the mid-sixties, moreover, just after the Wiemken tomb was completed at Jever, Floris built for German merchants their Hanseaten Huis in Antwerp,[66] while soon after that he provided the wall-tomb of Duke Albrecht I of Prussia in the Dom at Königsberg (Kaliningrad) in East Prussia where that dated 1549 of Duchess Dorothea, his first German commission, already stood.[67] Floris's tomb of Frederik I of Denmark in the Cathedral of Schleswig of 1551-1555, carved as usual in Tournai marble and alabaster, is much less architectural.[68] The tomb of Christian III of Denmark at Roskilde was carried out by Floris in Antwerp rather later, over the years 1569-1576, for Frederik II.

The Hanseaten Huis, that late parallel in Antwerp to the Fontego dei Todeschi in Venice of two generations before, was unfortunately burned down in 1893. Old views (Pl. 204) nevertheless make evident that, though much simpler, it was not dissimilar to the Antwerp Stadhuis (Pl. 175)—which was, of course, erected in precisely the same years as the Wiemken tomb. It would seem, from the relatively severe style of the Hanseaten Huis, that Floris, at least when

---

[66] The date of the Antwerp Hanseaten Huis is given sometimes as c.1565, sometimes as 1564-1568. Pieter Kraus, Hendrick van Paesschen or Peeter Frans are also mentioned rather than Floris as the responsible builders, and doubtless one or several of them did carry out the work: Gerson-ter Kuile, *Belgium*, p. 178, n. 103. Old photographs exist showing this vast utilitarian edifice in a decrepit condition and almost totally devoid of surviving architectural character.

[67] Osten-Vey, *Germany*, p. 280: Floris's tomb of Christian III of Denmark, dated 1569-1574, is in Roskilde Cathedral. Unlike most of the others, this is freestanding, perhaps because of French influence. That of Albrecht I is more like Andrea Sansovino's tomb of Cardinal Ascanio Sforza in Santa Maria del Popolo in Rome.

[68] Dehio, *Hamburg*, p. 581.

working for Germans at architectural scale, emphasized the more restrained and Academic side of his personal style rather than the Northern Mannerism of his published designs of 1556-1557. This is true also of his tombs in Königsberg, at least as compared with the one by a follower at Jever.

At Jever the splendid coffered wooden ceiling of the Audienzsaal in the Schloss (Pl. 205), begun for the same client a bit earlier probably than the Wiemken tomb but completed in the same year,[69] is closer to Floris's own work in architecture than is the tomb. This ceiling with its simple plan of repeated square coffers separated by deep beams must seem, indeed, to twentieth-century eyes more Italian than Netherlandish in character, and even early cinquecento, so to say, rather than Mannerist.

Another big monumental tomb of the 1560s, more than rivalling the ones by Floris in Königsberg if not quite the one at Jever, is that of the Landgrave Philipp of Hessen-Kassel and his original wife Christina of Saxony—his bigamous second wife died earlier and was buried elsewhere. This was begun by his successor Wilhelm IV in 1557,[70] the year Philipp died, in St. Martin, the cathedral-like principal church of Kassel. The Kassel tomb (Pl. 206) is not freestanding like that of Edo von Wiemken; yet it originally dominated the eastern end of the church all the same, rising high against the central window of the Gothic apse dating from the mid-fourteenth century. In the postwar restoration of the church it has now been installed against another one of the mediaeval windows in the tall north aisle.

The design of Philipp's tomb was prepared and the work begun by Elie Godefroy, a Walloon from Cambrai in what is today northern France. Long in Philipp's employ, Godefroy had also worked for Erich of Brunswick-Calenberg at Münden in the early sixties though his work cannot be identified there. Well before that, however, he was already mentioned in 1557 as "architectus" in connection with the Kassel Schloss. The Kassel tomb is constructed of the characteristic imported materials that were so much used for similar work: black Tournai marble as regards most of the architectural elements and alabaster for the sculpture. The sculpture includes among the various figural elements standing portraits of Philipp and Christina, all that Godefroy himself completed, and a large relief of the Ascension in the center, as also much orna-

mental detail. The following year 1568 Godefroy died and the work was carried to completion in 1572 by another Walloon, a pupil of his, Adam Liquir Beaumont, who modified the design of the upper storey.

Godefroy's lower storey takes the form of a triumphal arch as on several of Floris's tombs. The figures of Philipp and Christina stand in arched niches at either side flanked by fluted Doric columns. The sarcophagus, carved with the Brabant and Wettin arms of the Hessian and Saxon princely houses, is set in a deep niche of rectangular section. On the rear wall of the niche is the relief of the Ascension—from which, since the last war, the figure of Christ is missing; that is flanked by other equally high reliefs at either side. There is very little of the new Northern Mannerist ornament here except, as at Jever, on the coffers of the barrel-vault over the central niche and in the framing of the inscription within the lunette, all more probably designed by Beaumont than by Godefroy. The upper stage, certainly all by Beaumont, is much closer to the Jever tomb, for caryatids take the place of an order above the inner pair of freestanding columns in the lower storey. These carry a projecting pediment on whose top Michelangelesque figures recline. Composite columns frame the reliefs at either side, while figural sculpture at large scale occupies the spandrels of the arch capping the central niche in the lower storey. Obelisks and lions rise above the upper entablature and, still higher, there floats an elaborate polychromed armorial achievement flanked and crowned with figures.

Philipp had been a great Protestant leader before the scandal of his bigamous second marriage, and Maria Wiemken was a Lutheran like most of those for whom the big Schlösser described earlier in this chapter were built. Although he lived until 1592, the Protestant ruler of another princely house, the Welfs, Wilhelm of Brunswick-Lüneburg, never built a new chapel in his Schloss at Celle. Among the various carved grave-slabs in the Stadtkirche there which he commissioned, none compares at all with the elaborate tombs at Jever and at Kassel. Rather, they follow the modest pattern of the ones dating from the time of Franz Otto whom Wilhelm had succeeded in 1559. However, the surviving Gothic chapel in the southeast tower (Pl. 207) of the Celle Schloss was most elaborately refurnished and redecorated for Wilhelm beginning in the mid-sixties. About that time also a large *Fürstenstuhl* (prince's pew) was installed by him at the west end of the Stadtkirche under the organ. The pulpit in the Schlosskapelle, dated 1565, is as Early

[69] Reclams *Niedersachsen*, p. 415.
[70] Dehio, *Hessen*, p. 451.

Renaissance in scale and in most of its ornamental detail as that—actually of a few years later—in the Augustusburg chapel, and consonant work continued in the Celle chapel well into the seventies.

The *Fürstenprieche* (prince's loge) in this Celle Schlosskapelle is carried on segmental arches, running all along the north wall, that in turn repose on heavy molded brackets. There are two galleries also across the west end, one higher than the loge, the other slightly lower. These rest on pairs of broader segmental arches supported by heavy columns. The western galleries and the loge, which dates from 1576, occupy together rather more than a third of the volume of this tiny vaulted chamber. But the loge is as delicate in scale as is the pulpit, if rather more fanciful in detail.

The panels of the parapets of the Fürstenprieche in the Celle chapel and of the galleries as well were decorated in the seventies with carved reliefs of Christ, the Prophets and the Apostles. The panels before the ordinary pews below, however, are filled with miniscule Biblical and allegorical scenes. These are close in style to the painting of the Crucifixtion on the altar, by Maerten de Vos or a follower,[71] that is, probably some years earlier as it carries the date 1569. The great interest of the altarpiece, as already noted, is in the side wings which show the Celle Schloss and the Gifhorn Schloss as of that date and thus provide *termini* for the sixteenth-century construction carried out by Ernst, Franz, Franz Otto and Wilhelm.

Screens of grillwork and glass protect the Fürstenprieche in the Celle chapel and part of the upper gallery to the west. These elements half mask in the former case the fluted and gilded composite colonnettes behind and the very restrained and elegant foliate decoration, also all gilded, on the inner wooden ceiling. Higher overhead, there is barber-pole polychromy on the round ribs of the fifteenth-century vaulting and stars are spattered all over the severies, while from the intersections of the ribs hang jewelry-like pendants of metal terminating in tassels. These seem to be unique today, but may once have existed in other chapels and churches.

This Celle chapel, so dainty in detail and so satiatingly cluttered, is out of key with the more characteristic stylistic modulation of the sixties and seventies as illustrated by most of the major Schlösser

of the period; only the earliest work of 1558-1560 at Horst (Fig. 29, Pl. 180) at all resembles it. It is hard to believe, indeed, that the furnishing, though the work of at least a decade and more, is effectively contemporary with the interior architecture of the chapel in the Augustusburg (Pl. 201). The Augustusburg chapel, however, is manifestly by a trained and experienced designer, whether the designer was van der Meer, Lynar or some other. Even in that chapel, moreover, the altar and the pulpit August installed are not remote from what the painters, carvers and other craftsmen at Celle, working to no over-all architectural scheme one must suppose, carried out piecemeal for Wilhelm much as they might have decorated pieces of elaborate court furniture. One cannot, certainly, recognize here the hands of those who were active on the Celle Rathaus in the sixties and seventies (Pls. 230, 231) whose work there will be discussed in the next chapter.

Indeed, in the Celle chapel the pulpit of 1565, the organ of about 1570, and the screens of the Fürstenprieche, not to speak of the cassone-like panels fronting the pews below, are best considered not as interior architecture but as decorated furniture. Only the massive masonry work of the brackets on the north side, the columns at the west end and the segmental arches of marbled masonry that these carry are architectural in scale (Pl. 207). From the thick proportions of those elements, moreover, one might hazard the guess that they were introduced by Ernst shortly before his death in 1546 or in the next decade by Franz Otto. They certainly resemble in their detailing the corresponding members of the gallery in the Gifhorn chapel (Pl. 129) built for Ernst's brother Franz in 1547.

August of Saxony included, as we have seen, no major sculptural works in his Augustusburg chapel. At Freiberg, however, in the mediaeval Münster, he erected at the crossing a large cenotaph to the memory of his brother the Elector Moritz who had died in 1553. This freestanding monument, the first such in Saxony, was begun in 1563[72] shortly, that is, after the Wiemken tomb at Jever and several years before that of Philipp of Hesse at Kassel. If the Freiberg cenotaph hardly rivals either of these as architecture, it nonetheless includes much ornamental craftsmanship of a high order with which both Italians and at least one Netherlander were concerned.

The general design of the cenotaph at Freiberg was provided by the brothers Benedetto (†1572) and Ga-

---

[71] More particularly, the small Biblical scenes on the parapets would seem to be by de Vos's assistants rather than by Maerten himself, whether or not he painted the altarpiece.

[72] Dehio, *Dresden*, p. 104; Piltz, *D.D.R.*, p. 470.

briele de Thola (†?1569) from Brescia who had been responsible for the painted decorations on the walls of the court in the Dresden Residenzschloss in Moritz's time. From this design a wooden model was made by Georg Fleischer, a Dresdner. The goldsmith Hans Wessel (†1587) from Lübeck supervised the execution, but he assigned the actual work to an Antwerp sculptor, Antonis van Zerroen, casting himself only the brass griffins that support the sarcophagus. Wolfgang Hilliger (1511-1576), who had cast here in Freiberg, the wall-tablet dated 1545 in the Torgau chapel, carried out the bronze crucifix on a model provided by Fleischer.

The monument to Moritz at Freiberg (Pl. 208) rises above a stepped base in three stages and is all of imported black Tournai marble and alabaster like the one at Kassel. On the third step of the base are seated twelve allegorical figures of the Arts and Sciences and on the two set-back stages of the superstructure there are twenty panels filled with inscriptions. In the lower stage these are separated by pairs of Tuscan columns; in the upper stage, between the inscriptions —all framed by scrolls at this level—the arms of the various lands of the Wettins are carved. Above this ten of Wessel's brass griffins carry an empty sarcophagus on which a life-size effigy of Moritz kneels surrounded by angels carrying an hourglass, a helmet, a shield and so forth. Shouldering the electoral sword, he prays before Hilliger's crucifix.

The year before his own death in 1586, August planned a more considerable modification of the east end of the Freiberg Münster. As executed over the years 1588-1594 by his successors from a design of the Italian-Swiss G. M. Nosseni, the remodelling eventually turned the choir and apse into a sort of Wettin pantheon (Pl. 270). In conception, at least, this project—which will be described in detail in a later chapter—was August's. It concluded an exceptionally productive electoral reign in which such church-work as the completion of the Schlosskapelle at Dresden, the erection of that at the Augustusburg and the funerary monument at Freiberg outshone his concurrent secular building activity in Saxony to a degree quite exceptional in sixteenth-century Germany. To posterity, however, August's fame is overshadowed by that of his eighteenth-century descendant, August der Starke (the Strong), who became king of Poland and built a great deal both there and in Saxony.

Of neither August's secular work at Dresden in Saxony nor that of his contemporary, the Wittelsbach Duke Albrecht V of Bavaria at Munich—who suc-

ceeded in 1550 a few years before August—does anything of much consequence survive from the sixties in the extensive remains of the two Residenzschlösser. Construction of the Antiquarium in the Residenz at Munich began in 1569 under the direction of Wilhelm Egckl (†1588), since 1559 Albrecht's electoral *Hofbaumeister* (court architect), from designs prepared by Jacopo Strada (†1588) who came from Milan. However, this was so much modified by Frederik Sustris (1524-1590) in the eighties for Wilhelm V, and so completely redecorated by Sustris's Italian and German associates (Pl. 280), that little need be said about it yet. It is, all the same, already of rather special historical interest at this point. The erudite Strada, in projecting this long, low, barrel-vaulted crypt to hold Albrecht's collection of antiquities—mostly supplied by Strada in his role as agent or dealer—evidently had in mind semi-subterranean Roman chambers. Thus, except for triumphal arches (which were usually only temporary constructions), the Antiquarium is the first instance of the direct imitation of an Antique building-type in the north of Europe. The surviving design for the exterior (Pl. 209), on the contrary, gives evidence rather of Strada's intimate knowledge of Giulio Romano's work at the Palazzo del Te, of which he had made drawings for Albrecht, and his own distinctly Mannerist sympathies. Little, if any, of that design seems to have been executed; none at least survives.

Another building by Egckl, designed by him—not by Strada—and erected a few years earlier in 1563-1567,[73] housed among other things the ducal *Marstall- und Kunstkammerbau* (stables below and Albrecht's collections above). This is largely extant as regards the arcaded court, though the exterior was remodelled and refronted by Andreas Gärtner, the father of Friedrich von Gärtner, at the opening of the nineteenth century for King Maximilian I. The structure, now the *Münze* (mint), stands near the Residenz, a short distance southeast of the Max Joseph-Platz.

The present exteriors of the Munich Münze are extremely simple, with plain stuccoed walls broken only by rows of moderate-sized windows. These may well be merely nineteenth-century replacements of Egckl's. Such simplicity would certainly have been appropriate for a building that housed horses, cows, carriages and a wine-cellar below, even though above there were, in addition to rooms for the display of

[73] Lieb, *München*, pp. 86-87.

works of art, a ballroom, a small chapel and other rooms for the use of the elector's family and their close associates. The architectural interest originally was confined to the court (Pl. 210) as it is still today except for Gärtner's handsome Neo-Classic facade on the front.

Irregularly oblong in shape, the court of the Munich Münze is surrounded by three levels of arcading, with three bays at the ends, eight on the south and nine on the north. If Albrecht and Egckl had a particular model, it must have been Alberlin Tretsch's lately completed court in the Altes Schloss at Stuttgart (Pl. 158); but the segmental arches are even lower and broader here and the columns stumpier except in the top storey. The capitals in that range are rather elegantly Tuscan; those below are of a vaguely Composite sort, however, with volutes at their corners that are almost crockets. The ground-storey arches are faced with smooth rusticated voussoirs, though the ones in the first storey have heavily molded archivolts. Those over the Tuscan columns, however, are quite flat and unmolded. A solid parapet, broken by podia carried on scroll brackets, guards the first-storey gallery; above, there is a balustrade consisting of plain rectangular members.

Despite Albrecht's building activities, Munich's days as a center of advanced architectural design still lay fifteen years ahead, following on the accession of Wilhelm V in 1579. Remembering the Saxon elector's Augustusburg, begun the year after Egckl's Marstall was finished, one might expect more from August at Dresden. Unhappily, both the *Zeughaus* (arsenal) that Melchior Trost, architect of the earlier Residenzkapelle, built for August beyond the stable court of the Dresden Schloss beginning in 1559, and the *Kanzlei* (chancery) of 1565-1567 by Hans Irmisch (†1597)[74] were destroyed by the bombing of 1945, though August's *Jägerhof* (hunting lodge) of 1568 in suburban Altendresden is partially extant.

The biggest and most impressive of these Dresden structures must have been the Zeughaus (Pl. 211), a rather plain, nearly square block with a large interior court. Its sides were long enough to carry four broad cross-gables, widely spaced, though the outer end had only three and the inner but a single one over the principal entrance. Others faced on the court, two on each side and one at each end. Those on the exterior rose above a tall single storey broken at the inner and outer ends by arched portals. These

were flanked by rusticated pilasters and capped with pediments. Ranges of small horizontal openings, set high in the wall, could be solidly shuttered for protection, thus emphasizing the military functions of the Arsenal.

The gables on the Dresden Zeughaus, as usual, were the principal architectural features. They were all of four stages, with the lower two framed by pilaster orders. The first stage was of four bays and each bay held a pair of rectangular windows; the second stage was of two bays and had only two windows. This stage, however, was framed by rather bold vertical S-scrolls; the much lower third stage had in each gable a pair of oculi and, at the edges, smaller S-scrolls under a very short terminal stage outlined by C-scrolls at the sides and topped by a plain pediment. Though broader and with a more regular use of pilasters, these gables of around 1560 were thus quite similar to the ones in the main court of the Residenz Schloss as built for Moritz, chiefly in the late forties (Pl. 131).

The Dresden Zeughaus was completed in 1563. Two years later Irmisch, a pupil of Voigt von Wiegerand just settled in Dresden, began the considerably smaller and less regular Kanzlei on a site nearer the main portion of the Schloss. This was three storeys tall with regular paired rectangular windows like those in the Zeughaus gables. The big gables here on the inner end rose in three stages, the lower two flanked by bold S-scrolls, the third by C-scrolls, and were capped like those in the main court and on the Zeughaus by plain pediments. The lowest stage of the cross-gable at the other end was a continuation of the walls below, while the upper two repeated the design of the end-gables.

The Jägerhof at Altendresden was built in 1568,[75] contemporaneously with the beginning of the Augustusburg, on the site of an Augustinian monastery outside Dresden that had been demolished in 1546. This consists today of only a single low block, the west wing of the original structure, punctuated on the court side by three octagonal stair-towers crowned with *welsche Hauben*. The surviving decoration is confined to the gables at the ends. These are not dissimilar to the ones on the Kanzlei but the scroll-work at the sides of their two stages is much more elaborate. Additions were made to the Jägerhof from 1582 to 1611, to which period the gables may well belong, but most of the sixteenth-century structure was

---

[74] Loeffler, *Alte Dresden*, pp. 404, 411.

[75] *Ibid.*, p. 403.

demolished after 1877 when it became barracks for cavalry. What still exists is now occupied by a Museum of Folk Art.

Some of the smaller Schlösser that followed a few years later after the Jägerhof are, on the whole, of greater architectural interest than any of Albrecht's or August's work of this period in Munich and Dresden. Even more worthy of attention, moreover, are many of the surviving town-houses and civic buildings. Those that date from the sixties and seventies will be described in the next chapter, following on a continuation into the seventies of the account of Schloss-building of the third quarter of the century that has been the principal subject of this one.

Five

LESSER SCHLÖSSER
AND CIVIC ARCHITECTURE,
1560-1580

THE ambitious Schloss-building previously described that was undertaken in the 1560s outranked earlier sixteenth-century secular construction in Germany except for Schloss Hartenfels at Torgau among extant works and the Joachimsbau in Berlin among those which are gone. In the next decade there was much less activity. Certainly no new German Schlösser were erected in the seventies of the size and splendor of Frederik II's Kronborg Slot[1] at Helsingør in Denmark; nor do rivals survive in Germany of such grand English mansions as Burghley House, near Stamford, which Sir William Cecil was still extending at this time, or even the more "prodigious" Wollaton, outside Nottingham, which Robert Smythson designed about 1580 for Sir Francis Willoughby. Building in German towns, however, both private and municipal, was much more interesting in these years than in Denmark or England, to judge at least by what survives today and by what is known to have existed.

The arcaded court facade of Schloss Isenburg, at Offenbach on the Main just east of Frankfurt, carries the inscribed dates 1570, 1572 and 1578.[2] Though modest in size, it is far richer than the Saxon Elector August's Jägerhof outside Dresden; nor is it unworthy of comparison with his much grander but very plain Schloss at Augustusburg (Pl. 200), begun in 1568, as that was carried to completion by 1573. For that matter, what is extant of this Schloss at Offenbach is more comparable to Frederik's Kronborg or Cecil's Burghley than are August's Schlösser. Schloss Isenburg retains various simple elements, especially on the side toward the river, of fifteenth- and sixteenth-century date[3] that had survived a fire of

1564; what is remarkable here, however, almost rivalling in the amount of carved decoration the Schöner Hof of the Plassenburg (Pl. 193) as completed a year or so before, is the three superposed galleries of eight bays running across the court front between two octagonal stair-towers (Pl. 212).

It seems most likely that it was Conrad Büttner, a master-mason from nearby Büdingen in southern Hesse, who executed for the local ruler, the Count of Ysenburg-Büdingen, this impressive facade as one side of a projected rectangular court. Pedimented portals, flanked on the left by pilasters and on the right by half-columns, occupy the canted facets of the two towers and would have provided corner accents had the other sides of the court been erected. Above each of these doorways a vertical line of windows, four on the left and five on the right, marks the half-storey twists of the spiral stair within. Though rather small, these windows are of distinctly High Renaissance character. Their plain pediments crown eared architraves quite in the way of those dated 1559 surviving at Uslar (Pl. 194).

The severe style of these windows at Offenbach contrasts with the carving in high relief occupying the fields between the arches and the entablatures of the portals, not to speak of the profusion of other carved work, much of it armorial, on the long fronts of the gallery parapets. Though the ground storey has a rather severe range of compound piers of the Roman arch order fronted by fluted Ionic pilasters, the bold ornament that fills the spandrels and the somewhat daintier foliate scrollwork in the frieze is more in the spirit of Daniel Engelhardt's carving at the Plassenburg (Pl. 193).

The next two storeys of the court facade of Schloss Isenburg are trabeated, and both are precisely three-quarters the height of the ground-storey, a Serlian

---

[1] National Museum, *Kronborg; the Castle and the Royal Apartments*, 2nd ed. [Copenhagen], 1964 (henceforth cited as National Museum, *Kronborg*).

[2] Dehio, *Hessen*, pp. 666-667.

[3] The date 1528 is inscribed inside the northern tower, but

a more complete renewal of the Schloss was carried out in 1556-1559 not long before the fire, *ibid.*

proportion already employed on the Ottheinrichsbau. Above each of the ressauts of the entablature over that the parapet of the first storey is phrased by podia. These are decorated with figures personifying the Planets, the Virtues and so forth; while narrow vertical panels, filled with foliate scrolling, separate the pairs of coats of arms on the broader horizontal panels. This first storey has no columnar order but, instead, a range of herms set against plain piers. Little volutes beside the heads of these figures support the long members of the second entablature. That is executed, despite the considerable spans, in monolithic blocks of red sandstone like most of the rest of the facade.

The podia and parapet of the second storey at Offenbach repeat those of the first storey almost exactly; but the piers at that level—rectangular in section and with fewer flutes than on the lower portions of the herms below—taper upward to carry wooden beams rather than stone lintels. The fourth storey and the mansard roof were added in the eighteenth century and the whole was restored in 1952-1953.

The site of Schloss Isenburg is flat and thoroughly urban, separated today from the Main by both a broad and much-travelled street and a modern embankment. Very different is Burg Trausnitz,[4] high above Landshut, where Wilhelm von Wittelsbach, later Duke Wilhelm V of Bavaria, and his wife Renée of Lorraine whom he married in 1568 had the old wings of the mediaeval castle faced in the seventies with ranges of galleries on the court side and added also a new wing at the south end (Fig. 37). Here on the Isar, the material is brickwork, roughly stuccoed in the local way to suggest, as on the Stadtresidenz in the town below, rustication, not the fine sandstone ashlar of the Main valley. All the same the result is impressive by reason of its rather grand scale and a consistent severity of treatment approaching the Academic restraint of advanced work done after 1600. The international Late Renaissance flavor of these arcades, round in the first storey above a plain ground storey and semi-elliptical in the second, should be no surprise. The designer, Frederik Sustris, though a Dutchman born in Amsterdam, had been thoroughly trained in Florence under his father and others; and the execution was carried out by the team of Italian craftsmen he had brought north with him in 1569 to work for Hans III Fugger in Augsburg.

There was little opportunity, however, for *stuccatori* to work on the arcades at Burg Trausnitz (Pl. 213). The regular rhythm of the arches and of the plain Tuscan pilaster-order on the supporting piers is varied only by the smaller arches, with oval oculi above, that flank the central bay on the west side and by the slanted faces of the staircase rising in the southwest corner. Opposite, on the court side of the inner gatehouse block, however, the rusticated stucco trim of the five rows of windows in the upper storeys and on the gable is slightly elaborated. Yet, on this gable, Sustris already eschewed the boldly scrolled and finialled outline characteristic of gables on German secular structures since the 1530s which would still continue in common use elsewhere well into the next century. Here, at the top, there is only a rounded crowning element, following exactly the curvature of the big clock, and tiny segmental pediments rather than *welsche Gebel* rise over the rusticated corners.

Inside Burg Trausnitz Sustris and his Italians covered the walls and the flat panelled ceilings of the old Dürnitzbau (Pl. 214) and the new Fürstenbau, the south wing, with both large figural compositions and a profusion of arabesque decoration. The work in the Fürstenbau was done in 1578-1579, just before Wilhelm moved to Munich on his accession as duke of Bavaria. Soon he began commissioning there rather more important things from Sustris.

The decoration in the Fürstenbau was mostly destroyed in a fire in 1961, but the famous *Narrentreppe* (Fool's Staircase) in the south wing still preserves its frescoes by Alessandro Scalzi (Il Padovano) illustrating episodes from the *commedia dell'arte*. In these, life-size figures follow the visitor up or down the stairs—an Italian conceit that is thoroughly Mannerist.

As has just been mentioned, it was from the service of Hans Fugger that Wilhelm called his artists for the work inside and out at Burg Trausnitz. Sustris, assisted by the painter Antonio Ponzano and the *stuccatore* Carlo Pallago (†1604), had just completed the decoration, in a most elaborate version of late Italian Mannerism,[5] of the *Badezimmer* (bath) and

---

[4] Aretin, *Landshut*, pp. 23-25; Reclams *Bayern*, pp. 450-453.

[5] Comparison with Francesco de' Medici's famous Studiolo in the Palazzo Vecchio in Florence, decorated under Vasari's direction in much the same years 1570-1573, indicates distinct differences in taste between Augsburg Fuggers and Florentine Medicis at this point, but these differences are considerably less than in the "Stübchen" of Anton Fugger dating from the mid-century (Pls. 172-174), difficult though it is to determine the stylistic source of that unique interior and even precisely when it was executed, much less by whom.

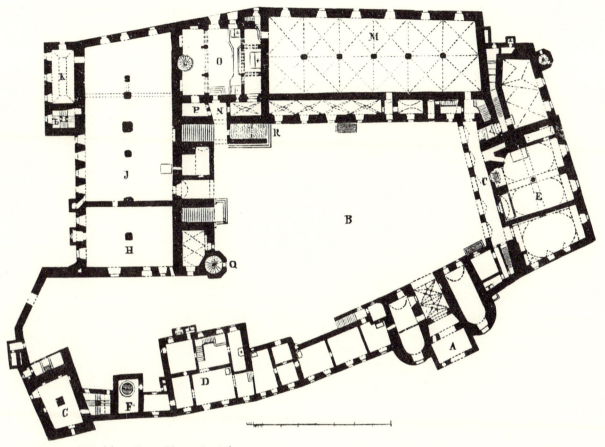

Fig. 37. Landshut, Burg Trausnitz, plan

Bibliotekzimmer (library) in the Fuggerhäuser at Maximilianstrasse 38 in Augsburg. These rooms, alas, were totally demolished in the war though they are known today from photographs (Pls. 215, 216). They must have had the most important works of decoration of this later Renaissance period in Augsburg, if not in all Germany. This Fugger, who lived until 1598, was a patron of art worthy of his family name.

In 1575, two years after Sustris's departure for Landshut, Hans Fugger acquired the Schloss at Kirchheim-a.-d.-Mindel, halfway between Augsburg and Memmingen, and began to reconstruct it in 1578.[6] What Jacob Eschay (†1606) built for him there survives in considerable part today.[7] Though very big and regular in its original quadrangular form, before the entire north wing and half the west wing were demolished in the nineteenth century, the Fuggerschloss is so very plain and so truncated as to be of very little

interest today from the exterior. But the Cedar Hall (*Cedernsaal*) within occupying most of the upper half of the east wing, with its decorations of 1582-1585, initiates the cycle of German *Festsäle* with magnificent wooden ceilings. Although a relatively modest one is extant in the Stadtresidenz in Landshut dating from around 1540 (Pl. 119), that in the Jever Audienzaal of the early sixties (Pl. 205) was probably the first example of such a feature in Germany to approach the one in the Cedernsaal of the Fuggerschloss. These halls will be considered as a group in Chapter VII since they are mostly of the eighties or later. In its lack of architectural elaboration on the outside, the Kirchheim Schloss resembles Schloss Augustusburg of a decade earlier (Pl. 200). It is unlikely, however, that Hans Fugger himself or Eschay—from 1594 the City Architect of Augsburg—who presumably designed as well as executed it, intended to emulate August of Saxony and Hieronymus Lotter.

It should be noted in this connection that the Fuggers, like the Bavarian Wittelsbachs, were still Catholics in a period when Protestants were generally much

---

[6] Dehio, *Östliches Schwaben*, p. 147.

[7] The interior of the church here at Kirchheim, however, was entirely remodelled in a Neo-Gothic vein in the nineteenth century, *ibid*.

more addicted to Schloss-building; but the Wittelsbachs were always great builders from Duke Ludwig X in the sixteenth century to King Ludwig II in the nineteenth. The employment of foreigners, moreover, was with them a well-established tradition. It was to Landshut in Bavaria, it will be recalled, that Italians had first been summoned from Mantua by Ludwig X in the late 1530s to execute and even to design the Stadtresidenz (Pls. 114-120). The employment of Sustris and his Italian collaborators by Hans Fugger in Swabia indicates that the Augsburgers had by this time[8] lost the leadership generally recognized as theirs in the days of the painters Burgkmair and Breu and the sculptors Dauher, Loscher and Hieber. In architecture the old prestige would return only after 1600 with the maturity of Elias Holl (1573-1646), the most productive and also the ablest German architect associated with the international Academic reaction of the early decades of the seventeenth century.

In the third quarter of the sixteenth century it was not Catholic Bavaria and Swabia but rather the largely Protestant lands along the valley of the Weser, where it flowed from Hannoversch-Münden through eastern Westphalia toward Bremen and the North Sea, that were most productive architecturally. It will be recalled that on the death of Unkair in 1553 Cord Tönnis took over the completion of the Schloss of the counts of Lippe at Detmold (Pl. 137). A decade later Tönnis, unrecorded in the intervening years, built in 1565[9] for Hilmar von Münchhausen at Rinteln, on the Weser halfway between Hameln and Minden in Westphalia, the *Archivhäuschen* (a small pavilion to hold the family's records). Today only the ground-storey oriel survives (Pl. 217).

Wholly out of key with both the contemporary "Dutch High Renaissance" and Northern Mannerist modes coming from the Netherlands which were then most influential in Germany, this exquisite oriel at Rinteln belongs to a quite special late aspect of the autochthonous Early Renaissance, yet it almost suggests also in its dainty elaboration the Rococo of the eighteenth century. Though almost nothing on it is still Gothic, there is also very little that is Italianate other than the medallion-like heads carved in low relief on the outer panels at the base and in the spandrels of the windows as well as on the crowning lunettes. The "curtain-tops" of the three lights of the window—which are almost horizontal, as already at Torgau in the thirties and forties (Pl. 78)—are ingeniously outlined by small cylindrical moldings that intersect. These delicate members are identical in section with the pairs of ringed vertical elements on the mullions below. Despite their extreme attenuation, the latter may have been intended by Tönnis to represent candelabrum-shafts, but they seem today idiosyncratic inventions that are neither of Late Gothic nor of Renaissance character. A link with Unkair, if not with Saxony, is apparent all the same in the trilobe *welsche Gebel*. Except in the very personal flavor of the whole, however, the Rinteln oriel is not at all premonitory of Tönnis's mature work of the following decades.

By the year the Archivhäuschen was begun at Rinteln Hilmar was home at last from campaigning in Sweden and elsewhere in northern Europe as a leader of mercenary troops in the emperor's service. That year he was ready to start developing also his other inherited estate at Schwöbber southeast of Hameln, and some time before he died in 1573[10] he employed Tönnis to build the manor-house there. Today this consists of three wings surrounding a court that opens to the east. Only the west wing (Pl. 219)—which carries the dates 1574 and 1575 on the north and south gables, respectively, and 1576 on the kitchen fireplace within—was even begun by Hilmar, but that was completed not long after his death by his widow, born Lucia von Reden. The south wing of 1588 and the north wing of 1602-1604 were added by their son, also named Hilmar, to match the earlier work.

Compared with the greater Schlösser of the sixties, Tönnis's original block at Schwöbber is modest in size and has no feature comparable to the oriel at Rinteln. The rectangle of the plan (Fig. 38) contains a front and a back range of rooms of varying size. These are so disposed that the spiral staircase is not in the center of the east front but rises just to the left of the entrance. Its presence is indicated externally only by two small slanting windows that cut across the string-courses between the storeys. Otherwise the extensive fenestration, all of plain two-light rectangu-

[8] All the major sculptural commissions of the Augsburg city authorities went to outsiders in the eighties and nineties: Breuer, *Augsburg*, pp. 97-98. In architecture, the Swiss-born and Italian-trained Joseph Heintz (1564-1609), designer of the royal stables in Prague for the emperor Rudolf II, although primarily a painter was the most important figure in Augsburg just after 1600 and provided paintings as well in two Augsburg churches. For his Prague stables, see J. Zimmer, "Iosephus Heinzius, Architectus cum Antiquis Comparandus," *Umění*, XVII, 1969, pp. 219-243. His architectural work in Augsburg will be discussed in Chapter IX.

[9] Kreft-Soenke, *Weserrenaissance*, pp. 273-274.

[10] *Ibid.*, pp. 278-279.

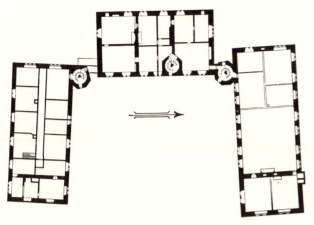

Fig. 38. Cord Tönnis: Schwöbber, Herrenhaus,
plan

lar windows, is quite regular in the three storeys. The oriels that project from the upper storey are symmetrically disposed, moreover, with the one on the right immediately above the round-arched entrance. Except for the simple portal, these oriels are the only ornamented elements of the facade. Supported on bold brackets and with coats of arms carved on the two panels below the triple lights, these oriels have plain mullions dividing the lights—carved strapwork is introduced only on the flanking pilaster strips where arabesques would have been used earlier.

There is also at Schwöbber a suggestion of such up-to-date decoration on the cross-gable rising against the main roof; at least it has none of the delicacy of Tönnis's work at Rinteln (Pl. 217) though it is not as heavy-handed as his earlier dormers at Detmold (Pl. 137). Moreover, where the three stages of the gables on the ends offered more space for decoration, he used several sorts of scrolled edging that is even closer in character to Netherlandish strapwork, as well as the familiar German pilaster-strips on the surface between. Various small obelisks and spheres also punctuate the outline against the sky in the usual way. The segmental lunette, or miniature *welsche Gebel*, that crowns each gable provides a very modest conclusion, it should be noted, less noticeable than the round balls beside it and the crocket-like members projecting from its extrados. These last are already premonitory of the "horns" so common on gables in Westphalia from the seventies onward well beyond 1600.

The later north and south wings are linked almost symmetrically by the polygonal stair-towers on either side to the original block. Thus extended, this manor-house (*Herrenhaus*) in its final form is often called, not improperly, a Schloss. In contrast a much more modest and rather earlier Herrenhaus in Westphalia dated 1550,[11] Haus Aussel at Batenhorst (Pl. 218), just south of the Autobahn near Gütersloh, may be cited. Of Fachwerk with infilling of brick, this is more similar to contemporary town houses—even to the characteristic fluted lunettes that provide most of the carved and painted ornament—than to the Schlösser and Herrenhäuser that are built of stone or stuccoed brick. The nearby town of Wiedenbrück has Fachwerk houses dated 1549, 1559 and 1576[12] which distinctly resemble, and even rival, Haus Aussel in their decoration.

From the first some at least of the richer citizens of towns and cities, beginning with Jakob Fugger, had been ambitious patrons of Renaissance architecture in masonry. By the sixties the extent of their patronage was already beginning to balance that of the princes who were erecting or enlarging their Schlösser and, indeed, to outrank at least in pretention most contemporary Herrenhäuser. By the seventies, indeed, such building, even in rather small places comparable to Wiedenbrück, was more considerable in quantity and often more ornate than even the grandest Schlösser of the princes whether the material was stone, brick or Fachwerk. In any case the appetite of princes for building seems, for economic or other reasons, to have diminished in the seventies though it would revive again in the eighties. The new production in the towns consisted, as earlier, both of houses built for individuals and of structures serving civic purposes; for these the leading citizens were responsible in their corporate capacity as members of the Council.

In towns where most of the houses were of Fachwerk there was, however, little significant stylistic change in the third quarter of the century. Indeed, such an exceptionally large timber-framed structure as the Siebendächerhaus (Pl. 220), built as late as 1601 for a tanner in Memmingen in Bavarian Swabia,[13] is almost totally devoid of the post-mediaeval ornament that had begun to appear on many houses in

---

[11] Dehio, *Westfalen*, p. 36.
[12] *Ibid.*, p. 601.
[13] Neither Dehio, *Östliches Schwaben*, p. 159, nor Reclams *Bayern*, p. 495, attempts to date this house. T. Breuer, *Stadt und Landkreis Memmingen*, Munich [1959] pp. 35-57, describes innumerable Fachwerk houses in Memmingen but does not give dates for many of those that must belong to the relevant period.

the north of Germany—as, for example, at Brunswick and at Celle (Pls. 102-103)—already in the second quarter of the century. Because of the practice of carving inscriptions that include dates above the entrance of Fachwerk houses, with such inscriptions the most conspicuous decorative features of the facades these houses are often clearly and precisely dated.

At Höxter in Westphalia, in the upper Weser valley, the *Dechanai* (deanery), built by Christoph von Amerlunxen in 1561,[14] is exceptionally picturesque. Here two quite different elements are balanced one against another: on the left an "oxheaded," i.e. truncated, gable; on the right a polygonal oriel (Pl. 221). Moreover, the Dechanai is as richly carved with fluted semi-circles brilliantly polychromed as any of the houses of the forties in Einbeck (Pl. 170). Rivals in their profuse decoration, though lacking the varied massing of the Dechanai, are the house called "Zur gute Quelle" of 1565; the Stadtschenke of the same year—this with an oxhead gable like the Dechanai; and two more of this date at Nikolaistrasse 10 and Marktstrasse 15.[15]

Everywhere, the vernacular decoration of Fachwerk houses tended to be repeated, as at Höxter, with little change. However, the Bokelman Haus[16] at Rinteln, probably of the early seventies, already reflects in the flat patterns used over most of the surface—on the panels as well as on the stiles—the new Northern Mannerist ornament. Of that there was as yet no trace on Tönnis's Archivhäuschen, also in Rinteln, of the mid-sixties (Pl. 217). On the other hand, a modest house of 1578[17] at Langestrasse 22 in Bückeburg (Pl. 223), which lies to the south of Stadthagen, has elegant quattrocento features of a sort rarely seen on surviving facades of Fachwerk though such decoration may well have existed once in some profusion.

Town houses of masonry reflected much sooner and more distinctly than those of timber the changing modes of the sixties and seventies; often they were stylistically abreast of contemporary Schlösser and civic buildings. For example, the front of the house called the "Roter Ochse" at Erfurt in Thuringia, which is dated 1562,[18] has above the ground storey a somewhat overscaled but otherwise not incorrectly detailed entablature suited to the engaged Doric columns that flank the portal, while in the first storey there is a range of five pedimented windows rather like those on Gromann's Französische Bau at Heldburg (Pl. 190) erected in the same years. Here, however, the windows above are separated from one another by delicately fluted Ionic pilasters carrying a second, unbroken entablature that rises to the sill-level of the plain second storey. It would, therefore, be less exaggerated to characterize this house as "German High Renaissance" than most contemporary Schlösser since the main storey is thus pseudo-structurally articulated in a quite up-to-date way. This can be compared to the ground storey at Schloss Rheydt (Pl. 198) which is actually five years or so later in date.

The cross-gable on the Roter Ochse, however, occupying most of the front, is of distinctly Netherlandish character, but Dutch rather than Brabantine. Its two stages, the lower three bays wide and the upper only one, resemble particularly those of the gable on the no longer extant Burgerweeshuis of 1560 in Amsterdam. Just as there, these bays are flanked and separated by Corinthian pilasters, but the fenestration at Erfurt is different: three small arched windows below and an oculus above. The panels of the pilaster-shafts and the imposts and archivolts of the window-frames, likewise panelled, are decorated only with modest bosses and the entablatures are unbroken by ressauts. As at Amsterdam, the crowning member is a plain pediment, carrying on the Roter Ochse a figure with a banner, perhaps even here a *Landsknecht*. Both the Dutch and the Saxon examples have elaborate sculptural decoration at the sides of the top stage combining heraldic and foliate elements. At Erfurt further figural sculpture also flanks the lower stage, thus providing a livelier and more broken silhouette than the rectangular panels carved with coats of arms at Amsterdam.

Another much later Erfurt house, the so-called "Breiter Herd" of 1584,[19] repeats the pedimented windows, unbroken entablatures and two-stage gable of the Rotor Ochse. But on this caryatid-herms take the place of an order on the first storey—as already at Offenbach in the early seventies on Schloss Isenburg (Pl. 212)—and the ornamental carving is much bolder and more profuse. The elaboration of the top storey on this facade and the repetition of

---

[14] Dehio, *Westfalen*, p. 241.

[15] Dehio, *loc. cit.*, lists three more dated houses in Höxter of 1554, 1571 and 1598, giving their street numbers; all are of Fachwerk.

[16] This actually carries the date 1570 but is not mentioned in Dehio, *Westfalen*, or in Reclams *Niedersachsen*.

[17] Reclams *Niedersachsen*, p. 99.

[18] Piltz, *D.D.R.*, p. 304.

[19] DKD, *Thüringen*, p. 371.

the large pedimented windows in the two stages of the gable produce that rather choked look of ornamental excess generally, and not incorrectly, associated with Northern Mannerism. This sort of architectonic congestion, it will be recalled, had first appeared in Germany in the late fifties on the Heidelberg Ottheinrichsbau (Pl. 177).

The earlier Heeremannscher Hof at Münster in Westphalia, restored since the last war for use as the *Landesverwaltungsgericht* (State court of equity), is rather different. This German facade (Pl. 222), which carries the date 1564[20] on its small central dormer, has a stylistic severity that might, with less impropriety than anything surviving from these decades of the mid-century in Holland, be called "Dutch High Renaissance." It is more comparable to Pasqualini's much earlier tower at IJsselstein or to Vincidor's arcading in the court of the Breda Kasteel, both of some thirty years before. Plain panelled Tuscan pilasters separate the exceptionally wide unframed windows here; above them heavy brackets, flattened in the outer bays, carry a central two-bay oriel capped by a fluted pediment. Over the compressed entablature of the upper storey a high blocking course carries a balustraded parapet. In the center, the single dormer is flanked by very restrained double S-scrolls and crowned with a fluted lunette.

The simplicity, regularity and strong horizontality of this modest facade in Münster lend it an Academic air that is more characteristic of the 1610s than of the 1560s. All the same, the few carved features, the plain fluting and the modest scrolling retain a rather Early Renaissance sort of delicacy. There is, moreover, no apparent influence yet from Antwerp, despite some slight resemblance in the character of the fenestration and the handling of the orders to the just completed Stadhuis there (Pl. 175).

Münster, being in western Westphalia, is not very far from the Dutch border. Moreover, the look of much of its sixteenth-century civil architecture is at least superficially Netherlandish because of the characteristic combination of stone and brick, though that does not include the stone-fronted Heeremannscher Hof. However, the *Krämeramtshaus* (merchant's guild house) of 1588 has a very late example of a stepped gable (Pl. 156). Each step of that gable is topped by a pierced lunette, a motif which is certainly

more German than Dutch. On the other hand, the very large stone-mullioned and transomed windows set in the brick wall and the engaged columns on the gable resemble features of such Dutch facades as that of the Kardinalshuis of 1559 at Groningen more than does most German work of so late a date.

In another, more largely brick-built town, Lüneburg, some distance southeast of Hamburg on the road to Celle, many late mediaeval houses with arcaded gables survive on the sides of Am Sande, the long market square before the Rathaus, and in other streets. Some of these were rebuilt or elaborated in the mid- and late sixteenth century but—as also in the north at Lübeck—it is the local vernacular, established long before, that gives Lüneburg its special character[21] and not any new influence from the Netherlands.

Exceptional, however, and again illustrating—or so it must seem—German emulation of the "Dutch High Renaissance," is the house (Pl. 225) dated 1574 at Lünertorstrasse 14[22] in Lüneburg. Yet the scrolled cartouches on the podia of the giant order joining the two lower storeys and the varied treatment of the fluting of both that lower order and also the upper one are more Mannerist than proto-Academic. But the composition as a whole, with the two ranges of engaged columns, the unbroken entablature at the top and the absence of the tall gables so ubiquitous locally, is not dissimilar to the facade of the Heeremannscher Hof in Münster of ten years earlier (Pl. 222).

For the architecture of the later sixteenth and early seventeenth century the town of Hameln, on the Weser southwest of Hannover, is more important than Lüneburg or even Gdańsk. Not only do some of the finest works of the period survive—several houses now handsomely restored and one major civic structure—but architects from Hameln were much employed in eastern Westphalia and, indeed, set the pace for what is called, with more justification than for most such regional terms, the "Weserrenaissance."[23] It was at Schloss Neuhaus in this district that Unkair seems to have introduced *welsche Gebel* in central Germany, whether or not he was following the model provided by those on the Halle Münster, and he was working at nearby Detmold at the time of his death

---

[20] Dehio, *Westfalen*, p. 391; W. Hager, *Münster in Westfalen*, 2nd ed. [Munich] 1966, p. 40, attributes the facade of the Heeremanscher Hof to Hermann tom Ring.

[21] J. Matthaei, *Lüneburg*, 2nd ed. [Munich] 1965, provides many illustrations of both mediaeval and Renaissance houses.
[22] *Ibid.*, p. 25.
[23] Kreft-Soenke, *Weserrenaissance*, deals with this subject in great detail; K. E. Mummenhof, *Wasserburgen in Westfalen*, 3rd ed. [Munich] 1968, pp. 24-33, provides additional material on minor Schlösser.

in 1553. Moreover, at Detmold it was the man who would be the leading Hameln architect for several decades, Cord Tönnis, probably a native of the town, who carried forward the work on that Schloss long before he was employed by Hilmar von Münchhausen at Rinteln and Schwöbber, both also in the Weser region. As has already been noted, however, no other building activity at Hameln or elsewhere can be plausibly attributed to him before the Archivhäuschen of 1565 at Rinteln.

The grandest house of earlier date in Hameln, for example, the wrongly entitled "Stiftsherrnhaus"[24] in the Osterstrasse (Pl. 318), is almost certainly not by Tönnis. A three-storeyed Fachwerk structure presenting nine bays to the street, this seems quite devoid of Renaissance features, at least at first sight. But there is evidence on the end walls that the upper storeys once carried the characteristic fluted-lunette decoration and, on the beam ends that project below the overhangs of the upper storeys, there are carved masks not dissimilar to those Tönnis introduced in elaborating the *welsche Gebel* at Detmold (Pl. 137). Moreover, the stone bench-ends at the sides of the stoop are not only crowned with shell-filled lunettes but carry pairs of herms flanking the allegorical figures of Justitia and Fides. The house was erected for Friedrich Poppendieck, a member of the Hameln city council, in 1556-1558.

At about the same time a Gothic house of stone at Bäckerstrasse 16 was adapted for Johann Rike, a local patrician, but the surviving facade of this (Pl. 227) was remade by Tönnis in 1568-1569.[25] As the earliest example of his mature style, that facade is also one of the first monuments of the later Weserrenaissance. Unlike the Stiftsherrenhaus, which has lost its original top storey and its probable cross-gables, the facade of this Rike house—there is a second one built later for Jost Rike—is very tall, with four stages in the gable above the two storeys below. The fenestration, moreover, is very extensive in the lower walls. That recalls more than a little the Netherlands. However, the windows are not subdivided in the somewhat Dutch way of those on the Schloss at Hannoversch-Münden further up the Weser—where Netherlanders were in fact most probably employed—or the Münster houses of the period.

Especially typical of the maturing Weserrenaissance is the simple two-storeyed oriel on the Johann Rike

house to the right of the older Gothic portal that Tönnis retained. A similar one had already been provided earlier, in 1540, on the Kavalierhaus at Gifhorn (Pl. 99). The quadruple lights in this Hameln oriel are nearly identical with those to the right of the entrance, though elsewhere on the facade the windows are slightly shorter and differently subdivided —at least they are so today. Plain flat bands rather than pilaster-strips separate the windows in the lower storeys, as also the panels flanking the transitional top storey and those on the three lower stages of the gable. For all the great height of the facade, however, the recurrent broad entablatures, crossing the wall unbroken between the tops and the sills of the successive ranges of windows, produce an almost obsessive horizontality little tempered by the vertical lines of the pilasters.

There is not much ornament of any sort on the Johann Rike house, though two very underscaled edicular features, both capped with fluted lunettes and framed by colonnettes, carry armorial carving in the spandrels of the pointed arch of the portal. The oriel, however, is crowned by a gable in the form of a larger and simpler edicule. This last is supported at the sides by quite vigorous S-scrolls and topped by a plain pediment.

Larger pediments, equally plain, are silhouetted against the sky over the panels at the sides of the top storey of the Johann Rike house. Thus they initiate at that transitional level the varied outline of the gable much as scrolls so often do elsewhere. But S-scrolls, of a curvature both more generous and more horizontal than those over the oriel, flank the second, third and fourth stages of the gable. At the center of the third stage is set a small arched window similar to the blind arch in the gable of the oriel; while the single panel of the topmost stage carries a scroll-edged cartouche with a bold central lozenge. The terminal is a sharp-pointed pediment with akroter-like elements at its base; both above this and also beyond the scrolls at the sides there is evidence other finials once existed. Presumably these were quite like those still present above the pediments of the second, or transitional, storey of the facade. Finally one should note the long Roman—but very un-Classical—inscription on the frieze at the top of the first storey. This includes at its end the date, 1568, of construction.

This Hameln town house is considerably more elaborate than the Schwöbber Herrenhaus (Pl. 219) as built by Tönnis some few years later for Hilmar von Münchhausen and his widow. But Tönnis

[24] Kreft-Soenke, *Weserrenaissance*, p. 247.
[25] *Ibid.*, pp. 247-248.

achieved on its street façade a rather special architectonic effect, not with a profusion of carved decoration, but chiefly by the especially harmonious ordering of the various parts. Extremely subtle, for instance, is the asymmetrical but balanced arrangement of the windows in the storeys below the gable in contrast to the vigorous, but not monotonous, reiteration of the strong curves of the S-scrolls above. The Johann Rike house has little in common with the "Dutch High Renaissance" of the houses in Münster and Lüneburg of this decade that have been described earlier in this chapter. The Hameln architect was by this time already the mature master of a personal style, one of which his own work of only three years before at Rinteln (Pl. 217) had offered no recognizable premonition.

The next considerable commission by a citizen of Hameln was for the other Rike house at Osterstrasse 12 (Pl. 228). Built for Jost Rike, like Poppendieck a member of the Rat, this carries the date 1576 and is not by Tönnis. But well before that time a much more extravagant, though provincial, example of a Weserrenaissance house, begun like the Johann Rike house in 1568,[26] had been completed in 1571 in the considerably smaller town of Lemgo, just to the north of Detmold.

Like Görlitz, further east on the Neisse, Lemgo was very active in the textile trades—woollens, linen and yarn—in the sixteenth century and also the seat of the printer and publisher Meyer Longo. Moreover, as has Görlitz, Lemgo has retained far more buildings of this period than Hameln because of the especially severe commercial decline that followed here after the Thirty Years' War. Other than the local Rathaus, of which the Renaissance transformation continued intermittently down to 1612, the most prominent structure in Lemgo is the Hexenbürgermeisterhaus (Pl. 226). This was built for Hermann Kruwel, mayor of the town from 1579 until his death in 1582, who was notorious for his persecution of witches (Hexen). The responsible craftsman was most probably the local master-mason Hermann Wulff. He had begun in 1565[27] the remodelling of the mediaeval Rathaus

by building a porch, which he signed and dated, facing the Mittelstrasse at the north end. Over that an upper storey of more advanced design was eventually added in 1589.

The façade of the Kruwel house occupies a central place in a long but uneven series of house-fronts surviving at Lemgo on which provincial Renaissance types of gable alternate with retardataire Late Gothic ones.[28] The mid-century group begins with a curious example built in 1556 for Johann Koch, an earlier mayor of Lemgo. This stands at Mittelstrasse 16 across from Wulff's porch. The gable of the Koch house has four stages, each flanked by fluted lunettes tipped sidewise so that the scalloped outline at the edges approaches a sequence of S-scrolls. Yet the gables over the house at Mittelstrasse 58, dated 1559, and even the Wippermann Haus at Kramerstrasse 5, of as late as 1576, are still entirely—and rather elegantly—Late Gothic. Over the house at Mittelstrasse 40-42 of 1574, which has an oriel dated 1580, the gable is framed by meandering S-curves in seven steps, each curve outlining a fluted fan, a type of decoration still repeated on top of the later oriel. As is so often true of provincial work, this motif varied without significant development one of the formulas of the preceding quarter-century.

The Hexenbürgermeisterhaus (Pl. 226) is elaborated beyond all other surviving sixteenth-century work in Lemgo except the Rathaus. Its façade is considerably more overloaded by the gable at the top than are any of the others, not to speak of the Jost Rike house at Bäckerstrasse 16 (Pl. 228) in Hameln which was its exact contemporary. Above three storeys—or perhaps one should say two and a half, since the second storey here is only a sort of mezzanine—the gable rises in four stages, each stage containing mullioned and transomed windows of three lights separated by widely-spaced engaged columns arranged in a syncopated sequence. These columns have fluted shafts and Corinthian capitals. Five of them subdivide the third storey into four bays; the lowest stage of the gable has four; the following one three; and the penultimate stage two.

Fluted Ionic columns frame the ground storey of the Hexenbürgermeisterhaus at its edges and also flank the round-arched portal; but there is no continuous entablature associated with this order nor is there one above the mezzanine. At that level, how-

[26] Ibid., p. 261; O. Gaul, Schloss Brake und der Baumeister Hermann Wulff, Lemgo [1967] (henceforth cited as Gaul, Brake), pp. 36-41. He does not hesitate to attribute the Hexenbürgermeister Haus to Wulff.

[27] Kreft-Soenke, Weserrenaissance, pp. 259-261; Gaul, Schloss Brake, pp. 29-32. Kreft-Soenke note and also illustrate (their fig. 244) the appearance here of bands of chip-carving below the podia on the Rathaus porch at Lemgo six years after their earliest identifiable use at Uslar (Pl. 194).

[28] Kreft-Soenke, Weserrenaissance, pp. 261-263; Dehio, Westfalen, pp. 288-290.

ever, herms are inserted over the entablature blocks at the edges and under the string-course from which the columns of the next storey spring. Neither do entablatures link the successive ranges of Corinthian columns above, but only cornice-like string-courses. These are broken by ressauts over the columns in each storey and also under the columns in the next one above.

The most striking characteristic of the facade of the Hexenbürgermeisterhaus in Lemgo is the very bold scalloping of the sides of the gable. In each stage there are slightly irregular half-circular protuberances that are fluted internally, quite like those on the Koch house of 1556. These features are framed by C-scrolls in high relief projecting below short straight elements, somewhat as on the west gable of the Schloss at Hannoversch-Münden (Pl. 195) but much coarser in scale. At their bases the scrolls are turned inward in big tight spirals; at the top of the gable, however, the fourth stage is capped by a small triangular pediment with a fluted field. This rises above a small oculus and an arched niche in which a standing figure of Christ is set.

The gable of the Hexenbürgermeisterhaus is quite symmetrical, but in the lower storeys of the facade the organization of the various features is irregular: In the second bay from the right the broad arched portal is flanked, as already noted, by Ionic columns that are repeated only at the outer corners·of the front; then, as on Tönnis's Johann Rike house in Hameln (Pl. 227), there is in the end bay on the left a two-storey oriel, here of four lights, capped with a tall gable which rises through the second storey. A second oriel that does not match, since it has only three lights, is also bracketed out from the first storey to the right of the portal almost as if it were an after-thought. Yet this last is capped with an earlier and simpler, not a later, sort of gable than the one to the left, providing a further disparity between the two.

Both oriels are decorated with much more carving than the rest of the facade; moreover, this carving is executed at a considerably daintier scale than the Corinthian order above and the scalloped enframement of the main gable. Small Corinthianesque pilasters, fluted like the engaged columns above, separate the lights on both of them, much as the pilasters do on the oriel of the Regensburg Bischofshof of a half-century earlier; while between the podia of this sub-order the arched panels are carved with coats of arms and with figures of the Virtues.

The oriel on the left of the front of the Hexen-bürgermeisterhaus has a panelled Ionic order on the ground storey that is not consonant with the one used at the portal and on the edges of the facade. Carved on the panels of these pilasters are no arabesques such as were usual earlier, but instead a pinched sort of misunderstood strapwork more or less of the new Brabantine sort. Such ornament appears also on the podia of the upper order, both on the oriel and on the lower portions of the herms so awkwardly inserted at this mezzanine level. The herms define the edges of the facade between the Ionic half-columns of the ground storey and the Corinthian ones of the second storey without really constituting a first-storey order themselves.

The blank gable of the lefthand oriel of the Hexen-bürgermeisterhaus is crowned, like the main gable, with a fluted pediment over a rondel set in a square top-stage. Below this, however, there are tall S-scrolls at the sides. Like those on the main gable, these scrolls are considerably coarser in execution than the pilasters below, yet they are also flatter here than the comparable elements higher up. On either side of a blank arch on this lower stage Classical heads project from rondels, much as on the Rathaus porch dated 1565 that Hermann Wulff signed. This motif, though hardly exceptional, seems to provide evidence of Wulff's responsibility for much of the carved decoration on this house, if not for the whole design. The crown of the righthand oriel consists of three fluted lunettes such as Unkair had introduced at Stadthagen some forty years earlier (Pl. 93). Here in Lemgo, however, that detail follows rather from a nearly identical one on the house built for Franz von Kerssenbrock around 1562 at Papenstrasse 24—a house that may well be not by Wulff, but by some follower of Un-kair active here before him.

The still almost quattrocento character of the low-relief carving on the archivolt and the wreath-deco-rated spandrels of the entrance portal of the Hex-enbürgermeisterhaus should be noted. Over the portal, in loose correspondence with the herms at this level on the edges of the facade, appear also Adam and Eve in high relief with the fateful Tree, heavily fruited, rising between the lights of the window over the cornice of the flanking Ionic order.

The total effect of this eclectic mixture of features on the Hexenbürgermeisterhaus, some continuing a mode introduced two generations earlier, others that reflect motifs still arriving fresh from Antwerp, is more coherent in its rather *volkisch* way than an analytical description suggests. Alien ideas had presumably been brought to Lemgo by the native-born stone-mason Georg Crossmann (†1612) who had been trained in Antwerp and even brought home a Brabantine wife. Whether or not Crossmann worked, alone or with Wulff, on the Hexenbürgermeisterhaus, its facade displays such a medley of architectural elements and such a profusion of inconsistently scaled carved work as to suggest several hands were, indeed, involved. It is, all the same, almost as premonitory of the later and riper stages of the Weserrenaissance as Tönnis's so much more carefully designed Johann Rike house in Hameln (Pl. 227) of the same years.

On balance, therefore, one ought to consider the Hexenbürgermeister house as advanced rather than retardataire even for the Weser Valley region. It has been noted already, for example, that the Wippermann house at Kramerstrasse 5 here in Lemgo is still entirely Late Gothic in its detailing though built as late as 1576.[29] Nonetheless, the considerably greater sophistication of the architects who were working in Hameln in the seventies is very apparent in the facade of the house at Osterstrasse 12 there (Pl. 228). This carries the date 1576[30] up under the pediment crowning the gable and the client was Jost Rike, though who the architect-builder was is uncertain. All the same, much on this facade does recall Tönnis's Johann Rike house of 1568-1569 (Pl. 227). The careful organization of the fenestration is similar, as also the simplicity of the intervening panelling, not to speak of the continuous horizontal entablatures—used here again without any corresponding Classical orders—over the first and second storeys and on the two lower stages of the gable. Even the slight disparity between the two oriels is closer to the other Rike house here in Hameln than to the much stronger asymmetry of the facade of the Hexenbürgermeisterhaus (Pl. 226) in Lemgo; while the pointed arch resembles in shape, if not in detail, the Gothic portal Tönnis retained on the earlier Rike house.

What is new on the Jost Rike house, and rather more premonitory of the later Weserrenaissance than the elements that flank the gable of the Hexenbürgermeisterhaus at Lemgo, is the sort of scrolling used

on the outer edges of the gable. Only the top stage actually recalls the latter in its pedimented conclusion and in the short vertical members set above large convex C-scrolls at the sides; but the intersection of curved and straight bands is more distinctly in an advanced Northern Mannerist vein than anything at Lemgo. So also is the enframement of the lozenge-shaped niche in the top stage from which projects a "Neidkopf" (image of Envy). Other elements of the terminal feature also animate the silhouette in a rather new way, above all the horn-like crockets projecting from the slopes of the pediment and the upper curve of the C-scrolls. These were presaged, it will be recalled, on the west wing at Schwöbber (Pl. 219) but are unknown in Holland. More common in northern Europe are the prominent obelisk-finials at this level, perhaps derived from those on the Antwerp Stadhuis (Pl. 175) and, in Germany, the round balls like those Unkair used from the first to stud his welsche Gebel. Such balls reappear both on the large scrolls of this stage of the Jost Rike gable and also on the richer and more complicated framing of the lower ones. That framing, which includes as at Hannoversch-Münden S-scrolls and C-scrolls that are both concave and convex, is thus already quite characteristic of the mature Weserrenaissance and, indeed, of German secular architecture generally in the later decades of the sixteenth century and the opening decades of the seventeenth.

Comparable maturity of scrolled gable design can be found in extant work in Holland but only a year earlier—1575—on the house known as De drie Haringen at Deventer in Overijsel[31] and south of the Schelde at Antwerp on the Sint Joris Gildehuis (archers' guildhall) in the Grote Markt as rebuilt in 1579-1582 after the fire of 1576. The Deventer facade is also the first anywhere to use chip-carved banding profusely.

Despite such parallels, and the inclusion in the ornament of strapwork elements of the Netherlandish sort that had only very lately become available in the published designs of Vredeman, the gable on the Jost Rike house—as architectonic as Tönnis's earlier one on the Johann Rike house (Pl. 227) yet much more varied—is no import from Holland or Brabant, but rather in the German line of descent[32] from

---

[29] The broad gable of the Rathaus of Nienburg, north of Stadthagen, carries no scrolling and is still crowned by seven fluted lunettes in echelon. It is thus very like the west gable on the Halle Münster of the mid-twenties though it was not built until the eighties: Kreft-Soenke, Weserrenaissance, p. 268.

[30] Ibid., p. 248.

[31] Kunstreisboek, p. 155.

[32] This is, of course, a moot point. But earlier chapters should have established a predominantly autochthonous descent for the scalloped gable in Germany down to the sixties, much as Unnerbäck has done for the simpler welsche Gebel.

Knotz's of 1534-1537 on the north wing at Neuburg (Pl. 90). Whoever the designer was, Tönnis was ready to follow his lead in the next decade, most notably on the house he built here in Hameln for the merchant Gerd Leist in 1586-1589 (Pl. 318) which will be discussed in Chapter VIII.

The style of a quite different architect comes to mind in the case of a gable of even livelier outline than that of the Jost Rike facade over the house built for Jobst Wulfert, a member of the Herford town council, at Neuer Markt 2 (Pl. 229) in that larger Westphalian town northeast of Bielefeld in 1560.[33] But this gable, rising above the very plain original facade, must date from considerably later, around 1577-1578. The fluted pediments atop the windows here could be of the earlier date; but the bold geometrical patterns in relief on the three main stages of the gable closely resemble those Laurens von Brachum introduced on the corner pavilions of Schloss Hovestadt in western Westphalia only in the midsixties (Fig. 31). More remarkable are the open scrolls of decorated bandwork that flank all three stages of the gable, particularly the way in which a larger and a smaller S-scroll cross each other in the second and third stages. On the third stage these even have something very like the "horns" of the gable on the Jost Rike house (Pl. 228). Small mermaids and large fluted shells, however, introduce here maritime notes more appropriate to Holland than to inland Westphalia. Doubtless these may be considered definite evidence of influence, direct or indirect, from the Netherlands, resulting either from the employment of itinerant aliens or from emulation of engraved plates in the books published in Antwerp by a German craftsman.

In the small town of Horn, south of Detmold, Haus Weweler at Mittelstrasse 50 preserves a two-storeyed oriel, dated 1563-1564,[34] with a triple crown of fluted lunettes still in the Unkair manner. But the two lower stages of the main gable, remodelled in 1579, are flanked by very bold S-scrolls of coarse bandwork. The lowest pair of these scrolls also have horn-like projections, here closer to those on the Jost Rike house (Pl. 228) than to the ones on the Wulfert house at Herford (Pl. 229). This indicates how rapid was the spread of this "horn" motif in Westphalia toward 1580.

This does not exclude the possibility of direct influence from Serlio's publications on the Dresden gables of the late forties.

[33] Kreft-Soenke, *Weserrenaissance*, p. 255, pl. 52.

[34] *Ibid.*, p. 257.

In the third quarter of the century, when many *Bürgermeister* and other members of the local town councils were erecting fine houses for themselves in towns both large and small, it is not surprising that such citizens should in their corporate capacity also build, renew, rebuild or enlarge the structures that served the public business and the pleasures of their towns. From the Rathaus at Celle (Pls. 230-231), begun in the early sixties but much embellished in the late seventies, to the considerably larger and better known one at Rothenburg-o.-d.-Tauber (Pl. 243), designed and built through the mid-seventies and completed in 1578, and the modest but extremely picturesque one at Marktbreit (Pls. 249-250) on the Main south of Würzburg, which was begun in 1579, many such civic structures were now erected. Equally interesting, and sometimes at least as large, were other public edifices such as the Hochzeitshaus (Pl. 233), for weddings and other festivities, of the mid-sixties at Alsfeld in Hesse. Alsfeld already had a Weinhaus of masonry of the thirties, but never rebuilt its Fachwerk Rathaus of the second decade of the century. The Hochzeitshaus will shortly be described in some detail. A quite different type of structure serving a public purpose is the quadrangular college (Pl. 245) that the Nürnberg authorities built at Altdorf, a village rather remote from their city, in the early seventies.

With these structures can be grouped the quite similar buildings erected by princely rulers as adjuncts to their principal residences to house administrative offices. Such are, dating from the sixties, the chanceries of the Elector of Saxony at Dresden and that of the Landgrave of Hessen-Kassel at Marburg, the one destroyed in 1945, the other still surviving. More followed later and several of those that are extant will be described in following chapters. Far more representational, however, are the portals, porches and such added to existing Rathäuser in great cities, particularly that of the end of the decade in Cologne and another some ten years earlier in Lübeck. Even in modest Lemgo the Rathaus received a significant addition in the sixties, it will be recalled, and there were more in 1589 and in 1612 (Pl. 389).

These civic and administrative buildings varied in purpose and also in style, from the simple and still largely Gothic college at Altdorf (Pl. 245) to the almost High Renaissance dignity of the *Doxal* (porch) of the Cologne Rathaus (Pl. 237) and the Northern Mannerist exuberance of the *Laube* (gallery) on that at Lübeck (Pl. 238). All the same, these may best be considered approximately in chronological order, as Schlösser and town houses were above, rather than subdivided according to type, mode or region. Certain Austrian civic buildings in Styria and Carinthia to the south and east that were built between the late fifties and the early eighties, however, will only be briefly discussed together and out of sequence.

The Rathaus of Celle, with its tall and ornate northern gable (Pl. 231) facing the marketplace, is a conspicuous feature on account of its considerable length. In this otherwise largely timber-built town, moreover, it stands out because it is of stuccoed brickwork like the Stadtkirche just behind it and the big Schloss in its nearby park. As lately restored, with bright painted accents of red and green on the white end gable and the dormers that rise above the pale ochre-colored walls of stucco, the Celle Rathaus also contrasts with both the ashlar masonry usual in the Weser region and the exposed brickwork of Gdańsk and Lüneburg.

The existing structure at Celle has a rather complicated history[35] as is evident from the disparity between the small gabled dormers and the tall end-gable. The rebuilding on top of mediaeval vaulted cellars—still surviving as a Ratskeller—started in 1561 in Duke Wilhelm's time. The original intention of Frederic Soltesburg, the *Ratsmaurermeister* (master-mason to the Council), and his successor, the *Ratsbaumeister* (architect to the Council) Jakob Riess, or those of their clients, the members of the Council, seems to have been to reflect the architecture of the local Schloss. As was noted earlier, Soltesburg was, indeed, employed at the Schloss from his arrival from Stadthagen in the mid or late thirties until 1553. He was then succeeded by Michael Clare who had been working at Gifhorn for Duke Franz until 1549. The relationship of the Celle Rathaus (Pl. 230) to the local Schloss is particularly evident in the gable of the central dormer added in 1562, a triple *welsche Gebel* such as was used earlier on the east front of the Schloss (Pl. 98). It is of the sort Unkair had employed at Stadthagen (Pls. 92, 93) very likely while Soltesburg was working there, and such multilobed gables continued to be used elsewhere even very much later than this (Pl. 94).

Soon two more gabled dormers were added on the Celle Rathaus, that on the right, crowning an oriel carried on heavy brackets, probably around 1564-1565. With their vertical pilaster-strips and horizontal entablatures, these later dormers on the long side of the

Celle Rathaus—whether designed by Soltesburg or by Riess—are still of the type that was possibly first introduced in simpler form on the Saalfeld Rathaus (Pl. 70) rather than based on *welsche Gebel*. The ones at Celle, however, are framed by relatively bold S-curved scrolls of later character. That to the left, moreover, carries tiny obelisk-finials as well and thus approaches in vivacity of outline the gables of the new Hameln houses. Indeed, it may well have been executed under Riess's direction by Hameln masons. The oriel below, however, is decorated with two portrait medallions that are still of quattrocento delicacy. These have been thought to represent Emperor Maximilian II and his wife but are quite possibly merely a mythical king and queen.

The three small dormers on the east side of the Celle Rathaus are completely overshadowed by the tall and very elaborate gable over the north end of the main block (Pl. 231). Executed in sandstone by masons from Hameln who arrived in 1577, this is the richest surviving example up to that date of a Weser-renaissance gable. Not surprisingly, it follows rather closely the one on the Jost Rike house of 1576 in Hameln which these men may well have executed (Pl. 228). But, on this, the whole surface is covered with flat geometric motifs, thus closely resembling the gable on the Wulfert house (Pl. 229) in Herford as decorated probably in these same years and, not impossibly, by the same stone-masons, though the motif had been introduced in Germany early in the previous decade at Horst and Hovestadt by Johannssen and Brachum, whether or not it came originally from the Netherlands.

Instead of the plain vertical bands of the Jost Rike house, the four stages of the north gable at Celle are phrased by fluted pilasters—first Doric and Ionic, then somewhat fanciful, and finally Corinthian—arranged in complicated counterpoint to the windows and the raised decoration on the surface. Though the entablatures of these orders are broken by ressauts, they provide relatively strong horizontal accents on the surface of the gable. The successive stages are also framed at the sides by various combinations of scrolls detailed as bold bandwork in the Vredeman manner. The three lower stages are further ornamented at their edges both by small obelisks and fruit-like elements recalling details in Vredeman's plates and also by the plain balls that Unkair had begun to use so long before at Schloss Neuhaus and at Stadthagen. The edicular top stage is flanked, as on the Rike house (Pl. 228), by concave quadrants rather than by

[35] *Ibid.*, pp. 239-240.

scrolls and by taller obelisks than those at the sides of the first stage. More notably, the horn-like crockets of the Jost Rike gable, not found in Vredeman's plates, also appear here as well as on the quadrants and on the slopes of the pediment over the terminal edicule. Quite as on that Hameln house, this gable carries in the entablature the date, here 1579, of its completion.

Thanks largely, perhaps, to the bright and high-keyed paintwork with which postwar restorers have covered the sandstone, the general effect of the 1577-1579 gable at Celle is extremely cheerful and gay as may well be correct for the period. This sort of poly-chromy, it may be noted, is very similar to what has been renewed on Elizabethan tombs in England. The latter are mostly somewhat later, however, and no dynastic tie yet linked England and the Welfs of Celle.

In 1580, the year after the Hameln masons completed their gable, a southward extension of the Celle Rathaus was begun, presumably by Riess himself, to serve as a Hochzeitshaus. As extended in 1938, this is now rather longer than the earlier block. The original facades and gables, moreover, had already been stripped of their sixteenth-century decoration in 1785, thus producing an exterior that here in Celle, may not improperly be called "Georgian"—by that date the ruler of Celle was George III of England as elector of Hannover and heir of the dukes of Brunswick. After the south wing was completed an arcade of three low arches carried on very thick stubby columns was introduced in 1599 to provide a more impressive approach to the exiguous stairs leading down to the Ratskeller. The armorial achievements in the spandrels of Duke Wilhelm and his wife date probably from 1576, however, while the ground-storey oriel to the left was added nearly a hundred years later in 1661.

The next important civic building to be begun in Germany, at least among those that survive largely intact, was the Rathaus at Altenburg (Pl. 234), north-west of Karl-Marx-Stadt (Chemnitz) in Saxony. This was designed by Nickel Gromann, the Saxon ducal architect, who was then also busy at Heldburg, and built 1562-1564.[36] It is very different from the one at Celle both in size and in consistency of character. Indeed, except for the gables added later at the sides —which are not conspicuous from the front—nothing at Altenburg resembles either the early work of Soltes-

burg and Riess or the later gable by the Hameln masons at Celle, much less the remodelled Hochzeitshaus at the south end (Pls. 230, 231). But Gromann, a more sophisticated architect than either Soltesburg or Riess, had by this time evolved a mature personal style, as noted in connection with his work of these years at Heldburg (Pl. 190) since he assisted, and eventually succeeded, Krebs at Torgau so long before.

The Altenburg Rathaus follows in the main a tradition for such civic structures that had long been established in Saxony (Pls. 70, 234). Indeed, Gromann's squarish block, crowned—exceptionally—with a hip-roof, is more like that at Šaalfeld, built a generation earlier than like Lotter's larger one at Leipzig of the previous decade (Pl. 163) or even its more modest brother at Pegau. In the middle of the front at Altenburg a very tall octagonal tower rises, much as at Saalfeld, Leipzig and Pegau, above a rectangular projection in which the front entrance is set. The main stage of this tower, starting just above the ground-storey portal and reaching almost to the main cornice of the block behind, is cut by slanting windows that light the spiral stair within. This stage is followed by four more, the first and third somewhat shorter, but the second as tall as the ground storey.

Entablatures mark off the stages of the tower at Altenburg and their angles are bound by slender cylindrical members. These last are not detailed as columns but seem rather descendants of the curious corner-shafts Unkair used on his stair-towers (Pl. 51). The intermediary cornices project very little, but over the fifth stage—which now carries clocks on its cardinal faces—a range of very plain and heavy modillions supports a balcony. The terminal stage is somewhat smaller and has a less assertive cornice, while above that the S-curved roof is crowned by a small open lantern.

There is a curious lack of coordination between this giant tower at Altenburg and the hip-roofed mass against which it is set. Though the central portal in the ground storey of the tower is not dissimilar in design to the other two that open asymmetrically to the left, it is scaled to the ground storey of the tower, not to the rest of the front. Moreover, the corbel-supported balustrade above it does not quite coincide with the sills of the first-storey windows of the main block, while the walling of this central portion of the facade is of diamond-rusticated ashlar, a plastic treatment of the surface not seen elsewhere on the building that slightly recalls Güstrow (Pls. 188, 189).

It is in the handling of the main block of the Al-

[36] DKD, *Sachsen*, p. 356.

tenburg Rathaus that various resemblances to Gromann's Französischer Bau (Pl. 190) at the Heldberg are recognizable. For example, except for the portals on the left and the squaring off of that end, the Altenburg facade is symmetrical. Pairs of framed and pedimented windows are regularly disposed on either side of the tower in each of the two lower storeys and similar windows, but without pediments, are set higher up under the crowning entablature. Stringcourses at the sill and cornice-levels of the windows continue across the wall, as also between the somewhat less evenly spaced windows on the right side of the block. Moreover, these are also carried around the two oriels, cantilevered out at first-storey level, that flank the main facade.

The rounded oriel at the righthand corner of the front of the Altenburg Rathaus is approximately three-quarters of a circle in plan; the other is but a small curved segment because of the slight extension of the main block beyond it. In both the first and second storeys of the oriels there are windows, four on that to the right and two on the other. These are identical in their framing with the ones on the flat walls but set tightly side by side.

Above the delicately carved bottom of the oriel on the righthand corner half-length portraits of Saxon rulers carved in low relief alternate with angel figures to form a frieze under the first-storey windows. Above these last another frieze has similar figures separated by scrolled cartouches. Next comes a band decorated with a bold range of circular bosses and then, below the second-storey sills, another more delicate band in which vertical fluting alternates with pairs of rectangular diamond bosses. The architrave of the main entablature and the lower portion of its cornice are carried without change around the oriels. But, in the frieze between, more diamond rustication replaces the scrolled modillions and rosette-like bosses used over the flat portions of the walls. Despite the entablature, the oriels are continued as cylinders well above the level of the eaves of the main block. At their tops the terminal stage on each carries another frieze of vertically-set diamond-rusticated rectangles below S-curved *welsche Hauben* of a shape and size consonant with that crowning the tower at the front.

As already noted, the prominent gables on the east and west sides of the Altenburg Rathaus—that on the right centered, but that on the left set at the southeast corner just behind the cap of the oriel—are not original but date from some twenty years later. When first completed, following Gromann's design, by the

master-builder Caspar Böschel of Karl-Marx-Stadt—probably, with the collaboration of the sculptor Hermann Werner from Gotha—the main block with its continuous horizontal cornice line, broken only by the oriels at the corners, and its pyramidal roof, not to speak of the regularly-spaced and pediment-crowned windows, was at least as advanced as Gromann's other work of these years at Heldburg and Weimar. Like them, moreover, it was hardly at all affected by the new Netherlandish influences that were beginning to arrive in Germany to the west and to the north of Saxony just at this time.

The relatively Academic character of the *parti* of the Altenburg Rathaus is evident. The execution of the detail, on the other hand, though refined as regards the moldings and boldly realistic as regards the ducal portraits, is neither proto-Academic nor particularly Mannerist by international standards but seems rather somewhat provincial. The crude Ionic capitals of the fluted columns flanking the main portal at Altenburg, for example, and those of the stumpy fluted pilasters above that frame the inscription in the frieze contrast curiously with the Roman elegance of the longer and more legible inscription carved on the two flat bands of the broad archivolt surrounding the arch.

Also provincial, and not unfamiliar in earlier German work, is the way the pediment over the very heavy and plain cornice of the portal does not extend the full width of the edicule—in order, one must suppose, to leave room for the lions that hold scrolled shields at each end—and also fails to repeat on the raking cornice the moldings used on the horizontal one below. Even more idiosyncratic stylistically is the great variety of figural and abstract motifs introduced on the oriels. What is unclear is whether such details were elaborated already in Gromann's original design or were "invented," so to say, by Werner or whoever executed the carved decoration.

In the mid-sixties when the Altenburg Rathaus was reaching completion, a different sort of civic building was rising at Alsfeld in Hesse and, in the great northern port city of Bremen, another was being much extended and embellished.

At Celle the dining facilities for the Rat occupied the usual location under the building in the vaulted Ratskeller, a mediaeval survival. At Alsfeld there could be no cellar, old or new, below the modest Fachwerk Rathaus of 1512-1516, since the ground storey was an open market surrounded by stone arches. So, already in 1538, the Rat of this ambitious town had brought in Hans von Frankfurt to build a separate Weinhaus across the northwest corner of the market-place from the Rathaus (Pl. 95). In 1564[37] Hans Meurer began a larger and more monumental structure, the Hochzeitshaus (Pl. 233), not like the one at Celle a mere extension of the Rathaus—here free-standing on all sides—but by itself at the southeast corner of the market square. The town came under the rule of the neighboring landgraves of Hessen-Marburg after construction of the Hochzeitshaus had started; it was not completed, perhaps for that reason, until 1571.

Though the taste of the Council at Alsfeld was not as advanced relatively in the 1560s as in the 1530s when their Weinhaus was commissioned, the Hochzeitshaus is a remarkably elaborate civic structure for such a small town. Occupying a corner site, this presents its northwest corner to the marketplace, and Meurer recognized the special location by treating the north and the west facades nearly identically, from the asymmetrically placed portals in the ground floor to the broad three-stage gables above the two main storeys. Even more strategic visually was the placing of the two-storeyed diagonal oriel on the corner toward the marketplace. Cantilevered out at first-storey level, this feature recalls more than a little Rosskopf's oriel on the Schönhof in Görlitz (Pl. 63) of a generation and more earlier.

Topping the corner oriel of the Alsfeld Hochzeitshaus are four lunettes carved with coin-like medallions; but their simple shape has been partially disguised, as are also the broader *welsche Gebel* that crown the two main facades, by an outer frame of scroll-work. Below the terminal lunettes the gables have the usual panelled pilaster-strips between the windows. Of these pilaster-strips there are three in the lowest stage; two in the next; and a smaller one in the third. The windows are arranged in groups of two or of three lights in the first and second storeys. All of them are rectangular and framed with moldings cut back from the wall-surface. That surface now consists of large blocks of raw rubble, but doubtless was once smoothly stuccoed and perhaps even decorated with painting.

While Meurer was content to flank the first and third stages of the gables of his Alsfeld Hochzeitshaus with elements of plain concave curvature, in the second stage he used S-scrolls with something of the

new boldness characteristic of this period elsewhere. On the whole, however, his design must be considered rather retardataire even for this provincial town. Retardation is particularly evident in the design of the arched portals. These are flanked by panelled pilasters and capped by fluted pediments with rosettes at either side. The busts in the medallions have no very Classical air, moreover, and the quality of execution is no more advanced than in Rosskopf's so much earlier work at Görlitz (Pl. 63) that Meurer's corner oriel here especially recalls.

Altogether more sophisticated is the *Schütting* (merchants' guild house) in Bremen on which Carsten Husmann rebuilt completely the northeast gable in 1565[38] (Pl. 232). The original building as erected by Johann de Buscheneer in 1536-1538 was Late Gothic. He came from Antwerp, and the facades he designed were quite Brabantine in their extensive fenestration and the stepped and finialled gables at the ends, of which that on the right survives in its early form.[39] Two ranges of nine windows, each of three lights and divided at half-height by transoms, run regularly across the front and there are similarly grouped lights on the ends. But except for the windows and the smooth large-scaled ashlar of the walls between little remains on the front that is original —if, indeed, the windows themselves were not later enlarged. The somewhat inappropriate crowning cornice and balustrade, as also the central dormer, date from 1594. These are thought by some to be the work of Lüder von Bentheim who later remodelled so sumptuously the Rathaus on the opposite side of the marketplace, but the attribution is not very persuasive. The conspicuous main portal and the steps before it date from 1895; the applied decoration over the front windows is also of the nineteenth century but earlier, perhaps of 1849 when the Schütting was taken over by the *Handelskammer* (chamber of commerce).

Other than the extensive and regular fenestration, the most impressive feature of the Bremen Schütting is Husmann's gable (Pl. 232). That is unequalled in elaboration for the date either in Hameln or in Gdańsk though it was rivalled a little later at Celle (Pl. 231). The gable rises in three stages and in each stage windows set in shallow blind arches alternate with plain stretches of wall between panelled pilasters

---

[37] D. Groszmann, *Alsfeld* [Munich, 1960] (henceforth cited as Groszmann, *Alsfeld*), pp. 26-30.

[38] Kreft-Soenke, *Weserrenaissance*, p. 233.

[39] Though larger and executed in stone rather than brick, this must have closely resembled the Stadhuis of Culemborg in Gelderland erected from a design by Rombout Keldermans in these same years 1534-1539: *Kunstreisboek*, p. 202.

of the Ionic order. The windows are double in the first and second stages but there is only one in the second above the central window of the stage below; the third stage has one window also, but that is single and quite small. Boldly projecting heads, somewhat like those on the Altenburg Rathaus (Pl. 234), occupy medallions in the tympana of the blind arches of the first and second stage, but in the third stage there is the key of the Bremen arms. Both the first and the second entablatures carry foliate carving on their friezes between ressauts decorated with rosettes that are set above the pilasters.

In the lowest stage of the Schütting gable in Bremen the line of the impost of the blind arches now continues to the right as the top member of the 1594 balustrade and also to the left. Over these extensions there is on each side a small C-scroll, doubtless an emendation of that later date. In the second stage also the impost line is continued beyond the outer pilasters, with a big-foliated S-scroll below and a smaller one above, both presumably original, on either side. The two-level treatment of the scrolling, rather unusual on earlier German gables and not yet apparently in use in the Netherlands, is repeated at the sides of the third stage. That last stage is, somewhat unexpectedly, capped by a fluted lunette of which the extrados turns outward in a scroll on either side. Thus the terminal feature is not much like previous *welsche Gebel* but exemplifies rather the newer and bolder ideas maturing to the south of Bremen in the upper Weser region. On top of the lunette two small S-scrolls support a finial-like square pier on which a human figure—a *Landsknecht*?—carries both a shield with the key of the Bremen arms and an iron banner that serves as a lightning rod.

This elaborately organized gable on the Schütting could have provided the model for the less Classical but equally subtle ordering of those on the two Rike houses at Hameln of 1568 and 1576 (Pls. 227-228) though that is not very likely. Here in Bremen, Husmann's competence as a designer—whatever may have been his origin—seems of a somewhat Netherlandish order, though his gable does not depend at all on advanced Dutch or Flemish models of these years.[40] The pilaster order, in particular, is rather a belated echo of that sort of "Dutch High Renaissance" still influential in Münster. Moreover, if Husmann already knew up-to-date Brabantine ornament from Floris's

and Vredeman's publications or even, perhaps, visits to Antwerp, he was certainly not yet employing it to the degree architects a generation younger working in Bremen after 1600 would be doing.

In the years around 1570 two big cities embellished their town halls with very elaborate porches or galleries, while Schweinfurt, north of Würzburg in Franconia, erected a large new Rathaus, as did also Brieg (Brzég) in Silesia. The Rathaus in Cologne dates from the mid-fourteenth century and still extends, as restored since the war, all along the east side of the present Rathausplatz. Rather than rebuild it, the Council[41] decided in 1567 to mask the front almost completely as commonly seen from the Portalgasse which enters the square from the west. Their new Doxal or open two-storeyed porch is five bays wide and two bays deep, large enough to provide room for all fifty-one members of the Council in the sixteenth century. Thus this feature is quite considerable in itself. Until its removal in a nineteenth-century "restoration," the Doxal contained a double flight of stairs leading to the Hansesaal, the big hall in the upper storey which had survived from the fourteenth century. Originally the *Bürgermeister* came out into the open upper storey to announce to the public the decisions of the Council.

The Council's chosen executant, appointed in 1569, was Wilhelm Vernukken (†1607). As he came from Kalkar, a town southeast of Kleve and like that very near the Dutch border, he may almost be considered a Netherlander. He was not, however, the original designer. There exists in the Historisches Museum in Cologne an earlier head-on perspective drawing (Pl. 235) which is certainly not by Vernukken. This is dated 1557, more than a decade before his employment by the Cologne Rat. Since this is signed "C.F.," it is most probably by Cornelis Floris. The drawing makes even more evident than does the surviving structure as carried out by Vernukken the proto-Academic quality of the design. The upper storey, in any case, was rebuilt later. In an even purer High Renaissance taste is a trabeated design for the Doxal, also signed "C. F." and submitted at the same time, which is presumably by Floris too[42] (Pl. 236). Both the designs were in existence to serve as models and

---

[40] Enkhuizen: *Kunstreisboek*, p. 354; *Niederlanden*, pl. 91; Gorinchem: *Kunstreisboek*, p. 407.

[41] K. Goettert, *Das kölnische Rathaus*, Mönchen-Gladbach [1959] (henceforth cited as Goettert, *Kölnische Rathaus*).

[42] *Ibid.*, pp. 50-51. It is interesting to note that no trace of Northern Mannerist ornament, for the origination of which Floris is often credited, appears in this project and very little in the other.

the arcuated one, indeed, was very little modified in execution. The porch as built, however, is quite unexpected for Vernukken in the light of his earlier work elsewhere. It will be recalled that he had been employed for at least five years, beginning in 1559, at Schloss Horst. At first he worked there with his father Heinrich and under the Arnhem architect Arndt Johannssen and his associate Laurenz von Brachum, later with the Frenchman Joist de la Cour who arrived at Horst only in 1563. What Vernukken did at Horst has no High Renaissance character at all (Pl. 184).

The employment of Netherlandish artists in Cologne in the Renaissance period had begun early, around 1518, with the edicular *Epitaph* of Jacques de Croy, Bishop of Cambrai, in the Treasury of the Cathedral; following that came Jan van Roome's screen in St. Maria-im-Kapitol (Pl. 58), imported from Mechelen by the Hackeney family in the mid-twenties. Then there are two much later black and white tombs of Tournai marble in the Cathedral. One is that of an elector-archbishop for whom Rüttger von der Horst was lay-deputy, Adolf Graf von Schauenburg, executed in 1561,[43] the other that of his brother Anton. Both are of the years when Rüttger began to rebuild his Schloss at Horst and Wilhelm Vernukken was kept busy there. These tombs are not by Vernukken. If not by Cornelis Floris himself they must, as surely as the contemporary Wiemken tomb at Jever (Pl. 203), be by one of his pupils or assistants such as Hagart. The two Schauenburg tombs in Cologne closely resemble four more modest examples of nearly contemporary date—one of them is dated 1555[44]—in the Onze-lieve-Vrouwekerk at Breda in Holland. Executed by followers of Floris, these Dutch tombs differ as markedly in their Mannerist elaboration from the nearby Early Renaissance tombs carried out, presumably by Italians, before the death of Hendrick of Nassau-Breda in 1538 as from Floris's Doxal projects of 1557 (Pls. 235, 236) or, for that matter, the Breda Kasteel of the same years of the thirties.

Of Northern Mannerist ornament resembling the designs in Floris's *Inventien* of 1556-1557 there is little or no trace on the Cologne Doxal as executed (Pl. 237) nor are there any conspicuous borrowings that might have come from Vredeman's plates of 1563.

On the contrary, more aptly than most other Netherlandish or German work of the third quarter of the century except the alternative trabeated project by C. F., the loggias as executed might be called "High Renaissance," though they reflect Sansovino's Venice rather than San Gallo's Rome. This is even more true for the other project of the previous decade, the arched one that must have been Vernukken's immediate model.

The lower storey of the Doxal—which survives, though restored, almost exactly as Vernukken built it—consists of a range of bays of the Roman arch order and, in front of the central bay, additional freestanding columns, consonant with the engaged columns used throughout, to carry the projecting sections of the entablature. The upper storey, as proposed in the arched project of 1557, was to have been taller and lighter, with only columns as supports like the other 1557 project and no arches, since this was not intended to be vaulted like the ground storey. There is no evidence, however, that the original upper storey as carried out by Vernukken was, in fact, based on the earlier design.

In the just-mentioned project for the Doxal (Pl. 235) spheres are shown lined up with the two outer columns on either side above a second entablature with rather plain modillions in the frieze. Over the projecting central bay the drawing also indicates, first, a plain rectangular panel for an inscription and then a large oval carved with the arms of Cologne. Some additional carved decoration was also proposed for the spandrels of the ground storey and the solid section of parapet in the center of the upper storey. That last takes the place of the balustrade which was to run between the podia below the upper order and also across the rest of the top. The element joining the base of the terminal oval to the top of the attic would also have carried carved decoration.

In the executed ground storey of the Doxal Vernukken followed this project closely. Moreover, the existing upper storey is not very dissimilar, despite the pointed arches and the ornament of a Brabantine character that is carved on the lower section of the columns, a motif Vernukken may well have drawn from Vredeman's engraved plates. The differences can be explained, presumably, by the reconstruction of the whole first storey when the upper vault was carried out in 1618. In the rebuilding, however, Vernukken's columns, or parts of them, may well have been reused for the order.

[43] Dehio, *Rheinland*, p. 318.
[44] *Kunstreisboek*, pp. 547-548.

The shape and proportions of the executed arches and the Corinthian order of Vernukken's ground storey on the Cologne Doxal are as "correct" as in the arched project of 1557 (Pl. 235). However, all the columns stand free, as was not proposed in the drawing, even the pair to the rear flanking the central bay. Above them, the entablature breaks forward in single ressauts over the end bays and in two steps above the central one. The ornament in the spandrels indicated in the project was reduced in execution to human heads, small in scale but in high relief, and there are other rather more coin-like heads framed in disks on the frieze, one over each of the columns. The sole suggestion—and it is no more than that—of the new Netherlandish ornament in Vernukken's ground storey is very inconspicuous: the scrolled edging of the cartouches on the podia below the columns. But such edging is a detail not unknown in sixteenth-century Italy and need not derive from Floris or Vredeman. Later, in the Schmalkalden Schlosskapelle (Pls. 267, 269), Vernukken would use Vredemanian ornament almost exclusively, but that was around 1590.

The Lübeck Laube (Pl. 238) provides, somewhat in the manner of the Cologne Doxal, a frontispiece toward the marketplace for the Rathaus, but it could hardly be more different in character from Vernukken's porch. Built in 1570-1571,[45] this is a glazed gallery above an open arcade, all in carved sandstone, set against the tremendously tall Gothic front on the south side of the old brick-built town hall. It was executed, and presumably designed, by two masons from the Netherlands, Hans Fleminck or Flemming and Herkules Midow (†1602)—very probably the "Klaus" Midow who later completed Schloss Güstrow in Mecklenburg. Their Laube is as characteristic an example of Northern Mannerist architectural design, as exported in this decade and the following from the Netherlands, as the slightly earlier Cologne Doxal is of the more Academic sort associated especially with Floris. Only in the gables of the dormers does any reflection of that "High Renaissance" aspect conspicuously appear: A pair of well-proportioned arches is introduced in the central one and identical single-arched windows, flanked by plain shell-topped niches, occupy the other two dormers, a combination that at least suggests the Serlian or "Palladian window" motif.

Each dormer of the Lübeck Laube rises over two bays of the first storey; however, the fluted Corinthian pilasters at their sides line up, not with the Ionic ones below, but with the caryatids that alternate with them. Thus the facade has little vertical coherence and the resultant syncopation may be considered almost exaggeratedly Mannerist in its uneasiness. The ground storey is perfectly regular since the six bays of the open arcade are identical. The arches are carried, however, not on proper columns but on clumsy square piers with chamfered shafts and rather plain, impost-like capitals. The molded archivolts above are broken by diamond-rusticated bosses that also band the intradoses, while a flatter sort of rustication, textured on the surface, fills the spandrels.

In the main storey of the Lübeck Laube the rhythm doubles, with the fluted Ionic pilasters, as already noted, directly over the piers below and the caryatids between them. Beneath the sill-level a wide band of diamond rustication is broken by the recurrent podia of the order. The podia over the ground-storey arches rest on molded brackets, serving also as keystones, in alternation with the ones centered above the spandrels between. Despite pedimented heads, the large windows of the main storey, all subdivided by central mullions and transoms, press against the vertical elements between them. Thus they provide, much as on the Antwerp Wewershuis of the early forties, maximal illumination for the gallery within. Above them the frieze of the order, wholly disproportionate in depth to the pilasters it crowns, carries the most profuse carved decoration on the whole facade. Moreover, the horizontal cartouches surrounded by scrolled strapwork are even more distinctly of the sort Vredeman had been offering since the early 1560s (Pl. 176) than any of the ornament on the Cologne Doxal. In Germany, as in the Netherlands, the use of such Northern Mannerist detail became common only as the 1570s advanced, so that the Laube provides a rather precocious example internationally.

Above this ornate Netherlandish frieze on the Lübeck Laube are the dormers of which the somewhat Academic character is contradicted by flanking members decorated with heavy strapwork. Each of these members consists of a good-sized convex quadrant from which straight arms extend both sidewise and upward to end in tight scrolls, a theme more Dutch than German. The side gables are then capped, as often in Holland, by relatively simple pediments, also filled with strapwork, and have pairs of obelisks

45 Dehio, *Hamburg*, p. 382.

at their base. Above another disproportionately broad frieze, carved with shields of arms, that runs across all three dormers the middle dormer has a second stage in which a tiny order frames a reduced version of the Serliana motif used on the other two. The bold scrolls and straight vertical elements at the sides of the second stage are framed by taller obelisks than those on the other dormers. All the same, by contemporary German standards these distinctly Netherlandish gables are relatively simple in outline, especially as compared with the Weserrenaissance gables of these years in eastern Westphalia. Before the end of the decade, however, those would be introduced as far north as Celle on the righthand end of the Rathaus there (Pl. 231) by masons who were actually brought from Hameln.

Of the characteristic brickwork of the German north, which often looks more Netherlandish than it really is, there is no trace in the representational splurge of this Lübeck frontispiece built entirely of imported stone. However, in the tiny town of Krempe in Schleswig-Holstein, near Glückstadt to the northwest of Hamburg in the valley of the Elbe estuary, a small Rathaus survives (Pl. 239) of 1570[46] which might be considered to be, not Dutch, but Danish in character rather than German. Modest though it is, this town hall may well, at least for contrast, be described here. The lower storey and the ends of the Krempe Rathaus are of brickwork varied only by the white stucco of the segmental tympana over the three-light windows. On the long sides the construction is Fachwerk with the fenestration almost continuous between the vertical stanchions of timber.

There is at Krempe no elaboration of the outline of the gables, neither that over the center of the front nor the larger ones at the ends of the main roof. But an arrangement of short and shallow arched niches —first five, then three, then one—each arch of triple round-edged orders executed in molded brick like the jambs and arches of the larger opening of the entrance below—provides a patterned surface on the front. This front is thus neither recognizably Late Gothic nor Italianate, but rather a continuation of the special brick vernacular of such German towns as Lübeck and Lüneburg, not to speak of Denmark, that goes back to the high Middle Ages. A small shingle-covered hexagonal lantern riding the ridge of the roof at one end provides in its slated *welsche*

Haube the only echo of the more sophisticated contemporary architecture of the German lands to the south and east.

In another border area, far to the east at Brzég in Silesia, a much larger Rathaus (Pl. 240), rising at the same time, is more typical of the period. Its mediaeval predecessor burned with the rest of the city in 1569, and the next year[47] the Council employed Giacomo Parr (†1575) and his son-in-law Bernardo Niuron to build the new one. Completed in the main within two years, a striking feature was added in 1577 when the open crowning stages of the main octagonal tower, which is asymmetrically placed, were considerably increased in height to dominate the whole.

Parr's Milanese origin is apparent here at Brzég in his work of the mid-century on the Portalbau of the Schloss (Pl. 136). By the seventies, however, he was thoroughly acclimated, thanks to his intervening employment[48] on two local school buildings: One was the Stadtschule begun in 1548; later came the Gymnasium of 1564 where he was first assisted by Niuron. There is nothing specifically Italianate about the Rathaus except for the loggias that run between the two square stair-towers on the front and the generous size and the vertical proportions of the architrave-framed windows. Both the loggias and the window-type are still of essentially quattrocento character, however, not at all "High Renaissance," nor yet Mannerist. The loggias, moreover, had German precedent in Saxony in the shorter ones—no longer extant— that Nickel Hoffman built on the front of the Halle Rathaus in 1558, not to speak of G. B. di Quadro's very broad and tall ones on that of Poznań in Pomerania (Pl. 241), dating from the fifties, which are so much grander and more "High Renaissance" in character. On the other hand, the general composition of the Brzég Rathaus is of an advanced character hardly approached to the west even in the contemporary design of the Augustusburg. It was already rivalled, however, by Parr's son Franz's work at Güstrow (Pls. 186-189) to the north in Mecklenburg.

Hitherto the impressive piling up of the various elements of which German Renaissance building complexes such as Schlösser—if not so much town halls —were composed had mostly resulted, not from any architectonic intention, but because of the inheritance of mediaeval work and its piecemeal replacement.

---

[46] *Ibid.*, pp. 286-287.

[47] Łozinski-Miłobedzki, *Guide*, p. 52.
[48] Article "Jacobo Pahr" in ThB.

Moreover, even on such more ambitious Schlösser of the sixties and seventies as those at Horst and at Hovestadt (Fig. 31, Pl. 181), the prominent pavilions marking the corners seem to have been imitations of French models and, at least Horst, were actually afterthoughts. At Brzég, however, all the parts except for the main tower were organized by Parr into a coherent mass-composition. That tower, however, being asymmetrically placed at the rear, does recall in some degree the big mediaeval keeps and the tall new watchtowers that dominated so many earlier Schlösser from that of the thirties at Torgau onward (Pls. 80, 82). On the other hand, it is not much like the ones that rise, more or less in the center, on the fronts of Saxon town halls, from the one at Saalfeld of the late twenties and thirties to Gromann's at Altenburg of the early sixties (Pls. 70, 234), nor does it rival such a Dutch *speeltoren* (carillon tower) as Daniel Dirksen erected in Gdańsk ten years before.

Most of the individual elements of the Brzég Rathaus are familiar except for the bulk of the square stair-towers that project at the ends of the main block to frame the loggia. However, their octagonal upper stages, similar to the taller crown of the main tower, are exceptional and, like that, possibly later additions. The high gables at the ends of the main block are scalloped, and so are the gables on the three dormers rising above and behind the trabeated upper storey of the loggia, which is of wood like the one at Offenbach. But the scalloping does not approach the liveliness of outline of the Westphalian gables of the late sixties and seventies (Pls. 227, 228).

Though the lowest stage of each dormer on the Rathaus at Brzég is framed by pilasters, these are not repeated on the stages above; moreover, on the bigger gables at the ends of the main roof plain vertical strips replace any proper order at all. Under the flanking strips in each of the four stages of the end-gables, however, the podia are extended outward below simple S-scrolls. These scrolls, moreover, are doubled vertically in each stage much as on the left gable of the Bremen Schütting (Pl. 232). This treatment is repeated with the terminal member capping the fourth stage. Similar podia also flank the third stage of the dormers—in this case not associated with vertical strips—above the single S-scrolls of the stage below. Over that third stage, as at the base of the top stage on the bigger gables, molded strings, identical with those topping the podia, are carried all the way across below the crowning feature which is better described

here as a tiny segmental pediment than a *welsche Gebel*.

The treatment of these gables and dormers at Brzég thus displays something of the sophisticated originality of the ones in Hameln (Pls. 227, 228) by Tönnis and the unidentified contemporary who designed the Jost Rike house. Yet there is not the same variety of relief and of outline here: No "horns" or obelisks, not even plain balls, stand out against the sky, and the scrolls at the edges are not elaborated. The soft curves of these last contrast with the boldly spiralled ends characteristic by this time in several of the German districts to the west and most particularly in the Weser valley. Unfortunately, restoration since the last war has not yet proceeded any further on the Rathaus than on the Schloss at Brzég.

The loggia across the front of the Brzég town hall was still a rather novel feature at this date, though those on the front of the one at Poznań (Pl. 241) of 1553-1560 antedate them by a decade or more. Both lie in this same eastern region beyond the Neisse and the Oder which is now in Poland.[49] In a southeastern area far nearer Italy, at Klagenfurt beyond the Alps in Carinthia, some unknown builder-architect—doubtless an Italian—provided in the mid-seventies, shortly after the Rathaus at Brzég was first completed, the design for the *Landhaus* (provincial capitol) which Hans Freymann carried out over the years 1574-1580.[50] In the court at the rear of this there is a two-storeyed loggia, perhaps planned from the first, running between two tall towers. These towers were begun by Freymann's successor, Giovanni Antonio Verda, an Italian or Italian-Swiss who had been active in Graz since 1558, and completed in 1588 by Christoph Windisch. Similar arcaded courts, often very simply detailed, were by this time common in Schlösser in this region. Moreover, grander and more correctly proportioned arcades with a High Renaissance arch-order had already been erected a good deal

<hr />

[49] J. Kowalczyk, *Sebastiano Serlio a Sztuka Polska*, Breslau, 1973 (with résumé in Italian, pp. 287-303), figs. 76-78, illustrates Quadro's dependence on Serlio's *Quarto libro* for the design of the *stucchi* on the vault of the great hall at Poznań in Pomerania which dates from 1555. His arcades are not so Serlian and, indeed, for the most part Serlian influence only reached Poland a good deal later than this: *ibid., passim*.

[50] KDÖ, *Kärnten Steiermark*, p. 345; Baldass, *Österreich*, p. 25. Baldass illustrates the arcaded court of the Klagenfurt Landhaus and also that of 1568-1577 at Linz by Christoph Canevale, which is similar but less advanced, pls. 6, 9.

earlier at the rear of the Styrian Landhaus at Graz by the Italian-Swiss Domenico dell'Allio (†1563), who came from Lugano, in 1557-1565.[51] The arch-order contrasts with the plain, still rather quattrocento, Tuscan columns used on the Klagenfurt Rathaus and on such Schlösser as Spielfeld in Styria or Hartheim in Upper Austria.[52]

The existence of these arcades in Silesia—and also in Carinthia and Styria, not to speak of Moravia—is further evidence of the relatively greater employment of aliens from the south, such as the Milanese Parr and dell'Allio from Lugano, to the east and southeast of the central German lands. Such consistently Italian design as is already to be seen in the court of the Salamanca Schloss at Spittal-a.-d.-Drau (Pl. 112) in Carinthia and later in the arcades of the Graz Landhaus in Styria hardly seems to belong at all to the German Renaissance in the way that even the loggias (Pl. 240) by Parr do at Brzég for all his Milanese origin. Those by the Saxon Nickel Hoffmann at Halle, which were dated 1558, were less Germanic and actually more Italianate than Parr's; their trabeated design, indeed, almost rivalled that of one of the contemporary projects for the Cologne Doxal (Pl. 236) in its High Renaissance "Classicism." Such Classicism, so to call it, was now entering Germany from the west, not the east or southeast. The Carinthian and Styrian civic buildings provided no favored alternative in the central German lands to the models provided by Saxon Rathäuser: That must justify the brevity of the references to them here.

The Rathaus at Schweinfurt, on the Main in Lower Franconia, is nearly as large as Parr's at Brzég. It was built in the same years 1570-1572,[53] after the Graz Landhaus but before the Klagenfurt town hall, and like the Halle loggias it is by Hoffmann. Not surprisingly, he followed here Saxon rather than Austrian models. Since it occupies a corner site at the south end of the big market-place, this civic monument (Pl. 244), now restored after a fire in 1959, is more conspicuous than the one at Brzég, but not so interesting architecturally. Long an imperial free city, Schweinfurt became Lutheran early and in 1554 it suffered, like the Plassenburg at Kulmbach, serious

damage in the so-called War of the Margraves. Fifteen years later the Council called Hoffmann from Halle to design and build the new Rathaus. Hoffmann had by that time been active at Halle for some twenty years.[54] In the mid-fifties he worked on the completion with galleries of the Marktkirche (Pl. 37) for Lutheran use and then, recurrently, on additions to the Rathaus. These include the trabeated loggias on the front that have just been mentioned and the tower, which he began ten years later. In that year, 1568, he was also collaborating briefly with Lotter on the Augustusburg. But he did not imitate at Schweinfurt the long facades of Lotter's Leipzig and Pegau Rathäuser (Pl. 163), much less the mode—at once simpler and more symmetrically regular—of the Augustusburg (Pl. 200) as it was being carried out in these years by others.

The prototypes for Schweinfurt were other relatively new Rathäuser in Saxony that had their main gabled—or at Altenburg (Pl. 234) hip-roofed—block set parallel to the main square or marketplace on which they faced and a tall polygonal tower rising at the center of the front. By their prominence in the *Stadtbild* such towers were, like contemporary Dutch *speeltoren*, recognized symbols of civic authority in German lands. The Perlachturm at Augsburg in Swabia and the one Hoffmann added to the Halle Rathaus are good examples. He introduced here, however, a major variant to this scheme by using a T-shaped plan. Thus the Schweinfurt tower—which is not especially tall—rises, not directly in front of the main facade, but against the gable of a projecting wing. This produces a more complex mass composition than was common earlier, somewhat as Parr was then doing so differently at Brzég. At the base of the tower there is a low rectangular projection in which one would expect to find the principal portal; instead, there are—at least today—only four small arched openings on the front. The main entrances are to the left and right on the sides of the central wing and lead into a cross-passage.

These two portals of the Schweinfurt Rathaus, and also the slightly smaller ones at each end of the facade of the main block, are consistently "Early Renaissance" in character; so, for that matter, is most of the detailing elsewhere. Moreover, as in the case of the parapets with which he had fronted the tribunes in the Halle Marktkirche fifteen years before (Pl. 37), Hoffmann continued to use Late Gothic tracery in

[51] Dehio, *Steiermark*, pp. 94-95, 277; Baldass, *Österreich*, pls. 14-15.

[52] Dehio, *Steiermark*, p. 388, pl. 314; Kunstdenkmäler in Österreich, *Oberösterreich, Niederösterreich, Burgenland* [Munich, 1967] (henceforth cited as KDÖ, *Oberösterreich*), pp. 387-388, pl. 93.

[53] Reclams *Bayern*, p. 812.

[54] See article "Nikolaus Hoffmann" in ThB.

the open one that runs all the way along the base of the tall roof.

If, indeed, Hoffmann first worked under Nickel Gromann at Torgau in the early forties, he certainly did not follow the line of Gromann's later development. Nor did he really compete here at Schweinfurt with the latter's Altenburg Rathaus of some ten years earlier except in the tower—as also, for that matter, in the one he was adding at this point to the Halle town hall. In addition to the Late Gothic parapet here, finial-like figures topping the steps of the gables still animate the outline in a rather Late Gothic way quite as on the retardataire *Kanselarij* of 1566-1571 at Leeuwarden in Holland.[55] There are two pairs of these on the gable of the front wing and four pairs, with a single figure at the crown of each, on those at the ends. Scrolls, on the other hand, play only a minor part in elaborating the outline of the gables against the sky. Two *welsche Hauben*, one above the other, terminate the clock-tower rather than the more Italianate arcaded lantern under a single domelet on his Halle tower.

Below, the walls of the upper storeys of the tower of the Schweinfurt Rathaus are rather simply panelled between rows of windows. These walls, moreover, are all of ashlar masonry, while only the trim of the portals and windows is executed in cut stone on the stuccoed rubble walls of the main block. Because a major street enters the marketplace at the left end of the Rathaus the whole of that end is exposed and appropriately elaborated. A five-stage gable rises over this front against which a subsidiary projection, covered at gable level with a curved hip-roof, is set asymmetrically. Thus the mass composition is distinctly varied, but without approaching the architectonic order of Parr's at Brzég.

Hoffmann was also slightly involved in these years in the complicated story of the design and construction of the Rathaus at Rothenburg-o.-d.-Tauber, further south in Franconia (Pl. 243). The surviving rear half of the mediaeval Rathaus here, begun in the thirteenth century, presents a very plain, tall front to the street, with a steep gable that is topped by a slim tower and an array of Gothic finials. To the right the equally tall gable of the later Renaissance Rathaus rises beside it. This is at the south end of a long block filling all of one side of the irregularly oblong marketplace. The setting provides still what has been, ever since the day of the Austrian theorist Camillo Sitte,

the most generally admired example of German urban design of the later Middle Ages and the Renaissance.

In 1501 a bad fire had cleared the site in the marketplace beside the old building. Only in 1568,[56] however, did the Council of Rothenburg—like Schweinfurt an imperial free city that had turned Lutheran very early in 1524—call on Leonhard Weidmann to provide a *Visierung* (project) for a new front wing on the Rathaus. Weidmann, who had earlier been employed as a mason and stone-carver in Brandenburg and in Saxony, received his citizenship in Rothenburg that same year. Then, in 1570, Hoffmann was called in to pass judgement on Weidmann's design. Construction now began, first under the supervision of Wolf Löscher (†1577) from Nürnberg down to 1573 and later of a Saxon, Hans Helwig, known as Hans von Annaberg. Most of the carved work, however, was executed by Weidmann. Indeed, he eventually became in 1574 or 1575 *Stadtbaumeister*. In 1574-1578 he built the *Spital* (hospital), in 1589-1591 the Gymnasium for the city authorities, and in 1596, for a private client, the so-called Baumeisterhaus (Pl. 320), prominently located in the Obere Schmiedgasse just below the marketplace.[57] Thus, in the end, Weidmann contributed more than any other to the distinctive character of the sixteenth-century Rothenburg that so largely survives.

Like Hoffmann's Schweinfurt Rathaus, the one at Rothenburg is retardataire in design; however, its latent mediaevalism is partially masked by the heavily rusticated loggia erected in 1681 at the base of the facade that extends along the marketplace. Thanks to its corner site, the building has like Hoffmann's two principal fronts: a gabled one beside the old Gothic wing, and the longer one, broken by a short octagonal stair-tower, facing the square. Because of the rising site and the disposition of the streets, the visual emphasis is on the corner where an oriel projects. Indeed, that oriel is, like Gromann's on the corners of the Altenburg Rathaus (Pl. 234), the most richly decorated feature of the whole. Thus the composition is markedly picturesque and quite asymmetrical in contrast to Parr's carefully balanced massing at Brzég (Pl. 240) or even Gromann's approximation of a similar sort of order at Altenburg.

Most of the detailing on the Rothenburg Rathaus that can be attributed to Weidmann is quite as idio-

[55] *Niederlanden*, p. 384, pl. 190.

[56] Reclams *Bayern*, pp. 773-774.
[57] *Ibid.*, pp. 766-775.

syncratic as Gromann's at Altenburg, but much simpler. A conspicuous exception, however, is the portal in the ground storey on the south end with its correctly detailed Ionic columns and plain crowning pediment. This portal is centered between two identical oblong windows in a well-organized Academic composition that might be thought beyond the competence of either Weidmann or Hoffmann: Perhaps it was the work of Loscher or Helwig; even, like the loggia on the long side, it could be a later interpolation. Above the lowest level the many windows on the south front are unevenly grouped two and four in each of the upper storeys; they have, all the same, continuous cornices above heavily molded frames. These cornices repeat the horizontal emphasis of the bold string-courses that cross the facade at both floor and sill-levels in sharp contrast to the almost mediaeval verticalism, reflecting that of the Gothic wing on the left, of the composition as a whole.

Except for the impingement of the corner oriel on the right, however, the design of the gable over the south end of the Rothenburg Rathaus reverts to the symmetry of the ground storey but there is nothing Academic about its detailing. Rather the four stages of the gable display a sort of grid-pattern very like that on many German gables of the thirties. Here this grid is in exceptionally high relief because of the substitution of rounded members—no more columnar than Unkair's corner shafts—for the more usual pilaster-strips between the windows and the introduction of continuous molded strings at the levels of the top and bottom of the many small windows. On the other hand, the S-scrolls flanking the first, second and third stages and the concave C-scrolls on the top stage are more vigorous in their curvature and more heavily modelled than Parr's at Brieg, not to speak of Hoffmann's at Schweinfurt (Pls. 240, 244); the terminal element, moreover, is a plain pediment. But this last is more pointed than the Academic one over the portal below and on it stands a tall figure—a *Landsknecht?*—with lance and shield. Finally, ball-topped finials animate the whole outline still in a somewhat Gothic way, so that the general effect is rather hybrid by the contemporary standards of larger towns in this decade.

On the long side of the Rothenburg Rathaus the fenestration and string-courses are identical with those of the middle storeys on the end; but the windows are here mostly in pairs except for one of three lights beside the corner oriel. Because of that irregularity the stair-tower is not quite in the center and the

slanted windows in its sides provide a further break in the ordonnance of this front. The *welsche Haube* at the top of the tower, with fluted lunettes over each of the eight faces just below, recalls at enlarged scale the turrets, perhaps fifty years earlier in date, on Jakob Fugger's remodelled house at Maximilianstrasse 38 in Augsburg (Pl. 8). More relevant comparisons might be with those of the 1530s on the Gifhorn and Celle Schlösser (Pls. 56, 98) or the crown added in that decade atop the much larger tower of St. Elisabeth at Wrocłav, though it is not likely the Rothenburgers knew any of these particular examples.

An even more conservative work of these years is the small quadrangle, somewhat like an Oxford or Cambridge college, that the Nürnberg Council built, not in or near the city itself, but at the small village of Altdorf, to the southeast on the way to Amberg, in the early seventies. The Nürnbergers had acquired Altdorf in 1505 in the War of Bavarian Succession from the Wittelsbachs of the older Neuburg line, the so-called "rich dukes," who had possessed it since the end of the fourteenth century. In 1565 the Council had decided to move the Gymnasium Aegidianum, a high school founded in 1526, to a more rural and peaceful location. In 1571 the construction of the building began, and it was brought to completion in 1575.[58]

Toward the street the Altdorf college is protected by a wall with a central gateway; on the west side of the court a long block rises three storeys; to north and south two-storey wings advance to meet the wall in front (Pl. 245). The principal feature is a six-storey square tower with clock-faces set in the top storey. This is crowned by an S-curved roof so steep that it barely approaches a *welsche Haube*. The second stair-tower in the north wing at Altdorf is octagonal and has an even steeper roof. The only element in the whole complex of Italianate character is the arcading in the ground storey, open along the western block but mostly blind on the side wings. Yet the arches of this arcade are so plain and low and broad, and carried on such heavy square piers above blunt impost capitals, that the effect is more Romanesque than either Late Gothic or Renaissance. The windows, which are arranged in regular, or nearly regular, rows in the upper storeys all have segmental arches still of the sort often used in the 1530s. These are here detailed with jambs and archivolts so deeply chamfered and molded that they have no Renaissance character at all.

[58] *Ibid.*, p. 19.

The marked stylistic retardation of this college at Altdorf probably resulted more from the laggard taste of the Nürnberg Council than the fact that the building served educational purposes. Yet it is not much more retardataire than various English colleges of somewhat similar quadrangular plan built well into the next century such as Wadham at Oxford of 1610-1613 and Peterhouse at Cambridge, built 1625-1634, to mention two vary late examples.

Saxon taste in architecture was, as it had long been, much more advanced than that of the Nürnbergers. Bahrmann's brewery, An der Frauenkirche 3 in Meissen (Pl. 246), is a striking example of town architecture, dated 1569-1571,[59] that rivals in distinction contemporary houses in Hameln (Pls. 227, 228). The two rows of squarish windows in the upper storeys of the tall narrow front have bevelled stone jambs and lintels decorated with big hemispheres. The asymmetrically placed portal below has similar ornamentation at the top and in the spandrels of the arch, while Corinthian columns of correct proportion flank it at either side. Higher up, a sort of attic above the equally correct entablature carries a carved relief of Samson and the Lion and is framed by modest scrolls under a plain pediment.

All this detailing on the Meissen brewery suggests in its delicacy a somewhat earlier date than 1570. On the other hand, the big scale and the elaborate treatment of the gable is rather advanced for that date, even though the same windows as below are used at smaller size in both the first and second stages. At the base of the gable, above the main cornice, there comes first an attic-like stage subdivided by five podia. These are set under the three stubby pilaster-strips on the lowest stage of the gable and also under the centers of the two windows. A second run of podia, unexpectedly, was also introduced above this stage beneath the pilaster-strips. But both on this stage and on the next it is the boldness and the verticalism of the S-scrolls at the sides that is particularly striking. Moreover, the angels placed beyond the scrolls in the lower stage and, even more, the urns in the parallel positions at the sides of the next stage above are most unusual and perhaps unique. The strong horizontals of the lower stages are repeated, however, in the short terminal one even though, above its broken pediment, a third angel silhouetted against the sky provides a finial vertical accent.

Naturally, Rathäuser more generally received elabo-

rate architectural treatment than breweries. There are two in Saxony that date, the one partially, the other entirely, from the early seventies. At Wittenberg, on the north side of the marketplace, the big Late Gothic Rathaus (Pl. 247) of 1522-1540, as begun in the time of Friedrich der Weise, with its absolutely regular rows of curtain-arched windows in the first and second storeys, was not rebuilt at this later time. But its most conspicuous features, the gables at the ends and the ranges of four big stone dormers on either side date from 1570-1573.[60] So also does the two-storeyed porch projecting in the center of the south facade. This has two sets of freestanding Doric columns, plain below and fluted above, supporting three pediments loaded with elaborate figure sculpture, one in front and two at the sides.

The gables on the Wittenberg Rathaus, effectively of four stages at the ends and of three on the dormers along the sides, are much less assertive than that on the Meissen brewery. Above the plain rectangular stages at their base the flanking S-scrolls are less vertical and the crowning pediments are enlivened only by short ball-topped finials. As on the front of Parr's Rathaus at Brzég or earlier on the Joachimsbau in Berlin, the reiteration of these regularly spaced features is most effective. Though these update the whole exterior they are all the same not inharmonious with the simpler and even more regular treatment, already so "modern," of the wall-surfaces below. Thus the stylistic continuity of sixteenth-century German civil architecture, early and later, is here very evident.

As in the case of the Meissen brewery, no architect can be named for the work at Wittenberg as a whole, either in the twenties or in the seventies. However, the porch with its rich figural decoration was executed in 1573 by Georg Schröter, the sculptor from Torgau who had provided the pulpit in the chapel at Schwerin in 1562. In the intervening decade he had moved well away from his Early Renaissance beginnings.

The Rathaus at Gera, the biggest town between Karl-Marx-Stadt and Weimar, was built in 1573-1576[61] (Pl. 248). This has been attributed to Nickel Gromann and he may well, as at Altenburg, have supplied the original design for execution by another, perhaps N. Teiner. The overpowering octagonal clock-tower here, projecting through a full half of its diameter from the front and rising to con-

[59] Dehio, *Dresden*, p. 273; Piltz, *D.D.R.*, p. 526.

[60] DKD, *Sachsen*, p. 394; Piltz, *D.D.R.*, p. 251.
[61] DKD, *Thüringen*, p. 373; Piltz, *D.D.R.*, p. 383.

siderably more than twice the height of the main block, is not symmetrically placed as on the Rathaus at Altenburg; but the portals and the two-light windows in the upper storeys, two to the right and three to the left of the tower, have pediments resembling those Gromann used at Heldburg and also at Altenburg ten years before. All the windows in the tower, moreover, even the slanted ones in the third and fourth storeys, have pediments too, but here these are segmental.

Furthermore, the diamond rustication of the rectangular projection in which the main portal is set at the base of the Gera tower recalls Altenburg. On the other hand, the curious attempt to assimilate the shafts at the corners of the tower, regardless of the varying height of the storeys, to Ionic columns, somewhat as Hieber had attempted to do fifty years earlier on the corners of his model for the Augsburg Perlachturm (Pl. 23) seems, like the rather *volkisch* figural carving on the portals, too provincial to have been proposed at this late date by Gromann. As regards the main portal at Gera one might further note how closely herms are associated on that with a chamfered arch of the autochthonous kind, first introduced at Görlitz in the 1520s (Pls. 64, 69), that had been widely popular ever since in Saxony at a vernacular level. These herms were, of course, a much later import and one already handled at Wismar in the early fifties with greater competence (Pls. 146, 147).

With this Saxon Rathaus one far to the west may be contrasted. In the Rathaus at Emden (Fig. 39), across the Dollart estuary from Dutch Friesland, more up-to-date use was being made of Netherlandish forms by Laurens I van Steenwinckel. This architect had come from Antwerp and settled in Emden in 1567 long before the Rathaus was begun in 1574.[62] He may have been assisted by his son, Hans I (†1601), who was also Antwerp-born. In 1578, two years after the Emden Rathaus had been completed, Hans went to Helsingør in Denmark to work with, or under, Anthonis van Opbergen (1543-1611)—who came from Mechelen, it will be recalled—on the Kronborg Slot eventually, in 1585, succeeding Opbergen. His son, Hans II (1587-1639), who was born in Copenhagen and later employed on the Frederiksborg Slot at Hillerød that Christian IV of Denmark began in 1602.[63] Even in the third generation, moreover, the

Steenwinkels had not lost touch with the Netherlands for Hans II was sent in his youth to study with Lieven de Key (1560-1627), one of the two leading Dutch architects of the day.[64]

Well before Laurens came to Emden, most of the houses in the city were thoroughly Netherlandish, indeed rather specifically Dutch, in character. Among those that once stood in the marketplace but were destroyed in the last war were excellent examples of what was earlier called "Dutch High Renaissance." These had engaged columns of stone between the windows and several even were without visible gables above their horizontal crowning cornices.[65] Others, one of them dated 1548, evidently looked more typically Dutch, since they were built of brick interlaced with stone and had gables flanked by modest scrolls and capped by fluted segmental pediments. The ones with orders on the facade must have been very like such Westphalian houses under strong Dutch influence as the undated one at Ägdienstrasse 11 in Münster or the much later Krameramtshaus there of 1588. Here in Emden they may well have been considerably earlier.

Though Laurens van Steenwinckel came not from Holland but from Antwerp—being almost certainly a Protestant fleeing from Philip II's Inquisition—and obviously knew the Antwerp Stadhuis well, the Emden one was in some respects more Dutch than Brabantine. The eaves gallery, though here cantilevered out from the face of the wall, does reflect that on the Antwerp town hall (Pl. 175), but otherwise it was much simpler than the presumptive model. But that was evidently also true of Floris's own Hanseaten Huis in Antwerp (Pl. 204) as that was carried out in the mid-sixties shortly after the Stadhuis was finished. No proper orders were used on the Emden Rathaus except for that on the single cross-gable over the entrance. This gable, moreover, was not only off-center but much lower than that on the Antwerp town hall. The main entrance, perhaps marking the location of an earlier side street, was covered by a slightly flattened arch, very plain except for the rusticated voussoirs and ashlar of the spandrels.

Across the facade at Emden—which was all of

[62] Horst, *Architektur*, pl. IX, shows the Emden Rathaus before the war.

[63] Reclams *Niedersachsen*, p. 155; D. F. Slothouwer, *Bouwkunst der Nederlandsche Renaissance in Denemarken*, Am-

sterdam, 1924 (henceforth cited as Slothouwer, *Denemarken*), pp. 22-43. J. A. Skovgaard, *A King's Architecture: Christian IV and his Buildings*, London [1973] (henceforth cited as Skovgaard, *Christian IV*), pp. 131-132, lists five van Steenwinkels with brief biographical notes.

[64] Skovgaard, *Christian IV*, pp. 17-25.

[65] Horst, *Architektur*, pp. 196, 233-237, fig. 162.

Fig. 39. Laurens van Steenwinckel: Emden,
Rathaus, 1574-76, elevation

Rathaus zu Emden [99]).

stone, not of stone and brick as one might have expected—the windows ran in regular rows, with seven
to the left of the three bays above the entrance and
ten to the right. All were very large, with only the
narrowest piers of ashlar masonry between. The
ground storey together with its mezzanine corresponded closely with the height of the asymmetrically
placed main entrance, but the basic regularity of the
composition was further broken by a subsidiary entrance, arched and flanked by an order, which was
rather wider than a normal bay. This opened just
to the right of the still broader principal portal. The
first storey, defined just above its base by a modillioned string-course at sill-level, rose all the way up
to the eaves gallery. Since this storey was taller than
the combined height of the ground storey and its
mezzanine the enormous windows were not only divided vertically by mullions but also horizontally by
transoms at half-height in a distinctly Netherlandish
way.

Behind the front gable at Emden, riding the ridge
of the tall hip-roof, was a massive square block from
which an octagonal lantern rose in three stages. In
the lowest stage, which carried clock-faces on the
cardinal sides, the corners were marked by engaged
columns; the next stage was arched and carried a
welsche Haube out of which rose a final open stage
capped by a tiny "onion." Unlike the front facade,
the very big and tall chimneys, one at either end and
four to the rear, were of brick with stone bands, very
much in the Dutch manner.

There is no good reason, all the same, to call this
Emden Rathaus "Dutch," much less "Dutch High
Renaissance." Its author was from Antwerp, but the
proto-Academic aspect of mid-century Brabantine architecture, as illustrated in the Antwerp Stadhuis, is
reflected only in the *parti*, yet the characteristic ornament of Vredeman appeared only in the carved panels of the gable. The outline of that, moreover, was
by current German standards relatively simple and
static. It recalls, rather, Pasqualini's Serlian one at
Buren (Pl. 43) a little but it is nothing like those of
the forties on the Dresden Moritzbau (Pl. 131) that
Steenwinckel might more likely have known.

The Emden Rathaus provides further evidence that the current of Northern Mannerism only rarely flowed eastward across the borders of the southern and the northern Netherlands into contiguous German districts. Rather, the new ornament was widely but unevenly distributed in Germany by the books, issued in Antwerp from the mid-century onwards, with plates of Floris's and later of Vredeman's designs. Also—though one suspects less ubiquitously than is often supposed—it was brought in more directly by those two artists and by the other travelling sculptors and craftsmen from the Low Countries who were occasionally employed in Germany.[66] The Emden Rathaus, having been designed by an Antwerp architect rather than a craftsman, was in fact less markedly Northern Mannerist in character than most work of the day in eastern Westphalia and in the Brunswick electorate or even in Saxony.[67] But it was hardly very proto-Academic either as contrasted with its Antwerp model.

The Rathaus at Rothenburg-o.-d.-Tauber and, *a fortiori*, the college at Altdorf were both retardataire compared with contemporary practice in the German districts just mentioned. By the end of the decade, however, a somewhat humbler new structure in Franconia was more up to date. The Rathaus (Pl. 249) of the small town of Marktbreit, on the Main southeast of Würzburg, was begun for the prince-bishop of Würzburg Julius Echter in 1579[68] by Hans Kessebrot, a stone-mason from nearby Segnitz. The front of this he topped by gables with the bold new outline characteristic of the house facades by Tönnis and others (Pls. 227, 228) in contemporary Hameln. These gables at Marktbreit rise in three stages with each stage flanked by heavy S-scrolls. On the east and also beside the contiguous Maintor, the city gate erected only in 1600, the scrolls are tightly spiralled outward at their tops and closely, even rather awkwardly, associated in each stage with a columnar order. The entablature of that order carries on its two projecting ends spheres of stone to punctuate the outline. In the very plain lower walls of rubble, on the other

hand, the paired windows in the upper storey are still of the "curtain-topped" sort as, indeed, are even those on the later gate. Internally, the amount of light such fenestration admits is much reduced by the depth of the reveals in the thick stone walls and the dark wood of the wainscoting (Pl. 250).

Externally, the many windows are set nearly regularly along the left side of the Marktbreit Rathaus, but slightly off-center on the gabled front. Also off-center are the two portals. On the larger one bevelled blocks of rustication cut across both the fluted pilasters at either side and the archivolt of the semicircular arch of the doorway; the smaller one to the left has, instead, engaged columns and a slightly flattened arch. Both are capped above the entablature with the same sort of banded scrollwork.

Similar, but much coarser, scrollwork edges the three stages of the tall gables on the town hall at Marktbreit and obelisks rise, as so often, from the ends of the cornice-like string-courses between the stages. The four windows of the first stage of the gables and the two of the second are separated by pilaster-strips in the manner first introduced in German gable-design in the early thirties. Despite the experienced client, this must be considered provincial compared to contemporary work in Bremen and Münster, not to speak of Hameln. The Rathaus and the Maintor beside it are rather less hybrid all the same than most examples of the "Juliusstil." That will become evident in later chapters where Julius's commissions of the decades 1580-1620 are described. The Maintor belongs in date, of course, with the later work, but its close association with, and similarity to, the Rathaus next door suggests its mention out of sequence at this point where it is incidentally illustrated (Pl. 249).

A modest city gate, earlier in date but of much more sophisticated design, survives at Amberg, which lies well to the east of Nürnberg on the way to Schwanndorf. The walls that surround it were begun in the fourteenth century by Emperor Ludwig the Bavarian, continued in the next century and, as so often, further strengthened and modernized in the sixteenth by the Electors Palatine. In the fortifications four of the five original gates still survive. Of these only the Wingershofertor of 1576-1580,[69] however, be-

---

[66] Later, the Netherlanders active in Germany were usually Italian-trained. This is true of Frederik Sustris, Peter Candid (Pieter de Witte) and Adriaen de Fries, to mention three of the most important. Artistically, therefore, they count as Italians, not northerners.

[67] This reinforces the conclusion that the development of the scalloped gable in the third quarter of the century in Germany was largely autochthonous despite probable Dutch influence at Schloss Horst in the early sixties.

[68] Reclams *Bayern*, p. 491.

[69] *Ibid.*, p. 40.
The design of the rusticated archway at Ritthem gateway, so vigorously Serlian for its early date, 1547, is incorporated in fortifications carried out for the Viceroy Mary of Hungary, the sister of Charles V, by Donato de Boni and a northerner,

longs largely to this period. The other three, all the same, were in fact modified and extended in 1574, 1581 and 1587, respectively, by Friedrich III and his successors Ludwig VI and Johann Kasimir, the regent for young Friedrich IV.

The inner arch of the Wingershofertor is mediaeval and of brick; the outer Torbau, however, is all of stone and rusticated. A central square tower rises over the broad segmental archway and lower wings extend at either side. The tower is capped with a pyramidal hip-roof, resembling at much smaller scale Gromann's on the Altenburg Rathaus, and the wings are also hip-roofed. Squarish openings for artillery framed by heavy curb moldings, six on the tower and two on each wing, interrupt the bold surface pattern of chamfered ashlar blocks. Two armorial panels, one lined up with the lowest pair of openings just above the arch and the other centered between the four upper openings, provide the only carved ornament on this small but impressive example of military architecture. The gateway was very likely designed by some Italian military engineer.

A more appropriate conclusion to this account of buildings other than major Schlösser and churches, large and small, erected in the sixties and seventies than the city gate that has been discussed is the *Alte Hofhaltung* (old bishop's palace) in Bamberg (Pl. 251), or at least that portion of it occupied by the *Ratstube* (council room). In fact, this was as much a princely town house as a center of diocesan administration. The prince-bishopric of Würzburg, often held jointly with that of Bamberg, was ruled through the centuries by a series of ecclesiastical magnates who were great builders. It was, for example, the climactic activities of the Schönborn bishops in the eighteenth century that produced the famous Residenz at Würzburg as also the Neue Hofhaltung here. In the late sixteenth and early seventeenth centuries their predecessor Julius Echter, who has just been mentioned, set a pace in Würzburg itself and the vicinity.

At Bamberg, somewhat earlier, Prince-Bishop Friedrich von Wurssberg commissioned in 1570[70] from Caspar Vischer designs for the edifices flanking the entrance to the galleried mediaeval court of the Alte Hofhaltung. Construction was completed by 1577 by the local builder Erasmus Braun with the assistance

of the stone-carver Pankraz Wagner (†1584). It will be recalled that Vischer was an architect long employed by Georg Friedrich of Brandenburg-Kulmbach. He had indeed been working on the margrave's grand scheme for the Schöner Hof at the Plassenburg above Kulmbach since the early sixties. Also by Vischer was the less ambitious Burg at Streitburg, on the Wiesin between Bayreuth and Forchheim. A ruin since 1811, this was erected in 1563-1565[71] for Georg Friedrich, the same years as the Schöner Hof.

It is interesting that this Catholic bishop employed as architect one so long in the service of a Lutheran magnate—a magnate who was, moreover, a foe of the Würzburg and Bamberg bishops—to provide plans, but that was hardly exceptional in this period. Moreover, after his employment at Bamberg, Vischer may have worked again for Georg Friedrich from about 1576 at Schloss Weinstein, which is in Upper Franconia a little to the west of Kulmbach.

What was built by Braun from Vischer's designs at this point consists of two parts, contiguous but not closely related in character. On the right is a double portal leading into the fifteenth-century Fachwerk court; on the left, in rivalry with the Romanesque north transept of the cathedral nearby, rises the tall but narrow rectangular block of the Ratstube. This has a stair-tower set back on its northern side, that is away from the church and inside the old court. Neither portion has much resemblance to anything at the Plassenburg. The two arches of the portal, one narrow and one wide, are flanked by herms. Such had found no place earlier in the Schöner Hof and may well be not of Vischer's but of Wagner's design. Higher up a many-figured frieze, which was more certainly executed by Wagner, is flanked by recumbent nudes—these latter strangely out of scale—and then crowned with the episcopal arms surrounded by intricate three-dimensional scrollwork. That scrollwork is the most advanced element of the whole composition.

The Ratstube at Bamberg has three main storeys below a very steep three-staged gable. The stair-tower, semi-octagonal for three storeys, has a squared-out top storey with a cantilevered corner. The most ornate feature is the oriel, also cantilevered, that projects from the right side of the front in the first and second storeys. Both storeys of this have paired windows framed by half-columns and much armorial carving above and below the first-storey windows.

Pieter Fransz., on Fort Rammekens near Zeeburg in Zeeland: *Kunstreisboek*, p. 513.

[70] H. Mayer, *Bamberger Residenzen: Eine Kunstgeschichte der Alte Hofhaltung . . .* , Munich, 1951, pp. 26-43.

[71] Reclams *Bayern*, p. 841.

Panelled pilaster-strips frame the front and there is an additional vertical element running up through the two lower stages of the gable. The first and third stages of the main gable, as also the single stage of the smaller one over the stair-tower, are flanked by very boldly curved S-scrolls, their fields filled with carving. The second stage of the main gable substitutes convex quadrants for the S-scrolls, and both are topped by fluted *welsche Gebel*.

The windows throughout the Bamberg Ratstube are relatively large, close-set and of squarish shape. Yet their frames of fillets that cross at the corners are still Late Gothic rather than Renaissance. Indeed, the whole design in its flat linear organization shows no such reflection of the new modes of this third quarter of the century as does the sculpture on the portal. Though Vischer did not die until 1580 he must by this time have been fairly old and somewhat out of touch with the new currents of Northern Mannerism that were reaching by the end of the decade even such a small town as Marktbreit under the aegis of Friedrich von Wurssberg's successor Julius Echter.

The Schlösser, the town houses and the other buildings described in this chapter and the one before are, of course, by no means all that survives from the 1560s and 1570s. But most of the more conspicuous monuments, whether or not of much individual distinction, as well as those especially significant for the main line of development of German Renaissance architecture in the third quarter of the century, have been discussed. Included are a few badly damaged or destroyed in the last war of which good old photographs or other visual documents are available for the exteriors if not, usually, the interiors. One monumental interior which does survive is in Schloss Ambras near Innsbruck of the early seventies, far to the southeast. That will be described later in connection with various German examples of great halls in Chapter VIII. An even more sumptuous, though much smaller, interior of a totally different sort is still largely extant in Lübeck. Though this is dated loosely 1572-1583, it is illustrated (Pl. 441) much later here and briefly described, out of sequence because of its relevance to similar work in the north at Schloss Gottorf in Schleswig that is of still later date: 1609-1613.

Subject to extraneous circumstances such as wars, depressions or epidemics it is natural, as any stylistic episode in the history of architecture approaches maturity, that the number of buildings illustrative of the new mode increases despite the very many that continue some earlier phase still in favor with those who undertook to erect new buildings. Statistics have no real meaning in this connection since what one might profess to be counting can hardly be precisely defined. In any case, extant monuments represent only a portion of those that once existed, even if the ones which have been demolished but about which historians may—or may not—be adequately informed at secondhand be added.

Thanks to the religious peace of 1555 in Germany the following quarter-century saw a very considerable increase in building both secular and ecclesiastical. In the remaining decades of the sixteenth century after 1580, however, secular production seems at least to have levelled off. This impression, all the same, could well be due to unconscious selection within the increased volume of work which survives. However that may be, only a few things as notable as the Fuggerkapelle of 1510, Schloss Hartenfels of 1530, the Landshut Stadtresidenz of 1540, the Schöner Hof of the Plassenburg of 1560 and the Hameln houses of the 1570s were erected in the 1580s and 1590s. Even so, a generally higher standard of production was perhaps achieved, at least in some parts of Germany. Schloss Hämelschenburg (Fig. 50, Pls. 299-305) is of a quality rarely exceeded either in Germany or in other northern countries in those decades.

Six

THE REVIVAL OF
CHURCH-BUILDING AND
MAJOR SCHLÖSSER OF THE
LATE SIXTEENTH CENTURY

As has already been indicated in earlier chapters, it was under Lutheran sponsorship that church-building in Germany revived in the mid-sixteenth century. To recapitulate: first in the new cycle came the construction of the Marienkirche at Marienberg in southern Saxony in 1558-1564, a few years after the religious peace of 1555. Then, in the 1560s and early 1570s, the Schlosskapellen described in Chapter V were either newly built or provided with up-to-date furnishings in the new taste. For the most part these chapels survive today in their original condition as the Marienberg church does not. In areas ruled by Catholic princes, the old mediaeval *Pfarrkirchen* (parish churches) continued in use through the later decades of the century with little or no modification. Where Protestants were in control, for that matter, few changes were made in older edifices either except for the removal of subsidiary altars. Yet elaborate new main altars were often introduced in such churches and, in some, even more monumental tombs of Lutheran potentates clog up the east ends. There were also many new pulpits. By this time all these features were of either Renaissance or Mannerist character, many of them very richly carved and polychromed. Except for the Saxon Elector August's chapel in the Augustusburg of 1568-1573 (Fig. 36, Pls. 200-202), however, no new edifice either Catholic or Protestant erected in the third quarter of the century was of consistently post-mediaeval design.

The situation changed markedly after 1580; in the next two decades more churches, both Catholic and Protestant, rose in Germany than in any other northern country. In Elizabeth I's contemporary England there was no new church-building of any importance, though a few edifices begun much earlier were carried forward, most notably Bath Abbey. The college chapels erected for Jesus and Lincoln at Oxford closely followed mediaeval prototypes as did even that for

Wadham dating from James I's reign. At Peterhouse in Cambridge, moreover, built as late as 1628 in Charles I's time, the plan of the chapel was still traditional.

In France only one early Protestant church survives.[1] That is because resurgent Catholicism led in the seventeenth century to the demolition even of those that had survived the preceding wars. In the headquarters of the major new branch of the Reformed church in Geneva, where Jean Calvin ruled as a sort of Protestant pope, there was no church construction at all. Calvin himself was content with the mediaeval Cathédrale St.-Pierre, since 1532 a Protestant parish church, suitably but not drastically purged of Catholic fittings. Ulrich Zwingli in Zurich had gone further than Calvin in removing images and even organs from churches; but neither did he sponsor new church-building, nor were any churches erected elsewhere in Switzerland before the last quarter of the century.[2]

In two northern countries where Calvinism was almost as dominant as in Geneva—Holland and Scotland—no churches were built before the 1590s, though

[1] The exception is St.-Martin at Montbéliard (Doubs) in eastern France (see Chapter X). But Montbéliard was an enclave, called Mömpelgard in German, belonging to the Lutheran dukes of Württemberg. Furthermore, Duke Friedrich received there many Anabaptist refugees from Calvinist Holland.

[2] The earliest surviving Reformed churches built in Switzerland, the ones at Aarwagen and Ardez, date only from the 1570s: the former, which is in Canton Bern, from 1576-1577; the other, in the Lower Engadin, is probably of the same years. Both are modest rectangles with polygonal apses, but that at Ardez has an aisle with tribune over on one side only and both have western galleries: G. Germann, *Der protestantische Kirchenbau in der Schweiz*, Zurich [1963] pp. 43-48.

The columns at Ardez are crudely Tuscan and the balustrade of the tribune Italianate; the raised patterns on the vault are geometrical, moreover, not Gothic ribs.

the existing mediaeval churches were emptied of Catholic altars and often of sculpture and stained glass as well. The Burntisland church in Fifeshire in Scotland, begun in 1592,[3] is the oldest new-built edifice that survives in its original form. It is a good-sized square in plan and has a central tower carried on four plain pillars that define a central area. This makes the interior somewhat like that of the Huguenots' circular "Temple de paradis" completed in 1564 at Lyon in organization,[4] but it is all built of stone, not mostly of wood like the internal structure and the surrounding galleries of the French example. It differs more markedly from mediaeval churches in Scotland or elsewhere than anything built up to that time in Germany except Chiaramella's Wolfenbüttel chapel (Fig. 26). One might almost call the building a "meeting-house" or note, at least, that a Scottish "kirk" is usually no "church" in plan. The oldest Protestant church in the Netherlands was the equally modest one, begun in 1597 by Prince Maurits,[5] son and successor of William of Orange, for the new town of Willemstad in Noord Brabant. The octagonal plan of this recalls not so much the circular edifice in Lyon as the somewhat later polygonal *Temple* at La Rochelle.

The next Protestant edifice of consequence outside Germany, the Zuiderkerk in Amsterdam by Hendrik de Keyser, is more a church and less a *Temple*, "kirk" or "meeting house." Since that was not begun until 1603, it will be described in a later chapter. In Scandinavia, however, the chapel within the Kronborg Slot at Helsingør in Denmark was consecrated in 1582 a decade before the independent edifices at Burntisland and Willemstad were begun. In its present condition (Pl. 253) this resembles a rather small German Schlosskapelle, but it was refurbished in 1631 after a fire of 1629 by Hans II van Steenwinckel (1587-1639)[6] for Christian IV and once again—very attractively, if not altogether accurately—in 1838-1843 by the leading Danish architect of the day, M.G.B.

Bindesbøll. Like the Slot as a whole—at least as refaced in stone for Frederik II over the years 1578-1585[7]—the chapel was originally the work of Antonis van Opbergen (1543-1611) from Mechelen. The much larger and grander chapel in the Frederiksborg Slot at Hillerød, carried out for Christian IV, will be briefly discussed later since it dates from after 1600 like the Zuiderkerk in Amsterdam.

From the terminal decades of the century, as earlier, almost all surviving ecclesiastical edifices that were built by and for Protestants are in Germany. More than balancing this production, however, there now ensued a revival of Catholic church-building also. This revival was a major manifestation of the increased vigor of the Roman Church which had resulted from the concluding decisions of the Council of Trent in the 1560s. Even more effective were the militant activities of new religious orders, above all the Society of Jesus founded by St. Ignatius of Loyola.

The church that was the Jesuits' headquarters in Italy, the Gesù, begun by Vignola in the late 1560s and completed by Giacomo della Porta and others in the early 1580s, is generally accepted as the first architectural monument of major importance of the Counter Reformation. With its nave flanked not by aisles but by chapels, its domed crossing, short transept arms and apsidal east end, the Gesù has often been considered the basic model for Counter-Reformation churches everywhere. German historians and critics have long seen in the first great church built under Jesuit auspices in the north of Europe. St. Michael in Munich, an initiatory work of comparable significance for German church architecture of the next two centuries. As Hauttmann put it in 1923:[8] "Wie in einer Kernzelle finden sich hier die lebensfähigen Energien der Vergangenheit vererbt und alle Möglichkeiten der Folgezeit vorgebildet." Yet it is, in fact, rivalled in historical significance by the Münster of Sts. Peter and Paul (Pl. 255) at Klagenfurt in Carinthia, begun a year earlier by the Protestant authorities of that town and later taken over by the Jesuits. All the same, the Jesuits' church in Munich may be described first since it is rather unlikely that a Protestant church far to the south at Klagenfurt in Carinthia influenced the Catholic one in the Bavarian capital in the way it may well have a generation later a Lutheran one, the

[3] G. Hay, *The Architecture of Scottish Post-Reformation Churches 1560-1843*, Oxford, 1957, pp. 32-34, pl. 2.

[4] The construction of the "Temple de Paradis," as it was called, followed on Catherine de Medicis's Edict of Toleration of 1562.

[5] Maurits was named for his uncle Moritz of Saxony, but he was apparently more influenced by his French stepmother, born Louise de Coligny, the daughter of the Huguenot leader Admiral de Coligny. Maurits's half-brother Frederik Hendrik, Louise's son, was a godson of Henri IV.

[6] Slothouwer, *Denemarken*, pp. 40-41, 66; Skovgaard, *Christian IV*, pp. 19, 75.

[7] National Museum, *Kronborg*, pls. 33-34; Slothouwer, *Denemarken*, pp. 62-88; 18 pls.

[8] M. Hauttmann, *Geschichte der kirchlichen Baukunst in Bayern, Schwaben und Franken*, 2nd ed., Munich, 1923 (hereafter cited as Hauttmann, *Kirchliche Baukunst*), p. 16.

Hofkirche at Neuburg-a.-d.-Donau, in the Upper Palatinate.

The St. Michael we know today, either as restored since the war in 1946-1953 or from earlier photographs showing the original decoration on the vaults, was the result of two building campaigns: the first in 1583-1587 (Fig. 40) and the second, after the collapse

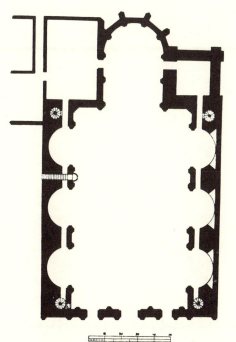

Fig. 40. ? Frederik Sustris *et al.*: Munich, St. Michael, plan as built, 1583-87

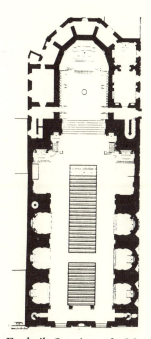

Fig. 41. Frederik Sustris *et al.*: Munich, St. Michael, plan with crossing and "east" end of 1593-97

of the tower made necessary the reconstruction of the choir, in 1593-1597 (Fig. 41).[9] The last date is that of the consecration. Though the church was erected for the Jesuits, it was Wilhelm V, Duke of Bavaria since 1579, who financed the construction. In the preceding years of the mid-1570s, before his accession, it will be recalled that Wilhelm had undertaken the modernization and redecoration of Burg Trausnitz at Landshut. As noted, that work was carried out by a group of Italians, previously employed by Hans Fugger in Augsburg, under the direction of Frederik Sustris (1524-1599). It is natural to suppose therefore

that Sustris would have been the choice of Wilhelm, if not of the Jesuits, to design the great new church in Munich; indeed, he is recorded as the responsible architect for the second campaign in the 1590s when the crossing and the "east" end—actually toward the north—were rebuilt and extended. Alternatively the Jesuits, who had been established in Munich since 1559, might well have called on one of their own members for plans even though the duke was providing the funds. That was frequently what happened with edifices the Order erected both in Italy and elsewhere. Neither supposition, however, is supported by the surviving documents.

At the hearing in 1590 after the collapse of the tower, the master-mason Wolfgang Miller (1537-?), who had been in charge of the construction of the church over the years 1583-1587, attempted to reduce his responsibility for the disaster by claiming that Sustris (whom he called Friedrich "Maler"—i.e. the painter) and Wendel Dietrich (c.1535-1621/1623) had both neglected to provide adequate supervision. Dietrich, a woodcarver from Augsburg, was later responsible for the magnificent ceiling (Pl. 350) over the great hall in Hans Fugger's Schloss at Kirchheim-a.-d.-Mindel and also in the 1590s for the high altar here in St. Michael (Pl. 256). He had evidently provided some drawings, most probably following Sus-

[9] Dehio, *Oberbayern*, pp. 20-23; Hauttmann, *Kirchliche Baukunst*, pp. 110-116; J. Braun, *Die Kirchenbau der deutschen Jesuiten*, 2 v., Freiburg-i.-B., 1908-1910 (henceforth cited as Braun, *Jesuiten*), pp. 49-95, figs. 8-10 (plans). Parallel with St. Michael the Jesuits also built the Salvatorkirche in Augsburg in 1582-1584 of which no trace survives: Braun, *Jesuiten*, pp. 43-49, figs. 6, 7.

tris's ideas since he had apparently no previous architectural experience and certainly lacked first-hand knowledge of the new churches then in construction in Italy. Sustris, Miller testified, had only visited the site "bisweilen" (sometimes) and Dietrich only three or four times a year. No mention is made of any Italian or any Jesuit. Sustris in these years was certainly responsible for even more extensive additions and alterations to the ducal Residenz here in Munich than he had earlier carried out at Burg Trausnitz[10] and that, as a more direct commission from Wilhelm, may well have preëmpted his attention. It remains, nonetheless, likely that he was the effective designer of St. Michael rather than either Miller or Dietrich.

Sustris's training, of course, had been primarily as a painter; but that he was already competent—and fairly up to date even by Italian standards—as an architectural designer the arcades and the Torbau of Burg Trausnitz make evident (Pl. 213). By 1569, when he left Italy, the Gesù was already under way and, through the Munich Jesuits or otherwise, he could have had access to Vignola's published designs for the Roman church. However, the earliest extant plan for the Munich church, probably prepared before Sustris's presumed intervention, shows a nave flanked not by chapels but with continuous side aisles. Thus it resembles the Gesù only very slightly in the crossing and at the "east" end.

The executed nave of St. Michael (Pls. 254, 256, 257) is very different, yet neither the three bays of that which date from the 1580s nor the new transepts and choir of the 1590s depend on the Gesù except for the dome Sustris intended, at least, to erect over the crossing. Indeed, the differences from the Gesù both in the nave and in the choir are far more notable than the few similarities. There are, for instance, no clerestorey windows of which the heads intersect the barrel vault of the nave in the Vignolan way. Rather, tribunes as deep and tall as the chapels below provide a complete second storey flanking the nave. Moreover, the choir, though apsidal-ended, is very much longer than that of the Roman church and pierced with windows as that is not.

In fact, as regards the nave, though not the later crossing and choir, St. Michael seems much closer to possible models that are both northern and Protestant, particularly the chapel of the Augustusburg (Pl. 201), completed ten years before the Munich church was begun, and also the Klagenfurt Münster (Pl. 255), the construction of which was under way in the same years of the 1580s. Of course the dimensions both of height and of breadth are much larger than those of the Augustusburg chapel—indeed the breadth is even greater proportionally than in the Gesù—and the wide piers, framed by pairs of fluted pilasters between the chapels and, again, above in a second order with panelled shafts between the bays of the tribune, do not at all resemble the Roman arch orders of the Saxon interior. At least August of Saxony's chapel would have provided a rather more accessible source than Serlio's sectional view of the Basilica of Maxentius which Hauttmann proposed because the chapels in Munich are all rounded as in the church-plan Serlio published in 1547 (Fig. 42). Only

Fig. 42. Sebastiano Serlio: church project, plan, 1547

the central bay of the hypothetical Classical model[11] is rounded. But a closer analogue, whether or not actually a real source, should now be described even though it has no rounded side chapels at all.

Despite its historical importance the Dreieinigkeits-

---

[10] In 1584-1586 Sustris remodelled the Gothic parish-church of St. Jakob at Dachau. Of his work there nothing remains: Dehio, *Oberbayern*, p. 98.

[11] Hauttmann, *Kirchliche Baukunst*, pp. 111-112, with illustrations. Serlio's church plan with rounded chapels flanking the nave is in his *Architectura*, Quinto libro, Paris, 1547, pl. 26 recto.

kirche or Münster in Klagenfurt[12]—since 1787, when the bishop moved his seat here from Gurk, the cathedral of Sts. Peter and Paul—is a disappointing church to visit. Although the contiguous structures have of late been partially cleared away it has no architectural exterior. Inside, the rich investiture of stucco and fresco decoration of 1725 by Kilian and Marz Josef Pittner overhead and the tall high altar with its painting of 1752 by Daniel Gran, not to speak of the elaborate pulpit of 1726 and the balancing Glorification of St. John Nepomuk, both carved by Johann Bacher, at the entrance to the choir, and the series of side altars of 1725-1726, create a Rococo interior of such consistent character that it is hard even to notice the surviving nave elevations of the 1580s.

Spacially the original, relatively short, rectangular nave of the Klagenfurt church as built 1582-1591, with aisles below and tribunes of the same height above, now opens to the east into a three-bayed choir, only slightly narrower, that is dominated by the high altar. Decoratively the veil of early Rococo ornament in low relief covering the spandrels of the arches of the aisles and the tribunes, their intradoses and the vaults behind distracts attention from the structural scheme, quite as the larger-scaled *stucchi* and the frescoes effectively obliterate the basic form of the barrel vault with its ranges of pointed intersections, as in the Gesù, over the clerestorey lunettes. Today, the view to the west (Pl. 255), where the two-storeyed elevation is carried across the end, gives a better idea of the original character of the interior, even though the tribune arches there are not round but pointed to make up for the relative narrowness of the three bays.

A two-storeyed interior elevation as in the nave at Klagenfurt—which had been introduced first in the oldest Protestant edifice in Germany, the Schlosskirche at Torgau (Pl. 125) of 1543-1544—was also used in Munich for St. Michael, but without the giant order of Klagenfurt. The next northern European example of an internal giant order appeared in the Collegiate Church of Zamošč[13] in Poland. Zamošč, which lies southeast of Lublin near the present Russian border, was the new town being planned at his birthplace

by Chancellor Jan Zamoyski. The Zamošč church was begun by an Italian architect in 1587, a few years after the one at Klagenfurt; the earliest example in Germany of an internal giant order is in the Hofkirche at Neuburg-a.-d.-Donau of 1607-1618 (Pl. 436). It is most unlikely that Bernardo Morando, Zamoyski's Italian architect—who was, as usual, primarily employed as an expert on fortifications to lay out the new town—was influenced by the Klagenfurt Münster, or even the Gesù. He came to Poland in 1578 from Padua in the Veneto and may rather have had Palladio's Venetian churches in mind. But Joseph Heintz (1564-1609), almost certainly the responsible designer at Neuburg, might well have followed a Protestant model for this Protestant church, especially as he came from Basel or Bern in Switzerland before he was trained in Italy. Ironically, the Klagenfurt Münster had already been taken over in 1604 by the Jesuits, just as the church at Neuburg would be a decade later.

What changes the Jesuits may have made at Klagenfurt so early remain uncertain; but in 1661 they added the Chapel of St. Francis Xavier on the south side and, in 1665, the deep choir. In that extension they repeated the two-storey elevation, introducing blind arches below and glazed loges above, but reduced the height of the latter compared to the tribunes in the nave in order to introduce a full entablature. There are also large semicircular clerestorey windows in the lunettes at the base of the choir vault since no light could come in here through tribunes. Of the Jesuits' decorative programme of this period only some *stucchi* of 1668 survive at the west end of the nave (Pl. 255).

To discount the likelihood of influence from Klagenfurt in Munich is to increase the possibility that the chapel of the Augustusburg (Pl. 201) was the model. However, the architectonic sobriety and plastic articulation of the compound piers and arches here —"High Renaissance" rather than "Protestant" in spirit—is not echoed in the Munich church. Instead, two ranges of niches with statues were introduced, one between the pairs of fluted pilasters in the lower storey and a second between the pairs of panelled ones above. The statues were executed in terra cotta from Sustris's designs by the Dutch-born sculptor Hubert Gerhard (c.1540/50-1620) and Sustris's son-in-law Hans Krumpper (c.1570-1634) from nearby Weilheim, both trained like Sustris in Italy.

Moreover, the barrel-vault of St. Michael is neither undecorated, as was that of the Gesù until the late

[12] KDÖ, *Kärnten Steiermark*, pp. 342-343. For historical background, see G. Mecenseffy, *Geschichte des Protestantismus in Österreich*, Graz-Cologne, 1956.

[13] J. Kowalczyk, *Kolegiata w Zamosciu*, Warsaw, 1968 (henceforth cited as Kowalczyk, *Kolegiata*). This elaborate monograph provides many measured drawings and illustrations of details.

seventeenth century, nor provided with a continuous pattern of simple geometrical bandwork as was that of the Augustusburg. In the Munich church pairs of panelled ribs rise from the upper pilaster order between the arches of the tribunes and, originally, quite rich ornamentation occupied all the surface between (Pl. 254). This stucco-work, probably executed by Gerhard, was organized on the main barrel-vault of the nave in an alternation of large circles with longitudinal panels of rectangular shape, both surrounded by moldings. The first and third bays had three circles and two rectangles separated by irregular spandrel-panels that were similarly framed; the second bay syncopated this arrangement, using two circles and three rectangular panels. The restorers have repeated the pattern, though with no subsidiary decoration such as once existed in some profusion (Pl. 256).

The pseudo-structural articulation of the interior of St. Michael is made more vertical visually, despite the absence of a giant order, by the omission of the entablature of the lower order above the arches of the side chapels and by the absence of any continuous horizontal member over the arches of the tribunes above at the base of the main vault. This membering, however, is not repeated on the inner wall of the "west" front (Pl. 257). There, the three arches that carry the shallow organ gallery are not separated by paired pilasters and the tall windows above do not correspond with the tribune arches along the sides of the nave. A circular window at the top once echoed more directly the shape of the round panels on the vault overhead than does the restored window now.[14]

As this arrangement of the fenestration in the "western" wall inside St. Michael makes evident, little or no attempt was made on the facade (Pl. 258), based on a design by Krumpper—who was Sustris's professional heir as well as his son-in-law—rather than by Sustris himself, to do as advanced architects were then doing in Rome and follow either of the two variant models that had been provided by this time: Vignola's published project for the Gesù and the facade as now nearly completed by others from a design of Giacomo della Porta. Thanks to the great width of the upper storey in Munich, made necessary by the tall tribunes inside—so different from the tiny balconettes above the arches along the nave in the Gesù—there was no room over the outermost bays

of the ground storey for great Albertian S-scrolls or even for Vignola's concave C-quadrants.

Furthermore, the entablature of the Doric order of pilasters in the ground storey of the facade of St. Michael does not break forward at the center as Vignola proposed for the Gesù, presumably because there is in Munich no axially placed main portal. Instead, two identical portals of red marble, designed by Sustris, each capped by an oculus opening between the horns of a broken segmental pediment, flank a large central niche. That niche contains a statue of Michael the Archangel modelled by Gerhard and cast in bronze by Martin Frey.

The next storey of the Munich facade has no continuous order; at the ends, however, truncated pilasters topped by plain obelisks are set outside the line of the taller ones framing the slightly narrower wall at this level. Between the three big arched windows shorter niches holding statues of early Wittelsbachs, with plain sunken panels over them, model the surface quite differently than in the storey below, much as if someone other than Krumpper had become involved in the design as well as in the execution. Even the ground storey, moreover, was not carried out quite as Krumpper planned it.

Above, a rather tight arrangement of niches and panels fills the much shorter top storey of the facade of St. Michael in order to display more of Wilhelm's ancestors. The gable capping this is not Italianate at all but faintly echoes in its bandwork secular German gables of the preceding decade. Hitherto such gables had appeared only rarely in Bavaria despite the very early introduction of their presumptive prototypes on the north wing of the Neuburg Schloss in the contiguous Upper Palatinate. Moreover, the use of bandwork decoration of the sort introduced, however timidly, here had been avoided by Sustris earlier on the gable of the Torbau at Burg Trausnitz (Pl. 213), it will be recalled, as also in his contemporary Grottenhof in the Residenz (Pl. 282) that will shortly be described. Internal evidence thus supports the suggestion that it was neither Sustris nor Krumpper who provided the uncoordinated design of this facade above the ground storey. Though the church was consecrated in 1597 some of the embellishment in any case, such as the range of statues in the upper niches which includes three Habsburg emperors as well as more Wittelsbachs, is probably considerably later than Sustris's death in 1599.

To the years 1592-1597, however, certainly belong the choir and the transepts of St. Michael, as also the

[14] In the postwar restoration the circular window was replaced by a short rectangular one with curved top and bottom.

modest domed Kreuzkapelle to the east of the choir. The transepts open into the crossing through wide arches that rise directly from the entablature of the lower nave order. Their barrel-vaults were decorated with a variant of the treatment used over the nave. Above the crossing, however, a much larger circular panel at least suggests the missing dome. To the "east" the lower walls of the deep choir, against which the choir stalls carved by Dietrich are set, were quite unarticulated up to half the height of the lower storey of the nave, perhaps to provide space for frescoes or tapestries. The plan of the terminal apse at this lower level is five-sided, not semicircular as in the Gesù, and the entablature of the main order of the nave is continued all around but without fluted pilasters, except for one pair at the choir arch. Just below this, arched openings and niches with statues alternate. That treatment is then repeated between the clerestorey windows in the next zone, but this time with ressauts breaking the terminal entablature above each of the niches.

The arches of the conspicuous clerestorey windows in the choir and apse of St. Michael intersect slightly the base of the barrel-vault, as in the nave of the Gesù, and also the half dome. This vaulting in the choir, now restored merely with simple flat ribbing in place of Gerhard's rich original decoration, is concentric with the barrel-vault of the nave but lower, since the width of the choir is rather less. At the "east" end of the nave, above the flanking pairs of fluted pilasters against which the two major subsidiary altars are set, the panelled pilaster order of the sides is repeated under the decorated bands of the archivolt of the choir arch. In both storeys of the exiguous "east" wall niches holding statues are set between the pairs of pilasters above the altars. These statues, like the ones in the nave and most of those outside on the front, were modelled in terra cotta by Gerhard and Krumpper after designs provided by Sustris.

At the rear of the apse the very tall high altar by Dietrich, first executed beginning in 1586 from Sustris's designs, has been very completely restored since the last war and reinstalled in the new choir of the 1590s. This rises in three stages and carries a large arch-topped painting of St. Michael and the Fall of the Rebel Angels by Christoph Schwarz (c.1545-1592). He was a Munich-born artist who started as a pupil of Melchior Bocksberger (†1587)—Johann Bocksberger's nephew it is supposed—and then studied in Venice, possibly with Titian. Three orders of paired columns flank the lower and middle stages

with angels carved by Andreas Weinhart on either side. The top stage of the altar, up in the zone of the half-dome, is narrower and linked to the entablature below by carved S-scrolls. In this stage an edicule frames a glory set within a vertical oval. Above, the horns of a broken segmental pediment embrace a pedestal carrying a sort of monstrance. Thus this crowning stage of the high altar resembles in outline considerably more than does that on the front of the church the "scalloped" gables on contemporary secular buildings. In its Germanic elaboration the altar seems to conflict, indeed, with the spacial clarity of the apse vault, especially now that Gerhard's stucco decoration is gone. This contrast provides a strong argument against assigning to Dietrich any architectural responsibility for the earlier design of the nave of the church or even the original choir.

The lefthand side of the church has always been largely masked by the Jesuits' Kolleg next door, now known as the Alte Akademie, though the upper portion of it can be seen from the court. The righthand side, however, is extremely interesting. The outer plane of the lower wall is that of the buttress-like elements projecting between the chapels while their curved plan (Fig. 40) is revealed between. Over the transept on the "south" a gable of very special character, surely of Sustris's design, contrasts not only with the clumsy gable on the front but also with the scalloped ones so common elsewhere. The gable consists of distinctly Academic elements—three pedimented windows, in particular—so combined that the pitch of the roof is approximated without recourse to scrolling. All but unique, this gable recalls only that of the Wewershuis in Antwerp of forty years before, which is unlikely to have been known to Sustris. It provides better evidence of Sustris's architectural sophistication than anything else he designed in Munich except the interior of the church—if, indeed, he was responsible for that from the first, not after 1592 only and just for the rebuilding of the crossing and the choir.

The other great new Catholic church of the early eighties was associated with the university at Würzburg. In Munich St. Michael stands to the right of the Jesuits' Kolleg, built 1585-1597,[15] which surrounds

[15] Lieb, *München*, pp. 93-95. As with the church next door, the usual assumption is that Sustris provided the design for the Kolleg with a Roman model, Bartolomeo Ammannati's Collegio Romano, in mind. Here also, however, resemblance to the presumptive Italian model is not close and the latter was not erected until 1583-1585, much too late to have been

large courts behind the street front. That street front (Pl. 260) is severely plain with regular ranges of pedimented windows. Though four-storeyed, it is topped by the uppermost storey and the high gable of the church facade. In Würzburg the *Templum academicum* or Neubaukirche—to give it the old name that the street on the south still carries—overtops even more the Juliusuniversität on the north, thanks particularly to the tremendous west tower solidly rebuilt after it threatened to collapse in 1628 and completed by Antonio Petrini (1624/1625-1701) after 1696. Moreover, except for its comparably great size and its tribunes, even the interior does not resemble that of the Munich church, much less the Gesù in Rome.

In the eighteenth century the building activities of the prince-bishops of Würzburg who were members of the Schönborn family rivalled those of the Wittelsbach electors. As was mentioned earlier, the Schönborns had a worthy predecessor in Bishop Julius Echter von Mespelbrunn,[16] who ruled Würzburg from 1573 to his death in 1617. So many buildings were commissioned by him, indeed, that a distinct "Juliusstil" is recognized by some German authorities. This *Juliusstil* is characterized particularly by the late retention of such Gothic features as the cross-ribbed vaults and the window tracery in this church. In 1576-1580 Julius erected the Juliusspital, his first important commission, but this was rebuilt by Petrini after a fire of 1699 in 1700-1714 and still later restored and refronted after another fire by Johann Balthasar Neumann in 1746-1749. Julius's architect for the hospital was Jean Robÿn from Ypres in southern Flanders, usually called Johann Robin, concerning whom more will be said later.

At Julius's Würzburg seat on the Marienberg,[17] a hilltop fortress across the Main from the city whose origins go back to the earliest Christian centuries and perhaps before, his work included the eastern part of the southern wing, begun in 1578 the year before the Marktbreit Rathaus; the whole north wing of around 1600, the date of the Marktbreit Maintor; the Marienturm on the northeast corner; and the Vorburg. In this complicated range of constructions on the Marienberg—dating, as regards the round church in the inner court, from Carolingian times and, as regards the outer bastions, from after the close of the Thirty Years' War in 1648—Julius's contribution is not easy to distinguish today since it is so intimately involved with earlier mediaeval elements and the whole is now partially ruinous.

Much has been entirely lost at the Würzburg Marienberg, notably the characteristic gabled dormers on the court side of the Hauptburg to the east, but a good deal is extant (Pl. 259). The rectangular choir of the church in the court was added by Julius and the elaborately carved wellhead nearby. Then there are the southeast and northeast towers—the latter mediaeval but restored by Julius—and the three rather plain wings of the court of the Vorburg to the west. Above all, the entrance gate to this court of 1607 (Pl. 363), which will be described in a later chapter, testifies still to the grandeur that once resulted from the many decades Julius's building activity continued here.

In the city of Würzburg itself the upper two storeys of the Rathaus also belong to Julius's time: 1593-1594.[18] The family Schloss of Mespelbrunn, however, between Würzburg and Aschaffenburg, had already been enlarged by Julius's father. He himself added only the Rittersaal on the ground storey and the chapel, this last in 1566,[19] well in advance of becoming bishop of Würzburg. He had also commissioned a fine set of tapestries two years before that, indicating his taste for the arts developed early. Nineteenth-century restoration has exaggerated the mediaeval picturesqueness of this moated grange and little survives from Julius's time except for the alabaster altar in the chapel carved by the younger Michael Kern (1580-1649) around 1610.

For most of his projects Julius employed one architect, Georges Robÿn, better known as Georg Robin or Robbin.[20] He came originally from Ypres in southern Flanders, like Johann Robin who built the Juliusspital, and had begun his professional career there by building dams and fortifications. Although Georg Robin may actually have visited Italy in the 1570s, his trip was doubtless undertaken more to study up-to-date fortifications than formal architecture. In 1575, however, the elector of Mainz appointed him

---

known at first hand to Sustris. The Kolleg can be better appreciated historically in relation to Hans Alberthal's Klerikalseminar (Pl. 419), built later for the Jesuits in Dillingen in 1618-1627 beside their Studienkirche.

[16] M. H. von Freeden and W. Engel, *Fürstbischof Julius Echter als Bauherr*, Würzburg, 1951.

[17] M. H. von Freeden, *Festung Marienberg*, Würzburg, 1952. See especially the keyed block-plan inside the rear cover and pl. 30, Leypold's engraving of 1603/1604.

[18] M. H. von Freeden, *Würzburg*, 2d ed., Munich [1961], fig., p. 6.

[19] Reclams *Bayern*, p. 496.

[20] See the article "Georg Robin oder Robbin" in ThB.

Erzstiftesbaumeister (architect of the archdiocese) and had him build an electoral Kanzlei that has not survived. While still in Mainz he also erected the church of St. Gangolf, likewise no longer extant. He was further consulted, at least, by Count Wolfgang von Hohenlohe in 1576 as mentioned earlier. His documented works in Würzburg include principally Julius's university, the construction of which started in 1582, and the contiguous church, begun the next year and consecrated in 1591.[21] Wolfgang Beringer, of the city's office of works, was also involved in the execution of the church.[22]

The Würzburg Neubaukirche has suffered more from war damage than the university and, unlike that, is not yet restored. But there had been from almost the first a history of recurrent damage followed by repair and remodelling. Already in 1628, as was noted, it became necessary for statical reasons to begin the reconstruction of the tower that occupies nearly the full width of the west front. At that time a range of tremendous pier-buttresses was also added along the south side toward the Neubaustrasse. These are treated as panelled Doric pilasters raised on double podia. The podia are also panelled in the lower section but horizontally rusticated above. Whether the heavily molded round archivolts, richly carved spandrels and bold segmental pediments over the first and second rows of big windows are also of this same date is not clear, but they are certainly of the seventeenth century, early or late, not original. The full height, with three ranges of traceried windows, was provided from the first by Robin and Beringer, but the grandiose scale of the projecting elements, and even more that of the tower, surviving still to dominate the Würzburg skyline, is already Baroque.

The northern side of the Neubaukirche, closing the quadrangle of university buildings, preserves its original character (Pl. 330). There the three rows of big windows are set flat in the wall with no buttresses between them. The hybrid character of Robin's *Juliusstil* is here very apparent. The windows are rather elaborately traceried in a Late Gothic way above triple lights, just as on the southside, and they have pointed heads here in both the middle and upper ranges lighting the tribunes, though those of the aisles are semicircular. Internally also, mediaeval ele-ments are present, as was noted earlier, but there they are less conspicuous. Though the plain transverse ribs separating the eight bays of the nave are semicircular, the oblong vaults between have simple quadripartite cross-ribbing of a sort that is still essentially Gothic.

As the height and the three ranges of windows of the exterior walls of the Neubaukirche suggest, what is most unusual about the interior is the high and narrow spacial volume that results from the inclusion of two levels of tribunes above the side aisles. This provides the sort of interior space Pevsner considers characteristically Mannerist. It also recalls St.-Eustache in Paris where the tall proportions of the old High Gothic churches of the Ile de France were even more strikingly maintained in campaigns of construction that continued through the sixteenth century. The interior elevation at Würzburg, moreover, has little in common with that in St. Michael in Munich, for the Roman arch order of the Augustusburg chapel is used here in all three storeys. The resultant repetition of the elements, particularly the fluted engaged columns: Doric, Ionic and Corinthian in correct sequence, produces an effect which suggests —much as did dell'Allio's court of the Graz Landhaus a generation earlier—the High Renaissance. This is in marked contrast to what may be recognized as the Counter-Reformation, or even proto-Baroque, character of the interior of the Munich church. The church in Würzburg, unlike the one in Munich, has not been reopened since the war. In any case, the apse had been entirely renewed in 1851, with no regard for the original design, when the church was returned to religious use after secularization in 1803.

The next important Catholic church to be begun after those in Munich and in Würzburg was the Petrikirche in Münster, the first in the Rhine Province of the Jesuit Order, which dates from 1590.[23] The master-builder responsible for the design and construction of the church, which was completed in 1597, was Johann Rosskott, a local mason. He was advised by one of the Jesuits, P. Michaelis, as regards the ritual organization of the interior; but there is even less resemblance than in the Jesuits' Munich church to the Gesù in Rome. Carefully restored since the war, and hence somewhat bare and new-looking today, the church seems at first sight totally mediaeval both externally and internally (Pl. 261).

Inside the Petrikirche the five-sided apse has large windows of which the arches conform to the pointed

[21] Reclams *Bayern*, pp. 951-952; the east and south wings of the Juliusuniversität were completed by 1584; the north wing was under way a year later.

[22] Hauttmann, *Kirchliche Baukunst*, pp. 37-38.

[23] Dehio, *Westfalen*, pp. 383-385; Braun, *Jesuiten*, I, 10-32.

curvature of the vaulting and the tracery is almost Flamboyant. However, this east end is largely occupied by an elaborate two-stage altar. That altar includes Corinthian columns of black Belgian marble, four below and two above, and carries an edicule capped with a broken segmental pediment. The edicule is flanked, like a highly decorated gable of the period, by three-dimensional strapwork which is distinctly Brabantine in character. The figural sculpture, of which only the alabaster statues of St. Peter and St. Paul and four reliefs of the Latin Fathers survive, is by the local sculptor Johann Kroess (†c.1607) and dated 1599-1601. The pulpit and the confessionals are early eighteenth century. Though the sparse net-ribbing of the vault is still Gothic, in section it is semi-elliptical, not pointed, while the arches of the nave arcade are half-round and those of the tribunes segmental. At the west end the organ gallery is carried on a broad segmental arch also and behind it the big west window is round-arched, though it has Gothic tracery in the head.

The structural organization of the interior elevation of this Münster church is complex and the proportions neither Gothic nor Renaissance. Columns that are exceptionally thick and stubby, yet crowned with Ionic capitals, support the arches of the nave arcade, the rib-vaulting of the aisles, and the broad flat strips running up to the vaults above the tribunes. The ribs actually rise, however, from rather Gothic angels' heads serving as consoles. Since the plane of the clerestorey wall is set well back from the piers, the balustrade at the front of the tribunes introduces a strong horizontal note; moreover, this balustrade is detailed in a hybrid Renaissance way. Equally hybrid in character are the statue-filled niches along the nave. These are cut into the piers just below the string-course that connects the railings of the balustrades in the individual tribunes.

The interior of the Petrikirche is all white today. Lacking frescoes and stucco decoration, it does not at all resemble the characteristic Jesuit churches of southern Europe of the next century and probably never did though the walls were, of course, freshly plastered by the restorers. Externally it has rather a Netherlandish Gothic—or even English Tudor—look thanks to the exposed red brick of the walls and the contrasting stone trim (Pl. 262). Such trim frames the buttresses flanking the side walls, the slim octagonal turrets at either side of the apse and all the windows.

The windows in the clerestorey at Münster are set very high in order to clear the roofs of the tribunes;

they are also very small and have no tracery. The half-round top of the big west window has been mentioned, contrasting with the pointed windows at the east end. But the aisle windows consist, quite in the Tudor way, of three plain lights merely cusped at the top under flat lintels. On the other hand, the segmental heads of the somewhat larger windows of the tribunes, which provide most of the illumination inside the church, are filled with tracery. This is, however, simpler and rather less Gothic in design than the tracery in the east and west windows. On the exterior, the molded jambs of these tribune windows descend on either side of the aisle windows below and thus mask externally the three-storey elevation of the interior.

Just as the elaborate and slightly later altar in the apse of the Petrikirche seems quite out of key with the predominantly mediaeval look of the interior, so the round-arched western portal, flanked by fluted Corinthian columns and crowned by the Jesuits' IHS framed, like the altar, both by strapwork and by figural sculpture, contrasts with the near-vernacular simplicity of the exterior as a whole. This feature is probably the work of Rosskott; the sculpture on the north portal, however, is attributed to Bernt Katman.

The stylistic ambiguity of their Münster church remained for several decades characteristic of those the Jesuits built in the Rhineland. Sometimes described as examples of *Nachgotik*, as was noted earlier, they totally belie the supposition that the Order was imposing the model of the mother-church in Rome on Counter-Reformation church-building throughout Europe. Actually, indeed, except for the distinctly Gothic polygonal apse, the interior of this Jesuit edifice comes far closer to that of the oldest surviving edifice erected for Protestant use, the chapel of Schloss Hartenfels at Torgau (Pl. 125) which Luther consecrated almost half a century before, than to the Gesù in Rome or even to St. Michael in Munich.

One reason for this similarity is not hard to seek. In the programme of those religious who were the most militant opponents of the Reformation, sermons were of great importance. As in the mediaeval churches of preaching orders, the provision of space for large congregations within hearing range of the pulpit was a prime functional requirement. The pulpit was therefore usually set—as here in the Petrikirche and long before that, of course, in various Lutheran chapels in Schlösser, beginning with the one at Torgau—high against a central pier at the side of the nave and visually accented by a treatment as rich as that of the altar. Furthermore, both in Catholic and Protestant edifices tribunes and galleries provided for much larger congregations than could occupy the nave. One can say, therefore, that the differences between Protestant and Catholic church architecture in sixteenth-century Germany are very slight.

Except for some aspects of their iconography, therefore, the confessional uses of churches and chapels could easily be changed; in fact that seems to have happened fairly frequently. At Neuburg-a.-d.-Donau, for one instance, the shift was from Catholic to Lutheran in the case of the Schlosskapelle in 1543; later, in the case of the Hofkirche there, it was from Lutheran to Catholic in 1614. At Heidelberg the Lutheran Elector Palatine Friedrich III turned Calvinist in the sixties; but his brother Ludwig VI, who succeeded in 1576, was once more a Lutheran. Then after Ludwig's death in 1583, his brother Johann Casimir as regent brought back Calvinism, and to that confession Friedrich IV continued to adhere until his death in 1610. However, Friedrich IV's moderate Calvinism had no apparent effect on the architecture of the chapel in the Friedrichsbau (Pl. 425) that he built in 1601-1607, nor was that modified by his Lutheran successor, Friedrich V. On the other hand, the shift from Lutheran to Calvinist of the Brabants of Hesse in 1608 did have an iconoclastic result in the chapel of Schloss Wilhelmsburg above Schmalkalden, a Hessian enclave in the Lutheran Thuringia of the Wettins.[24]

Two interiors of the late 1580s, both completed before the big Munich and Würzburg churches—and indeed before the Petrikirche was even begun—one of them Protestant, the other Catholic, are of a decorative elaboration that even St. Michael in Munich did not approach, despite the contribution of Sustris's team of Italian-trained artists, much less the university church at Würzburg and the Jesuit church in Münster. The more sophisticated of the two, the Lutheran—later Calvinist—chapel to which reference has just been made in Schloss Wilhelmsburg, may better be discussed a little later; the Franciscan church at Hechingen deserves detailed description first.

Hechingen lies southwest of Tübingen in quite a different part of Germany from Schmalkalden, and

was ruled not by the Protestant dukes of Württemburg but by the counts of Hohenzollern. Unlike the members of the northern branches of the family after the time of Cardinal Albrecht these had remained Catholic. There at Hechingen a small monastery church dedicated to St. Luzen was begun in 1586[25] by Franciscan monks who had come from Munich to revive a mediaeval foundation. It was completed in 1589, as also the greater part of the decoration, by two Württembergers—Wendelin Nufer from nearby Herrenberg and Hans Ammann from Ulm—together with a certain Meister Michael V. from Petershausen, south of Ingolstadt in Bavaria. Externally the church is a very modest stucco-covered structure with a low nave four bays long and no aisles, but flanked by deep buttresses. There is also one low-gabled chapel that opens off the third bay on the south side. Beyond this chapel the choir, narrower and even lower than the nave but almost as long, ends in a three-sided apse. A few rather small windows with pointed arches are cut into the lower walls while above them are widely spaced oculi.

Nothing about the exterior of St. Luzen—at first sight a very ordinary parish church such as exist in innumerable German villages—prepares the visitor for the interior (Pl. 263), a virtuoso fantasia in stucco of the most extravagant sort. Later, in the eighteenth century, south German Stukkateure would similarly transform the interiors of many churches, both Gothic ones and Baroque ones, into Rococo decorative entities, but nothing approaching this had hitherto been seen in northern Europe except the extravagance of the carved decoration in the Brugge Vrij of fifty years earlier—or, at least, nothing now survives. In the meantime Netherlandish designers, particularly Floris and Vredeman, had developed and distributed through their travels and their publications of the third quarter of the century the vocabulary of Northern Mannerist ornament, but no German had yet exploited this as enthusiastically as did Nufer. The earliest considerable stucco decoration in Germany, that executed by Italian stuccatori in the Stadtresidenz in Landshut (Pls. 114-116), was small in scale, geometrically ordered and, for the most part, subordinated visually to Bocksberger's and Postumus's associated fresco painting. Later, in the Poznań Rathaus of the fifties (Pl. 242), the Augsburg Fuggerhäuser around 1570 (Pls. 215, 216) and even more in the newly completed nave of St. Michael in Munich

---

[24] The paintings contrasted what Lutherans considered the "true story" of the life of Christ with the papal version. See Note 28. The Calvinist objection, however, may have been to figure-painting of any sort, i.e. essentially iconoclastic.

[25] Dehio, *Baden-Württemberg*, pp. 186-187.

(Pl. 256) Sustris's associates Pallago and Gerhard were still handling the stucco decoration of the walls, and more particularly the vault, in a thoroughly Italian way. Their stucco-work was characteristically organized in large, fairly simply shaped panels filled either with frescoes or with delicate ornament of a distinctly Italianate cast. Indeed, there seem to be no Northern Mannerist elements at all in the work of these men.

In what they were executing at Hechingen for these Franciscans from Munich, Nufer and his associates may well have intended to rival St. Michael, the Jesuits' headquarters there, by the luxuriance of the *stucchi* despite the plain and still predominantly Gothic character of this small monastic church. Thoroughly Gothic certainly, with no resemblance to the ceiling decorations of Sustris's team, is the lierne cross-vaulting overhead even though, as with most sixteenth-century work of this sort, it is half-round in section rather than pointed like the arches of the windows. If inherited near-Gothic elements dominate in the Münster Petrikirche and Roman arch-orders in the Würzburg Neubaukirche, it is the pseudo-architecture carried out in stucco on the upper walls of the nave and choir and the profusion of figural modelling and up-to-date strapwork ornament, all also in stucco, that distinguish the decoration of the interior here.

The lower walls in St. Luzen are quite plain. At their top the order of the upper walls—half-columns in the nave (Pl. 263) and pilasters in the choir—is carried on very large scrolled brackets. The surfaces of these are covered, around central projecting bosses, with flat strapwork of a sort that seems to derive, almost as directly as that on Robert Smythson's screen at Wollaton in England of these same years, from the plates of Vredeman. Similar decoration fills the panels of the pilasters in the choir, but this still suggests the quattrocento in its small scale despite the substitution of strapwork for arabesques. The ornament on the half-columns in the nave is much more plastic. The upper two-thirds of their shafts, being fluted, conform well enough to a recognizable Doric norm even though the capitals are enriched by an egg-and-dart molding. But on the lower third of the shafts round and diamond bosses in high relief alternate with small flat elements of undefinable shape in a thoroughly Northern Mannerist way.

Above the columns along the sides of the nave of St. Luzen the entablature is continuous, with a frieze filled with strapwork and other ornamentation,

though only its cornice is bowed up over the choir arch and over the respond of that at the other end of the nave. There are, in addition, ressauts above the columns separating the bays, presumably to support visually the clusters of ribs that spring from these points. The regularity of the wider inter-columniations on the south is broken by the introduction of broad and deep-sunk arches at the three windows. The jambs of these are filled with flat ornament above the scrolled cartouches at their base.

A striking irregularity at St. Luzen is the omission of the central half-column on the north side of the nave. This was evidently done to provide a place for the pulpit (Pl. 264). Attached to the wall just below one of the ressauts in the entablature, the pulpit was executed in 1589 by Amman in a hybrid Late Gothic-quattrocento taste very different from Nufer's stucco-decoration.

On the south side of the nave of St. Luzen an arch in the lower wall opening directly opposite the pulpit leads into the chapel of St. Anthony, where there is an altarpiece of 1757 by J. B. Enderle (1725-1798). Like the window reveals, both the wide jambs of this arch and its intrados carry flat strapwork decoration. The gallery and organ that fill most of the westernmost bay of the nave are, like Enderle's altarpiece, eighteenth-century additions and the high altar dates from 1743. However, this altar and the ones flanking the choir-arch do incorporate some original figural sculpture and other elements, most notably in the upper stages of the two side altars, that were carved by Hans Ulrich Glöckler in 1588.

In all of the sub-bays created by the half-columns in the nave at Hechingen, except the wider one on the north from which the pulpit projects, shell-topped niches frame more than life-size figures of the Apostles. These are in high relief but not full round. In the choir, where the entablature above the pilasters is unbroken by ressauts, the three sides of the apse and two of the sub-bays on the south are occupied by windows. The other sub-bays have shallower shell-topped niches than those in the nave. These are occupied by figures in low relief of the patron saints of the Seven Basilicas of Rome.

Below the continuous impost moldings of the niches in the nave of St. Luzen the portions of the walls flanking the half-columns carry scrolled cartouches and flat strapwork much like that on the window jambs; bolder strapwork fills most of the spandrels. Above and behind the pulpit (Pl. 264), however, the spandrels of the broad segmental blind arch are filled with flat pattern-work at the rather smaller scale of the decoration on the brackets below the half-columns. Perhaps this is by Ammann rather than by Nufer.

Over the entablature in the nave of St. Luzen the lunettes framing the oculi are rather differently ornamented than the lower walls. The intrados of each circle is decorated with pattern-work like the decoration on the spandrels below, but the edges of the large cartouches in their centers are cut into strap-work that scrolls outward in quite high relief (Pl. 263). Above the choir-arch similar scroll-work surrounds a large oval relief of the Stigmatization of St. Francis. From this, conspicuous S-scrolls descend at either side, somewhat as on contemporary gables. In the lunette at the top of the west wall, now largely obscured by the organ, the stucco decoration is nearly identical, but with an oculus in place of the central relief.

Originally this interior at Hechingen was further enriched with color. This was applied in 1595 by Hans Depay, who came from Riedlingen in southern Württemberg, in much the same bold polychromatic way as the gables of the Celle Rathaus have been restored (Pl. 231); today it is mostly just white-washed. In the equally rich, but wholly different chapel of St. Felix in the Schloss of the Counts of Fürstenberg—Catholics like their Hohenzollern neighbors—at Heiligenberg well to the south of Hechingen, the original color and much gilding survives —or was restored when the chapel was altered in 1878 (Pl. 265). This may well be described at this point before the Protestant one at Schmalkalden since it is not only Catholic, like Hechingen, but also located in the present state of Baden-Württemberg not far from Überlingen on the Bodensee. The mediaeval castle here was superbly located on a naturally fortified site projecting southward high above the plain that continues southward to the lake. Of this a partial reconstruction was begun by Count Joachim in 1546 and continued intermittently during more than thirty years. After 1562 the architect in charge was Hans Schwarz and later, from 1575, Jörg Schwartzenberger from the nearby town of Messkirch.[26] It

was Schwartzenberger specifically who was responsible for the great Rittersaal of 1580-1584 here to be described in the next chapter.

The Heiligenberg chapel rises through three storeys of the west wing which dates structurally from the fifteenth century. This was remodelled, still for Joachim, in the late 1580s and 1590s. As in the Lutheran chapel of the Celle Schloss, where Duke Wilhelm's elaboration of the fittings of the interior, begun in the sixties, probably extended into the eighties, this Catholic chapel includes a large, partially screened *Fürstenloge* (lord's pew), here suspended above the south end of the narrow rectangular space, and also a gallery that is set equally high. This last runs along the south wall and is also provided with a double-arcaded screen. The gallery serves as the only connection between the south wing of the Schloss, largely built by Schwarzenberger in the 1570s, and the western end of the north wing on this side of the rectangular court.

These spacial intrusions at Heiligenberg are both at second-storey level, two storeys above the floor of the court and the main body of the chapel. From below, the presence of such large and conspicuous elements high overhead, combined with the organ gallery on the west at first-storey level under the Fürstenloge, produces almost as oppressive an effect of congestion as in the chapel at Celle (Pl. 207). Moreover, most of the carved and polychromed decoration, carried out by Glöckler, who executed the altars at Hechingen, is up above on the under-surfaces and the parapets and screens of the Fürstenloge. In the open lower arches of the screen are half-figures of Christ as Salvator Mundi and the Apostles. These are less securely dated than Glöckler's reliefs of 1593-1596 of scenes of the Passion carved on the front of the organ gallery. Still higher, the ceiling, though designed to look like three parallel ranges of small square cross-vaults, is necessarily executed in wood since there are, in this long interior no internal supports of full height. The ceiling was carved, gilded and polychromed by Hans Dürner (†1613), from Biberach-a.-d.-Riss in southern Württemberg, beginning in 1589-1590.

The present restored condition of the Heiligenberg chapel makes uncertain just what it was actually like when the campaign of redecoration reached completion shortly before Joachim's death in 1598. The fourteenth and fifteenth-century glass in the Gothic windows, themselves presumably of fifteenth-century date, was brought here from the Dominican church

---

[26] *Ibid.*, pp. 206-207. Schloss Heiligenberg as a whole is too confused an amalgam to be readily described though it is not unimpressive, in good part because of its site. Most notable are the four-storeyed loggia of 1594-1604 in the court and the tall freestanding bell-tower of the same date beside the lower buildings in the base-court to the north. Both are presumably the work of Schwartzenberger.

in Konstanz (Constance) in or after 1878. To drastic nineteenth-century remodelling belong also the arches supporting the organ gallery below the Fürstenloge and the extension of the choir-stalls on the ground floor. These last include, however, various elements that survived from Schwarzenberger's joinery of the late 1590s on which the new work was modelled.

The Schloss of the Lutheran Landgraves of Hesse, the Brabants, in Kassel as extended for Philipp der Grossmutige's son Wilhelm IV in the 1570s may well have rivalled the cumulative pile of the Fürstenbergs' Schloss in size, but it seems to have resembled more closely in design the Berlin Joachimsbau of the late thirties. Of the Schloss at Kassel no more is extant than of the one in Berlin. As surviving drawings indicate, however, the three storeys of both the southwest and southeast ranges of the Kassel Schloss were evidently quite as regularly fenestrated as Theiss's (Pl. 100); indeed, they even approached symmetry in the placing of the cross-gables at the ends and, on the southeast range, of the dormers in between.

There is no evidence of the intervention, here on the Kassel Schloss, of the Walloon sculptor Adam Liquir Beaumont who was at this time completing for Wilhelm the tomb of Philipp; nor yet of Wilhelm Vernukken, who followed him as head of the local court-sculptor's atelier in 1577. Elsewhere in these decades Vernukken was sometimes involved in the design or execution of architectural projects. Most lately, there was at Cologne the Doxal and, after this, at Schmalkalden the decoration of the Schlosskapelle, where he worked also for Wilhelm IV. Doubtless, however, it was Christoph Müller from Saxony, appointed *Hofschreiner* (court cabinetmaker) and *Hofbaumeister* by Wilhelm a year after Vernukken became court-sculptor, who was in charge of the extension of the Kassel Schloss, as he was later of the construction of Schloss Wilhelmsburg at Schmalkalden.

Related buildings in Kassel housing various aspects of Wilhelm IV's well-organized administration survived intact to the south of the former monastery of the Carmelites until the bombardment of 1943. But of the Kanzlei or Renthof of 1579-1580 and the Zeughaus of 1581-1583, very probably both by Müller, the restorers in 1959 salvaged only a wall-fountain, perhaps by Vernukken, of around 1600 and a doorway inscribed 1618;[27] more has been rebuilt since.

Fortunately good examples of such structures still exist in other places and there is much finer late work for which Müller and Vernukken were responsible at Wilhelm's other major seat above Schmalkalden. Even though the characteristic gables on Schloss Wilhelmsburg there are long gone, most of the interiors survive and have lately been well restored.

The line of the counts of Henneberg, who shared the rule of Schmalkalden in Thuringia with the Hessian landgraves, died out in 1583. Two years later Wilhelm had the mediaeval castle on the hill east of the town demolished. He then began, with Vernukken's advice, a new quadrangular Schloss (Fig. 43)

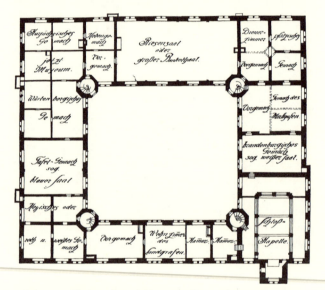

Fig. 43. Christoph and Hans Müller: Schmalkalden, Schloss Wilhelmsburg, begun 1585, plan

with a most splendid chapel completed according to an inscription in 1588.[28] Somewhat resembling the Augustusburg (Fig. 36, Pl. 200) despite the very different character of the site, the erection of the Schloss

---

rebuilt in 1963-1964; the design of the Zeughaus, not yet restored, is attributed to Rochus von Lynar from Dresden. Probably, that was carried out by Christoph Müller and completed by him—or more likely his son Hans—after 1600.

[28] DKD, *Thüringen*, p. 399; Piltz, *D.D.R.*, p. 363; [E. Badstübner] *Stadtkirche und Schlosskapelle zu Schmalkalden* [Berlin, 1972] pp. 21-29. The keystone of the middle bay of the vault is inscribed: W(ilhelm) L(andgraf) Z(u) H(essen) Anno Domini 1588.

H. Baier-Schröcke, *Der Stuckdekor in Thüringen vom 16. bis zum 18. Jahrhundert*, Berlin, 1968, pp. 8-9, has little to add, but her figs. 3-9 offer various details of the *stucchi*.

---

[27] Reclams *Niedersachsen*, p. 425; Dehio, *Hessen*, p. 456. The *Marstall* (stables) of 1591-1593, now a market-hall, was

was carried through by the elderly Christoph Müller and his son Hans. Without its original gables the exterior is now rather uninteresting and, like the earlier Saxon Schloss and Eschay's contemporary Fuggerschloss at Kirchheim, remarkable chiefly for its size and regularity (Pl. 268). But among the many interiors that preserve their original decoration the tall chapel (Pl. 267), rising through three storeys at the west end of the south wing, and the associated Weisser Saal are among the finest northern interiors that survive from the sixteenth century. The contrast between the cumulative redecoration of the Catholic Schlosskapelle at Heiligenberg and this example of a new-built Lutheran chapel is striking. But Wilhelm was continuing here a German tradition that goes back to the building of the Torgau chapel by the Saxon Elector Johann Friedrich and to the decoration of that at Neuburg for Ottheinrich von der Pfalz, both more than forty years before.

The Schmalkalden chapel, though probably built by the Müllers, was decorated with polychrome stucco executed by Hans Becher under Vernukken's supervision in the late 1580s. In plan and organization it follows, up to a point at least, the chapel at the Augustusburg of fifteen years earlier. Doubtless Christoph Müller knew that well. But, as in Julius Echter's big new Catholic church at Würzburg, there are here two tall ranges of tribunes on the south and north sides above the aisles and across the east end, the last providing on the intermediate level a generous Fürstenloge adjoining the Weisser Saal. This structural articulation is not continued at the "east" or altar end—the chapel is counter-orientated. There only the gallery for the organ is carried across on heavy rounded brackets, but this has also a central projection to provide room for the console. Apparently an innovation here, though common in later Protestant usage, is the removal of the pulpit from the center of the left side to the far end immediately above the altar as was first done, probably, in the *Temple* at Lyon in the early 1560s.

Of what was in earlier chapters called, perhaps exaggeratedly, the "High Renaissance" character of the interiors of the Augustusburg chapel (Pl. 201) and the Würzburg Neubaukirche, not to speak of the Doxal Vernukken himself added on the Cologne Rathaus (Pl. 237), there is very little here. The arch-order has pilasters, not half-columns, and the arches are three-centered, not semicircular, thus recalling a little the segmental arches used so long before in the Torgau chapel (Pl. 125). The awkwardly high parapets

in the openings of the tribunes once carried the figural paintings—probably somewhat like those surviving on the pews in the Celle Schlosskapelle (Pl. 207)—that were removed or covered up in 1608 under Calvinist influence,[29] leaving only broad blank areas that distract the attention from Vernukken's membering (Pl. 269). Overhead, the semi-elliptical cross-vaults are so low they would hardly have stood but for the sturdy iron ties at the base of the third storey and at the haunch of the single transverse rib in the center. These vaults of 1588, therefore, contrast as much with the unexpectedly "Classical" barrel-vault of the Augustusburg chapel of twenty years before as with the belated Gothic rib-vault of the Neubaukirche in Würzburg which is more nearly contemporary.

What is most remarkable about the Schmalkalden chapel, though by this date hardly new, is the consistent use of strapwork and other Northern Mannerist ornament over the whole stuccoed surface of the vault and also on the three ranges of pilasters, the archivolts of the aisle and tribune arches, and the spandrels. This decoration is of a delicacy of relief and harmony of scale quite unlike Nufer's rather coarse *stucchi* at Hechingen (Pl. 264). Moreover, figural sculpture, which is so prominent there, is here mostly restricted to the carved relief of Christ and the Apostles on the pulpit and the saints, modelled in stucco, that repose so awkwardly, like parodies of Michelangelo's figures on the Medici tombs, in the shallow wall-areas over the arches of the upper tribunes just below the vault (Pl. 269). Further minor figures are all but lost in the strapwork on the vault surface. Sculpture in the round is introduced only in the symbols of the Evangelists that support the corners of the altar slab—a very curious item this, with a font hollowed out of its center which is provided with a drain like a wash-basin.[30]

The tonality of the interior of the Schmalkalden chapel is high-keyed, but the predominantly white, so disturbingly plain, parapets—where the paintings were—are elsewhere varied by jewel-like accents of color and gilding. These are most profusely introduced on the vault. In the contiguous Weisser Saal, however, to the east in the upper storey, the ceiling and the frieze at the top of the walls—once hung

---

[29] The exceptional location of the pulpit, mentioned above, is not a Calvinist emendation.

[30] The curious, and perhaps unique, altar-*cum*-font supported by Vernukken's carved Evangelists seems to be original, not a feature introduced under Calvinist influence.

with tapestries—are, as restored in 1956-1957, almost all white (Pls. 267, 269).

The Wettins of the Albertine line in Saxony, well to the southeast of the Hessian Wilhelm's realm, had been using the Münster at Freiberg, halfway between their Dresden capital and Karl-Marx-Stadt, for family burials since the death of Duke Heinrich der Fromme, Georg der Bärtige's successor, in 1541. There the Elector August, the builder of the Augustusburg, had erected in 1563 at the crossing the big freestanding cenotaph (Pl. 208) described in a previous chapter to honor his brother Moritz, Heinrich's successor and his own predecessor, who had died ten years before. Now, in 1585,[31] just before the work on the chapel at Schmalkalden began, August employed Giovanni Maria Nosseni (1544-1620) to undertake a drastic remodelling of the east end of the church in order to make of it a sort of Wettin Pantheon.

Nosseni was an Italian-Swiss sculptor from Lugano who had settled in Dresden ten years before after working in Italy—probably in Venice—for several years. Though he was required to retain the Gothic structure, including the tall pointed windows on the five sides of the late fourteenth-century apse (Pl. 272), the ultimate result of the transformation was almost totally Italian in character. Moreover, the particular modulation of the later German Renaissance that Nosseni initiated in the Freiberg choir in Saxony is in several respects more significant for the great church-interiors of the following Baroque and Rococo periods than St. Michael in Munich which has long received so much attention from scholars. There is, indeed, little relationship between Nosseni's work at Freiberg and Sustris's other production of the 1580s and 1590s, doubtless because the former had come north from Italy nearly a decade later than Sustris and his Italian team; nor does that of either, at Freiberg and in Munich, at all resemble the Northern Mannerist interior architecture that Vernukken's chapel at Schmalkalden (Pl. 267) illustrates so ripely in the same decades.

The employment of the foreigner Nosseni marked a change in Saxon patronage from the predominant dependence of the dukes and electors earlier on German administrators such as Dehn-Rothfelser and

master-masons such as Krebs and Kramer. Whether such Italians worked in the thirties at Torgau or on the Georgenbau in Dresden is not established though it is not unlikely. But certainly nothing at all comparable to the Stadtresidenz at Landshut was erected for the Wettins of either the Ernestine or the Albertine line before the time of August. Even then, in Saxony only the portal of the Dresden Schlosskapelle (Pl. 130), projected by the Italian Johann Maria in the mid-fifties, had really echoed the High Renaissance even loosely before the Augustusburg chapel. In the design of that, however, the Tuscan-born Lynar seems to have been involved, at least from 1572, though he was not one of those responsible for the work initiated at the Schloss four years before.

After the Dresden portal and the Augustusburg chapel, August's employment of the alien Nosseni in the mid-1570s at Freiberg is understandable. However, for August, local precedent from before his own time will hardly have been so important as in the case of Wilhelm of Bavaria's use of Sustris and his team to remodel Burg Trausnitz at Landshut in the seventies more or less along the Italian lines of Duke Ludwig's Stadtresidenz there of thirty years before. Indeed, at the Dresden Schloss the additions of the eighties and nineties: the Stallhof, the Langer Gang and the Kanzlei, which will be described later in this chapter, offer more evidence of continuing control by the local architects and master-builders, Paul Büchner (1531-1607) and Hans Irmisch (†1597), than of any intervention by Nosseni. Even here at Freiberg, moreover, Irmisch was the executant of Nosseni's architectural design.

The advanced character—advanced not alone by German but by international standards of the 1580s —of Nosseni's architecture and the associated decoration in the Freiberg choir is very evident, especially as contrasted with Büchner's and Irmisch's work of the period in Dresden (Fig. 47). More appropriately than the nave of St. Michael, not completed in Munich before Nosseni began work at Freiberg, his east end as recast may even, as was suggested above, be called "proto-Baroque." Yet there is in this Lutheran monument no historical likelihood—nor internal evidence either—of influence from Vignola's Gesù in Rome or from churches by Palladio that Nosseni may have known from the plates in the *Quattro libri* if not, as Morando probably did, first-hand in Venice. Nor is there any such similarity to the organization of earlier German churches as has been noted in the nave of St. Michael at Munich to the Augustusburg

[31] Dehio, *Dresden*, pp. 102-105; Piltz, *D.D.R.*, p. 470. The frieze of the entablature on the exterior of the choir carries the date 1594 of completion of the work and the initials both of Nosseni—further identified as L(uganensis) I(talus), i.e. Italian from Lugano—and of Irmisch, with a B standing for *Baumeister* in his case.

chapel though Nosseni, being in Saxony, is more likely than Sustris to have known it. His tall fluted pilasters in strong relief, moreover, will hardly have been modelled on the very flat ones in the nave of the Klagenfurt Münster, in any case just under way in the mid-eighties, much less on Morando's at Zamošč, where work began only in 1587.

The Freiberg choir is, of course, like the Fuggerkapelle in St. Anna at Augsburg or the Wiemken choir at Jever, a burial chapel in a church, not an independent structure, and a remodelling at that. Nosseni's remodelling was, all the same, so thorough and so architectonic that the underlying Gothic structure, and even the traceried heads of the tall Gothic windows, are all but unnoticeable now in the interior (Pl. 270). Whether the design as executed is largely of 1585, before August's death in 1586, or was evolved gradually is not clear; but it may well be essentially of that early date, with only minor changes made as the work progressed to completion in 1594. The *parti* is relatively simple despite all the elaboration in detail. Between the windows in the two straight sides fairly broad three-storey edicular structures rise to the base of the vault. In the angles of the polygonal apse the broken plan of the narrower but similar feaures is largely masked, while in their top storeys the curved heads of the statue-filled niches, corresponding to those at this level along the sides, are much more conspicuous than the Gothic heads of the windows between.

At ground-storey level on the straight sides of the Freiberg choir kneeling statues of two dukes on the right face similar statues of their wives on the other side. These are Heinrich der Fromme, who died as noted in 1541, paired with his wife Katherine, who lived till 1561; and August with his wife Anna, whose death in 1585, a year before August's, may well have provided the original motive for the mausoleum project. In the angles of the apse Christian I is balanced by his successor Johann Georg, who lived till 1656. Christian was most responsible for the execution of the work planned by his predecessor August though he himself died in 1591, only five years after August and several years before the work was completed. In the remaining angles, allegorical figures of Faith and Hope take the place of grave monuments on either side of the sculptured figure of the Risen Christ in the round which is silhouetted high up against the central east window.

At the sides of the Freiberg choir Heinrich and August and their wives across the way are framed by pairs of freestanding columns of colored marbles that carry boldly projecting ressauts in the entablatures. At the angles of the apse, however, there is room only for single columns. Between the edicules and beneath the windows are large white marble panels with longer inscriptions than the similar panels inserted below the kneeling figures. There is thus a striking alternation between the warm tones, large scale and high relief of the bronze statues that the colored elements frame at the base of the piers and the chaste flat panels above with their small-scale lettering. There is also a sort of syncopation between the latter and the more modest inscribed panels under the figures below.

The middle storey of the Freiberg choir provides, above the tomb edicules, an attic-like member on top of which small silhouetted figures are set at the bottoms of the windows. On the podia under the figures are carved the actual epitaphs, each flanked by very large and boldly elaborated armorial shields of one of the dukes or his wife. These are linked forward to the plane of the ressauts below by putti holding swags of drapery. Behind the putti, pairs of big vertical scroll-brackets rise to support the top storey of each of the edicules. In this storey tall fluted pilasters flank plain niches in each of which is the stucco figure of a Prophet, eight in all. Above the pilasters the richly decorated entablatures with their ressauts offer a strong, but broken, horizontal line in high relief. This is precisely at the level from which the pointed arches of the windows spring and thus helps to obscure the surviving Gothic tracery in their heads. The ressauts each carry, moreover, a music-making angel seated just in front of the lower edge of the vault (Pl. 270). The architectonic complexity of the total conception certainly approaches the mature Baroque of Italy of a generation and more later though German scholars have usually considered it to be Mannerist.[32]

What is most premonitory of the later German Baroque and Rococo in the Freiberg choir, however, is the treatment of the vault (Pl. 271). The structural ribs were covered with plaster, as so often in eighteenth-century remodelling[33] and the whole surface

[32] "In den Plastiken und Ornamenten wie in der Gesamtkomposition [are] die Formprinzipien des Manierismus deutlich," Dehio, *Dresden*, p. 105.

[33] See H. R. Hitchcock, *Rococo Architecture in Southern Germany* [London, 1968] for various examples from Freising (pls. 43-49) in the 1720s to Rottenbuch in the forties (pls. 136-142); and Andechs in the fifties: H. R. Hitchcock, *Ger-*

filled with a big illusionistic figural composition, partly frescoed, partly stucco in relief, of Christ and the Archangel Michael as they announce the Last Judgement amid heavenly hordes of angels and cherubim.

On the exterior of the Freiberg choir (Pl. 272) great cornice-crowned piers mask or replace the Gothic buttresses of the choir and apse, crowding the pointed windows much as do the edicules in the interior. Here also the effect is somewhat proto-Baroque, resembling a little the south side of the Würzburg Neubaukirche as that was remodelled by Petrini or others in the seventeenth century. Here, moreover, the buttresses seem directly premonitory of those on the sides and rear of the Lutheran Marienkirche in Wolfenbüttel (Pl. 432), begun in 1608, which will be described in the terminal chapter. It is quite possible Paul Francke (c.1538-1615), the architect of that church, actually knew Nosseni's remodelled choir at Freiberg.

In German church architecture there are few conspicuous external features recognizable as dating from these terminal decades of the sixteenth century to compare with the boldly massed Freiberg apse. However, the exceptional west tower on St. Gumbert at Ansbach in Franconia (Pl. 273) should at least be mentioned. This was heightened in 1594-1597 for the Kulmbach Landgrave Georg Friedrich by the Ulm-born architect he was employing in this period, Gideon Bacher, at the same time Bacher was erecting the contiguous Kanzlei.[34] He had lately been assisting the Wallbergers, Caspar and Wolfgang, in remodelling or rebuilding the city gates of Nördlingen,[35] but the work at Ansbach was his first of much architectural interest. The two upper stages of the tower of St. Gumbert compose not inharmoniously with the surviving mediaeval turrets of the Gothic *Westwerk* that flank them, but they also incorporate four large round-arched windows, their heads filled with Renaissance tracery; while between them the horizontally channelled ashlar walling seems almost proto-Baroque in its heavy scale. However, Nosseni and his work merit more comment at this point than Bacher and what he did for Georg Friedrich.

As has been noted, Nosseni's transformation of the Freiberg choir was planned for the Elector August

in 1585, the year before August's death. Although Nosseni had arrived in Saxony a good deal before that, hitherto he had apparently worked—at Torgau from 1576 and at Dresden from 1583—chiefly as a designer of sculpture. His presumptive association with Paul Büchner in the design of the Lange Gang at the Dresden Residenzschloss dated only from the year after he was commissioned to redesign the Freiberg choir. The most advanced and personal work of architecture for which he was responsible in Dresden, the Lusthaus on the Brühlsche Terrasse, was not begun for the Elector Christian until 1588. At that time the transformation of the east end of the Freiberg Münster was being actively continued for the same prince. Unhappily, the Dresden pavilion was demolished in 1747, but a description follows below which is based on extant drawings; in any case the interiors were later and not by Nosseni.

There is really, then, no earlier surviving work by Nosseni to prepare one for his architectural innovations at Freiberg, much less for the mausoleum at Stadthagen (Pl. 442), which he designed and began early in the new century. Furthermore, though he had worked at least as much, and probably much more, as a designer of sculpture than for architectural work up to this point, the figural sculpture at Freiberg, the element of highest individual quality in the whole ensemble, is the work of another Italian, Carlo di Cesare from Florence. Cesare, a pupil of Jacopo Sansovino and of Giovanni da Bologna, was in the service of Francesco de' Medici until he came north just before Francesco died. Though he is considered by critics both then and later to have been one of the most accomplished artists of his generation working in the tradition of those great cinquecento sculptors, he is not represented today by any surviving sculpture that is identifiable in Florence but chiefly by the statues in Freiberg.

As toward 1540 at the Landshut Stadtresidenz, at Augsburg around 1570 in the Fuggerhäuser, and in these years of the 1580s and 1590s at Munich in the Residenz, decorative ensembles in Germany of thoroughly Italianate character were less the responsibility of single artists than of teams. Earlier in the sixteenth century it is possible to distinguish, at least loosely, what German master-builders were responsible for from what foreign designers contributed. Later, in Nosseni's time, the distinction in elaborately decorated interiors between individual inclusions of sculptures, frescoes or *stucchi* by particular Italians or other foreigners and the intentions of the "architects"—so to

man Rococo; the Zimmermann Brothers, London, 1968, pls. 47-50.

[34] Reclams *Bayern*, pp. 51-53, 58; A. Gebessler, *Ansbach* [Munich] n.d., pp. 17-18, pl. 1.

[35] Reclams *Bayern*, pp. 616-617.

beg the question by calling them—of the settings is not so clear. In any case, the execution was usually still in the hands of German master-builders even where the designers were aliens from the south or the west.

Nosseni's architectural capacities were probably first put to the test at Freiberg, but his later production long continued to be of a similar distinction although quite different in character. For example, his other principal surviving work, the polygonal mausoleum at Stadthagen (Pl. 442) has nothing in common with the Freiberg choir except its function as a princely burial chapel. Attached to the east end of the *Stadtkirche* (town church) there, this was commissioned in 1608 by Count Ernst von Holstein-Schaumburg, an especially enthusiastic builder. Since it is so late, this mausoleum will be discussed in Chapter X together with other examples of early seventeenth-century Academic design.

The Schaumburgs and others had, however, a generation before Ernst commissioned the mausoleum already introduced various Renaissance features in the mediaeval church of St. Martin at Stadthagen. The wainscoting, of which some portions were retained in the restorations of 1893 and 1908, dated from 1587.[36] In the northwest corner a sixteenth-century Fürstenloge still survives. This is much simpler than the one at Celle (Pl. 207), with which it must be roughly contemporary, but quite similar in general character. At the rear of the apse on the left is the very large tomb of Ernst's predecessor Otto IV, who died in 1576, and his two wives. This was executed a few years later by Jacob Kölling and Arend Robin and it quite overshadows the altar the chancellor of the Schaumburgs, Anton von Wietesheim, donated in 1585. Both, however, are characteristic examples of the very rich features Lutherans commissioned in the last quarter of the sixteenth century even for erection in small mediaeval parish churches.

The altar of the fifteenth-century Stadtkirche at Lauenstein near Dippoldiswalde combines, more coherently than the one at Stadthagen, a broad centerpiece rising in three stages up to the Gothic ribbed vault of the polygonal choir with the tombs of R. and A. von Bünau (†1592; †1591) by Michael Schwenke (1563-1610) from Pirna. He worked here in 1594 and 1602.[37] The kneeling figures of the Bünaus, as also the statues of Moses and Aaron higher up, are probably

later, around 1615, and like the pulpit here, by Lorenz Horning (†1624).

At Bristow, east of Güstrow in Mecklenburg, the modest *Gutskirche* (estate church) was built by the local landowners, the Hahn family, at the end of the century—the east gable carries the date 1598.[38] Under the low, round-arched cross-vaults of the choir the altar at the east end with its flanking portals (Pl. 275) is almost as elaborate as that at Lauenstein. With its many carved reliefs, its three successive orders and its framing of open bandwork, this matches the pulpit, font and organ gallery, all brought to completion by 1601. Such a contrast between simple, almost vernacular, architecture and a multiplicity of prominent carved and polychromed furnishings is very typical of Lutheran practice at this time. More usually, however, such features were introduced, as at Stadthagen and Lauenstein, into edifices inherited from the middle ages.

There are also in the Stadthagen church several more modest *Epitaphien* executed in wood which are also of this period. That of Christoph von Landsberg of 1584 is at the west end of the south aisle, and to the right of the altar is another, dated 1590, of Anna and Engel von Landsberg. The total effect rather resembles an English Gothic parish church cluttered up by the introduction in these same years of various sorts of tombs. It seems, therefore, to belong to a different artistic world from Ernst's mausoleum, begun in 1609 (Pl. 442) immediately behind the apse, as much as the similar funereal aggregations in Elizabethan England do to Inigo Jones's severely Academic Banqueting House for James I. There in fact the Baroque ceiling by Rubens was designed twenty years after Nosseni's burial chapel.

Not all Protestants were as content as the princes whose seats were at Kassel, Celle and Stadthagen merely to crowd their inherited Schlosskapellen or the churches in the towns that were their principal seats with Fürstenlogen and other galleries, elaborate carved altars, pulpits, fonts and vast sculptural tombs. New churches sometimes were built, often in close association with manor houses quite as in England before the Reformation. At Breese-im-Bruch, in the Elbe valley southeast of Lüneburg, the *Gutskapelle* (estate chapel) is a more modest example than Bristow of a small late sixteenth-century Lutheran parish church. It was begun a little earlier in 1592.[39] The

[36] Reclams *Niedersachsen*, p. 706.
[37] Dehio, *Dresden*, pp. 219-220; Piltz, *D.D.R.*, p. 531.
[38] DKD, *Mecklenburg*, p. 358.
[39] Reclams *Niedersachsen*, p. 65.

rather broad un-aisled interior (Pl. 274) is covered with a wooden ceiling of segmental section panelled with decorative cross-ribbing as if it were a vault. On its surface are large painted medallions surrounded by brightly polychromatic strapwork of the Netherlandish sort that was by this time in general use in Germany. The biggest of the medallions contain major religious subjects, while others have single figures of Prophets on the north side and of Apostles on the south; in between, still smaller ones resembling lockets carry paired coats of arms.

A much larger and more pretentious painted ceiling, dated 1594-1595,[40] exists in St. Nikolaus, the Stadtkirche of Geithain northwest of Karl-Marx-Stadt. The nave and aisles of this were begun as a hall-church in 1504, but it was never vaulted as had been originally intended—this intention the stubs of vaulting ribs at the tops of the piers make evident. Instead, the ceiling is quite flat and geometrically panelled (Pl. 276). The figural paintings within the panels were the work of Andreas Schilling from Freiberg. Most of the religious themes he illustrated are not, to twentieth-century eyes, appreciably different in their iconography from what might have been expected had the paintings been commissioned by Catholics. However, the half-length portraits of the Protestant "saints" Luther and Melancthon, rivalling in prominence St. Nicholas to whom the church was dedicated, should be noted.

Breese has, all the same, a more complete if less ambitious church interior (Pl. 274) of the 1590s than Geithain. Along the north side and across the west end are galleries carried on very flat segmental arches. These are supported, much as in the chapel at Celle, by short columns with simple capitals that are again more Romanesque than Renaissance in their proportions. The parapet of the galleries is decorated with ranges of arched panels between short pilaster strips. These panels are painted, again as at Celle, with scenes of the Youth and the Passion of Christ at very small scale. Fronting the *Herrenloge* (lord's pew) in the north gallery are plain wooden grilles. At the west there is also a second gallery split by the later organ. This gallery again has painted panels on the parapet and is flanked, under the edges of the ceiling to left and right, by seated figures of St. Paul and of David. Everywhere, in addition to the figural and decorative painting, the profusion of Scriptural texts provides the most obviously Protestant aspect of the church.

Despite all the rich, if provincial, decoration lavished on the interior Otto Grote (†1616), lord of the manor of Breese, who built the church, was content externally with a plain brick box elaborated only by pilaster strips on the multi-staged gables at the east and west ends. His alabaster tomb slab was executed much later, in 1651, and the carved altar dates from 1717.

The Woldenhorner church at Ahrensburg, northeast of Hamburg, lately restored, is more impressive externally than Breese because of its good-sized west tower, provided with brick quoins on the corners, and the hexagonal lantern that rides the roof. All the large windows still have pointed arches and inside, curiously enough the ceiling (Pl. 277) is a simpler version of the rather Late Gothic one over the Heiligenberg chapel (Pl. 265) of the Catholic Fürstenbergs. This Lutheran church was built in 1594-1596[41] by Peter Rantzau, the local lord. He was the heir of a general in the service of Frederik II of Denmark who had acquired the property of the Cistercian monastery at Renfeld in 1567. The combined pulpit and altar at the east end is as at Breese much later, here of 1716.

The parish church at Žŏrawina, a village just south of Wrocław in Silesia, has a longer and more complex history than the Breese and Ahrensburg churches. This fourteenth-century edifice was much enlarged and adapted for Lutheran use over the years 1597-1602;[42] then, in 1654, it became Catholic once more. But the interior still retains very late sixteenth-century painted decoration on the mediaeval vault and a raised *Herrschaftsbühne* (lord's pew), as well as galleries at the sides of the nave, of the same period (Pl. 278). As regards the exterior, several additions to the Gothic shell, all dating also from around 1600, are most striking (Pl. 279). The west front retains its plain early tower, but against it is set on the north side a tall projecting element in brick containing stairs as the levels of the large squarish windows make evident. At the base of this is a simple, almost Serlian, portal with rusticated imposts and arch. The gable in two stages has a succession of C-scrolls and S-scrolls as varied as those on German secular gables

[40] Dehio, *Dresden*, pp. 121-122; Piltz, *D.D.R.*, p. 449. The altar setting of around 1611 is by M. Grünberger and the pulpit of 1597 is by P. Besler, both Freibergers.

[41] Dehio, *Hamburg*, p. 90.

[42] Łozinski-Miłobedski, *Guide*, p. 285; Grundmann-Schadendorf, *Schlesien*, p. 117; G. Grundmann, *Der evangelische Kirchenbau in Schlesien*, Frankfurt, 1970, pp. 13-14.

of the late sixteenth century. The balancing one over the transept-like projection at the northeast is even more intricately scalloped, and a third gable in three stages rises from the roof between to crown a sort of enlarged dormer. More delicate and repetitious scroll-work outlines the one on the eastern end of the main roof.

Except for its inherited tower and the very tall roof of the nave, also inherited, the Žŏrawina edifice might easily be taken for a small Schloss or a fair-sized Rathaus rather than a church. As in earlier decades, indeed, so in the 1580s and 1590s, it is the amount and the elaboration of secular construction which is notable that overshadows in Germany all but such major ecclesiastical works as St. Michael in Munich, the Würzburg Neubaukirche and the Freiberg choir.

At Munich Wilhelm V, the year after his accession as Duke of Bavaria in 1579, undertook several building projects at the Residenz (Fig. 44), continuing the

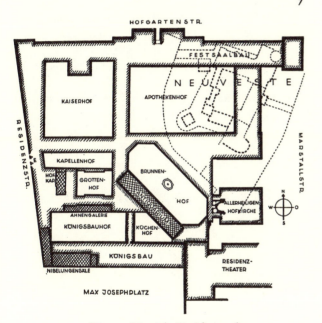

Fig. 44. Munich, Residenz, plan

transformation of the old fortified seat of the Wittelsbachs into a Renaissance *palazzo* as Albrecht V had begun to do in the 1560s. The work was directed, as had been Wilhelm's earlier remodelling of Burg Trausnitz above Landshut, by Frederik Sustris and carried out by Sustris's team of Italians and Italian-trained northerners. The immediate occasion for the new construction was a fire in 1580 that destroyed the fourteenth-century Neuveste. The principal additions

of this period[43] down to Wilhelm's abdication in 1597 were the wings round the *Grottenhof* (grotto court) that extend toward the present day Residenzstrasse from the northwest corner of Albrecht's Antiquarium. Sustris's new work occupies the east, south and west sides of this court (Pl. 282). The wing on the north side, replacing a simple wall, was only built in the eighteenth century; moreover, the facades of the south and west wings were also remodelled to match in 1729 after a fire by François Cuvilliés for the Elector Karl Albrecht. Much survives from the 1580s all the same. The work for which Sustris was responsible includes the arcade carried on red marble columns at the base of the eastern wing and the storey over that in which niches holding statues alternate with large rectangular windows. The similar upper storey at the other end of the court is also essentially of this period.[44]

More remarkable is the Antiquarium (Pl. 280) as deepened and redecorated by Sustris and his associates beginning in 1586, two years before the work in the Grottenhof reached completion. When first erected from Jacopo Strada's design in 1571 by Wilhelm Egckl, it will be recalled, this was a sort of vast vaulted crypt, very broad and low, under Albrecht's library. Even after Sustris's modification and even with the added height he achieved by lowering the floor, it remains crypt-like in feeling despite its great size and sumptuous decoration. A plain red marble base corresponds to the stairs that descend from the ground level of the Grottenhof at the northwest end. Above that ranges of panelled podia on either side support chunky pilaster-like piers set under the vaulting conoids between the bays. Into the faces of these piers are cut niches that contain full-length Antique statues while, among the seemingly endless profusion of Classical busts that Strada had supplied to Albrecht, the most conspicuous and what seem to be the finest in quality are those arranged in threes at the base of the deep-sunk window-frames. But more busts flank the bases of the piers and others are even set in the short niches that are cut deep into the vault surface above the capitals of the piers. The remainder of the interior is smoothly decorated in fresco.

Down the center of the vault of the Antiquarium (Pl. 280) runs a series of large panels alternately of

[43] Lieb, *München*, pp. 90-93.

[44] Horst, *Architektur*, fig. 215, shows the Grottenhof with the garden that once surrounded the fountain. Many small beds of geometrical shapes were punctuated with clipped trees also of diminutive size.

square and of circular shape somewhat as on the vault of the nave of St. Michael, but filled here with figural paintings by Pieter de Witte (c.1548-1628). This artist was a southern Netherlander, trained like his associate Sustris in Italy where his painter father had settled, and known in Munich as Peter Candid, a corruption of his italianized name Pietro Candido. Wilhelm invited him up from Florence where he had been, like Carlo di Cesare, in the service of Francesco de' Medici in 1586, the year before Francesco's death. In executing this very extensive fresco programme, which includes illusionistic *genii* in pairs floating against clouded skies on the faces of the vaulting conoids and a vast quantity of arabesques on the cross-vaults, Candid had Italian assistants. The Bavarian scenes introduced in small panels above and beside the windows were done by a German, Hans Thomaner, however. There was originally much similar painted decoration under the arcades around the Grottenhof also. Candid carried this out with the aid of Il Padovano (Alessandro Scalzi), who had painted the Narrentreppe at Burg Trausnitz for Wilhelm in the 1570s, and another Italian named Viviani. The work went on until 1595 when Candid left the ducal service two years before Wilhelm's abdication and well before the decorations were finally completed.

The openness of the polychromatic arabesques against a white ground on the vault of the Antiquarium resembles a little the painted wooden ceiling of the Gutskapelle at Breese-im-Bruch (Pl. 274). But there the result is distinctly provincial and the elements of the ornamentation are not Italian but of Netherlandish origin. The quality of the painted vault of the Antiquarium is also distinctly superior to that of Schilling's ceiling at Geithain (Pl. 276), a work more comparable in scale. Despite the northern birth of both Sustris and Candid the Munich frescoes are as wholly Italianate in a late Mannerist vein as the interiors Sustris had decorated for Hans Fugger in Augsburg a decade earlier just after his arrival in Germany. They might almost as well have been produced for a Medici as for a Wittelsbach though the result hardly rivals in elegance Francesco's Studiolo in the Palazzo Vecchio in Florence as decorated by Vasari and his team in the early 1570s.

Since the decorating of the Antiquarium was still not completed when Wilhelm abdicated in 1597 his successor Maximilian, co-regent since 1594, carried on with the programme down to 1600. He also built, in the years 1597-1601, the chapel to the west of the Grottenhof. However, both the nave and the choir of this were enlarged in the second decade of the seventeenth century when Maximilian extended the Residenz to the west and north. Nothing of the original very late sixteenth-century work in the chapel now survives in recognizable form.

The Elector of Saxony, Christian I, for whom Nosseni was carrying on the remodelling of the choir of Freiberg (Pl. 270) and Ludwig, the contemporary duke of Württemberg, were almost as active builders at Dresden and at Stuttgart in these terminal decades of the sixteenth century as Wilhelm and Maximilian at Munich. Of the magnificent *Lustspielhaus* (pleasure pavilion) in the Schlossgarten at Stuttgart, built by Georg Beer (†1600) in 1580-1593[45] at a cost of 54,670 gulden, only a few portions of the exterior arcading survive, set up now in the park beyond the railway (Pl. 281).

Beer, a born Württemberger, lived at Bönninghein between Ludwigsburg and Heilbronn over the years 1552-1568. In 1575 he was called to Stuttgart as ducal architect in succession to Alberlin Tretsch and the Berwarts, who had built the Altes Schloss for Duke Christoph in the fifties and sixties. The Lustspielhaus was his principal work though he also erected the *Collegium Illustre,* now the *Katholischer Konvikt* (Catholic boys' school), in 1588[46] in Tübingen, a large but rather plain quadrangular structure, and in 1589 supervised for the duke the rebuilding of the town of Schiltach near Freudenstadt in the Black Forest after a disastrous fire. The houses at Schiltach are mostly of Fachwerk, but the *Jagdschloss* (hunting lodge) that he erected in 1586-1594[47] for Ludwig at Hirsau, to the west of Stuttgart just north of Calw, was of masonry. This still survives in part as a picturesque ruin.

The Stuttgart Lustspielhaus was awkwardly close to the vast eighteenth-century Neues Schloss and so, after being remodelled to serve as an opera-house while the new Schloss was rising from 1744 to 1806, it was demolished in the nineteenth century. Thus the pavilion is known only from engravings and drawings[48] and, as regards its quality, from the re-

---

[45] Merian, *Schönsten Schlösser*, pl. opp. 65, shows the Stuttgart Lusthaus in its extensive garden setting some distance from the Altes Schloss. Fleischhauer, *Württemberg*, pp. 54-59.

[46] Fleischhauer, *Württemberg*, pp. 75-76, pl. 127.

[47] *Ibid.*, p. 74, pls. 43, 46, 233, 240. The towers of Schloss Mömpelgard at Montbéliard (Doubs) were also rebuilt by Beer in 1589: *ibid.*, p. 76, pl. 44.

[48] *Ibid.*, pls. 29-39, 241.

mains re-erected in the park. Ludwig's and Beer's model was very possibly the Prague Belvedere (Pl. 111), begun more than forty years before, for an arcade was carried all around the exterior (Pl. 283). Yet the surviving elements of this arcade make evident that it was far from having the advanced character of the Bohemian model. As in Tretsch's loggias surrounding three sides of the court of the Altes Schloss, the arches are segmental. But the more elegant proportions of the fluted Ionic columns and the small scale of the carved decoration on the archivolts and in the entablature have an almost quattrocento delicacy that contrasts with the clumsiness of the detailing of the earlier work in Stuttgart. On the long sides stairs rose from left and right over two central arches set in front of the main arcade; above, two more arches carried on Corinthian columns provided a porch at the first-storey level of the circumambient terrace and the principal interior.

A sort of echo of the court of the Stuttgart Altes Schloss was provided on the nearby Lustspielhaus by four short round towers. Placed at the outer corners of the arcading, these were much more conspicuous than the ones behind the arcades in the corners of Tretsch's court. The windows of the principal storey, three on either side of the porch and two at each end, were of complex design. They had double lights below that were topped by pairs of smaller openings above transoms and then by oculi over the upper lintels. There was nothing Italianate about these windows nor the gables at the ends and over the porches; these last were elaborated with decorated pilaster orders, in four stages on the big ones and in two on the smaller, but also had rather modest scrolls on their edges.

The low ground storey of the Stuttgart Lustspielhaus contained three square pools of water around which rose stubby fluted piers, as also from the middle of the fountains at their centers, to carry the net-ribbed vaulting. That was mostly in oblong bays, though the four larger bays over each of the pools and the small ones at the corners were square.

The upper storey was undivided and covered with a segmental ceiling suspended from the roof-trusses. The character of its decoration, as seen in an engraving of 1619 (Pl. 284), may be summarily indicated here. Above a continuous entablature broken by ressauts the lunettes at the ends were elaborated both with sculpture and with architectural elements around a large central oculus and two smaller oval windows. These windows occupied the tall lowest stage of each

of the end gables externally. Along the walls, wainscoting that was panelled by pilasters rose nearly to the top of the lower lights of the windows. The heads of these lights were narrowed just below the transoms by concave curves that were visible also on the exterior. Around the window-heads above, which were set deep into segment-topped niches, there was small-scale scrollwork. This sort of ornament was even more conspicuous above and below the frames of the painted panels on the upper walls. Most of the figural sculpture was concentrated at the portals in the centers of the long side walls.

The decoration, or at least the painting on the ceiling, was the work of Wendel Dietterlin (1550-1599),[49] well known as "Ditterling" to his English contemporaries. Dietterlin, who had been a citizen of Strasbourg since 1571 though born at Pullendorf on the Bodensee, came to Stuttgart in 1590 by which date the Lustspielhaus must have been structurally complete. It was in Stuttgart, moreover, that he published the first part of his *Architectura* in 1593; in that year, however, he returned to Strasbourg and brought out there the second part the next year. Concerning him there will be more to be said in Chapter IX, for his major influence in Germany, as elsewhere in northern Europe, followed after the appearance of the much enlarged second edition of his book in Nürnberg in 1598 (Pls. 354, 355). Beer's pupil Heinrich Schickhardt (1558-1634),[50] about whom more will also be said below, worked with or under him on the Lustspielhaus.

Less coherent in any case than Sustris's treatment of the Munich Antiquarium, the main interior of the Stuttgart Lustspielhaus, whether Beer or Dietterlin was mainly responsible, owed little or nothing to Italy. The result must rather have been one of the richest apartments ever decorated in a Northern Mannerist vein. Certainly, moreover, the exterior will have outshone the other work of this period in Stuttgart, of which three or four examples[51] survive—at least as drastically restored since the last war—around the square north of the Altes Schloss. The most notable of these sixteenth-century buildings in the present Schillerplatz are the *Stiftsfruchtkasten* (granaries) behind the Stiftskirche, of which the present facade

---

[49] A drawing in the Hamburg Kunsthalle of the Glory of the Lamb may be a project by Dietterlin for the ceiling: *ibid.*, pl. 40.

[50] *Ibid.*, pp. 276-299, provides the latest account of Schickhardt's architectural career.

[51] Dehio, *Baden-Württemberg*, pp. 468-469.

with its exceptionally plain four-staged gable was added in 1592 to a fourteenth-century building, and the *Merkursäule* (Mercury column) of 1598 across from the northeast corner of the Schloss, both very likely by Schickhardt rather than by Beer. The last is a tall tower-like shaft that originally served as a water-tank for the Schlossgarten, crowned now above its capital with a sculptured figure of Mercury added in 1862. The Kanzlei of 1543 and 1566 shows the effect of the "restoration" of 1684 by Matthias Weiss (1636-1707) even more than that of the present post-war period while, of the facade of the contiguous *Prinzenbau* (princes' wing), only the ground storey is Schickhardt's work of 1605; the rest was originally by Weiss, but drastically remodelled by J. F. Nette (1672-1714) in 1708. Schickhardt's visit to Italy in 1598 has been considered to initiate a new phase in his career; his late work (Pls. 335, 336) hardly supports this view of the older German historians, except perhaps in the case of his church of 1602-1605 (Pl. 438) at Montbéliard in France.

Of the buildings undertaken at Dresden by the Elector Christian I in the 1580s and 1590s while work on the Freiberg choir continued, quite as much is extant as at Stuttgart despite the notorious bombing of 1945. The Lusthaus was totally demolished long ago. Designed by Nosseni, it was begun[52] after the decorating of the Munich Antiquarium, if not of the Stuttgart Lusthaus, had been under way for several years. The surviving construction of this period at and around the Schloss is not by Nosseni but by Paul Büchner (1531-1607) and Hans Irmisch (†1597), who had been in the ducal service since 1565 when the former arrived in Dresden from Nürnberg.

From a painting in the Dresden Stadt Museum (Pl. 285) a good idea can be obtained of the character of the Lusthaus as executed under Nosseni's direction by Carlo di Cesare and Sebastian Walther (1576-1645). Having been begun in 1589—though it was not entirely finished internally even by 1645 when Walther died—this may be described first. Much smaller than the Stuttgart Lustspielhaus (Pl. 283) or even the Prague Belvedere (Pl. 111), the Lusthaus sat high on the Jungfernbastei, one of the corner bastions of the new fortifications of Dresden Rochus von Lynar had built in 1569 for the Elector August. This bastion provided a balustraded podium surrounding the squarish pavilion on all four sides. The ground storey of the pavilion, all that was of Nosseni's de-

sign, had a column-flanked doorway at the center of each side with a continuous entablature above surrounding the whole structure. Over the ressauts capping these portals there was carved armorial decoration. On the narrow ends the portals were flanked by single-arched windows topped by pediments; on the long sides each of the flanking pairs of arched windows was linked by a single pediment.

An iron balustrade crowned the ground storey of the Dresden Lusthaus to protect a roof-terrace. On that stood an attic storey of very plain character begun by Sebastian Walther in 1617; but this was crowned, rather like the Prague Belvedere, by a very assertive roof of cyma section with a delicate metal cresting on top not unlike the balustrades over the lower storey. Perhaps it is the contribution of the artist who painted the picture, but the general look, and particularly Walther's mansard-like roof, seem almost to prefigure the special Saxon Rococo of M. D. Pöppelmann (1662-1736), whose masterpiece is the early eighteenth-century Zwinger here in Dresden. As the decoration of the interior of the Lusthaus was not completed by Christian Schiebling (1603-1663) until the mid-seventeenth century that need not be described here.

These vanished ducal pleasure-houses at Stuttgart and Dresden were exceptional works for their date, standing apart from the other structures such as arsenals, chanceries and stables built in these decades at or near Schlösser to serve more practical needs. Far more characteristic are a varied lot of Schlösser both big and little, many of them erected for much less potent lords and landowners. One of the largest, and yet one of the least interesting, must have been the very plain one (Pl. 310) Count Jakob Waldburg, hereditary lord chamberlain of the Empire, rebuilt in 1580 at Wolfegg, northeast of Ravensburg in southern Württemberg, which will be briefly described later.[53] On the other hand, a much smaller example, Holtfeld (Pls. 315, 316) off the Bielefeld-Osnabrück road near the village of Halle-in-Westfalen, though only a modest oblong Herrenhaus or manor rather than a Schloss, has a very positive character and will receive more attention. It was erected by a Herr von Werndt just at the turn of the century.

Several of the Schlösser of the 1580s and 1590s more than rival, both in size and in elaboration, the

[52] Löffler, *Alte Dresden*, pp. 24-25, 350.

[53] The Schloss that survives today is not the one of 1580 but the nearly identical result of a rebuilding after a fire in the seventeenth century.

earlier-mentioned Schloss at Schmalkalden of 1585-
1589. There the interior of the chapel (Pl. 267) is far
and away the most remarkable feature and one without its sixteenth-century equal except for the more
"High Renaissance" one at the Augustusburg. Perhaps
the grandest new Schloss is that at Weikersheim
(Pl. 294), built in 1586-1598 by Count Wolfgang von
Hohenlohe. This lies just to the west of Mergentheim
in Hohenlohe, today northwestern Bavaria. The most
interesting group of Schlösser, however, consists of
those at Barntrup and Brake, both begun in 1584;
the one at Hämelschenburg of 1588-1597; and that at
Varenholz of 1591-1600. All of these are in the district around Hameln along the upper Weser. It was
in this district that Unkair had worked down to his
death some thirty years earlier. Tönnis, also, had prac-
ticed in the region from the 1560s and was still active
at Hameln. Both Brake and Varenholz were built,
the one completely, the other largely, for Count Simon VI zur Lippe, who was the principal local ruler.

Barntrup, however, the earliest and smallest of these
prime examples of the "Weserrenaissance," was not
erected by a great lord like Wolfgang von Hohenlohe
or Simon zur Lippe. The client was the widow, born
Anna von Canstein, of Franz von Kerssenbrock who
had grown rich like Hilmar von Münchhausen by
serving as a sort of *condottiere* in the French Wars of
Religion. Some incidental construction here may have
been begun already in the 1570s before Hilmar's death
in 1576 to judge from the date 1577[54] on the entrance
to the outer court; but it was only in 1584 that Anna
called on the Hameln builder-architect Eberhard Wilkening to design and erect the Schloss itself. This is
Wilkening's earliest documented work; it is also the
earliest extant example of the ripe Hameln mode, destined to continue in use in the upper Weser district
well beyond 1600, of which the so-called Ratcatcher's
House of 1602-1603 in Hameln (Pl. 390) is the most
famous example. Records of payments to Wilkening
in 1585 and 1588 survive for Barntrup and the latter
date, which is inscribed at the top of the western gable, presumably indicates the completion of the work
three years before Anna's death.

The rectangular plan (Fig. 45) of Schloss Barntrup
with its corner towers may have been suggested by
chateaux Franz von Kerssenbrock had seen in France
—that at Nevers, for example. Moreover, it was in
these years that Dietrich von Fürstenberg, bishop of
Paderborn, added the round towers at the corners of

[54] Kreft-Soenke, *Weserrenaissance*, pp. 225-227.

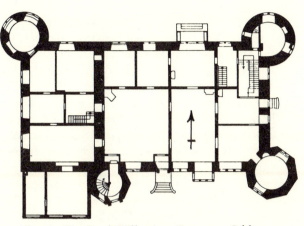

Fig. 45. Eberhard Wilkening: Barntrup, Schloss,
1584-88, plan

the Schloss at Schloss Neuhaus (Pl. 44) which make
it resemble somewhat the so much earlier French
chateau of Bury.

The "garden front" of the Schloss, which occupies
the northwest corner of the fortifications of the town
of Barntrup, has two ranges of irregularly placed rectangular windows grouped in twos and threes. Above
the plain portal, asymmetrically placed in the facade,
is an oriel carried on stone brackets. Below the pilasters which divide the three lights of the oriel a broad
field carries carving in low relief. The south front of
the Schloss is even less regular. Perhaps because a
projecting wing was planned at the left, the octagonal
stair-tower, at the base of which is the principal entrance on this side, rises neither at the center nor at
the far end. Moreover, its small size does not match
the dimensions of either the round towers on the
north front or the octagonal one on the southeast
corner though it is capped like them with a sharply
pointed *welsche Haube*.

Into the short south front of Schloss Barntrup
(Pl. 286) various features are crowded. The main
entrance at the base of the tower is flanked by engaged Doric columns with fluted shafts. To the right
of that and at a lower level a pedimented cellar-door
opens; then there is another portal that has both columns and a pediment. Finally, near the eastern corner tower, a two-storey oriel that is quite similar to
the one above the entrance on the north front rises
up from the ground. The carved decoration includes
lions' heads on the ressauts of the orders; diamond
bosses on the podia; and arms above the stair-tower
portal as well as under the upper lights of the oriel,
in both cases flanked by tiny herms. Over the broad

flat string-course at the top of the ground storey there is a very small bust of Anna, while in the pediment of the cellar door a cellarer pours out wine.

The portals and oriels on the Barntrup Schloss are all handled merely as casual incidents, not as major constituents of an architectonically ordered facade. Otherwise, the interest of the exterior is largely confined to the two ends. Doubtless this was because Wilkening was used to designing such gable-fronted townhouses as had become increasingly prominent in Hameln since Tönnis erected the Johann Rike house there in 1568-1569. However, the south front is not entirely without membering. The broad string-course, really a flattened entablature, at the top of the ground storey is repeated below the first and second storeys and carried round the two octagonal towers at its ends. On the towers the uppermost string provides a terminal cornice at the base of the *welsche Hauben*. Pilaster-strips join these horizontal elements at the corners of the towers and on the faces of the east and west walls between, though there are none on the north and south fronts.

Thus, in the manner of the fronts of the Hameln houses, architectural elements are used at Barntrup to organize the whole wall-surface on the two ends (Pl. 287). Moreover, the pilaster-strips are decorated in a manner that would henceforth be increasingly popular in the Weser region and not without echoes elsewhere, for across the fluted verticals run slightly projecting blocks of random width elaborated by all-over chip-carving.

Unless relevant earlier examples have been even more completely destroyed than the Schloss at Uslar (Pl. 194) or—as is unlikely—have escaped the sharp eyes of Kreft and Soenke,[55] Wilkening at Barntrup

was the first to use chip-carved blocks profusely in Germany though they appeared little if at all later on Schloss Brake. This was a decade after the early employment of chip-carved decoration extensively on the stone banding of the brick facade of De drie Haringen in Deventer, in the Dutch province of Overijssel, and twenty-five years after the first recognizable appearance of the motif at Uslar. Moreover, Wulff had introduced it inconspicuously below the podia of the porch he added in 1565 at the north end of the Rathaus at Lemgo in this same region of the upper Weser valley. The chip-carved blocks he used on the Schloss at Brake (Pls. 288, 289), moreover, may well have preceded Wilkening's at Barntrup if only by a year or two.

On the east end and the octagonal corner tower to the left at Barntrup the flat stone bands framing the windows are carved with a simple flat pattern of scrollwork. Thus, in contrast to the plain stucco of the walls, all the stone trim is enriched in one way or another. Here Wilkening was already demonstrating the *horror vacui* that would later be so characteristic of this region, but still in a quite modest way. Also to be noted is the way the windows are carefully set inside the wall panels formed by the grid of horizontal and vertical stone membering. There is, however, no such subtle ordering of the elements here as on Hameln house-fronts even of earlier date (Pls. 227, 228). For the most part the windows in the wide central panel, all the way up through the lowest stage of the two gables, have three lights while the ones in the side panels have only two. Moreover, most of the windows are irregularly spaced, though not in the rather casual way of the short and long chip-carved blocks of the vertical strips between them.

The two gables at Schloss Barntrup are not iden-

[55] In the appendix, added in their 3rd ed., which deals with this sort of decoration, "Der Kerbschnitt-Bossenstein, das Ornament der späten Weserrenaissance," Kreft-Soenke, *Weserrenaissance*, pp. 291-303, illustrate many examples including several already mentioned here (their figs. 242ff.: 245, Uslar; 243, Hannoversch-Münden; 244, Lemgo) and also other German examples earlier than Barntrup. Such survive at Bäckerstrasse 16 in Hameln of 1569 (fig. 242), on the portal of the Rathaus at Brackel south of Hamburg, dated 1573 (fig. 254), and at Schloss Grevenburg, which Kreft-Soenke date in the mid-seventies (fig. 257). Later specimens, most of them after 1600, are also included (figs. 246-277). Especially significant is the example at Hameln, which was certainly known to Wilkening and possibly of his design. These particular bosses, however, are exceptional since they have diamonds in relief as well as chip-carving on their surfaces. The voussoirs at Brackel, however, are the ones most similar to the chip-carved bands and voussoirs of two years later on De drie

Haringen at Brink 55 in Deventer in the Dutch province of Oberijsel, the earliest identifiable examples in Holland.

The treatment is almost certainly of Dutch origin, yet it seems to have been little used in Holland before its exploitation at Deventer in 1575 and on the Nieuwe Oosterpoort at Hoorn in Noord Holland in 1578; *Niederlanden*, p. 380, pl. 167.

A simple pattern of plain dots regularly spaced appears on many of the bands in relief which often striate Vredeman's published elevations; that graphic device may have been interpreted as chip-carving by craftsmen more used to working in wood than in stone. It is curious no Dutch examples older than the German one at Uslar seem to have survived, but it is possible such have not yet been identified by date. The question also remains whether Wilkening from Hameln or Wulff of Lemgo has priority in Germany after Uslar and Hannoversch-Münden.

tical. That on the west is the simpler and even, perhaps, the earlier by a year or two. The pedimented crowning element on this is nearly identical to the one dated 1576 on the Jost Rike house at Osterstrasse 12 in Hameln (Pl. 228); that may, indeed, be an earlier work of Wilkening though no chip-carved blocks or bands are introduced there. Below the pediment, much wider convex C-scrolls at the sides make almost a lunette of the entire second stage of the gable. The outlining of the stage below with a concave C-scroll under an S-scroll resembles more the treatment of the second stage of the gable on the Jost Rike house. The framing of the lowest stage—absent on the left because of the overlap of the top storey of the corner tower—is not quite so much like the Hameln example. All these bordering elements, moreover, are elaborated by small jewel-like bosses in addition to the plain fillet-edging of the bands that was used previously on the house in Hameln.

Because of the impingement of the tall flanking towers, the gable between them at the east end of Schloss Barntrup is effectively only of two stages beneath the pedimented terminal. That is topped by an obelisk rising between the sharp crocket-like members earlier called "horns." In the stage immediately below, S-scrolls come together at the top, just beneath the moldings at the base of the crowning edicule. These scrolls are punctuated by stone balls on their extradoses as at the other end of the Schloss. The outlining of the lowest stage is more varied and, for this date, exceptionally bold. The upper C-scrolls kick out in bold concave "horns," while the nearly vertical S-scrolls below are linked to the C-scrolls by strapwork and further elaborated by balls, as on the upper stage, and even by tiny "onions." Once more the surfaces of the jewelry-like scrolled bands are enriched with bosses resembling precious stones set as cabochons.

Even though its west wing of 1603 was demolished in 1820 Schloss Brake,[56] just outside Lemgo, is a much larger and more impressive structure (Fig. 46) than that at Barntrup as befitted the princely client. The east wing here, however, dates only from 1666 in the time of Casimir zur Lippe and the south wing was then remodelled also. But the big six-storey tower at the west and the long three-storeyed north wing extending eastward at its side, both original, are most impressive in size and considerably more coherently

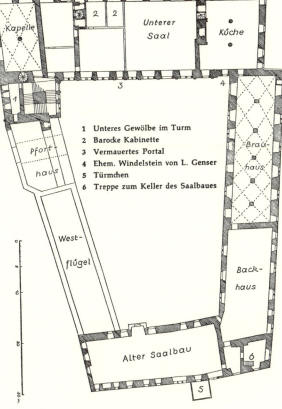

Fig. 46. Brake, Schloss, plan

designed than the facades of Schloss Barntrup. Simon zur Lippe not surprisingly employed as his architect Hermann Wulff,[57] who had been active in Lemgo for some twenty years ever since he added the north porch to the Rathaus. The contract for Brake survives but is unsigned and carries no date. The Schloss was evidently habitable by 1587, however, when Simon moved in and a payment of 500 taler to Wulff on 19 April 1592, as also the date 1591 on the portal of the tower, indicate when the work was finally completed four or five years later.

The design of the tower at Schloss Brake (Pl. 288) is of almost Academic severity with full entablatures capping the basement and all six storeys. The front is two bays wide and, beginning with the first storey, a pair of plain rectangular windows occupies each bay. Up through the fourth storey, pilasters divide the bays, but in the two top storeys there are only plain vertical strips. On the ground and first storeys the pilasters have broadly spaced bands of chip-carving such as Wilkening was then using so profusely

---

[56] Kreft-Soenke, *Weserrenaissance*, pp. 230-231; Gaul, *Brake*, pp. 60-103, plan, p. 59.

[57] Gaul, *Schloss Brake*, pp. 27-85.

The figure labels read:
1 Unteres Gewölbe im Turm
2 Barocke Kabinette
3 Vermauertes Portal
4 Ehem. Windelstein von L. Genser
5 Türmchen
6 Treppe zum Keller des Saalbaues

Kapelle · Unterer Saal · Küche · Pforthaus · Westflügel · Brauhaus · Backhaus · Alter Saalbau

at Barntrup (Pl. 287) and Wulff himself had already introduced rather tentatively in 1565 on the porch of the Lemgo Rathaus.

To the right of the Brake tower nothing survives; to the left is the contiguous end of the surviving north range. Broader than the tower, that has considerably wider bays on the end except in the center. But above its first storey there is a gable of which the two principal stages line up with the second and third storeys of the tower. The pilaster-orders on these are identical with those on the tower; however, the windows are not paired but grouped in threes. The top stage of the gable above is capped with a plain pediment of rather steep pitch corresponding to that of the main roof; the edges of the other two stages, all the same, are very boldly scalloped with pairs of S-scrolls set one above another. The upper end of those in the lower stage and the lower end of the first pair in the upper stage turn outward in sharp-pointed "horns" much as on the lowest stage of the east gable at Barntrup. Balls and tiny obelisk-like finials further enliven the outline.

The long north front (Pl. 289) of Schloss Brake echoes the rather orderly and almost "proto-Academic" western face of the tower rather than the animated Northern Mannerist design of the end gable. Although not completely symmetrical as regards the terminal bays, this is firmly organized as a five-part composition with blind bays, occupied by privies, projecting on either side of the three in the middle. These last are varied in width much as on the west end. That variation is the more noticeable here, however, since the central bay has only a single pair of windows while those that flank it each have two pairs. Beyond the western projection the first two bays have three-light windows in the first storey but there are no openings at all in the bay at the corner. At the other end, a wider bay contains a single pair of windows above and one window only below.

So different from the gable at the west beside the Brake tower is the one over the east end that it may quite probably be a good deal earlier in date. With its ball-studded quadrant edges in all three stages and fluted *welsche Gebel* above, it distinctly recalls Unkair's. Perhaps it was designed before Simon called in Wulff in 1584. However, as has been noted earlier, the treatment of the gables on Lemgo houses in these decades was often even more retardataire.

The court facade of Schloss Brake (Pl. 290), which faces the south, contrasts with the west front in a rather different way than the one on the north. That

is because of the almost continuous fenestration in both storeys and the very delicate detailing of the pilaster-orders and the window-frames. Because of its modest scale the detailing here resembles Wulff's on the upper storey of 1589, above the porch of 1565 on the north end of the Lemgo Rathaus, and also his double oriel of the same date facing the marketplace at the southern end; but the orders at Brake are more carefully designed and there is none of the purely ornamental carving Wulff used so profusely on his Rathaus additions of this later period.

The upper storey of the court facade at Schloss Brake has eight identical bays; then, toward the east end, a single blind bay; and finally, beyond that, a ninth standard one. Ionic pilasters rise from plain podia at sill-level, with the fluting of their shafts interrupted, as on the west and north facades, by chip-carved blocks. These pilasters separate the paired windows and carry a rather thin entablature. This entablature includes, however, a frieze on which are carved a few heads, placed apparently quite at random. The window-frames here unexpectedly recall those on the Meissen brewery (Pl. 246), for their narrow chamfered members are decorated both with small raised hemispheres and with diamond bosses.

At the base of the upper storey of this south front of Schloss Brake a continuous balcony runs. This is partly supported by the wall of the lower storey and partly carried on heavy brackets, two to a bay. These are of scrolled section and decorated again with diamond bosses. The ordonnance of the lower storey, which has a Tuscan pilaster-order with fluted shafts and window-frames identical with those above, is much less regular than that of the upper one. The fourth bay from the left, for example, is narrowed to match an entrance arch which is now filled up. Over this is a carving of Adam and Eve in low relief, not unlike the group over the entrance to the Hexenbürgermeisterhaus—which may well be by Wulff also (Pl. 226). In the next bay the low arch of the cellar door truncates the base of the windows; while two bays further to the right a wide doorway was introduced in the early nineteenth century, perhaps replacing one of sixteenth-century date.

Inside the Brake Schloss two rooms in the tower retain some ornamental stucco-work, dated 1586, which was executed by Conradt Rotermund. Far more and far richer decoration of this sort, dating also from the late eighties, survives in Schloss Wilhelmsburg above Schmalkalden and the most notable interior there, that of the chapel with its *stucchi*, has already been described and illustrated. At Schmal-kalden, however, the exterior facades (Pl. 268) it may be noted, although much longer, quite regular and all but absolutely symmetrical except for the tower at the southwest corner—a survival, as regards its shank, from the thirteenth century—are very dull compared to those of Brake or Barntrup.

The coupled windows of Schloss Wilhelmsburg are small and very simply framed, with painted wooden shutters providing today a rather domestic note. Though probably anachronistic, the colored shutters are not without visual appeal against the bare rubble of the walls. As has been noted earlier, the cross-gables were all removed after the Thirty Years' War except for the ones in the centers of the facades. Even those lost their scrolled decoration around 1820 when the *welsche Hauben* over the octagonal stair-towers in the corners of the court were also replaced with plain pointed roofs. The original carved stone portals in the court are somewhat elaborated, it is true, but they are very clumsy in their proportions. That to the west carries the arms of the Landgrave Wilhelm IV of Hessen-Kassel, the builder, while his portrait bust is set in an edicule over that to the east. The local red sandstone, used for the walling as rubble and still partially covered with stucco, did not lend itself to such delicate carving of exterior detail as Wulff was able to provide in these years at Lemgo and at Brake. Wilhelm made up for his plain exterior with exceptional internal richness.

The one prominent external feature of Schloss Wil-helmsburg above Schmalkalden is the crowning oc-tagon of the mediaeval southwest tower which is associated with the contiguous Schlosskirche to the east within the main block. Colonnettes of stubby proportions, with plain arches between, elaborate somewhat its belfry and, above that stage, the S-curved *welsche Haube* rises to a tiny open lantern.

Inside Schloss Wilhelmsburg there are two sorts of decoration. The most elaborate of the secular in-teriors is the Weisser Saal (Pl. 291) opening off the east end of the chapel. The *stucchi* on the walls of this room, executed under Wilhelm Vernukken's gen-eral direction by Hans Becher, are almost as rich, if not as continuous overhead, as the decoration for which the same men were responsible in the chapel next door. These are even lighter in tone, however, since only a very few details are touched with gilt or color, at least as lately restored. The allegorical female images of Prudence, Justice, Peace and so forth have a curious lack of consonance with the bold

and intricate strapwork that surrounds them. These reliefs almost suggest provincial work of 1800 in the fragile way they contrast with the somewhat rustic—yet Michelangelesque—vigor of the stucco figures in the chapel. The character of the strapwork, however, is a reminder that Vredeman's designs had continued to appear and to be circulated through the seventies as, indeed, they would be even beyond 1600. On the other hand, Vernukken, it may be recalled, had hardly yet been influenced by them in an unmistakable way when he was executing the Cologne Doxal fifteen years before.

Elsewhere in Schloss Wilhelmsburg the decoration is two-dimensional. Painted surrounds consisting of quadratura and strapwork elements frame the win-dows and doors in various bright colors that stand out sharply against the plain white plaster of the walls between. The largest room, the Riesensaal (hall of giants), rivals in size but not in height nor in the decoration overhead the other great halls of the end of the sixteenth century that will be discussed to-gether in the next chapter.

More prosperous or, at least, more spendthrift as well as more powerful than the Hessian Landgraves, not to speak of the Lippes, were the Saxon Electors. In Dresden the Elector August's successors, first Chris-tian and then Johann Georg, both undertook various extensive additions to the Residenzschloss in the 1580s and 1590s[58] employing, like August, Paul Büchner (1531-1607) and Hans Irmisch (†1597). Chris-tian's first commission on his succession in 1586 was for the *Stallhof* (stable court) and the *Langer Gang* (long corridor), connecting with the Georgenbau of the 1530s, which were completed by 1591 (Fig. 47). Remodellings in 1729, in 1744 and in 1872-1876 had denatured the original interior of the Langer Gang long before the bomb damage of 1945. There followed in 1592-1593 the Kleiner Schlosshof[59] (Pl. 293) which lies behind Moritz's big court of the 1540s. None of these extensions and additions, being the work of Germans long in local practice and little influenced by Nosseni, show much stylistic development beyond the earlier Kanzlei, which the same men had built in 1565-1567 when they first entered August's service a decade before Nosseni reached Dresden.

Along the north side of the Stallhof of the Dresden Residenzschloss an arcade twenty bays long, above which is the Langer Gang, was built across from

[58] Löffler, *Alte Dresden*, pp. 20-24, 349-350.
[59] *Ibid.*, pp. 22, 349.

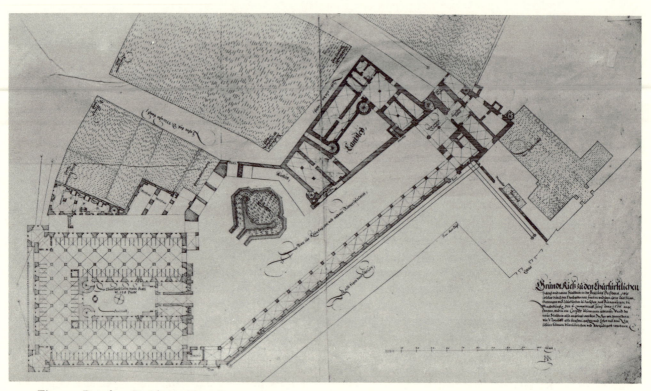

Fig. 47. Dresden, Residenzschloss, Langer Gang
and Stallhof, plan, 1586-91 (engraving from
Chronik Anton Weck, 1679)

the Kanzlei to link the old Torbau of Georg der Bärtige with August's Zeughaus of 1559-1563 (Pl. 211). This range was primarily, it would seem, of Büchner's design like the Chancery over the way, and carried out by Irmisch as just stated. There is at least a possibility, however, that in this case Nosseni offered some advice. The arches, for example, rest on sturdy but well-proportioned Tuscan columns such as the Büchner-Irmisch team had never previously designed or executed. In the earlier German way, however, vertical members capped with scroll-framed shields rise between the spandrels. Above the ressauts in the molded string-courses, moreover, inverted scroll-brackets are set against the base of the first storey, a motif for which there is no obvious Italian precedent—nor, for that matter, any surviving German one. However, the windows, one pair to each bay, are framed by architraves and capped by plain pediments as on the Lusthaus (Pl. 285) that Nosseni designed two years later.

The three small gables that once rose at each end and over the middle of the arcade along the Langer Gang (Pl. 292) of the Dresden Residenzschloss are no longer extant. These had obelisk-topped scrolls flanking rectangular windows with pedimented heads. Of these there was one only in the middle gable, but pairs in the gables at the ends. Also all gone is the original *sgraffito* decoration, as elsewhere at the Residenzschloss. Flowing scrollwork filled the continuous band beneath the sills of the first-storey windows and between the windows were the Labors of Hercules. More delicate scrollwork crowned these panels linking together the pediments of the windows. On the outer side of this range facing north boldly rusticated portals, arched and flanked by heavy Tuscan half-columns, were set in the more smoothly rusticated wall of the ground storey. Otherwise this wall was ornamented only by a row of painted figural panels. The paired and pedimented windows of the first storey repeated those on the other side, so that the long gallery within is exceptionally well lighted.

The last remains of the original internal decorations of 1588-1589 in the Langer Gang, painted by Heinrich I Gödring (1531-1606) with the probable assistance of his young son Heinrich II (c. 1571-1621)—much modified already when the Langer Gang later came to be used as a museum of arms—were destroyed in the holocaust of 1945. In the two-aisled lower storey the plain cross-vaults are carried on a central row of Tuscan columns just like those of the outer arcade. This very architectonic interior, like the arcade outside, suggests the hand of Nosseni in its simple and massive Italianism, while the external *sgraffiti* were very likely the work of the German Gödring.

The *Kleiner Schlosshof* (small court) behind Moritz's principal court in the Dresden Residenzschloss, built in 1592-1593 for the Elector Johann Georg, showed little evidence of Nosseni's possible intervention and must have been predominantly the work of Büchner and Irmisch (Pl. 293). The arches of the superposed galleries were once more segmental, not semicircular, and the Tuscan columns were short and stocky. Thus they resembled those in Tretsch's court of the Altes Schloss in Stuttgart (Pl. 158) or on Egckl's building (Pl. 210) that is now occupied by the Mint in Munich, both of thirty years before. Diamond rustication in low relief occupied the archivolts of the ground-storey arches and also the vertical members that rose between the spandrels.

A certain *tenue* evident here and there in this smaller court of the Residenzschloss—for example in the cornice-topped window-pairs of the upper storey —might possibly reflect Nosseni's earlier involvement in the design of the Langer Gang. Indeed, even the cross-gables here could have been the result of an attempt further to "classicize," so to say, the model provided by the somewhat Serlian ones on the Moritzbau (Pl. 131) in the larger court of a generation and more before. They certainly contrast markedly with the Northern Mannerist elaboration characteristic of the gables and dormers of these decades in Westphalia of which so many have been described in this chapter.

The Kleiner Schlosshof in Dresden was one of the latest arcaded courts of the German Renaissance. This feature, introduced early in the Fuggerhäuser, reached its climax in the fifties and sixties in the court of the Altes Schloss at Stuttgart and the Schöner Hof of the Plassenburg at Kulmbach. As indicated already, completely arcaded courts were rather more common, however, to the east and southeast in Poland, in Bohemia and Moravia, and in Styria and Carinthia than in the central German lands. They are, of course, all but unknown in sixteenth-century England except for the Royal Exchange, but that was modelled on the Antwerp Beurs, itself unique for this period in northern Europe and a public not a private

building. The arcades in the court at Burghley House are not continuous and have been filled in, while that fronting the rear block at Somerset House was a later emendation.

The counts of Hohenlohe were minor magnates compared to the Lord Protector Somerset, effective ruler of England in the brief mid-century reign of the youthful Edward VI, if not to William Cecil, later Lord Burghley and a principal minister of Queen Elizabeth, or to the electors of Saxony in Germany—on a level, say, with the Lippes and the Fürstenbergs. All the same, soon after his accession in 1575, Wolfgang II von Hohenlohe, the son of Ludwig Kasimir, who began the remodelling of Schloss Neuenstein, was at least considering a building campaign at Schloss Langenburg. Five years later he obtained plans for extending with a very large new wing another family Schloss at Weikersheim,[60] lying between Rothenburg-o.-d.-Tauber and Mergentheim, which was mentioned earlier in this chapter. The result of Wolfgang's activity there, which continued down to 1605, is far more impressive in its present well-preserved condition than what is now extant of Christian's and Johann Georg's late sixteenth-century constructions at the Dresden Residenzschloss. Partly, however, this is because of the survival here of various major elements, some of them older, some newer (Fig. 48).

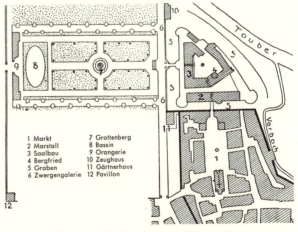

Fig. 48. Weikersheim, Schloss, plan

The Schloss at Weikersheim is approached, for example, from the formal marketplace, laid out in 1719 by J. C. Lüttich, across a bridge over a moat and through the cross block of stable buildings, dated

[60] Dehio, *Baden-Württemberg*, pp. 521-523.

1679-1684, to the inner court. Roughly triangular in shape, this court is dominated on the right by the tall mediaeval keep, circular in plan and now crowned with a *welsche Haube*, and further enclosed by lower structures of minor interest. To the left rises the main Renaissance front which is flanked on the right by an octagonal stair-tower of generous dimensions and a plain three-storey wing slanting inward.

The question of responsibility for the design of the new facade fronting on the court at Weikersheim is somewhat complicated. The Fleming, Georg Robin, Julius Echter's architect at Würzburg, was the first to be involved with Wolfgang even before his major works in Würzburg were underway. After a possible visit to Italy about 1575, the archbishop-elector of Mainz as earlier noted had him build an electoral Kanzlei there which is no longer extant. Then, in 1576, the year after his appointment as official architect in Mainz, he was consulted by Wolfgang von Hohenlohe concerning the Schloss at Langenburg, on the road from Rothenburg to Schwäbisch-Halle, and finally in 1580 he was asked to provide plans for the one at Weikersheim. The wooden model based on these plans, made by Georg Stegle from Stuttgart, has not survived. But Stegle next prepared plans of his own, probably not unrelated to Robin's, that Wolfgang Beringer, the city-architect of Würzburg who had a few years earlier been associated with Robin there, carried out chiefly just before and just after 1600.

Work may have begun as early as 1586, however, and the new wing at Weikersheim was presumably already roofed by 1596 when Beringer began the chapel that was completed four years later in 1600. Yet the gable over the court facade is inscribed with the date 1598, while the rusticated arcade that carries an open terrace at first-storey level along the court front is of 1603 and the great Rittersaal (Pl. 351), the rich decorations of which will be described in the next chapter, was not completed until 1605. The tall mullioned and transomed windows lighting this vast interior and the quatrefoiled oculi above them make this facade exceptionally vertical in its proportions, almost as if there were here a giant order joining the first and second storeys.

The garden front at Weikersheim (Pl. 294) is even grander in scale, for it also rises three storeys, with no loggia at the base, and is sixteen bays long. Rows of almost evenly spaced rectangular windows, paired like those on the righthand wing in the court, occupy three bays to the left and five to the right, since the great hall is not centered in the plan. The two-

storey height of that is again evident, as on the court side, thanks to the special fenestration. Above, however, the three great cross-gables, identical with that of 1598 on the court side, and the larger ones on the ends of this main block are quite symmetrically disposed, with no relation to the ranges of windows below. Broad rather than tall, these gables are all of three stages separated by horizontal "friezes." These run below the sill-level of the windows on the two lower stages and above the windows in the third.

The lowest stage of each of the gables at Weikersheim on the court and on the garden front is divided into three bays. The broad central bay, exactly the width of the second stage, is occupied by a pair of windows as that is also. The two side bays contain single windows set off by stubby panelled pilasters. Pairs of scrolls frame each stage, the lower ones S-curved and horizontal in extension, the upper ones also horizontal but of C shape. The outer ends of these last flip sharply upward like the "horns" on so many Westphalian gables. A single oculus, connected by bandwork with the scrolls at the sides, opens in the third stage of each gable and over that is a tiny pediment with three ball-topped finials. How serious is the loss of the decorated gables at Schmalkalden this impressive facade—so plain below, so rich above —rising behind the extensive Baroque garden of 1709 can well suggest.

The small chapel at Weikersheim, dated 1596-1600, should at least be briefly described. It is square in plan (Fig. 48) with Emporen on all four sides. The parapets of these are decorated throughout their entire length with stucco reliefs of Biblical subjects, presumably executed by Gerhardt Schmidt who later worked in the Rittersaal here in 1601-1605, and so the main interest is the figural modelling rather than the architectural setting.

Despite the extensive building activities of Julius Echter and Wolfgang von Hohenlohe in Franconia, which went on in both cases beyond 1600, the finest extant architecture of this period is mostly in Westphalia. The modest Schlosskirche at Hämelschenburg, in the valley of the Emmer between Hameln and Bad Pyrmont, was mentioned earlier; being freestanding, it does not at all resemble the Weikersheim chapel and the galleries that clog the interior are later intrusions with no stucco decoration like that of Gerhard Schmidt at Weikersheim. With this work of 1563 (Pl. 299) are closely associated some stone farm buildings dated 1556. Almost vernacular in their simplicity, with plain gables capped and framed by stone balls, these are completely overshadowed by the Schloss that Jürgen von Klencke built in the late eighties and nineties. Two other Westphalian Schlösser of the nineties may well, however, be described before Hämelschenburg—one of them the Schloss at Schloss Neuhaus near Paderborn already discussed as regards its earlier portion in Chapter III—though neither of them is of comparable interest. Nor, for that matter, is the even larger Schloss at Wolfsburg, further to the east and north. That also will be described before Hämelschenburg with which it must be almost precisely contemporary.

In the discussion of Unkair's initial work of the 1520s at Schloss Neuhaus which is so important historically it was noted that the corner towers there (Fig. 9, Pl. 44) were added—probably around 1590 when the north wing at Hämelschenburg was also under construction—by Dietrich von Fürstenberg, no relation to the lords of Heiligenberg, who had become prince-bishop of Paderborn in 1585. It is likely that he employed as his architect Hermann Baumhauer, who later built the Paderborn Rathaus in 1613-1618. The cross-gable on the north side of the court of this Schloss though remodelled, probably in 1720, by F. C. Nagel for Clemens August—the Wittelsbach elector-archbishop of Cologne who was also bishop of Paderborn—still carries the date 1590. These round towers have paired windows in their upper storeys and are crowned by *welsche Hauben* topped with blind octagonal lanterns. The north and east wings between the towers are of two storeys (Pl. 295), one less than the towers, like Unkair's earlier wings, and the rectangular windows on their outer sides, are all grouped in threes. These windows are linked vertically and horizontally by very thin stone membering on the stuccoed walls, as are also the narrower ones on the towers. The north facade is nine bays long; that on the east also has nine regular bays but it extends further to the south to include the end of Unkair's original front.

Three-stage gables rise over every other bay of the later wings of the Schloss at Schloss Neuhaus, each with pairs of windows in the first and second stages. At their edges are C-scrolls above S-scrolls on the second stage, S-scrolls on the third stage and above that a scrolled and round-topped terminal feature out of which rises a sharply pointed finial. The eighteenth-century portal—a rusticated elliptical arch with iron balcony above—is not inharmonious with the flatness and regularity of the north front. That differs very markedly in its restrained simplicity and delicacy of

scale from the south front of Hämelschenburg as built in the nineties (Pl. 303) and does not much resemble Baumhauer's Rathaus (Pl. 385) in Paderborn either; yet it agrees very well with Unkair's work of a half-century and more earlier: further evidence of the continuity of sixteenth-century German architectural design.

More precise information is available concerning the extension of another Westphalian Schloss, Varenholz, which lies in the Weser valley southeast of Münden. The new work here was carried out over the years 1591-1600[61] for Count Simon zur Lippe, the builder of Schloss Brake just before this. But the old square keep at the northwest corner was never demolished and the transformation of the mediaeval castle had, in fact, been begun much earlier. The southwest wing across the court from the keep, as built by Simon de Wendt in 1542-1543 for an earlier Lippe, is Late Gothic in all its detailing. It was in 1581 that Simon zur Lippe called from Lemgo Hermann Wulff, whom he would a few years later be employing also at Brake, to execute the elaborate armorial achievement above the main entrance. Flanked by fluted Corinthian columns and capped by a pediment filled by a fluted shell, the portal carries the inscribed date 1582.

For the extensive transformation of Schloss Varenholz, however, Simon employed not the experienced Wulff but the more obscure Johann Bierbaum. A master-mason from nearby Salzuflen, Bierbaum had worked, presumably under Unkair, at Petershagen much earlier in the mid-forties. However, the *parti* (Fig. 49) was very likely decided by Simon himself with some advice—technical, and even perhaps also architectural—from a Dutch expert on fortifications, Johan van Rijswijk (†1612), who soon after was working in Bremen. The big bastions at the northeast and southeast corners which have such an important place in the composition of the southeast side are presumably of Rijswijk's design, not Bierbaum's.

That outer front of the longer of the new wings of 1591-1600 (Pl. 296) provides, indeed, the most impressive aspect of Schloss Varenholz. Whether or not also designed by Rijswijk, the broad squat towers rising from the corner bastions, square in the second storey and octagonal above, with two-stage *welsche Hauben*, somewhat resemble those flanking the front of Giacomo Parr's Rathaus (Pl. 240) of the early

---

[61] Kreft-Soenke, *Weserrenaissance*, pp. 286-287; Gaul, *Brake*, pp. 35-36, 50-51.

234

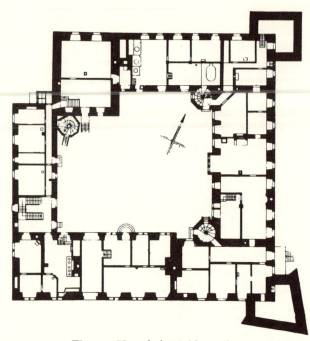

Fig. 49. Varenholz, Schloss, plan

seventies at Brieg in Silesia. Two tall four-stage gables, with very lively scalloped outlines but no membering other than string-courses on their faces, are overlapped by the inner sides of these towers. Between them three smaller gabled dormers, each of three stages, are symmetrically disposed. As so often, even as late as this, the dormers are not lined up with the somewhat irregular ranges of plain two-light windows in the three storeys of the main wall below. Thus the exterior here, with its minimal stone trim and roughcast stucco, has little of the grandeur of Brake (Pl. 288) and also lacks the even and extensive fenestration of the new wings of this period at Schloss Neuhaus (Pl. 295).

In the court at Varenholz the stucco of the portions built in the nineties is, all the same, banded decoratively in a reversing herringbone pattern carried over from the work of the 1540s. The principal feature, a tall oriel inscribed with the date 1599, rises just off the center of the northwest side (Pl. 297). This has four storeys, with five fluted colonnettes framing the four lights in each storey. Though very crudely executed, the orders are successively Doric, Ionic, Corinthian and—more loosely—Composite. In the ground and third storeys segmental arches replace lintels at the base of the compressed entablatures.

On the Varenholz oriel armorial carving decorates

the panels below the first-storey windows and allegorical figures those on the next. There is only simple strapwork with flower-like bosses, however, in the ones on the third storey. This last is crowned with a two-stage gable rather heavily ornamented with additional short fluted colonnettes of indeterminate character and scrolls along the edges. As on the housefront in Herford (Pl. 229) small human figures are locked into these scrolls. The chip-carved blocks so profusely used by Wulff at Brake (Pls. 288-289) are here as roughly executed as the rest of the detail. They appear as keystones in the various archivolts and also, very broadly spaced, on the strips that mark the angles of the octagonal stair-turrets at the northeast and southwest corners of the court. The flat window-frames in the court, however, have the same sort of very low-relief strapwork decoration as those Wilkening had employed at Barntrup (Fig. 45, Pl. 287) a decade before this. All this suggests the provincial hand of Bierbaum, with no influence of consequence from any Netherlander such as Rijswijk.

In quite a different and more advanced style is the portal, with the earlier date 1594, at the base of the northwest stair-tower of Schloss Varenholz. This is flanked by herms, considerably better proportioned than those beside the portal on the other tower. It is also crowned with heavy strapwork which is carved in high relief around a ringed lion's mask. On this tower, moreover, the angles have cylindrical members. These are much in the old Unkair manner, but are banded here with chip-carved rings. Altogether this portion of Schloss Varenholz is more comparable to Hameln work of the period in quality and presumably neither by Bierbaum nor by Rijswijk.

The Schloss at Wolfsburg, to the northwest of Brunswick near the present interzonal frontier, is even larger than that at Varenholz though not as well documented. As was noted above, it must, however, be of approximately the same years.[62] This was lately acquired by the municipal authorities of what has been, since the war, the most productive and prosperous small urban entity in Germany because of the Volkswagen works, even though it was founded as a city only in 1946. Eventually that ownership should assure a thorough restoration, for Wolfsburg is not as well maintained as Neuhaus or Varenholz, nor are its present varied uses altogether appropriate. Wolfsburg's sophisicated interest in architecture of

[62] Kreft-Soenke, op. cit., pp. 289-290.

the twentieth century is reflected in the employment of Aalto and Scharoun for public buildings, if not in its disappointing urbanism.

The rebuilding of the mediaeval *Wasserburg* (moated castle) at Wolfsburg, protected by two arms of the river Aller, was very possibly begun by the local lord Hans von Bartenstein who died in 1583. It is only known that the stone-mason Johann Edeler from Hameln, who died in 1592, was employed there after 1588 by Hans's heir Günther. After Edeler's death it is thought that Heinrich Rumpf from Helmstedt—not far away to the southeast where Paul Francke was then building the Juleum—took over in 1593 when his name is mentioned in a document. Above the entrance passage leading to the court is the date 1598, which may well indicate when the work, or a large part of it, was completed.

Like Varenholz, Wolfsburg is quadrangular, but the low west wing was erected over mediaeval vaulted cellars only in 1840. The south and north wings have three storeys above the ground storey (Pl. 298). Because of the four storeys of the one to the east, however, each taller than those of the other wings, that portion of the Schloss rises considerably higher. Throughout there are regular ranges of two-light windows. These are quite unframed; but, as on the exterior at Varenholz, the end-gables and cross-gables are all boldly, though not very elaborately, scrolled. The biggest, those at the ends of the east wing, are backed by cross-gables facing east and, over the south end, one facing west as well. At the base of these gables on the two ends of this rather grand range stone brackets project. These once carried a *chemin de ronde*, an exceptional mediaeval survival on a Schloss of so late a date.

The end gables at Wolfsburg are crossed by three vigorous string-courses, the cross gables by two. The lowest stage on all of them is framed by rising, convex C-scrolls above which are short vertical members. In the next stage further convex C-scrolls come first and then concave ones of which the lower ends project as modest "horns." In the third stage of the end-gables these paired C-scrolls are repeated at smaller scale between obelisk-topped urns, and both end-gables and cross-gables terminate in tiny *welsche Gebel* topped by obelisk-finials. The gables are the principal features of the skyline, but behind those at the north end rises the square top of the *Hausmannsturm* (keep) which is asymmetrically capped with a tall *welsche Haube*.

Other smaller and less elaborate Schlösser of these terminal decades of the century may better be discussed, together with secular work in towns of similar character, in the next chapter. There also the great halls, new features of the years before and around 1600, will also find a place. The climactic work of this period, however, the Schloss at Hämelschenburg of 1588-1599[63] should now be described in some detail to conclude this chapter.

Unlike the quadrangular Schlösser just discussed, Hämelschenburg is a broad, slightly irregular U in plan (Fig. 50) rising high above a pond, lying to the east of the open side of the court, against a tree-clad hill. West of the pond a bridge, set diagonally to road and Schloss, leads up to the level of the court. That level is well above the narrow moat, connecting with the pond, that runs between the road and the basement of the south wing. The free-standing arch at the bridge (Pl. 299) was erected, not by Jürgen von Klencke, who has already been mentioned as the builder of the Schloss, but by his heir Ludolf von Klencke in 1608, curiously enough a year before Jürgen's death: This is much in the style of the south wing, though by that date Tönnis, probably, and Hundertossen, certainly, one or the other of whom has been proposed as Jürgen's architect, had died.

The north wing of Schloss Hämelschenburg (Pl. 300), begun twenty years earlier and completed in 1592, is much more delicately detailed. In particular the ground-storey oriel—once on the court side of that wing but now set against the west wing beyond the corner stair-tower—closely resembles the contemporary one of 1585-1589 that Tönnis was just completing on the Gerd Leist house in Hameln (Pl. 318). It is also not unlike Hermann Wulff's upper porch of 1589 on the north end of the Lemgo Rathaus. The Ionic colonnettes between the three windows, fluted above but with delicate carved decoration on the lower third, are very similar to those used both by Tönnis and by Wulff; but they stand here on podia that are carved with masks flanked by very bold diamond bosses. Further such bosses, moreover, project from scroll-edged cartouches on the panels between the podia, and there are also raised bands decorated with somewhat simpler reticulated patterns above and below.

The north wall of the court at Hämelschenburg is nearly three times as long as Tönnis's Hameln house-

[63] *Ibid.*, pp. 150-151.

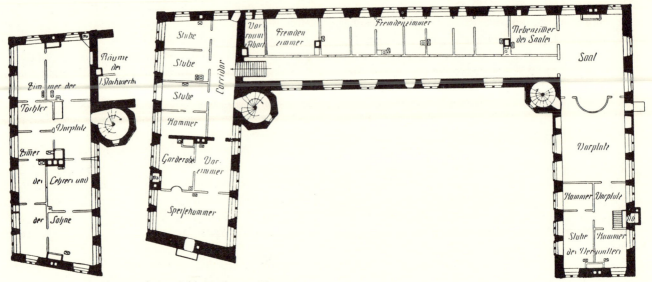

...enburg, Schloss, plan, 1588-97

front is broad; thus it resembles rather more the court side of the north wing at Brake (Pl. 290), though the fenestration here is neither so continuous nor so regular. The windows are paired throughout, but toward the left end they are narrower and less evenly spaced. Their framing resembles that of the triple windows on the first storey of the Leist house (Pl. 318). Above the entablature of the ground storey and below the sills of the next storey above, narrow podia, carved with plain bosses and other simple ornaments, were introduced. Moreover, in the frieze of the terminal entablature, the cornice of which is at eaves-level, human heads in high relief project over each of the delicately detailed colonnettes, somewhat as on the court facade at Brake.

A gable decorated in a rather different spirit (Pl. 300) rises over the east end of this northern wing at Hämelschenburg and there are also two big gabled dormers on the court side. These features are all elaborated to a degree approached hitherto only by the gable, dated 1579, on the Celle Rathaus (Pl. 231) which was executed by Hameln craftsmen. The treatment of the pilaster-strips on the end-gables, interrupted by projecting blocks of chip-carving alternating with round bosses, seems a mere variation of that of the vertical members on Wilkening's slightly earlier gables at Schloss Barntrup (Pl. 287) and of the pilaster order that Wulff was using at Brake (Pl. 288) at just this time. In the lowest rectangular stage the pairs of windows are framed, not by colonnettes as on

the wall facing the court, but by strips of blocks and bosses. These vertical strips flank a bare middle bay and are bounded at the edges by additional projecting members broader than they are.

In the next stage of the northeast gable at Hämelschenburg narrow paired windows are set over the inner ones of each of the pairs below. The latter are flanked by the above-mentioned extremely decorative strips; and two more of these strips subdivide the solid middle section at this level which was left quite plain below. Above the strips is an entablature carved with heads in high relief like those over the upper storey on the court facade. The third stage is not as tall as the second and has two single windows only. These are located over the outer bays of the windowless section in the middle of the one below. The vertical strips and horizontal entablatures are identically treated at this level, as is true also of the narrow fourth stage which has no window at all.

The complication of the scrollwork framing the three upper stages on this Hämelschenburg gable almost defies description. In the second stage C-scrolls are set over S-scrolls, and the broad, slightly concave, surfaces of both are carved with alternating disks and batons in low relief. The fields these scrolls enclose are elaborated with similar disks and with small bosses, some hemispherical, some diamond-pointed. Panelled obelisks and plain balls further elaborate the outline against the sky. In the next stage the upper end of each of the S-scrolls is flipped out in a "horn," much as on the Barntrup gables, and the lower spiral is repeated in a second spiral that is not part of a scroll. This stage is also flanked by panelled obelisks.

The topmost stage of the northeast gable at Hämelschenburg has two small S-scrolls on each side and is capped by a pediment with a heavy cornice. From the slopes of this, horn-like crockets project, much as on the Jost Rike house at Hameln of 1576 and at Barntrup a decade later (pls. 228, 287). This is not the final element, however, for above the pediment an open square of entablature is carried on brackets over which a sort of four-armed open crown carries a finial that is set diagonally. Probably such a terminal feature had never been introduced before over a Renaissance gable either in Germany or elsewhere in the north; here it is actually the top of a chimney, however, as later on the south wing also, and elaborate chimney caps of one sort or another are not unknown in the sixteenth century, especially in France.[64]

The two rather shorter gables of the dormers on the court side of the north wing (pl. 302) of Schloss Hämelschenburg are neither symmetrically disposed nor coordinated with the bays of the wall below. Their decoration is also considerably flatter, except for the stubby fluted Corinthian colonnettes beside the paired windows in the lowest rectangular stage of each of them. The friezes of the entablatures again have heads in high relief, but the pilaster-strips are mostly decorated with thin motifs of simple strap-work rather than with chip-carving. Such textures, here executed in lower relief than on the end gables, are restricted to four horizontal bands of ashlar, quite unrelated to any of the other members, that run all the way across the rubble faces of the gables. Paired C-scrolls with sharp outer ends, one above another, enclose the second stage and bigger single S-scrolls the third. The terminal pediments with their bold "horns" are again of the sort that had been used, perhaps for the first time, on the gable of the Jost Rike house (Pl. 228) ten years before.

Before describing the stair-tower in the northwest corner of the court that provides the only vertical communication inside the north wing a tentative, if rather complicated, answer may be hazarded to the difficult question of attribution here at Schloss Hämelschenburg. The oriel and the court facade, except

perhaps for the gabled dormers above the roof line, might well be the work of Tönnis. If these minor gables, mixed as is their character, are in fact not of his design, then it would seem that the tall end-gable is not by him either but by some other hand. If none of the gables were added later when the south wing was built in 1597-1599, they could all have been a slightly earlier contribution by Hundertossen or whichever other Hameler or Lemgoer was responsible for that later wing. Wilkening from Hameln need not be entirely excluded in the eighties—nor, indeed, in the nineties. He is, at the least, still a rather more likely candidate than either Herman Wulff or Georg Crossmann from Lemgo.

The northern stair-tower at Hämelschenburg might well be the work of the hypothetical "other hand" even though the entablatures of the court facade of the wing to the right are continued around it and, indeed, across all the gables of the dormers on this west side as well. Yet the portal at the base of the tower with its fluted Corinthian columns seems to accord more with the underscaled detailing on the oriel despite the frieze over it which was much widened to provide space for armorial decoration. The unrelated pediment, carried on carved lions' heads, is rather sharply pointed in shape and shorter than the cornice below. God the Father on the first day of Creation, as carved in the field of this pediment, and the Archangel Gabriel above the apex suggest a rather different taste. That taste does not seem to accord with the other details. For example, the chip-carving on the blocks banding the pilaster-strips at the corners is quite in the more abstract manner of Wilkening's work at Barntrup and Wulff's at Brake (Pls. 287, 288). But is that different taste Tönnis's? Paradoxically, it seems closer to Wulff's and, as was noted earlier, the oriel also somewhat resembles his at Lemgo.

Above the level of the eaves of the main roof, the northwest stair-tower at Hämelschenburg continues upward in five more short stages. The topmost of these is provided with little arched openings of which the jambs and archivolts are varied with chip-carved banding. Above is a rather heavy *welsche Haube*.

The principal interior in the north wing of Schloss Hämelschenburg is a great hall, not now accessible, that occupies a large part of the first storey. In the main storey of the west wing a string of guest rooms opens off a broad corridor along that side of the court (Pl. 302). Except for the oriel, moved here from the

[64] Venetian chimney-tops are often somewhat elaborated and those of Schloss Ambras, outside Innsbruck in the Tyrol, probably of the 1560s, actually rival French ones: DKDÖ, *Tirol*, pl. 3.

north wing, the court side of this wing is very plain (Pl. 301). The windows are mostly pairs of simple oblong lights while the ones on the ground storey have transoms also. Above the eaves-line, however, there are on this wing three gabled dormers facing the court and three more on the outer side. These gables are all narrower and flatter than those over the court side of the north wing but there are scrolls flanking the upper stages below little terminal pediments accented by "horns." The surfaces of the dormers on the west wing are actually broken in the lowest stage only by small windows, but there is also banding of the sort already tentatively introduced on the ones around the corner of the court to the north. This treatment of the western dormers is so consonant with that of the walls of the north wing that they must be by the same hand; but one might surmise that the plainer work below is rather a survival, perhaps from the sixties, well before Jürgen von Klencke started rebuilding the Schloss in 1588. On the outer side, however, the windows have heavy flat frames banded with chip-carved blocks like those on the pilasters of the northeast gable. The octagonal stair-tower in the southwest corner, up against the south wing built in the late nineties, is almost identical with the northerly one.

If Jürgen von Klencke had been content with building anew only the short north wing at Hämelschenburg and then merely remodelling the longer one on the west, his Schloss would have been no more impressive than Brake in its present truncated state. It is very largely because of the south wing Jürgen added in 1597-1599 that Hämelschenburg outranks in interest all other German secular work surviving from the terminal decades of the century—not least what the electoral princes of Bavaria and Saxony were adding to their so much more extensive Residenzschlösser in Munich and Dresden. It even rivals, indeed, the earlier Schöner Hof of the Plassenburg. Between the moat at its base and the earlier subsidiaries across the way that date from before Jürgens's time—the farm buildings of the fifties and the chapel of 1563—there is barely room for the modern road to pass. This grandiose block must, therefore, be viewed in sharp perspective, either from the southeast (Pl. 303), with the later arch in the foreground, or from the southwest, rising high above the big trees that grow on top of the medieval bastion at this corner.

Even so, two aspects of the exceptional grandeur of this portion of Schloss Hämelschenburg are at once apparent, the great height and the total symmetry of

the south front, quite eclipsing the more modest and irregular facades that flank the court behind it. The battered mediaeval foundations raise the base of the ground storey—ground storey, that is, on the north side toward the court—the equivalent of a storey and a half; two storeys then follow that are equal in height to those of the north wing. But there is an additional storey here and, over that, the lowest stage of the four cross-gables provides what is in effect still another. Higher up, the second and third stages of the cross-gables are very nearly as tall and even more richly decorated than those at the east and west ends of the main roof of this block.

Though the elements of which the facades of this south wing at Hämelschenburg are composed are quite different from the arabesqued arcading of the Plassenburg (pls. 191-193) there is a certain similarity to the Schöner Hof in the combination of a general ordonnance at very large scale with nearly continuous decoration at much smaller scale on the surface of the walls. In the over-all grid of horizontal and vertical elements, moreover, the former dominate as much as they do in the Schöner Hof, at least below the gables, which are in any case lacking at the Plassenburg. Each of the three storeys has an entablature and these are punctuated, like the ones on the north wing here, by heads in high relief. In addition, the string-courses at the level of the sills, quite as in the Schöner Hof, are very nearly as prominent as the cornices of the entablatures.

What gives the south facade of Schloss Hämelschenburg its exceptional character, however—the treatment was not yet fully developed on the court side—is the repeated bands of chip-carved blocks. Such, it will be recalled, had been only tentatively introduced on the gables of the north wing (Pl. 302), though they were somewhat more consistently applied to the dormers of the west wing (Pl. 301). However, in each main storey and in each stage of the gables of the south facade except the topmost there are two such bands, so that the whole wall-surface is texturally striped in a manner analogous to bichromatic Netherlandish banding in brick and stone.[65]

Crossing these horizontals on the south facade of Hämelschenburg, and crossed by them, are the re-

[65] By this time in Holland textured bands of stone, introduced a quarter-century or more earlier, were in increasingly common use as they would, indeed, continue to be well into the new century. Especially relevant among early examples is the earlier-mentioned Nieuwe Oosterpoort at Hoorn of 1578 on which the many bands of stone are all chip-carved.

peated vertical elements. Here these are pilaster-strips, like those on the northeast gable (Pl. 300), not colonnettes as on the court facade, and rather widely spaced on the storeys below, though more closely set on the gables. Beside the central group of three bays, moreover, the vertical strips are doubled as also at the sides of the lowest stage of the gables of the dormers.

Even more than the still slightly asymmetrical north side of the surviving wing at Brake (Pl. 289), the south facade of Schloss Hämelschenburg is a balanced composition. This is made up below of five elements of varying breadth but shifts above to a range of only four identical dormers. Where at Brake two rather broad flat sections housing the privies come forward on either side of the middle bays, here the only projection is the deep three-light oriel cantilevered out from the center of the ground-storey.

With its delicate colonnettes between the windows and the carved panels below them this oriel on the south side of Hämelschenburg seems an almost anachronistic repetition of the one that was once on the north wing and is now on the west one. Similar oriels, however, were used even later in Hameln. This feature is certainly not consonant with the decorative plaiding of horizontal and vertical members characteristic of the south facade as a whole, yet the disparity is no greater than on the Rattenfänger Haus of 1602-1603 (Pl. 390) or the Dempstersches Haus of 1607 (Pl. 391).

On the court side of this south wing at Hämelschenburg (Pl. 304), which was presumably finished first, the plaiding of the wall surface is not yet altogether consistent. It is as if the designer, whoever he may have been, was feeling his way gradually from the very restricted use of chip-carved blocks on the window-frames in the ground storey here, much as on the outer front of the contiguous west wing, to the wholly regular banding he eventually employed on the second storey, as well as on the two gabled dormers on this side, and then all over the outer front. Moreover, the portal on this court facade is placed with no regard for the pattern of fenestration—very irregular in any case—of the ground storey. The Ionic half-columns at the doorway are heavier and more coarsely fluted than on either of the oriels or on the doorway at the base of the northwest stair-tower, and the pediment above actually overlaps the ground-storey entablature. Around the door-opening boldly over-scaled architectural elements contrast with very flat surface-patterns that are much like the patterns on the dormers of the north wing across the court (Pl.

302), which may possibly be by Tönnis. Perhaps the portal is an interpolation dating from after the south wing was completed in 1597 and by a different designer. It does not, however, at all resemble the gate of 1608 (Pl. 299).

The outlines of all the six gables (Pl. 303) above the facade of this south wing at Hämelschenburg are almost the same as that of the gable at the east end of the north wing (Pl. 300). These gables are also much more characteristic of the work of the same decades in Hameln than is the portal. On the gables at the ends, the curious openwork crowns above the terminal pediments repeat that on the northeast gable and are, once again, actually chimney tops; while the smaller gables of the dormers terminate with the horned pediments of the Hameln house of 1576. It is, indeed, the horns on the pediments and the sharp flipped-up ends of the C-scrolls on the penultimate stage of the gables on the south wing that make the whole skyline so animated. The more conventional obelisks, so like Tönnis's on the Leist house of 1585-1589 at Hameln (Pl. 318), of the northeast gable were omitted on all those of the south wing in favor of the bolder curved elements common at this later date in Westphalia.

It is in this south wing at Hämelschenburg that the family living quarters are—and presumably always were—with the dining room at the eastern end of the first storey and the principal bedrooms in that above. The interiors now retain only a portal or two and a few chimneypieces that seem to be original. But an exceptional feature of the court of Schloss Hämelschenburg remains to be mentioned: this is the *Pilgerlaube* (pilgrims' gallery) of which the three bays run northward from the stair-tower at the left end of the west wing (Pl. 305). The brackets at the top of the openings, now glazed, are identical with those of the somewhat anomalous portal in the court front of the north wing just on the other side of the stair-tower. Like that, the loggia, which was intended to provide accommodation for pilgrims and other passing travellers, may well be an interpolation by a later hand. It could date from after 1597, when the south wing was completed in the main, carried out for Ludolf like the gateway of 1608, rather than for Jürgen.

Hämelschenburg concludes the remarkable group of great Schlösser dating from the last decades of the sixteenth century. These more than balance in size and in originality of design the most notable secular productions of the day in other Protestant parts of

Europe. If they lack the symmetry of the "Prodigy Houses" of Elizabethan England that Robert Smythson designed and built and are none of them as Italianate as Wollaton nor as "modern" as Hardwick, Jürgen von Klencke, whoever his architect may have been, was a builder of the caliber of Sir Francis Willoughby and Bess of Hardwick, nor were Wolfgang von Hohenlohe and Simon zur Lippe much less ambitious.

The grand Danish castles of Frederik II and Christian IV at Helsingør and at Hillerød, Slot Kronborg and Slot Frederiksborg, were respectively somewhat earlier and somewhat later, but are more comparable in character to the German Schlösser. In France, however, the wars of religion had brought chateau construction to a halt and revival awaited the political consolidation of the state under Henri IV after his accession in 1589.

Seven

DOMESTIC AND CIVIC
ARCHITECTURE OF THE
LATE SIXTEENTH CENTURY

I N the years toward the end of the sixteenth century many more Schlösser beside those described in the previous chapter were being built, remodelled or extended. Because of grand scale or idiosyncratic design, certain of them rival in interest, at least as regards particular features, even the finest, Weikersheim and Hämelschenburg, that have already been discussed and illustrated. Several contain principal interiors—*Rittersäle* (knights' halls) is one name for them—of such exceptional size and richness of decoration that they are more than comparable to the surviving one at Weikersheim, mentioned earlier but not yet described, if hardly—or so it may be surmised—to the lost Lustspielhaus in Stuttgart (Pl. 284).

These "great halls," so to call them in English, represent a significant innovation, and one most characteristic of this period, though there were some forerunners. The most notable early examples in Germany are the ones at Landshut and at Jever which were briefly described in earlier chapters; but the largest of all is Austrian, the so-called *Spanischer Saal* (Spanish hall) at Schloss Ambras outside Innsbruck in the Tyrol, built around 1570 by the Archduke Ferdinand,[1] of which there will shortly be an account. However, before dealing with the later monumentally-scaled German interiors which followed only well after that something should be said concerning the exteriors of several more Schlösser of these decades as well as such ancillary structures as arsenals and chanceries. Of particular external features which survive on minor Schlösser, two at least should also be mentioned that are as impressive as anything at the grander princely seats.

At Schloss Fürstenau, which rises out of the Mumling at Steinbach, just outside Michelstadt in southern Hesse, the great arch of 1589[2] (Pl. 306) that joins the south and north wings on the west side of the court has no equal at the larger Schlösser—compare, for example, the modest later arch at Hämelschenburg (Pl. 299). Built by Count Georg III von Erbach, this quite overshadows the mediaeval and earlier sixteenth-century elements of the modest Schloss. The arch itself is plain but very thick, since it was cut through the existing defensive wall on this side. Above, however, there is a broad parapet of open strapwork interrupted in the center by armorial carving and crowned by two statues of *genii*.

Five years later, in 1593,[3] that prelate ever active at building, the Prince-Bishop of Würzburg Julius Echter, made much more considerable additions to Schloss Grumbach at Rimpar, just north of Würzburg, which he had lately bought than he had, before his elevation, to the Schloss he inherited at Mespelbrunn. To the existing south wing with its curtain-topped windows he attached a new east wing known as the *Juliusbau*. Except for three round towers, two of them flanking the entrance, the exterior of this new wing is very plain, with many rather small rectangular windows somewhat unevenly disposed. On the court side, however, the entrance portal is heavily rusticated and ornamented above with Julius's arms framed in a cartouche.

The whole Schloss at Rimpar, moreover, is dominated by another round tower, mediaeval as regards its base, located at the southeast corner. That tower Julius's architect—presumably here Georg Robin rather than Lazaro Augostino or Wolfgang Beringer—

---

[1] A son of the emperor Ferdinand I, this Habsburg archduke was made Statthalter of the duchy of Tyrol in 1564 by his father and surived until 1595. That his first wife was Philippine Welser, daughter of the Augsburg banker, has been mentioned earlier. Presumably the hall was called "Spanish" because by this time even the Austrian Habsburgs were thought of as members of a Spanish royal house.

[2] Dehio, *Hessen*, pp. 780-781.
[3] Reclams *Bayern*, pp. 759-760; 496.

carried up five storeys, well above the eaves of the new Juliusbau, spacing the windows quite regularly and marking the storey lines with molded string-courses. At the bottom of the topmost storey of the tower a balcony, carried on boldly scrolled brackets, introduces a more truly Renaissance note in its spindled balustrade, but one still of quattrocento delicacy. Yet even this balcony still recalls a mediaeval *chemin de ronde*. Concerning the Rittersaal within, of which the decoration is more advanced in style, something will be said later in this chapter.

At Giessen in Hesse, on the road from Frankfurt to Marburg, the modest Schloss that the Landgrave Philipp of Hesse built in 1533-1539, all of Fachwerk above the ground storey, is quite overshadowed by the nearby Zeughaus[4] (Pl. 307). Not only is this arsenal building constructed of stone, it is also three or four times as large. The Zeughaus was erected by Ebert Baldewein in 1586-1590 for Ludwig IV of the Marburg line of the Hessian Brabants. The long three-storeyed block has rather small rectangular windows in pairs in the upper storeys and large mullioned and transomed ones for the ground floor—these last replaced, or perhaps even first introduced, in the restoration of 1959. But the regularity of the facade on the west side is broken by a broad projection and beside it a somewhat narrower one. At the base of the former a heavily detailed double portal opens. Over that the panel of armorial carving is capped by a pediment.

The C-scrolls that frame the carved arms above the portal repeat the theme of the gables and gabled dormers which provide, as so often, almost the only other decoration on the Giessen Zeughaus. The bold strapwork banding, the "horns," and the concave and convex C-scrolls are all by this date familiar enough; but the curious incurved "bites" out of the sides of the lowest stage of the larger gables are exceptional as also the carved bears set on top of the ends of these stages.

At Ansbach the builder of the Schöner Hof of the Kulmbach Plassenburg, the Hohenzollern Margrave Georg Friedrich, obtained something rather different from the architect he was employing in these years, Gideon Bacher.[5] The Kanzlei Bacher erected at Ansbach (Pl. 308) in 1594-1597,[6] occupies the site of a mediaeval cloister to the north of the church of St. Gumbert of which, it will be recalled, Bacher was then heightening the main western tower (Pl. 273).

Three-stage gables, seven of them altogether, with those on the sides as broad and high as the ones at the ends, provide characteristic crowning features on the Ansbach Kanzlei. These all have panelled pilasters on the two lower stages and S-scrolls and C-scrolls of exceptional thickness at the sides, while the top stages are capped with tiny pediments. This rather heavy-handed treatment of the outline is balanced by the more delicate panels of sgraffito bandwork that cross the gables at the base of each of the three stages. A similar band of sgraffito decoration is also carried across the facades between the first and second storeys.

All three storeys of Bacher's Kanzlei have rather closely set windows, those in the ground storey divided only by mullions but with transoms as well in the upper storeys. Quite exceptional is the black and white rendering, vaguely suggesting voussoirs, that surrounds all the windows. This creates a pseudo-relief pattern over the entire wall surface to emulate economically the channelled masonry of Bacher's new upper storeys on the nearby tower of St. Gumbert (Pl. 273); but the effect in this case can hardly be described as proto-Baroque.

In the court of the Ansbach Kanzlei, where there is no sgraffito decoration, the upper storeys have low arcades with very broad segmental arches carried on stubby panelled pilasters. Diamond bosses in the podia of the pilasters, repeating similar elements below those in the gables on the outer sides, provide the only decoration. Very like the Kanzlei is the more modest Neuer Bau in the lower market. That was built by Bacher at much the same time to house the margrave's guests.

Although these late examples of Georg Friedrich's building activity lack the distinction of the Schöner Hof of the Plassenburg (Pls. 191-193) for which he had been responsible thirty years earlier, the relatively great size of the Kanzlei, rising beside the tall tower of St. Gumbert as remodelled and completed in the same years by the same builder-architect, is evidence of the seriousness with which the margrave took the administration of his lands.

A few years later the painter-architect Peter Senge-

[4] Dehio, *Hessen*, pp. 312-314.
[5] Bacher did not work on the Schöner Hof of the Plassenburg; doubtless he was too young to have been employed there in the sixties. Later, in 1590, he had done some building for the margrave of Baden at Schloss Hochburg, south of Freiburg-i.-B. in southern Baden, and, as was noted earlier, he was associated with the Wallbergers at Nördlingen on

the reconstruction of the town's gate-towers in 1592: See the article "Simon Bacher" by M. Bach in ThB.
[6] Reclams *Bayern*, pp. 58-59.

laub (1558-1622) provided for the Wettin Duke Johann Casimir of Sachsen-Coburg nearly as extensive
administrative premises at Coburg in the Kanzlei
(Pl. 309) he began to build in 1597.[7] Of the external
wall-paintings Sengelaub executed no trace remains
though they can be seen in eighteenth-century prints.
Their absence explains the barren look of the ground
storey as restored since the war, with tiny low-arched
shop-windows along the front and even smaller
square windows above them at mezzanine level.

The upper storeys of the Coburg Kanzlei, however,
still provide a fine show the whole length of one side
of the big square marketplace. Two rows of generous
rectangular windows in pairs, each pair pedimented,
extend between the polygonal oriels cantilevered out
on the two front corners. Under these, plain cylindrical members rise from the ground to support sculptured consoles. Each facet of the oriels has a single
pedimented light on both the first and the second
storeys. The cornices of the oriels continue the one
which tops the wall between and are crowned with
bell-shaped *welsche Hauben*. Below the sills of the
windows of the oriels there is low-relief carving,
chiefly scrolled cartouches but with some small figures
as well.

The entrance to the Coburg Kanzlei, set asymmetrically in the left end facing the Spitalgasse, has
more elaborate armorial carving in higher relief. But,
as usual, most of the ornamentation of the exterior
is concentrated on the gables, both the broad ones at
the ends and those of the three dormers symmetrically
disposed above the long front facing the marketplace.
All the gables are of three stages with pilaster-framed
and pediment-topped pairs of windows in the lowest
stage. Of these pairs there are two in each of the end-
gables and in that at the center of the long front, but
only a single one in those flanking it. On the end-
gables alone this stage is bounded by complex flat
scrolling; all of the gables, however, have such scrolling at the edges of the second stage. The three larger
ones also have single pedimented windows in the
second stage, but only pairs of oculi in the other two,
a motif repeated in the third stage of the big gables.
The third stages on all five have similar S-scrolled
edges, but they are alternately terminated by round
pediments and by pointed ones.

What adds to the vivacity of the gables on the
Coburg Kanzlei as provided by their scrolled outlines and introduces also a note of verticalism bal-

ancing the horizontality of the main storeys below
is the over-all apparatus of pilaster-orders. The way
the median pilasters are threaded up through the
pediments of the coupled windows should be particularly noted, moreover, since that is most unusual
and highly Mannerist. To the elaborate treatment of
the wall-surfaces, the multiplicity of statues of *Landsknechte* with pikes and the needle-like obelisk-finials
at the sides of the several stages of all the gables and
at their tops give further piquancy.

Obviously only potentates whose territories were of
considerable extent had need of such administrative
buildings as the Ansbach and Coburg chanceries.
With these proud structures at the seats of princely
Hohenzollerns and Wettins, certain smaller Schlösser
—manor-houses rather than mansions—built in these
decades in widely separated districts may be effectively contrasted. Such naturally lack the large scale
and the considerable extent of the major Schlösser,
and even of their appendages. They are likely, moreover, to be rather retardataire in style. Yet the excellent unrestored form in which they have often survived, their rural settings and their lack of pretension
have a real charm quite different from the impressive—and at times oppressive— visual impact of such
grand works as the Schlösser at Hämelschenburg and
Weikersheim or the Coburg Kanzlei. However, the
minor Schlösser, of these decades, it should be real-
ized, are by no means all so small. Schloss Wolfegg,
for example, as rebuilt in 1580-1583 after a fire of
1578 for Truchsess Jakob von Waldburg,[8] rivalled in
size Hans Fugger's at Kirchheim-a.-d.-Mindel and, to
judge from surviving paintings, resembled that in its
quadrangular plan and the extreme plainness of the
exterior. The most notable features of the Schloss,
as rebuilt again with little change over the years 1649-
1690 after burning by Swedish troops in the Thirty
Years' War and lately restored, are still the pavilions
at the corners. These massive elements, here hip-
roofed, provide a later example of a French motif
introduced in more elaborate form at Horst (Pl. 181)
some twenty years earlier, but not much employed
in the years between except by Laurenz von Brachum
at Hovestadt (Fig. 31). The most conspicuous example, however, rivalling in size any so far described,
is Schloss Johannisburg (Pl. 367), at Aschaffenburg
on the Main, as erected in the early years of the sev-

---

[7] *Ibid.*, p. 200.

[8] Johannes Graf von Waldburg-Wolfegg, *Schloss Wolfegg*,
Munich [1961]. The Waldburgs were hereditary Lord High
Stewards of the Empire; this author was a descendant.

enteenth century by Georg Ridinger for the arch-bishop-elector of Mainz. That will be described at some length in the next chapter.

The much more modest Schloss Friedrichsburg (Pl. 311) at Vohenstrauss, a village northeast of Amberg near the present Czechoslovak border, also has at first sight somewhat the air of a French chateau, but one of a considerably earlier period, even though it was actually built in 1586-1590[9] shortly after Wolfegg. The solid rectangular block has round cone-roofed towers on each of the corners that are not unlike those added to the Schloss at Schloss Neuhaus at about this time (Pl. 44). There are additional similar but slightly lower ones, somewhat as at Rimpar, one in the middle of the north end and another on the south; this last, however, is a nineteenth-century addition. Except for plain stone string-courses between the storeys on the towers that throw sharp shadows on the yellow-painted stucco and the simple moldings round the rather regularly disposed rectangular windows, the only worked stone is a portal flanked by fluted Ionic pilasters and crowned by an armorial panel under a fluted lunette. This is set at the base of one of the towers on the east or entrance side.

The gables at Vohenstrauss have a simple wavy outline of the sort that goes back some two generations. Such a treatment had still been in common use through the mid-century but was not often repeated so late on buildings of any consequence. Each of the four stages is framed by a thin S-curved member and capped by a sort of impost that is not continued across the face, somewhat as on the gables of the Brzég Rathaus (Pl. 240). Associated with these imposts are short, very plain pilaster-strips and at the crown a small *welsche Gebel*. The builder of the Schloss was Friedrich von Vohenstrauss, of the Zweibrücken line of the Wittelsbachs, and the work was supervised—and doubtless designed—by Leonhard Greneisen from the small town of Burglengenfeld southeast of Amberg.

The Herrenhaus of Gut Hoyerswort (Pl. 312), at Oldenswort southeast of Schleswig, was erected in 1591-1594[10] by Caspar Hoyer to whom Duke Adolf

of Gottorf had given the estate in 1564. This has even plainer gables, bordered with S-curves only on the second and third stages, and one asymmetrically placed octagonal stair-tower. That last, however, has a *welsche Haube* rather than the simpler cone-shaped capping used at Vohenstrauss. The windows, subdivided by wooden mullions and transoms, are much taller here and set closer together in the white-washed brick wall. A stone string-course caps the ground storey and other strings cross the gable, but the only carved decoration is around the portal, in any case possibly not original. Like the Rathaus at Krempe (Pl. 239), this manor-house might well be considered Danish rather than German.

Two Schlösser of this period in the same border district are more considerable. Both built of brick, they are very similar to each other in other ways also. The one at Glücksburg, on the coast northeast of the present border-town of Flensburg, was built for Duke Johann II of Schleswig-Holstein by Nickels Karies in 1582-1587; that at Ahrensburg, on the old road from Hamburg to Lübeck, was erected by Peter Rantzau in 1594-1598[11] at the same time the church described in the previous chapter was in construction. Both are square with polygonal corner towers (Figs. 51, 52; Pl. 313), but that at Glücksburg is a *Wasserburg* rising out of a lake; the moat at Ahrensburg is neither so close nor so defensive (Pl. 314). Both also are three-storeyed and have regularly spaced windows, of two lights with wooden transoms at Glücksburg, of three at Ahrensburg. The Glücksburg towers have plain octagonal pointed roofs and the gables between, two to a side, are quite undecorated. The Ahrensburg towers, taller and slimmer than the earlier ones at Glücksburg, are capped with lanterns between upper and lower bell-shaped elements, and the gables there are delicately outlined with continuous scrolling and terminated by short horizontal elements. There are, furthermore, tiny obelisk finials on the tops and half-way down the curved edges at the sides as so often elsewhere on scrolled gables. Like Hoyerswort, the walls are white-washed, not left plain as on the church; however, the stone portal of the entrance is much simpler here than at Hoyerswort, merely a plain arch on molded imposts with squared-off spandrels.

Glücksburg has an unexpectedly formal plan (Fig. 51), almost like that of a Venetian *palazzo*. A great hall extends through the middle in each storey, with

---

[9] Reclams *Bayern*, p. 881.

[10] P. Hirschfeld, *Herrenhäuser und Schlösser in Schleswig-Holstein*, 3rd ed. [Munich] 1964 (henceforth cited as Hirschfeld, *Schleswig-Holstein*), pp. 75-76. *Ibid.*, pp. 11-44, provides all that can be established from documents concerning Renaissance work in Schleswig before the last quarter of the century; not much of consequence survives earlier than what is described in Chapter VIII.

[11] *Ibid.*, pp. 63-64; 71-73.

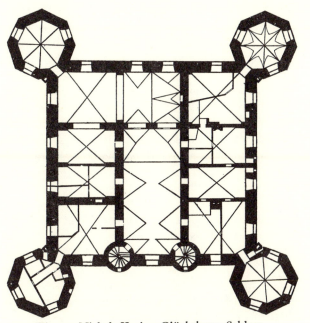

Fig. 51. Nickels Karies: Glücksburg, Schloss,
1582-87, plan

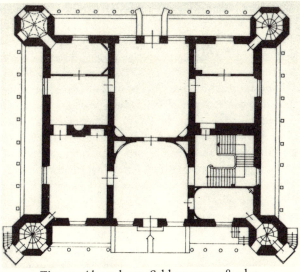

Fig. 52. Ahrensburg, Schloss, 1594-98, plan

pairs of large rooms on either side and smaller ones in three of the towers. Inside another tower on the northeast an exceptionally generous stair rises. Though still a spiral, the scale of the stair is unusual this early in northern Europe, though broad stairs are not unknown in contemporary England as, for example, at Hardwick Hall and Hatfield.

Schloss Holtfeld is far from Schleswig in the countryside southwest of the village of Halle-in-Westfalen

on the main road from Bielefeld to Osnabrück. This Westphalian Herrenhaus is quite different from the half-Danish Schlösser just mentioned but follows right after the one at Ahrensburg in date.[12] Modest in size and simple in plan, Holtfeld is a rectangle with a short square tower, later truncated, attached to the rear on the left end. Though largely of stuccoed rubble and brick, it has one very original decorated gable executed in cut stone and is also notable for the extent and the regularity of the fenestration throughout.

Above a high plain base, rising at the rear from a moat, the two storeys of Schloss Holtfeld have rather close-set windows subdivided by stone mullions and transoms (Pl. 315). Each of these is capped in the ground storey by a blind arch, all semicircular on the front, but elsewhere with some that are semi-elliptical. The latter, it might be noted, would seem quite Netherlandish if the brickwork were exposed as in certain examples in western Westphalia mentioned earlier. Continuous string-courses mark the line of the ground floor and that of the sills, the lintels and even the transoms of the windows. Otherwise the walls are plain except for small inserts of stone carved with strapwork. These are set into the zone of the upper half of the ground-storey windows and also that of the lower half of the first-storey ones. Above, tiny carved heads project boldly from the wall-surfaces, perhaps an echo of Hämelschenburg which is not very far away to the north.

Both of the gables of Schloss Holtfeld are much decorated but in quite disparate ways, neither resembling at all closely those at Hämelschenburg. The one on the north end repeats in its lower stages the windows of the ground storey, even to the semi-elliptical bearing arches. In the first stage there are four of these window-frames, the two outer ones blank; in the next stage there are only two. The lowest stage is framed by two big vertical S-scrolls with short vertical members over them in the zone of the bearing arches. In the next stage convex quadrants rise only to the level of the transoms of the windows, but there are again straight sections above them. The third stage, which has carved panels inset between pilaster-strips but no window, is framed by concave members reaching the full height. The terminal stage is no more than a sort of podium, supported at its base by two tight S-scrolls, that carries the figure of a *Landsknecht*.

[12] Kreft-Soenke, *Weserrenaissance*, p. 256.

All this has, like the walls below, a rather vernacular air. The cut-stone gable at the other end is of quite a different order, one of the minor decorative masterworks of the Weserrenaissance (Pl. 316). Three stages of equal height are subdivided into a series of nearly square panels by pilaster-strips carved with bold but simple strapwork. Two of these panels in the first and second stages are occupied by mullioned and transomed windows. The upper pair of these is capped, much like the ones at the other end, by flat blind arches; over the lower pair there are tiny round arches above each of the individual lights.

The solid panels on the south gable at Holtfeld are carved all over with flat strapwork and the edges of each stage are elaborately scalloped in a similar spirit. The considerable variety of small S-scrolls and C-scrolls used here recalls somewhat those on the left-hand gable of the Schütting in Bremen (Pl. 232) though that was thirty years or more earlier in date. Between the stages there are entablatures with friezes of strapwork varied by raised inscriptions. The third entablature is crowned by a shallow segmental element with scrolled ends; over this the plain horizontal podium is actually the top of a chimney somewhat as on several of the Hämelschenburg gables (Pl. 300).

An additional feature at Holtfeld was originally a *welsche Haube* capping the southwest tower beside the gable. At the rear (Pl. 315) a simple oriel still overhangs the moat; and some at least of the rather plain interiors, now used for a restaurant, are in fair condition despite remodelling in 1937-1938 and in 1966.

The Holtfeld property had belonged to the Wendt family since the end of the fifteenth century. The new Herrenhaus was built a hundred years later in 1599-1602. The character of the decoration of the southern gable has led some to attribute that portion, at least, to Johannes von Brachum, Laurentz's son, who had settled in nearby Widenbrück in 1579. However that may be, the crisp chiaroscuro of the all-over carved decoration here and the total absence of recognizably Italianate elements other than rather faintly suggested pilaster-orders characterize a special sort of Northern Mannerism which seems to be autochthonous. It resembles distinctly, however—and not least in its *horror vacui*—the sort seen on the facades of such a grander and more extensive Westphalian Schloss as the one at Hämelschenburg. Moreover, for all its small size, provincial flavour and remote location, Holtfeld certainly compares in quality also with

the south wing at Hämelschenburg (Pl. 303) as completed just when Holtfeld was begun. Such Westphalian monuments are not readily matched elsewhere in northern Europe around 1600. But another similar gable, dated 1609,[13] survives in Westphalia also on Haus Thienhausen (Pl. 317), at Sommersell on the road from Horn to Höxter. That is an even more splendid specimen of Weserrenaissance decoration despite its late date, a decade after the one at Holtfeld.

German town mansions had long more than rivalled in size and pretension such Herrenhäuser as Hoyerswort and Holtfeld, and nowhere more notably than in Westphalia. In Hameln at Osterstrasse 9, to the right of the Fachwerk front of the Stiftsherrenhaus of a generation earlier, rises the tall gable of the house of the merchant Gerd Leist (Pl. 318). This was built in 1585-1589[14]—the latter date is carved on the gable—by Cord Tönnis, whose mason's mark and initials appear on the chimneypiece in the principal room. The asymmetry of other house-fronts in Hameln that were erected or remodelled in the sixties and seventies is still maintained but now ordered more coherently than earlier on Tönnis's Johann Rike house (Pl. 227). Almost precisely half the facade in the two lower storeys is occupied by an oriel three lights wide. To the right of this in the ground storey is the entrance arch with a boldly rusticated archivolt carried on canted imposts.

The righthand edge of the oriel of the Leist house is in the exact center of the facade, an axial line taken up again in the first and second stages of the gable. The minor axes of the oriel and the entrance, equidistant from the center, are also carried upward. Above the entrance three somewhat narrower windows correspond to the lights of the oriel and are decorated identically with delicate engaged Corinthian columns, much in the way of the oriel on the south front at Hämelschenburg (Pl. 303) of a few years later. In the second storey identical windows echo the triplet motif, though with no framing order, and such are repeated behind the edicule crowning the oriel at this level. This last, a decorative feature not used at Hämelschenburg, is the most elaborate element of the whole composition. It rises the full height of the first storey, like the one over the lefthand oriel on the Hexenbürgermeisterhaus at Lemgo, so that its terminal entablature lines up with the one

[13] *Ibid.*, p. 284.
[14] *Ibid.*, pp. 248-249.

on the main wall behind. The deep central niche contains a statue, while beyond the flanking colonnettes there are very free arrangements of C-scrolls and S-scrolls. Tall, slim obelisks rise over the corners of the oriel and a very vigorously modelled pediment crowns the niche, its slopes enlivened with minor horn-like protrusions.

In the next storey of the Leist house at Hameln, really the lowest stage of the gable, the engaged order is somewhat stockier than the Ionic one on the ground storey of the oriel and the Corinthian one framing the windows of the first storey. A central column in this range is on axis; the other two are set a little in from the edges so that they line up with the frames on the outer sides of the triple windows of the first storey. At this level, however, the windows are in pairs only, corresponding to the two inner lights of the triplets of the first storey. The next stage again has an engaged order flanking a single pair of windows. Above that a tiny square attic has a *Neidkopf* like that on the Jost Rike house of 1576 (Pl. 228), set here in a deep-sunk circle framed by heavy strapwork. As usual, however, the greatest elaboration of the gable is at the edges.

In the lowest stage of the gable of the Leist house a tight spiral scroll caps each of the bands of plain flat rustication framing the sides of the main facade below. Over that on either side the lower ends of a concave double-C-scroll project outward and upward as rather delicate "horns" below tall slim finials. Such finials recur over the outer engaged columns of the next two stages. At the base of the second stage the spiral scrolls are repeated, but curved inward instead of outward, and over them are small S-scrolls. In the terminal stage concave C-scrolls with "horns" as their upper terminations flank the attic and smaller ones elaborate the outline of the pediment.

The Leist house in Hameln carries a good deal of carving of various sorts, mostly on the oriel (Pl. 318). A freestanding statue of Lucretia with her suicidal dagger stands in the shell-topped niche and a low-relief frieze of allegorical figures set in a range of shallower niches occupies the podium zone of the Corinthian order. In addition there is jewelry-like enrichment on the lower third of the shafts of that order. This last is as out of scale with the bold enframement of the main gable above as is that of the oriels on the Hexenbürgermeisterhaus in Lemgo (Pl. 226) of some fifteen years earlier.

Very close to the Leist house in date were two other houses, one surviving in Detmold and another, destroyed in the last war, in Hildesheim. That in Detmold at Lange Strasse 14, dated 1587,[15] is not in good condition, moreover, especially the ground storey which now contains shops. Above, the two oriels—that on the left somewhat wider than the one on the right—and the main gable still retain their continuously scrolled framing of strapwork in which fluting alternates with raised disks. In the first storey the original windows also have flat carving on their frames as at Brake, Varenholz and the west side of Hämelschenburg.

Much more sophisticated in design though more typical, despite its elaboration, of earlier decades was the contemporary house in Hildesheim of 1586-1589[16] called, because of the portraits of the Caesars on the facade, the Kaiserhaus (Pl. 319). Built sidewise to the street, this was quite unlike the Hameln houses with their tall front gables. So also, although the lowest course of the stone sheathing on the long front was decorated with strapwork, that was in rather low relief. It was thus consonant with the still very quattrocento triple range of coin-like circular medallions that rose to the sills of the ground-storey windows.

Above, on the facade of the Kaiserhaus in Hildesheim, came an almost freestanding minor order of columns which was scaled, not to the storey-height, but to that of the windows. Statues in the round were set in the edicules, framed by pairs of the small columns, between the windows. This treatment was of somewhat more "High Renaissance" character on account of its orderly plastic articulation. The rather small scale of the elements, however, echoed that of the quattrocento sort of decoration below. Over this storey the upper one was absolutely plain; but at the right hand end of the main storey there was a single oriel carried on heavy carved brackets. This oriel was ornamented with herms and other detail recalling neither quattrocento nor High Renaissance Italy; on the contrary, it was of the Northern Mannerist sort, coming from the Netherlands, that had been increasingly popular in Germany since it was first introduced some twenty-five years before.

Happily, there survives on the fifteenth-century Tempelhaus in the marketplace at Hildesheim a comparable oriel dated 1591.[17] That is not so retarda-

[15] *Ibid.*, p. 242.
[16] Horst, *Architektur*, p. 244.
[17] Reclams *Niedersachsen*, p. 391.

taire or, at least, it is less ambiguous stylistically. Herms again frame the two double lights in each storey, and the carved work in the panels below the first-storey windows, here in relatively high relief, is Mannerist in a rather more Netherlandish way than anything on the Kaiserhaus. The edicule at the top is not unlike the one over the oriel of the Leist house in Hameln (Pl. 318) but it has a full-size window in the middle instead of a niche with a statue. This Tempelhaus oriel has lately been restored, doubtless correctly, with much polychromy and gilding. The very elaborate timber-framed Wedekind Haus of this period[18] that once stood next door was one of a great many that were destroyed in the war, including all the other buildings in the marketplace here except the Rathaus.

Not all towns and cities were even as advanced as Hildesheim in their house architecture of these decades. The characteristic retardation of Nürnberg architecture through the entire sixteenth century, for example, was illustrated before its wartime destruction by the Topler house on the Oberer Panierplatz, built as late as 1590[19] and with additions of 1597. Segment-topped windows, as on the Altdorf college buildings (Pl. 245); panels filled with Late Gothic tracery; and, at the corners and all over the gables, cylindrical members that made no attempt, any more than those on the gable of the Rothenburg Rathaus of twenty years before, to approach Classical orders— all combined to produce a picturesque structure that might well have been thought a hundred years or so older.

More attractively retardataire, and happily extant, is the Hagereiterhaus in Rothenburg built by the local city-architect Leonhardt Weidmann in 1591.[20] This stands beside the tall and very plain hospital he had erected in 1574-1578 while the Rathaus was in construction. Neither resembles the Rathaus but the small square house, intended for the director of the hospital, has a fairy-tale look. This has no more to do with the Renaissance than with the Gothic but is typical of what so charms the innumerable visitors to

Rothenburg today. Its roof rises from the square block below in a concave curve to a sort of flattened octagonal spire and is casually broken by one or two small dormers and chimneys, perhaps not all original. On the main front the cylindrical stair-tower continues two stages above the main eaves to terminate in a tiny open lantern capped with an even tinier "onion."

There is almost no detail on the Hagereiterhaus. But the round-arched doorways and the rectangular windows, some double but mostly single, have flat stone trim molded inward from the stuccoed rubble of the main wall-surfaces. Projecting string-courses mark the first-storey line and set off the upper stages of the tower.

The so-called Baumeister Haus (Fig. 53; Pl. 320), however, that Weidmann built in 1594[21] for Mi-

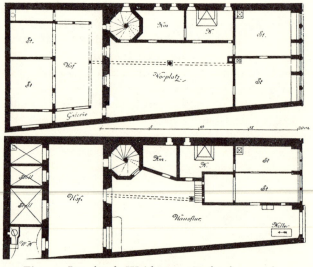

Fig. 53. Leonhardt Weidmann: Rothenburg-o.-d.-Tauber, Baumeister Haus, 1594, plan

chael Wirsching, a member of the local Council, at Schmiedegasse 3, just out of the marketplace, has the most elaborately decorated house-front in Rothenburg. The facade of this house is also the most up-to-date in design. As on the Tempelhaus oriel in Hildesheim rows of herms separate the windows on the first and second storeys instead of columns, and the four stages of the gable, all framed by panelled pilaster-strips, have tall vertical S-scrolls at their edges ending in open spirals at top and bottom. Thus this house rivals in pretension those in Hameln though Weidmann— even by this late date—was by no means so subtle

[18] Strange, *Deutsche Baukunst*, fig. 78. The richest of all these facades decorated with carved woodwork, so treated that the structural members were invisible behind the ornamental cladding, was that of the Salzhaus in the Römer at Frankfurt-am-Main: Horst, *Architektur*, pl. XIII. This did not survive the war. Stange, *op. cit.*, p. 284, dates it "um 1600."

[19] Horst, *Architektur*, p. 282.
[20] Reclams *Bayern*, p. 772.

[21] *Ibid.*, p. 774.

and consistent a designer as Tönnis and his contemporaries in Westphalia. The big pediment over the portal on the left, almost as severely "correct" in design as the one on the end of the Rathaus (Pl. 243), hardly accords, for example, either with the ornate membering of the windows or with the steep pitch and the boldly scrolled outline of the gable.

Many extant town-houses of the nineties in other towns are quite as comparable as the Baumeister Haus to those in Hameln and one of them, to be described later in this chapter, is actually in Nürnberg (Pl. 324), otherwise so retardataire architecturally. Especially pretentious is the Haus zum Ritter at Heidelberg (Pl. 321), a survivor of the fire that destroyed most of the town in 1693. That house is, indeed, more richly decorated than any other German sixteenth-century house now extant. It was built in 1592[22] for Charles Bélier, no German but a Walloon merchant from Tournai on the upper Escaut (Schelde). Presumably he was a Protestant who had fled from the Inquisition in the Spanish Netherlands. However, there is nothing about the design of the facade to recall surviving sixteenth-century work in the district of southern Flanders from which he came. Client and designer seem rather to have sought to exceed in elaboration the Ottheinrichsbau (Pl. 177) of the Heidelberg Schloss as completed some thirty years earlier. Engaged orders of fluted columns, Doric, Ionic, Corinthian and Composite, are used on the three main storeys and the two lower stages of the gable. However, only those in the gable have the Serlian proportions of the ones at the Schloss. The windows in all five storeys are capped by pediments like those over the lower windows of the Ottheinrichsbau; but the two oriels, rising symmetrically through the first and second storeys above the asymmetrical ground storey, have no local precedent in other existing house-fronts or on the Schloss.

What most distinctly resembles the earlier work at the Schloss on the Haus zum Ritter is the profusion and the eclectic variety of the ornament. The gable especially evinces a real *horror vacui* and throughout, not surprisingly, there is much strapwork decoration in relief of the rather bold sort that had only become common in Germany since Ottheinrich's time. The outline of the gable, moreover, is exceptionally vigorous, with very big and heavily molded S-scrolls in the two lower stages. Prominent also are the rusticated obelisks at the sides, and there are

many other embellishments both abstract and figural. Finally, for example, the terminal stage of the gable consists of two large S-scrolls that are joined at the top by a horizontal element on top of which is the half-length figure of the *Ritter,* Saint George.

Two almost equally ornate but much better organized house-fronts of this decade survive at Minden in Westphalia: Haus Hagemeyer in Scharn (Pl. 322), carrying the date of completion 1592;[23] and Haus Hill, which is some seven or eight years later.[24] The facade of the former, begun for the Bürgermeister Thomas von Kampen, who died in 1586, and continued by his widow Wobbeke Claren, who lived twenty years longer, rises in three storeys above an exceptionally tall ground floor—unfortunately remodelled into shops around 1900—to a three-stage gable. Several earlier German facades, especially in Münster and in Enden, had reflected in the very regular use of the orders what has, in describing them, been called the "Dutch High Renaissance" in marked contrast to those just described at Rothenburg and at Heidelberg (Pls. 320, 321). Here evenly spaced engaged orders are used on each of the six levels, though the way these are detailed may best be defined as "Provincial Mannerist."

The four storeys of Haus Hagemeyer are six bays wide with very large unframed rectangular windows in each bay. In the top storey, which is really the lowest stage of the gable, the windows are arched and the outermost bays solid, as also in the next one. In the two-bay stage above that the single arched window is set behind the central column and the terminal stage also has one such column. Though the recurrent entablatures give a certain rectangular crispness to the general effect, much as on the Baumeisterhaus at Rothenburg, the open scrollwork at the sides of the three upper stages of the gable is exceptionally fantastic in outline and even has human figures in the round seated against the outer columns. The designer of this facade—or, perhaps more probably, only the executant of the sculptural decoration—may have been Johann Robin, who came originally from Ypres in southern Flanders. Before this, it will be recalled, he had completed the Juliusspital in Würzburg in 1580 and later, in the mid-nineties, is recorded as being employed not far from Minden on the Rathaus at Stadthagen (Pl. 341). Nothing there, however, much resembles the carved decoration on Haus Hagemeyer.

[22] Reclams *Baden-Württemberg,* p. 210.
[23] J. Soenke, *Haus Hagemeyer, Minden* [n.d.].
[24] Kreft-Soenke, *Weserrenaissance,* pp. 264-265.

Of Haus Hill in Minden only the gable survives in its original form, for the lower storeys were re-modelled in the eighteenth century. Fluted half-col-umns take the place of the nearly freestanding ones on the Hagemeyer house, but the intertwined naked figures and open scrolled bandwork flanking the three stages of the gable are all but identical. A very high-keyed polychromatic restoration, however, now pro-duces a more two-dimensional and less articulated effect. One should note also the chip-carved bands crossing the columns and the window-frames, for these are of the sort that was being so profusely used in the eighties and nineties on Schloss Hämelschenburg (Pl. 303). Such do not appear on the Hagemeyer house which has, indeed, very little in common with the more typical work of the Weserrenaissance in this period. Despite the similarities of the two Minden house-fronts they may well have had different de-signers and executants, whether or not one was Robin.

Very like the gable of Haus Hill is that of the house of the former mayor Johann von Barkhausen (Pl. 323) in the marketplace at Bad Salzuflen, just to the southeast of Herford. This must be of the eighties,[25] a decade or so earlier than the one in Minden. On the Salzuflen facade, which is also now polychromatically restored, carved figures are inter-twined with the scrolling only in the top stage of the gable. Below, in the two middle stages, the fields of the S-scrolls are fluted, as so often at nearby Lemgo, and there are also tight C-scrolled "horns" just above the entablatures. The order here consists of fluted pilasters rather than half or engaged columns as on the Minden facades.

Beside these rather frivolous Westphalian house-fronts, made more conspicuous today by the restora-tions lately carried out by the *Denkmalpflegeamt* (agency for maintenance of monuments) of the state of Lower Saxony, the big Fembohaus (Pl. 324) of the nineties,[26] one of the very few of this period in Nürnberg that survived the war, seems very severe and dignified. It is also, for sixteenth-century Nürn-berg, exceptionally up-to-date in style. The Fembo-haus, now a museum, rises in four storeys, all of fine ashlar in pink sandstone, above the sloping Burg-strasse. The lowest storey is quite unbroken on the front except by the broad entrance arch, molded but

unframed, and one plain arched window to the left. The next three storeys, both on the front and along the Burgstrasse on the right, have regular ranges of large rectangular windows. These are close-set and also quite unframed. The only adornment of the fa-cade below the gable is the one-bay oriel over the entrance; that is flanked by Corinthian pilasters and capped with a broken segmental pediment. Like the entrance arch below, the oriel is not centered, in large part doubtless because another house originally over-lapped what would have been the two outer bays of the front on the left-hand side.

The four-stage gable of the Fembohaus, only slightly masked at its base on the left by the neighboring house, is quite symmetrical, with the axis strongly marked by the pairs of half-columns—Ionic, Corin-thian (set diagonally) and Tuscan—that flank the central windows. These last are very little smaller than the ones of the main storeys below. Five of them occupy the lowest stage; three, the second; and a single one between two oculi the third; in the fourth there is only an oculus. At the sides of the lowest stage of the gable of the Fembohaus there are S-scrolls wound into tight spirals at top and bottom. In the next stage very bold convex C-scrolls project be-low less assertive concave ones. The next stage has on each side, above short rusticated obelisk-finials, two concave C-scrolls of which the upper kicks out at its base into a very sharp "horn." Unusual features in the terminal stage are the urns with flowers in them beside the concave C-scrolls; then come convex scrolls with horn-like upper ends and, between them, a bronze figure of Fortuna standing on a plain po-dium.

The relative simplicity of this Nürnberg facade is worth noting. Figural decoration is restricted to the small horizontal panels between the podia of the or-ders and the terminal statue. However, thanks to its great absolute height, the ashlar masonry and the scalloped silhouette, made up though that is of rather coarse elements, the Fembohaus is one of the more impressive lesser works of the later German Renais-sance. In Nürnberg it seems to have been rivalled only by the slightly later Pellerhaus (Pl. 396), a work of the elder Jakob Wolff, of which very little is ex-tant today. That will be described in the next chapter.

The Fembohaus was completed in 1598; how long before that it was begun is uncertain, perhaps as early as 1591; nor is the architect known any more than for the Topler Haus. One completely wood-panelled

---

[25] Dehio, *Westfalen*, p. 32, dates the gable "um 1580"; Kreft-Soenke, *Weserrenaissance*, p. 275, "erst nach 1580," not-ing that Barkhausen lived until 1605.

[26] Reclams *Bayern*, pp. 641-642.

interior survives that is characteristic of the years around 1600, and there are also several later stucco ceilings of 1674 and of 1734-1735. Whether it is relevant that Nürnberg had remained Catholic, while the clients for most of the fine town houses in other towns were Protestant, is uncertain—probably not.

Though Paderborn, for example, was ruled from 1585 to his death in 1618 by a Catholic prince-bishop, Dietrich von Fürstenberg—the client for whom the Schloss at Schloss Neuhaus was completed—the city had a Protestant mayor most of the time from Fürstenberg's accession to 1602. Around 1600[27] this official, Heinrich Stallmeister, built a prominent house in the Marienplatz now known as the Heisingsches Haus. His architect may well have been Hermann Baumhauer who built later, in 1613-1618, the nearby Rathaus. Certainly the handling of the four-staged gable on the house is very similar to the main gable of the Rathaus (Pl. 385). As has been noted, Baumhauer very likely also worked at Schloss Neuhaus around 1590 and, more certainly, also for Fürstenberg at the Wewelsburg. What he did there in 1604-1607 will be described in the next chapter.

The facade of the Heisingsches Haus is quite symmetrical, with ranges of rectangular triplet windows flanking the central features. The rather flat four-light oriel over the arched entrance may well be a later addition; otherwise the regularly spaced windows are repeated without change throughout the three main storeys. The pilaster-strips that frame the triplets in the upper storeys and those in the lowest stage of the gable are closer to the plain vertical strips of the nineties at Schloss Neuhaus (Pl. 295) than to the colonnettes Baumhauer later used so profusely on the Rathaus here (Pl. 385). The prominent arch of the central portal, which has infilling of a much later date, rests on wide imposts, however, decorated with flat bandwork and the archivolt is interrupted by chip-carved blocks of the sort so characteristic of the Weserrenaissance. At the ends of the broad flat frieze of the entablature above the portal there are ressauts related to the flanking columns. The nether portions of the shafts of these Corinthian columns are carved with ornament below plain fluting, as so often in these decades at the end of the sixteenth century in Germany and also in England just after 1600.[28] Their

usual source was probably Vredeman's engravings, but they were already inconspicuously present on the Kardinalshuis in Groningen of 1559 in Holland even before his *Architectura* was first published.

In the gable of the Heisingsches Haus in Paderborn no such decorated shafts but rather herms were introduced two to a stage, a motif long familiar since it had appeared on the title-page of Serlio's *Quarto libro* in 1537. These herms and the ones on the oriel most resemble, however, Weidmann's on the Baumeisterhaus of 1594 at Rothenburg (Pl. 320) and contrast with the simple panelled strips deemed sufficient to frame the windows between. Beyond the terminal herms in each stage the outline consists of various combinations of broad C-scrolled and S-scrolled bandwork. Conspicuous here, as on Tönnis's Hameln houses, are the horn-like S-curved elements that run across the short vertical members in the two lower stages and those that project from the upper S-scrolls in the third and fourth stages. Equally piquant are the stubby but sharp obelisks set on the ends of the three lower stages just above the outer herms.

One more masonry town-house may be mentioned here in conclusion: the Gasthaus zum Engel at Bergzabern, also of around 1600;[29] for in localities where Fachwerk remained the usual form of construction there was in general little modulation of design in these latest decades of the sixteenth century. Bergzabern (or Zabern) lies west of the Rhine on the road from Karlsruhe to Pirmasens in the Saarland. However, the house with its diagonally-set oriels on the two front corners recalls rather such things as the Schönhof at Görlitz (Pl. 63), far to the east in Saxony, of some seventy years before or the more nearly contemporary Hochzeitshaus at Alsfeld (Pl. 233) in Hesse than anything in this region, which in any case is not rich in Renaissance architecture. All the same, the ornament on the Gasthaus zum Engel is mostly of up-to-date character. Strapwork panels are introduced over the windows on the oriel and fluted bands, not unlike those on the contemporary house in Detmold, decorate the simple S-scrolls outlining the successive stages of the gable.

In the last years of the sixteenth century the private houses of leading citizens and the buildings erected to serve public needs differ very little in style and pretension. In small towns there is not even much difference in size. At Bad Salzuflen the Rathaus (Pl.

[27] Kreft-Soenke, *Weserrenaissance*, pp. 269-270.

[28] The richest examples are at Hatfield, dating from about 1603.

[29] Reclams *Baden-Württemberg*, p. 39.

326), originally erected in 1545 by Hermann Edeler —who moved in that year from Bielefeld to nearby Herford—differs from such a contemporary house as that of the mayor (Pl. 323) chiefly in being free-standing on three sides. The gable, dating probably from the later eighties,[30] over the plain two-storeyed Late Gothic structure is all but identical with that on the house at Markt 7, also of uncertain date, beside the mayor's. The crisp strapwork scrolls on the Rathaus gable are set outside simply panelled vertical strips at the edges of the three lower stages and also on the top. Today they are chiefly notable for the sharp contrast of their restored polychromy with the smooth white stucco of the walls and the plain frames of the windows. The three buildings seen together provide an exceptionally attractive urban center in this small Westphalian watering-place.

At Rinteln the Rathaus (Pl. 327), newly built in 1583,[31] was equally modest in size and, while wholly Renaissance in style, more characteristic of a considerably earlier period because of its rather plain stepped gable. Each step of this, all the same, is crowned by a small *welsche Gebel*, still quite in the manner of the twenties and even more like those on the gable of the Alsfeld Weinhaus of 1538 (Pl. 95). Each of the simple oriels over the round-arched entrances is also capped by a triplet of fluted lunettes. These last are exceptional at this date. This is not so much because of their retardataire design, still recalling that of the oriels on the Stadthagen Schloss (Pl. 93) not far away to the northeast of forty or fifty years earlier, but because of their being an identical pair. Thus they seem to reflect the rising demand for balance in facade design toward the end of the century even though they are not quite symmetrically placed.

Beside this rather simple facade of the early eighties, facing the main square in Rinteln, a wider and taller wing of much more up-to-date character was added on the left some fifteen years later. This extension of the original structure has one centrally placed two-storeyed oriel, a large rectangular entrance to the right and a tall gable. The outline of the gable is varied by C-scrolls and S-scrolls, horn-like projections and pairs of obelisk-finials capped by slim elements of iron. The contrast between the two gables summarizes neatly the general modulation of style in this middle section of the Weser valley through nearly three-quarters of a century. Neither, however, has

much in common with the finest Renaissance survival in Rinteln, the oriel of Tönnis's Archivhäuschen (Pl. 217) of 1565.

With this Westphalian Rathaus of mixed date, an example from further south and east in Saxony may well be compared, especially as Saxony had earlier been more advanced stylistically, though it was no longer consistently so this late in the century. The prominent, asymmetrically-placed portal of the Rathaus at Kronach—which lies to the east of Coburg, just on the inner or "west" side of the present interzonal frontier—was inserted twenty-five years later. Otherwise the facade, like the earlier portion of the one at Rinteln, is dated 1583.[32] The narrow but monumental front (Pl. 328) toward the main street, however, has more in common with the Fembohaus of the next decade in Nürnberg (Pl. 324) than with either of the two parts of the Rinteln Rathaus. Like that, it is built of ashlar masonry, not of rubble, and the detail is mostly massive in scale and tightly organized, especially on the edges of the gable.

Doubtless the ground-storey windows on the front of the Kronach Rathaus with their broad chamfered architraves are of the same period as the heavy rusticated arch of the later portal. In the first storey of the front, however, and also along the flank to the left, the large squarish windows, rather closely set and regularly disposed, must be original. These and the ones on the gable—two pairs in the first stage and one pair in the second, with a single one at the top—each carry, above very flat friezes, pediments that barely project from the wall surface. These are very likely late echoes of Gromann's of twenty years before, also in Saxony, at nearby Heldburg and Altenburg (Pls. 190, 234). In the field of each pediment, moreover, there is a carved rosette that hardly accords in its delicate scale with the other, so much heavier, detailing.

In contrast to the relatively advanced yet essentially linear treatment of the pediments over their heads, the windows in the first storey of the Kronach Rathus are still framed in the old Late Gothic way with fillets in relief intersecting at the corners. On the other hand, the string-courses over and under the first storey, as well as those at the sill-level of the simpler windows in the upper stages of the gable, are neither flat and linear nor hybrid in character, but all heavily molded. So also the pilaster-strips beside the pairs of windows in the two lower stages of the gable have

[30] Kreft-Soenke, *Weserrenaissance*, p. 274.
[31] *Ibid.*, p. 273.
[32] Reclams *Bayern*, p. 428.

rather deep-cut panels and, at mid-height, projecting masks in high relief. With that sort of emphatic membering go the chunky scrolls at the sides of the gable, mostly convex and concave Cs with tightly spiralled ends, but including also some short vertical elements and, as accents, five squat obelisks. Pairs of these flank the bases of the two upper stages and another rises as a terminal feature through the broken pediment crowning the whole.

Altogether, indeed, this facade at Kronach begins to have a weight and a *tenue* that is almost proto-Baroque. This is as different from the lighthearted "Provincial Mannerism" of the gable of the Salzuflen Rathaus (Pl. 326), which must be nearly contemporary, or even that on the left at Rinteln (Pl. 327), as from the "Early German Renaissance" understatement—so to put it—of the one in the direct line of descent from the twenties on the right at Rinteln. Certainly Gromann himself was never as advanced as the unknown designer of the Kronach Rathaus.

Arnstadt is a town in this region lying to the north of the mountains on the Welde Gera above Erfurt in Thuringia. Despite its considerably greater size and the coarse scale of the flat bandwork on the two front gables, the Rathaus there has little of this premonitory quality. It was built in 1581-1583, just before the one at Kronach, by Christoph Junghans[33] from the small town of Schwarzburg on the Schwarza, south of Arnstadt and to the west of Saalfeld. The righthand wing of this Rathaus, much remodelled in the nineteenth-century to provide a great two-storey hall at first-storey level within, presents a tall gable to the market-place. In the first stage of this the presumably original frames of the two oval oculi are linked to the S-curves of the flanking scrolls by heavy strapwork punctuated at the intersections by small round bosses like bolt-heads. The central semi-elliptical window in the next stage, however, like the three tall windows of the hall below, appears to have been modified in the nineteenth-century remodelling. This second stage is capped, not by a mere string-course, but with a full entablature from which two ressauts project to support statues on either side of a big clock in the center. Very generous C-scrolls, linked again by strapwork around and over the clock, flank the sides at this

level. Except for a flat horizontal band, there is no division between the second stage of this Arnstadt gable and the terminal one. That has a tiny central niche linked like the oculi below to flanking scrolls, again of S-shape but reversed. A miniscule pediment with an obelisk on top provides the crowning feature.

Nearly identical is the gable over the other end of the facade of the Arnstadt Rathaus except that there is no clock and no niche. What is surprising with regard to this second gable is its total lack of relation to the three nearly continuous bands of rectangular windows below, or even to the column-flanked portal of the entrance in the ground storey. There must be a suspicion, at least, that this utilitarian front was the work of another designer than Junghans or whoever was responsible for the two gables above. Yet it is not necessary to assume at this late date, as some have done, the actual intervention here of the Netherlander Erhart van der Meer, who had worked considerably earlier on the Arnstadt Schloss, as also at the Augustusburg in the preceding decade. The flat strapwork, though surely derived directly or indirectly from Vredeman's Antwerp publications of the sixties and later, is not so different from what had been introduced in Germany on the court gable at Horst (Fig. 30) all of twenty years before, probably by the Netherlander, Johanssen.

Moreover, the one feature of the Rathaus at Arnstadt that is really unusual for this date, the capping of the roofs just behind the gables with tall lanterns rising in three diminishing stages, only remotely suggests Netherlandish architecture of this period. The more complex culmination of the tower of the Gdańsk town hall, added in 1559-1560 by the Dutchman Daniel Dirksen—the grandest example of a Netherlandish *speeltoren* outside Holland—is not likely to have been the model for Junghans or the Arnstadt Council. However, they may well have known of others still existing then in Holland before so many burned in the seventeenth century. The way these lanterns at Arnstadt draw the visual emphasis away from the gables, so frequently the sole architectural feature of interest on mid- and later sixteenth-century German secular buildings, to the three-dimensional organization of the whole composition is certainly not un-German. Even if, at a date so early, the three-dimensional massing of Giacomo Parr's Rathaus at Brzég in Silesia (Pl. 240) of some fifteen years before is rather exceptional, that does in some degree match already the plastic complexity of the Arnstadt Rathaus. Moreover, the top of the building at Arnstadt is still

---

[33] DKD, *Thüringen*, p. 356. Junghans may have worked under Erhart van der Meer on the Schloss at Arnstadt, demolished in the eighteenth century, which could explain the Netherlandish influence that has been recognized in his Rathaus. Van der Meer's chapel at Augustusburg, however, is hardly Dutch or Brabantine in character.

further complicated by small slanted dormers breaking out of the roof and by larger gabled ones, consonant with the gables on the front, running along the righthand side (Pl. 329). There is here, all the same, no such architectonic order yet as Parr had provided in the town hall at Brzég or Gromann in that at Altenburg (Pl. 234), both of the early sixties.

Turning westward from Thuringia to Franconia and specifically to Würzburg, a city ruled by a Catholic prince-bishop, it should be recalled that, of the two big edifices whose construction initiated the revival of Catholic church-building in Germany in the 1580s, one was the Neubaukirche (Pl. 330) as undertaken by the first of the Würzburg "building bishops," Julius Echter. Closely associated with this both functionally and physically is the university that Julius founded; indeed, the Neubaukirche is better known as the Universitätskirche, and the institution is still called the Juliusuniversität. The three wings of the university form a very large quadrangle (Fig. 54) of which the church provides the enclosure on the south, and the architect was the designer also of the church.

Construction of the university buildings began in 1582[34] two years after the Juliusspital in Würzburg was completed by Johann Robin—just mentioned in connection with the houses of this period at Minden—and a year before the other Robin, Georg, assisted by the Würzburg city-architect Wolfgang Beringer, began to erect the contiguous church. It was Georg Robin who once more was the responsible designer of the university building rather than Beringer. The longest section of that extends at a slight angle northward from the west front of the church for no less than 19 bays of which four extend beyond the outer front of the north wing. The ten bays at the west end are occupied by a very large vaulted hall with a central row of columns. This is of about the same length as the nave of the church but broader. The east wing is not quite parallel with the west wing and projects only slightly beyond the north front.

The whole structure of the Juliusuniversität has a very institutional look because of the endless rows of paired rectangular windows in all four storeys. In the court (Pl. 330) this monotony was broken by introducing in the ground storey of both the east and west sides rusticated blind arcading in which segmental-headed windows are set. There are also the three ranges of big windows of the church on the south to vary the general effect—round-arched

ones, as noted earlier, in the ground storey, but pointed ones above that light the two ranges of tribunes. The rustication of the arcades, moreover, like some of the contemporary membering at Kronach and Gideon Bacher's channelled ashlar on the tower of the nineties at Ansbach (Pls. 273, 328), already has a proto-Baroque vigor in marked contrast to the graceful Late Gothic tracery in the church windows and the delicate receding moldings that frame the standard pairs of windows. This eclectic mixture is typical of the *Juliusstil*.

Two soberly detailed portals break the north front of the university building (Pl. 331) which was erected in 1588 after the east and south wings were completed the previous year. These are identical, but one of them is in the center and the other at the righthand end. Very different from them is a third much more elaborately decorated entrance on the left. Evidently this has always been the principal portal, even though it is right up against the slightly advanced end of the east wing. On the first two portals widely-spaced pairs of Corinthian columns carry broad ressauts projecting from continuous entablatures above the doorways. The arches of these have plain imposts and molded archivolts. On that to the left, however, pairs of Doric columns are set in two planes and the cornice only of the entablature is carried across over the broad and rather low arch. Here, moreover, the imposts are panelled pilasters and the arch has a greater range of varied rustication on the voussoirs than on the arcades in the court.

There is also figural carving in the spandrels of the principal portal of the Juliusuniversität, something quite lacking elsewhere on this rather utilitarian structure. Over the cornice comes a high attic occupied by a relief of the Pentecost, with Julius in the round kneeling in front of it. This relief, framed by flat pilasters with delicately carved decoration on their shafts, is sheltered above by a thin penthouse roof. The two Ionic colonnettes that support the roof are much too small in relation to the Doric columns over which they are set; but the most conspicuously un-Classical element is the intricate scrolled bandwork, for that is of the most advanced Northern Mannerist sort. Such ornament also flanks the pilasters and continues behind and beyond the Doric columns to the outer ends of the main entablature. The final twirlings, indeed, extend still farther.

This main portal of the Juliusuniversität may well be several years later than the completion of the rest of the north wing, yet still before 1592; in any case,

---

[34] Reclams *Bayern*, p. 952.

it was not executed by Robin but by Erhard Barg (born 1544) and Johann von Deundam. The roof these men put over the attic to protect the relief of the Pentecost cuts off almost the whole of Robin's pair of first-storey windows immediately above. As if to make up for this, the wall-panel between the first and second-storey windows, here framed together vertically, was very richly carved with a triple cluster of coats of arms framed by intricate scrolling in which putti cavort almost in the eighteenth-century Rococo way.

Especially characteristic of the hybrid *Juliusstil* as illustrated by the university buildings in Würzburg is the vault covering the entrance passage within the main portal. This has boldly projecting ribs arranged in a Late Gothic pattern of intersecting curves. Moreover, the gables on the north ends of the east and west wings, as well as the smaller gables of the dormers at the center of the north front and on the court, are rather conservative in design, though not to such a degree. Entablatures run across them between the stages and the vertical edges are crisply framed, while plain pediments cap the oculus-filled squares at their tops. The scrolled bandwork decorating the sides of the upper stages is quite subsidiary and much simpler than that over the main portal. Despite their late sort of ornament, these features still resemble the dormers over the Dresden Moritzbau (Pl. 131) of some forty years before. Certainly they quite lack the exuberance of contemporary examples in the Weser valley region and elsewhere to the north and east. All the same, Julius's university buildings are a great advance in size, in regularity and in their decoration over the college the Nürnbergers had begun to erect at Altdorf (Pl. 245) ten years earlier.

The Würzburg university was, of course, Catholic. In 1576 the Welf Duke Julius of Brunswick-Wolfenbüttel had already founded the Protestant Schola Julia at Helmstedt. This town lies at the eastern edge of his territories, just inside the interzonal frontier today and off Autobahn E8 leading to Berlin. The Schola Julia long served as a university but was ultimately closed in 1810. In 1577-1578 Paul Francke (c.1538-1615)[35]—who would begin much later the Wolfenbüttel Hauptkirche for Julius's son Heinrich Julius—erected at Helmstedt a pair of modest blocks

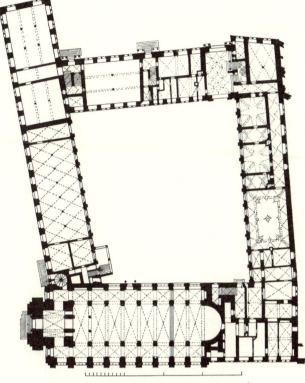

Fig. 54. Würzburg, Juliusuniversität and Neubaukirche, plan

facing one another across a narrow "campus," each with an octagonal stair-tower. Though less retardataire in detail than the wings of the Altdorf quadrangle, these are all the same exceedingly plain, except for the decorated portals at the base of the towers. Facing the north end of this campus, however, Francke added in 1592-1597 for Heinrich Julius,[36] who had succeeded his father in 1589, a new structure. That was shortly after the university had acquired international prestige from the presence of Giordano Bruno in the year of Heinrich Julius's accession, evidence of the new ruler's up-to-date intellectual interests, which were evidently scientific as well as literary. This block (Pl. 333) has little in common with the simple ones built earlier for Julius, Heinrich's father; on the contrary, it more than rivals the lately completed Juliusuniversität at Würzburg in the splendour of its adornment though not in size.

Francke's freestanding rectangular edifice, called the Juleum, at Helmstedt is accented, rather in the man-

[35] Reclams *Niedersachsen*, pp. 366-367. The principal reference for Paul Francke is K. Seeleke's article in the *Braunschweigisches Jahrbuch*, 3 F. I (1940), pp. 29ff. By this time Francke, like other German designers, surely had access to Vredeman's publications.

[36] Heinrich Julius was the first German to write plays in prose and maintained a team of English actors at Wolfenbüttel.

ner of Gromann's contemporary Rathäuser, by the very tall slim stair-tower in the middle of the long south front toward the campus which echoes those on the inner sides of the earlier blocks. Otherwise, however, it does not much resemble other comparable structures of the day here or elsewhere. Francke was a very original designer and he was called on to provide at Helmstedt a type of building for which there was little relevant precedent in Germany. His block, for example, is only two storeys tall, but the storeys are each of double normal height. So also the windows, although few in number—five in each storey on the north; but only four, because of the centrally placed tower, on the south—are unusually large for a secular building. Their design is even more exceptional, especially in the upper storey later occupied by the university's library.

The ground-storey windows of the Helmstedt Juleum are round-arched. Thus they bear some resemblance to the proto-Renaissance church-windows of two generations before, the earliest probably those that light the aisles of St. Martin at Lauingen. But the pattern in each window-head of three circles set tangent to a transom and linked by straight members closely approaches, like the decoration on the Arnstadt gables (Pl. 329), strapwork of the Netherlandish sort. With such ornament Francke had perhaps first become acquainted in the seventies while working on the Heinrichstadt fortifications at Wolfenbüttel in association with Willem de Raet from Antwerp.[37] The base-line of the pediments over the arches of these windows is continued as a vigorously molded string-course all around the building.

In the upper storey of the Juleum the windows, though only slightly wider than those below, become vast rectangles of seven lights, rivalling in extent Netherlandish fenestration of the second half of the sixteenth century. The strapwork decoration of these, which is both richer and more delicate than the tracery in the heads of the ones below, fills completely the top lights at either side in each window and also runs across over the seventh central light. Rather than Francke, the sculptor Jakob Meyerheins (†1615) was responsible for the main portal of the Juleum, occupying the place of one of the ground-storey windows to the right of the stair-tower. But the stair-tower also has its own rather modest portal.

Much more extravagant than any of these portals,

however, are the end-gables and the gabled dormers. Of these last there are three on each side, though the one in the center on the south is almost completely masked by the third storey of the tower. All of them are of a distinctly later stylistic character than the portals, approaching that of Francke's work of 1608-1615 on the big church at Wolfenbüttel. Thus they contrast with the relatively severe treatment of the stair-tower. That carries only bands of rustication on the corners and three string-courses. The lowest of these is a continuation of the one that surrounds the whole building; the next corresponds to the upper moldings of the cornice at the eaves of the main block; while the third is a sort of entablature with a narrow flat frieze as well as a crowning cornice. Above the fourth level, moreover, as often on the watchtowers of sixteenth-century Schlösser and the clocktowers of contemporary Rathäuser, a balustraded gallery is cantilevered out on big scrolled consoles. The next stage is only slightly diminished in size, while the clock-faces occupy tiny pedimented dormers on the cardinal faces of the *welsche Haube*. This terminal feature is here elongated upward in a sort of bell-shape and capped by a needle-like circular spire.

Returning to the gables of the Juleum, it should be noted that the treatment, though unusually elaborate, of those at the two ends and of the three dormers on each side is by now of a quite familiar sort, with orders on each of the main stages and scrollwork at the edges. Rather exceptional here, however, are the pediments over the two paired windows in the lowest stage and the gesticulating figures that are silhouetted against the roof and the sky over the ends of the first three stages of each of them and on top of the terminal ones.

The structural elements in the hall (Pl. 334) that occupies most of the ground floor of the Juleum are also richly decorated. The ceiling is of wood, but it is supported by heavy square piers of masonry linked by semi-elliptical stone arches running both east and west and north and south. The strapwork carved on the piers and arches is closer to that on the frames of the upper windows of the exterior than to the pilastered and scalloped treatment of the gables.

A special feature of the Juleum, unusual in an educational building, was the provision of the equivalent of a Ratskeller and wine-rooms in the basement. There the duke hoped the students would learn that "Baccus von ihnen mit Füssen getreten werden muss" (Bacchus should be trampled on). A quite Bacchic

[37] Reclams *Niedersachsen*, p. 776; Karpa, *Wolfenbüttel*, pp. 8-11.

exuberance however, sharply contrasting with the predominantly plain institutional character of the Würzburg university building, is evident here in much of the ornamentation both inside and out.

The strapwork tracery of the big windows at Helmstedt is quite as intricate as the Late Gothic sort in those of the Neubaukirche along the south side of Julius Echter's quadrangle (Pl. 330); while the plastic decoration on the faces of the end and side gables, as also the figures that punctuate their edges like finials, are of a very different character from the sober flat membering of the Würzburg ones. Those last are in any case a decade earlier in date and, as has been noted, they still represent except for the increased variety of the flanking scrollwork a type more common in the mid-century. The special exuberance of Francke's detailing, rivalling that of the Hameln and Lemgo architects who were his contemporaries, is enhanced, indeed exaggerated, by the characteristic polychromy as revived—or introduced—by present-day restorers in the spirit of that on such considerably earlier exteriors in the state of Lower Saxony as those already described at Celle, at Minden and at Bad Salzuflen.

During the ten years or so between the completion of Julius Echter's university buildings at Würzburg and the Helmstedt Juleum, from the mid-eighties to the late nineties that is, a considerable number of Rathäuser and other civic buildings were either built new or received notable additions in various regions to the south, to the north and to the east. At Esslingen on the Neckar, just southeast of Stuttgart, the Rathaus of Fachwerk was first built around 1430 and the original character is still preserved in the rear half of the existing structure. In 1586,[38] however, the ducal architect of Württemberg, Heinrich Schickhardt, also busy at this time in Stuttgart, drastically remodelled and extended upward the front that faces the marketplace (Pl. 335). In the ground storey on this side, all of ashlar masonry, a rather correct range of Tuscan pilasters frames two plain arched entrances and, between them, two smaller arched windows, the whole symmetrically disposed. The next two storeys, the second one overshot like the first storey of the older portion to the rear, are timber-framed but here covered with stucco—at least they are so covered today.

Like the designers of most other pretentious buildings erected in German towns Schickhardt, who had not yet visited Italy, concentrated his architectural efforts at Esslingen in the well-established way on the tall four-stage gable. Exceptionally complete cornices mark its storey-levels; but the moldings that edge the rather simple C-curves and straight vertical elements at the sides are mitered into the architraves below these cornices in an unusual, and possibly unique, way.

As on the righthand gable at Arnstadt (Pl. 329) a clock, and here also a calendar dial, both by Jakob Diehm from Tübingen, occupy the center of the lower stages of the Esslingen gable. This clock is dated 1586-1589. Very much flattened consoles in pairs flank the clock-face and support slim engaged Corinthian colonnettes, two on either side of the upper dial. These in turn carry figures set in shallow niches, while a third framed niche, this capped by a semicircular pediment, is hollowed out between them.

The really original feature of the Esslingen Rathaus, however, which gives this facade its strikingly vertical silhouette is the two-storeyed open lantern of octagonal plan that rises out of the topmost stage of the gable. A three-dimensional treatment of this sort was approached at Arnstadt (Pl. 329), but it is more boldly handled here. This makes up to a large extent for the inconsistencies of handling in the lower storeys and the rather heavy-handed scalloping of the edges of the gable below. Otherwise the outline is enlivened only by single plain balls; these long-familiar accents are set on the ends of the successive entablatures and repeated also over the corners of both entablatures of the lantern.

A similar heavy-handedness is also evident at Esslingen in the vaulted entrance hall (Pl. 336) that Schickhardt provided under his new front toward the marketplace. In this a range of very stubby spirally fluted columns, raised high on cubic podia decorated with lions' heads, runs down the center. Half- and quarter-columns also serve as responds at the sides and corners to help carry the Gothic net vaulting. This is of depressed segmental section with coarsely molded ribs. In this markedly hybrid interior,[39] moreover, the voluted capitals are almost as much Romanesque as Renaissance in design and the foliate carving on them and on the intradoses of the main

---

[38] R. Lempp, *Das alte Rathaus in Esslingen*, Esslingen [1969] pp. 4-47. This excellent monograph includes measured drawings of the front and side elevations, Lempp's figs. 15, 16, 36.

[39] The interior of the Esslingen Rathaus probably gives a fair idea of what the ground storey of the contemporary Lusthaus in Stuttgart was like.

ribs is of a peasant-like crudity. Schickhardt had much to learn when he visited Italy a decade later!

In the great port of Bremen the front of the Stadt-wage in the Langestrasse (Pl. 332), built in 1587-1588,[40] is much more consistent in design than that of the Esslingen Rathaus, being all of one period. In several respects, all the same, it might be considered less advanced; yet the recurrent use here of chip-carved blocks of stone set in the brickwork relates it to such a major and nearly contemporary work of the Weserrenaissance farther to the south and east as the Hämelschenburg Schloss (Pls. 299-305). Such blocks are used on the entrance arches; again to provide a sort of quoining at the edges of the lower storeys; and finally across the paired pilasters of the upper stages of the gable. Of these stages there are no less than six if the transitional one which is also the second storey of the main block is included. The predominant use of exposed brickwork of good quality, on the other hand, and the strong horizontality of the seven successive entablatures, in contrast to the height and the steepness of the gable, suggest the Netherlands. The paired windows, however, are very small by current Dutch or Brabantine standards and the fluted lunettes over them were retardataire in Germany, if not to the west, by a generation or more.

The scalloping of the edges of the gable of the Bremen Stadtwage is also somewhat timid compared to the work of the Hameln architects higher up the Weser and thus closer to Dutch or Flemish gables of the second half of the century. On each stage there are only modest convex spiralled C-scrolls and then more open concave ones set above short vertical elements. As on Dutch gables, no "horns" break the outline; but eleven obelisks, five to a side and one at the top, provide a vigorous, if somewhat repetitious, enlivenment of the skyline. Considering the generally conservative character of this front and its lack of any marked individuality it seems unlikely—though it has been suggested—that it was a very early work of Lüder von Bentheim (p. 1550-1612/1613), the best

recorded Bremen architect-builder of the years just after 1600. His major work, the remodelling of the Bremen Rathaus, will be discussed in the next chapter and his involvement in the construction at least, if not also in the design, of the Leiden Stadhuis will come up later in this one.

Though not a great port like Bremen but an inland city, Brunswick had been since the early Middle Ages an important place. At least nominally ruled by the Welf dukes of Brunswick, whose principal seat was not far away at Wolfenbüttel, the pride of the citizens had long found expression in impressive civic structures much as had happened in Bremen. All the same, the two facades of the Gewandhaus (drapers' guild hall) there, though differing markedly from one another, both seem provincial for the late sixteenth century. The simpler and better organized one (Pl. 337) was added as the front of an extension to a surviving fourteenth-century structure of Fachwerk. That was the work of a Meister Wolfers from Hildesheim and it was built in 1589.[41] The taller, broader and much more elaborate east front (Pl. 338) was erected a little later in 1590-1591.[42] The design for it was provided by the city-architect Hans Lampe (†1604) and—among others—the masons Balthasar Kircher (†p.1598) and Jürgen Röttger (1550-1623) carried it out.

Wolfers's west front has, in the center of the ground storey, a round-arched entrance surrounded by a broad flat frame of hewn stone. This is set between two moderate-sized windows in a wall otherwise all of rubble. Since these windows have pointed arches and the rest of the facade is not of rubble but of fine ashlar, the lower storey may also be in part a survival like the timber-framed section behind it. The first storey, however, is almost entirely open since it has three very large and close-set windows. These are each divided into three lights under segmental heads by stone mullions, and they also have transoms of stone a little above mid-height. As on the facade of the Kronach Rathaus (Pl. 328), the frames of the windows are all detailed in the Late Gothic way with small cylindrical members that intersect at the corners.

The same detailing is used on the much smaller segment-headed windows in the second storey of this western front of the Brunswick Gewandhaus as also in the lower stages of the gable. In contrast to this retardataire treatment of the openings, however, is

---

[40] R. Stein, *Das Bürgerhaus in Bremen*, Tübingen [1970] (henceforth cited as Stein, *Bremen*), p. 44. Stein's elevations of the sixteenth- and seventeenth-century houses, his figs. 27-41, and his pls. T22-T43, provide an extraordinary profusion of gabled facades, all too many of them destroyed in the war. These range from simple early ones with stepped *welsche Gebel* to the most elaborate sort of scrolled Weserrenaissance work rivalling that on local public buildings, with some examples dating well down into the mid- and later seventeenth century.

[41] Reclams *Niedersachsen*, p. 58.
[42] Stelzer, *Braunschweig*, p. 15. The statue of the Angel of Justice that crowns the gable was installed in 1592.

the heavy C- and S-scrolling at the edges of all the stages of the gable; in the first two stages, indeed, there are on the upper elements even "horns" in the Hameln manner. Very plain pilaster-strips with flat panels phrase the second storey of the lower wall and all three stages of the gable above. Neither the usual obelisk-finials nor a terminal pediment complete the outline; instead, at the apex a small block-like podium supports a winged figure carrying a thin metal cross.

Although the east front of the Brunswick Gewandhaus (Pl. 338) is much more advanced stylistically, it quite lacks the consistency of scale and the simple dignity of that toward the west which has just been described. Engaged columns on all four storeys support full entablatures, while various sorts of herms and herm-like members are introduced in the four stages of the gable above. The squat proportion of all eight levels, resulting from the shortness of the columns and the height of the entablatures, is most exaggerated at the base in the open arcade—a rather exceptional feature for the date, incidentally—and in all four stages of the gable above. The heavy horizontal membering used throughout is interrupted, however, by diamond-bossed podia above and below the line of the windows in each stage.

As unusual in German town architecture of the sixteenth century as the loggia at the base of the eastern facade of the Brunswick Gewandhaus are its very flattened three-centered arches. This shape seems to be a belated echo of the French *anse de panier*[43] that was first used in the north at the Palais de Savoie around 1520. Here it is repeated in the arch over the sunken balcony in the center of the first storey and again, at smaller scale and with squarer proportions, in the central windows of the next two storeys and the two lowest stages of the gable. The rest of the fenestration is more generous, but quite unrelated to these accented openings in shape and handling.

So profuse and heavily modelled are the various elements of architectural decoration on the east front of the Gewandhaus at Brunswick, especially in the gable, that the large size of the paired windows in the side bays of the first, second and third storeys, and even the close setting of the smaller windows on the gable, passes almost unnoticed. In the elaboration of the edges of the gable the recurrent small S-scrolls

quite fail to produce a vigorous outline like that of the west gable, for the alternating human figures and obelisk-topped urns are petty in scale and indecisive in silhouette.

With this civic structure in Brunswick, ornately pretentious in a way that recalls the princely Ottheinrichsbau at Heidelberg (Pl. 177) of a generation earlier even more than the contemporary Haus zum Ritter there (Pl. 321), may be contrasted certain utilitarian edifices that are simple and regular in design with only modest decoration of an up-to-date character on their facades. At Ulm, for example, the *Kornhaus* (granary)[44] presents a very broad and tall gabled front to the street with three storeys below and five stages in the gable (Pl. 339). This gable has a rippled edge produced by eight plain S-shaped members on either side, by no means an advanced treatment for 1594 when the Kornhaus was built. But the flat rustication both of the whole ground storey and of the broad frames of the small paired windows above has a grandeur of scale lacking on more richly ornamented facades of this period such as the one at Brunswick (Pl. 338). Comparison with Sustris's somewhat similar detailing of the Torbau at Schloss Trausnitz (Pl. 214) in the seventies or Bacher's more nearly contemporary Kanzlei at Ansbach (Pl. 308)—both by relatively well-known designers and one of them Italian-trained—emphasizes the exceptional taste and ability of the city-architect Caspar Schmid (†1619) who, together with Matthäus Gaiser, presumably designed and certainly erected the Ulm Kornhaus.

In Lübeck the building near the Rathaus that now serves as the main police station was probably also built by the local city-architect Hans Rode as a Kornhaus in the same year 1594;[45] later it served as the city's Zeughaus. It is more modest in its dimensions than that at Ulm and has lacked since 1822, except for the pediment on top, the original edging of the three-stage gable. But this generously fenestrated brick facade has an unmistakably Netherlandish air that is, indeed, almost of mid-century vernacular character because of the segmental bearing-arches over the windows and their subdivision in the outer plane of the wall by sturdy wooden transoms.

On the Lübeck Kornhaus only a few flat bands of stone, some narrow string-courses between the storeys and occasional carved voussoirs in the bearing arches over the side windows of the ground storey relate

---

[43] Could there actually be French influence here? It seems very unlikely. Stelzer, *Braunschweig, loc. cit.*, notes the geometrical ordering of the proportions of this facade, but it cannot be said the result is very persuasive of the aesthetic, as distinguished from the intellectual, value of that procedure.

[44] Dehio, *Baden-Württemberg*, pp. 495-496.
[45] Dehio, *Hamburg*, pp. 387-388.

the Dutch simplicity of the treatment of the brick walling to the wide arch of the portal. Like the arches of the loggia at the base of the east front of the Brunswick Gewandhaus this is three-centered. The frame, moreover, is all of stone with alternate chip-carved and diamond-bossed blocks cutting across the bevelled jambs and the archivolt. Above the keystone, which carries a lion's head in relief, stands a statue of Mars—a modern copy of 1922—in front of a tiny niche. This niche is squeezed rather awkwardly into the narrow strip of wall in the first storey between two of the evenly spaced windows.

Only the entrance doorway on the Lübeck Kornhaus prepares one for the decorative extravagance of the outside staircase on the east side of the Rathaus there that leads up to the principal hall inside. This was built originally in 1594[46] also, probably by R. Coppens; what survives today (Pl. 340), however, is a copy made in 1893-1894, itself restored since the last war. The spirit is that of the Laube on the court side of the Rathaus (Pl. 238) as executed by the Netherlandish stone-carvers Hans Flemming and Herkules Midow in the early seventies. The archivolts of the three supporting arches are banded; textured rustication fills the spandrels; and herms separate the mullioned and transomed windows that follow the slope of the stair inside. Further herms decorate the shallow oriel at the top beneath a small gable. This last is faced with intricate scrollwork and capped by a tiny semicircular pediment.

At the lower end of the outside stair on the Lübeck Rathaus there is a quite different edicule on which fluted Ionic columns flank an arch facing the street. This and another arch to the left are filled with scrolled iron grillwork and both carry pediments set against a square attic. The attic is capped by a somewhat simpler gable than the one over the oriel at the top of the stairs. The carved ornament used in profusion throughout is of the current Netherlandish sort. At this late date such carving was by no means necessarily executed by Netherlanders as the decoration on the Laube fronting the south side of the Rathaus had been earlier (Pl. 238). But that was some twenty-five years before, when the mode was new and relevant publications of engraved designs were not yet so accessible in Germany.

Among the more considerable civic structures outside Germany built, or drastically remodelled, in the 1590s, the central portion of the Stadhuis (town hall)

at Leiden,[47]—though much lengthened later—remains especially conspicuous. It occupies a very long site on the Breestraat, the main street of this considerable city, an old port near one of the original mouths of the Rhine, which is here called the Waal. The fact that the material came from Germany and that quite probably the execution was directed by a German has led to its inclusion in this account of the German Renaissance. In stone-less Holland it is not surprising that the preparation of the blocks of Bückeburg sandstone used to reface the mediaeval exterior, though worked in general accordance with a design provided by the leading Dutch professional of the day Lieven de Key (1560-1627), city-architect of Haarlem, was under the direction of Lüder von Bentheim of Bremen, for he supplied the stone by water from quarries he controlled near Minden in Westphalia. Thus in contradistinction to the sixteenth-century German buildings designed by Netherlanders and, at least in part, executed by Dutch or Brabantine craftsmen, on this prominent monument in Holland, though built from a project by a Dutchman, the stone-cutting was carried out by Germans, or so the documents seem to suggest.

The long facade of the Leiden Stadhuis on the Breestraat has a somewhat artificial homogeneity as restored in this century. De Key's original project for modernizing the mediaeval predecessor was made in 1594 and the tall fourteenth-century tower to the rear received its crowning stages in 1599, dates that provide *termini* for the original construction. In 1604, however, the front was extended to the east and much later, in 1662 and 1735, two gables were added over the western end. After a fire in 1929 the main facade was lengthened eight bays to the left and the tower rebuilt more or less in the form it had at the end of the sixteenth century.

From the first, de Key's design for the Leiden Stadhuis was longer and lower than most German Rathäuser of the day except Lotter's at Leipzig (Pl. 163). But the complex central features below and above the main entrance in the first storey dominate even today the much extended front. These are set over and in front of the plain ashlar wall with its two widely-spaced ranges of mullioned and transomed windows. From the street two balancing flights of stairs parallel to the facade lead up to a *perron* before the portal. Vertical fluted members with reverse entasis and crossed by textured bands frame a banded

46 *Ibid.*, pp. 384-385.

47 *Kunstreisboek*, p. 436.

arch below the *perron* and also mark the half-landings at either side. Balustrades follow the upward slope of the flights of stairs and reclining putti top the podia between the upper and lower sections of that.

At the rear of the *perron* of the Leiden Stadhuis the actual entrance into the first-storey is also through an arch. On the archivolt of that diamond-bossed blocks alternate with textured ones and, at its sides, engaged Ionic columns carry a projecting portion of the entablature that crowns the whole facade. To left and to right two windows, slightly taller than those on the rest of the front, are framed by fluted pilasters of the same Ionic order and capped with pediments. These last are at the level of the balustrade running the entire length of the facade. Between the columns and the pilasters are short statue-filled niches and over them, as also over the entrance arch, are tablets carved with inscriptions and framed with scrollwork. Bolder scrollwork, with elements rather like the "horns" of the Weserrenaissance, flanks the three stages of the gable. Strapwork that is more delicate in scale surrounds the oculi in the side bays of the first stage and in the center of the second one, while six sharp obelisks accent the ends of the entablatures and a seventh tops the terminal pediment.

There are a good many differences between de Key's surviving drawing for the facade at Leiden and the Stadhuis frontispiece as executed. The horn-like protrusions on the scrolls at the sides of the gable as built suggest particularly that these changes were more likely to have been made by the German Bentheim than by the Dutch de Key. Such architectural features as boldly scrolled gables had by this time been so far developed in Germany, especially in the Weser valley, that they were exportable to the Netherlands, or so it would seem, as also to Scandinavia.[48]

[48] Except for the special Leiden situation, this must remain a moot point as regards Holland, if not England and Denmark. That Hans I van Steenwinckel (probably) came to Helsingør in Denmark in 1578 from Emden, not directly from his birthplace Antwerp, and in 1585 succeeded Opbergen in general charge of the work on the Kronborg Slot (Skovgaard, *Christian IV*, p. 131) suggests the gables there could have been influenced by earlier German examples. Certainly little precedent exists for them, at least on surviving facades, in the southern Netherlands before the eighties except for the very different ones on the Palais de Savoye (Pl. 41) in Opbergen's native Mechelen which are, at the latest, two generations earlier.

In England influence from Dietterlin toward 1600 has long been recognized, but there are few surviving examples of elaborately scalloped gables—not, in any case, a Dietterlinesque motif—after the ones, doubtless of the 1570s, at Kirby Hall,

After the Nürnberg edition of 1598 of Wendel Dietterlin's *Architectura* appeared, that became a common vehicle of transmission for German influence—if hardly specifically that of the Weserrenaissance—all over northern Europe. Here in Leiden, however, the particular circumstances were exceptional in the mid-nineties and no specific inspiration from Dietterlin is evident. Circumstances elsewhere had usually been different even where building material was obtained, as for the Leiden Stadhuis, from German quarries. It has been thought, for example, that Stadthagen might have been peculiarly open to Netherlandish influence since the stone for the Antwerp Stadhuis was quarried nearby in the early 1560s and the workmen employed on the job were not Germans but from Brabant. Yet the Stadthagen Rathaus,[49] as created by extending along the south side of the marketplace an older structure, the Rhumhus, previously serving the town as an arsenal, shows no evidence of early contact with ideas from Antwerp.

On the Rhumhus as it existed before 1595—essentially now the eastern half of the present Stadthagen Rathaus (Pl. 341), across the main street from a modest earlier one—the decoration seems to have had a local source. The original treatment, which survives on the gable at the end and on one gabled dormer over the long facade toward the marketplace, includes stepped *welsche Gebel* accented on the edge with balls, which are very similar to those on the gables and dormers of the Stadthagen Schloss as begun by Unkair in the mid-thirties and later extended.

When the length of the old Stadthagen Rhumhus was doubled in the mid-nineties, both the end-gable and the dormer were repeated on the western half without change, probably by Cord Reineking. Only on the tops of the oriels in the upper storey, three of them symmetrically disposed on the front toward the marketplace and one around the corner facing the main street, does scrollwork of advanced design appear. This seems to be the work of Bishop Julius

and probably there never were. Those at Kirby must derive from the engravings of Vredeman, for relevant executed work on the Continent is not likely to have been known in those years to English designers—if, indeed, the designer here was not, in fact, some craftsman from the Netherlands. The gable-like crestings of the early eighties on the corner towers at Wollaton were definitely borrowed from Vredeman by Robert Smythson, along with other decorative motifs in the interior, as Mark Girouard has made evident: M. Girouard, *Robert Smythson . . .* , South Brunswick, N.J., n.d.

[49] H. and A. Masuch, *Das Rathaus von Stadthagen; ein Renaissancebau*, Bückeburg, 1964.

Echter's architect, the Walloon Johann Robin and his helpers, to whom payments are recorded from May 8 to December 12, 1596. Yet the open, jewelry-like cresting is of the sort German craftsmen had long been borrowing from Vredeman or other Brabantine sources, not something Robin would have brought with him many years before from his native Ypres; in any case, he had already been working in Germany for some fifteen years, it will be recalled, and even probably nearby in Westphalia at Minden shortly before this. The cresting includes helmeted watchmen's heads projecting from sunken circles between flanking scrolls, these last topped by fruit-baskets and banded obelisk-finials. The tallest gable is the one now flattened against the old Rhumhus wall at the east end. This has two stages with an inscribed panel including the date 1596 in the lower stage. Rather exceptionally, it was closely followed as a model when the oriel was doubled to the right in 1612.

At Bad Hersfeld on the Fulda, however, just off the Autobahn northeast of Alsfeld in Hessen-Kassel, something quite parallel occurred. There the mediaeval Rathaus was drastically remodelled in 1597 (Pl. 342), the date on one of the gables, and then doubled to the same design—even more exactly than the oriel at Stadthagen—in 1612, the date inscribed on the portal. Three storeys tall, both portions of this Rathaus have paired rectangular windows in the two upper storeys, regularly but not symmetrically disposed, and column-flanked portals with arches that open onto a small and informal square. Otherwise the decoration is confined to the gables which are all identical.

A string-course marks the start of the Hersfeld gables just above the second-storey windows, and three more mark off the upper stages. Pilaster-strips, banded with plain stone courses, frame the lowest stage in which the windows are grouped in twos and threes. Similar strips flank the pair of windows in the next stage but not the oculus in the top one. Tight S-scrolls and C-scrolls, some of the latter concave and others convex, are associated in the upper stages with broad bandwork on the wall surfaces much as at Arnstadt (Pl. 329). The terminal feature in each case is a fluted lunette, a motif somewhat retardataire for this late date. So also the outline is accented both by up-to-date obelisk-finials and, as on the gables of the Rathaus at Stadthagen executed in the nineties (Pl. 341), by stone balls of the sort Unkair had introduced some seventy-five years earlier.

Well to the southwest of Stadthagen and Hersfeld, the Rathaus at Darmstadt,[50] the principal city of Rhenish Hesse, is very different (Pl. 343). That incorporates no mediaeval core like the one at Hersfeld, nor did it extend an earlier Renaissance structure as at Stadthagen or Rinteln. Moreover, the clean white stucco of the walls and the bright brown-red paint on the stone trim, as restored in 1952-1953 after war damage resulting from a fire-raid in 1944, contrasts with the rubble walling and untreated cut-stone trim common to both the latter and to that at Hersfeld as enlarged.

The Darmstadt Rathaus stands free at the south end of the marketplace, opposite the early eighteenth-century wing of the Schloss, and only the conspicuous principal portal, dated 1676, is not as originally designed in 1588 and completed in 1590 by Jakob Wustmann, a local builder-architect who later worked on the Schloss. The original main entrance is the modest doorway at the base of the stair-tower, a tall asymmetrically-placed feature that partly overlaps the lefthand cross-gable.

Except for that overlap, the design of the facade of this conspicuous civic monument in Darmstadt is quite regular with three storeys of coupled rectangular windows and two further pairs in the lowest stage of each of the gables. Panelled pilaster-strips separate the bays in this stage below a compressed entablature very similar in character to the eaves-cornice below. Vertical S-scrolls, with rather stiff internal fluting, flank this lowest stage on all the gables. The next stage of the gables has no windows and is framed below a second, slightly narrower, string-course by horizontal S-scrolls. At their outer ends these project well beyond the obelisk-finials above the flanking pilaster-strips, while their inner ends extend inward on the wall-surface like the bandwork on the Hersfeld gables (Pl. 342). The terminal stage of the ones at Darmstadt is simpler, with two quadrant C-scrolls capped at the top by a broken pediment through which another obelisk-finial rises.

The two-stage gable of the Darmstadt stair-tower is narrower and simpler. Small quadrants and longer vertical elements frame a clock-face below; above, concave C-scrolls rise to a fluted *welsche Gebel* capped by still another obelisk-finial.

At Konstanz (Constance), south of the Bodensee at the present Swiss border, the rear wing of the Rath-

---

[50] Dehio, *Hessen*, p. 132.

haus faces a court behind a plainer block on the street which was remodelled in 1589-1594.[51] This inner facade (Pl. 345)—presumably of the following years, since the date 1598 is inscribed on one of the ceilings inside—is compositionally more elaborate than that of the Darmstadt Rathaus, yet considerably less advanced in its detailing. Two round towers occupy the inner corners of the court, while between them in the ground storey is an open loggia of three wide segmental arches, quite unmolded, carried on very sturdy Tuscan columns. Above each of these arches a pair of arched windows with rusticated voussoirs is carried on smaller colonnettes sunk into the wall-plane. Over the first storey rises a single gabled dormer which has one pair of plain arched windows between panelled pilasters in the lower rectangular stage. Over that, there are C-scrolls and S-scrolls on the edges of the next stage and, terminally, a fluted welsche Gebel above a single window arched like those below.

The two towers in the court of the Konstanz Rathaus have identical portals at their base, both of them slanted inward. These portals are segmental-arched and framed by arabesqued pilaster-strips under rather flat entablatures. Small windows at this level have a similar treatment; while on the tower to the right more such windows, set unevenly, trace the spiral path of the stair within. On the lefthand tower, however, there are four arched windows in line with the windows in the central portion. These are separated only by broader pilaster-strips with disk ornaments at mid-height. Three more, identical with the isolated ones on the righthand tower, are similarly lined up in the second storey.

Everything about this Rathaus facade in Konstanz is a bit disjointed. The loggia is not quite centered between the towers; the coupled windows of the first storey are not coordinated with the arches below; and the dormer is so little related to the rest of the facade that it may well be a later addition. Konstanz is, of course, far from the central German lands; perhaps the location accounts for the distinctly provincial character of this court facade—surely no Italian or Italian-Swiss designer was employed. The retention of some sections of earlier walling may well be, as so often elsewhere, the explanation of the irregularities, however.

The Rathaus at Bad Gandersheim, for example, just to the west of the Autobahn near the somewhat larger town of Einbeck in Hessen-Kassel, includes the mediaeval Moritzkirche as adapted after a fire in 1580.[52] But there are several Renaissance features here that date from the late sixteenth century. The most prominent is a two-storeyed oriel, and beside it, an outside stair that rises to a pedimented portal at the base of the surviving rectangular church-tower. Of the two additional oriels, both cantilevered out at upper-storey level, one is at the extreme right and the other on the end. That by the stair is very similar to those on the portion of the local convent—famous in the middle ages as that of Hroswitha, the playwriting nun—built by Heinrich Overkatte in 1599-1600[53] (Pl. 344). It is doubtless also by him and of approximately the same date. On the new wing of the convent both of the small gables on the two oriels and also the main gable are framed by bold S-scrolls confining fluted fields as on several housefronts of the preceding decades at Lemgo (Pl. 226) associated with Hermann Wulff. Overkatte had been working as an assistant to Wulff before coming to Gandersheim, possibly even completing himself Schloss Brake (Pls. 288-290) outside Lemgo in this decade.

Beyond the righthand oriel on the Gandersheim convent the upper storey is of Fachwerk; indeed, in this town almost all the houses are timber-framed, at least as regards their superstructure. But even in towns such as Gandersheim, Celle, Brunswick or Hersfeld, where Fachwerk predominates, the churches always—and the civic buildings usually—are of masonry. However, the Esslingen Rathaus, that at Hersfeld and the Brunswick Gewandhaus, do preserve at the rear or in the core earlier portions built of timber as has been noted. At Alsfeld, moreover, the early sixteenth-century Rathaus is of Fachwerk above the stone arches of the open ground storey, but the Weinhaus of the late thirties is of stone and so is the Hochzeitshaus of the sixties.

The town of Einbeck, however, not far from either Alsfeld or Gandersheim, is all timber-framed except for the Rathaus[54] (Pl. 346) in the marketplace which has a lower storey of rubble, here stuccoed. In this the narrow single windows have flattened curtain-tops as did those on the Alsfeld Weinhaus originally. The upper storey is of Fachwerk carved and poly-

[51] Dehio, Baden-Württemberg, p. 264.

[52] Kreft-Soenke, Weserrenaissance, p. 245.

[53] Ibid., pp. 244-245; [K. Kronenberg] Gandersheim, das Reichstift und seine Kunstwerk [Munich, 1969] pp. 20-22.

[54] Reclams Niedersachsen, pp. 148-149.

chromed like that of the houses across the way and in the Tiedexerstrasse (Pl. 170). The projecting bays that flank asymmetrically the open wooden porch recall a little the turreted front of the Alsfeld Rathaus of 1512.[55] Each of them rises from the ground storey, above a transitional hip, into a sharp pointed spire covered with slate. The dating of these various elements is uncertain, but the bowed section on the right is of 1593 and the other would be a bit later. It should also be noted that the wooden porch is round-arched in contrast to the curtain-topped windows, probably several decades earlier in date, that light the hall within. Though the Einbeck Rathaus is rather modest, even in the context of this small town, among surrounding houses that are mostly of rather regular reticulated Fachwerk, its tower-like vertical accents are very striking. Their fairy-tale flavour recalls Weidmann's Hagereiterhaus of the nineties at Rothenburg with its tall pointed roof and round stair-turret.

In Wolfenbüttel south of Brunswick, always a fairly large place and since the thirteenth century the seat of the Welf dukes of Brunswick and Lüneburg, even the Schloss was, and still is, principally of Fachwerk though now covered with stucco. However, most of the older house-fronts—some 500 all told, extending in date down through the eighteenth century—are less picturesque in composition and less richly decorated than in smaller places such as Einbeck and Höxter. Moreover, the Rathaus, as extended in 1599 beside a marketplace that was laid out in 1590, differs little from the nearby houses and, indeed, part of it was originally built as a house.[56] That part, now occupied by the Ratskeller, was taken over by the Council in 1602; the other wing was added in 1609. The carved and polychromed decoration on the 1599 front differs, however, from that of the inherited Early Renaissance vernacular, still in common use at Einbeck and elsewhere in Westphalia and Hesse, since there is some faint reflection of contemporary German strapwork instead of fan-like fluted lunettes. That is also true of certain houses surviving in Hameln and Rinteln, to be described in the next chapter, which are rather later in date (Pls. 391, 392).

Little has been said hitherto concerning the city-planning of the later sixteenth century in Germany beyond the occasional mention of new fortifications. Often, these were still designed by Italians, as earlier

for Hendrick of Nassau at Breda in Holland and for Charles V in the southern Netherlands, as also in the same years of the thirties and forties in Nürnberg. Even before Wilhelm von Kleve called Alessandro Pasqualini from Holland to Jülich in the late forties Duke Heinrich II of Brunswick-Wolfenbüttel was already fortifying Wolfenbüttel with walls and a moat. That was shortly before 1542 when the town was taken, all the same, by the forces of the League of Schmalkalden.

Wolfenbüttel flourished rather later, particularly under the cultivated Heinrich Julius, builder of the later portion of the Juleum at Helmstedt (Pl. 333). The population actually increased tenfold in the decades following the battle of Mühlberg in 1547. However, the major improvements were only begun in the seventies, though well before Heinrich Julius succeeded his father Julius in 1589. The bastions of the new system of earthworks protecting the town—mentioned in passing earlier as the work of the Brabantine military engineer Willem de Raet assisted by Paul Francke—were the first built east of the Rhine. Rather more significantly for sixteenth-century city-planning, Julius required in the new Heinrichstadt quarter "gleichformige Häuser einer Weite und Höhe, auch räumige schnurige Strassen," that is, "houses all of the same width and height, and spacious straight streets."[57] This was the original programme of 1571 which was carried out mostly in two campaigns, one beginning in 1577, the other in 1590 after Heinrich Julius's succession.

Two towns, one wholly new, the other much extended, were developed in the nineties specifically to receive Protestant refugees from the east and the west. Duke Friedrich of Württemberg laid out Freudenstadt high in the Schwarzwald, south of Baden-Baden on the road that runs from Tübingen to Strasbourg, to receive the Lutherans—some two-thirds of the population of Styria!—expelled by that bigoted Catholic, the Archduke Ferdinand, later the Emperor Ferdinand II. This was not purely philanthropic: the refugees were expected to work in the newly opened silver mines. However, these mines never rivalled the earlier ones in the Saxon Erzgebirge; worse, they soon ceased to be profitable when, as the seventeenth century wore on, more and more silver reached Europe from the New World. As a

---

[55] *Deutsche Kunstdenkmäler, Hessen* [Munich, 1964] (henceforth cited as DKD, *Hessen*) pl. 3.

[56] *Ibid.*, pp. 775-776; Karpa, *Wolfenbüttel*, pp. 6-19.

[57] S. Busch, *Hannover, Wolfenbüttel und Celle, Stadtgründungen und Stadterweiterungen . . . , vom 16. bis 18. Jahrhundert*, Hildesheim, 1969, pp. 24-27, 48-51, 65-69, 80-83, figs. 24-30; plan, fig. 2.

result the town was not fully built up. Since the destruction of the last war, however, it has now been restored and is today a flourishing resort. New arcades around much of the central area repeat those that once existed or were at least intended by Schickhardt.

In 1597[58] Count Philipp Ludwig II von Solms, the ruler of Hanau, extended that old town on the Main, just east of Frankfurt, to receive religious refugees from the southern Netherlands. The Neustadt (new town) that Nicolas Gillet then laid out was polygonal and surrounded, in the new way lately established as most defensible against artillery, with broad-pointed bastions. Within, it was organized on a checkerboard plan including two rectangular open squares, one where the Rathaus was to rise, the other with a new church in its center (Fig. 55).

The original scheme of the Württemberg duke's architect, Heinrich Schickhardt, for Freudenstadt[59] (Fig. 56) was more utopian and unrelated to any surviving older town. It was to be square in shape with gates at the four cardinal points and round towers and bastions at the corners. A main street was to lead at each cardinal point to a very extensive open space in the center where a big Schloss was to be set lozenge-wise. Other parallel streets filled the L-shaped spaces between the main arteries. As carried out mostly after 1600, this plan was considerably simplified. The principal surviving public building, Schickhardt's church begun in 1601, is of a most exceptional L-shaped plan to fit the predetermined layout (Fig. 57). This will be discussed in the next chapter as also the equally exceptional church at Hanau of which the cornerstone was laid a year earlier. The architects of that were Walloon refugees.

Though very little else is extant either at Freudenstadt or at Hanau, the plans are the most remarkable of a considerable group that were made for towns similarly built or extended especially to receive religious refugees, mostly at a rather later date. Throughout this period, however, it was the modernization of the fortified enceintes of cities and towns that represented the most active aspect of city-planning. Generally, where places that long remained strongholds are partially extant, what survives today consists of an accumulation of elements—some mediaeval, some Renaissance and some dating from after the Thirty Years' War. Over-all they are more interesting for

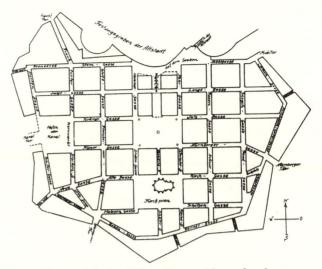

Fig. 55. Nicolas Gillet: Hanau, Neustadt, plan, 1597

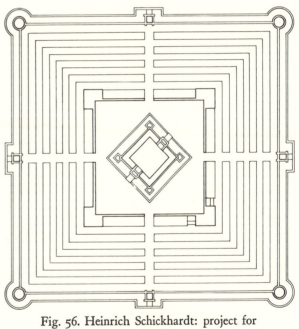

Fig. 56. Heinrich Schickhardt: project for Freudenstadt, 1599

the picturesque *Stadtbild* they provide than for particular portions that were erected in the later sixteenth century in the way of the Frazösischer Bau of the Heldberg or the Schöner Hof in the Plassenburg. On the complex pile of Veste Rosenberg above Kronach,[60] for example, only one section has decorated gables; but several round towers, if not actually new-built

[58] Reclams *Niedersachsen*, pp. 332-334.
[59] Fleischhauer, *Württemberg*, pp. 291-294.

[60] Reclams *Bayern*, pp. 426-427; *Geschichte und Rundgang durch die Veste Rosenberg* [Lichtenfels and Kronach, n.d.].

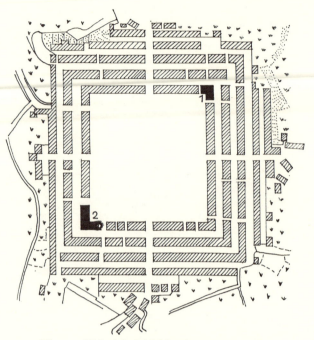

Fig. 57. Heinrich Schickhardt: Freudenstadt,
plan as of c.1850

in the 1590s, probably received then their *welsche Hauben*. The more extensive *Veste* (fortress) above Coburg is largely nineteenth-century reconstruction, but it does include some work of the 1550s by Nickel Gromann and of the 1610s by Gideon Bacher.[61]

These new strong points only rarely have impressive entrances added in this period in the way even such a modest older town as Amberg does. One exception, however, is the main portal at Wülzburg,[62] lying to the east of Nördlingen and north of Eichstatt, which was like Rosenberg more fortress than town. The late sixteenth-century fortifications here were begun for the Margrave Georg Friedrich of Brandenburg-Kulmbach, the builder of the Plassenburg, by Blasius Berwart, one of the Württembergers he had long employed at Kulmbach. They occupy the site of a Benedictine monastery secularized in 1537 when the Kulmbach Hohenzollerns turned Protestant. Laid out in 1588, the Wülzburg fortress was five-sided like the Kasteel at Antwerp on which it was modelled. Following on Berwart, the Brandenburg architect Kaspar

Schwab took charge and then, down to 1601, Gideon Bacher,[63] who was working for Georg Friedrich at Ansbach on St. Gumbert and the Kanzlei there in the nineties. Ironically, Wülzburg fell without a struggle to the Catholic forces of the Emperor Ferdinand II in 1631, but that ill fate may have saved it from destruction.

Since the rather grand outer portal at Wülzburg dates from around 1600, it would probably have been designed by Bacher rather than by Berwart or Schwab even though it does not at all resemble his Kanzlei in Ansbach (Pl. 308). For example, there is a San-michelian sort of boldness in the main storey that contrasts with the crudely Northern Mannerist membering on the attic which frames an intricate armorial panel.

So different that it is hard to believe it can also be of this period, however, is the *Nordertor* (North Gate)[64] of Flensburg, which is dated 1595. Located at the present Danish border on the northern edge of Schleswig-Holstein, this might better be considered Danish than German perhaps, like several of the Schlösser and Herrenhäuser north of Hamburg (Pls. 312, 313, 314) described earlier in this chapter; certainly there is nothing about it typical of the German Renaissance. Rather it represents a belated continuation of the brick-built Baltic Romanesque of several centuries earlier.

So far little has been said about interiors of the last two decades of the sixteenth century. This realm, in which the later German Renaissance achieved autochthonous distinction, includes most notably the monumentally scaled secular *Festsäle* (great halls) that survive in various Schlösser. These vast rooms parallel chronologically—and also in their large dimensions, if not their broad rectangular shape—the long galleries that are so characteristic as a new feature of English country-house planning under Elizabeth I. Like the English galleries, the German great halls are generally located in an upper storey so that their vast flat ceilings can be suspended from the main roof-trusses, thus freeing the floor area from obstructive pillars. They are like Elizabethan galleries also in the general character of the sumptuous decoration. While in England that usually consists of carved wooden wainscoting around the walls, such

[61] Reclams *Bayern*, pp. 202-205; DKD, *Bayern nordlich der Donau* [Munich, 1960] (henceforth cited as DKD, *Bayern*), p. 367, pl. 93.

[62] Reclams *Bayern*, pp. 933-934. The *Haupttor* (main gate) *durch die Veste Rosenberg* [Lichtenfels and Kronach, n.d.]. be considered Baroque.

[63] In 1601 Bacher restored the Schloss at Hof-a.-d.-Saale in eastern Franconia; in 1604 he was at Ulm working on the fortifications, and then—as just mentioned above—a decade later, in 1614, on the Coburg Veste: See Note 5.

[64] Dehio, *Hamburg*, p. 186.

as was frequently used in more modest interiors in Germany, with chimneypieces of marble, stone or wood and ceilings of pargetted plaster, in most of the German great halls the walls are plastered and the ceilings of wood. The ceilings provide, moreover, the principal field for decoration—carved in wood, inlaid or polychromed—though there are usually stone or marble chimneypieces also and sometimes quite monumental portals of carved stone to match.

An early example in Lower Bavaria of such a wooden ceiling over a large interior, contrasting with the very Italianate vaulted rooms on the far side of the court of the Landshut Stadtresidenz, is the one there dating from the late 1530s over the large hall that occupies most of the top storey of the front wing, the Deutscher Bau (Pl. 119). At Neuburg, nearby in the Upper Palatinate, the approximately contemporary Rittersaal in the north wing, completed in 1538, of Ottheinrich's Schloss is considerably larger than the rooms in the earlier west wing that Ottheinrich himself principally occupied. As in the principal rooms in the Fuggerhäuser (Fig. 4), earlier by twenty years or more it may be recalled, there are two stone piers in the Rittersaal (Pl. 105), though they do not carry vaults like those in the ground-storey at Augsburg but a flat ceiling. The elaborate wooden wainscoting in this hall was only installed later, shortly before Ottheinrich left permanently for Heidelberg in 1556, but may have replaced simpler wood panelling of the late thirties. In the Heidelberg Ottheinrichsbau no great hall survives intact inside the extant walls of the ruin, but in the main storey there are some remains of the vaulting that once covered it.

At Jever, in the northwest, the *Audienzsaal* (audience hall) of 1560-1564 in the Schloss (Pl. 205), though not especially large in area[65]—c.38 by 22 feet—is of a height approaching that of Italian *sale* in contrast to the relative lowness of previous German examples. So also the deep coffering articulating the wooden ceiling certainly looks Italianate. All the same, it seems likely the craftsmen employed here were not Italians; rather they will have been Netherlanders strongly influenced, like the sculptor then executing the Wiemken tomb in the church here, by Cornelis Floris—if, indeed, "H. H." himself was not in control as he may well have been. The Jever ceiling certainly differs considerably from the flatter treatment of the one over the hall in the Deutsche Bau at Landshut

(Pl. 119), a treatment maintained in most later great halls in Germany.

The great hall at Schloss Ambras, far distant in the Tyrol from the central German lands and thus much nearer Italy, deserves particular mention at this point. It is, not surprisingly, even more Italianate than that at Jever. Because of his marriage to Philippine Welser, the Augsburg banker's daughter, the Archduke Ferdinand who ruled in the Tyrol as Statthalter[66] was better supplied with spendable funds than most Habsburgs. Schloss Ambras, which lies just outside the provincial capital, Innsbruck, to the south where the Autobahn leading to the Brenner Pass into Italy now begins, was almost completely rebuilt for Ferdinand in 1564-1567.[67] It is interesting externally chiefly for the sgraffito decoration executed in grisaille on the walls of the enclosed quadrangular court. This was the work of Ferdinand's court-painter Heinrich Teufel (†1570) in 1566-1567 and has lately been completely restored (Pl. 347). As noted earlier, this court gives a good idea of what the west and south sides of the one in Ottheinrich's Schloss at Neuburg must once have looked like, as doubtless various others also that have by now lost all trace of external murals.

More remarkable, however, is the nearly freestanding great hall (Pl. 348). This is set just below the main block of Schloss Ambras, at middle level beside the much larger open court. It was built in 1570-1571 after Ferdinand, by then a widower, had married an Italian wife, Anna Gonzaga. This vast hall is c.140 feet long, c.33 feet broad and c.16.5 feet high, thus larger as was noted earlier than any in more northerly German lands. Although called the Spanischer Saal because of its Habsburg builder, it is thoroughly Italianate in design except for the northern character of the flat wooden ceiling. That was executed in 1571 by the Innsbruck joiner Konrad Gottlieb. Gottlieb had earlier extended Hans Waltner's ranges of choir-stalls decorated with intarsia in the Hofkirche, subsidiary features of the church which were not mentioned in the earlier account of it.

---

[66] Not the same as his nephew Ferdinand, from 1596 ruler of Inner Austria, who succeeded as Emperor Ferdinand II in 1619.

[67] Dehio, *Tirol*, p. 77. The name of the Schloss is there given as "Amras" though not in Kunstdenkmäler in Österreich, *Salzburg, Tirol, Vorarlberg* [Munich, 1965] (hereafter cited as KDÖ, *Salzburg*), p. 307. Merian, *Schönsten Schlösser*, pl. opp. 23, shows the exterior of the Spanischer Saal above a formal Renaissance garden and below the plain old Schloss as remodelled in the sixties with its four regular ranges of good-sized rectangular windows.

---

[65] Reclams *Niedersachsen*, p. 415. Some additions on the south side date from 1836.

Along the right wall of the Spanischer Saal, away from the main block of the Schloss, the very broad rectangular window embrasures are set close together. Over each of these is an oculus in the frieze that runs around above the lower cornice. Repeating the rectangular shapes of the windows on the other three walls are big portraits of earlier Tyrolean rulers. Arabesques by the Netherlander Dionys van Hallaert fill the narrow panels between the windows and between the portraits; while in the frieze there are *stucchi* by Anton Brack interrupted by pairs of real antlers before each of the oculi along the sides. Except for these last, there is nothing Germanic or northern about the wall treatment. Gottlieb's panelled wooden ceiling, moreover, is no rival to those in Germany, whether earlier or later, nor is it consonant with the Italian character of the wall decoration. The exterior was entirely renewed in 1954.

A new scale of splendour in German princely apartments designed for large-scale entertainment, rivalling that of the Spanischer Saal, was reached in Beer's Stuttgart Lustspielhaus (Pl. 284), begun in 1580, which has already been described in this chapter. But that was hardly characteristic since it was an independent structure and did not have a flat ceiling even though it was not vaulted either. Later, in the last decades of the seventeenth century, and more particularly in the early and mid-eighteenth century, the *Kaisersäle* and *Fürstensäle* (emperor's and princes' halls), the principal secular interiors in the monasteries in southern Germany and Austria, would be among the grandest rooms of northern Europe. They often approached those at Versailles in size and architectural scale and, above all, in the richness of their decoration with *stucchi* and frescoes. Not much of interest survives in monasteries, however, that dates from the time before the destruction of the Thirty Years' War ceased and the economic blight which was its aftermath came to an end around 1680.

Still, at Ochsenhausen in Swabia, between Memmingen and Biberach, some early interiors remain intact in the big Benedictine abbey. The *Prälatur* (abbot's residence), which had first been built together with the cloisters below in the mid-fifteenth century, includes an audience hall which probably dates from the enlargement in 1583-1585[68] of this portion of the monastery to the south of the nave of the fifteenth-century church destined later to be thoroughly baroquized. Though not very high, this Au-

dienzsaal has a fine beamed ceiling and also three elaborate wooden portals. These last, however, seem to be related to work executed by the Memmingen craftsman Thomas Heidelberger for the Benedictines at Ottobeuren, their more famous abbey on the other side of Memmingen, considerably earlier in 1547-1548. These doorways at Ochsenhausen are so awkwardly related to the ceiling in their asymmetrical placing and so different in style that they may well be some twenty or thirty years older, and only retained or reinstalled in the 1580s.

The beaming of the ceiling of the hall at Ochsenhausen is almost as heavy as at Jever (Pl. 205) but the design is more complicated, even though decorative carving is almost totally lacking. Within the square shape of the room a great octagon is defined by heavy modillioned members. At the center of that is a cruciform panel which is somewhat more richly ornamented than the rest of the ceiling; elsewhere the surface is merely subdivided into interlocked hexagonal and rhomboidal panels somewhat in the Serlian way of the Neuburg Grosser Flez which is around twenty-five years earlier. Julius Echter's hall at Rimpar of the mid-nineties[69] is also low and even subdivided by columns. The wooden panels of the ceiling were marbled—at least that is their condition today—and the armorial frieze painted white, though picked out in color. This is a rather modest example of a great hall, more domestic than monumental and doubtless designed by Georg Robin.

The Rittersaal of the Fürstenbergs far to the south at Schloss Heiligenberg (Pl. 349)—of which the chapel, as remodelled in this period, has been described in the previous chapter—is the earliest of the series of truly monumental secular interiors created in Germany in the last decades of the sixteenth century which quite overshadow those at Ochsenhausen and Rimpar. To begin with, the hall at Heiligenberg is not only much bigger, it is in fact the largest in Germany, though not as large as the Spanischer Saal of Schloss Ambras in the Tyrol. It occupies the entire top storey of the south wing of the Schloss as rebuilt and extended for Count Joachim von Fürstenberg beginning in 1569.[70] The builders principally responsible for the work were two brothers, Benedikt and Hans II Oertlin. They had, most lately, been employed nearby in Überlingen on the Bodensee but came originally from Radolfzell. That lies further to the

[68] Dehio, *Baden-Württemberg*, pp. 364-365.

[69] Reclams *Bayern*, p. 759.
[70] Dehio, *Baden-Württemberg*, pp. 206-207.

south and west on the Zellersee which provides the present Swiss border. There in Radolfzell Hans had become *Stadtsteinmetz* and *Werkmeister* (city stone-mason and work-master) in 1559.

Over an area 36 by 11 meters the unsupported flat ceiling at Heiligenberg is hung from the roof-trusses at a height of 23 feet. Along the southern side ten big windows, subdivided by mullions and transoms and with an oculus over each, are set in deep niches. Identical niches, with windows opening on the court, occupy the center of the north wall and a pair of them flank each of the elaborate sandstone chimney-pieces at the ends. One of these last, carrying the date 1584, was most probably executed by Hans Morinck (†1616), a Netherlander who had settled across the Bodensee in Konstanz. A full entablature, with a carved frieze that is also gilded and polychromed, provides the imposts for the niches and is also carried across the walls between the tall lower lights and the oculi above them. Today the fronts of the piers are occupied by an endless series of large framed ancestral portraits of various dates doubtless initiated for Count Joachim and long continued by his princely successors.

Not the least of the attractions of this great gallery at Heiligenberg is the splendid view southward from the many windows toward the Bodensee and the Alps. But the real glory is the carved and polychromed ceiling of linden wood, executed not by Morinck or the Oertlins, but by Jörg Schwartzenberger from Messkirch who also worked in the chapel. The matching marquetry floor was installed only in 1842, however, and the whole was restored in the 1880s, when the chapel was last remodelled, and again in 1953. The ceiling is by no means completely flat, though the relief of the membering is considerably less than at Ochsenhausen, Rimpar or Jever and the pattern more intricate.

Four square areas that are slightly dished upward, with various interior subdivisions and much painting and gilding in subsidiary panels, run the length of the Heiligenberg hall. Each of them is framed, beyond a nearly continuous border of delicate strapwork, by four curved segments outside the corners. These are, however, cut off in the long direction of the hall by cruciform panels with octagons in their centers and also linked at the sides by rectangular panels. Thus, for the regular rhythm of the ten wall-bays on either side, there is substituted overhead a much more complex pattern but the whole composition is tightly bound together by flat white strips decorated with

gilded strapwork, which are very like those around the square and cruciform central areas. The restoration of the 1880s seriously coarsened the original coloring.[71] However, the delicate scale of most of the ornament in relation to the great extent of the whole ceiling effectively reduces the nineteenth-century garishness of the arabesques on the large central and flanking panels so apparent when those panels are examined closely.

Perhaps in actual emulation of the Fürstenbergs' Rittersaal far away in southern Württemberg, Hans Fugger introduced in the large but dull Schloss Jakob Eschay built for him at Kirchheim-a.-d.-Mindel in Swabia in 1583-1585[72] the *Cedernsaal* (cedarwood hall), a very grand room indeed (Pl. 350). If not quite so large as the one at Heiligenberg—about 98 by 40 feet—this has at least as gorgeous a ceiling, here all of carved wood and intarsia with no painting or gilding, and it occupies the full width and a good part of the total length of the south wing. The walls below, however, are quite differently treated than at Heiligenberg. Once again two ranges of windows, here rectangular below and square above, are set in deep niches of oblong section, but the sides and elliptically-arched tops of these niches are quite undecorated. Between them the sections of wall are occupied by smaller niches of semi-cylindrical section.

These niches in the Kirchheim Cedernsaal are capped by plain segmental pediments and occupied by over-lifesize figures modelled in plaster.[73] Representing famous men and women, these were executed in 1583-1585 by the Italian-trained Dutch sculptor Hubert Gerhard and the Italian *stuccatore* Carlo Pallago ten years or so after their earlier work, together with Frederik Sustris, for Hans Fugger in the Fuggerhäuser in Augsburg was completed. By this time, of course, Sustris and several of his associates, both Italians and Italian-trained northerners, were in the service of Duke Wilhelm V of Bavaria, first at Landshut and then at Munich. It will be recalled that Gerhard worked again with Sustris in Munich later on St. Michael. He also modelled the Augustusbrunnen in Augsburg for the city authorities in 1589 which Peter Wagner eventually cast in bronze some time before

[71] At least it seems probable that it was the earlier restoration and not that of 1953 and following years which had such a deleterious effect on the polychromy.

[72] Dehio, *Östliches Schwaben*, p. 147.

[73] The material looks like terra cotta but is actually *gebrannte Gips*, that is, plaster colored brown before being modelled instead of being painted afterward.

1594. Like Carlo di Cesare's slightly later statues at Freiberg (Pl. 270), the ones at Kirchheim are all completely Italian in style whichever of the two sculptors was responsible for them individually.

Earlier Hans Fugger had, in 1580, commissioned the great Venetian sculptor Alessandro Vittoria (1525-1608) to provide a bronze altar for the chapel of his Schloss; but for Hans' own monument Gerhard made the wax model from which it was carved in marble by Alexander Colin at Innsbruck. Gerhard completed in 1594 a large sculptural group of Mars and Venus and a putto for the center of the court at Kirchheim which is now preserved in the Bayrisches Nationalmuseum in Munich. This complicated work is mounted on a tall pedestal decorated at the corners with winged and scrolled herms. It easily rivals the latest compositions for fountains and such that were then being executed by leading sculptors in Italy. Probably, moreover, the statutes of Hercules, Mars and Minerva in the niches on the east wing by the main entrance are also by Gerhard.

Other prominent features at Kirchheim beside the ceiling of the Cedernsaal (Pl. 350) are the tall marble chimneypiece in the middle of the north side of that hall, with its Michelangelesque figures in terra cotta by Gerhard, and the wooden portal at the west end which leads in from the stairs. Despite the profusion of figural sculpture loaded onto the chimneypiece, the architectural framework is simpler and larger in scale than that of Morinck's almost precisely contemporary one at Heiligenberg or that at Weikersheim of fifteen years or so later, which will soon be described. The assured handling of the Classical members of the portal, their big scale and, most particularly, the aggressiveness of the plain but boldly curved "horns" of the broken pediment above the canonic entablature already have, to later eyes, almost a Baroque look. It seems at least as premonitory as much work carried out in the second and even the third decade of the new century.

The portal in the Kirchheim hall is the work not of Gerhard but of the Augsburg woodcarver-architect Wendel Dietrich. As noted already, Dietrich was also involved in these years of the mid-eighties in the original campaign of construction and decoration at St. Michael in Munich and he continued to work there, at least on the high altar (Pls. 254, 256), until the church was completed.[74] His use on the Kirch-

heim portal of various woods of different tones provides a limited polychromatic range of dark and light browns; the same woods were employed by him in the ceiling. That is a greater decorative tour-de-force than the one at Heiligenberg, in good part because of the less strident coloring. Photography, however, exaggerates the tonal contrast of the light and dark wood at Kirchheim and fails to suggest the over-all tonal harmony achieved by Gerhard.

Three great square areas surrounded by modillioned cornices occupy the center of the Kirchheim ceiling. These provide a rather more structural sort of organization than the nearly flat panel-work on that at Heiligenberg. Each of the squares has a dished octagon at its center, again surrounded by a modillioned cornice. Within the octagons, Fugger lilies are framed in ovals that alternate with masks in higher relief. The four square panels that surround each of the octagons also carry at their corners bigger and still bolder masks. These are also set in ovals that are here elaborated by scrollwork. Around the edge of the ceiling, above the modillioned cornice at the top of the walls, as also between the big square areas, there are smaller panels. These are, alternately, of square, of circular and of round-ended rectangular shape, but all of them are framed and filled with similar ornament.

Comparison with the detailing of the stucco-work of these years in St. Michael in Munich (Pls. 256-257) appears to confirm that that was designed as well as executed by Gerhard. Exceptionally fine in its own way as is the work of Dietrich at Kirchheim, it does not support the theory that he provided the plans for the Munich church in these same years. His son's work in the 1620s in the Augsburg Rathaus, very late though it is, will be mentioned in the terminal chapter.

The rich decoration in stucco, also of the eighties, in the Weisser Saal at Schloss Wilhelmsburg above Schmalkalden has been mentioned earlier. That room is not comparable in size to the halls at Heiligenberg and Kirchheim, but the Riesensaal (hall of giants) there, occupying almost the whole of the top floor of the east wing, is similar in area. All the same, this is only one storey high, while the great halls just described rise through the equivalent of two full storeys. The painted decoration, probably of the later

---

[74] In its premonitory character and bold scale the Kirchheim portal differs markedly from Dietrich's high altar in St. Michael in Munich (Pls. 254, 256) it should be observed. Its high quality lends some support, however, to the theory he was the original designer of that church.

years of the decade,[75] framing the windows and door-ways in the Riesensaal is of the sort seen in many other interiors in this Schloss that are now occupied by the town's natural history collections. But there are also along the side walls at the top tremendous scrolled consoles carved with strapwork; carried by similarly decorated tapering elements, these provide support for the invisible roof-trusses from which the ceiling is hung.

The wooden ceiling in the Wilhelmsburg Riesensaal is somewhat disappointing by the highest German standards of the day. A broad beam, running from south to north, with two suspended square elements —suggesting that internal piers were originally intended as in the Neuburg Rittersaal and at Rimpar—emphasizes the length and the lowness of the hall by dividing the surface directionally. On either side of that very heavy beam, much flatter ones further subdivide the surface of the ceiling into a sequence of broad square and rectangular panels flanked by narrower ones. The painted decoration on these beams and panels has by now become very faint so that it contrasts both with the excessive brilliance of the restored colors at Heiligenberg and the studied restraint of Dietrich's intarsia of various woods at Kirchheim. However, it would seem that the polychromy on this ceiling was never really consonant either in scale or in vigor of treatment with the painted decoration on the walls. That has, in any case, survived very much better or else has been more plausibly restored.

Of two very large halls in the Schlösser of the Hohenlohes at Weikersheim and at Neuenstein, the first, which occupies the greater part of the two upper storeys of the south wing, dates structurally from the nineties as already noted.[76] It was decorated a little later, however, over the years 1600-1605, still for Count Wolfgang. The other is probably also of early seventeenth-century date but was drastically "restored" by Bodo Ebhardt in 1906. The Weikersheim hall (Pl. 351) accumulated in a short period of years a remarkable—many might consider an excessive—profusion and variety of decoration but the post-war restoration there has been much more discreet. The wooden ceiling, by Elias Gunzenhäuser from Stuttgart, has a regular pattern of alternating large octagons and small squares framed by beam-elements of relatively slight

width and projection. But on these wooden panels Balthasar Katzenberger painted in 1600-1601 neither decorative Italianate arabesques nor Brabantine scrolled strapwork but a series of realistic hunting scenes treated as if they were easel pictures.

Along the walls of the Weikersheim hall, however, at the top of the segmental-headed niches in which the taller rectangular windows are set on both sides, as also around the big oculi over them, there is a great deal of polychromed strapwork in stucco. This is quite in the spirit of the somewhat earlier decoration of the Weisser Saal at Schmalkalden. Being rather coarser, it is more like the pargetting of the nineties in Hardwick Hall in England. All down both sides, moreover, a startling series of life-sized stags reposes in the areas below and between the oculi. Their bodies are in low relief, but their necks and their heads, crowned with real antlers, are fully three-dimensional. In one instance, moreover, above the entrance from the terrace on the north side, a life-size bear seems to be leaping into the hall out of a circular niche framed with strapwork. Below this is inscribed the date 1605. At the ends more exotic or heraldic beasts, including an elephant and a lion, supplement the stags. The craftsmen responsible for this stucco-work were two men from northern Germany, Gerhard Schmidt, who had worked at Wolfenbüttel in 1587 and at Königsberg (Kaliningrad) the year after, and his assistant Christoph Limmerich. Schmidt had come to Weikersheim in 1597 and there decorated in stucco the parapets of the Emporen in the chapel in 1600 as noted earlier. Later stucchi of 1606 by Schmidt also survive in the church at Freudenstadt (Pl. 424) to which attention will be called in the terminal chapter.

At the east end of the Weikersheim hall the main portal of stone is set against the front of a musicians' gallery protected by a later scrolled balustrade (Pl. 351). The heavily molded round arch of this portal is framed by pairs of armored figures and more military references appear in the Classical armor and weapons carved on the frieze of the entablature. Above, the attic contains a big pictorial relief of a battle with foreground figures that are almost freestanding. The relief is flanked by slightly smaller carved figures than the archway below. Over a second richly decorated entablature two rampant lions rest their paws on armorial shields while above, standing on a low podium carved with drums, St. George in the round spears the dragon.

The chimneypiece at the other end of the Weikers-

[75] See Note 20 to Chapter VI.
[76] See Note 50 to Chapter VI. The dimensions of the Weikersheim hall are 38 x 12 meters and 9 meters high; the Neuenstein hall is somewhat smaller.

heim hall is rather similar. The lower rectangular opening is again flanked by three-dimensional figures, some nude, others armoured like those beside the entrance portal. The rather tall over-mantel, corresponding to the attic above that portal, again has a battle scene, here in low relief, and also figures in the round at either side. The true attic here is shallower and capped with a segmental molding over which lions support a crown; the field just below has oval shields of arms surrounded only by scrolled decoration. Beyond the decorated vertical strips that frame it, however, are seated figures with flags. At either side of this chimneypiece the stags of the long side walls give place to what might be called a Hohenlohe "Tree of Jesse," even though inverted, which branches out into innumerable genealogical subdivisions, each indicated by a small shield of arms, from the sides of recumbent figures—Wolfgang on the left, his wife on the right.

In the much more modest Schloss[77] of the counts of Ortenburg, which lies west of Passau and south of Vilshofen on the Danube, one room at the north end has a relatively plain wood-panelled ceiling perhaps dating from the time of Count Joachim von Ortenburg. He acceded in 1559 and, in 1574 and 1575, commissioned from the Regensburg sculptor Hans Petzlinger (†1603) his own tomb and that of Count Anton which survive in the local parish church. To that period could well belong also the fairly simple marble chimneypiece and the marble door-frame here. The faded wall-paintings, however, must be of much later date, perhaps even eighteenth century. This Rittersaal in the deserted Schloss is little remarked because visitors come primarily to see the magnificent ceiling of the Festsaal (Pl. 352), later adapted as a Lutheran chapel, at the top of the south wing.

Neither especially large in area nor more than moderately tall, that hall at Ortenburg—now surrounded on the north and the west by simple, almost makeshift, wooden galleries quite in the "meeting-house" manner—has a ceiling that rivals those commissioned by the Fürstenbergs, the Fuggers and the Hohen-

lohes. This is perhaps not so surprising when one learns that Joachim, though he had become a Protestant in 1563, nonetheless was married to Ursula, Countess Fugger, and the next Ortenburg count, Heinrich, married Anna Jakobea Fugger.

In the center of the oblong field of the Ortenburg ceiling is an oval filled with an armorial shield in high relief. This is flanked by putti and framed with three-dimensional scrollwork. Over that a peacock in all its glory is unexpectedly exquisite in its naturalistic coloring, for the polychromy here, unlike that of the Heiligenberg ceiling, has never been renewed. Otherwise this ceiling, like that at Kirchheim, owes its harmony solely to the intarsia in wood of related tones.

At the four corners of the Ortenburg ceiling dished octagons rise well above the main plane of the ceiling. These are joined to one another and to the central oval by other dished areas of cruciform shape filled with three-dimensional scrollwork. There is thus on the ceiling a very great variety of relief, color and scale from the flat, textile-like patterns on the surface of the relatively large subsidiary panels to the sharp elements projecting downward from the centers of the octagons and the cross-shaped areas, not to speak of the polychromed peacock in the center.

The date of the Ortenburg ceiling is uncertain, but must be not far off 1600: Joachim died in 1600, Heinrich in 1603, so either might have commissioned it, if not so probably one of their widows. Thus it falls within the period of years that saw the erection and the completion of the decoration of the hall at Weikersheim. Whether of the very end of the sixteenth century or of the opening of the seventeenth, such superb decorative work would hardly be equalled in quality before the great Baroque and Rococo halls of the early eighteenth century. Even the considerably later decoration of 1620-1623 in the destroyed Goldener Saal of the Augsburg Rathaus (Pl. 420), projected by Peter Candid and executed by Matthias Kager—both Italian-trained—was really no rival. That, however, may be considered already to initiate the German Baroque in this sort of grand interior some score of years after the hall at Ortenburg and the larger one at Weikersheim were finished.

[77] Reclams *Bayern*, pp. 658-659.

Eight

NORTHERN EUROPE
AND MANNERISM IN THE
EARLY SEVENTEENTH
CENTURY

BEFORE embarking on the principal subject of this chapter, the culminating—if not quite the concluding —phase of Northern Mannerism in Germany, something should be said about the broader European scene in order to place the German episode in relation to better-known aspects of international architectural history in the first quarter of the seventeenth century. At the outset it should be stated that the date 1600 does not mark a major stylistic turning point in northern Europe.[1] In the years that immediately precede and follow the turn of the century no such modulation of architectural design can yet be recognized in the north as was already pregnant, if not yet actually under way, in Italy.[2] There Carlo Maderno in 1598-1603 at least initiated the earliest phase of the Baroque with his facade of Santa Susanna in Rome—or so many scholars, if not Howard Hibbard, have agreed.

However, very soon, by the second decade of the century, when late Northern Mannerism in Germany was approaching its close, a few buildings to which the term "Baroque" can be loosely applied were already in construction in Poland and in the southern Netherlands. Several of these may be briefly discussed here even though they will be a little out of exact chronological sequence. The most famous is the house

that Rubens—often considered the first Baroque painter—designed and built in Antwerp in 1613-1617,[3] just after his return from Italy. This is, all the same, more properly to be considered as Mannerist still, if Italian Mannerist rather than Northern. Even earlier, at least in conception, and more advanced in certain respects was the polygonal pilgrimage church known as the Basiliek at nearby Scherpenheuvel (Montaigu). That was planned and at least begun by a good friend of Rubens, Wencelas Coebergher (1554/1561-1634), in 1609[4] though it was not completed until 1627. The Antwerp-born Coebergher, a pupil of Maerten de Vos, had been active as a painter from 1583 in Paris, in Naples and in Rome. He returned to Antwerp in 1604 ten years before Rubens, becoming architect of the Emperor Rudolf II's brother, the Archduke Albrecht, then viceroy, and his wife Isabella, who succeeded in 1621.

Three other big new churches, two in Antwerp and one in Brussels, may also be mentioned in this connection. The most imposing is the Sint-Carolus Borromeuskerk, erected in 1614-1621[5] by the Jesuit P. Aguilon and Pieter Huÿssens (1577-1637). On the facade of this elements of decoration provided by Rubens survive and it contains no less than three of his major altarpieces. The other Antwerp church is the Sint-Augustinuskerk of 1615-1618.[6] This was designed by Coebergher, like the Scherpenheuvel Basiliek, as was also the somewhat later Sint-Augustinuskerk in Brussels, commissioned by the Archduke Albrecht just before his death in 1621 and completed in 1624. In the Antwerp church a great painting by Rubens again tops the high altar. Despite their altarpieces, Coebergher's other churches are much more

---

[1] This general statement does not apply very well to the France of Henri IV. The political stability he brought allowed a revival of building there after the unproductive reigns of the later Valois; real renewal, all the same, began only under his widow Marie de Médicis.

[2] Some German scholars—mistakenly, one may well believe —used to consider extreme late examples of Northern Mannerism in Germany as approaching the Baroque. In this book certain aspects only of German work of around 1600, and as regards only a few monuments, are associated at all with the succeeding Baroque, usually when those monuments seem premonitory of the mature German Baroque of the later seventeenth and eighteenth centuries rather than the international sort of Baroque based on Roman works of the mid-century.

[3] Baedekers *Benelux*, p. 133. Only Rubens's garden gate and garden-house survive; the rest has been rebuilt.
[4] *Ibid.*, pp. 84-85.
[5] *Ibid.*, p. 132.
[6] *Ibid.*, p. 134.

debatably Baroque than his Basiliek, particularly as regards their basilican interiors; the similar interior of the Jesuits' church in Antwerp was, in any case, completely renewed after a fire in the eighteenth century. Now the story should return to Germany.

For all the local precedent which the Order's grand church in Munich provided—itself quite probably more dependent on northern than on Italian sources —the Jesuits in Germany rarely evinced in the early seventeenth century that respect for Roman models, whether of the late sixteenth century or contemporary, which is often evident in other countries both in the south and in the north of Europe. A notable, if exceptional, example in the north is the Gesù-like church of the Jesuits at Kraków in Poland, planned by P. Giuseppe Briccio, S.J., in 1596 and built in 1605-1619[7] by Giovanni Trevano, with *stucchi* of 1619-1633 by G. B. Falconi. However, their biggest German church of this period, Mariä Himmelfahrt in Cologne (Pl. 452), begun as late as 1618, is even more Gothic— or at least *Nachgotik*—than their Petrikirche in Münster (Pl. 261) of the 1590s. So also, just before that, was the modest Jesuitenkirche of 1613-1617[8] at Koblenz on the Rhine of which only the west front survived the last war. Moreover, the rather grander pilgrimage church of St. Michael at Violau (Fig. 58), northeast of Augsburg in Swabia, though not built for the Jesuits, follows in cross-section the mediaeval hall-church model. This was erected in 1617-1619 by David and Georg Höbel and consecrated in 1620.[9] The later investiture of Rococo *stucchi* and frescoes, however, dating from the mid-eighteenth century, quite disguises today the interior.

It was the Hofkirche at Neuburg-a.-d.-Donau (Pl. 436), begun in 1607 as a Protestant edifice though completed after 1614 for the Jesuits, which seems to have provided more definitely than the Order's St. Michael in Munich the usual precedent for the Baroque church-architecture of the next two centuries in Germany. The Neuburg church will be described at some length in the terminal chapter.

In German secular work there were two other sty-

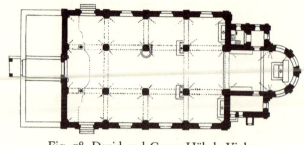

Fig. 58. David and Georg Höbel: Violau, St. Michael, plan, 1617-19

listic currents, neither of them either *Nachgotik* or early Baroque, that dominated architectural design in the opening decades of the seventeenth century. The less novel of these was a special sort of late Northern Mannerism parallel to, rather than derivative from, what was then being built in Holland. There the long continuance of the armistice with Spain and the increasing prosperity the uneasy peace had brought were notably encouraging ambitious architectural production.[10] In Germany Late Northern Mannerism was often much more escalated in scale, however, and carried even on churches to extremes of plastic fantasy hardly to be matched in Holland. The alternative was a new kind of disciplined design[11] similar to what Inigo Jones was soon introducing into England and, a decade later, Jacob van Campen (1595-1657) into Holland.[12] No Germans were so humbly dependent as they on Palladio and Scamozzi, however.

On the Mannerist side, the engravings published in the nineties (Pl. 355) by Dietterlin exerted a major influence internationally for two decades and more beyond his death in 1599, and not least in Germany. However, Dietterlin himself was less an architect even than Vredeman or Cornelis Floris; primarily, at least in his early maturity, he was a painter of external quadratura frescoes. Those he executed in the mid-seventies on the former Jesuit College in Strasbourg were reputedly still somewhat in the manner of the Holbeins. Later he was more concerned with various aspects of interior decoration than with building projects. Thus there was mention earlier of the vast coved ceiling he painted in the nineties in the Stuttgart Lustspielhaus (Pl. 284).

The first part of Dietterlin's *Architectura* was issued as early as 1593 while he was employed in Stuttgart, as has been noted. It was followed by the publica-

---

[7] Łozinski-Miłobedzki, *Guide*, pp. 118-119; Knox, *Poland*, pl. 14. An earlier exception would have been the Jesuits' modest church, St. Paulus in Regensburg, an existing edifice remodelled by an Italian beginning in 1591: Braun, *Jesuiten*, I, p. 1; II, pp. 105-109, fig. 11 (plan). Braun, p. 107, writes ". . . sie war kaum viel mehr als ein schlichte Nutzbau." St. Paulus was largely rebuilt after 1715 and destroyed in 1809, so its possible relevance here cannot be checked.

[8] Reclams *Rheinlande und Westfalen*, p. 300.

[9] Dehio, *Östliches Schwaben*, p. 36.

[10] See Hitchcock, *Scrolled Gables*, chapters VI, VIII.

[11] See Note 2 to Chapter IX.

[12] See Hitchcock, *Scrolled Gables*, chapter VII.

tion of the second part in Strasbourg the next year. But the most significant date for the proliferation of Dietterlin's plates of heavily ornamented architectural features—there are in all over 200—is 1598. That was when the second edition,[13] with much additional material, was brought out in Nürnberg the year before his death. The Dietterlin influence modified and eventually supplanted that of Vredeman's publications, even though one of those came out as late as 1601. A generation earlier, in the seventies, at least three were issued. Another is dated 1583, not long before Vredeman's influence reached its peak. Moreover, there seem to have been undated editions and collections of designs as well.[14] He himself kept turning up not only around the Netherlands but also in various other places in northern Europe. Little or nothing survives of his decorative work, however, or else it has not yet been disentangled from what others borrowed from his plates.

Certain works, on the other hand, that the city-architect of Augsburg, Elias Holl (1573-1646), began to build there and outside Eichstätt (Pls. 405, 406) around 1510 make evident a significant shift away from Northern Mannerism was under way in Germany. Several crucial dates of construction may be noted here though detailed descriptions of the various buildings involved follow only in the next chapter. The shift was already incipient a few years earlier in the design of the demolished Augsburg Siegel Haus (Seal House: i.e. where the city's seal was kept), particularly the side elevation, opposite the Fuggerhäuser in the Weinmarkt, and the surviving *Wertachsbruckertor* (Wertach bridge gate) (Pls. 400, 403) in the circuit of the city's walls. These were both erected in 1605, a few years after construction of the east front of the Zeughaus started in 1602 but before its completion in 1607 and the erection of the south facade of the *Stadtmetzg* (city slaughterhouse or, more accurately here, butchers' guildhall) in 1609. These two especially important monuments of this period in Augsburg are both happily extant. All four of these signal commissions were carried out by Holl for the city

authorities. But, in the case of the Zeughaus, the Siegel Haus and even the rather more advanced Stadtmetzg, he was executing designs provided by the Swiss-born but Italian-trained painter Joseph Heintz (1564-1609).[15]

Even more novel at this point than the facade of the Stadtmetzg is the severity of those of Schloss Willibaldsburg outside Eichstätt (Pls. 406, 407). The portion of that known as the Gemmingenbau was designed in or around 1609 by Holl without assistance from Heintz and carried out over the next ten years by Johann Alberthal. It is not irrelevant that the latter is sometimes known as Giovanni II Albertalli. He was possibly born, like his father Pietro, in the Italian-Swiss Grigioni rather than in Eichstätt where he was trained by the father. There Pietro had long been employed by successive prince-bishops. From that time on, Holl in Augsburg and Alberthal at Eichstätt, at Dillingen, at Neuburg and elsewhere, not to speak of others—most notably the younger Jakob Wolff at Nürnberg down to his early death in 1620—continued to follow this line even for a few years after the beginning of the Thirty Years' War in 1618. In the same way John Webb and Roger Pratt, it might be recalled, continued to work in Jones's Anglo-Palladian manner well beyond the outbreak of the so much shorter Civil War in England in the 1640s and fifties.

Well through the second decade of the century the two quite different types of design—one still late Northern Mannerist and the opposing sort of which Holl was the most productive practitioner—flourished in Germany. That both could sometimes have had the support of the same clients, and even in the same years, must seem surprising because of their contradictory character. As already mentioned, for example, Ernst von Holstein-Schaumburg commissioned in 1608 from the Italian-Swiss Nosseni the distinctly Academic family mausoleum behind the parish church at Stadthagen. Two years later some other architect—certainly German and most probably Hans Wolff from nearby Hildesheim—began for him the Bückeburg Stadtkirche of which the facade (Pl. 435) is the grandest work ever carried out in the Dietterlin vein. The year 1615 saw both the completion of this church, with its font by the Italian-trained Netherlander Adriaen de Fries of this same date, and that sculptor's model for the figural group on Ernst's tomb in the mausoleum (Pl. 442) that he executed a few years later in 1618-20.

---

[13] Reprint: W. Dietterlin, *The Fantastic Engravings . . .* , A. K. Placzek, ed., New York, 1968.

[14] Most of this Vredeman material exists in the Print Collection of the Metropolitan Museum of Art in New York, though much of it was photographed for use here in the Royal Library in The Hague.

It should perhaps be recalled here that 1577 was the year the inhabitants of Antwerp rebelled against Spanish rule though that rule was soon renewed.

[15] See Note IX, 11; see also Note V, 8.

German writers of previous generations often considered the facade of the Bückeburg church and, with somewhat more justice, the one designed by Heintz and begun in 1602 by Holl which fronts the Augsburg Zeughaus (Pl. 399) to be already Baroque. The Northern Mannerism of the later sixteenth and early seventeenth centuries in Germany was much admired and imitated in the decades following 1870 under the new empire. But such architecture was hardly then recognized as representing a specific international phase of style. Rather, thanks to contemporary nationalism, it was vaunted as a specifically Germanic or Teutonic one, seen as distinguishable from the imported Early Renaissance mode, obviously Italian in origin, of the early decades of the sixteenth century throughout northern Europe, which is roughly true. In fact, it seems to have been the opposing Academic current that led the way, already early in the new century, toward the eventual triumph of the Baroque in Germany. That triumph came, of course, only a good deal later, well after the Thirty Years' War was over.

It will, therefore, be more intelligible stylistically, though inaccurate chronologically, if the work of the first quarter of the seventeenth century is not, like that of earlier decades, presented here in a single year-by-year sequence. This chapter, for the most part, deals rather with the bulk of characteristic late Northern Mannerist secular production in German lands. There are also occasional references to work elsewhere in the north. It is only in the next chapter that the almost precisely contemporary manifestations of the other sort of design—the sort here loosely called Academic—in the secular work of such northerners as Heintz, Holl and Wolf who knew the contemporary production of Italy at first hand, will be described and discussed. Certain prominent buildings elsewhere in northern Europe which seem to have been equally or more premonitory will also be mentioned. The terminal chapter however deals, in recurrent comparisons, both with the major late Northern Mannerist churches—not discussed at this point in the narrative —and with the notable contributions to church architecture of the Swiss-born Heintz and that other architect Johann Alberthal, who was also Swiss, at least in origin, but like Nosseni Italian-Swiss. Thus detailed accounts of the two major Protestant churches in Germany, at Wolfenbüttel and at Bückeburg (Pls. 433, 435), both begun in the first decade of the century, can be paralleled with analysis of contemporary monuments that illustrate a quite different and more advanced international current in architectural design. Moreover, the Wolfenbüttel Marienkirche and the Bückeburg Stadtkirche do not, in fact, even slightly resemble the other Mannerist works initiated for the very same Welf and Schaumburg clients in these years which are described in this present chapter. Yet the architects each employed for both their churches and their secular commissions may well, in the two cases, have been either the same or at least very closely related.

In size and magnificence it is rather with the other big new churches of the day, both Protestant and Catholic, that these structures range. Among the former, some of the most prominent still follow the model provided by the Jesuits' Petrikirche of the nineties at Münster. Thus they are examples of *Nachgotik*. This, in their case, is not so much a survival of *Sondergotik* as a sort of premature, though more generic, revival. By contrast, other churches that are more in the line of descent from the Klagenfurt Münster and St. Michael in Munich may rather be considered to be on the way, at least, towards the Baroque.

An account of the later German secular architecture of the Northern Mannerist sort may well begin with some description of several of the new or, more frequently, rebuilt and enlarged Schlösser of the early decades of the seventeenth century. Schloss-building, it would seem, was pursued less energetically now than in the last decades of the sixteenth century. But most of the great building families, such as the Wittelsbachs of Bavaria and of the Palatinate, the Saxon Wettins of both the Albertine and the Ernestine lines, the Brunswick Welfs, the dukes of Württemberg, the Hohenlohes, the Schaumburgs and, among prelates, Julius Echter, prince-bishop of Würzburg, continued their activities; these activities were, moreover, rivalled by those of others of Julius's ilk at Aschaffenburg and at Eichstätt. The paragraphs in the previous chapter devoted to the Festsaal at Schloss Weikersheim, which was completed in 1605, extended into the new century the story of the building production of Count Wolfgang von Hohenlohe who lived, indeed, until 1607. At another Hohenlohe Schloss, Neuenstein, Heinrich Schickhardt from Stuttgart, assisted by the local architect Georg Kern (born 1583), finished in much the same years the remodelling and enlargement an earlier Hohenlohe, Count Ludwig Casimir, had begun in the 1560s.

At Langenburg,[16] a third Hohenlohe Schloss, the court dated from the fifteenth century but was rebuilt for Count Wolfgang in 1583-1586. All the conspicuous features there (Pl. 356), however: the two-stage gables, the colonnaded galleries, and the corbelled balconies, were added by Wolfgang's successor Philipp Ernst a good deal later in 1610-1616. For this work he employed the Thuringian architect Jakob Kauffmann. Kauffmann seems to have been involved in some capacity, doubtless rather minor, before this in 1595 with the extension of Weikersheim for Wolfgang. At Langenburg, where the gables are as prominent as at Weikersheim, these are flanked in both their stages by bold C-scrolls, yet the scrolls terminate in small fluted lunettes of distinctly earlier character. It is unlikely, all the same, that the gables go back thirty years or so to the 1580s, before Kauffmann came to Langenburg, since they are topped by little onions rather than plain stone balls.

More exceptional in the court at Langenburg than either the not unfamiliar sort of cross-gables or the two storeys of conventional arcades is the pierced parapet that extends around all four sides at main-storey level crowning, on one side only, a range of plain round arches below. This parapet is visually most striking where it is not interrupted by the columns of the gallery but fronts an open balcony carried on very heavy stone brackets. The balcony was evidently introduced to provide continuous circulation at this level. In particular, the identical parapeted balconies, twice repeated across the narrow end of the court on the upper storeys, produce a boldly vertical composition of voids not matched elsewhere in the court of a Renaissance Schloss.

Count, later Prince, Ernst von Holstein-Schaumburg—a brother-in-law of Wilhelm der Weise of Hesse, who had been responsible for the Wilhelmsburg at Schmalkalden—more than rivalled as a builder in these early decades of the seventeenth century his contemporary Wolfgang von Hohenlohe and the latter's successor Philipp Ernst. The Schaumburg church of 1610-1615 at Bückeburg and the Mausoleum at the earlier family seat, Stadthagen, which Ernst commissioned in 1608 and began the next year to erect behind the parish church of St. Martin, are in their contrasting ways more considerable productions than anything at Neuenstein or Langenburg, if not the great hall at Weikersheim. The one is perhaps the culminating work of late Northern Mannerism, as already suggested; the other, though commissioned two years earlier, is one of the first and finest examples of the new sort of Academic design. These will be discussed at length in the next chapter along with other contemporary churches of comparable importance.

Ernst von Schaumburg's secular work at Bückeburg was not as considerable as that undertaken by Wolfgang von Hohenlohe at Weikersheim and Philipp Ernst at Langenburg though, as regards interiors, it was even more sumptuous than the former. Some civic building, however, also went on at this time in the town of Stadthagen: Johann Schwartze's oriel on the end of the Rathaus, for example, emulating Johann Robin's of 1596 beside it, carries the date 1612, as was noted earlier. The handsome stone house-front at Markt 4, with its scrolled gable, is perhaps of a year or two before that.[17] In the Schloss, on the other hand, there survives from this period only one chimney-piece, dated 1604, in the so-called "Fürst-Ernst-Zimmer" at the southwest corner. This is carved with a relief of the Triumph of Bacchus based on a Georg Pencz print of 1528 but has little of the extravagance of Ernst's contemporary work at Bückeburg.

It was in Bückeburg he left a real mark on the Schloss.[18] Very extensive construction of a still later date there—the eastern block of 1732 and the quadrants facing it of 1894-98—mask what was erected for Count Otto in 1560-1563. Otto's builder, Heinrich Schrader from Stadthagen, worked here in the manner of Unkair, one of whose assistants he had probably been on the earlier Schaumburg commission of the thirties at Stadthagen. Ernst's emendations in the opening years of the next century, however, were largely confined to the interior. In the chapel (Pl. 359), which was redecorated over the years 1603-1608, the Gothic vaults were retained but completely covered, like the walls, with painted decoration incorporating quadratura details taken from Dietterlin's plates.[19] The carved and gilded reredos and the altar of 1606 in front of it, as well as the balancing compo-

[16] Dehio, *Baden-Württemberg*, p. 275; [R. Schlauch] *Langenburg in Hohenlohe*, 4th ed. [Gerabronn, 1965] pp. 20-36. Merian, *Schönsten Schlösser*, pl. opp. p. 19, shows the whole of the Langenburg Schloss in the landscape with its five towers and one big gable on the exterior.

[17] Kreft-Soenke, *Weserrenaissance*, p. 282.

[18] *Ibid.*, 237-239; J. Habich, *Die künstlerische Gestaltung der Residenz Bückeburg . . .*, Bückeburg, 1969 (henceforth cited as Habich, *Residenz Bückeburg*).

[19] Habich, *op. cit.*, pp. 80-135; pls. 17-44b provides many

sition that fills the west end—all executed by the sons of Ebbert I Wulff from Hildesheim and more particularly, it is probable, by Ebbert II (†c.1608)—are only the most conspicuous of the interpolated fittings. These are by far the richest of the period in northern Europe, more than rivalling the earlier ones at Lutheran Celle and Catholic Heiligenberg (Pls. 207, 265). Like the chapel at Celle, this was Protestant though that is hard to believe!

Ernst's Bückeburg chapel, in its turn, is outclassed by the sculptured portal (Pl. 357) in his Goldener Saal.[20] As a whole, however, the hall is disappointing, for it lacks the great dimensions and, like that at Schmalkalden, the tall proportions of those at Kirchheim, Heiligenberg and Weikersheim. The flat wall decorations, moreover, suggesting wallpaper, must date almost in their entirety from the restoration carried out in the late nineteenth century. But the portal, as glitteringly gold and white because of that restoration as when it was new, shows that the Wulffs, in this case probably Ebbert II and Jonas (†1618/1619), were late Mannerist artists of a very high rank. Against a three-dimensional setting as fantastic and indescribable as any design published by Dietterlin (Pl. 355)—and largely based once more on his plates—nearly life-size statues of Mars and Venus, related to works by Giovanni da Bologna, flank the actual door; while above, at half-scale, a Mercury even more directly derived from the Italian sculptor's than the Mars leaps into the hall. The paintings on the ceiling by Hans Rottenhammer (1564-1625) from Munich, who had returned from Italy to Augsburg in 1606, are perhaps a decade later in date and by no means of equal interest.

The portal in the Bückeburg Goldener Saal, after all, like what was carried out in the chapel, is decoration not architecture and the work of sculptors, not of men who were experienced at architectural design. Of the same years that saw first, probably, the beginning of the elaboration of the interior of the chapel in 1603 and then, in 1604-1605, the execution of the Goldener Saal are the three contiguous structures (Pl. 358) that Ernst had built facing the marketplace in order to provide an honorific approach to the Schloss. The fantasy of the new decorations inside the Schloss is here somewhat tempered, but there is no

approach to the Academic severity of the Stadthagen mausoleum as begun for Ernst by Nosseni only a few years afterward. Academic design appears first at Bückeburg in the modest Rentenkammer, but this long low block inside the grounds of the Schloss, with a range of engaged Tuscan columns on the ground storey, dates probably from after 1610.[21]

On the gateway[22] of 1605-1607 in the center of the group of buildings in Bückeburg at the entrance to the grounds of the Schloss, the Ionic columns carrying the bold ressauts of the entablature are flanked by flatter decorative members similar to what the Spanish call *estípites*, a motif recurrent in Dietterlin's engraved plates. Above, between balls and obelisks, a broken S-curved pediment carries two dragons against the sky, both gazing fiercely upward at a figure that is perhaps Bellona. Quite different in its delicate all-over carved decoration, so flat that it suggests peasant embroidery, is the little two-bayed Kammerkasse or *Rentenamt* (rent-office)[23] of 1609-1610—not the same as the Rentenkammer inside the grounds—on the right (Pl. 360). This is capped, not with a gable, but by a flattened domical roof, actually a sort of broad, square *welsche Haube*. In its elegance and almost total lack of familiar architectural elements the rent-office resembles a little the Münchhausen oriel at Rinteln (Pl. 217) of half a century earlier and, even more, the remarkable gable of Haus Thienhausen (Pl. 317), at Sommerzell between Horn and Höxter, which is also dated 1609.

The larger Kanzlei to the left of the entrance gateway at Bückeburg (Pl. 358) is plainer and more conventional in design but no more Academic. Low arches on squat imposts run around the base below a tall first storey lighted by large rectangular windows with central mullions. The broad gable, rising in three stages over the front, has pilaster-strips that are banded, like those on the smaller Kammerkasse, in the typical Weserrenaissance manner with chip-carved blocks. These pilasters are associated in the two lower stages with flattened entablatures. The edges of all three stages have a succession of S-scrolls, mostly with out-flipping ends, and small obelisks; while a central oculus and, over it, a lunette of a rather early sort, somewhat like those at Langenburg, elaborate the terminal element.

Ernst lived until 1622, but except for the mauso-

---

examples of direct copying of Dietterlin's engravings in the interiors in the Bückeburg Schloss.

[20] *Ibid.*, pp. 147-161, pls. 50-55. The plates again illustrate specific sources for various details in the Bückeburg great hall in the plates of Dietterlin's *Architectura*.

[21] *Ibid.*, p. 71, pl. 9.
[22] *Ibid.*, pp. 62-69.
[23] *Ibid.*, pp. 69-71.

leum, which was not completed until after his death, his building activity all falls in the first decade and a half of the century. Another great Protestant church at Wolfenbüttel, however, was actually begun in 1607/8 before his major work here in Bückeburg, the Stadtkirche, was erected in 1610-15.

A younger contemporary of Ernst von Schaumburg, Heinrich Julius, duke of Brunswick-Wolfenbüttel, was as ambitious a builder as he and, as has been indicated, a more interesting personality. His principal architectural monument, the Haupt- or Marienkirche in Wolfenbüttel (Pls. 431-433), though far from complete at the time of his death in 1613, overshadowed even more than Ernst's at Bückeburg other construction there of the period and will be discussed together with the latter in the next chapter. The same architect, Paul Francke, was responsible for the notable Juleum he built earlier at Helmstedt (Pl. 333).

Like Ernst at Bückeburg, Heinrich Julius inherited a Schloss that had been partly rebuilt, in this case first by Francesco Chiaramella in and after 1558 (Fig. 26) and then more extensively, over the years 1569-1575, by Francke.[24] Even less sixteenth-century work is now visible here than at the Bückeburg Schloss because of the drastic late seventeenth- and eighteenth-century remodelling which covered the whole exterior, including the walls of the court, with stucco. However, Francke's tall *Hausmannsturm* (keep), dominating this enormous but extremely dull Schloss, was probably projected by Heinrich Julius but erected only after his death in 1613 for his successor Friedrich Ulrich. The tower is of stone, unlike the rest of the Schloss which had always been, like most of the houses in the town, timber-framed. Carried up from a mediaeval—perhaps thirteenth-century—base, only the great height of Francke's tower and the elaborate ironwork crowning the *chemin de ronde* make it impressive today.

Except for the church that Francke began here at Wolfenbüttel in 1608, his principal surviving work of these decades is the Zeughaus[25] across the Schlossplatz from the Schloss (Pl. 362). This was begun just before the Hausmannsturm in 1613. Carried forward by Friedrich Ulrich, it has on the portal the date 1619 when it was completed four years after Francke's death. Broad gables at the ends and, along the flank, three tall cross-gables—identical as regards their upper

stages to those at the ends—produce a characteristic edifice of the period. This has, however, little of Francke's vividly personal style as that is seen in the Juleum at Helmstedt (Pl. 333) and the Stadtkirche here (Pls. 431-433). The Zeughaus is built, not of Fachwerk like the Schloss, but of stucco-covered rubble. Cut-stone trim is restricted on the main walls, as on the tower across the way, to plain, long-and-short chains of rustication at the corners. Similar rustication, rather than pilasters, frames all four stages of the gables.

Francke paired his rectangular windows throughout the exterior of the Zeughaus except in the upper stages of the gables. The extreme simplicity and total regularity of this fenestration contrasts with the rather coarse scrolling, executed in cut stone, that scallops the outlines of the gables. The scrolls have tightly rolled ends, with "horns" only on the third and fourth stages. However, the surfaces of these stages are elaborated by decorative elements in relief and tall finials topping the upper scrolls accent the skyline.

Another Protestant prince much addicted, like his predecessors, to building was Duke Friedrich of Württemberg who founded Freudenstadt in 1599. He died, however, in 1608 well before Heinrich Julius and Ernst von Schaumburg. Of the various works his court-architect Heinrich Schickhardt undertook for him in Stuttgart and elsewhere late in his life after 1600, very little of consequence now survives except for the churches at Freudenstadt in the Schwarzwald and at Montbéliard in France, where Friedrich was count of Mömpelgard—to give the enclave its German name—which will both be discussed in the next chapter. At Tübingen, however, the outer gate to the Schloss (Pl. 361), dated 1606,[26] is a masterpiece. Not designed by Schickhardt, who was never much of an ornamentalist, this was executed either by Christoph Jelin, a Tübingen stone-carver who had worked earlier on the Lusthaus in Stuttgart, or by Hans Braun, also from Stuttgart. Possibly it was the invention of one of the Württemberg craftsmen happily inspired by Vredeman's engravings. Hardly reflecting that source, however, is the relative correctness of the Doric order of the engaged columns and the faint suggestion of a Roman triumphal arch. But, below under-scaled fluting, the lower halves of the shafts of the columns are covered with flat strapwork. Above, around Friedrich's arms—which are set in the English Garter, of which he had been the proud recipient—a

[24] Karpa, *Wolfenbüttel*, pp. 14-15; see also Note IV 2.
[25] *Ibid.*, p. 16.

[26] Fleischhauer, *Württemberg*, pp. 295-297.

broad cadenza of three-dimensional strapwork is flanked by the freestanding figures of two soldiers, one with a gun and the other with a flag. The wall of the bastion against which all this decoration backs is very plain, though two little boxes of stone are cantilevered out at the corners on boldly carved egg-and-dart and other moldings.

With this Tübingen portal—over-restored in the present century, alas—may be compared two others of the period, now in better condition, that are less extreme examples of Northern Mannerism. The fortification of Wülzburg, which lies between Nürnberg and Eichstätt, was first undertaken in 1588[27] for the Margrave Georg Friedrich of Brandenburg-Kulmbach by the elder Blasius Berwart. Berwart, who came from Stuttgart, had been employed earlier, it will be recalled, by the margrave on the Plassenburg at Kulmbach together with Alberlin Tretsch, also from Stuttgart, in the 60's. He had then been active at Königsberg (Kaliningrad) in East Prussia and may have returned there in the nineties. The work at Wülzburg continued beyond 1600, however. The pentagonal lay-out, with sharp-pointed corner bastions, is a model of advanced organization in the construction of fortresses at the end of the sixteenth century. The portal is an equally notable example of contemporary architectural design, dating most probably from just after 1600. The designer may have been either Gideon Bacher, in charge here until 1601, or more likely his successor, the younger Blasius Berwart. A son of the elder Berwart, he had probably been briefly employed before this at Ansbach under Bacher in 1597[28] on the margrave's Kanzlei and on the west tower of St. Gumbert. A likelier possibility, however, is Georg Ridinger (born 1568) from Strasbourg, who started working for Georg Friedrich, with or under Bacher, at Ansbach in 1595 even before the younger Berwart and may have been associated with Bacher from 1599 at Wülzburg. There is at least some similarity here to the portals of Schloss Johannisburg at Aschaffenburg which Ridinger began to build in 1605.

Whoever was the designer, the heavy columns on this gateway at Wülzburg, arranged in triplets, are banded like the arch at the center with more than

Sanmichelian boldness. The Doric order is very correct in its proportions, from the podia below to the cornice above, even if somewhat coarse in execution. However, over the central bays a sort of *estípites*, quite like those on the gateway at Bückeburg (Pl. 358), carry a second entablature. These flank rusticated arches within which are carved elaborate armorial achievements. The resultant contrast between the Northern Mannerist character of the upper storey and the Academic design of the lower one somewhat parallels the mixed style of Joseph Heintz's facade, begun in 1602 by Elias Holl, on the Zeughaus in Augsburg (Pl. 399), which must be almost precisely contemporary. A far more important work historically, since it initiated a major stylistic modulation, this facade will be discussed in detail in the next chapter.

At Würzburg, Prince-Bishop Julius Echter continued building down to his death in 1617. Since 1578, at least, he had gradually been turning the mediaeval fortress on the Marienberg,[29] across the Main from the city, into something approaching a Renaissance palace. Later destruction, unfortunately, has made it difficult to appreciate what his "palace" was really like in its prime. Among the various features that do survive, however, one of the best preserved is the portal of the outworks (Pl. 363), built the same year 1606 as that at Tübingen. This is of similarly mixed design but much cruder than the latter or even the one at Wülzburg. Particularly after 1610, various considerably larger works than this gateway, undertaken at several of the major Residenzschlösser, illustrate a comparable stylistic ambiguity.

The Wittelsbach duke of Bavaria, Maximilian, who succeeded Wilhelm V in 1597, and also his relatives, the Electors Palatine Friedrich IV and Friedrich V—whose electorship he acquired in 1623 after the defeat of the last as "Winter King" of Bohemia—more than maintained the building traditions of their forebears in the early decades of the seventeenth century, at least down to Friedrich V's debacle in the earliest stage of the Thirty Years' War. Maximilian went on building in the diluted and somewhat Germanized Italian Mannerist mode associated with Frederik Sustris whom his predecessor had been employing. Indeed, Sustris himself survived until 1599. Of the other two, Friedrich IV preferred a much more northern sort of design, but his successor Friedrich V turned

[27] Reclams *Bayern*, pp. 933-934.
[28] As often elsewhere in northern Europe in this period, the names mentioned in documents confuse rather than clarify the question of authorship; while the stylistic evidence provided by a single gate such as the one at Wülzburg is rather limited.

[29] M. H. von Freeden, *Festung Marienberg*, Würzburg, 1952.

early to the Academic on his return from England in 1613.

Neither Maximilian nor Friedrich IV employed architects of any great originality. Maximilian, however, kept on doggedly with the transformation of the Munich Residenz into a Renaissance palace. That programme Egckl had begun for Albrecht V in the sixties; after a hiatus, Sustris then carried on more concertedly for Wilhelm V in the eighties and nineties after the latter's accession in 1579. Finally, Maximilian concluded the work considerably more successfully than Echter was able to do at the Marienberg if with little more distinction.

There is some question whether structures so very Italianate and so little Northern Mannerist as what Maximilian sponsored should be discussed at this point rather than in the next chapter. Yet what resulted does not, for the most part, exemplify the new German Academic mode very well either—if, indeed, the client and his designers actually intended that it should. Such an intention is not very likely even though all of them—client and architects alike—presumably knew the prominent buildings Heintz and Holl were then designing and erecting in Augsburg, and perhaps the Willibaldsburg at Eichstätt. Neither Augsburg nor Eichstätt were far away from Munich in neighboring Swabia.

It was Maximilian who built the conspicuous wing on the western edge of the Residenz complex. The very long facade of this still extends along the present-day Residenzstrasse (Pl. 365). However, the construction of that only followed after the creation of the Kapellenhof to the north of Sustris's Grottenhof (Fig. 44). Associated with that small court were the *Hofkapelle* (court chapel), begun in 1601 but much broadened in 1630, and the Reiche Kapelle, consecrated in 1607.[30] The long half-octagon-ended Brunnenhof (Pl. 364) is of c.1610.[31] In its center stands the

elaborate Wittelsbach Fountain of 1611-1614. That was designed and executed by Hubert Gerhard, the Dutch-born sculptor of the Sustris team, who had worked at Kirchheim in the nineties for Hans Fugger as well as at St. Michael here in Munich, and his workshop. This Brunnenhof runs along the northeastern flank of the Antiquarium, where the interior decoration planned by Sustris had finally been completed by Peter Candid and others only in 1600, just after Sustris's death.

The west wing of the Munich Residenz with its facade on the present Residenzstrasse was not initiated until 1612.[32] This portion of the work was followed in 1613-1615 by the considerable addition of four more wings to enclose another court, the Kaiserhof, to the east of the range along the street and to the north of the Kapellenhof (Fig. 44). Inaccessible today, in the range on the north side of this court, which is only now being restored, is the monumental staircase, known as the *Kaisertreppe*. That once led up to the great rooms called the Kaisersaal and the Vierschimmelsaal where Maximilian received the Emperor Ferdinand II on his visit to Munich after his accession in 1619.

These consecutive constructions of Maximilian's in the second decade of the seventeenth century run all the way from the west end of Leo von Klenze's Königsbau of the mid-1820s, which fronts on the present Max-Joseph-Platz, to the same architect's even longer and more varied Festsaalbau on the north which faces the Hofgarten and masks the north wing of the Kaiserhof. What Maximilian built is impressive today chiefly because of its great extent, however, and must always have been somewhat incoherent in organization. Moreover, campaigns of remodelling and redecoration under Maximilian's successor, the Elector Ferdinand Maria, in the later seventeenth century and again under Max Emanuel, Karl Albrecht and Max III Joseph in the early and mid-18th century left few interiors untouched. Finally in the last war both interiors and exteriors suffered very seriously and restoration, as has been noted, is still far from complete. The facade toward the Residenzstrasse and those that surround the Brunnenhof are already in good, if renewed, shape as also the walls of the Kaiserhof, but

[30] Lieb, *München*, pp. 99-102. The Reiche Kapelle was destroyed in 1944. Lieb's plate on p. 101—from a prewar photograph—illustrates the interior with both real marble and *Stuckmarmor* (scagliola) intarsia on the walls and delicate *stucchi* with much gilding on the vault. The interior of the Hofkapelle has been restored as of 1630: *ibid.*, pl. opp. p. 109.

[31] *Ibid.*, pp. 103-104. It is not clear why the restorers of the Munich Residenz have painted the date 1540 on the northern gable in the Brunnenhof. The scrolls, exceptionally flaccid and extended, on the sloping sides of this gable and its mate at the other end might be noted. Their timid character em-

phasizes how little elaborate gables with bold multiple scrolling of the Weserrenaissance sort were ever acceptable in Munich.

[32] *Ibid.*, pp. 104-108.

not yet the once magnificent Kaisertreppe and associated rooms to which it provided access.

Eighteenth-century prints of the Munich Residenz (Pl. 365) show what appears to be a monumental near-Academic facade on the west side of the Residenz extending all along the present-day Residenzstrasse. The giant order indicated as set against a rusticated wall seems already in these views to prefigure the well-known early Baroque facade, begun as late as 1664 by Abraham Leuthner von Grundt, on the Černin Palace in Prague. But the giant order and the rustication were in fact only quadratura paintwork on a stuccoed brick wall; while tall gables with single pairs of bold scrolls below segmental pediments rather than Academic hipped roofs then terminated the northern range which was eventually masked in the 19th century by Klenze's Festsaalbau.

Klenze did not touch the western facade which extends monotonously for thirty-six identical bays. This has been re-stuccoed since the war and the quadratura decoration repainted, doubtless with basic accuracy. The focal features, two portals and a niche executed in red marble and elaborated with sculpture, all survive, but the whole is dry and dull today. Perhaps it always was even though the sculpture is more proto-Baroque than Mannerist in its derivation from Giovanni da Bologna. Between the two big portals that rise to left and right through the two lower storeys, the high-placed niche in the center holds the most considerable adornment, a famous statue: the Virgin as *Patrona Bavariae*, which is dated 1616. This is by Hans Krumpper, and the portals are doubtless of his design also. More modestly scaled but similarly restored, is the Brunnenhof (Pl. 364) where Gerhard's large and complex fountain with its profusion of figural statuary is also very Italianate, though in a more delicate and rather Cellinian way. Gerhard may have been involved in other ways also as he was earlier at St. Michael.

It is harder to characterize the architecture than the sculpture of Maximilian's additions to the Munich Residenz, though it does appear somewhat proto-Baroque, at least in the old views, as has already been suggested. There is also considerable uncertainty as to who was responsible for the general design of the work carried out over the years 1600-1616. Of what was done earliest, before 1612, very little is recognizable in the present state of the Residenz. Sustris, of course, had died in 1599; but Peter Candid, even though he had left Wilhelm's service as early as 1595, actually lived until 1628 and may well have continued

to advise those in immediate charge of the project whenever he was in Munich. The most identifiable of the men who supervised the construction was Hans Krumpper, Sustris's son-in-law, who was named *Fürstliche Baumeister* by Maximilian in 1613, though he probably had already succeeded to some of his father-in-law's broader professional responsibilities much earlier on Sustris's death in 1599. Moreover, it was certainly he, as has already been noted, not Gerhard who provided the statue of Virgin in the niche at the center of the western facade as well, probably, as the design for the two widely spaced portals to either side of it. Krumpper, because of his position, probably at least supervised also the execution after 1612 of Gerhard's Wittelsbach Fountain in the Brunnenhof—he had as a young man been apprenticed to Gerhard.

Born around 1570, Krumpper had appeared at Wilhelm's court in Munich first, it will be recalled, when he was about 20 years old, formally entering the ducal service as early as 1590. It is also relevant to remember that in his youth he had been in Venice for a while, and even worked in Florence in Giovanni da Bologna's studio. Though primarily a sculptor, Krumpper was certainly quite familiar at first hand with Italian late 16th-century architecture. At Polling in 1605 it was he who built the tower (Pl. 454) of the Stiftskirche. Though he was not able to finish it, this tower is all the same certainly finer than anything architectural now surviving at the Residenz he may have executed.

Both the Brunnenhof and the long west facade on the Residenzstrasse (Pls. 364, 365) in their dry regularity do have something in common with such nearly contemporary works as Elias Holl's Stadtmetzg in Augsburg and his Schloss Willibaldsburg outside Eichstätt (Pls. 405, 406), both of which will be discussed at length in the next chapter. Whether or not those initiatory works of Academic design in Germany were already as well known in Munich so soon after their completion as they are to scholars today, the actual execution of the new portions of the Residenz in this period is documented as the work of men presumably rather less well-trained than Krumpper, the builders Hans II Reiffenstuel (†1620) and Heinrich I Schön (†1640), both of whom belonged to the electoral *Bauamt* (Office of Works) and the designing may well have been their responsibility also. Schön, moreover, was definitely the designer in 1615 of a project for a tower attached to the Brunnenhof and for the Altes Schloss at Schleissheim (Pl. 408), north of Munich, which he began for Maximilian in 1616. Though at least semi-Academic in character, this last is so coarsely executed that it quite lacks the *tenue* of the work of Holl with which it will be compared in the next chapter. All the same, these facts make Schön at least as plausible a candidate as Krumpper for the over-all design of the work at the Residenz carried out after 1612.

The partially surviving quadratura decoration of the walls of the Kaiserhof in the Munich Residenz, lately restored, is somewhat more elaborate than that in the Brunnenhof because of rhythmic alternation of paired windows and paired pilasters. It is thus somewhat less routine and monotonous than the Residenzstrasse facade of the west wing. But the most interesting later work attributed to Krumpper, other than his sculpture on the Residenz, is the extension and decoration of the interior of the church at Polling (Pls. 453, 455), near his native Weilheim, in the 1620s—if, indeed, he was in charge there again as for the erection of the tower in 1605. That will be described below also, at the conclusion of the terminal chapter. Certainly, moreover, the Kaisertreppe in Munich, once it is restored, whether it was designed by Krumpper, by Schön, or by some other hand, should again take the initiatory place it deserves in the development of the monumental stair-hall in Germany, a development that would eventually produce such remarkable interiors in the eighteenth century as those, largely from J. B. Neumann's hand, at Bruchsal and at Brühl.

In its present condition, part over-restored, part ruined, even the work of the Wittelsbach Electors Palatine Friedrich IV and Friedrich V on the Heidelberg Schloss, carried out in 1601-1607 and 1613-1615 respectively, though suffering even more from earlier wars than did the Munich Residenz from the last, remains today more interesting. Specifically, moreover, what Friedrich V erected for his wife Elizabeth, the daughter of James I of England, was a rather early example of then-novel Academic design (Fig. 63; Pl. 410), well in advance of what Maximilian's designers —though one of them had actually been trained in Italy—were able to achieve in Munich.

The Friedrichsbau (Pl. 366), to the west of the Gläserner Saalbau Friedrich II had completed in 1549 (Pl. 140), was clearly intended by Friedrich IV to match, up to a point, and even to rival the Ottheinrichsbau of 1556-1559 at right angles to it on the southeast (Pl. 177). Friedrich III had turned Heidelberg into a "German Geneva" in the catch-word of contemporaries by shifting his religious allegiance and his

support of theologians from the Lutherans to the Calvinists. Doubtless in part because of his doctrinal preoccupations he had not been more of a builder than Calvin himself. Friedrich IV succeeded him in 1592. Nine years later[33] he began his new wing, employing as electoral architect Johannes Schoch (†1651). Schoch came from Königsbau near Pforzheim in northern Baden but, like Dietterlin, he was associated professionally with Strasbourg. He had long been city-architect there until called to Heidelberg in 1601.

The existing wing on the site (Fig. 23) where the Friedrichsbau was to be built, including the Elector Rupprecht I's old chapel of 1346, had to be demolished because it was in dangerous condition. This site runs from east to west, not from north to south like that of the Ottheinrichsbau, and is bounded on the court side by the Gläserner Saalbau to the right, as has been said, and on the left by the Frauenzimmerbau. That last had been largely rebuilt by Ludwig V earlier in the sixteenth century and still includes the first examples at Heidelberg of such internal features of Renaissance design as chimneypieces. Of what Ludwig built, however, little else eventually survived the seventeenth-century wars.

The site of the Friedrichsbau was considerably lower than that of the Ottheinrichsbau; where that is raised on a high base, the ground storey of Friedrich IV's wing, occupied by his chapel, is well below both the median level of the court and the ground-storey arcade of the Gläserner Saalbau. On the north side, however, the new wing rises directly from the terrace. The relatively low level of the terrace doubtless determined that of the floor of the chapel, awkward though this is on the court side where the ground rises sharply upward a few feet to the south of the new front.

The cornerstone of the Friedrichsbau was laid June 3, 1601, and the roof was on by the spring of 1604. Work went on inside for a year or so more and the whole was finally completed in 1607 as stated in two carved inscriptions. Despite the vicissitudes of the later history of the Schloss which brought so much destruction, the Friedrichsbau is physically in good condition today. It was twice necessary to replace the roof in the eighteenth century because of fires; but the present roof, designed by Professor Karl Schäfer as part of a drastic restoration undertaken in the 1890s, undoubtedly follows the original closely. The later restoration of 1954 made minor changes only in the in-

---

[33] Oechelhäuser, *Heidelberger Schloss*, pp. 63-72.

teriors, but otherwise these are predominantly new work of the 1890s except for that in the chapel.

Both facades of the Friedrichsbau follow fairly closely the court front of the Ottheinrichsbau (Pl. 177) surely at Friedrich's insistence. But Schoch, designing nearly fifty years later than whoever was Ottheinrich's architect, produced a tighter, better coordinated and more consistently scaled composition. Like the earlier wing, this is of three storeys with the lowest, which fronts the chapel, nearly twice the height of the first and second. Throughout, the windows are arranged in paired lights, here provided with pediments in both of the upper storeys as well as below. There are four double bays instead of the five of the Ottheinrichsbau and once again statue-filled niches in the middle of each bay. These niches are, however, more comfortably adjusted in height and width to the window-frames between them than Colin's of the late fifties.

The pilaster orders of the three storeys of Friedrich IV's new wing are more proportionally related than on Ottheinrich's and, like the entablatures they carry, in much bolder relief. The lowest order is set on podia so tall that the bases of the pilasters correspond with the transoms of the chapel windows. This lowest order is neither fluted nor rusticated as a whole, but two bold bands do cross the lower half below a plain upper shaft that has very marked entasis like the upper order at Hovestadt (Pl. 185) of forty years before. The order provides only just enough room under the capitals for the ends of the pediments topping all the windows. At this level these last are round-headed and traceried in subtle reference to the chapel within. Of that the windows are tall enough to light both the aisles and the tribunes. Again the decorative theme is an old one, for such window heads were already used at Lauingen (Pl. 12) a half-century earlier.

The shafts of the order on the middle storey of the Friedrichsbau, while shorter, have equally strong entasis. They also carry strapwork ornament on their lower portion as is so often the treatment in these years around 1600. Rather richer ornament occupies the same position on the order of the storey above recalling the contemporary order on the arcade at Hatfield in England; over that decoration the shafts are fluted like the half-columns of the top storey on the Ottheinrichsbau.

How the cross-gables[34] on the Heidelberg Fried-

richsbau compared with those that originally rose over the earlier facade of the Ottheinrichsbau it is now impossible to say. Here their own two-bay width is syncopated in relation to the regular double bays below. Thus, in the lowest stage of each a single pilaster marks the center and niches occupy the sides. The next stage has an almost Baroque boldness of scale. There are heavy C-scrolls at the base and cornices that are bent to a horizontal S-curve above much like those on the contemporary gate leading to the Bückeburg Schloss (Pl. 358). Then comes a full entablature and, over that, a lunette carrying a terminal statue. The double windows in each of the middle stages repeat those below at smaller scale. The oculus that pierces the lunette is again a feature of German gable-design that had long been very common.

The sixteen statues of Friedrich's ancestors in the niches, replaced by copies in the restoration of the 1890s, were probably the work of Sebastian Götz, a Swiss sculptor from Chur. He was employed from 1604, after the structural work was largely complete, much as Colin had been by Ottheinrich.

There is no greater difference between the Ottheinrichsbau and the Friedrichsbau than in the treatment of the entrances. On the earlier wing with its five double bays the portal could be centered (Pl. 177). Moreover, it is there elaborated almost as an independent entity rising through the entablature of the lowest order up into the first storey (Pl. 179). The Friedrichsbau has no central bay and the principal portal, though it leads to the chapel, is barely visible from the higher ground of the court (Pl. 366). For all the pious inscription carved with phrases from the 118th Psalm in Latin and Hebrew—"This is the Lord's gate; the righteous shall enter here"—which occupies a tablet set at the transom level of the ground-storey windows, the arch of the main portal, which occupies the fourth half-bay from the right, merely repeats that of the window above, omitting the tracery. It is not even symmetrically framed, since the podium of the pilaster on the right carries, like all those of this lowest order, a lion's head in high relief, while that below the statue of Ludwig VI on the left is plain. The other portal at the far right on the south side, almost hidden by the projecting wing of the Gläserner Saalbau, is equally inconspicuous from the court.

Thus neither of the facades of the Friedrichsbau—

---

[34] What one sees today of the Heidelberg Friedrichsbau

must be in good part the result of Professor Schäfer's restoration of the 1890s in any case.

for that on the north is effectively identical with the one on the court—offers much evidence that the ground storey is entirely filled by the big new chapel that replaced Rupprecht's, except for the great height of the transomed windows and their arched and traceried heads. The inscription with the date MDCVII over the main portal states that Friedrich had this "Palatium" erected and ornamented "divino cultui et commodae habitatione." It seems evident that a desire to have a comfortable dwelling (so to translate the Latin) rather than the intention to make appropriate provision for the divine cult determined the architectural character of the structure as a whole.

No more than most of the earlier Protestant examples incorporated in Schlösser beginning with that at Torgau—except the one at Augustusburg—does this chapel have an exterior of its own. The surprisingly spacious interior (Pl. 425) may better be discussed later along with other churches of the opening decades of the seventeenth century. So also the account of Friedrich V's Englischer Bau of 1613-1615 (Pl. 410), so notably early an example of Academic design when considered internationally—and not improbably, indeed, of non-German authorship—finds its proper place in the next chapter in relation to other similar work of the years 1610-1620. Much as the Gläserner Saalbau (Pl. 140), this is overshadowed in the total Schloss complex by the more elaborate work of Ottheinrich and Friedrich IV. Like the great Dicker Turm at its farther end that Friedrich V heightened in 1619, moreover, it was reduced to a ruin by the French bombardment of 1693 and has never been restored.

Of the mid-sixteenth-century Schloss of the Wettins at Weimar in Thuringia Nickel Gromann's so-called Bastille, which was begun in 1545 for the Saxon Elector Johann Friedrich, the builder of Schloss Hartenfels at Torgau, survives considerably better, but is not very impressive compared to the Cranach house nearby (Pl. 168). The rest, however, burned in 1618 and, the following year,[35] a new Residenz, like that at Munich more palace than Schloss, was begun on a quadrangular plan provided by Giovanni Bonalino. Bonalino came, most probably, from the Italian borderland in the Tyrol originally, but he had been court-architect to the prince-bishop of Bamberg since 1615 and later, in 1628, began St. Stephen there.

This vast Weimar project of the Wettin dukes of the Ernestine line was intended to exceed in size, not only the relatively modest constructions of the Wittelsbachs of the Palatinate at Heidelberg, but also the much more extensive additions made by Maximilian to the Munich Residenz. Construction proceeded very slowly, however, during the Thirty Years' War. Some time after 1650 the elder J. M. Richter (1620-1667) took up the work again after a long hiatus, omitting the south side of the quadrangle that Bonalino had planned; in 1664 construction halted once more, with the west wing still incomplete. After a fire in 1774 the whole was "restored" under Goethe's direction. By its date as also by its style the Weimar Schloss of the seventeenth century belonged originally to the Early Baroque already and in its present late eighteenth-century form need hardly be further considered here. Bonalino's churches are more significant historically, but these were all begun after 1620[36] as were his Early Baroque loggias of 1623-1629 in the Ehrenburg at Coburg.[37]

The Weimar project had been initiated just too late. The long religious truce, initiated in the 1550s, was coming to its end in 1618 and not until well after the Peace of Westphalia in 1648 were conditions in Germany generally conducive to ambitious architectural production. Destruction had been all too common, moreover, and many earlier buildings suffered more from the woes of seventeenth-century wars, the result both of internecine strife and of foreign invasion, than from the wars of the twentieth century and were rarely repaired until long afterward.

One great quadrangular Schloss, however, had already been brought to completion, that at Aschaffenburg on the Main for the archbishop-elector of Mainz, Johann Schweickhardt von Kronberg, a prince-prelate whose realms exceeded those of any of the lay electors. Another (Pl. 406) had been largely carried out for the prince-bishop of Eichstätt, Johann Konrad von Gemmingen, before his death in 1612, an important initiatory example of Academic design. To this some reference has already been made and it will be further discussed in the next chapter. But Schloss Johannisburg at Aschaffenburg,[38] begun in 1605 and completed by 1614, despite its very regular quadrangular plan (Fig. 59), continues almost as characteristically as the Friedrichsbau at Heidelberg the late Northern

[35] DKD, *Thüringen*, pp. 405-406; Piltz, *D.D.R.*, p. 314.

[36] Hauttmann, *Kirchliche Baukunst*, pp. 38, 39.

[37] Reclams *Bayern*, pp. 196-197.

[38] E. Bachmann, *Schloss Aschaffenburg und Pompejanum*, 2nd ed., Munich, 1965. A. Stadtmüller, *Aschaffenburg nach dem zweiten Weltkrieg*, Aschaffenburg, 1973, pp. 167-170, deals with the postwar restoration only.

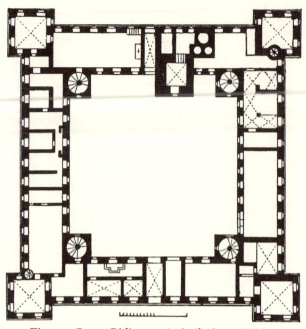

Fig. 59. Georg Ridinger: Aschaffenburg, Schloss Johannisburg, plan, 1605-14

Mannerism of the preceding decades. Indeed, as was noted earlier, the architect, Georg Ridinger, came like Schoch from Strasbourg, where he was born in 1568.

As the international influence of Dietterlin particularly emphasizes, Strasbourg was replacing Antwerp around 1600 as the fountainhead of the continuing architectural current to which the rise of Academic design in northern Europe was opposed. From the Alsatian city came several architects to work for various German princes who were neither employing such Italians or Italian-Swiss as Nosseni and Bonalino, nor Italian-trained northerners like Sustris and Krumpper. Thus Ridinger, after training under Jörg Schmidt in Strasbourg, was already called in 1595, when still quite young, to Ansbach to assist Gideon Bacher and, as noted earlier, he may well have worked also with Bacher for the same client at Wülzburg. Aschaffenburg is his masterpiece and also the most considerable surviving secular work of the first decade of the seventeenth century in Germany.

There is an innate stylistic ambiguity about the Aschaffenburg Schloss which is most characteristic of the period. This vast pile on the bank of the Main (Pl. 367)—so plainly visible today at a considerable distance from the Autobahn to the north—may be considered in several of its larger aspects already somewhat Academic. In the decoration of the gables,

on the other hand, it displays something of the fantasy associated with Dietterlin's engraved designs, designs presumably well known to the Strasbourg-trained Ridinger. The one breach in the symmetrical regularity of the massing was caused by the retention of the old mediaeval *Burgfrit* (keep) that had survived a disastrous fire in 1552 (Pl. 368). However, to have laid out the court in such a way that this was centered on the north side would have truncated the chapel at the eastern end of that wing.

The dominant orderliness results particularly at Aschaffenburg from the location of the identical eight-storeyed towers at the four corners—for towers they are, rather than pavilions of the French sort such as had been introduced in Germany at Horst in the early 1560s (Pl. 181). Moreover, the regularity of the long rows of evenly spaced windows—twelve in each of the three storeys of the east and west sides, though only eleven on the south—is far more noticeable than the asymmetrical location of the partially remodelled Burgfrit. Then, for all the fantasy of their outline and the turgidity of the strapwork decoration along the edges, the few gables are centered, both above the exterior walls and above those in the court; so also the axes are strongly marked on the south externally, and on the south and east in the court, by heavily detailed portals. These recall a little the slightly earlier Wülzburg gate with the execution of which Ridinger had probably been associated even if he did not design it himself.

There is about the portals at Aschaffenburg a truly proto-Baroque boldness of scale, and the same is true of the rusticated quoins on the corners both of the tall external towers and the shorter polygonal stair-turrets in the court (Pl. 368). Furthermore, the S-curved *welsche Hauben* over these last, echoing the larger ones over the octagonal eighth storey of each of the outer towers, lend a massive sort of plasticity to the angles that contrasts with the monotonous planar extension of the walls.

Perhaps the most impressive view of the Schloss at Aschaffenburg, now thoroughly restored externally after damage from bombing in the last war, is from across the Main (Pl. 367). If the survival of the Burgfrit produces a slight irregularity in the silhouette, the retention also of the mediaeval fortifications along the river's edge provides a high terrace as a podium that greatly increases the monumentality of the whole. Holl used the old fortifications at Schloss Willibaldsburg outside Eichstätt in a similar way (Pl. 406).

On the north side of the court of Schloss Johannis-burg, by contrast, various irregularities on both sides of the keep provide a more picturesque composition recalling earlier Schlösser (Pl. 368). The open loggia that once ran around the northeast corner is gone, but the two-storey height of the chapel to the left of the keep is indicated by the very tall windows, some-what as at the Heidelberg Friedrichsbau. The elabo-rate portal of the chapel, moreover, is flanked by pairs of fluted columns. Above, there is a relief of the Bap-tism of Christ between the "horns" of a broken seg-mental pediment. This whole composition, however, is awkwardly jammed up against the simpler portal of the stair-tower with its bold rusticated bands and no other decoration. The chapel portal is—as it looks —an interpolation by another hand. The hand is that of the sculptor Hans Juncker (b. 1582), also respon-sible for carving the altar and the pulpit inside the chapel between 1609 and 1618. But this Catholic chapel, like the Protestant one at Heidelberg, may better be discussed, independently of the present ac-count of the Schloss, together with other churches of the period.

Not until the grandiose monasteries of the mature Baroque rose in the late seventeenth and early eight-eenth centuries is there another secular work in Ger-many as large and impressive as this Schloss at As-chaffenburg. It eventually cost 900,000 florins to build, a vast sum even for the rich ruler of the extensive elec-torate of Mainz. That was certainly well beyond what most German princes of the day who were not high ecclesiastics as well as lay rulers could afford. Schloss Johannisburg has therefore seemed to many especially premonitory of what would be built in central Europe only much later. That productive time would come when the three decades of war that began so shortly after the Schloss's completion and the long, barren aftermath that followed were finally over.

But this Schloss at Aschaffenburg may also, and rather more justly, be considered a culminating work of the German Renaissance. Already, in the 1520s and 1530s—to recapitulate a little—Unkair seems to have projected nearly regular quadrangles at Schloss Neu-haus (Fig. 9) and Stadthagen (Fig. 13); in the early sixties, square corner pavilions, an idea then first im-ported from France, had made an appearance at Horst and Hovestadt (Fig. 31; Pl. 181). Later in that dec-ade, the raised corners were less prominent at the Augustusburg Schloss, as also somewhat earlier on the Altes Schloss at Stuttgart. But the Augustusburg

plan (Fig. 36) is a true square externally, though cruciform as regards the court. Thus it was already more totally regular and symmetrical than that at Aschaffenburg could be because of the off-center loca-tion of the keep. The chapel at Augustusburg, more-over, is in the exact middle of one side, not pushed toward a corner as at Aschaffenburg.

There is an almost Baroque escalation of scale in the treatment of the entrances at Schloss Johannis-burg. In this respect the portals resemble several of those in fortifications carried out in these years. They are particularly like the one at Wülzburg, for exam-ple, with the construction if not the design of which Ridinger himself may actually have been involved, not to speak of that of the outer works of the Marien-berg (Pl. 363).

Other equally prominent elements, however, re-mained characteristically Northern Mannerist at Aschaffenburg in their detailing. The window-frames in the main storeys are elaborated with miniscule broken pediments and there is strapwork around those in the upper storeys of the towers. Higher still come the gable fronts articulated both with pilasters and with arched niches. Such niches had first ap-peared in the early thirties on the west wing of the Neuburg Schloss (Pl. 75). That seems to indicate at so late a date an actual stylistic stasis, not as yet to call it retardation. The stasis here is evident even if the Schloss be compared with additions to the Munich Residenz (Pls. 364, 365) that are nearly contemporary, less impressive though those are. But at the Residenz a good part of the work carried out for Maximilian was, in fact, of a few years later than Ridinger's. Very possibly, moreover, the work in Munich was designed by Krumpper, who had been trained in Italy. As sug-gested earlier, he could also have known the current work of Heintz and Holl in Augsburg as Ridinger in 1605, or even later after the Stadtmetzg was erected in 1609, presumably did not.

All the same, the boldly scrolled outlines, heavy strapwork ornament and obelisk accents on Ridinger's gables illustrate the continuing vitality of a major theme of German Renaissance architecture, one that flourished especially in the Weser region in the termi-nal quarter of the sixteenth century. The *welsche Gebel* that crown the gables at Aschaffenburg had, of course, a still longer history, extending back to the twenties in Saxony and Westphalia as was described in Chapter II. The ensuing stage of stylistic develop-ment, at least as regards work in this district done for the archbishop-electors of Mainz, would open only some twenty years later with the initiation of the Mainz Schloss in 1627.[39] Even that, moreover, though its construction dragged endlessly on as at Weimar because of the war—in this case until 1678—is still at least as much "Late Renaissance," so to say, as Early Baroque in character.

Another rather smaller and less regular quadrangular Schloss, begun in 1603[40] two years before that at Aschaffenburg, is the one at Bevern (Fig. 60),

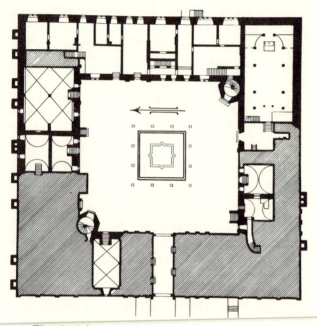

Fig. 60. Johann Hundertossen: Bevern, Schloss, 1603-12, plan

north of Höxter in the Weser valley. The culmination in this district of Renaissance Schloss-construction had been reached already before 1600 at Hämelschenburg (Fig. 50; Pls. 299-305), but the Bevern Schloss has something of the terminal stylistic character of that at Aschaffenburg. The client was Statius von Münchhausen, a son of Hilmar von Münchhausen, for whom Tönnis began Schloss Schwöbber in the early 1570s. Hilmar's original designer-builder was Johann Hundertossen, since 1592 city-architect of Hameln and possibly one of those involved at Hämelschenburg. Hundertossen died in 1606, however, some six years before Hilmar could finish his Schloss.

The entrance front of Schloss Bevern (Pl. 369) ap-

[39] Reclams *Rheinlande und Westfalen*, pp. 426-427.
[40] Kreft-Soenke, *Weserrenaissance*, pp. 227-228.

pears at first sight symmetrical, though it is neither as regular nor as monumental as that at Aschaffenburg. There are only two storeys above a half-basement and no pavilions or towers at the corners. Instead, the facade is flanked by three-stage gables with the typical decoration of the district. This is distinctly more delicate and also more idiosyncratic than on the gables of the Schloss on the Main, for the pilaster-strips are banded with chip-carved blocks and the strapwork has jewelry-like detailing. Narrower and simpler dormers subdivide the long range of roofs between the cross-gables at the ends of this front and also on the rear; the sides have dormers only.

On a closer view various disparities become evident on the entrance front at Bevern. The lefthand cross-gable is wider and taller than that on the right, and the spacing of the windows—some single, some double and two triple—is irregular in the lower walls. The pilaster-strips on the dormers of this entrance front line up with those that flank the windows below, but that is otherwise true only of the middle bays of the cross-gables at the ends. Under the outermost edges of the scrollwork on the lowest stage these gables carry additional pilasters that have no counterparts on the wall below. On the east or rear side, moreover, though the cross-gables are nearly identical with that at the righthand end of the west front, there are no pilaster-strips at all on the wall below, and such appear only under one of the dormers on the south.

The most conspicuously asymmetrical feature on the west front at Bevern, however, is the portal with its broad-banded arch and slender flanking columns. These support a simplified entablature that, in fact, rings the whole exterior at the top of the ground storey. The entablature incorporates a cornice much more modest in its projection than the one at the eaves above, but the continuity of the repeated horizontals counters the off-center location of the portal.

In the court at Bevern (Pl. 370) it is rather surprising to find that only the ground storey is of masonry and the upper storey all Fachwerk. Unexpected also is the variety of features within a basically regular ordonnance. In the northwest and southeast corners only, for example, polygonal stair-towers rise two storeys above the eaves-line and are capped with "onions," i.e. bulbous *welsche Hauben*. Elsewhere in the upper storey, however, the timber-framing creates a continuous grid, quite as on the facades of contemporary town-houses at Hannoversch-Münden and elsewhere, and wherever convenient for the interiors one, two or even three of the units are glazed. Similar rectangular lights in ones and twos are inserted in the masonry wall of the lower storey. On the north side near its western end there is also a sort of flattened oriel decorated with stone half-columns below and carved wooden pilasters above. This is capped by a triangular gable in which two small pilaster-framed windows open under a fluted lunette.

The other decoration on the court facades at Bevern is less Italianate and rather casually placed. Strapwork, interrupted by the characteristic chip-carved bosses of the Weserrenaissance, appears only on a few of the vertical elements, as if there had been no fixed general programme. Moreover, the elements below which are executed in stone are often not lined up with the regularly spaced stanchions of the Fachwerk above, presumably because no one in over-all charge after Hundertossen's death in 1606 had coordinated the work of the masons and that of the carpenters. Such verticals, three to the left and three to the right, flank the entrance arch of the west side, but not symmetrically: thus the arch, as on the exterior, is way off center. All of this detailing, just the same, is notable for the delicacy of its scale and the elegance of the workmanship. This contrasts with most earlier carved work in the Weser district. Elsewhere, it is usually only on oriels that ornament is of jewel-like elaboration, as if more finical and accomplished carvers were responsible for its execution than were employed on the larger structural elements.

Several more or less richly decorated portals are inserted at quite irregular intervals in the lower walls of the Bevern court, suggesting still more the lack of an over-all design. Some lead down to the cellars, much as at Barntrup and Hämelschenburg, others lead up to the rooms in the raised ground-storey. The most conspicuous are those at the bases of the stair-towers and between the northwest tower and the flattened oriel, here not especially rich and delicate. A few are arched like the broad and simple one at the entrance; others, such as that beside the oriel, are flanked by columns; while one or two have heavily molded rectangular frames and crowns of strapwork.

In comparison to the very considerable amount of decoration on the Fachwerk of many town-houses of this and the previous period the treatment of the wooden elements at Schloss Bevern, other than occasional verticals, is very simple. Moreover, it is predominantly rectangular like the structural grid. The rectangularity of that is varied only by the X-bracing

of the square panels at the bottom with no merely ornamental use of diagonal or curved members. At least as restored, the polychromy is equally restrained.

All told, Schloss Bevern is somewhat anticlimactic after Hämelschenburg, but in no other large new Schloss is the later German Renaissance vocabulary handled with so graceful a casualness. Elsewhere in the north of Europe, to mention a few contemporary works, such great English houses of these years as Audley End, begun in 1603, and Hatfield, begun in 1607, are much larger, not to speak of Slot Frederiksborg, begun in 1602 at Hillerød in Denmark. Audley End and Frederiksborg were—in the one case completely, in the other largely—the work of men probably or certainly of Netherlandish origin or training: Bernard Janssen, known as Johnson in England, and among several, particularly the youngest Steenwinkel, Hans II, in Denmark. By contrast, Bevern was entirely autochthonous. It was, moreover, the house of a minor *Herr* (landowner), not a king like Christian IV who commissioned Frederiksborg, or a great lord such as Robert Cecil the younger, first Marquess of Salisbury, for whom Hatfield was built. However, Cecil seems to have employed only English designers: Simon Basil, probably, who had become King's Surveyor the previous year, and definitely Robert Lyminge. Inigo Jones's intervention at Hatfield at this early date seems most unlikely though it has been suggested.[41] It is sad to record that, because of his accumulated debts, Statius von Münchhausen lost possession of his Bevern property to the dukes of Brunswick[42] in 1619, only seven years after the Schloss was completed and long before his death in 1633. Cecils still live at Hatfield.

Of the Schlösser built or much remodelled and enlarged during the years Bevern was in construction and shortly thereafter, several have been referred to already in one or another connection. The most conspicuous features of the earliest of these, the triangular one at Wewelsburg of the prince-bishop of Paderborn, as rebuilt 1604-1607,[43] are great round corner towers. These do not quite match but are all simpler versions of the ones the same client, Dietrich

[41] It is of largely coincidental interest that Inigo Jones may well have seen Frederiksborg in construction. Skovgaard, *Christian IV*, pp. 122-123; see also Note IX 31.

[42] One wonders if it was ultimately inherited in the eighteenth century by the Hanoverians who were kings of England as ultimate heirs of the dukes of Brunswick.

[43] Dehio, *Westfalen*, pp. 597-598.

von Fürstenberg, had added some ten or more years before at Schloss Neuhaus. Between the towers on the south and the west extend two long blocks that are fairly regular. These are all but devoid of architectural features. There is, however, a single modest dormer, set off-center over the south front, and a small oriel projecting somewhat nearer the middle of the other. The main gables are absolutely plain except for string-courses between the storeys; and the south front, thanks to the inclusion of earlier construction, is not even in one plane.

The latest of the Schlösser already at least briefly discussed were that at Overhagen near Lippstadt in Westphalia, and the Residenz, usually known as the Rotes Schloss, at Weimar in Thuringia. Both were begun in 1619. The one belongs stylistically, despite its late date, to the 1560s while the other, as has been noted, is effectively of a period nearly a hundred years later, despite its actual initiation early in the seventeenth century by Bonalino.

Of early seventeenth-century Schlösser not hitherto mentioned the prior's lodging at the great Benedictine Abbey at Ellwangen, near Biberach in Swabia, as rebuilt in 1603-1608, belongs to the Academic current; so also to some degree does even the very exceptional polygonal Schloss at Darfeld, in Westphalia northwest of Münster, which was projected and partly executed in 1612-1616.[44] Even Schloss Schwarzenberg at Scheinfeld, southwest of Würzburg in Franconia just off the main road to Nürnberg, as rebuilt after a fire in 1607 over the next decade—possibly from a design Elias Holl supplied—by Jakob I Wolf (c.1546-1612) from Nürnberg or his son is at least proto-Academic. Several of these are discussed in Chapter IX.

But there are various other Schlösser of these decades that also illustrate, if not for the most part so impressively as those at Aschaffenburg and at Bevern, the latest phase of Northern Mannerism. The Schloss at Haddenhausen (Fig. 61),[45] just southeast of Minden in Westphalia, already once rebuilt in the 1530s after war damage, was thoroughly remodelled in the

[44] Horst, *Architektur*, pp. 91-94, figs. 63, 64; Klapheck, *Schloss Horst*, pp. 333-352, figs. 244-259. Only a considerable portion of the court arcades of this ambitious octagonal scheme for the Darfeld Schloss survives as originally planned and built; even this is today usually inaccessible. Earlier scholars such as Horst and Klapheck gave this belated fragment of "High Renaissance" central planning, partially executed by the sculptor Gerhard Groninger from Münster for Jobst von Voede, the local lord, perhaps excessive importance.

[45] Kreft-Soenke, *Weserrenaissance*, pp. 245-247.

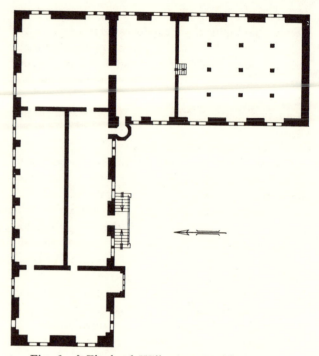

Fig. 61. ? Eberhard Wilkening: Haddenhausen, Schloss, c.1613-16, plan

second decade of the seventeenth century by another Münchhausen, Hilmar II. He also completed Schwöbber for his daughter Lucia and her husband Johann von der Bussche, who had paid 37,000 taler for the property. One bay-window at Haddenhausen carries the date 1616, but the work actually began some three years earlier. The architect may well have been, not Hundertossen as has been suggested, but that other builder-designer from Hameln, Wilkening, who was responsible in the 1580s for Barntrup. The L-shaped plan of the Schloss at Haddenhausen was doubtless that of the earlier structure on the site dating from the 1530s, but the most conspicuous feature is an arched gateway, which must be of about 1616-1620, leading into the court (Pl. 371). This is decorated with such a virtuoso mixture of variously chip-carved voussoirs it more than rivals the earlier one of 1608 at Hämelschenburg (Pl. 299). That might also be by Wilkening as was earlier noted.

The Schloss at Wendlinghausen, in this district but lying between Lemgo and Barntrup, was also built in much the same years 1613-1616[46] by Hilmar II von Münchhausen for his son Heinrich Hilmar. Over the portal appears the date 1614. Whether or not the archi-

[46] *Ibid.*, pp. 287-288.

tect was again the elderly Wilkening, this *Wasser-burg* must be by the same hand as Haddenhausen: the rather restrained treatment of the gables on both certainly suggests such common authorship.

The Wendlinghausen Schloss is a modest two-storeyed rectangular block with a much taller octagonal stair-tower at the left end of the court front. Both sides have prominent dormers that rise a storey above the eaves and are capped with two-stage gables. These gables are decorated with S-scrolls and C-scrolls and also with much chip-carving very like that on the Haddenhausen arch. Except on the ends, the fenestration, predominantly paired rectangular windows, is rather irregular, as also the location of the five projecting *Garderoben* (privies), two in each storey and even one in the basement!

In a quite different district much further to the west and south the Schloss of the counts of Nassau-Hadamar at Hadamar, north of Limburg-a.-d.-Lahn at the eastern edge of the present-day state of Hesse, is considerably larger than the manor-houses—for that is what they really are—built or remodelled by Hilmar II von Münchhausen for his children. The original structure at Hadamar, purchased by Count Emich I in 1323 from the Cistercian abbey of Eberbach, burned in 1540 but rebuilding began only in 1566.[47] Moreover, the work was not carried to completion until after 1612 for Count Johann Ludwig, first by an obscure, doubtless local, builder M. J. Hederich Sprenger, and then from 1616 by Joachim Rumpf, court-architect at Hanau down to the death of Count Philipp Ludwig II von Solms in 1612. Plans by Rumpf of 1617 and of 1620 survive. The lay-out at Hadamar is U-shaped. The north and east wings are still basically Late Gothic in the ground storey but of early seventeenth-century character above. That on the south is also dated 1614-1617, and subsidiary buildings, including stables of 1622-1629, enclose the court to the west.

The three wings of Schloss Hadamar (Pl. 372) are all of stuccoed rubble with cut-stone trim like most of the Schlösser further north in Westphalia. The three storeys of the tall and rather narrow blocks are crowned with exceptionally steep three-stage gables. These are sparsely decorated with the usual scrolls at the edges and some pilaster-strips in the middle stage. The scrolled edging of the gables is less elaborate than on those in the Weser district by, or attributed to, Wilkening, and the principal accent on the Schloss is

quite different. A very tall octagonal stair-tower rises four more storeys above the three storeys of the wings, thus recalling some of the towers on Rathäuser in Saxony. Here, the tower is crowned with receding stages covered with slates below, first a large and then a small *welsche Haube*. Though much simpler, this terminal treatment somewhat resembles that of such contemporary Dutch towers as the one dated 1613 on the Nieuwekerk in Haarlem by Lieven de Key and the Munttoren at the center of Amsterdam, as heightened by Hendrick de Keyser (1565-1621), a little later in 1620,[48] more than it does any examples further east. An exception would be that of 1559-1560 on the town hall of Danzig by the Netherlander Dirk Daniels. Sixteenth-century *speeltoren* in Holland may well have been known to Rumpf, moreover, if hardly Daniels's remoter one.

This sampling of German Schloss architecture of the opening seventeenth century may conclude with a Torbau (gatehouse), far to the north at Husum, carrying the date 1613.[49] That lies west of the city of Schleswig, and actually on the coast of the North Sea, in a district that was architecturally, as also politically, as much Danish as German in the past. Of brick, like the Schlösser at Glücksburg and Ahrensburg (Pls. 313, 314), with only the trim of stone, the whitewashed Husum Torbau (Pl. 373) seems at first sight much less similar to the Westphalian Schlösser than does that at Hadamar. However, its three-stage gables, edged with C-scrolls and carrying plain strapwork elements on the face of the topmost stage, are not really so different. The other feature somewhat elaborated here, the entrance portal, has a rusticated arch flanked by paired pilasters which are also rusticated. This is capped by an inscribed panel between two statues set in niches. Though hardly to be considered even proto-Academic, the Husum gatehouse is all the same more formally Italianate than the very nearly contemporary freestanding arches at Hämelschenburg and Haddenhausen (Pls. 299, 371).

In these decades the new architecture in the principal German cities and towns exemplified, like the Schlösser, both the continuance of Late Mannerist exuberance and the arrival of the international Academic current. It was in 1609, on the one hand, that Holl carried out from Heintz's design on the Stadtmetzg at Augsburg a facade (Pl. 405) almost as severe

---

[47] Dehio, *Hessen*, pp. 349-350.

[48] *Kunstreisboek*, pp. 362, 325.
[49] Dehio, *Hamburg*, p. 252.

as those he was then designing himself for the exterior and the court of Schloss Willibaldsburg outside Eichstätt (Pl. 406). On the other hand, older Hameln architects were still as active in the service of their fellow-citizens as for the Münchhausens and in the same Weserrenaissance vein of Northern Mannerism.

Nowhere is the continued florescence after 1600 of the ripe manner characteristic of the 1580s and 1590s more conspicuous, moreover, than in the great ports on the estuaries opening into the North Sea and the Baltic. Cities such as Gdańsk, Lübeck and Bremen celebrated their commercial prosperity by building public edifices of unparalleled richness. Since the merchants by their trade were more closely tied to Holland and the other Dutch provinces than to Catholic Poland in their culture and by their Protestant religion, if not to the same degree to Brabant and Flanders, they continued not surprisingly to employ for civic monuments and for their own houses Netherlandish architects. None were yet ready, however, to echo the advanced design of the Waag in Haarlem of the late nineties, or the still somewhat transitional mode of the extensions of the Gent Stadhuis, as begun in 1595 and carried out over the years down to 1618; rather they rivalled or exceeded in much of their Gdańsk work the picturesque elaboration of the contemporary Haarlem Vleeshal of 1602-1603 by Lieven de Key.

In Germany, however, in the lower Rhineland, though just east of the Dutch border, the modest Rathaus at Meppen, as remodelled in 1601[50] the year before the Vleeshal was begun, shows little of the Northern Mannerist exuberance of de Key's work. As was noted earlier, this repeats an early sort of stepped *welsche Gebel*, modifying the motif only by piercing the flutes of the crowning lunettes as had been done earlier on the Krameramtshaus of 1588 in nearby Münster (Pl. 156). More similar in these opening years of the seventeenth century to the Haarlem Vleeshal is the lively outline of the contemporary gables on Peter Sengelaub's Casimirianeum at Coburg (Pl. 374), built 1601-1605,[51] and the bold relief, at least, of the architectural features on the eastern facade of the Augsburg Zeughaus (Pl. 399), as designed by Joseph Heintz in 1602 and executed by Elias Holl.

The Casimirianeum, however, bristling with obelisks and framed by scrolled elements of multiple curvature, is still like Sengelaub's earlier Coburg Kanzlei (Pl. 309) in the characteristic German mode of the 1580s and 1590s; the Zeughaus leads forward, not so much to the Academic sort of architecture that those responsible here—Heintz and Holl—would be introducing at Augsburg and Eichstätt two years after it was completed in 1607, but towards the High Baroque, and to a degree hardly matched even in Italy in these years just after 1600 except by Maderno at S. Susanna. For all its early date and ambiguous character, therefore, the Augsburg Zeughaus may better be discussed in the next chapter together with the demolished Siegel Haus there, for which Heintz and Holl also share credit, and Holl's extant Wertachsbruckertor (Wertach bridge gate), both of 1605 (Pls. 399, 400, 403).

What is relatively exceptional at this date about the Coburg Casimirianeum is that it housed a school, the Gymnasium Academicum, which Duke Johann Casimir had been planning to establish since 1598. Thus the structure may properly be compared—and to Paul Francke's advantage—with the even richer one, the Juleum (Pl. 333) described in the previous chapter, that Franke had just completed at Helmstedt in 1599 for Duke Heinrich Julius of Brunswick-Wolfenbüttel.

Another far less interesting building serving a novel purpose is the former Ottoneum, now the Kunsthaus, that Wilhelm Vernukken erected in 1603-1606[52] just before his death in 1607, for the Landgrave Moritz of Hessen-Kassel in Kassel, for this was the first theater built in Germany. At least in its present condition, as remodelled first in 1696 by Paul du Ry (1604-1714) to hold the prince's art collections and again in 1709 for the scientific departments of the Collegium Carolinum, later the university, the Ottoneum does not at all resemble earlier work by Vernukken at Horst, Cologne and Schmalkalden (Pls. 184, 237, 267); but then those other things with which his name is associated seem to have little or nothing in common anyway! Doubtless, moreover, the postwar restoration, though conscientious, has exaggerated the composite character of the rather dull facade which du Ry's portico now dominates below the chastened remains of the original gable.

The Wettin and Brabant clients for the structures just mentioned in Coburg and Kassel were princely magnates, not town councils; yet at this point even the burghers of such a small town in southern Hesse

[50] Reclams *Niedersachsen*, p. 564.
[51] Reclams *Bayern*, pp. 200-201.

[52] Dehio, *Hessen*, pp. 456-457.

as Gross Umstadt, between Darmstadt and Aschaffenburg, were providing themselves with a Rathaus (Pl. 375) successfully rivalling Moritz's theater if not Johann Casimir's school. There the portal is column-flanked and the end and cross-gables are elaborately decorated with scrolled strapwork at the edges and many tiny obelisks. Carried out by the master-mason Hans Marian from nearby Darmstadt, this modest civic edifice may have been begun as early as 1596.[53] However, the principal years of execution were more probably 1604-1606—thus overlapping the initiation of the vastly greater work on Schloss Johannisburg (Pl. 367), not far away at Aschaffenburg, by Ridinger in 1605, and finally completed only in 1625.

In larger towns individual citizens often competed in these years with Herren, if not with princes, as patrons of architecture; but the structure most comparable to the Great Arsenal in Gdańsk is also a civic one, the Rathaus in the equally large and prosperous port of Bremen on the Weser estuary. The history of this prominent structure[54] (Pl. 376), facing the Schütting across the marketplace at an oblique angle to the front of the mediaeval cathedral, is rather complicated. The Gothic Rathaus of brick, dating from the early fifteenth century, was never wholly rebuilt as the big traceried windows with their pointed arches that survive high up on the ends make evident.

Already in 1551, however, equally broad rectangular windows of four lights, stone-mullioned and pedimented, were introduced on either side of the pointed portal in the lower storey on the left end of the Bremen Rathaus. In 1595 somewhat similar windows, but much taller, with those on either flank of two lights and the rest of three, were cut into the front. These windows are also capped by pediments, in this case alternately pointed and segmental. The rather drastic modification of the inherited mediaeval facade of the Rathaus represented, very probably, a response to the addition the previous year of the balustrade that crowns the facade of the Schütting across the way.

The even more conspicuous features that make the facade of the Bremen Rathaus as it exists today the most sumptuous of all German examples of Renaissance civic design were added only in 1608-1612. These features are the open arcade that runs across the whole

front towards the marketplace and the three-bayed central projection on this side—almost all window—as well as the five-stage gable which crowns it (Pl. 378). The last, moreover, is echoed by two equally elaborate three-stage stone dormers at either side. These rise above and behind a balustrade that closely resembles the one across the square on the front of the Schütting.

Just what the relation this remodelled facade at Bremen had to contemporary architecture in the Low Countries is hard to say. Even far to the east in Gdańsk, as well as nearer at hand in Emden, directly across the Dollart from Friesland, Netherlandish architects—some from the south and others from the north—were often employed. But that was not so common in Bremen except, much earlier, for Buscheneer and, at this point, Johan van Rijswijk. Moreover, Simon zur Lippe, it will be recalled, consulted Rijswijk around 1600 concerning his Schloss at Varenholz higher up in the Weser valley. It is recorded that Rijswijk received payments from the Bremen authorities in 1601 and again in 1603—on both occasions for work on fortifications as at Varenholz. Despite the important architectural activities of Italian military engineers in the north, first at Jülich two generations earlier, then at Wolfenbüttel, and later at Zamość in Poland—to mention only the most conspicuous instances—an engineer from Holland would hardly have had the broad background in the arts of Pasqualini, Chiaramella or Morando. He is not likely, therefore, to have been able to provide the basic programme of architectural design for such a representative civic work of the day as the remodelling of the front of the Bremen Rathaus. Another Dutchman, Heronimo van der Elst, is recorded as having worked on the Rathaus, but only as a sculptor.

What is certain is that the Oberkirchner sandstone quarried at Bückeburg, used for all the new work of the early 17th century on the Bremen Rathaus, was provided by Lüder von Bentheim (†1613) and still for three years after his death by his son Johannes (†1643). Several earlier Bremen buildings have been attributed wholly or in part to Lüder on no real evidence: the Wage of 1587 (Pl. 332), the Kornhaus of 1591, and the balustrade and front dormer on the Schütting of 1594 (Pl. 232). However, his first documented association with a major architectural work is the contract of 1595 to provide stone from Bückeburg for the Stadhuis at Leiden which resulted from his meeting with the Dutch architect Lieven de Key.

---

[53] *Ibid.*, p. 339.

[54] E. Waldmann, *Das Bremer Rathaus*, Burg bei Magdeburg [1931], bibl., p. 50; H. Adamietz, *Das Bremer Rathaus* [2nd ed., Bremen, 1966]; Kreft-Soenke, *Weserrenaissance*, pp. 232-234.

This known relationship between the German and the Netherlander has led some writers to attribute the design of the Leiden facade as a whole or in great part to Bentheim. Others, contrarily, would assign what was done on the Bremen Rathaus in this period to de Key!

Neither exclusive attribution seems likely. But it is not plausible, either, to recognize in Bremen specific influence from the Antwerp Stadhuis (Pl. 175), already more than forty years old, or even from the Rathaus at Emden (Fig. 39) as built by the Antwerp-born Laurens van Steenwinckel in the mid-seventies. That last is evidently somewhat nearer both chronologically and geographically; yet the Bremen facade resembles it even less than it does the one in Antwerp.

Regardless of the authorship of the remodelled facade of the Bremen Rathaus—which in any case may well have changed over the years—there is considerable disparity in date, though little in style, between the tall, but fairly broad and widely set, windows of 1551 on the ends and those dated 1595 in the side bays of the front, as also the smaller but more closely set ones of 1608 and later in the three projecting bays at the center. These last, moreover, are repeated almost identically in the lower three stages of the broad gable above, which carries the date 1612, and also in the bottom stage of each of the two dormers on either side. Moreover, the contrast between the Italianate arcade with its profuse figural carving that runs across the front below and the northern spikiness of the gables above is also very marked.[55] All the same, there is a sort of visual harmony in scale and in degree of elaboration throughout all the profuse decoration. That decoration was more largely the work of the local sculptor Johann Prange, it seems, than of the Netherlander van der Elst.[56]

The great size and near-continuity of the glazed areas on the front of the Bremen Rathaus give it a distinctly Dutch look. Paradoxically, that look is stronger here than in the case of such comparable, but less typically Northern Mannerist, public buildings in the Netherlands as the Antwerp and Hague town halls (Pl. 175) that date from a generation and more earlier. Fenestration so extensive was matched, however, in various sixteenth-century guildhall facades both in the southern and in the northern Netherlands. Among extant examples there are the house called De Zalm of the 1530s in Mechelen and the *Wewershuis* (drapers' guildhall) of the early forties in Antwerp. Most notable, however, for its generous fenestration must once have been the Burgerweeshuis of 1560 in Amsterdam. On the other hand, the lively outlines of the gables at Bremen conclude a major architectural development more characteristic of late sixteenth and early seventeenth-century Germany than of the Dutch provinces, much less Brabant and Flanders.

Almost the whole of the main floor inside the Bremen Rathaus is occupied by a single great hall (Pl. 377). This is more spacious than any of those in Schlösser. Like them, however, it is roofed with a wooden ceiling that is suspended from the roof-trusses. The ceiling of the Bremen hall is heavily beamed as in several minor German examples, not panelled and painted as at Heilingenberg and Weikersheim nor yet decorated with intarsia as at Kirchheim and Ortenburg. Moreover, the treatment of the walls is confusingly episodic, with elaborate portals of various sixteenth- and seventeenth-century dates interrupting the wooden wainscoting along the inner side. On the other side the two-storeyed projection that corresponds to the three central bays of the facade is closed off internally from the main space. This contains, below, the Güldenkammer for privy meetings of the Council and, above, a musicians' gallery that is glazed towards the hall to match the big windows in the outer wall.

The doorway to the Güldenkammer in the Bremen Rathaus and the spiral stair leading to the chamber above provide virtuoso cadenzas that conclude late Northern Mannerism. They were completed only towards 1620 by the wood-carvers Evert Lange and Servaes Hopperstede (†1652). The wainscoting all around the great hall, which is doubtless somewhat earlier, displays a similar character though it is for the most part somewhat simpler and less plastic. In the recurrent pilasters and arched panels, as also in the mixture of flat strapwork and bossy elements in the ornament, this distinctly resembles contemporary interior woodwork in England. Much of that, reputedly executed by craftsmen from the southern Netherlands, dates from the last years of Elizabeth's reign and the

---

[55] The arcade contrasts equally with the "High Renaissance" severity of a prominent earlier example in Austria, the Stallburg in Vienna, begun in 1559: H. Kühnel, *Die Hofburg zu Wien*, Graz-Cologne, 1964, pp. 36-40; Baldass, *Österreich*, pl. 6. However, that in the Stallburg and also the ones at Graz and Klagenfurt were, after all, the work of Italians.

[56] Prange, coming from nearby Oldenburg, began to work on the Bremen Rathaus in 1609; van der Elst provided a project, for the facade only, in 1612 by which time the remodelling of the exterior was complete.

first of James I's, that is the decades immediately before and after 1600. The inspiration, however, often
came from Dietterlin's *Architectura*, as doubtless also
here in Bremen, a German rather than a Brabantine
source.

In Germany, as in England, the end of this stylistic
phase was already in sight just as the most extravagant examples were being finished. The Academic
facade of the Stadtmetzg in Augsburg (Pl. 405) rose
in the years after the major remodelling of the front of
the Bremen Rathaus got under way and, in England,
Inigo Jones was designing the Queen's House in 1616
or 1617 just as the lush decoration of the interior in
Bremen was approaching completion. The southern
Netherlands was the ultimate, if not the immediate,
source of most late Northern Mannerist extravagance
in the north of Europe. Yet the extension of the Stadhuis at Gent in Flanders, in a vein already rather
more Academic than the better-known one of the
early 1560s in Antwerp, was begun in 1595 and completed around 1620 before much of the decoration of
the Bremen interior was actually executed. Only the
simply scrolled gables, now battered, still echo Northern Mannerist ones of the previous decades of the
late sixteenth century above the regular ranges of
pilasters and windows of the walls. Even earlier, yet
more Academic still, are the coupled engaged columns
of the contiguous Bollaertkamer on the Hooge Poort
of 1580-1582 despite the chip-carved rustication which
is carried across the entire basement and also used on
the bands crossing the shafts of the ground-storey's
Doric order.

In Bremen there is another public building of the
same period as the remodelled front of the Rathaus.
Now known as the Krameramtshaus (Pl. 379), this
was completed by Ernst Crossmann from Lemgo in
1622[57] after Johann Nacke, who had begun the work
in 1619, died in 1620. This *Kost-und Hochzeitshaus*
(house for weddings and other festivities) was built
at the expense of the cloth-merchant Dietrich Diek-
hoff for the Tailors' Guild. The Krameramtshaus
facade provides a slightly later and almost equally
extreme example of Northern Mannerism—as regards the special character of the ornament, indeed,
it is somewhat more advanced than the Rathaus. Necessarily restored drastically in 1954 after serious war
damage, the front of the Krameramtshaus has two
storeys with very tall windows, each of two lights

under the left gable but of three lights under the
wider one to the right. All mullioned and multiple-
transomed, as those of 1608-1612 on the Rathaus are
not, the two rows of windows here are separated from
each other at first-storey level by a double band of
carved ornament that is repeated above at the eaves-
line.

Over the relatively severe facade of the Bremen
Krameramtshaus rise the two gables, both of four
stages, though that on the right is wider than the one
on the left as was indicated above. In both of the
gables shallow shell-crowned niches, those in the center occupied by statues, alternate with small two-light
windows. These last are framed by architraves and
crowned with various sorts of conventional scrollwork. Narrow string-courses in high relief define the
successive stages and carry obelisks on their ends in
the familiar way. But the scrolling at the edges of the
gables, particularly that of the second stage, is of a
strange, almost biomorphic, character quite different
from the crisply organized strapwork on the central
Rathaus gable of ten years before (Pl. 378).

If the term "decadent" may ever be descriptively,
though not moralistically, applied to any architectural
work, even one carried out in a mode as consistently
over-ripe as Northern Mannerism, it might be used
for Crossmann's decoration—so unlike that on his
father's somewhat earlier Rathaus at Hannoversch-
Münden (Pl. 383)—on the exterior of the Bremen
Krameramtshaus. However, ornament similar to his
appears also on Francke's Marienkirche in Wolfenbüttel (Pl. 433), a major church commission well under way by this date.[58] It is also to be seen on some
other surviving works in this region: There is, for
example, the Bürgermeister Hintze house of 1621[59] at
Stade, which is not far away on the Bremen side of
the Elbe estuary. This sort of ornament—which apparently began to spread only after 1620—has a particular name in German: *Ohrmuschelstil* (conch-style).
The name suggests the human ears that conch-shells
somewhat resemble.

The Rathaus at Bocholt (Pl. 380), near the Dutch
border across the Rhine from Kleve, was begun in

---

[57] Kreft-Soenke, *Weserrenaissance*, pp. 234-236. Stein, *Bur-
gerhaus in Bremen*, fig. 38, provides an elevation of this
facade as it was originally.

[58] It is not possible to date the various elements of the
decoration of the Wolfenbüttel church closely enough to establish priority for Francke's ornament, but it is not likely
that Crossmann's is dependent on it. Both sorts are probably
parallel developments from a common, probably Netherlandish, source.

[59] Reclams *Niedersachsen*, p. 704. The house in Stade was
drastically "restored," using old elements of decoration, by
O. Kiecker in 1932.

1618,[60] a year earlier than the Bremen Krameramts-haus. On that there is no ornament of this peculiar sort. For the most part the exterior is by contrast rather quiet, and Netherlandish in a retardataire way. The windows of the upper storeys, opening between engaged orders, for example, are topped by semi-elliptical brick bearing-arches, as on De Zalm of the 1530's in Mechelen. However, the loggia along the base of the front is at least as Italianate as that on the Bremen Rathaus, and more up-to-date in having compound piers of the Roman arch order. Such an arch order, moreover, cannot readily be matched in external arcades of this date or earlier surviving in either the northern or the southern Netherlands. The motif was, of course, long established in Austria and already used in Germany inside the Augustusburg chapel and the Würzburg Neubaukirche.

On the other hand, the detailing of the *estípites*-like order of the top storey of the Bocholt facade and also that of the extravagantly rich two-light oriel, project-ing asymmetrically in the second from the left of the eight bays of the middle storey is distinctly Northern Mannerist. The balustrade masking the base of the high roof recalls that of 1594 over the Schütting in Bremen (Pl. 232) and the one on the Bremen Rathaus (Pl. 376), which just preceded this one at Bocholt. The end gables of brick, however, with only rather simple broad scrolls of stone at the edges, are dis-tinctly Dutch rather than German. A good example in Holland for comparison is the gable of the house at Rijnstraat 41 in Arnhem, which is probably ten or twenty years earlier in date.[61] They can, however, be equally closely matched in Denmark on King Chris-tian IV's more nearly contemporary Rosenborg Slot in Copenhagen and on Jens Bangs' Stenhus in Aal-borg of 1623.[62] The cross-gable on the front, on the other hand, rising over the two central bays of the facade across the balustrade, is almost entirely of stone except for the bearing arches of the windows, and thus rather characteristically German.

At Münster in Westphalia, not far to the east of Bocholt, the Stadtweinhaus (Pl. 381) was built by a Bocholt master, Johann von Bocholt in 1615,[63] several years before the Bocholt Rathaus and in a much less Netherlandish vein. Although, like the earlier one at Alsfeld (Pl. 95), this is beside rather than under the Rathaus, the name "Ratskeller" would be more fa-miliar to English or American ears for the sort of civic amenity once provided here. The Münster exam-ple is, indeed, quite overshadowed visually by the tall and spectacular fourteenth-century facade of the Rat-haus side of it in the Prinzipalmarkt and, in fame, by the Friedenssaal inside the Rathaus where the Peace of Westphalia that ended the Thirty Years' War was signed in 1648.

Considered for itself, however, the Münster Stadt-weinhaus ranks high among civic works of the period. It is considerably more dignified, if far less sump-tuous, than the contemporary public works in Bremen (Pls. 376, 379), yet without any of the new Academic character of the Augsburg Rathaus (Pl. 415) as begun in this same year by Holl. Rather exceptional, and recalling slightly the much larger Doxal on the Cologne Rathaus (Pl. 237) Wilhelm Vernukken be-gan in 1569, is the two-bay porch projecting from the center of the ground storey. The carved ornamenta-tion is richer here and more plastically intricate, con-trasting with the plain smooth ashlar of the rest of the facade. Simply detailed and rather closely spaced rec-tangular windows, however, quite without mullions or transoms fill most of the upper wall-surface almost as on the Bremen Rathaus.

A flattened entablature, continuing the line of the top of the porch, crosses the facade of the Münster Stadtweinhaus at that level as do similar ones above the first storey and over each of the four stages of the tall gable. These quiet and markedly horizontal ele-ments on the gable provide visual support for the tall banded obelisks that rise from their ends and at the top. The scalloping at the edges of the flat planes of the gable, bold in scale but crisply detailed, consists mostly of ordinary C-scrolls paired one above the other, with those in the second and third stages termi-nating in projecting "horns" of the Weserrenaissance sort. Exceptionally, however, heart-shaped openings between the scrolls, just below the penultimate obe-lisk, vary the otherwise familiar pattern.

Two additional facades rebuilt in the Prinzipal-markt at Münster were of uncertain date,[64] but prob-ably a few years after the Weinhaus. One of them is five bays wide, another has three bays, and they are

[60] Reclams *Rheinlande und Westfalen*, p. 74.

[61] *Kunstreisboek*, p. 193.

[62] Skovgaard, *Christian IV*, pp. 67-74, 96. The building history of the Rosenborg Slot is very complicated and need not be detailed here.

[63] Dehio, *Westfalen*, p. 387.

[64] *Ibid.*, pp. 387, 391. The gabled house at Prinzipalmarkt 48 in Münster, however, the only facade there that survived the war intact, is dated as late as 1627. Jahn, *Deutsche Renais-sance*, pl. 60, shows the Prinzipalmarkt in color, as restored, from a photograph by Klaus Beyer.

crowned, respectively, with a three-stage and a two-stage gable. These gables are more elaborately decorated with pilaster orders and whorled scrolling than that on the Stadtweinhaus, perhaps because they are later. Thus, despite all the destruction of the last war, the Prinzipalmarkt as restored now offers a rather consistent image of early seventeenth-century civil architecture in western Westphalia.

As was true of Schlösser in this period and the immediately preceding one, however, the finest work was being done in other Westphalian districts lying well to the east of Münster along the Weser, more particularly the upper reaches of the river around Hameln. Bremen, of course, is on the Weser estuary, but far to the north. No longer did the regions further east beyond the Oder and the Neisse maintain their leadership. The Waga of 1604[65] (Pl. 382) at the town of Neisse (Nysa) is in Silesia south of Brzég (Brieg), thus very near the present border between Poland and Czechoslovakia. If one compares that with the Rathaus (Pl. 383) begun the previous year at Hannoversch-Münden—where, as noted earlier, the Fulda and the Werra join north of Kassel to form the Weser—the great superiority of the latter in quality is very evident. The comparison, however, is now hardly fair, since the former was largely destroyed in the last war and rebuilt only in much simplified form in 1947-1948 while the other is intact. Though more up-to-date than the membering at Hannoversch-Münden, the full entablatures on the Neisse gable always over-weighted the top of the facade. Except for the rusticated piers and arches of the ground-storey loggia, moreover, nothing else at Neisse at all approaches the sort of restrained and formal design Holl would soon be introducing at Augsburg and Eichstätt far to the southwest in Swabia.

By contrast, the decoration of the rooms in the top storey of the north wing of the Wawel Zamek in Kraków, not far from Neisse, rebuilt around 1600 for the Swedish-born King Zygmunt III of Poland, is more than a little premonitory of the lost interior of the Goldener Saal in the Augsburg Rathaus (Pl. 420) as that was carried out in 1620-1623 by Italian-trained artists. Like the once-magnificent interior at Augsburg, these rooms already approach the Baroque in their luxury. Though rebuilding began as early as 1596, the decoration in Kraków dates not from the late 1590s but, like the Neisse Waga, from 1604.[66] At

that point the Italian Giovanni Trevano, who had arrived the previous year to erect the Jesuits' Kraków church, took charge. What he provided naturally reflects work in Italy of the turn of the century as the earlier Waga—which must in any case be by a local northern builder-architect, not an Italian—of course does not.

The front facing the marketplace of the Gothic Rathaus in Hannoversch-Münden (Pl. 383) is almost precisely contemporary with the Neisse Waga. It was remodelled and extended in 1603-1609,[67] at first by Georg Crossmann (†1612) from Lemgo, the father of Ernst Crossmann who later worked in Bremen. Then, after he left, the local master-mason Friedrich Weitmann took over but soon gave up on the job also. It was eventually carried to completion only in 1619 by Simon Högel from Göttingen. In payment for the designs of the cut-stone trim on the gable and the oriel Crossmann received from the local Council 200 taler, another 220 for that on the main portal, and finally 112 for the chimneypiece, inscribed with the date 1605, in the upper *Hochzeitsaal* (hall for weddings)—there was no separate Hochzeits- or Weinhaus at Münden. It should be noted that the activity in Bremen of Georg Crossmann's son Ernst, who might have assisted here, provides evidence of a definite professional link between the upper and the lower Weser valley. That link seems, however, to have no recognizable stylistic significance as regards the particular structures in Münden and in Bremen of the two Crossmanns.

Portal, oriel, gables: these are the features generally elaborated in German Renaissance architecture, and of them the most important for the total architectonic effect are the gables. Despite the approximate symmetry of the plan of the Münden Rathaus, with two large halls on each of the principal storeys, this symmetry is made evident on the lower portion of the facade only by the axial location of the portal. Above, however, the three gables, that in the center only slightly wider and taller than the other two, are carefully matched and connected by freestanding bandwork elements below a continuous string-course. The Netherlander Anthonis van Opbergen, who had earlier worked on Slot Kronborg in Denmark, was joining together the gables on the Great Arsenal at Danzig in a similar way at much the same time.[68] Four

<hr>

[65] Łozinski-Miłobedzki, *Guide*, p. 170.
[66] *Ibid.*, p. 116.

[67] Kreft-Soenke, *Weserrenaissance*, pp. 253-254.
[68] There were probably comparable examples in Holland. The facade of the Amsterdam Arsenal at Singel 423 of 1606,

tall obelisks, two of them above the links, punctuate the top of this stage, while rather smaller ones flank the narrower stages above.

Scrolls, mostly S-scrolls, edge the successive stages of the Münden gables. In the third stage these are tied by flat bandwork in the side gables to the oculi and in the central one to the square opening. All three gables are crowned with human figures standing on molded cross-elements that rise above the scrollwork. Projecting "horns" are quite lacking, however, so that the outline of the gables is not otherwise very lively, at least by contemporary German standards.

Similar scrollwork, projecting well in front of the rubble wall-plane, flanks the central portal of the Münden Rathaus framing as well the armorial panel over it, and there is more scrollwork on the small gable that rises well above the level of the main eaves on top of the oriel. Ionic columns in pairs, their shafts fluted above and with vertical bosses below, support the entablature over the arch of the portal, while on the voussoirs of the arch oblong bevelled bosses alternate with lions' heads. The more characteristic chip-carved blocks of the Weserrenaissance are introduced here only on the sides of the broad podia of the Ionic order in place of the masks in high relief that ornament their fronts.

This detailing at the entrance of the Münden Rathaus has for the most part the same bold scale as that of the gables. The oriel, however, is more delicately treated; indeed, as so often, the mullions are almost too narrow for the herms carved on their faces. Yet this tall, thin feature, flanked by unbroken surfaces of rubble masonry, once perhaps stuccoed, balances very effectively the generously fenestrated lefthand section of the facade. In that the three paired windows in each of the storeys are set almost closely enough to equal the openness of the Fachwerk facades of which this town is so full.

Two other important civic buildings in the Weser region, both in rather larger towns than Hannoversch-Münden, were built in the second decade of the century: the Hochzeitshaus in Hameln of 1610-1617 and the Rathaus in Paderborn of 1612-1618 (Pls. 384, 385).[69] Neither resembles at all closely Crossmann's work, in part at least because the one at Hameln was entirely new-built and incorporated no

surviving mediaeval work at all while, at Paderborn, only the old vaulting of the cellar was retained. As mentioned earlier, the architect of the latter, Hermann Baumhauer from Wewelsburg, had remodelled the Schloss there for the prince-bishop of Paderborn, Dietrich von Fürstenberg, in 1604-1607 and was probably responsible well before that for the round towers Fürstenberg added on the corners of Unkair's Schloss at Schloss Neuhaus (Pl. 44) around 1590. It was the Catholic ruler Fürstenberg, moreover, who ordered the Protestant Council of this sharply divided town to build the new Rathaus at a cost of some 8,000 taler. At Hameln it was probably Eberhard Wilkening, whose best authenticated work is the Barntrup Schloss of 1584-1588 (Pls. 286, 287) who provided the design of the Hochzeitshaus for the city authorities.

Though neither of these terminal master-works of the Weserrenaissance rivals the Bremen Rathaus in elaboration, they are both much more coherent in design than that and they occupy equally prominent positions in their respective towns: the one in Paderborn at the upper end of the Marienplatz; the other in Hameln at the inner end of the principal street, the Osterstrasse. Of the two, the former is at first sight the more impressive, because of its very tall front gable and two lower gables that flank it. These cap the short projecting wings which rise above open loggias at the sides. At Hameln the Hochzeitshaus (Pl. 384) presents to the main street its long flat side elevation crowned by three identical cross-gables; owing to a break in the building line, however, the end-gable is also very conspicuous as one advances along the Osterstrasse.

Baumhauer combined three unrelated themes on the Rathaus at Paderborn (Pl. 385). Most striking are the gables with their scrolls, two to each stage, with the lower end of the upper scroll in each case flipped out in a bold "horn." Then there are the many identical window groups, with close-set lights separated only by delicate colonnette-mullions. More exceptional are the paired loggias at the base of the projecting wings. These last do not share the dainty scale of the window-framing and the gable edgings; they are instead massively tectonic. The columns of the loggias, three to a side, are short and sturdy below heavy Tuscan capitals and their archivolts are wide and flat, though banded with typical chip-carved voussoirs.

The windows of the Paderborn Rathaus are, exceptionally, all of eight lights on the front of the main storey of each of the wings; elsewhere on the ground and first storeys they are grouped in threes and then

attributed by some writers to Hendrick de Keyser, may be considered to be analogous, though the horizontal "binder," so to call it, is above rather than below the scrolled gable tops. Hitchcock, *Scrolled Gables*, Fig. 88.

[69] Kreft-Soenke, *Weserrenaissance*, p. 269.

in twos in the gables. The groups are linked at sill-level by continuous string-courses and again at their heads by the unbroken entablatures of the Ionic order of the colonnette-mullions. Below these last, small brackets repeat the reiterative pattern. This pattern is almost, but not quite, regular on the sides, though interrupted by the arches of the loggia at the front on the ground storey on both sides and by a projecting four-light oriel in the third bay from that end on the right.

Baumhauer's window treatment does, however, vary slightly on the gables. The string-courses at sill-level there are not continuous and the entablatures are punctuated by ressauts, not only over the colonnette-mullions, but also over the additional engaged colonnettes that flank each stage. Moreover, the grouping of the paired window-lights on the main gable is syncopated, with four in the lowest stage, then three, then two and finally only one in the penultimate stage, as also in the lower stage of the smaller gables.

Considering all that has happened to it—"renewal" in 1725-1726; restoration and remodelling of the interior in 1870-1878, when the present portal was introduced; bombing that gutted the building completely in 1944—the exterior of the Paderborn Rathaus is in surprisingly good condition today. That is because of the conscientious restoration carried out over the years 1947-1958.

An evident echo of the Paderborn Rathaus, especially as regards the window treatment, is the present Hotel Vialon at Horn on the main road to Detmold. Most probably it was Baumhauer who built this in 1616-1617 for Johann Hermann von Kotzenberg; the richly carved portal toward the marketplace was added by another Kotzenberg, Adam Heinrich, only in 1680. The exterior looks, all the same, to be of some two generations earlier. Thus it provides an exceptional but not unique example of continuing respect for earlier Renaissance work down into the late 17th century.

Testimony to the marked individualism of the builder-architects of the Weserrenaissance is the Hameln Hochzeitshaus (Pl. 384). It is surprising that a civic structure so different as that could have risen in another Westphalian town near Paderborn in almost exactly the same years—in this case 1610-1617[70] —as Baumhauer's. All the same the two do have in common their regular fenestration and vigorously horizontal entablatures topping the storeys, two at

Paderborn, three at Hameln. Moreover, their staged and scallopped gables are not dissimilar. They definitely share the same set of stylistic ideas, ideas that by this time had been developed through a generation and longer. Baumhauer concentrated his decoration at the openings, however, and even made that decoration mostly columnar, though still in a rather quattrocento way; Wilkening—or whoever was actually the architect of the Hameln Hochzeitshaus—left his windows quite unframed. For the most part, however, these are arranged in pairs, though they are single in much of the ground storey. All have transoms and are subdivided only by single mullions in contrast to the more extended groups of shorter and narrower lights on Baumhauer's Paderborn Rathaus.

The decoration on the Hameln Hochzeitshaus consists chiefly of repeated bands of chip-carving running across the whole surface of the wall, very much as on the south wing at Hämelschenburg as carried out in the 1590's. Only on the gables is the marked horizontality of this treatment balanced—again as at Hämelschenburg (Pls. 300, 303)—by vertical pilaster-strips; but even across these the chip-carved bands are continuous. Other echoes of Hämelschenburg are the crowned chimneys rising above and behind the peaks of the end-gables and the character of the scrolling on all the gables. The broad scale and the tightly spiralled ends of the paired scrolls, S above C in each stage, are almost identical with those on the Schloss.

The rows of windows on the Hameln Hochzeitshaus are quite regular along the entire length of the Osterstrasse facade in both of the two upper storeys. In the ground storey, however, the three portals are unevenly spaced. Two of these, moreover, have pediments set above flanking Corinthian columns, while the third (Pl. 387) has only a broad arch. That is decorated, however, on the imposts and on alternate voussoirs with flat strapwork, and there is a great deal of chip-carving on the wall between the portals. Their asymmetrical placing expresses the original subdivision of the interior into a weigh-house, an apothecary's shop and a wine store. In the main storey is the great hall for weddings and so forth and in the upper storeys was the town's arsenal.

Hameln today is predominantly stone-built and most of the older house-fronts that are not of freestone are now stuccoed over brick or rubble rather than visibly timber-framed. At Hannoversch-Münden the Rathaus was of masonry like that at Paderborn and the Hameln Hochzeitshaus, though the contemporary houses in the town are all of Fachwerk, with

[70] *Ibid.*, pp. 249-250.

only the churches and the Schloss also of stone. In some places, however, timber-framing continued to be used after 1600, as earlier at Alsfeld and Einbeck (Pl. 346) among other towns, even for civic buildings.

The Rathaus of 1610[71] at Höxter, in the Weser valley above Bevern, has like that at Einbeck and the court facades of Schloss Bevern a basement and raised ground-storey of masonry. But the slightly projecting upper storey above is of Fachwerk. In that upper storey there is simple X-bracing, not unlike that in the Bevern court (Pl. 370), below single windows which alternate with solid plastered panels of the same width. The end-gables rise in three stages, each overhanging the one below, while the long front toward the marketplace is dominated by an octagonal stair-tower. This is all of masonry up to the main eave, but it carries a terminal storey in timber capped by a double *welsche Haube* covered with slate. A pilastered portal at the base of the tower and an oriel in stone on the lefthand end are the only decorative features, both of rather unpretentious character for the district and the period.

Quite different is the small Altes Seminar or *Lateinschule* (Latin school) at Alfeld-a.-d.-Leine (Pl. 388) to the north of Bevern. That dates like the Höxter Rathaus from 1610.[72] Both storeys here are of Fachwerk and the many windows on the long sides are arranged in pairs with the solid panels between filled with brick. The brickwork on the ends is in big diamond patterns of two colors though plain on the long sides. All four facades are wholly regular and symmetrical. What is exceptional is the amount of painted decoration, for this fills not only the narrow panels below the windows of the two storeys but also those above and below the windows in the end-gables.

Polychrome decoration, elaborately restored around 1951, appears also on the vertical members of the frame on the sides and on the ends in both storeys of the Alfeld Lateinschule. The designer, and presumably the executant, of the painted scenes—some Biblical, others Classical in subject—and of the carved and gilded inscriptions was Andreas Steiger from Hildesheim. Unfortunately no comparable work at Hildesheim itself survived the last war; but the very elaborate facade extant at Marktstrasse 13 in Einbeck is somewhat more like this than the houses on either side. Doubtless it is of about the same date even though that is rather late for Einbeck. However, the

rich decoration is carved, in this case, not painted, as is the common treatment for the more ambitious Fachwerk facades of the period.

Such similarities indicate the essential identity of design common to all secular building in this region in towns both large and small. This is evident regardless of whether the structures were freestanding and served like Rathäuser some public purpose or private habitations of individual citizens such as rose cheek by jowl on both sides of main streets. From these last decades of peace at the opening of the seventeenth century, as from the previous period, quite a few houses, such as that in Einbeck, survive which rival—in their elaboration at least—contemporary town halls and Hochzeitshäuser. Good examples in masonry are the just-mentioned Hotel Vialon at Horn, today a very modest place, and the Heisingsches Haus (Pl. 325) at Marienplatz 2 in Paderborn, which was and is a small city rather than a town. The former is somewhat more probably by Baumhauer than the other, though it has been attributed to him. Whoever the architect may have been, the client was the Paderborn *Bürgermeister* Heinrich Stallmeister. As stated earlier, he was a Protestant who was frequently and almost continuously in office after 1585, even possibly as late as 1602, despite the overlordship of the Catholic Prince-Bishop Fürstenberg.

The situation as regards survivals from this period varies a great deal in different towns because of the vicissitudes of the intervening centuries. Recurrent fires and the ravages of war, particularly in the seventeenth and twentieth centuries, have done the greatest damage. The replacement or drastic remodelling of earlier houses that necessarily followed urban disasters explains the considerable variation of character between one town and another at least as much as localized modes of construction and design, for the same architect-builders often worked in several places. There are, of course, other new buildings serving public needs beyond the conspicuous ones already described not to speak of prominent features added in this period to earlier Rathäuser which deserve more than the mere mention those at Celle have already received.

At Lemgo, for example, the big apothecary's oriel (Pl. 389) on the Rathaus, carrying the date 1612,[73] which faces the marketplace is the most conspicuous element of the whole structure. This oriel is around the corner to the right from the porch on the Mittel-

[71] *Ibid.*, pp. 257-258.
[72] Reclams *Niedersachsen*, p. 12.

[73] Kreft-Soenke, *Weserrenaissance*, pp. 259-261.

strasse front, which initiated the career of the local sculptor-architect Hermann Wulff. Not only does the later oriel as seen from the northwest effectively balance that other tall feature in an urbanistic way, it also echoes the double dormer at the southern end carrying also the date 1589. The sculpture on that, as probably on the precisely contemporary upper storey over the northern porch, is by Georg Crossmann who later designed and began the Rathaus at Hannoversch-Münden. The extremely ornate oriel of 1612, however, is not by Crossmann, who died that year, but largely the work of the local master-builders Hermann and Johann Roleff. They were possibly assisted in the execution of the decoration by Hans and Jonas Wulff. The Wulffs had been doing their finest work for Ernst von Schaumburg just before this at Bückeburg (Pls. 357, 359, 434, 435) it will be recalled, but still maintained a busy family workshop in Hildesheim. Georg's son Ernst Crossmann had already left Lemgo and will hardly have been involved.

Whoever deserves the credit, this two-storeyed six-light bay-window of the Lemgo apothecary's oriel is a minor masterpiece. At the corners of both storeys are very elegant slim columns, plain Ionic below and fluted Corinthian above, with carved mullions separating the lights. Between the storeys a frieze is introduced with busts in relief of appropriate worthies, from the Dioscurides and Aristotle among the Ancients to the sixteenth-century Vesalius and Paracelsus. The frieze culminates on the gable with a cadenza of jewelled strapwork. This is quite unmatched on any house even in this town where so many Renaissance facades have survived. It recalls rather the ornament, of uncertain authorship, over the outer gate dated 1606 at Schloss Hohentübingen (Pl. 361). It is certainly not very like the work of the Wulffs at Bückeburg (Pls. 357, 359, 434, 435), for that is heavier in scale and much more derivative from Dietterlin.

At the opposite extreme, in what may be considered public as opposed to private architecture despite a client who was a single individual, is the penurious simplicity and retardataire design of the University of Mainz. The four-storeyed block, twelve bays long, that housed the university was built, late in his life, for Archbishop-Elector Johann Schweikhardt. Construction began as early as 1614, just after Ridinger completed the great Schloss at Aschaffenburg (Pl. 367), which had cost Schweikhardt, as has been noted, nearly a million florins. In contrast to the Schloss, it is even plainer than Julius Echter's earlier university building at Würzburg (Pl. 330). The monotonous

ranges of two-light rectangular windows are varied only by a pair of modest portals placed symmetrically in the ground storey and above, over the same bays, by small dormers. These carry a minimum of scrolling on their second stages and have old-fashioned *welsche Gebel* decorated with fluting on top. Little or nothing in the way of contemporary work is now extant at Mainz for comparison; as already stated, the electoral Schloss there was not begun for another decade. That was in 1627, the year after Schweikhardt died.

Elsewhere, however, quite a few very striking house-facades survive which date from the early seventeenth-century decades, several of them more than equal in interest to the public work of the day. In Hameln, for example, which had long been the headquarters of the Weserrenaissance, there are two houses of this period which are notable. These continue a local series of handsome street-fronts which began with the one Cord Tönnis built for Johann Rike in 1568-1569 (Pl. 227) or even, one could say, that of the Stiftsherrenhaus ten years earlier. One of the two most conspicuous later Hameln facades is all of ashlar masonry like those of various houses of the sixties, seventies and eighties. Another is of similar construction below, but the top storey and the gable are of Fachwerk. Thus that facade is in the tradition of the Stiftsherrenhaus here and, elsewhere in the Weser region, the Höxter Rathaus and the court facades at Schloss Bevern (Pl. 370).

The town of Hameln is world-famous for the legendary Rattenfänger (rat-catcher) known in English as the "Pied Piper of Hamelin." The name of this ambivalent character has in modern times been given to the finest house in Hameln. For that there is even less justification than the name of the mediaeval Danish prince Hamlet when applied to the Kronborg Slot as rebuilt by Opbergen in Shakespeare's own day. This house in the Osterstrasse (Pl. 390), near the other end from the Hochzeitshaus, was built in 1602-1603[74] several years earlier than that. The client was Hermann Avendes, a member of the local Council, but the identity of the architect has not been established. As for Schloss Hämelschenburg—which, of all current construction in this region, the Rattenfänger Haus most closely resembles—either Hundertossen or Wilkening has been suggested.

As on Tönnis's facade of the Gerd Leist house (Pl. 318) on the opposite side of the street, the entrance arch of the Rattenfänger Haus is pushed off axis by

[74] *Ibid.*, p. 249.

the two-storeyed oriel on the left here topped with a small gable; indeed, only the three stages of the main gable above are actually symmetrical. But there is such a carefully organized balance in the location of the window-areas in the three bays and the three storeys that there is no lack of architectonic order. As usual, the ornament on the oriel is much more delicate than on the rest of the facade, but throughout the detailing is of a complexity comparable to that of the south facade as erected in the previous decade of the Schloss at Hämelschenburg (Pl. 303). The pilaster orders that link the storeys vertically divide the front into uneven units: There are first, on the left, two half-bays, these overlapped completely through the two lower storeys by the oriel; then one wide bay in which the broad entrance arch is set; next, another half-bay; and, at the far right, what amounts to a quarter-bay.

The windows on the facade of the Rattenfänger Haus vary surprisingly: a single three-light one similar to that of the oriel opens in the ground storey to the right of the entrance; lined up over that there is in each storey a pair of close-set two-light windows; then, in the bay above the entrance arch, each storey has a pair of single windows; finally, over the right-hand half of the oriel, comes one narrow two-light window.

Only the line of the pilaster to the left of the last-mentioned window on the front of the Rattenfänger Haus is carried up into the gable; instead, the symmetrical bay-scheme of the lowest stage of the gable is syncopated irregularly with the asymmetrical scheme of the main facade below. Though most of them are now walled up, the four bays of this first stage were originally occupied by two-light windows. The flanking ones, which are slightly wider, have frames but the sides of the three middle ones are up against the pilasters. The design of those three bays in the middle is repeated in the second stage and that of the central one again in the third. There, however, a blind oculus rather than a rectangular window occupies most of the field.

The architectonic grid provided by the pilasters and entablatures on the facade of the Rattenfänger Haus is made more vertical in effect by boldly sculptured ressauts; yet across the whole wall there also runs an almost independent set of repeated horizontal bands. These are decorated, as earlier at Hämelschenburg and later on the Hochzeitshaus, with various sorts of chip-carving. Similar patterns diversify alternate voussoirs of the entrance arch, much as on the slightly later freestanding arches at Hämelschenburg (Pl. 299) and Haddenhausen (Pl. 371). Flat strapwork, with central rosettes in relief, decorates the other voussoirs, a motif repeated between the ressauts on the friezes of the successive entablatures. Thus there is a minimum of plain uncarved ashlar. On account of the relatively slight projection of most of the individual elements and the texture of the chip-carved horizontal bands, moreover, the general effect is even more consistently textile-like here than at Hämelschenburg or on the Hochzeitshaus (Pl. 384). That effect is almost as unlike the usual Northern Mannerist treatments of wall-surfaces by Germans or Netherlanders as it is different from anything Italian of this period.

Though the scrollwork outlining the three stages of the gable of the Rattenfänger Haus is not quite as similar to that edging the Hämelschenburg gables (Pls. 300, 303) as it is to the scrollwork on the Hochzeitshaus, its character is much the same. Here, however, exceptionally perky "horns" shoot out and up between the C-scrolls and the S-scrolls of the lowest stage. The obelisks introduced halfway up the sides of the second stage are hardly more protuberant here than the round balls that punctuate, as at Hämelschenburg, the outer rims of all the scrolls, including even the very short ones over the terminal stage.

The other most interesting house in Hameln of these years, that diagonally opposite the farther end of the Hochzeitshaus at Am Markt 7 (Pl. 391), is somewhat anticlimactic after the Rattenfänger Haus. Built for the *Bürgermeister* Tobias von Deventer or Dempster (hence known as the Dempstersches Haus) in 1607-1608,[75] four years later than the other but before the Hochzeitshaus was begun, it has a similar *parti*. Once more there is a single three-light oriel, here topped by a column-flanked and pedimented edicule. As this oriel is set far to the left the arched portal, almost identical with that on the Rattenfänger Haus (Pl. 390), could here be centered. The ground-storey windows have unfortunately been enlarged for shops; the ones in the next storey are all of three lights, but somewhat narrower than the ones on the oriel. These first-storey windows do not, however, like those on the Rattenfänger Haus, count as the vertical elements of a grid. Here the masonry portions of the wall, which are striped with bands of chip-carved blocks like the walls of the Hochzeitshaus,

[75] *Ibid.*

have no pilasters as on the Rattenfänger Haus and earlier at Hämelschenburg to balance the horizontal elements.

The Fachwerk of the top storey of the Demptersches Haus has the usual panels of identical width occupied alternately by windows and by solid plaster quite as on the Höxter Rathaus. Both the lower stages of the gable are similar, but the windows in them are shorter and paired. In the two central bays these are, so to say, syncopated with the symmetrically placed ones below. As restored, doubtless correctly, the small panels under all the windows and those above and below the plastered areas are covered with flat patterns, more or less of strapwork character, in white on grounds of strong colour. Moreover, the horizontal elements of the Fachwerk, though not the vertical ones as on the Alfeld Lateinschule (Pl. 388), are carved with continuous scrolling in very low relief.

An even more extravagant example of such decoration on a Fachwerk facade can be seen in the Kirchplatz at Rinteln (Pl. 392). This fronts the four-storey house, now the Heimatmuseum, that Christian Bokelmann had built in 1620.[76] Here the vertical elements carry the same scrolled carving as the horizontal ones while the patterns—at least as restored—are in colour against white. The few panels that are not ornamented are filled, not with the undecorated plaster of the court of Schloss Bevern and the Demptersches Haus, but with patterned brick somewhat as at Alfeld.

Doubtless there were once many more comparable house-fronts of richly decorated Fachwerk[77] and even today these two are by no means unique. More characteristic, however, is the considerably plainer Palmhaus (Pl. 393), dated 1610,[78] at Mosbach-a.-d.-Eltz, east of Heidelberg in Baden. That is, however, exceptionally large. It is also ungabled, with three sides therefore of more or less equal importance below the hipped roof, though a single octagonal oriel at the principal corner, rising through all the three upper storeys, provides one strong vertical accent. In the Mosbach market-place the Palmhaus is surrounded by many other timber-framed houses, mostly of around 1600 and gabled. Compared to them, this tall broad block is most impressive—more impressive, indeed, if less elaborated architecturally, than even the finest stone-built houses of the day in Hameln (Pls. 390, 391). Similar but smaller is the Rosenberger Hof next door. This also has an oriel which is dated 1600,[79] but only on the first and second storeys, and it is now crowned not by gables or an ordinary hipped roof but with a sort of flattened mansard, presumably of much later date.

Even less than in the work of this period by Hundertossen, Wilkening or Crossmann and their fellow Westphalians who remain anonymous is there any debt at the Palmhaus to the international conventions either of the later Renaissance or of Northern Mannerism. However, the molded polygonal bracket of stone supporting the corner oriel is carved with a crude figure doubtless intended as Bacchus, as well as a series of egg-and-dart and other Classical moldings. That is all which now survives of the original masonry ground storey between the modern glazed shopfronts.

In the upper storeys of the Palmhaus, each with what in Anglo-Saxon timber-framing is called a "hewn overhang," both structural and decorative elements are prominent in the design of the rectangular grid. Great Xs and other diagonals cross the solid panels between the paired windows for reënforcement while under them the simple X and lozenge patterns are slightly elaborated with a sort of cusping. This was produced, presumably as in Elizabethan England, by filling in with plaster selective chamfering at the edges of the members. The result is, of course, different in the absolute flatness of the dark-and-light pattern from the stone facades at Hameln with their architectural elements executed in relief; all the same, there is a certain similarity of scale and expression in the handling of the predominantly structural elements throughout. The date, 1610, is given in a carved inscription as was so often done on houses of Fachwerk.

Remarkable in another way, since rivalry with the sculptural decoration on contemporary architecture in stone was evidently the rather exceptional intention here, is the house at Marktstrasse 13 in Einbeck of 1605[80] which was mentioned earlier. Mannerist herms are carved on vertical members, which are not unlike those on several of the oriels executed elsewhere in stone in these decades around 1600. Then, on the

---

[76] Deutsche Kunstdenkmäler, *Bremen Niedersachsen* [Munich, 1963] (hereafter cited as DKD, *Bremen Niedersachsen*), p. 396.

[77] Horst, *Architektur*, pp. 250-270; his figs. 172-189 illustrate a great many that did not survive the last war.

[78] Dehio, *Baden-Württemberg*, p. 326.

[79] *Ibid.*

[80] DKD, *Bremen Niedersachsen*, p. 369.

panels below the windows at the base of the first storey, there are portraits in relief of the Evangelists engaged in writing the Gospels and other activities. Though not dissimilar to the ones in early mediaeval manuscripts, these derive here as do the herms from contemporary prints. The total effect of pretentious excess is distinctly provincial, lacking both the sturdy vernacular qualities of the plainer Fachwerk houses filling the streets of this and various other towns and any real comprehension of contemporary "high style," even of the most Germanic sort.

Doubtless the stone architecture of this period in Westphalia must also be considered provincial by international standards; all the same, the characteristic work there is so positively original that an autochthonous Weserrenaissance "high style" can be recognized which is both distinctive and distinguished. Although there is difficulty, as has been recurrently noted, in attributing many of the individual buildings to particular designers yet, beginning with Cord Tönnis and Hermann Wulff in the sixties, master-masons of exceptional architectural competence were in active practice for nearly two generations at Hameln and Lemgo and their production constitutes a notable group achievement. That achievement was not approached in consistency nor equalled in quality elsewhere in German lands until the second decade of the new century when Elias Holl reached professional maturity. From that time on, Holl was master of an Academic style that conformed closely to the higher international standards of the day thanks to what he could learn from Joseph Heintz, or recall from his own Italian travels and confirm in published architectural books.[81]

Around 1600, however, neither foreigners like Sustris and Nosseni nor other Germans with some personal experience of Italy such as Schickhardt and Krumpper rivalled the Weser masters in innate talent. The only near equals of the latter at the opening of the seventeenth century were the Netherlander Opbergen and, among Germans, perhaps Paul Francke and Hans Wulff. In the Wolfenbüttel Marienkirche (Pls. 431, 433) Francke maintained down to his death in 1615 the promise of his earlier Juleum in Helm-

stedt (Pl. 333) as spectacularly as did Opbergen in the Gdańsk Arsenal that of the Kronborg Slot in Denmark; while the facade of the Hauptkirche at Bückeburg—if it is indeed Hans Wulff's work—crowns a comparable if shorter and less well-documented career. But architectural achievement in these years was no more confined than earlier to the Weser district, even though the survivals in what were then big and prosperous cities—in contrast to such smaller places as Hameln, Lemgo and Paderborn—are by no means as notable as might be expected.

Throughout the sixteenth century Nürnberg, for example, was far more important than any of the towns along the Weser except the remote seaport of Bremen. Yet despite the active presence in Nürnberg in the early decades of the century of such artists as Dürer and Hermann Vischer, who were certainly among the most accomplished masters of Renaissance design of their day southern or northern,[82] Italian ideas in architecture came to acceptance there only very tardily. The Topler house of the nineties was still more Gothic than Renaissance in character. The Fembohaus (Pl. 324), not completed until just after that in 1598, is the earliest among those now extant to carry, above plain lower walls, a gable elaborated with an order on each of its four stages and with bold horned scrolls at their edges.

Of the next important house to be built in Nürnberg, the Pellerhaus (Pl. 395), which exceeded in size and elaboration anything of the sort previously erected there, almost nothing of the broad facade survived the last war except a few courses of rusticated masonry.[83] The front section of the Pellerhaus was erected in 1602-1605[84] for the merchant Martin Peller. Peller had settled in Nürnberg in 1581, coming from Radolfzell on the Zellersee, not far from the Swiss border in Baden. His southern origin offers in this period no plausible explanation, as it might have done earlier, of his relatively advanced taste. Moreover, his architect was local, Jakob I Wolf (c.1546-1612), the mastermason of the Nürnberg Rat; Wolf had as his associate here Peter Carl (born 1541) who had worked with him earlier on the Veste at Lichtenau,[85] a Nürn-

---

[81] One must not forget—as is so well known in regard to the formation of the mature style of Holl's contemporary Inigo Jones—the increasing availability of architectural treatises of the mid- and later sixteenth century, not to speak of the improvement in architectural delineation by northerners, an improvement surely related to their growing familiarity with engraved plates of architecture.

[82] In the case of Dürer, moreover, an artist admired and even emulated in cinquecento Italy, it should be noted.

[83] Reclams *Bayern*, p. 642.

[84] R. Schaffer, *Das Pellerhaus in Nürnberg*, Nürnberg [c.1935]; W. Tunk, "Der Stilwendel im Spiegel der Entstehungsgeschichte des nürnberger Pellerhauses," in *Festschrift D. Frey*, Breslau, 1943.

[85] Reclams *Bayern*, p. 470.

berg dependency that is just west of Ansbach. A bit later, in 1608,[86] Wolf provided the design of the Neue Hofhaltung at Bamberg for the Prince-Bishop Johann Philipp von Gebsattel. This structure as executed is so much simpler and more regular than the Ratstube of the Alte Hofhaltung across the way (Pl. 251) that it looks more like a contemporary university building than a Residenz. Today it is quite overshadowed by the tremendous L-shaped palace of the later Prince-Bishop of Bamberg, Lothar Franz von Schönborn, who was also Archbishop-Elector of Mainz. This is by J. L. Dientzenhofer (1660-1707) and the dates are 1697-1703.

In the same years 1607-1608, while Wolf was adding the court to the Pellerhaus and also working in Bamberg, he became involved as well, down to his death in 1612, in the reconstruction of Schloss Schwarzenberg at Scheinfeld, which is southeast of Würzburg. That ambiguous pile will be briefly discussed in the next chapter in relation to Elias Holl and the beginnings of Academic design in Germany. For all Wolf's considerable activity elsewhere in Franconia in the first decade of the century, the Pellerhaus was his principal work and, before its nearly total destruction, the facade was unequalled in size and architectural pretension, if hardly in distinction, not just by those of other houses in Nürnberg of the period but by any elsewhere in Germany of these years. Various public buildings, of course, were both larger and more sumptuously decorated, as several of this chapter's illustrations (Pls. 376, 384, 385) should make particularly evident, not to speak of those in Augsburg and even in Nürnberg to be described in the next chapter.

The facade of the Pellerhaus (Pl. 395) already approached Academic regularity, especially in the rusticated ground storey, so like that of the Nysa Waga (Pl. 382), with its plain, almost but not quite, semicircular entrance arch and flanking pairs of small round-arched windows (Fig. 62). The seven bays of the next two storeys were occupied by ranges of large rectangular windows. In the principal storey these were capped by flat arches and framed by Doric pilasters with rusticated shafts; in the storey above, the Ionic pilasters were plain. The projection of the oriel in the center bay, however, and the bold modelling of the scrolled keystones over the upper-storey windows —not to speak of the anomalous baluster-and-lozenge decoration in the panels below them—conflicted with

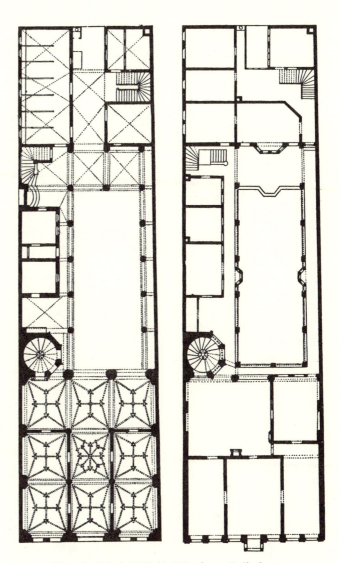

Fig. 62. Jakob I Wolf: Nürnberg, Pellerhaus, 1602-05, 1607-08, plan

the restrained character of the lower portions of the facade, a character which already suggests a little Holl's work in Eichstätt and Augsburg of 1509 and later. The still Northern Mannerist character of the three-stage gable, however, is comparable to that of many elsewhere which have been described earlier in this chapter, even if it is not of the high quality of the ones in the Weser valley region.

All the same, the fenestration in the gable of the Pellerhaus continued to be quite regular in the lower and middle stages. Moreover, the pilasters between the windows lined up with those below. That contrasts markedly with the complicated syncopation of the bays on the facade below the gable of the precisely

[86] H. Mayer, *Bamberger Residenzen*, Munich, 1951, pp. 63-71.

contemporary Rattenfängerhaus in Hameln (Pl. 390). The shafts of the pilasters, unlike those in the lower storeys, carried strapwork motifs in fairly high relief, while in the topmost stage herms were substituted for an order as on the Baumeisterhaus at Rothenburg (Pl. 320). Along the sides of the gable the scrolling was rather small in scale and restrained in curvature for this period in Germany; but the flat surfaces carried garlands in high relief and the globe-topped obelisks, three to a side, were hardly consonant in their almost Gothic spikiness with the decisive curved pediment supporting a statue that rounded off the top somewhat as with the crowning gables over the ends of the new wing of the Munich Residenz (Pl. 365) a decade later.

An even greater stylistic ambiguity marks the membering of the surviving court (Pl. 396). As noted earlier, it was in 1607-1608 that Wolf added this court behind the front section of the Pellerhaus. At first sight the arcading in the court may appear rather "High Renaissance," but that impression is soon dispelled. The piers in the ground storey are octagonal, not round, and brackets are clamped over the capitals below the corners of the abacuses. Truncated visually by the parapets at their bases, as so much earlier in the courts of the Altes Schloss at Stuttgart (Pl. 158) and the Dresden Residenz (Pl. 133), the arches of the upper storeys seem excessively broad and low in proportion while the tracery on the parapets is actually still Gothic. Finally the three oriels of prismatic plan introduce a note which is emphatically vertical if not quite so hybrid. The oriel at the end, moreover, rises against the front of a gable that is a coarse and abbreviated parody of the one originally facing the street.

The regularity of the facade of the Pellerhaus and the largeness of scale throughout offer some preparation for the advanced work by Jakob's son Jakob II in the vein of Holl that followed after his father's death in 1612. But because of the mixture of modes it is far less coherent in design than the work of Hameln and Lemgo architects in these years. It lacks, moreover, even the satiating but consistent richness of the Bremen Rathaus (Pls. 376-378) and resembles more Würzburg buildings in the *Juliusstil*, most of them considerably earlier in date if not in style.

Far to the east of Würzburg and Nürnberg, Erfurt in Thuringia had been a city of equal size and importance ever since the fifteenth century. The Erfurters had long been much readier than the Nürnbergers to employ Renaissance themes on the masonry facades of their larger houses. As early as 1538, it will

be recalled, the Haus zur hohen Lilie (Pl. 104) carried much delicate detailing of more or less quattrocento character around its portal and its windows. The Roter Ochse of 1563 (Pl. 224) and the Haus zur breiten Herd of 1584, both described in some detail in an earlier chapter, are among the most striking of German Renaissance town-houses and already quite as regular as the Pellerhaus except in their ground storeys.

Curiously enough, however, the house at Erfurt that corresponds most closely in date to the Pellerhaus, the Haus zum Stockfisch of 1607 (Pl. 397),[87] is not at all regular; moreover, the pilaster orders that are so conspicuous on the facades of the houses of 1563 and 1584 are here quite lacking. As on the Pellerhaus, the ground storey is rusticated, with plain blocks in relief alternating checkerboard-wise here with flat ones carved with various patterns of strapwork ornament. There is a similar alternation in the voussoirs of the broad arch at the far left end of the front leading to the court at the rear. On the principal portal, however, which is toward the other end of the facade, all the voussoirs of the arch carry strapwork ornament; and this arch, unlike the larger one on the left, is flanked by fluted columns. Above the entablature of the portal the *Stockfisch* (cod) that gives the house its name is carved on a panel set into an edicule. That edicule is flanked by colonnettes with strapwork carving on their shafts and capped, somewhat unexpectedly, by an oversize pediment.

Further to the right on the front of the Haus zum Stockfisch are two windows with flat stone frames decorated with simple scrolling and strapwork. Identical windows in the stuccoed wall above are arranged in three groups in each storey: There are two over the broader arch on the left; one on either side of the oriel; and three in the right half of the front. These last, however, are placed quite without relation to the main portal below. In the ground storey, under the tall oriel which is the most prominent feature of the facade, appear two more windows with pediments. Again these are not lined up with the ones above them. The rusticated ground storey is capped by a string-course continuing the sills of the first-storey windows and a similar one links the top-floor windows.

As usual, the oriel on the Haus zum Stockfisch is rather more elaborately membered than the rest of the exterior. Colonnettes rise at the corners of the two

[87] DKD, *Thüringen*, p. 371.

storeys and both the friezes of the related entablatures and the panels between the podia are carved either with arms in high relief or with flat strapwork. The main roof of the house runs parallel with the street so that no big gable was needed over the front. However, a small one of idiosyncratic character, for once quite unscalloped, tops the oriel. Thus no aspect of this front is even as proto-Academic as the facade of 1584 on the Haus zur breiten Herd here in Erfurt; the latter is more closely matched by a building of this period far to the south and west.

The very conspicuous house at one corner of the local marketplace later became the Rathaus in Gernsbach (Pl. 394), a small town just east of Baden-Baden in a district not otherwise rich in Renaissance architecture. This dates from 1617-1618[88] ten years later even than the Haus zum Stockfisch. It was built for J. J. Kast, a local shipper who controlled the timber traffic on the Murg, doubtless by an architect familiar with the Schloss at Aschaffenburg (Pl. 367) if not actually by Ridinger himself. Another Strassburger, Johann Schoch, Friedrich IV's architect at Heidelberg, has also been less plausibly proposed as the designer. Close-set rectangular windows, all divided by plain mullions, occupy the three storeys and also the lowest stage of the end-gables. These windows carry broken pediments resembling those on Schloss Johannisburg, which had been completed by this date. On the outer corner a polygonal oriel, rising through the first and second storeys, is supported on a simple rounded console and decorated only with three-dimensional strapwork. Very boldly plastic scrolls, Ss below in the first and second stages, and Cs with flipped-up "horns" at their lower ends above, scallop the edges of the gables. These are connected to the windows by flat strapwork executed at very large scale. The relative regularity and the strong horizontality of the string-courses and the crowning cornice, not to speak of the many pediments, broken though they are, combine to suggest as at Aschaffenburg some sort of Academic intention. The result, indeed, actually resembles a little the exterior of Heinrich Schickhardt's so much more advanced church of the previous decade, Saint-Martin at Montbéliard (Pl. 438).

The year the Kast house was finished was that when the Thirty Years' War began in Bohemia. Not all at once, but gradually and spottily, building activity in Germany came to a halt. In any case the latest

phase of Northern Mannerism, to which this chapter has been devoted, seems by this time to have been winding towards its end. Yet it is no more true in Germany that a general triumph of Academic design —much less a rapid acceptance of the Baroque—followed immediately after the completion of the Augsburg and Nürnberg Rathäuser in the early 1620s than was the case in England after Jones's Palladian Banqueting House in London was finished in 1621 and its Baroque ceiling by Rubens commissioned in 1629. The Queen's House, for example, which Jones had begun earlier, in 1617, was not finished until the mid-thirties under Charles I. It was only in 1635, moreover, that Rubens's paintings were finally installed in the Banqueting House, a few years before Orazio Gentileschi's on the ceiling of the hall of the Queen's House, so retarded was the initial impingement of even the Early Baroque upon England.[89]

This chapter might well have concluded—indeed, culminated—in an account of two Protestant churches, the largest and grandest yet erected anywhere. These are among the most considerable examples of late Northern Mannerism in Germany. But both the Marienkirche at Wolfenbüttel (Pls. 431-433), begun by Paul Francke in 1608 for Duke Heinrich Julius, and the Stadtkirche at Bückeburg (Fig. 68; Pls. 434-435), built for that even more ambitious builder Ernst von Schaumburg in 1610-1615, may be more effectively presented in the terminal chapter. There these can be considered in counterpoint, on the one hand, to the rising tide of Catholic church-building in these decades and, on the other, to certain nearly contemporary Protestant edifices that are much more advanced in style.

The increase in Catholic construction in Germany was a rather belated effect of the Counter-Reformation. It ensued well after the Council of Trent had concluded in the 1560s. Especially important as linking the two opposed sides is the Hofkirche at Neu-

---

[88] Dehio, *Baden-Württemberg*, p. 161.

[89] The north European parallels to the Banqueting House's ceiling by Rubens would be the rooms decorated earlier by Trevano, who came to Poland in 1603, for Zygmunt III in the north wing of the Wawel Zamek in Kraków and, later, the Goldener Saal in Holl's Augsburg Rathaus (Pl. 420) as painted by Matthias Kager following Peter Candid's designs in 1620-1623.

Charles I in England, on Lord Arundel's advice, employed artists of much higher international caliber than Zygmunt and the Augsburg Rat even if only some years after his accession in 1625.

The Gentileschi ceiling is now in Marlborough House in London, not at Greenwich.

burg-a.-d.-Donau. Begun by Duke Philipp Ludwig of the Upper Palatinate in 1607, this was designed originally for Protestant use. But it was only completed a decade later for the Jesuits after Philipp Ludwig's son, Wolfgang Wilhelm, who had been converted to Catholicism by his brother-in-law, Maximilian of Bavaria, succeeded in 1614. The Lutheran Philipp Ludwig was overt in his ambition to rival the Catholics' St. Michael in Munich and Wolfgang Wilhelm must have had a similar intention if for a contrary reason.

In church design more than in secular work stylistic difference can often be related, loosely at least, to non-architectural factors. The Catholic churches of the early seventeenth century in northern Europe, other than those of the Jesuits in the Rhineland, were mostly designed either by Italians or by men who had at least been trained in Italy; the architects employed by Lutherans were more usually Germans and the associated craftsmen often Protestant Netherlanders fleeing from the Spanish Inquisition at home. Yet too much weight should not be given to religion. The Neuburg church is quite different in plan and section from the slightly later churches at Wolfenbüttel and Bückeburg despite the fact that they were all three intended for Protestant use. The builder of the Bückeburg church, moreover, Ernst von Schaumburg, had called on the Italian-Swiss Nosseni to provide the very restrained Academic design of the mausoleum at Stadthagen (Pl. 442) already two years before he began his great Northern Mannerist church, as has been several times noted. It was, however, in the secular field and in buildings projected not by Italians but by northerners, that a new sort of architecture would most effectively develop in Germany, beginning rather gradually even before Nosseni was employed in 1608 at Stadthagen.

THE ACADEMIC TURN
AGAINST MANNERISM

Coeval with such extreme examples of Northern Mannerist architecture as the churches at Bückeburg and Wolfenbüttel, to be described at some length in the terminal chapter, came a sharply opposed reaction in much of northern Europe. This phase can be characterized as "anti-Mannerist," even though it is better not to name it so.[1] With it the German Renaissance concluded in the second decade of the seventeenth century, almost precisely a hundred years after its initiation around 1510 in Augsburg, and the locus was once more Augsburg. Moreover, it is the new restraint and formal order loosely called Academic here, not the latest excesses of Northern Mannerism, which prepared the way, or so it may be claimed, for the gradual acceptance of the Baroque.[2] That new current of architectural style soon began to flow northward from Italy, but only beyond the terminal boundary—around 1620—of this account of the German Renaissance.

In relation to preceding sixteenth-century developments in Italy the appearance in the north of the new stylistic discipline was a belated reflection of early Counter-Reformation architecture. That had largely superseded Italian Mannerism after the mid-century decades. Despite this Catholic background, such design in the early seventeenth century and after is at least as characteristic of Protestant England and Holland as of the various parts of the Continent that continued unreformed or were forcibly recovered for the Roman Church by the Emperor Ferdinand II and his Spanish cousins in the travail of the Thirty Years' War. Indeed, it was actually more accepted by the second quarter of the seventeenth century in the northern Netherlands of Frederik Hendrick and William II of Orange and in the England of Charles I and Cromwell than in the territories ruled by Habsburgs to the east of the central German lands and to the south of Holland.

The chronology of this architectural phase varies from country to country as do the particular sources of inspiration. Academic design of this general sort was introduced in Germany by Joseph Heintz and Elias Holl nearly ten years before Inigo Jones began the Palladian Queen's House at Greenwich in 1616-1617 for James I's Queen, Anne of Denmark, that is, about the time when Jones *may*, just possibly, have provided in 1613 a design for the Englischer Bau at Heidelberg which the Elector Palatine Friedrich V was planning to erect for his wife Elizabeth, the daughter of James and Anne.

Because of the Thirty Years' War, beginning in 1618, and its aftermath in the decades following the Peace of Westphalia in 1648 there could be no parallel in Germany to the mature Anglo-Palladianism of Jones, Webb and Pratt in the mid-century. The Civil War in England was much briefer nor did it exhaust the country to anything like the same extent; thus building could revive there by the late 1640s. Yet the Neuer Bau of 1614 in Augsburg (Pl. 414) is almost identical in design with the New Gallery that once existed at old Somerset House which was built for Charles II's French Queen only in 1661-1662 but reputedly followed a project by Jones that he might have prepared before the Civil War.

Even less is there any close analogy in German

---

[1] In early drafts of this text the adjective "academic," usually capitalized, was recurrently employed to describe this phase or sort of design. That usage is admittedly inaccurate—especially considering the way the word is most frequently employed by art-historians. At best it is no more precise than the negative term "anti-Mannerist" and it has been only sparingly used in this chapter. Its meaning for these years need not in the special context be ambiguous.

[2] As was noted earlier, German scholars have often considered extreme late examples of Northern Mannerism in Germany to be Baroque. Here only certain aspects of work of around 1600, and in a few instances, are presented as premonitory of the Baroque. A few precocious analogies to the "High" Baroque of the next generation in Rome, however, are occasionally noted.

lands with the Dutch Palladianism of Jacob van Campen (1595-1657) and Pieter Post (1608-1669). Holl's Augsburg Town Hall (Pl. 415), comparable in prominence, in size and in splendor to van Campen's in Amsterdam, was begun a full generation earlier, the one in 1615, the other in 1648; the Dutch architect's earlier Koymanshuizen in Amsterdam date from 1624, after the completion of the Augsburg Rathaus and Holl's other major works there, not to speak of Jakob II Wolf's new wing (Pl. 421) of the Rathaus in Nürnberg. But the Dutch story[3] starts much earlier, and its beginnings need not be summarized here.

In particular, however, it is the Haarlem Waag of 1597-1598[4] not the large and prominent extension of the Gent Stadhuis—still hybrid as regards the scrolled gables on top—which is the first nearly mature example of the new type of design in the Netherlands, though begun a year or two earlier. All the same, Lieven de Key's *Vleeshal* (meat-market) of 1602-1603, also in Haarlem, indicates that there was no immediate acceptance of this sort of architectural discipline in Holland.

In 1596 two painters, Willem Thybaut (c.1525-c.1598) and Cornelis Cornelisz. (1562-1638), who had both been trained abroad, were paid for providing three plans for the Waag. However, since Lieven de Key, the leading Dutch professional of the day, had been city-architect of Haarlem since 1593, it has been assumed by some writers that he really was responsible for the Waag as executed. In support of the attribution to de Key was the balustrade which once ran all around above the cornice, for this was evidently very like the one on the Stadhuis in Leiden. The latter, it will be recalled, had been in construction since 1594 under de Key's general direction though the work was probably executed in large part by Lüder von Bentheim from Bremen. Against this attribution for the Waag is the totally opposed character of de Key's Vleeshal of four years later, here in the Haarlem marketplace, with its ornate Northern Mannerist gables and dormers.

The use of stone throughout the Haarlem Waag, as at Leiden, rather than the more usual Netherlandish mixture of brick and stone on the Vleeshal, might explain in part the severity of the design; moreover, the portals on the two buildings, with their banded rustication, are very similar. On the other hand, except for the stone mullions and transoms, what might be called—rather prematurely—the "Jonesian" window-frames of the principal storey of the Waag, with their correctly Italian shape and their alternating pointed and segmental pediments, have no more in common with those of the Vleeshal than does the bold horizontal cornice crowning the walls of the Waag with the tall stepped gables over the front and rear of the Vleeshal.

Certainly, however, nothing so premonitory can be found that early in Germany. There, far more early seventeenth-century architecture resembles the Vleeshal than the Waag. Such facades as that of the Heeremanscher Hof of 1564 (Pl. 222) and the somewhat earlier one at Egidienstrasse 11 (Pl. 169), both in Münster—the latter apparently reflecting such contemporary Dutch work as the Kardinalshuis of 1559 in Groningen in its conspicuous use of applied orders—are rather offshoots from the earlier sort of design that has, doubtless exaggeratedly, here been called "Dutch High Renaissance." It is thus not necessary to consider them premature instances of the more mature architectural discipline which would eventually appear in Germany around 1610.

In the southern Netherlands the very considerable extension of the Stadhuis at Gent in Flanders is the one conspicuous work that might be considered relevant in this connection though not as notably as the contiguous Bollaertkamer erected by Joos Rooman in the early 1580s, twenty years before. Begun in 1595, the design of the Stadhuis extension must have followed only a year or two after that of the Haarlem Waag, though it was not completed for nearly a generation. On this, the almost total disappearance of the scrolling on the dormers above the long side because of the crumbling of the stone increases the monotonous severity of the design.

But what underlines most forcefully the contrasting character of the new portion is the marked difference between the regular rows of tall oblong windows on both the later facades, separated as they are only by plain pilaster orders, and the lush Brabantine Late Gothic of the contiguous earlier portion—which Waghemaekere and Keldermans had built almost a hundred years earlier. All the same, the ordonnance of the longer facade of the Gent Stadhuis was not so novel in the southern Netherlands. It follows that on the Antwerp Stadhuis of 1561-1664 (Pl. 175), though without repeating the hipped roof or the elaborate central frontispiece over the entrance.

[3] The Dutch story is best told in English in [H. E. van Gelder], *Guide to Dutch Art* (henceforth cited as van Gelder, *Dutch Art*), pp. 88-108. See also Hitchcock, *Scrolled Gables*, chapter VII.

[4] *Kunstreisboek*, p. 359.

In other words, there was not as in Haarlem any positive innovation to supplant effectively the continuing influence of earlier Netherlandish designers such as Floris and Vredeman. Much less, however, is there any reflection at Gent of the even more extravagant late Northern Mannerist ornament of Wendel Dietterlin. That became available by the mid-nineties in his publications of 1593 and 1594 from Stuttgart and from Strasbourg, respectively. It was more broadly distributed from 1598 onward by the second edition of *Architectura* which then appeared in Nürnberg.

A version of the new severely formal design appeared early in Switzerland at Luzern. The main facade of the Rathaus there was begun in 1599 by Antony Isenmann, only two years after the Haarlem Waag, and largely completed by 1606[5] long before the Gent Stadhuis. On this two regular rows of rusticated arches run along the quay of the Reuss, rather than pilaster-orders as in Flanders, and the result is equally advanced, except for the very heavy and clumsy Swiss roof with which the Luzern Rathaus is crowned. The Great Hall inside is dated 1604-1605 and the tower on the Kornmarkt side is still later— 1628—yet much less Italianate. Dietterlin certainly had no influence here and apparently little elsewhere in Switzerland and in Austria;[6] instead, contact with northern Italy continued in these years to be as close as it had been earlier.[7]

On the other hand, certain characteristics of Dietterlin's engravings (Pl. 401) offer a sort of parallel— if hardly a probable source—for the detailing of the transitional facade of the Zeughaus in Augsburg as built in 1602-1607[8] (Pl. 399). That was devised by a designer of Swiss origin, but carried out by the native Augsburger Elias Holl (1573-1646). Holl had returned from an Italian trip two years earlier in 1600 and had just taken on, in 1602, the professional heritage of his father Hans (†1594) as *Stadtbaumeister* (city-architect) of Augsburg.[9] He had already built

the modest *Giesshaus* (cannon-foundry) of the city in 1601-1602.[10] Construction of the Zeughaus had actually been started in 1600 by Jakob Eschay (†1606), who was the elder Holl's successor as *Stadtbaumeister* of Augsburg. Eschay's private work had included the big Schloss that Hans Fugger built at Kirchheim-a.-d.-Mindel in 1575-1585, within which is the Cedernsaal with its magnificent ceiling by Hubert Gerhard (Pl. 350).

No credit for the original design of the main or east facade of the Zeughaus goes either to Holl or to Eschay, though Holl may have modified it somewhat in execution, squeezing in rounded windows to light a mezzanine over the first storey. This impressive and original composition, as remote from most contemporary Northern Mannerist facades as from the Haarlem Waag or the Luzern Rathaus, is essentially the work of Joseph Heintz (1564-1609).[11] Heintz, a Swiss, was almost certainly a Protestant since he was the son of Daniel Heintz, *Stadtbaumeister* of Basel and later of Bern. He was trained in Italy where he studied painting in Rome in 1584 under Hans von Aachen (1552-1615). After eight years in the south he became in 1591 *Hofmaler* (court-painter) to the Emperor Rudolf II and settled in Prague in 1596.

A favorite of Rudolf, Heintz was employed both as painter and as architect, though Rudolf was never much of a builder.[12] He was kept busier elsewhere,

---

[5] *Kunstdenkmäler, in der Schweiz*, 2 vols., Munich, 1969-1970 (henceforth cited as *Schweiz*), I, pp. 136, 371.

[6] H. Aepli, *Der westschweizerische Profanbau der Renaissance, 1550-1680*, Fribourg, 1960, does not altogether support this opinion as regards the seventeenth century.

[7] Reclams *Schweiz und Liechtenstein*, pp. 435-436.

[8] Breuer, *Augsburg*, pp. 65-66.

[9] Holl has been much studied. Of the literature, in addition to his own *Selbstbiographie des Elias Holl*, Augsburg, 1873, there is J. Baum, *Die Bildwerke des Elias Holl*, Strasburg, 1908; H. Hieber, *Elias Holl, der Meister der deutschen Renaissance*, Munich, 1923; and J. Albrecht, "Elias Holl,"

in *Münchener Jahrbuch der bildenden Kunst*, XII (1937), 101 ff. W. Neu and Frank Otten, *Landkreis Augsburg*, Munich [1970] describe several examples of Holl's work on rural churches in the Augsburg district, none of much interest.

[10] Rauch, *Augsburger Baugeschichte*, p. 31, provides a section showing the vaulting; her p. 133 shows the Giesshaus as drastically restored in 1969-1973 to house the Stetteninstitut.

[11] J. Zimmer, *Joseph Heintz der Ältere als Maler*, Heidelberg, 1967.

[12] R.J.W. Evans, *Rudolf II and his World*, Oxford, 1973 (henceforth cited as Evans), Chapter 5, offers a not very thorough account of "Rudolf and the Fine Arts": ". . . local modifications of Gothic and Renaissance entered as a formative element in Rudolfine style. This is clearest in architecture. It has been said that Rudolf possessed no interest in building, perhaps because the medium was too 'solid' and impersonal for him. The observation is at best a half-truth: certainly no 'court' style emerged and there was no wave of palace-building by the emperor," p. 184. For the royal stables that housed the imperial menagerie or aviary, however, "architects like Heintz designed fitting accommodation," p. 177. See also J. Zimmer, "Josephus Heinzius, Architectus quam Antiquis Comparandus," *Umění*, 1969, pp. 217-243.

It is unfortunate that no work by Heintz seems to survive in Prague. One might note, however, that the building hous-

however, notably in Augsburg and at Neuburg-a.-d.-
Donau, from 1602 down to his death. He is represented in Augsburg as an artist by two paintings that
survive, signed and respectively dated 1607 and 1608,
in St. Anna and in St. Michael. He provided, moreover, the design for the demolished Siegel Haus there
(Pls. 400, 402) in 1605, and shortly thereafter that for
the front of the *Stadtmetzg* (butchers' guildhall),
though that was built by Holl only in 1609, the year
of Heintz's death (Pls. 404, 405). These last are crucial
works for the initiation in Germany in this decade of
the new sort of architectural design. Heintz was first
called to Neuburg early in 1603 to design the Rathaus
and also the Hofkirche, but the construction of that
very innovative church began only in 1607.[13]

Although a certain resemblance to Dietterlin's designs is evident on the Zeughaus facade in Augsburg
in the bold, even coarse, scale of the membering, any
influence from that source is unlikely considering
Heintz's training in Italy, if not his experience in
Bohemia. Somewhat similar is an abstract sort of plastic invention evident especially in the handling of the
window enframements. These actually recall some of
Michelangelo's detailing on the Porta Pia, a not impossible source in Heintz's case since he had certainly
been in Rome. The suggestion, at least, of a comparably heavy scale, combined with a rough stoniness of
texture produced by rather free shading, can be recognized in the series of engraved plates of columns,
entablatures and so forth that Dietterlin provided in
the first portion of his *Architectura* (Pl. 401) as published in Stuttgart in 1593. Figural, floriate and strapwork ornament is far less frequent in these plates than
in those that came out later in 1594 and 1598 (Pl. 355).
Heintz would hardly have depended on Dietterlin's
plates of the Tuscan order for an immediate model;
rather he was designing parallel to Dietterlin. But his
choice of the masculine Tuscan mode they would
both have considered appropriate for an arsenal must

have been a decision that was intentionally anti-Mannerist, if not proto-Academic.

On the ground storey of the Augsburg Zeughaus
(Pl. 399) the wall and the Michelangelesque pilaster
clusters, as well as the frames of the two square windows and the three-sided arch of the portal—so like
what Rubens would use for the garden gateway he
built behind his house at Antwerp some ten years
later—are all rusticated. The relief of the membering
in several planes throughout is most evident in the
repetition of the impost moldings of the arch on the
rear members behind the pilasters at the sides of the
facade. The projection of the half-columns in front
of the pilasters flanking the portal is still more boldly
three-dimensional.

In the main storey of the Zeughaus the pilasters are
again Tuscan and grouped, but rustication is restricted to the rear members. The big window-frames
at this level with their crowning fragments of broken
pediments—so much stronger in their relief and more
accented as verticals than Ridinger's of a few years
later (Pl. 368) at Aschaffenburg—were doubtless intended by Heintz to occupy alone the three bays. But
the introduction of the oculi, cutting up through the
entablatures and capped again by bits of broken pediment, distinctly enhances the proto-Baroque impression made by the facade. Moreover, the triglyph-
brackets below the entablature blocks of the windows
—fluted at the main windows, plain below the oculi—
seem a quite specifically Michelangelesque feature.

The second storey of the Augsburg Zeughaus, since
it is treated as an attic, is lower than the first; and the
windows, though identically framed, are square not
oblong. The principal members of the clustered vertical elements here are not really pilasters at all but
merely flat shafts elaborated with scale-covered scrolls
in relief at their tops.

The first stage of the Zeughaus gable is as tall as
the ground storey and has one central window just
like those below. At the sides plain S-scrolls attached
to a straight-edged rear wall reach out in great spirals
toward the modest balls over the outer verticals. The
members flanking the window in the central bay—
again not proper pilasters—are topped not by capitals
but by elongated triglyphs and the flat rear elements
of the wall behind them continue the plane of the
scrolls. The next stage repeats in simplified form the
second storey, with the single window here an oculus
like those in the mezzanine of the first storey. The
outer planes here recede in a rather complicated way
related to the flat rectangular element below. The

ing the *Micovna* (royal tennis court) on the Hrad, a late
structure of 1567-1569 by Bonifaz Wolmut who completed
the Belvedere, is distinctly "High Renaissance," not to say
Academic, in character: Knox, *Bohemia*, pl. 11a. Wolmut
actually survived until 1579 and worked for Rudolf in the
earliest years of his reign. The High Renaissance character
of what was erected in Habsburg territories in Austria under
Maximilian II and in the early decades of Rudolf's reign
has been discussed earlier, as also the arcaded courts of
Moravian castles of the mid- and late sixteenth century.

[13] J. Zimmer, *Hofkirche und Rathaus im Neuburg/Donau*,
Neuburg-an-der-Donau, 1971 (henceforth cited as Zimmer,
Hofkirche und Rathaus), pp. 10, 40-41.

crowning feature is more conventional, a very heavy broken pediment framing a pineapple set on a podium.

Somewhat surprisingly, analysis thus reveals in this remarkable facade rather more analogies with the still-unformulated Baroque of Italy than with the preceding work of the early decades of the Counter-Reformation there, at least as that is now best known in Rome and in the Veneto. The multi-planar treatment of the surface already suggests such a facade of the 1620s as Bernini's on the Propaganda Fide in Rome. The idea doubtless came from Vignola's plates published in 1563, or possibly from Ammannati's Collegio Romano of 1583-1585 in Rome, a work Heintz might well have known since it was in construction while he was there.

The total absence of foliate and strapwork ornament on the facade of the Augsburg Zeughaus seems to offer convincing evidence that Heintz was intentionally eschewing the decorative exuberance of Northern Mannerism in favor of a more architectonic sort of plasticity. The result is not without a rather remote similarity to the latest prominent church facade in Rome, that of Santa Susanna, built by Maderno over the years 1598-1603. Heintz's ultimate inspiration, however, even after his years in Prague must still have come rather from sixteenth-century work by such Milanese or Genovese architects as Tibaldi and Alessi, rather than from that of his own contemporaries, Maderno in Rome or Ricchino in Milan,[14] much less from Haarlem in Holland or in Luzern in his native country. As was true in the early decades of the century, once more advanced Italian influence seems to have been reaching Germany initially *via* the lands to the east not from the Netherlands to the west: at the opening of the new century, it was from Bohemia that Heintz came to Swabia not from Antwerp or Amsterdam.

Another most important architectural project with which Heintz was involved, from just after he designed the Zeughaus in 1602, was the Hofkirche at Neuburg-a.-d.-Donau (Fig. 66) which has already been mentioned several times. This will be discussed in the terminal chapter in relation to other major churches of the opening years of the century.

What adds the most intense note of a new and already almost Baroque vitality to the facade of the Augsburg Zeughaus is the large sculptural group in bronze above the portal. In intentional rivalry with Gerhard's St. Michael on the Munich Michaelskirche of the early 1590s (Pl. 258), Hans Reichle (c.1570-1642)[15] produced here his masterpiece in the precariously perched Archangel, the stricken Lucifer and the flanking subsidiary angels with their flags and lances. In 1605,[16] at the same time he was designing the St. Michael group, Reichle modelled and Wolfgang I Neidhart (c.1575-1632) cast in bronze—as he did also the group on the Zeughaus—the statues on the Kreuzaltar in the eastern bay of the nave of Sts. Ulrich and Afra in Augsburg, his other principal work. Reichle, who came from Schöngau in southern Bavaria, had been an assistant of Giovanni da Bologna in Florence over the years 1588-1593, coming north then to execute in 1595 a Magdalen in the Michaeliskirche at the base of the Crucifix that Wilhelm V had commissioned from Giovanni da Bologna. That naturally is in the latter's ambiguous style. But the forty-four terra cotta statues of Habsburg ancestors Reichle then executed over the years 1595-1601 for the palace of Prince-Bishop Andreas Cardinal Habsburg at Brixen (Bressanone) in the southern Tyrol have been considered by some to be Baroque.

Even before Holl had completed the Zeughaus and Heintz had painted the two pictures for Augsburg churches mentioned earlier, Heintz made his project in 1605[17] for the Siegel Haus of the city authorities of Augsburg. Of this nothing now survives except an elevation (Pl. 402) drawn by Holl; but there are prints showing the whole Weinmarkt before the Siegel Haus was demolished (Pl. 400). It was Holl who carried out the work and may have introduced certain relevant changes, though this seems rather less likely than his possible responsibility for the mezzanine windows on the facade of the Zeughaus.

However that may be, the end elevation of the Siegel Haus on the south was somewhat simpler and less plastic than is that of the Zeughaus. The three storeys, plus the lowest stage of the gable, were grouped by two superposed orders, Ionic below and Corinthian above. The entrance arch was round and had vermiculated[18] voussoirs. Above, triglyph brackets

---

[14] Ricchino started practice in Milan only after his return from Rome in 1603, and his San Giuseppe was not begun until 1607, the year the facade of the Zeughaus was completed in Augsburg.

[15] Osten-Vey, *Germany*, p. 328.

[16] Breuer, *Augsburg*, p. 44.

[17] Stange, *Deutsche Baukunst*, p. 141.

[18] Vermiculation may be considered Academic in contrast to chip-carving: That is characteristically Northern Mannerist despite its continued use well down into the mid-seventeenth century.

at the sides support a balustraded balcony. The windows were all square rather than oblong, with those in the ground storey capped by plain pediments. In the first storey, however, the windows had broken pediments that overlapped the architrave of the Ionic entablature, while thin cornices supported by more triglyph brackets topped the ones in the second storey. Above those, as over the ground-storey windows below, a subsidiary string-course split the total height of the two-storeyed order.

Over the upper storey on the Augsburg Siegel Haus the first stage of the gable was terminated at the sides by simple C-curves, quite unscrolled, below the extensions of the Corinthian entablatures to the left and right. These very plain elements recall Vignola's use of concave quadrants on his church-facades and facade projects of the mid-sixteenth century in continuation of Serlio's. These may, in fact, actually imitate them in even more intentional avoidance on Heintz's part of the richer Northern Mannerist sort of scrolling on gables than at the Zeughaus a few years before. The second stage, however, was flanked by S-scrolls, though these are also very plain. The scrolls were likewise much extended horizontally and also linked, above fluted blocks, by a heavy segmental pediment that was broken to provide space in the center for a Corinthian capital topped, as on the Zeughaus facade, by a pineapple. Except for the pediment, however, the somewhat Dietterlinesque bombast of the Zeughaus facade was largely absent. This was evidently even truer of the long side elevation with its giant Ionic order, continuing that on the ends, and its ranges of identical windows in each storey. A comparable ordonnance of tall Doric pilasters with pedimented windows between appears also on St.-Martin at Montbéliard (Pl. 438), begun from a project by Heinrich Schickhardt that is dated 1602, as also on the Neuburg Hofkirche (Pl. 437), for which Heintz was preparing not dissimilar external designs over the years 1603-1606 (Fig. 66).

Rather like the Siegel Haus but more plastically treated is the octagonal tower at Augsburg (Pl. 403) with which Holl, in this case on his own, crowned the mediaeval *Wertachbruckertor* (Wertach bridge gate) in the same year 1605[19] the Siegel Haus was built. On this also there is a giant order, here bent as on Nosseni's Stadthagen mausoleum at the eight corners, and two sets of plainly framed windows, one above the other. Only the rather coarse execution of the members, with no carved work at all, still seems somewhat tentative and without the assurance of the orders on the contemporary Siegel Haus, at least as that is known from visual documents that survive (Pl. 400). The absence of a *welsche Haube* is worth noting, especially since Holl used such terminations later over the top stage, dated 1614-1616,[20] he added on the Perlachturm by the side of the Rathaus and also on the towers of 1618 of the Rathaus itself (Pl. 415), all close variants otherwise of the one above the gate.

In 1607,[21] after the burning of Schloss Schwarzenberg at Scheinfeld in Franconia, southeast of Würzburg off the road to Furth, Holl rather than Heintz was asked by Count Schwarzenberg to provide plans for rebuilding. Construction—as mentioned earlier, not under Holl's supervision but that of the Wolffs from Nürnberg—was completed by 1616. A north wing was added in the 1650s and later, in 1672-1674, the dominating Schwarzer Turm shortly after the Schwarzenbergs became princes in 1670. There is, indeed, little about the Schloss today with its innumerable gables—four on each long side, three on the end—and its corner turrets to suggest Holl's hand except the regularity of the fenestration throughout. The windows, moreover, are mostly capped with cornices; while those in the gables—now plain but shown by Merian[22] as scalloped—are framed by flat rustication.

Unlike the Augsburg Stadtmetzg, carried out from a slightly earlier project of Heintz by Holl a year or two later in 1609,[23] Schloss Schwarzenberg, though rather simple, can hardly be considered to be properly formal in the new manner even though characteristic Northern Mannerist features are lacking, at least on the Schloss as it survives today. Comparison with Schloss Willibaldsburg outside Eichstätt (Pls. 406, 407), to be described shortly, for which Holl provided the design about 1609 suggests it was only in that year he turned firmly and consistently towards severe regularity and away from the three-dimensional elaboration of Heintz's Zeughaus facade or his own Wertachbruckertor (Pl. 403). Of that still transitional character there is more in an extant elevational drawing for the Stadtmetzg (Pl. 404) doubtless made by Holl rather than Heintz as a modification of the latter's design. This facade project is quite similar in the

[19] Breuer, *Augsburg*, p. 62; Rauch, *Augsburger Kunstgeschichte*, p. [104].

[20] Breuer, *Augsburg*, p. 64; Rauch, *Augsburger Kunstgeschichte*, p. [95].

[21] Reclams *Bayern*, pp. 794-795.

[22] Merian, *Schönsten Schlösser*, p. 8.

[23] Breuer, *Augsburg*, p. 66.

main to what was actually built, but it has rusticated pilaster strips between the bays and rusticated arches rather than pediments atop the windows of the first storey.

In the facade of the Stadtmetzg as executed (Pl. 405) the evenly spaced range of six pedimented windows in the first storey is even more characteristic of the new Academic mode than the pilastered ordonnance on the long side of the Siegel Haus. The plainer enframement of the windows in the storeys below and above, moreover, retains the emphasis on the main storey, despite the fact that the upper windows are oblong, not square as might by this time have been considered more proper for an attic. The two symmetrically placed portals, being more mid-sixteenth-century Italian in their architectonic elaboration than Northern Mannerist, do not seriously conflict with the greater severity of the storeys above.

Even in the gable of the Stadtmetzg, moreover, the segmental pediments of the windows of the lower stage, if not to the same degree the segmental arches of those in the second stage, accord well with the strong horizontal lines of the main entablature below the terminal entablature and the plain pediment above. The multiple planes of these stages suggest somewhat, however, as does already the similar treatment of the front of the Zeughaus as completed in 1607, the early Baroque of Italy. The side-pieces—scrolls in the first stage, C-curved cornices in the second—do not seriously compete with the calm rectangularity of the rest of the facade, so unlike the dynamic energy of the front of the Zeughaus as exaggerated by the already Baroque character of Reichle's St. Michael above the portal (Pl. 399).

Whether or not Holl modified Heintz's original project for this Augsburg facade, it was he who carried it out in 1609 the year Heintz died. For Schloss Willibaldsburg, moreover, on the heights across the Altmühl from Eichstätt, which lies to the north of Neuburg-a.-d.-Donau, Holl provided the ruling prince-bishop, Johann Konrad von Gemmingen, with a design probably in the same year 1609[24] that the Stadtmetzg was built. Construction there, however, was in the hands of Johann Alberthal (Giovanni II Albertalli).

As regards Alberthal—whose father Pietro I Albertalli (1542-1616) was certainly from the Italian-Swiss

Grigioni but may himself have been born in Eichstätt—there will be more to say in the next chapter concerning his later work for the Jesuits in Dillingen and in Neuburg. Like Holl, he had possibly been associated with Heintz several years before the latter's death. In his case, this would have been when he executed Heintz's design for the Lutheran church at Haunsheim,[25] a small village on the Eger west of Dillingen, for the local lord Zacharias Geizkofler. It was on the recommendation of Duke Philipp Ludwig of the Upper Palatinate, who was then erecting from Heintz's designs the Lutheran Hofkirche at Neuburg, that Geizkofler had consulted Heintz; in any case, he may have known him already at the court of Rudolf II in Prague since, though a Protestant, Geizkofler was imperial *Pfennigmeister* (financial officer), a responsibility that frequently required his presence in Prague.

Of the old mediaeval fortress outside Eichstätt dating from the fourteenth century little survives; but one of the interior courts of the Schloss Willibaldsburg, that in what is called because of the bishop the Gemmingenbau, which Alberthal brought to completion only in 1619—well after the bishop's death in 1612 —is extant as also the wings that enclose it, except for the tops of the corner towers. Upon the tremendous substructure of the earlier fortifications, treated as a terrace, Schloss Willibaldsburg presents towards the west a grand but rather barren front (Pl. 406). The main portion rises in three storeys above a basement with rows of widely-spaced rectangular windows in the two upper storeys and only slot-like openings below. The windows are all framed with identical architraves and have flat aprons below their sills. At both corners stand towers, somewhat as at Aschaffenburg (Pl. 367), rather than pavilions of the French sort such as were introduced at Horst (Pl. 181) in the 1560s; these rise a storey higher than the wing between and are broken only by one window in each of their faces. Quoins at the corners of the towers and string-courses at the bottom of the aprons under the windows provide the only relief. The towers each terminate, however, in a further octagonal storey, again with quoins on the corners rather than the giant order of Holl's gate of 1605 in Augsburg (Pl. 403) and single windows between. Today the octagonal stage is topped with battlements, but originally the towers carried swelling *welsche Hauben* approaching the onion shape of those crowning the features Holl

[24] Reclams *Bayern*, p. 257; T. Neuhafer, *Eichstätt*, 3rd ed., Munich [1969] cover, pp. 25, 46. The Bavarian elector's sculptor and architect, Hans Krumpper, was responsible for Gemmingen's tomb in the choir of Eichstätt Cathedral.

[25] Reclams *Bayern*, p. 343.

added in 1618 at the sides of the Rathaus (Pl. 415).

Toward the city the north front of Schloss Willibaldsburg, rising sheer from the hilltop, presents an even more barren appearance. The tall sub-basement here is quite unbroken and in the basement, as below the west front, two rows of slot-like openings line up with the ranges of fifteen regularly spaced windows in each of the two storeys above. The three bays side of the tower are carried up, like it, an additional storey. The general effect is more of a nineteenth-century factory than a seventeenth-century palace.

The court facades (Pl. 407) in the Gemmingenbau are equally regular but somewhat more elaborately detailed. The lower storey consists entirely of open arcades with molded archivolts carried by sturdy square piers that have plain panelled sides. The windows in the upper storey not only have the same flat aprons and molded architraves as those on the exterior but also pediments like those above the windows of the main storey of the Augsburg Stadtmetzg (Pl. 405). The only variation is that the pediments of alternate windows are broken. These recall faintly the earlier ones over the windows of the Augsburg Zeughaus (Pl. 399) not to speak of Ridinger's at Aschaffenburg (Pls. 367, 368), which must be almost precisely contemporary. Here, however, the motif is so discreetly handled than it does not detract from the regularity and severity of the court facades as a whole.[26]

It is as hard to believe the massive block of Schloss Willibaldsburg and its sternly elegant court are contemporary with the end gable on Haus Thienhausen (Pl. 317) and with the remodelled court of Schloss Langenburg (Pl. 356), as that the Augsburg Stadtmetzg was built a year after the remodelling of the Bremen Rathaus (Pls. 376-378) began and a year before the Hameln Hochzeitshaus (Pl. 384). However, the transitional character of the exterior of the west wing Maximilian had built on the Munich Residenz in 1612-1616 (Pl. 365) was noted in the previous chapter as also, in distinct contrast to that, the scrolls which crowned the gables at the ends of the northern front of that wing, a Northern Mannerist motif Holl abjured at Eichstätt. Following immediately after, the Altes Schloss at Schleissheim (Pl. 408), north of Munich, which Heinrich Schön (†1640) built for Maxi-

milian, beginning in 1616[27] when Schloss Willibaldsburg was nearly finished, though somewhat more consistent in design is still no real match for the advanced work by Holl of these years. All the same, it may well be described at this point.

The *parti* of the main front of the Altes Schloss at Schleissheim, with a single storey above a high half-basement, a central pedimented porch and a higher gable behind is, indeed, formal almost in Holl's way, as are the alternately pointed and segmental pediments of the windows of the main storey. But the pilasters, all of uncanonically broad proportions, which subdivide that storey, with flat blocks filling their panelled surfaces, seem as clumsy as the difference of pitch between the pediment of the porch, which is supported not on an order but on rusticated piers, and the pointed gable behind. These solecisms suggest either that the execution was not adequately supervised by Schön or that later restorations of the stuccoed surface of the brick walls have corrupted the original design. On the other side of the Altes Schloss there are certain minor variations: The window in the gable has a segmental pediment and there is no door at ground level on the left side. Moreover, the bays flanking the porch have paired windows of which the framing hardly matches the rest of the membering. Holl, however, had still used somewhat similar windows in pairs on the St. Anna Gymnasium in Augsburg as late as 1613-1615.

In the years soon after 1610, while work was continuing for the Bavarian Duke Maximilian at the Munich Residenz and before Maximilian began the Schleissheim Altes Schloss, at another Schloss of the Wittelsbachs a new wing was built far more comparable in design to Holl's Schloss Willibaldsburg. This is the Englischer Bau at Heidelberg. It was first projected by the Elector Palatine Friedrich V in 1612[28] at the time of his engagement to Elizabeth, the daughter of James I and Anne of Denmark, and erected 1613-1615. The site (Fig. 23) is bounded on the east by the Fassbau that the Elector Johann Casimir had

---

[26] But broken pediments are not outside the advanced repertory of this period in the north in any case: Inigo Jones, for example, in England did not disdain to use them though rarely on exteriors. One familiar example is his drawing for the "Great Door" of the Banqueting House, dated 1619.

[27] Dehio, *Oberbayern*, p. 46. Lieb, *München*, p. 116, however, gives the date as 1626 when Maximilian began to rebuild the *Herrenhaus* where his father had lived since his abdication in 1597. Reclams *Bayern*, pp. 799-800, agrees with Dehio, but even the 6th ed. of that precedes Lieb's book by five years and undoubtedly depends on the post-war Dehio. Earlier, G. Dehio, *Süddeutschland*, 2nd ed., Berlin, 1920, p. 492, gave the date as 1626.

[28] Oechelhaeuser, *Heidelberger Schloss*, pp. 82-83.

erected in 1589-1592[29] to house the famous *Grosser Fass* (big barrel). Reconstructed in 1727 for the Elector Karl Philipp, this monstrous object is still to many visitors the most fascinating thing in the whole Schloss complex at Heidelberg. On the other end the site abutted Ludwig V's tremendous Dicker Turm at the northwest corner of the Schloss, dating from 1533,[30] that Friedrich V himself would heighten a little later in 1619. Here, on a strengthened mediaeval substructure, Friedrich erected a new wing in total contrast to his predecessor's almost contiguous Friedrichsbau (Pl. 366) to the east of the Fassbau.

Of this wing, as of the Dicker Turm, nothing but the bare and ruinous walls now survive (Pl. 410). The wing deserves a detailed discussion here, all the same, as possibly erected from a design by Inigo Jones. If, indeed, the design is his, then it is his earliest surviving architectural work.[31]

The plan of the Englischer Bau is somewhat irregular in shape because of the older construction on which it stands. The south wall, rising out of the north end of the moat, runs diagonally northwestward and is therefore not parallel with the east-west line of the north front which conforms to that of the Fassbau and the Friedrichsbau on its left. The south wall is twelve bays long with two evenly-spaced rows of large rectangular windows framed by architraves. The windows are more closely set than those around the court at Schloss Willibaldsburg (Pl. 407) and have cornices over them but no pediments. The only break in the regularity of the fenestration is the portal at the far left. That is arched within a frame slightly broader than those of the other openings.

Though the general effect of the south facade of the Englischer Bau today is what one may, in this special case, actually call "Anglo-Palladian," that effect must originally have been partially contradicted above the eaves-line, as was true also of the extension of the Stadhuis at Gent which was still in construction in these years. Two large stone dormers,[32] of which only

the bottom stages survive, once rose high against the steep roof. All the same, to judge from the extant fragments, the dormers seem to have been rather simple in their outline and their detailing—not unlike, actually, a gable proposed or executed in London known only from a drawing attributed to Jones.[33] Especially relevant here, by contrast at least, must have been the earlier ones that once crowned the Ottheinrichsbau, in so far as their character can be determined, as also the gables that still exist on the nearby Friedrichsbau (Pl. 366) above both fronts. However, those on the Munich Residenz of this date were evidently not dissimilar (Pl. 365). The walls of the Englischer Bau also contrast with those of Ottheinrich's (Pls. 177, 178) and Friedrich IV's work here in that they are of rubble stuccoed, with only the window-frames, the flat string-course between the storeys and the terminal cornice of cut stone, with no decorative carving at all.

The shorter north wall of the Englischer Bau of the Heidelberg Schloss, only eight bays long, is differently treated from that on the south side. The windows in both storeys were arched and tall pilaster strips, almost the full height of the wall between them, supported a range of arches concentric with the tops of the upper windows (Fig. 63). Here also, as on the south side, there were originally two stone dormers with plain rectangular lower stages and, at their tops, pediments above scrolled side-pieces—what has earlier been called the Serlian sort of scrolled gable.

This north facade of the Englischer Bau cannot be considered as up-to-date as that on the south. Yet the presence of what amounted to a giant pilaster order in relief may seem to prefigure the Baroque more definitely than does the contemporary order of 1612-1616 on the west front (Pl. 365) of the Munich Residenz which was, and is today again, just quadratura painting. At any rate, the south side is certainly more characteristic of this kind of advanced early seventeenth-century design both in Elias Holl's Germany and in Inigo Jones's England. As various German writers

[29] *Ibid.*, pp. 72-73.

[30] *Ibid.*, pp. 84-87.

[31] It is unfortunate it could not be included, if only for comparison, in the 1973 exhibition, "The King's Arcadia: Inigo Jones and the Stuart Court," in the Banqueting House in London. The catalogue of this with the same title [London] 1973, by John Harris, Stephen Orgel and Roy Strong (henceforth cited as Harris, *King's Arcadia*), pp. 43-56, provides now the best account of Jones's early years and his travels on the Continent.

[32] Gabled dormers of this sort may not improperly be

called Serlian like Pasqualini's at Buren (Pl. 43) and the ones on the Dresden Moritzbau (Pl. 131).

[33] J. N. Summerson, *Architecture in Britain 1530-1830*, 1st ed. (henceforth cited as Summerson, *Britain*), pp. 99-101, pl. 34. Similar gables, moreover, called "Dutch" or "Holborn" in England, are well known to have crowned certain houses in London, including Fulke Greville's in Holborn that has been associated at least with Jones: Harris, *King's Arcadia*, fig. 189.

Fig. 63. ? Inigo Jones and ? Salomon de Caus:
Heidelberg, Englischer Bau, 1613-15, north
side, in the mid-17th-century

have remarked, it is the south side that most resembles the work of Jones of the next few years at Greenwich and in Westminster. However, it also parallels very closely Holl's contemporary buildings, particularly Schloss Willibaldsburg (Pl. 406), which was in construction at this time, and the Augsburg Rathaus (Pl. 415), which he was already designing by this date. The execution of the Rathaus actually began in 1615, the year the Englischer Bau was completed, it might be noted here.

No authorship for the design of the Englischer Bau has been, nor probably can be, firmly established. Certain circumstances associated with the Anglo-Palatine marriage of 1613 support, as does the traditional name,[34] the possibility—even the probability—that the

designer was English and, specifically, Inigo Jones, whose well-known later architectural productions it certainly brings to mind. In weighing such an attribution one should first review Jones's employment by the English royal family just before the engagement of Friedrich V and the Princess Elizabeth. To quote from Sir John Summerson:[35] "At the beginning of 1611 . . . [Jones] was appointed Surveyor to Prince Henry, the heir apparent to the throne. . . . Jones had

---

[34] It could hardly be called the Friedrichsbau since such

existed; one would have expected it to be known as the "Elisabethenbau" on the analogy of the nearby Elisabethentor. The actual name suggests that the alien character of its Academic design was recognized and that this led to the nomenclature: cf. the Französischer Bau at the Heldberg.

[35] Summerson, *Britain* [paperback ed., Harmondsworth, 1970], pp. 116-117. For another later account see Harris, *King's Arcadia*, as cited in Note 31.

already (1609-1610) designed the setting for 'The Prince's Barriers'. . . . [Also] he is supposed to have built a 'cabinet room,' for [the Prince's] collection of pictures, in Whitehall. . . .

"Around [Henry] revolved a number of young noblemen . . . and among these was Thomas Howard, 2nd Earl of Arundel. . . . But typhoid fever carried off [the Prince] on 6 November 1612.

". . . Arrangements were already in hand and could not well be postponed . . . for the marriage [of Elizabeth and Friedrich which] took place in February 1613, and it was on this occasion that the 'The Lords' Masque' [among others] was performed. Thomas Campion, the author, described his collaborator [Jones] as 'our kingdom's most Artfull and Ingenious Architect. . . .' On 27 April 1613 [Jones] was granted the reversion to the highest office in the [English] world of building—that of Surveyor of the King's Works [in succession to Simon Basil (†1615)].

"In April the bride and bridegroom [Elizabeth and Friedrich] . . . started on the journey to Heidelberg, which they reached in June. With them were Lord and Lady Arundel . . . and among [the Arundel] suite of thirty-six persons was Inigo Jones. [But] at Strasburg the Arundels made for Basel and then for Milan." From this account it might seem Jones never reached Heidelberg and that was what Summerson stated in his 1966 monograph on Jones. In a later edition of his Pelican volume, however, he changed his opinion and the authors of the catalogue of the Banqueting House exhibition of 1973 have reaffirmed the Heidelberg visit.[36] Even if Jones did not reach there, the possibility remains that he prepared for Friedrich one or more elevational drawings or, more probably, rather free sketches[37] as projects for the new wing.

Only the rebuilding of the mediaeval substructure of the wing was probably under way in 1612 before Friedrich went to England.

Another foreigner is even more likely to have played a part. Among the members of Prince Henry's household, in which Jones ranked high as surveyor, was a Frenchman from Dieppe, Salomon de Caus (1576-?1626). He was the prince's drawing master and also built for him a picture gallery at Richmond, something with which one would suppose Jones as Surveyor must also have been involved, as more certainly with the construction of the "cabinet-room" at Whitehall. After the Prince's death in 1612, de Caus left England the following year and is next heard of at Heidelberg as the designer of the Elisabethentor, the garden gate to the south of the Englischer Bau. That gate Friedrich completed in 1615, the same year as the Englischer Bau,[38] in honor of his "coniugi cariss," his dearest wife, as stated in an inscription. That Salomon, though primarily a designer of gardens, had some experience at building his work for Prince Henry at Richmond seems to attest. At Heidelberg, when the Elisabethentor had been completed, he laid out over the years 1616-1619 the extensive terrace garden to the east of the Schloss (Fig. 27), as seen in Merian's[39] and other views, just before Friedrich's ill-fated acceptance of the Bohemian crown.

De Caus's gate at Heidelberg (Pl. 411) has a touch of fantasy in the vine-carved semi-rustic columns and their capitals not unlike that of various details in Jones's drawings for the sets of masques, which were his principal production up to this time, and the scrolled broken pediment in particular can be closely matched in a masque project dated 1610/1611 for "Oberon's Palace."[40] Thus it is not extravagant to surmise that some sort of drawings for the Englischer Bau were prepared during the early months of 1613 by Jones in London—or, later, actually in Heidelberg—for the new wing and also, possibly, for the gate. In that year and the following de Caus would have developed Jones's drawings and supervised the execution, perhaps himself supplying the design for the less Jonesian north front as well, more certainly, as that for the garden gate.

Surely there were not more than two or at most three German architects, at least among those whose work is known today, capable in these years of pro-

---

[36] J. N. Summerson, *Inigo Jones*, Harmondsworth [1966], p. 35; Harris, *King's Arcadia*, p. 55.

[37] At this stage in Jones's career such drawings would hardly have been very professional; but they might have indicated clearly enough the *parti*, if not the details of the membering. See Harris, *King's Arcadia*, pp. 58-59, 95-115, for discussion and illustrations relevant to Jones's development as an architectural designer before the Queen's House was commissioned in 1616. The details could have been taken from any of several sixteenth-century Italian treatises. Jones owned and annotated the Venice, 1562, edition of Serlio, as also the Venice, 1601, Palladio; a Venice, 1567, Vitruvius; the Milan, 1584, Lomazzo; and by 1617, the Scamozzi of 1615, though that is not relevant here because of the late date. Moreover, Ottheinrich's copies of Cesariano's Vitruvius, his Serlios and Blum's work on the orders in German may well have been available in Friedrich's inherited library at Heidelberg.

[38] Oechelhaeuser, *Heidelberger Schloss*, pp. 80-81.

[39] Merian, *Schönsten Schlosser*, pls. opp. pp. 36, 37.

[40] Summerson, *Britain* (paperback ed.), fig. 75; Harris, *King's Arcadia*, figs. 62, 63.

ducing the design for the south front of the Eng-lischer Bau. Whether or not this is the earliest surviving architectural work carried out from a drawing provided by Jones it may be described as "prematurely Jonesian," even if it is actually by a German or by the Frenchman de Caus. The German architects are, of course, Holl and Alberthal, who were jointly responsible for Schloss Willibaldsburg as it was being erected in these very years, and possibly the younger Jakob Wolf of Nürnberg, who would soon extend the Rathaus there. There seems little likelihood that any of these was consulted in the brief relevant period running from late 1612 to mid-1613. For most of this half-year, Friedrich was in England, not in Germany, and almost certainly in recurrent social contact with the designer who had been his brother-in-law Henry's architect. Then, just before both left England together for the Continent, Jones was named by James, as Summerson noted, successor to Simon Basil as Surveyor of the King's Works though Basil still had two more years to live. It would have been natural enough for the elector to consult the famous designer of the masques he had been seeing in London especially as that designer was also a rising official, high in his father-in-law's favor as he had long been in that of the Queen—on the recommendation of Anne's brother Christian IV of Denmark according to John Webb.[41]

While Friedrich V's wing at Heidelberg was rising and the terrace garden being laid out, Augsburg[42] saw conspicuous new construction in a comparably up-to-date vein. Holl's Gymnasium St. Anna (Pl. 409), immediately behind that church, was built in precisely the same years 1613-1615 as the Englischer Bau. Badly damaged in the war though now restored, this is of somewhat less advanced character than the Englischer Bau—the pairing of the windows on this has already been noted. A better example of the new direction that architecture in northern Europe was taking at this particular point is the Neuer Bau of 1614 facing the main square of Augsburg across from the Perlach-turm.

As restored, the six bays of the lower storey of the Neuer Bau are framed by heavily banded Doric pilasters and have shop-windows at street level (Pl. 413). But the equally heavily banded arches between, with their keystones projecting in three overlaid planes, were there originally as also, presumably, the segmental-arched windows in the mezzanine. Above the capitals of the Doric pilasters—piers, they really are, though of taller proportions than those in the court of Schloss Willibaldsburg (Pl. 407)—there is only a very compressed entablature. In the upper storey the Ionic pilasters are more svelte but they are coupled at the ends above the broader piers below. Plain inner frames surround the wall planes of the bays between the pilasters and, in each of these, there are pedimented windows very nearly identical with those in the main storey of the court at Eichstätt though none of the pediments here is broken. Finally, a full entablature, scaled to the total height of the facade rather than to the upper order, crowns the whole. No high roof is visible and hence no gables or dormers were needed. Though the execution of the facade of the Neuer Bau—which, as was noted earlier, is quite as Jonesian as the Englischer Bau—was in Holl's hands, the design is attributed not to him but to Matthias Kager (1575-1634). Moreover, Kager certainly provided, a bit earlier, that for Holl's Kaufhaus in the Heiliggrabgasse which carries the date 1611.[43] He is another German who might have provided the design for the Englischer Bau, but not a very likely one.

Kager, like Heintz primarily a painter, was in Italy in 1598 though he had already come to maturity as an artist in Sustris's circle in Munich. In Augsburg he first appeared in 1605[44] when he executed the frescoes on the exterior of the Gothic *Weberzunfthaus* (drapers' guildhall) across from St. Moritz. Of those nothing remains[45]—the present external mural painting dates from 1935. Of the Kaufhaus little, except possibly the portals, survives in the totally rebuilt facade. As with the Stadtmetzg, it is difficult to refuse Holl all credit for the design of the facade of the Neuer Bau, especially as it is so superior in quality to the current work at the Munich Residenz that Kager must have known well and might have been expected to emulate. His major artistic contribution in Augsburg came later, from 1620 on, when he executed the decorations in the Goldener Saal in the Rathaus (Pl.

[41] Harris, *King's Arcadia*, pp. 43-56, gives credence to Webb's account of Jones's visit to Denmark. It is hard to see any stylistic connection between even a very early project of Jones's, such as that of 1608 for the Royal Exchange, and Christian's building operations in Denmark, even of the date Jones would have been there.

[42] Breuer, *Augsburg*, p. 66.

[43] *Ibid*.

[44] Reclams *Bayern*, p. 101.

[45] Rauch, *Augsburger Baugeschichte*, pl. on p. 26, shows this decoration as it once existed.

420) by which date that great structure had not only been begun but was already some five years in construction.

As early as 1610 the preparation of designs for the Rathaus had started, but the cornerstone of Holl's building was not laid until 1615. There survive, however, in the Maximilian Museum (Haus Boeck von Boeckenstein) in Augsburg various preparatory drawings and models, some certainly previous to 1615, for the Rathaus. This is the largest and most conspicuous of such civic structures now surviving in northern Europe from the hundred years between the completion of the Antwerp Stadhuis in 1564 and that of Amsterdam (the Royal Palace today) in 1665.[46]

Though the plans for Augsburg's Rathaus were already under discussion over a generation before Jacob van Campen and Pieter Post began the Amsterdam structure in 1648, Holl's Rathaus as executed is already more like the latter than the former in stylistic character. Only the moderately elaborate gables over the tall central portions of the east and west fronts, moreover, recall even faintly the Antwerp Stadhuis (Pl. 175); in fact, however, Holl's gables (Pl. 415) can almost be considered, if somewhat precociously, Early Baroque rather than still Northern Mannerist.

Moreover, the only features that seem unmistakably Germanic are the towers, projected only in 1618, that are attached to the middle of the north and south sides. This is particularly true of their swelling *welsche Hauben*, mentioned earlier, which approach the onion type that had not yet developed to maturity in Bavaria even though initiated in the mid-twenties atop the towers of the Munich Frauenkirche. The terminal octagonal stages, however, are similar to those of the towers of Schloss Willibaldsburg (Pl. 406), which date from this same second decade, and also to the one Holl had added earlier, in 1605, to the Wertachbruckertor (Pl. 403) although that had no *welsche Haube*. These are also echoed nearby at smaller scale in the terminal feature Holl built, at just this point in 1614-1616, to top the Perlachturm. The fact that Hans Hieber had projected the remodelling of this tower a hundred years before already with a crowning octagonal stage (Pl. 23) is interesting, if exceptional, evidence of a remarkable continuity in German Renaissance design through the whole sixteenth century and beyond.

What is exceptional about Holl's Augsburg Rathaus, as carried out from 1615 to 1620,[47] however, is quite different; its enormous size and its great height particularly as seen from the east or rear where the contiguous buildings were cleared away in the 1880s (Pl. 418) were not matched earlier. Counting the subbasement, which on this side is wholly above ground, the east front is about twice as tall as the largest German works of this period, Holl's Schloss Willibaldsburg outside Eichstätt (Pl. 406) and Ridinger's Schloss Johannisburg at Aschaffenburg (Pl. 367), and the other dimensions were comparable. The main rectangular block, fourteen bays wide and ten bays deep, is five storeys high without counting the mezzanines of the side bays; while the central portions on both the front and the rear, as also the towers, rise two storeys more to end, respectively, in gables and in the terminal octagons with their *welsche Hauben*.

The resultant mass of the Augsburg Rathaus more than equals that of the largest palaces in Rome of the Early Baroque period. It is, however, distinguished from the Palazzo Borghese, as continued by Flaminio Ponzio down to his death in 1613, or even the somewhat later Palazzo Barberini of 1628-1633, designed presumably by Maderno and executed by Bernini—to name the two palaces that are best known—by the complexity of the massing, especially after the addition of the towers, and the variety of the fenestration. Yet the frames of all the windows, except for the oval ones in the center of the third storey, are more severely canonical in their detailing than many designed by contemporary Roman architects. Even Holl's oval frames, for all their Early Baroque look, do not begin to approach the famous soft-eared ones that would be introduced, almost certainly by Borromini, on the front of the Palazzo Barberini some fifteen years later.

Such a "skyscraper," if one may so call it, was not at first intended. There are two wooden models in the Maximilian Museum that propose a much smaller edifice more consonant with the Neuer Bau. One of these, indeed, is only a richer version of that structure of 1614 (Pl. 413) though it may well have been pre-

---

[46] K. Fremantle, *The Baroque Town Hall of Amsterdam*, Utrecht, 1959.

[47] Breuer, *Augsburg*, pp. 63-64; L. Leybold, *Das Rathaus der Stadt Augsburg*, Berlin, 1886-1888; U. Christoffel, *Augsburger Rathaus*, Augsburg [1929] (hereafter cited as Christoffel, *Augsburger Rathaus*); R. von Walter, *Das Augsburger Rathaus*, Augsburg [1972]. The 93 plates in Leybold's publication provide rather complete visual coverage of a monument much damaged in the last war though now restored externally and to some extent within.

pared several years earlier. This has an open Roman arch-order below and Corinthian half-columns on both the upper and the lower storeys. Its main block is eight bays long with short wings, similarly detailed, projecting from the sides.

Another wooden model (Pl. 412) for the Rathaus now in the Museum in Augsburg has three wide bays on the front separated by paired half-columns carrying ressauts. Each bay in the ground storey, evidently intended again to be an open loggia, is filled with a Serlian or Palladian motif.[48] On the upper storey, however, the bays have four windows apiece, separated only by colonnette-mullions. Pediments, alternately pointed and segmental, cap the middle pair in each, a quite original treatment that has no conspicuous precedent in Italy though it is distinctly Italian Mannerist, not Northern Mannerist, in character. This model also carries an attic with four square windows in each bay that are set into the broad frieze of the terminal entablature. It is unlikely either of these projects is by Holl or, unless they date from before his death in 1609, by Heintz. Certainly neither much resembles their known works. Some writers, however, believe one or both of them to be by Kager because of their resemblance to the Neuer Bau.

There exists another model (Pl. 416)—this one presumably Holl's—which is dated 1615, the year the cornerstone of the Rathaus was laid.[49] Two drawings also in the Museum, one a rather poorly laid out perspective showing the west and north fronts, the other a more carefully drafted but incomplete elevation of the west front, both of them either by Holl or following closely his ideas, should also be mentioned. The second drawing agrees almost exactly with the executed work except for the absence of the towers, first planned in 1618, and the portals. These last, however, are already present in the perspective and even on the 1615 model.[50]

That wooden model of the Augsburg Rathaus (Pl. 416) is accurately scaled to the real dimensions of the executed building as several of the others in the Museum—not all of them by Holl presumably—are not. On it the central six bays are differentiated from the four on either side both on the west and on the east fronts. In execution, however, slight changes were made. Quoins, repeating those on the corners, frame the middle section; and this stronger emphasis on the central portion of the facade was further increased by adding pediments over the first-storey windows in these bays. So also, both in the Holl drawings and on the executed building, the central six windows—those indicated on the 1615 model as taller than the ones at the sides—are linked to the attic windows above. In the model none of the windows at this upper-storey level are pedimented, but in the drawings the pediments that were eventually executed are shown over the windows in the side wings. Those in the center, moreover, were already transformed into vertical ovals and capped with broken pediments. This detailing recalls the mezzanine windows on the Zeughaus (Pl. 399) and supports the suggestion made earlier that these were introduced by Holl into Heintz's projected elevation for the Zeughaus.

In the 1615 model of the Augsburg Rathaus and in one other—probably earlier—project the top two storeys form a unified cruciform element above the main oblong block in contrast to the two rather large gables capping only the outer ends shown on other surviving models. This cruciform element is four bays wide on the front and rear but, on the sides, only the width of the two bays occupied by the syncopated windows, here arched, that light the stair-landings within. On the front and rear, plain wall-areas flank two rows of squarish windows. The outer ends of the cruciform element that crowns the 1615 model have plain gables, as was perhaps already true at Schloss Schwarzenberg, and the roofs they would terminate are lowered to a proper pedimental pitch.

As has been noted, this model of the Augsburg Rathaus already shows the big central portal with its round arch and flanking columns. The executed portal, however, carries the date 1620. Also present al-

---

[48] Perhaps better called a "Serliana" as Italian scholars generally do. There are, of course, many possible sources beside Serlio from Giulio Romano's garden *loggie* on the Palazzo del Te in Mantua to Palladio's Basilica at Vicenza from which the usual English term derives.

[49] Breuer, *Augsburg*, pp. 63-65.

[50] Several more projects exist for the Augsburg Rathaus: Christoffel, *Augsburger Rathaus*, figs. 25-37. Since these cannot be precisely arranged in sequence as successive predecessors of the ones described here, only a few need be mentioned individually. The most interesting is a single unbroken oblong block in three storeys (Christoffel, *Augsburger Rathaus*, fig. 26) that follows much more closely than those mentioned above the Roman *palazzo* model. Inigo Jones in England, of

course, introduced the simple oblong block characteristic of many of Palladio's villas in his projects of 1619 for the Prince's Lodging at Newmarket and even before that, in a sense, in the Queen's House at Greenwich as begun in 1617—if not, indeed, still earlier at Heidelberg (Pl. 410); there, however, the west end of the block is a party wall shared with flanking structures as is most of the east end also.

ready on the 1615 model are the pairs of round-arched windows on either side of this and also the two subsidiary portals. Both on the model and in the drawings all these minor elements are simpler in design than they would be as executed around 1620.

The presumably somewhat later drawings for the Rathaus, moreover, show a distinctly different treatment of the central portions that rise above the main cornice on the front and rear from that indicated on the model of 1615 (Pl. 416). Two rows of six windows are linked in vertical panels formed by flat members. Over this, the upper cornice breaks back at the corners, a change of plane that is further emphasized in the executed building by the rustication of the rear element to continue upward that of the quoins below. Above, the first and only stage of each of the front and rear gables is elaborated by a Doric pilaster order. That breaks forward over the two central windows to frame a very large painted armorial achievement—originally an Imperial eagle apparently—while at either side are shallow niches. The framing of this stage is more like that of late sixteenth-century church facades in Rome than Northern Mannerist in character. It consists only of very large plain S-scrolls, one at either side—quite unrelated to the complicated multiple scrolling of most contemporary German gables—and a plain pediment above within which is set a smaller pediment capping the broad central edicule. Such relative simplicity had only been approached in Germany on the Siegel Haus here, at Munich on the Residenz, and at Heidelberg on the Englischer Bau before this (Pls. 365, 400, 410).

Except for the ultimate addition of the towers over the stairwells at the center of the north and south sides of the Augsburg Rathaus (Pl. 415) there is, therefore, only minimal animation of the skyline and that of a plastic rather than a two-dimensional character. Already in the elevational drawing, for example, the tall obelisks shown above the corners of the main block in the model were omitted and plain balls substituted like those that appear on the 1615 model on top of the crowning balustrade (Pl. 416). In execution similar stone balls were introduced on the ends of the entablatures of the gables on both fronts. By shortening this entablature slightly, these balls could be so placed as to terminate the vertical lines of the outer pilasters and their ressauts below. Finally a large pineapple carried on a capital crowns the peak of each pediment much as on the Siegel Haus (Pl. 400).

The severity of the exterior of the Augsburg Rathaus, its great size and the regularity of the fenestra-

tion might suggest it was conceived primarily as a municipal office-building. Actually, however, a very large part of the interior was given up to representational rooms, effectively the whole six bays of the center from front to rear. Thus the taller windows of that section suggest—though they do not in fact very clearly reveal—the great size of the principal apartment, for this so-called Goldener Saal[51] (Fig. 64) rises,

Fig. 64. Elias Holl: Augsburg, Rathaus, 1615-20,
transverse section

not only through the mezzanine above with its oval windows, but even into the next attic storey so that clerestorey lighting could be introduced along the sides (Fig. 65). The painted decorations in this great hall were designed by Peter Candid, by this date in his eighties, and executed by Matthias Kager in 1620-1623; the general layout was doubtless determined by Kager. Unfortunately the ceiling (Pl. 420), larger and more sumptuously molded, painted and gilded than the ones of the preceding decades at Heiligenberg, Kirchheim, Ortenburg and Weikersheim (Pls. 349-352) described earlier, was destroyed in the war, as also most of the wall painting. For that a basic qua-

[51] Christoffel, *Augsburger Rathaus*, figs. 4, 10, 40-48.

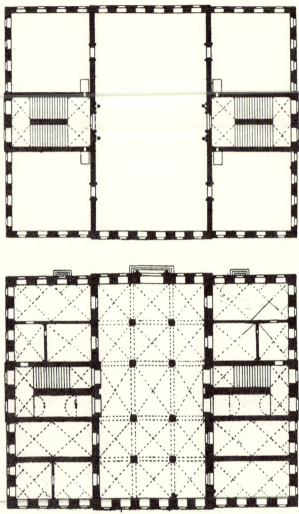

Fig. 65. Elias Holl: Augsburg, Rathaus, 1615-20,
plans

than what Candid and Kager provided, whether that be considered late Italian Mannerist, like Candid's frescoes of the eighties and nineties in the Antiquarium at Munich, or already Early Baroque. The ground-storey hall is divided by two rows of square marble piers carrying cross-vaults. Marble doorways, with plain broken pediments above them framing busts, and round arches in pairs, leading to the flights of stairs in the towers at either side, also survive. In the main storey another hall has marble columns supporting a panelled wooden ceiling, probably executed by Jakob Dietrich, a son of Wendel Dietrich. This is rather similar to wooden ceilings of the previous decades, such as his father's at Kirchheim (Pl. 350), but somewhat bolder in relief and simpler in detail.

In 1622[53] Holl provided one more notable civic ornament for Augsburg, the Roter Tor (Pl. 417), a gate in the city walls like his Wertachbruckertor (Pl. 403) of 1605. With its rounded corners under a square cornice, the raised bands that bind pilasters and wall-surfaces together, and the square and circular openings, this has a more Baroque sort of plasticity than anything by Holl of the previous decade except the earlier gate. Even for Holl, its latest distinguished and distinguishable figure, the German Renaissance was effectively over. Though he lived until 1646,[54] conditions in the war years of the second quarter of the century were not conducive to the production of new buildings. Destruction, rather than construction, became in Germany the order of the day, and even after the Peace of Westphalia in 1648 economic recovery followed only very gradually and tardily.

One or two more secular works under way in the second decade of the century are by no means unworthy of comparison with Holl's Rathaus though the new sort of design had elsewhere no such early success as at Augsburg. The Nürnbergers, for all their support of Dürer, had been slow to accept Italianate design in executed architecture, as was recurrently noted in previous chapters. The Fembohaus (Pl. 324) of the 1580s, among extant works, is the oldest mature example there of the German Renaissance. Even that is not really up-to-date by contemporary German standards. The Pellerhaus (Pl. 395), however, of a few years later is of rather more importance historically. Jakob Wolf's relative restraint as

dratura scheme was used in which niches and pedimented window-frames alternated; but the whole was very much elaborated with large figures in full color, putti and garlands above ponderously architectonic portals of real marble, three to a side, somewhat like that at Kirchheim (Pl. 350).

Had they survived, the Candid-Kager decorations of the Goldener Saal in the Augsburg Rathaus would in any case be already beyond the confines even of this penultimate chapter both in date and in style. Certain other interiors in the Rathaus[52] are in better condition today, thanks to postwar restoration. These are more characteristic in their restraint of the style of Holl

[52] *Ibid.*, figs. 4, 7-9, 11-12, 38-39, 49-54.

[53] Breuer, *Augsburg*, p. 60; Rauch, *Augsburger Baugeschichte*, p. [107] (col. pl.).
[54] For the relevant literature, see Note 9.

seen in the surviving lower half of the front is at this date more relevant stylistically than the facade as a whole ever was if considered as a late example of Northern Mannerism. A more significant step was taken in Nürnberg by Jakob's son, though only a decade later.

It was in 1616,[55] the year after construction of the Augsburg Rathaus was begun by Holl, that the younger Jakob Wolf (1571-1620)—who was probably associated earlier with his father in carrying out Holl's design for Schloss Schwarzenberg—undertook for the Nürnberg Council the addition to the fourteenth-century Rathaus of a very extensive west wing, which was brought to completion in 1622, two years after his death, probably by his brother Hans. This was attached to the structure Hans Beheim (†1538) had enlarged with north and east wings of wholly Late Gothic character a hundred years before. In this new wing Wolf already emulated Holl's latest work with notable distinction.

The exceptional quality of this extension of the Nürnberg Rathaus (Pl. 421) could be more readily recognized had the new wing faced open sites like the Augsburg Rathaus or risen, like Holl's, to exceptional height. In any case, the personal variants of the new sort of design as employed by Holl and by the younger Wolf are by no means identical. The differences are not to be explained by the two men's backgrounds and experience, for these were quite similar, especially as contrasted with their English contemporary Ingio Jones's. Augsburger and Nürnberger alike had established positions in civic bureaucracies—as foreign favorites of princes such as Sustris and Nosseni did not—and had even, in effect, inherited their official positions as *Ratsbaumeister*. As was noted earlier, however, Holl was so young—only twenty-one —at the time of his father's death in 1594 that he did not actually succeed until 1601 after the end of Jakob Eschay's intervening incumbency.

Both Holl and Wolf had been in Italy at least briefly: Wolf was sent there, indeed, by the Nürnberg Council. On the other hand, neither can be considered Italian-trained, nor would either have focussed his professional interest in Italy so largely on the work of Palladio and Scamozzi as Jones did during his tour with Lord Arundel in 1613-1614. Holl's most relevant practical experience had been as executant of Heintz's projects down to the latter's death in 1609; Wolf had

been the pupil and later the assistant of his father. For all his English birth and early appointment as Surveyor to Prince Henry, Jones in background resembled more such Italian-trained painters of foreign birth as the Dutch Sustris and the Swiss Heintz. Most of Jones's practical experience was acquired only after succeeding Simon Basil in 1615 as Surveyor of the Royal Works, not so far as is known by early and continuing association with actual construction.[56] Both the Germans were well-trained professional servants of their civic employers; while Jones, in the line of Alberti, was more like a modern architect and much less of a post-mediaeval craftsman, even though he can be considered also a sort of civil servant—not to say a bureaucrat—himself.

If the Augsburg Rathaus reminds one a little of nineteenth-century office-buildings thanks to its regular fenestration and its great height, that at Nürnberg is not unlike an early factory (Pl. 421). The two upper storeys consist of unvaried rows of very closely set windows, each framed by an eared architrave. The ones in the principal storey lack the cornices Holl used over his windows at this level, but in the upper storey here such are present, and there are also pediments over every other one. The almost syncopated rhythm was further elaborated by alternating pointed and segmental pediments, somewhat as plain and broken ones alternate in the court of Schloss Willibaldsburg (Pl. 407). These window-frames, moreover, are in much higher relief than any of Holl's. The crowning cornices of the windows project from the plane of the architraves on scrolled brackets and also continue as a strong horizontal line linking the unpedimented openings between. More vigorous also than at Augsburg are both the rustication at the corners—executed as is the whole facade in red freestone like the Englischer Bau, rather than in the stuccoed brick of Augsburg—and the heavy terminal cornice. This last is carried on chunky brackets and topped by a continuous balustrade which completely hides the low-pitched hip-roof.

Above and below the long rows of windows in the two upper storeys the monotonous regularity[57] of the

---

[55] Reclams *Bayern*, p. 640.

[56] Harris, *King's Arcadia*, pp. 28-55, broadens the picture of Jones's early architectural activities somewhat. However, this is mostly by hypothesis in contrast to the full and well-documented accounts of his work on festivals and masques for Queen Anne and Prince Henry down to the death of the latter in 1612.

[57] This extreme regularity might suggest the younger Wolf

facade of the Nürnberg Rathaus is sharply broken by certain architectonic accents. Three effectively identical portals at double scale stand out boldly from the solid flat plane of the ground storey, one under the pair of center bays and two under the eighth and ninth bays from each of the ends. Flanked by sturdy Doric columns, the portals all have heavy pediments. These are cut back at the outer edge of the ressauts and also interrupted in the middle. There an oval armorial achievement is connected by three-dimensional scrolling with the giant keystone of the arch below.

The portals of Wolf's facade of the Nürnberg Rathaus are dated in sequence from north to south 1617, 1616 and 1620, respectively; the earliest, that in the center (Pl. 421), carries on the slopes of the broken pediment very large and somewhat Michelangelesque reclining figures in the round. These were designed and carved by Christoph Jamnitzer (1563-1618), the last of a famous Nürnberg family of goldsmiths; the others have similar sculpture following the model Jamnitzer's provided. That was executed, not by Jamnitzer, but by a younger man born in the eighties, Leonhard Kern (†1662).

Considered in terms of the axes of the three big portals and the plain wall areas at the ends, the composition of the ground storey of Wolf's west wing of the Nürnberg Rathaus is of five parts in contrast to the front of the Augsburg Rathaus. That consists essentially of only three parts because of the modest character of the two side portals. The five-part organization of the features rising above the main cornice is even more notable in Nürnberg despite the absence of gables. As at the Altes Schloss in Stuttgart (Pl. 157) in the 1550s and over the center and ends of each of the two fronts of the Augustusburg Schloss (Pl. 200) around 1570, there are here only hip-roofed attics rising above the three terminal bays at each corner and the six bays in the center. The windows in these attics, identical in design with those below except that there are no ears on the architraves, are separated by pilasters carrying a full Doric entablature; while on the outer edges of the three raised bays at the ends the rusticated quoining of the main storeys below is continued upward. Over the square central attic there is a further stage only two bays wide on which the membering is slightly reduced in scale. The crowning ele-

ment is an octagonal arched lantern on top of which there is a rather tall *welsche Haube* and, above that, what may better be described as a parsnip than an elongated onion! On top of the attic storeys at the ends, however, one-bay arched loggias open under S-curved roofs.

These massive crowning accents at Nürnberg, though ungabled, are certainly in a northern rather than an Italian tradition; yet the resultant five-part composition against the sky is ahead rather than in retard of current Italian development. The composition in three dimensions is distinctly premonitory, indeed, of the five-part design, including both a raised central attic and also corner loggias, that Borromini proposed in the 1640s for the Palazzo Pamphili in the Piazza Navona in Rome and the elder Rainaldi executed in modified form. If Wolf had specific Italian models, however, they must have been Genoese or Milanese, not Roman; only in the court do the superposed arch orders of the arcades strike a recognizably Vignolan or Palladian note comparable to those in the court of the Graz Landhaus or the Stallburg of the Vienna Hofburg. Both of those, naturally, were two generations earlier in date and designed by Italians.

Transitional, of course, the great Nürnberg civic "palazzo" remains; but the facade, considered as a whole, is already more Baroque than Academic, despite the factory-like fenestration of the first storey. With this major monument, only completed four years after the Thirty Years' War broke out and a year before the Goldener Saal of the Augsburg Rathaus, the Renaissance in Germany came to its approximate end, a little more than a century after Jakob Fugger first had introduced Italianate design into Germany in his chapel at St. Anna in Augsburg.

Even later, however, is a much more modest structure which can be compared, stylistically at least, to the Nürnberg Rathaus. Though rather anti-climactic here (Pl. 419), it deserves at least a brief mention. The Klerikalseminar of the Jesuits at Dillingen, beside their Studienkirche of 1610-1617, was begun by Johann Alberthal in 1619 and completed, like the Nürnberg Rathaus, in 1622.[58] Working from his experience as Holl's executant at Schloss Willibaldsburg—and doubtless with Sustris's Jesuitenkolleg in Munich (Pl. 260) of a generation before in mind—Alberthal here provided another of the early models for a new institutional vernacular. That vernacular replaced the

as a third German who could have provided the designs for the Englischer Bau in 1613. He is, however, not a very likely candidate despite his possible assistance to his father before the latter's death in 1612 in carrying out Holl's designs for Schloss Schwarzenberg.

[58] Reclams *Bayern*, p. 220.

Juliusstil of Robin's university buildings at Würzburg (Pl. 330)—paralleled still in Mainz at this late date—and survived well into the next age when institutional building finally revived in the later seventeenth century. The churches of the first quarter of the seventeenth century are much more interesting than such things as the Dillingen Klericalseminar, however, as also more important historically. The revival of church-building in the later seventeenth century and through the mid-eighteenth century eventually produced many long-recognized masterpieces of German architecture. The early churches merit a chapter to themselves to bring the story of the Renaissance in Germany to a full close.

Ten

RELIGIOUS ARCHITECTURE
OF THE EARLY
SEVENTEENTH CENTURY

SOME general picture of the latest church architecture of northern Europe in the decades around 1600 should precede an account of the important churches in Germany begun just before the outbreak of the Thirty Years' War in 1618. Premonitions of German Baroque church architecture of the late seventeenth and eighteenth centuries have been recognized by some historians already in the 1580s in the nave of St. Michael in Munich. Not surprisingly at so early a date—despite Sustris's partial dependence on the Gesù in Rome a little later in that portion of St. Michael he was called on to rebuild in the nineties—there was no approach as yet to the Roman Baroque of the seventeenth century.

Moreover, as has been noted, the Jesuits in Germany,[1] unlike those in other countries, did not in the early decades of the seventeenth century follow the basic Counter-Reformation prototype provided by the Gesù. Instead, their half-Gothic Petrikirche at Münster (Pls. 261, 262), from the same years in the 1590s as Sustris's east end in Munich, offered an acceptable model followed for a generation by the Order, especially in their Rhineland province. This is evident not only in such a modest edifice as their church in Koblenz of 1613-1617,[2] but even in a major metropolitan monument, Mariä Himmelfahrt in Cologne (Pls. 451, 452), which was erected for them by the same architect in 1618-1627. That is the prime example, indeed, of what German writers call *Nachgotik*.[3]

At that point, as often before, evidence of formative Italian influence, considered as regards church architecture in terms of plan, of section and of interior elevation, is found earliest to the south and east; the Klagenfurt Münster (Pl. 255) in Carinthia, begun in 1582, may well be considered the first example of such influence, even though that was originally built for Lutheran use. Naturally, Catholics were more open to influence from Italy, if not from Rome and its new churches but rather from Lombardy and the Veneto, as had been true previously.

It was in 1584, while the Klagenfurt church was in construction,[4] that Bernardo Morando began the Collegiate Church at Zamošč in Poland for Chancellor Zamoyski, though the vaulting of the church was not completed until after Morando's death in 1600. The Paduan Morando had been called to Poland, it will be recalled, to lay out a new town for the chancellor and more particularly to design and supervise the fortifications which were in construction over the years 1587-1605.[5] Nothing approaching this Polish example of a Late Renaissance basilica survives in German lands to the west earlier than the Hofkirche at Neuburg-a.-d.-Donau begun in 1607 (Pls. 436, 437). Once again Poland was well ahead of Germany, though the original facade—very likely not of Morando's design—of the church at Zamošč was still hybrid, being crowned not by a pediment but with a scallopped gable.[6] Advanced work of the period in Rome, however, had no influence even in Poland before the building of the

---

[1] An exception may have been the demolished church of St. Paulus in Regensburg (See Note 7 to Chapter VIII). This long-lost monument is ignored by such standard authorities as Dehio, Horst, Stange and Hauttmann, however.

[2] Reclams *Rheinlande und Westfalen*, p. 300.

[3] The *Nachgotik* was certainly the favorite architectural mode of the Jesuits in Germany at this point. Gerstenberg, *Sondergotik*, at least *passim*, is a relevant reference. Braun, *Jesuiten*, I, moreover, devotes his first 400 pages to the Or-

der's churches of Gothic design in Germany dating from the decades just before and after 1600. A Tübingen dissertation of 1973 on the *Nachgotik* by Hermann Hipp is not yet available in print.

[4] Kowalczyk, *Kolegiata*, provides a very complete monograph on the church in Polish.

[5] *Ibid.*, fig. 78; Knox, *Poland*, pp. 36-37, fig. 25.

[6] Kowalczyk, *Kolegiata*, figs. 9, 36; Knox, *Poland*, fig. 26.

Jesuits' church in Kraków in 1605-1619[7] by Giovanni Trevano. These two churches, of course, were both for Catholic use.

Although no consecutive account of early Protestant church architecture has been provided in this book, the priority of the German examples in date and the grandeur and elaboration of certain of them, beginning with that at Klagenfurt, suggest that some reference should be made at this point to several more modest ones which were the first to be erected in northern Europe outside German lands. Relevant at least for contrast with contemporary work in Germany—where, as earlier, many of the most impressive new churches of this period, including the Neuburg Hofkirche, were erected by and for Protestants—is Reformed church-building in contemporary Holland. To the Dutch churches some attention was paid in Chapter VI, but these now merit further comment. All the same, none of them seems to have had any immediate influence across the Rhine except, perhaps, that at Willemstad or the one at Hanau in Hesse. The Amsterdam Noorderkerk was imitated at Emden only a generation later.

The first Dutch Reformed church was erected in Willemstad, southwest of Dordrecht, a "new town" beside the Hollandsche Diep built on the Ruigenhilpolder which had been created by damming in 1564. The town was planned by the Viceroy William of Orange in 1583 as a fortified octagon of slightly elongated shape. As at Zamość, the enceinte was provided with the latest sort of pointed corner bastions arranged somewhat more symmetrically than Morando's, but here in Holland it was set like an island in a star-shaped body of water.[8]

This modest octagonal "meeting house" at Willemstad, possibly following a French model, was erected in 1597-1607[9] for William's son Maurits—named for his uncle Moritz of Saxony—probably by Coenraent van Norenburch. It is thought, however, that Maurits himself may have dictated the octagonal plan to correspond with that of the town. The Willemstad church was soon followed by the Zuiderkerk in Amsterdam, built by Hendrik de Keyser in 1603-1611.[10] As mentioned earlier, that has a rectangular plan, like most German churches of the period, with

nave and side aisles, but the latter are interrupted here in a quite exceptional way by two pseudo-transepts, features de Keyser repeated in his later Westerkerk in Amsterdam begun in 1620 or 1621.

Further north in Denmark, one remarkable monument might be mentioned here also. The chapel in Slot Frederiksborg at Hillerød, built 1606-1620[11] for Christian IV, is quite as large as the Zuiderkerk, though that was the first Protestant church to rise in the richest Protestant city of the day. Like several chapels in Germany described in earlier chapters, moreover, that at Frederiksborg was very much more sumptuously decorated than the Zuiderkerk, though what one sees there today is largely nineteenth-century restoration, at least on the surface. Lutherans, whether Germans or Scandinavians, had even by this late date no such puritanical scruples as already restrained Calvinists in France and Holland as also in Scotland.

In Scotland the oldest surviving Protestant church in Great Britain, at Burntisland in Fifeshire, was erected in 1592.[12] As the plan indicates, this is a square meeting-house, but with a plain tower rising on four stone piers over the center and no decoration of any sort; of the slightly earlier "kirk" of 1588 at Pittenweem, also in Fifeshire, only the tower is in pristine condition. A somewhat comparable German example, much less original in plan, is the church at Nidda in Hesse (Fig. 73; Pl. 456) of 1616-1618 to be described below.

Dutch puritanism in architecture did not discourage great size and architectural elaboration as distinguished from figural decoration executed in paint or carved in stone and wood. De Keyser's other Amsterdam churches, the Noorderkerk of 1620-1623 and the Westerkerk of 1620-1631,[13] both begun just before his

---

[7] Knox, *Poland*, p. 18, pls. 14, 15.

[8] *Kunstreisboek*, p. 601, plan.

[9] *Ibid.*

[10] *Ibid.*, p. 339. The church is now used only for storage and is effectively inaccessible.

[11] Det Nationalhistoriske Museum, *Billeder fra Frederiksborg* [Hillerød, 1969], p. 31; Slothouwer, *Denemarken*, pp. 89-119. The contract with the Dutch mason Caspar Bogaert is dated late in 1601 and the Slot as a whole was in construction over the years 1602-1620, but Hans II van Steenwinckel not Bogaert was probably the responsible designer: Skovgaard, *Christian IV*, pp. 41-45.

[12] Summerson, *Britain* [paperback ed.], p. 537. The church was to be a "decent, honest and comely Kirk."

[13] *Kunstreisboek*, pp. 339-340. The Westerkerk is illustrated in J. Rosenberg, S. Slive and E. H. ter Kuile, *Dutch Art and Architecture 1600-1800* [Harmondsworth, 1972] pl. 188, and in *Niederlanden*, pls. 19-20. For the Zuiderkerk see Rosenberg *et al., op. cit.*, pl. 187. The Noorderkerk was published by Hendrik de Keyser in his *Architectura moderna*

death and with the tall tower of the latter completed only in 1638, are nearly as grand in their dimensions as the big Protestant and Catholic churches rising in Germany at the time the Thirty Years' War began that are to be described in this chapter; they are also more idiosyncratic in plan. The Amsterdam Westerkerk has two transepts like the Zuiderkerk, while the Noorderkerk is cruciform with the angles filled in to make an octagon externally. It thus recalls a little the more modest earlier church at Willemstad.

A special feature of the early seventeenth-century Dutch churches was such tall staged towers as the one on the Westerkerk. These were not matched or rivalled elsewhere on churches in the north of this period except for the Jesuits' Sint-Carolus Borromeuskerk in Antwerp of 1614-1621. Krumpper's at Polling, begun in 1605 (Pl. 454) also for a Catholic Order, is of a quite different character, and in any case was left incomplete by Krumpper. The oldest surviving Dutch example is that of the Haarlem Nieuwekerk which was added by Lieven de Key in 1613[14] to a mediaeval church that was otherwise entirely rebuilt in 1645-1649.

At this point the early history of Protestant church architecture may well be briefly recapitulated. The oldest extant examples, beginning with the chapel of 1543-1544 in Schloss Hartenfels at Torgau (Pl. 127) and the Marienkirche at Marienberg of 1558-1564, are in Germany. Those that once existed in France—the first probably the wooden one of 1562-1564 in Lyon—were all torn down in the next century, if not already destroyed in the religious wars of the later sixteenth century. The only exception is that begun in 1602 for the Duke of Württemberg at Montbéliard which can hardly be considered French. Early French Protestant architecture culminated eventually in the *Temple* that Salomon de Brosse (a.1562-1626)—favorite architect of Henri IV's widowed Queen Marie de Médicis though himself a Protestant—erected in the eastern Paris suburb of Charenton in 1623 after a previous one he had built there burned. Even the earlier Charenton *Temple* seems to have had still less influence in Germany than the Dutch churches. As noted earlier, only the Amsterdam Noorderkerk was copied, in the Neue Kirche at Emden, from the plates in de Keyser's

Architectura moderna. That was the work of the Emden city-architect Martin Faber (1587-1648). As it is so late, being dated 1643-1648,[15] it need not be discussed here.

The oldest Protestant churches extant outside Germany are those of 1588 and 1592 in Scotland mentioned just above. The next was Willemstad in Holland, begun in 1597. This was restored in 1791 and rebuilt after it was burned out in 1950 so that nothing is original now except the octagonal plan. Surviving edifices in Switzerland are of modest size and little intrinsic interest, nor did they have any influence abroad.

In Germany the Protestant churches closest in date to that at Willemstad were also erected in "new towns" as was earlier, among northern Catholic churches, the one at Zamošč in Poland. The church at Hanau, moreover, built for the use of Netherlanders, actually has some similarity to the Willemstad one, though the Netherlanders who were involved with it came from the south not the north. Hanau became Lutheran in 1530; later the local ruler, Count Philipp Ludwig II von Solms (1580-1612), turned Calvinist in 1593. For the many Protestants who were still fleeing from the Spanish Inquisition instituted by the Habsburgs in the southern Netherlands he then had a new town laid out,[16] south of the old one, as was mentioned earlier. The plan (Fig. 55) prepared by the engineer Nicolas Gillet is star-shaped like that of Willemstad, with five bastions at the edges. Otherwise it is arranged more or less like Zamošč with straight streets forming a regular pattern of square blocks. At the center the rectangular marketplace still survives with a later Rathaus serving the Neustadt quarter of the town in the middle of its north side. Opposite that a short street on axis leads to a second rectangular open space in which the new church was begun in 1600.[17]

The Protestant refugees at Hanau, like modern Belgians, lacked a common language, and so the new edifice had a quite exceptional plan (Pl. 422) with a small octagonal church for the French-speaking Walloons backed up against a much larger twelve-sided one for those who spoke Flemish. The pulpits were on either side of a dividing wall and both interiors had galleries all around. Externally, slim round stair-turrets linked the two unequal masses.

The Hanau church, completed in 1608, was very

---

and copied at Emden in Germany from his plates in the 1640s.

[14] *Kunstreisboek*, p. 362. Sixteenth-century Dutch towers usually were secular, not features of churches, and the grandest that survives, as earlier noted, is not in Holland but in Gdańsk.

[15] Reclams *Niedersachsen*, p. 155.
[16] Dehio, *Hessen*, p. 361.
[17] *Ibid.*, p. 364.

seriously damaged in the last war and the larger section survives only as a ruin with tall empty window-frames between the plain buttresses that project at the angles. The smaller octagon, however, was re-roofed and restored internally for use as the Evangelical parish church of the town by Wilhelm Lossow and Josef von Lanatsch in 1959-1960. Amateurs rather than experienced builders were responsible for the design of the original edifice. These men, René Mahieu, Jean d'Hollande (†1620) and Daniel Soreau (†1619), presumably followed French models in a general way, but nothing now survives of the period that is at all like this double-polygonal church elsewhere in northern Europe except, up to a point, the restored single octagon of the one at Willemstad.

Freudenstadt, it may be recalled, was laid out in 1599[18] for Duke Friedrich of Württemberg by his architect Heinrich Schickhardt in connection with the new silver mines in the Forchbachtal that were being exploited in rivalry with those of Saxony. The general shape of Hanau, as of Willemstad, was determined by the star-pattern of the fortifications, and the churches in both occupied open spaces at their centers to which principal streets led. Schickhardt's plan for Freudenstadt (Figs. 56, 57) belonged to another tradition, that of the square or rectangular town, which Morando had at least approached at Zamošč. How Schickhardt worked up this plan in a most original way, not at all like that of the Polish town, with public buildings occupying the corners of the big central space, has already been described.

Like Philipp Ludwig at Hanau, Friedrich had a charitable purpose as well as industrial development in mind when he founded Freudenstadt, for the town was intended to provide a refuge for exiled Protestants, in this case not from the southern Netherlands ruled by the Spanish Habsburgs, but from southern Austria. Thence the Habsburg Archduke Ferdinand, a nephew of the Ferdinand who built the Spanischer Saal at Schloss Ambras and later the Emperor Ferdinand II, after succeeding in 1595 as the ruler of Inner Austria, eventually expelled no less than two-thirds of the population. A large church suitable for Lutheran rather than Calvinist use was therefore needed at Freudenstadt, and this Schickhardt provided in 1601-1609[19] at the southeast corner of his central open space.

Another Protestant church of more advanced design, now in France—St.-Martin (Pl. 438) at Montbéliard—was built in these years for Friedrich by Schickhardt;[20] this will be described later.

Schickhardt had the rather Mannerist idea of placing the principal public buildings at Freudenstadt, not on the axes, but at the angles of the square facing the ends of the four wings of the diagonally-set Schloss at the center, itself never built. That suggested the use of an L-shaped plan, with the altar placed at the outer angle, and thus quite different from the plain rectangle of his Montbéliard church. Deep galleries are carried across both ends of the L on elaborately decorated supports and narrower ones rest on heavy scrolled brackets along the walls across from the altar (Pl. 424). Both arms of the church are covered with extraordinarily shallow cross-ribbed vaults decorated with carved medallions at the intersections of the ribs.

The Freudenstadt church was much damaged in the last war; externally, however, it has been very plausibly restored (Pl. 423). The organization of the masses is most exceptional, for there are towers at each end of the L and loggias of three widely-spaced segmental-arched openings run along the sides of the wings toward the square. Above the loggias are traceried windows of hybrid design. Two square towers project in front of the ends of the high roofs of the two branches of the nave and dominate the whole composition. But the transition from the plain square section of the lower storeys of each tower to the octagons of the upper stages is so clumsily handled that the plain pointed gables of the roofs appear to be merely affixed to the tops of the shafts. More familiar are the cantilevered galleries at the top of the lower octagons with their pierced parapets. Higher up, bell-shaped *welsche Hauben*, ending in tiny square lanterns under sharp spire-like roofs, provide a lively termination. The general flavour is almost vernacular in its simplicity and has little in common externally with the elaboration of contemporary secular work of the Northern Mannerist sort. There is even less reflection of Schickhardt's Italian trip of 1598; nor does it at all resemble the exteriors of the new Academic structures of Holl, rising at Augsburg and Eichstätt just when this edifice was completed in 1609. To those the contemporary exterior of the Montbéliard church of Schickhardt's design does, however, offer a parallel (Pl. 438).

[18] Fleischhauer, *Württemberg*, pp. 291-294.

[19] *Ibid.*, pp. 288-289; H. Rommel and G. Kopp, *Die Stadtkirche von Freudenstadt* [Freudenstadt, 1963], p. 6, plan; J. Baum, *Die Kirchen des Baumeisters Heinrich Schickhardt*, Stuttgart, 1905.

[20] The tower of the Stadtkirche in Cannstatt was also built by Schickhardt a bit later in 1612-1613: Fleischhauer, *Württemberg*, p. 287, pl. 140.

The great feature of the interior of the Freudenstadt church, extravagantly rich where everything else is quite plain, was once the polychromed stucco relief running the whole length of the parapet of the galleries. This was executed in 1606 by Gerhardt Schmitt who had finished his work at Schloss Weikersheim (Pls. 351, 353) the previous year. Of equal richness, but without figural elements other than the seraphs' heads at their tops, were the *estípites*-like supports. These were evidently minor masterpieces of Northern Mannerist architectural ornament and quite worthy of the alternating Biblical scenes and personages on the parapet above. The latter, one should note, provided what must have been, at least up to this time, one of the most extensive repertories of religious iconography in any Protestant edifice. Only the furnishings in the Celle chapel (Pl. 207) offer today so rich a repertory of early Lutheran figural art in church-decoration, since the painted religious scenes in the Schmalkalden chapel were early expunged because of Calvinist prejudice. Of course, innumerable altarpieces both carved and painted survive in churches and museums; several of the grandest will be mentioned later in this chapter (Pls. 427, 428).

Further decoration in the Freudenstadt church consisted of painted framing around the doors and windows in the white plaster wall much as in the secular interiors at Schmalkalden (Pl. 351) of a decade or so earlier. Unlike Schmidt's figural reliefs in stucco—which were in fact originally intended for another church and must always have seemed too ornate for this simple interior—the minor decoration accords well with the vernacular flavor of the exterior.

It was in the same years 1601-1607[21] that Schickhardt also built for the duke the more ambitious church of St.-Martin at Montbéliard. Rather forgotten today since Montbéliard (Mömpelgard), lying south of Belfort and just west of the Swiss border, has long been in the French *département* of Doubs, this is no rival in size or richness of decoration to the somewhat later Neuburg Hofkirche. That church was, however, projected by Joseph Heintz as early as 1603 though not begun, following a revised design, until 1607. The design for the exterior of St.-Martin (Pl. 438) was first presented by Schickhardt in a drawing of 1602. Both that and the executed exteriors are rather similar, as has already been noted, to those of Heintz's on the Augsburg Siegel Haus which are dated 1605, only a

few years later. A Doric order of pilasters, with those at the corners doubled, defines the bays along the sides of the church at Montbéliard quite as on the Siegel Haus and such members also frame the central projection on the east end above which the modest later tower of 1676 now rises in somewhat makeshift fashion. In each bay there is a single tall window. These are capped by broken pediments that are alternately pointed and segmental. In the second bay on the north and on the south there are simple entrance portals, but none in the middle of the west front.

Despite the crowns of the windows, which resemble Ridinger's at Aschaffenburg (Pl. 368) more than Holl's in the court of Schloss Willibaldsburg (Pl. 407), the ordonnance of St.-Martin is therefore at least as Academic as that of Heintz's side elevation of the Siegel Haus (Pl. 400). The gable over the east front, though simplified from the original project in later execution, is of a more hybrid and Germanic character. Yet, taken as a whole, Schickhardt's exterior can be considered to be as advanced in design as that of any church in France or Germany of its period, at least so far as is known today. The interior is of a Calvinist severity, however, a great barren rectangle with a flat ceiling, elaborated only by a U-shaped gallery to the west and the plain pulpit set against the wall in the middle of the east end.[22]

Though more full-size churches were being erected in these decades in Germany than earlier, princes both Protestant and Catholic were also building and furnishing chapels in their new or enlarged Schlösser as they had long been doing. It has already been noted that at Heidelberg a chapel of church-like dimensions occupies the two lower storeys of the Friedrichsbau (Pl. 425). Begun in 1601, the same year as St.-Martin, the chapel was completed, as that was also, shortly before the Freudenstadt church in 1607.[23] The Elector Palatine Friedrich IV and his master-mason, Hans Schoch from Strasbourg, offered here no originality of plan or design but were still content to provide, as in chapels at the Schlösser of various Lutheran princes for two generations and more, merely a larger version of the one at Torgau of 1543-1544 (Pl. 125). Although the Heidelberg chapel is even larger than that at the

[21] *Ibid.*, pp. 286-287, figs. 137-138.

[22] The Stadtkirche at Göppingen, begun for Duke Friedrich by Schickhardt in 1618, is very similar but lacks the external pilaster order: Horst, *Architektur*, p. 56, figs. 28, 30. According to Fleischhauer, *Württemberg*, p. 288, the church was designed a little earlier in 1615.

[23] Oechelshaeuser, *Heidelberger Schloss*, pp. 63-72.

Augustusburg of around 1570 and the one at Schmal-kalden of around 1590, the interior (Pl. 425)—as first restored in 1897-1900 along with the rest of the Friedrichsbau, and again since the last war in 1959—displays neither the "High Renaissance" structure and membering of August of Saxony's (Pl. 201) nor the Northern Mannerist decoration (Pl. 267) Vernukken and his associates executed so profusely in stucco for Wilhelm of Hessen-Kassel. This Heidelberg chapel is rather, for the most part, in the realm of *Nachgotik* though the arches of the nave arcade and the section of the main vault are round, not pointed, and some of the details are more than faintly Italianate.

The interior of the Heidelberg chapel, moreover, has been left as bare in the latest restoration—even though not sponsored here by a Communist regime—as the early one at Schloss Hartenfels; but old photographs indicate the effect was not very different when the vaults carried the painted decoration renewed, or quite possibly first introduced, in the 1890s. Thus Friedrich's chapel is closer in character to the Jesuits' Petrikirche of the 1590s at Münster and later Catholic examples of *Nachgotik* than to the most sumptuous of the princely chapels of these decades in northern Europe, the Lutheran one of Christian IV in the Frederiksborg Slot at Hillerød in Denmark. Heidelberg was no longer so much the "German Geneva" it had been under the Calvinist bigot, the Elector Friedrich III; but the chapel, all the same, was relatively simple as decorated and furnished by his successor, despite the fact that Friedrich IV's taste in exterior architecture was closer to Ottheinrich's.

Ridinger's Catholic chapel of 1605-1614 in Schloss Johannisburg at Aschaffenburg is similar to Schoch's, but smaller. Its altar and pulpit, however, executed in marble and alabaster by Hans Junckers as was earlier noted, had no parallels in style or in ornamental richness in the Heidelberg chapel even though, by contrast, the Swiss sculptor Götz's work on the outer walls of the Friedrichsbau is so profuse (Pl. 366).

The characteristic elaboration of late Northern Mannerism[24] is rarely more clearly manifested in these

years than in the design of the new altars and pulpits that were so often introduced into older churches. The three principal altars (Pl. 428) of the great Benedictine church of Sts. Ulrich and Afra in Augsburg[25]—still Catholic long after St. Anna became Protestant—one of them in the Gothic apse at the east end and two in the transepts flanking the entrance to the Gothic choir, dominate the eastward view in this very late, but still mediaeval, interior. The pointed vaulting in the eastern arm, it should be noted, was completed, probably by Konrad Stoss, only in 1603. The very tall high altar, which carries the date 1604 of the following year, is by two Bavarian wood-carvers, Johann Degler (†1637) from Weilheim and Elias Greither (†1646). These artists were responsible also for the only slightly smaller Afra altar set against the northeast pier of the crossing, dated 1607, and the Ulrich altar that matches it. The principal rival of these is the high altar by Jörg Zürn of 1613-1619[26] (Pl. 427) in the Nikolaikirche at Überlingen on the Bodensee that rises up so tall into the vault of the very late Gothic apse there. Few of them, moreover, owe much beyond quite probably their large paintings and staged composition to the prominent model provided by Wendel Dietrich two decades earlier at St. Michael in Munich (Pl. 256). Even less do they reflect those of the Early Baroque in Italy where the painters, at least, had often travelled and even studied.

Other features introduced in the principal church of Augsburg at this time, as in many others both Catholic and Protestant, include the pulpit of 1608 by Degler and the organ-case over the western gallery. Mathias Kager designed the latter in 1608 also and executed the paintings on the wings himself long before he worked in the Augsburg Rathaus; the carved work on the case is by Paulus III Mair (c.1540-1615/1619). There are, furthermore, a holy water basin of 1605-1607, possibly the work of Adriaen de Fries, and choir-stalls of 1604, probably by Hans Merz. Finally, two notable paintings of the period, one dated 1608 by

---

[24] German writers have been inclined to describe these features as "Early Baroque"; but they have, in fact, little in common either with Italian altars of this period or later Baroque ones in Germany. For all their profusion of sculpture and the large oil paintings on some of them, they seem in their many-staged elaboration rather to offer an analogue in church furnishing to the secular gables of the period. Such gables also appear on various churches, of course, even as

late and as far afield as the Franziskanerkirche in Vienna of 1603-1611. Something more Italianate, if not actually Academic, might have been expected there: Baldass, *Österreich*, pl. 3. More striking are the gables of around 1600 at Rotsürben in Silesia (Pl. 279).

[25] Breuer, *Augsburg*, pp. 43-44; [N. Lieb] *St. Ulrich und Afra/Augsburg*, 6th ed. [Munich, 1969] pp. 2-3, 6-10.

[26] Dehio, *Baden-Württemberg*, p. 485. Jahn, *Deutsche Renaissance*, pl. 151, a photograph by Helga Schmidt-Glasner, is the best view of this altar.

Hans I Rottenhammer (1564-1625) and the other of the following year by Kager, should at least be mentioned. As earlier noted, Joseph Heintz was also providing paintings for two other Augsburg churches at this point.

Because of the considerable number of elaborate furnishings added in the opening years of the century the interior of Sts. Ulrich and Afra overshadows in interest those of many, if not most, of the new churches begun in this decade in northern Europe. The grandest of these were mostly Protestant, moreover, except in Poland and the southern Netherlands. Several of the most architecturally ambitious Catholic edifices of the period are mausoleums in southern Austria dating from the very late sixteenth and early seventeenth centuries. The most notable is that of the Archduke Karl II at Seckau, near Graz in Styria, of 1587-1611 at least as regards the interior. As these structures need not, in the particular geographical and stylistic framework of this book, be considered German because of their remote location to the southeast and the usual employment on them of Italian architects and other artists, only the earliest and richest is illustrated here (Pl. 426), though there is further information about several of them in a Note.[27]

The next two important churches in the central German lands, both begun shortly after those at Hanau and Freudenstadt, were for Lutherans. The fourteenth-century Marienkapelle at Wolfenbüttel retained its Marian advocation as the Marienkirche, like the one at Marienberg of 1558-1564, even after it became the Lutheran parish church in 1568. A generation later Duke Heinrich Julius of Brunswick-Wolfenbüttel, for whom Paul Francke had completed the Juleum of the new university at Helmstedt by the late 1590s, began during the years 1601-1604[28] to consider rebuilding this as the Hauptkirche or principal church of Wolfenbüttel. By 1607 the first piles had been driven for the foundations and the next year, 1608, the cornerstone was laid with Francke in charge.

By 1607 also, Philipp Ludwig von der Pfalz, the Wittelsbach who not only ruled the Upper Palatinate but also, from 1609, the duchies of Jülich-Berg-Kleve in the Rhineland[29] of which his wife was the heiress, started building a *Hofkirche* (court church) at Neuburg-a.-d.-Donau in the upper town near the Schloss. For this he had been obtaining plans (Pl. 430) from Joseph Heintz since 1603.[30] Heintz, who was provid-

---

[27] Several mausoleums of 1590-1620 in Austria deserve at least short descriptions at this point. Especially monumental in size and scale is that of Ruprecht von Eggenberger at Ehrenhausen, on the Mur in Styria, of the same years as the one at Stadthagen. Begun in 1609 two years before Ruprecht's death and completed externally by 1614, it is a freestanding chapel with an octagonal dome and barrel-vaulted arms. Though a grand sight from a distance on its high embankment, the detail proves to be extremely heavy-handed when seen near to. The architect was Johann Walther, evidently in this case not an Italian, and that doubtless explains, at least in part, its character. The interior was only decorated toward 1690, however, possibly by J. B. Fischer von Erlach: KDÖ, *Kärnten Steiermark*, 365; Baldass, *Österreich*, pl. 32.

The slightly later mausoleum of the emperor Ferdinand II beside the cathedral of Graz, the Styrian capital—a considerably larger structure—is equally heavy-handed, but in a more Venetian Baroque vein somewhat resembling Alessandro Tremignon's much later San Moisé facade of 1668 in Venice. The cluster of two domes and a dome-topped round tower, however, provide a more traditional Venetian look. Begun by the Italian Pietro de Pomis in 1614 and completed externally in 1638 by Peter Valnegra, the interior, as at Ehrenhausen, was not decorated until 1687-1699 following designs definitely known to have been provided here by Fischer von Erlach: KDÖ, *Kärnten Steiermark*, p. 368; Baldass *Österreich*, pl. 33.

The somewhat earlier mausoleum of Ferdinand's father,

the Archduke Karl, which is mentioned in the text, is only a chapel occupying the north aisle of the choir of the great Romanesque abbey-church of the Benedictines at Seckau near Graz. Begun by Karl in 1587 before his death in 1590, it was completed in 1611. Alexander de Werda was first in charge, but the work was carried on after 1592 by the Italian Sebastiano Carlone: KDÖ, *Kärnten Steiermark*, p. 387. The frescoes, begun perhaps as early as 1583, are by another Italian, Teodoro Ghisi. This interior (Pl. 426), though modest in size, is one of the most elaborate decorative ensembles of fresco-painting and *stucchi* in northern Europe (Baldass *Österreich*, pp. 69-70; pl. 58) of the years just before 1600. None of these works, however, or the slightly later and more advanced ones in Salzburg that are mentioned below in Note 90, have much to do with the architecture of this period in the more central German lands, however premonitory they may be of the later Austrian and German Baroque. By contrast, at Montbéliard in the other direction the architect was German.

[28] Karpa, *Wolfenbüttel*, pp. 20-21, pls. 29-41.

[29] Philipp Ludwig's wife Anna was the second daughter of Wilhelm V of Kleve, the client of Alessandro Pasqualini at Jülich in the 1550s. On the death of her brother, Johann Wilhelm, who succeeded their father, she inherited the duchies, but Philipp Ludwig was in effect the ruler. Her older sister, Maria Eleonora, who had died the previous year, was married to Duke Albrecht Friedrich of Brandenburg. As a result of her early demise, the Hohenzollerns had to wait several centuries before they obtained control of these territories in the west.

[30] Zimmer, *Hofkirche und Rathaus*, pp. 18-19 and *passim*;

ing designs for the facade of the Augsburg Zeughaus and for the Siegel Haus (Pls. 398, 402) in 1602 and in 1605, respectively, also supplied in 1603 one (Pl. 429) for rebuilding the Neuburg Rathaus,[31] which had been badly damaged by the fall of the nearby church-tower. The grand new Hofkirche at Neuburg was to replace the Gothic church of a former nunnery that Ottheinrich von der Pfalz had secularized upon his conversion in 1542. This lay to the west of the Schloss on considerably higher ground facing an open square and at right angles to the Rathaus on the north.

As early as 1587, when he added a tower to the old church, Philipp Ludwig had proposed to erect a new edifice as a counterpoise to the Jesuits' St. Michael in Munich which had just been completed for the first time. In 1598, a year after Sustris finished rebuilding the east end of the Munich church, Philipp Ludwig eventually made a contract for the work with the local master-masons Heinrich Schäfer and Martin Traub, not with the Italian-Swiss Egidio Valentini (better known as Gilg Vältin), from Roveredo in the Grigioni with whom there were at this time only abortive negotiations. In March 1602, came the fall of the bell-tower that these Germans were erecting to replace the one of 1587, which had by 1599 already become dangerous. As a result of this disaster they were first imprisoned and then compelled to demolish the remains of their tower.

Soon, in 1603, it was Valentini who was set to work on the Rathaus diagonally across from the tower following designs Heintz supplied (Pl. 429); of this structure, however, on which he was assisted by one of the younger Pasqualinis,[32] little that is original survives today. On December 12, 1606, a new contract for the construction of the Neuburg Hofkirche was made with Valentini.[33] Work on that then went forward under his direction according to Heintz's somewhat modified design. Valentini had the assistance of another Italian-Swiss, Giovanni Bigaglie, but much of the cut-stone work was executed from 1611 onward by the local mason Georg Hain. The church was already

largely complete in the raw by 1609, however, and in 1613 the carpenter Jakob Bechtold from Spalt, a village in Franconia, erected the roof over the apse.

At that point Philipp Ludwig died and his son, Wolfgang Wilhelm, succeeded in 1614. Having lately become a Catholic under the influence of his brother-in-law Maximilian of Bavaria,[34] Wolfgang Wilhelm turned the church over to the Jesuits. For them the brothers Michele and Antonio Castelli, north Italians who were probably already on the job, carried out the extensive original stucco-decoration by the time of the consecration on October 21, 1618. Up to 1620 the church cost 100,077 gulden—roughly a tenth of the cost of the Schloss at Aschaffenburg. The west tower, however, was only built later by Johann Alberthal in 1624-1627, possibly with advice from Elias Holl, and definitely with the assistance of Antonio Serro. Also known as Krauss, Serro was like Valentini a Roveredan and he already had been employed by Wolfgang Wilhelm at Düsseldorf since 1619. His name is specifically mentioned in Alberthal's contract of 1624 for the construction of the tower, but not Holl's.

The construction of the Wolfenbüttel church, begun at almost the same time as that in Neuburg, proceeded for a while in parallel fashion: By 1613 the choir was completed with its vaults and the nave probably before 1621, the date on the inner portal of the west tower.[35] The cross-gables along the sides followed only rather later, however, several being of 1657-1660 and one as late as 1890, while the crown of the tower is dated 1751.

It is not easy to assign priority either to Philipp Ludwig's Neuburg church or to Heinrich Julius's Wolfenbüttel church as executed. The former was proposed first and also completed first. However, the edifice Valentini executed from Heintz's designs is more novel stylistically for Germany—in the light of later German church architecture, one may say that it is more "advanced." Yet in plan it is a hall-church (Fig. 66) and the decoration is distinctly Northern Mannerist. Even so, the Wolfenbüttel church may better be discussed before the one at Neuburg. The same applies to the Stadtkirche at Bückeburg though it was definitely several years later in conception and finished earlier.

Horn-Meyer, *Neuburg*, pp. 82-107. Zimmer is most detailed on the prehistory over the years before construction of the church began; Horn-Meyer are more concerned with the edifice as executed 1608-1624.

[31] Horn-Meyer, *Neuburg*, pp. 272-273; Zimmer, *Hofkirche und Rathaus*, pp. 16, 26-29.

[32] This was certainly not Alessandro (†1559) as given by Horn-Meyer, pp. 272-273, but Johann II (1562-1614/1615), a grandson, or possibly Alexander II.

[33] Zimmer, *Hofkirche und Rathaus*, pp. 20-24.

[34] His mother may well have been a Catholic since her father Wilhelm of Kleve had returned to the old faith in 1570.

[35] Reclams *Niedersachsen*, pp. 772-773; Karpa, *Wolfenbüttel*, pp. 20-21.

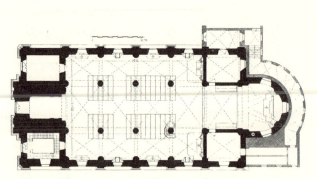

Fig. 66. Joseph Heintz; Egidio Valentini: Neuburg-
a.-d.-Donau, Hofkirche, 1607-18, plan

The Wolfenbüttel church, the cornerstone of which was laid by Heinrich Julius in 1608, was planned by Francke at that time or, possibly, a year or so earlier (Fig. 67). He supervised the construction until his death in 1615, two years after the duke's; then followed Johann Meier, who worked for Duke Friedrich Ulrich until his death in 1621; finally Johann Lange-lüddeke (†1657) carried the job to effective completion except for some of the cross-gables and the upper stages of the west tower. The west portal was carved by Heinrich Gottes before 1618 though the wooden doors are of 1645. In the years between the town suffered much war damage, some 420 houses being destroyed or ruined, so that the long delay in the campaign of construction at the church is not surprising and, indeed, was very common in the second quarter of the century in Germany.

In several ways Francke's Protestant church is as characteristic an example of *Nachgotik* as any that Catholics—and particularly the Jesuits who most favored the mode—were building in these years down through their Mariä Himmelfahrt in Cologne of 1618-1627 (Pls. 451, 452) and even considerably later. In its basic scheme Francke's Hauptkirche is a hall-church

with four oblong bays in the long nave, tall side aisles, broad transepts and a choir ending in a polygonal apse (Pl. 431). The arching of the ribs of the nave vaults, however, is half-round, not pointed, as already in the mediaeval Moritzkirche in Halle when finally vaulted in 1511, and in the Marktkirche (Pl. 37) there, begun in 1529, as also in many or even most later sixteenth-century German churches and chapels. All the same, the tall aisle windows still have pointed tops. Moreover, the piers carrying the vaulting, like those in the contemporary court of the Pellerhaus, are octagonal in section, not cylindrical as they were already, as early as the second decade of the century, in such advanced churches of that time as St. Martin at Lauingen and St. Katherine in Augsburg. The capitals of the piers, furthermore, are as remote from the recognizably Corinthian ones in St. Katherine (Pl. 14) of a hundred years before as from anything Gothic. Made up of various Northern Mannerist elements these capitals are, indeed, decorative confections of almost total originality. Additional carved decoration bands the columns approximately at eye-level.

Equally original at Wolfenbüttel, and rivalling Francke's work at Helmstedt (Pl. 333), is the detailing of the carved tracery in the heads of the tall three-light windows along the sides and on the west front (Pl. 433), as also the somewhat quoin-like elements that frame them at the sides. What are really the imposts of the pointed arches, for example, and also their archivolts are banded rather in the *Weserrenaissance* way. However, the ornament on the bands is not the familiar chip-carving. Rather it approaches the so-called *Ohrmuschelstil* as that can be seen, from this time or a little later, on the gable of the Bremen Krameramtshaus of 1619-1622 (Pl. 379), though both figural and animal elements are incorporated here. Soenke[36] rather begs the question of who was responsible for this detailing by dating the quoins at the corners of the west tower—not probably the earliest— "?1615," the year Francke died and Meier took over. He suggests that bosses so richly carved were Dutch in origin, noting that Lieven de Key used similar ones on the ground storey of the Haarlem Vleeshal as early as 1602-1603. In Germany they seem to have appeared first, at least in profusion, on the central portion of the remodelled facade of the Bremen Rathaus (Pl. 376) over which the gable is dated 1612. Those Francke may well have known.

Big buttresses project between the bays of the Wol-

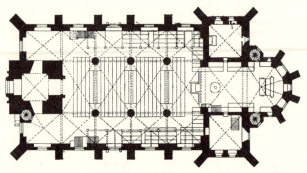

Fig. 67. Paul Francke: Wolfenbüttel, Marienkirche,
begun 1608, plan

36 Kreft-Soenke, *Weserrenaissance*, p. 294, figs. 281, 282.

fenbüttel Hauptkirche (Pl. 433). These are crowned, at a rather low level in relation to the height of the side walls, by heavily molded caps. Only the statues of the Evangelists, carved by Hans Röttgers (†1627) from Brunswick, standing on top of the buttresses break across the terminal entablature of the main masses of the church. The walls and the buttresses are, like the entablatures that crown them and in contrast to the *Ohrmuschelstil* tracery in the window heads, almost Academic in effect because of the monumental scale of the large areas of plain ashlar.

Like the pillars inside, the buttresses of the Wolfenbüttel church stand on high podia topped by a heavily molded string-course that runs all around the walls just below the window-sills. Like the octagonal pillars within, the buttresses also carry a single band of carved ornament set about a third of the way up their shafts. Because the buttresses at the corners of the nave and the transepts project diagonally, these are especially conspicuous and actually rather mediaeval-looking because of the visual emphasis on their essentially statical function. So also those, also projecting diagonally, at the angles of the apse still have a boldly mediaeval air in spite of the proto-Academic detailing (Pl. 432) of their crowning members that is in such sharp contrast to the fussily hybrid membering of the big pointed windows in between. The resulting similarity to the exterior of the east end of Freiberg (Pl. 272), as remodelled in the eighties and nineties of the previous century, is also worth remark and possibly relevant, for Francke may well have known it.

The most extravagant features on the outside of the Wolfenbüttel church are the cross-gables. Like the tracery in the windows, these may be of Francke's design but were mostly executed, as has been noted, well after his death in 1615. The four engaged columns which elaborate plastically the lower stage of each of them provide a quite standard Italianate motif of a sort that is rare on this stylistically ambiguous edifice; on many of the gables, moreover, there is also a second order in the upper stage. All are statue-crowned; but it is the flanking scrollwork, approaching the *Ohrmuschelstil* even more closely than do the carved blocks below, that sets them apart. These gables provide a climactic point in the long German line of development in gable design that began with the modest *welsche Gebel* of a hundred years before at Halle and Schloss Neuhaus (Pls. 44, 45). The character of the ornament also suggests a rather late date for the designing of the gables, well after Francke's and even Meier's death, as does the known fact that several were

executed only in 1657-1660, a decade after the Thirty Years' War was over.

The west portal at Wolfenbüttel, on the other hand, was certainly completed with its statues of the two dukes a bit before the war broke out in 1618, though it was doubtless begun by Gottes only after Francke's death three years earlier. With its broad arched doorway and two overlapping sets of engaged orders, this has in the lower stage a curious resemblance to the Romanesque portal of St.-Gilles-du-Gard. In the next stage an additional order appears between the statues of the dukes; above, *Ohrmuschelstil* scrolling supports a figure of Christ in front of the west window. Set in a broad field of plain ashlar and framed by carved blocks, this window is all but identical with those along the aisles in its detailing. Since it is cut off by the second storey of the portal at half-height, however, the proportions are considerably less vertical and Gothic-looking despite the pointed arch.

Because of the late date and inappropriate form of the tower as completed in 1751, the Wolfenbüttel church is disappointing as seen from the west. But another Protestant church with a most remarkable front, the Stadtkirche at Bückeburg begun in 1610, had already been completed by the time of Francke's death[37] (Pl. 435). Ernst von Schaumburg, who had commissioned from Nosseni two years before the very Academic mausoleum (Pl. 442) behind the church at Stadthagen, left no doubt as to his responsibility for the Northern Mannerist facade at Bückeburg: in his rather ironic inscription running along the frieze of the entablature: "*Exemplum Religionis Non STructurae*," five letters are gilded to spell out his name. This is, indeed, far more than the Stadthagen mausoleum (Pl. 442) already under way for two years, what one would expect from the work that Ernst had commissioned at the Bückeburg Schloss in the previous decade: the decoration of the chapel, the erection of the entrance gate and its flanking structures and above all the extraordinary portal in the Goldener Saal (Pls. 357-360). This Bückeburg facade represents the culmination of a major phase of German Renaissance architecture in church-design, while the Neuburg Hofkirche is significant rather because it initiated a new phase—providing the ecclesiastical parallel, one may say, of Holl's contemporary secular work at Augsburg and Eichstätt. Thus it seems better, as proposed ear-

[37] *Ibid.*, pp. 236-237; Habich, *Residenz Bückeburg*, pp. 73-80, 135-147. No west tower was completed here at Bückeburg, but the substitute crown of the facade is more concordant than the eighteenth-century tower at Wolfenbüttel.

lier, to discuss the Bückeburg Stadtkirche first. There is no ambiguity, however, as in the case of the Wolfenbüttel church, concerning relative priority. Ernst's church at Bückeburg was certainly not begun for some three or four years after the Palatine duke's at Neuburg, in 1610 or 1611, and still longer after the latter was first projected by Heintz in 1603.

There can be little question either that the construction of the Bückeburg church was directed by Hans Wulff (†1643) who had succeeded his brother Ebbert II in Ernst's service on the latter's death of the pest in 1609. Before their father Ebbert died in 1606 it will be recalled that Hans had already been employed from 1604 onward, together with his brothers Ebbert II and Jonas (†1619), on the decoration in the chapel of the Schloss and on the portal of the Goldener Saal. By the time the work in the chapel was completed in 1608 Ebbert II had returned to Hildesheim, but all the same he was commissioned by Ernst in that year to make a statue of Justitia for the Bückeburg Schloss. After Ebbert's death Hans took over that contract and received thenceforth a yearly salary of 50 taler. Jonas had taken on the control of the family workshop in Hildesheim after the father's death and was no longer employed at Bückeburg once the decoration and the furnishings in the chapel were completed.

It may be further noted here that the organ, dated 1615, which fills the east end of the Bückeburg church above the nineteenth-century altar, though heavily restored after serious damage by fire in 1902 was originally the work of Josias Compenius. The bronze font, commissioned in 1613 and signed and dated 1615, is by Adriaen de Fries. Neither of these names, however, has any probable relevance in attributing the design for the church. Credit for that must—with only slight doubt—be assigned to Hans Wulff.

The Bückeburg edifice is, like Francke's, a hall-church with ribbed cross-vaulting, but it is even less characteristically *Nachgotik* otherwise. There is no transept and the east end of the nave, filled with the vast organ, is blind and flat though the ends of the aisles are canted, somewhat as at Marienberg sixty years before (Fig. 68). The big piers are of cylindrical section and proper columnar proportions; indeed, they even have quite evident entasis (Pl. 434). Moreover, the capitals, for all their elaboration with cherubs' heads and strapwork detail, are recognizably Corinthian in their general form with vigorous volutes at the corners below square abacuses. There are even compressed entablature blocks between the abacuses and the springing of the heavily molded ribs. The

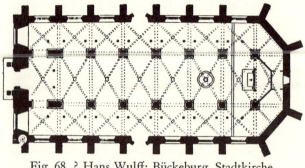

Fig. 68. ? Hans Wulff: Bückeburg, Stadtkirche, 1610-15, plan

curvature of these last, however, is pointed but so slightly as almost to escape notice.

At the west end of the Bückeburg church the glazed *Fürstenloge* (prince's pew) is carried on three round arches. This is entirely executed in wood and carved with a profusion of Northern Mannerist ornament polychromed and gilded like the portal executed by the Wulffs in the Goldener Saal (Pl. 357). There are here, however, no such large-scale figures as Ebbert II introduced on that. Against the middle pier on the north side the equally rich pulpit is suspended. Since Ebbert II died before the construction of the church began, this may have been the work of Jonas. Though he seems to have been continuously in Hildesheim through the relevant years down to his death in 1619, it could have been executed in the family workshop there and brought to Bückeburg for installation. Even if that be true, such an incidental contribution by Jonas need hardly negate Hans's general responsibility for the architecture of the church.

Because of the size and Classical character of the piers, the general impression made by the Bückeburg church internally is not without some suggestion of Academic intention, unlikely as that must seem as regards any of the Wulffs though not of their client. As earlier in the Torgau chapel or that of Schloss Augustusburg, for example, the elaboration of such features as the pulpit, the organ and here especially the Fürstenloge contrasts with the relative severity of the major architectural elements. However, the ornate detail of the Fürstenloge is quite consonant with that on the facade, though naturally much more delicate in scale. The facade, indeed, is grandly monumental to a degree unmatched by any other work in the Northern Mannerist vein, yet at the same time an extravaganza that calls to mind the later Iberian Baroque especially as modified in the New World.

Yet externally, also, there is at Bückeburg a marked

contrast between the plain walls of the sides and the amazing "west" (actually north) front of the Stadt-kirche (Pl. 435), rising so tall in the center of this small town at the head of the street leading up from the Schloss. The sides are broken only by bare stepped buttresses between tall and rather plain windows. These last have bevelled sides and tops, with no moldings at all, and in their round-arched heads simple tracery of the sort first used in German churches toward 1520. Only the side portals reflect the megalomania of the west front.

The heavily molded three-sided "arches" of these side portals of the Bückeburg church are crowned with bold scrollwork. That is at once so amorphous structurally and so assertive in scale that it resembles less Churrigueresque work in Spain than the overblown detailing of the nineteenth-century "Jacobethan" in England—that on Anthony Salvin's Harlaxton Hall in Lincolnshire, for example. All the same, to define the special character of the vertical members of the tall main storey of the front facade, as also the supports of the Fürstenloge within, the Spanish term *estípites* must be used again as already for the comparable elements on Ernst's entrance gateway (Pl. 358) to the Schloss here. More such members frame the west window above the main portal and also the clock in the lower stage of the broad gable (Pl. 435).

Despite the profusion of ornament on the Bückeburg facade, the basic organization is very clear and some of the principal elements are severely simple. Thus there are high bases of plain ashlar, broken only by the sub-podia of the *estípites*, on either side of the central portal. Vertical strips of ashlar also back the latter. Above, a full entablature, decorated only by Ernst's inscription in the frieze, is broken by ressauts that correspond to the strips below. From these, much bolder ressauts project about the *estípites*. Tall round-arched windows identical with those on the sides—i.e. framed only by plain bevels—occupy the flanking bays.

The heavy round-arched main portal of the Bückeburg church is also bevelled inside a plain rectangular frame in two planes. Before that stand full columns with Corinthianesque capitals of rather freer design than those in the interior. Above the ends of the boldly projecting entablature of the portal the wings of a broken pediment provide S-curved seats for *genii* on either side of a very big armorial achievement rising within an oval before the central window. The date of this would be c.1613. The frame of the window

is again bevelled, but its shape is quite special with a semi-elliptical arch occupying most of the horizontal top. Very simple tracery, framing four oblong lights below and an elliptical one above, subdivides the opening in contrast to the more delicate and retardataire sort, mostly made up of circles and semicircles, above the three lights of the windows at the sides. As noted earlier, shorter *estípites*, flanked at this level both by vertical S-scrolls and by obelisks, enclose the central window, while the subsidiary entablature above carries on top the flattened S-curved wings of a second broken pediment. These wings overlap the architrave of the main entablature of the facade and, between them, there is a scrolled and foliated finial that rises into the storey above.

That storey of the Bückeburg facade occupies most of the gable fronting the main roof of the church. The steep pitch of the roof is revealed by the slanting lines of the rear plane with a frankness rarely seen on Renaissance gables in Germany though common in England and France. Instead of scrolling the edges, as was usually done, Hans Wulff—or whoever was the designer—introduced large blind oculi on either side. The oculi are framed at their outer edges by C-scrolls, however, and capped by segmental pediments breaking out beyond the diagonal lines of the roof, thus providing as varied an outline as more conventional scrolling. These pediments in turn are flanked on their outer sides by finials of which the scrolls are "horned" almost in the Weserrenaissance way. Scrollwork of a similarly bold character, incorporating urns of semicircular section, fills the wall below the square sunken panel in which the big clock is set under its own pediment.

The entablature crowning the clock storey of the Bückeburg facade has a range of projecting scrolled brackets in the frieze to support a thin cornice. This cornice is actually the projecting edge of a balustrated gallery and on it two obelisks stand near the ends. The next stage of the gable is simpler and quite in the Serlian tradition, with just a pair of rather plain C-scrolls set back slightly from a rectangular plane that has a modest pediment-topped door in the center. Over that comes a small belfry which has an oblong opening for a single bell set under a simple pediment crowned by a cross. The relatively plain terminal stage, however, so out of key with the plastic elaboration of the rest of the facade, was only a substitute for an intended western tower that was never built.

Although the Bückeburg facade abounds in ambiguities, nonetheless there is a basic consistency in the bold scale of most of the elements not approached in other German work of the day except for the front of the Augsburg Zeughaus (Pl. 399). In any attempt to attribute this unique work to some architectural designer of higher repute than Hans Wulff one name comes first to mind, that of Wendel Dietterlin. He, however, had by 1610 been dead for over a decade. In the plates of Dietterlin's *Architectura*, all the same, many varieties of *estípites* and other ornamental members employed here—such as S-curved broken pediments and short, vigorously convex, C-scrolls—are already found. Moreover, the big scale suggested by Dietterlin's rather coarse style of engraving (Pl. 355) is even more like that of the details of the facade of the church than in the earlier interiors at the Schloss (Pls. 357, 359), executed by the Wulffs, which are more directly derived from his plates. Dietterlin-like also is the curious mixture of large, almost abstract, elements with relatively delicate figural and foliate ornament.

Nowhere is this similarity to certain of Dietterlin's plates more evident than in the side portals of the Bückeburg church, but it is almost equally to be noted in the woodwork of the Fürstenloge, though at a more modest scale. Dietterlin had died in Strasbourg in 1599 but his book, particularly in the enlarged second edition that appeared in Nürnberg in 1598, was still readily available. Evidence of its long-continued popularity in Germany, far beyond the years 1610-1615 when the Bückeburg church was being built and furnished, is the edition that appeared in Nürnberg as late as 1655.

So impressive an architectural work as the Bückeburg facade is hardly to be explained as just merely a compilation from engraved sources made *ad hoc* by a local master-mason. Moreover, the furnishings, if not all the Dietterlinesque painted decoration, of the chapel in the Bückeburg Schloss (Pl. 359) for which the Wulff brothers, Ebbert II, Jonas and Hans, are known from documents to have been previously responsible—not to speak of the portal in the Goldener Saal (Pl. 357)—are of comparable distinction, though not of such monumental scale. Surely these Hildesheimers should not be considered mere provincial craftsmen, with the usual limited capacity of such men for over-all architectural composition. Rather the Wulffs should be ranked as master-architects and compared with their more cosmopolitan contemporaries such as Heintz and Holl, by that time working already in the opposed Academic vein, as professional equals. Ebbert II may be rated that high also as a

sculptor in the tradition of Giovanni da Bologna, even if below such men actually trained in Italy as Hans Krumpper, Wilhelm Reichle and Adriaen de Fries, several of whom had actually studied and worked under that leading sculptor of the age.

As regards the Bückeburg church the ranking would apply specifically to Hans, for Ebbert had died the year before the church was begun and Jonas remained in Hildesheim. Hans must certainly have supervised the building of the church even if, as in the case of the Augsburg Zeughaus and the Neuburg Hofkirche, a *Riss* or *Visierung* (preliminary design) was first obtained by Ernst from some outsider.[38] Whoever that might have been, it was certainly not Heintz:[39] he, like Ebbert II Wulff, had died in 1609. Moreover, in the light of Ernst's recorded commission to Nosseni for the Stadthagen mausoleum several years earlier, the lack of a comparable contract among the surviving documents further supports the case in favor of Hans Wulff. Already in Ernst's service and receiving a regular salary, Wulff would have needed no new contract for work on the church.

When the original design for the Bückeburg church came into existence from the hand of Hans Wulff or some other, presumably in 1610 or 1611, the construction of the Neuburg Hofkirche,[40] also for Lutheran use, by Philipp Ludwig von der Pfalz was well under way. It was completed for the Jesuits by his successor Wolfgang Wilhelm a year after Ernst's church though not consecrated until two years later. Another church of at least equal historical importance, but known today only as elaborately redecorated in the eighteenth century, the Studienkirche of the Jesuits at Dillingen, had also been begun in 1610, most probably by Hans Alberthal, and was completed by 1617 shortly after those at Bückeburg and Neuburg.

These churches, at Neuburg and Dillingen, prefigure the two schemes favoured for German Baroque churches in the next hundred and fifty years. Moreover, the Castellis' *stucchi* at Neuburg provide a remote prototype for the characteristic decoration of German Baroque church interiors. It is to these

[38] This is most unlikely considering the many documents that are extant. Habich, *op. cit.*, pp. 13-29, summarizes the results of extensive archival research concerning the Bückeburg Residenz.

[39] *Ibid.*, p. 25, mentions Ernst's correspondence with Joseph Heintz, beginning in 1606, concerning a Last Judgement to be painted for the Bückeburg Schlosskapelle. The painting survives in Prague.

[40] Horn-Meyer, *Neuburg*, pp. 83-107.

early seventeenth-century churches, rather than to the grander and more conspicuous Munich one, that critical preëminence should be granted. All the same, St. Michael must have been better known to contemporary architects and their clients as it is to those twentieth-century scholars, both German and foreign, who continue to support its claims.

It is appropriate to describe first the Neuburg Hofkirche, turning to the Dillingen church later.

The mediaeval church of the Benedictine nuns that stood on the Neuburg site had been adapted for Lutheran use by Ottheinrich von der Pfalz after he became a Lutheran in 1542. That, of course, was Gothic. Except perhaps for the rounded apse—though that of the older church was actually polygonal—the new church has no characteristics even approaching *Nachgotik*. The four bays of the nave and the following single bay of the choir—which was walled in at the sides only in the eighteenth century—have unribbed rectangular cross-vaults supported on a giant order of square piers (Fig. 67). No more than the earlier Klagenfurt Münster (Pl. 255) is this a true hall-church, however, for over the aisles there are again generous tribunes. Such tribunes, of course, had been commonly provided since the Torgau chapel in edifices designed for Lutheran use. They were also introduced in two of the biggest Catholic churches of the 1580s in Germany, St. Michael in Munich (Pl. 256)—which the Neuburg Hofkirche was particularly intended to rival—and the Würzburg Neubaukirche. The resemblance to these, however, is rather slight as compared to the near identity with the surviving nave at Klagenfurt. All the same, Heintz, knowing Prague, might have been more influenced by the no longer extant church of sv. Trojice (Holy Trinity)[41] there, begun in 1577, about which little is known. A less likely source could have been the Jesuits' St. Paulus in Regensburg which was some fifteen years later in date.[42] As this church does not survive any more than sv. Trojice, little is known about that today either. The side elements at Neuburg are continuous aisles,[43] however, not separate chapels as at Klagenfurt and Munich, and there are no Roman arch orders as at Würzburg.

The Neuburg Hofkirche, even though it became Catholic only when Wolfgang Wilhelm handed it

over to the Jesuits in 1614, also resembles somewhat the church Bernardo Morando began at Zamošč in 1587,[44] some years after the one at Klagenfurt but before that was completed. This collegiate church in Zamošč had, in these years following Morando's death in 1600 but before that of his patron Zamoyski in 1605, just received its nave vault. There are no tribunes, so that the internal elevation is one-storeyed and the vault is continuous as in the Gesù, not subdivided into bays, as may already have been true from the first at Klagenfurt—it certainly is today. However, the cross-vaults required by the clerestorey windows at Zamošč nearly meet at the center of the nave as Morando doubtless intended from the first that they should. But the panelling of the surface with simple stucco moldings in a pattern of squares, circles, triangles and lozenges dates from after his death and initiated a long-lasting Polish mode of vault decoration. Beyond the five-bayed nave at Zamošč is a lower barrel-vaulted choir ending in a flattened apse. This last is polygonal rather than half-round like the one at Neuburg and that may well have been the case at Klagenfurt also before the later deep choir there was added by the Jesuits. The bays in the nave at Zamošč are separated by Corinthian pilasters of considerably greater projection than the flat ones at Klagenfurt. Between these are tall arches on imposts and over them bold ressauts break out of the heavy entablature.

The Neuburg interior is much less tectonically detailed than that at Zamošč and the internal elevation is two-storeyed, as at Klagenfurt, because of the tribunes. The giant pilasters applied on the four sides of the piers in the Hofkirche are in low relief like the Klagenfurt pilasters and neither they nor the imposts of the nave arches are of any definable order. The "capitals," so to call them, at the tops of the piers spread rather broadly to carry the clusters of vault ribs and are decorated only with triglyphs and a sort of foliate cornice just below the abacuses. The imposts of the nave arcade are crowned by seraphim and angels in higher relief occupy the spandrels. Neither at Klagenfurt nor at Zamošč was there any such figural decoration. In both of those instances, moreover, the giant order of pilasters is conventionally Corinthian.

As would be true later of most German Baroque and Rococo churches as well as many earlier ones that were redecorated like that at Klagenfurt in the eight-

[41] Not the existing church of the Trinitarians in the Spalena which was only built in 1712: Knox, *Bohemia*, p. 42.

[42] See Note 1 above and Note 5 to Chapter VII.

[43] According to Zimmer, *Hofkirche und Rathaus*, pl. 12, Heintz's original scheme had no tribunes.

[44] Kowalczyk, *Kolegiata*, pp. 26-47; Łozinski-Miłobedzki, *Guide*, p. 277. Knox, *Poland*, p. 36, gives 1584 as the date when Morando, at that time mayor of Zamošč, "began to raise the church."

eenth century, the richest ornamentation at Neuburg is on the vault: the *stucchi* of 1616-1618 by the Castellis (Pl. 436). The shapes of the molding-framed panels are much more varied than at Zamošč, including octagons, elongated hexagons and stepped squares. These fields, moreover, as well as the smaller panels on the intradoses of the flat transverse ribs, rival in their various infillings of figural or foliate ornament the consistent enrichment of all the many moldings. Because there is no polychromy here, such as the Mantuans had introduced in the earliest stuccoed vaults of Renaissance design in Germany, those in the Landshut Stadtresidenz (Pls. 114-116), what the Castellis provided at Neuburg is not so dissimilar to the decoration, dating from much the same years, that Maderno was providing overhead in the narthex of St. Peter's in Rome, though naturally it is much less sophisticated.[45]

For awhile after its completion as a Catholic church in 1614-1618 the Neuburg Hofkirche had three altarpieces by Rubens, as many as the Jesuits' Sint-Carolus Borromeuskerk of 1614-1621 in Antwerp. Rubens's Last Judgement, his Pentecost and his Fall of the Rebel Angels were taken to Düsseldorf in 1691, however, and are now in the Alte Pinakothek in Munich. The present early eighteenth-century altarpiece of the Ascension of the Virgin is by Domenico Zanetti and its vast architectural setting, rising up to the vault of the apse (Pl. 436), was erected still later by I. A. Breitnauer in 1753-1754. Rococo stucco-work of about 1725 covers the solid walls of the choir above the choirstalls and also the west gallery of 1699 as later extended, with its curved front on which stands the Baroque organ.

These posterior intrusions in the Neuburg Hofkirche are less awkward as elements of the early seventeenth-century interior than certain original features, notably the half-moon-shaped fields between the tribune arches and the edges of the nave vault required, as at Schmalkalden (Pl. 267), because of the much flattened curvature of the vaults of the tribunes. Considering the disparity of nearly a hundred and fifty years between the completion of the church and the latest and most conspicuous of these alien features, the framing of the high altar, the grand and unified impression the church offers today is somewhat surprising. Though by no means so famous, this interior does rival, as Philipp Ludwig intended, that of St. Michael in Munich (Pl. 256), at least as the latter is seen in its restored condition today with the vaults devoid of most of their original stucco decoration. The Jesuits lost the Neuburg church in 1772; in 1782 it became again the Hofkirche, The *stucchi* were "renoviert" (drastically repaired) in 1807-1808 and the whole church restored in 1900-1903, and again just lately.

The exteriors of the Zamošč Collegiate Church and the Neuburg Hofkirche cannot be compared in detail because the former was much remodelled externally in 1825-1827 and partially reconstructed in 1955. Surviving drawings, however, as noted already, indicate that the west front of the former was distinctly hybrid, especially as regards the curved enframement of the steep gable.[46] Doubtless, like the decoration on the vaults, this "scalloped" outline was not of Morando's devising. The exterior walls of the Neuburg church (Pl. 437) carry the giant Doric pilaster order that Heintz had intended for them from the first and had also used in his design of 1605 for the Siegel Haus in Augsburg (Pl. 400). Between the pilasters a round-arched aisle-window occupies each bay, as earlier proposed by Heintz,[47] and oculi light the tribunes above. Over the bold cornice of the external entablature there is also—but on the west front only—an attic. This carries pilaster-strips capped by ressauts which break the modest terminal architrave.[48] As has been mentioned, the tower is later, having been built only in 1624-1627 by Alberthal, though the projection of the central portion of the facade below it is original. Heintz was presumably echoing here late sixteenth and early seventeenth-century Italian church facades, models that Hans Krumpper, in designing the facade of St. Michael in Munich (Pl. 258) a decade or more earlier, manifestly did not heed—if, indeed, he was even aware of them. But there was already a relevant model then in construction in France of which Heintz might possibly have heard—Schickhardt's St.-Martin at Montbéliard (Pl. 438).

In 1617, ten years after St.-Martin was as much finished as it ever would be and while the Neuburg Hofkirche was still in construction, Alberthal completed a

---

[45] The Protestant church dated 1607-1609 at Zernez on the upper Inn in Switzerland has equally rich but quite different stucco decoration of this period. In plan, however, it consists of a square nave with a five-sided choir, where the stucco-work is concentrated, filled with a raised organ gallery: *Schweiz*, I, pp. 311, 391.

[46] Kowalczyk, *Kolegiata*, fig. 36, offers a detailed front elevation of the church as originally built based on drawings made in 1824.

[47] Zimmer, *Hofkirche und Rathaus*, pl. 14.

[48] The best view of the exterior of the Neuburg Hofkirche from the southeast is in Horst, *Architektur*, fig. 26.

Catholic church which can be considered of greater historical importance than either of the Protestant ones by Schickhardt and by Heintz. This was the Jesuits' church (Fig. 69) just mentioned, the Studienkirche at Dillingen,[49] a town in Swabia up the Danube from Neuburg and to the northwest of Augsburg. Since the middle of the sixteenth century[50] there had existed a university at Dillingen founded by Cardinal Otto Truchsess von Waldburg, bishop of Augsburg, who was the local ruler. It was handed over to the Jesuits in 1563; then Peter Canisius took it under his protection the following year. It was in 1606 that the Jesuits began to consider replacing the existing university church with a new edifice and, on April 13, 1610, they contracted with Alberthal to execute it with the assistance of his brother Albrecht (Alberto).

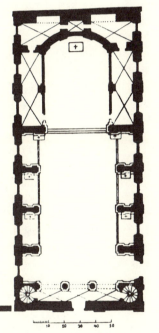

Fig. 69. Johann Alberthal: Dillingen, Studienkirche, 1610-17, plan

By this time Johann Alberthal[51] was already an experienced builder, having learned his trade, one may suppose, from his father Pietro in Eichstätt, whether

or not he was born there. After the thirteenth-century episcopal Schloss at Dillingen burnt in the mid-1590s, it was probably he who undertook the repairs rather than Pietro. The Rittersaal there was then built with its five piers, still extant, which carry the original panelled ceiling of 1595. A new top on the old mediaeval keep was also constructed, among other things, over the next few years. Alberthal erected as well the Dillingen *Rentamt* (rental office) of the Augsburg bishops in 1597 and the *Alter Wasserturm* (old watertower) in 1602. His later employment on Schloss Willibaldsburg down to 1619 indicates he did not lose touch with Eichstätt even though he had by then been a citizen of Dillingen for some years.

Another work, only attributed to Alberthal, is the hospital at Dinkelscherben, south of Dillingen and west of Augsburg, considerably enlarged in the eighteenth century, with its chapel, begun in 1604, which still contains an early seventeenth-century altarpiece by Hans I Rottenhammer.[52] More certainly he was responsible, beginning in 1603, for housing the Jesuits of Dillingen and also building a seminary there for forty students. If these utilitarian structures survive as at Dinkelscherben, they are now swamped by other university construction of the late seventeenth and early eighteenth centuries. The chapel of the seminary, completed in 1606, was consecrated September 30, the next year, when Alberthal was busy building for the bishopric the *Hofbrauhaustor* (gate of the court brewery).

More important, however, is the fact that Alberthal carried out in 1608-1609[53] the already mentioned Lutheran church at Haunsheim for Zacharias Geiskofler.[54] Haunsheim is a small village lying to the west of Dillingen and not far north of Lauingen—it was at Lauingen, one may recall, that the transitional church of St. Martin, possibly by Hans Hieber, had been completed almost ninety years before. The Haunsheim commission and his continuing work at Eichstätt brought Alberthal into contact with the advanced architectural designing both of Joseph Heintz and of Elias Holl.

[49] Dehio, *Östliches Schwaben*, pp. 79-80; Braun, *Jesuiten*, II, pp. 126-141, pl. 4c.

[50] Dehio, *op. cit.*, p. 78.

[51] A. M. Zendralli, *I magistri grigioni*, Poschiavo, 1958, pp. 56-59; Hauttmann, *Kirchliche Baukunst*, p. 36. There seems to be little reason to associate Matthias Kager with Dillingen, but see Note 78.

[52] Dehio, *Östliches Schwaben*, p. 34.

[53] *Ibid.*, p. 87.

[54] As mentioned earlier Geiskofler, though a Protestant, was *Reichspfennigmeister* (an Imperial financial officer) and *Kaiserlicher Rat* (Imperial councillor): Zimmer, *Hofkirche und Rathaus*, n. 27 and *passim*. He was much consulted by Philipp Ludwig von der Pfalz at Neuburg and also an important figure in the Emperor Rudolf II's court: Evans, *Rudolf II*, p. 76. His tomb-slab, dated 1617, is behind the altar in the Haunsheim church.

The historical importance of Holl's Eichstätt Schloss, which represents together with the facade of the Augsburg Stadtmetzg, also of 1609, the effective initiation of Academic design in Germany, has been sufficiently stressed already. The contemporary church at Haunsheim is less significant historically since this small edifice is posterior both to Schickhardt's early project for the one at Montbéliard by a half-dozen years and even to the beginning of construction of the Hofkirche at Neuburg by a year or so. On the Haunsheim church the ranges of giant pilasters that are applied all around Schickhardt's St.-Martin and the Hofkirche (Pls. 437, 438), as also already in 1605 along the side of the Augsburg Siegel Haus (Pl. 400), are repeated on the exterior and also within on the broad piers that support the vault. These piers are set tight up against the walls with no aisles or tribunes outside them. The workmanship both inside and out may be considered summary, as if by local labor. Academic proportions seem to have been muffed throughout, but especially in the pedimented windows on the sides. These are certainly very clumsy as compared to Schickhardt's, as executed at Montbéliard several years earlier, or those Alberthal himself was carrying out following Holl's design at Eichstätt (Pl. 407) very soon after this.

It can well be accepted, despite the various solecisms, that Heintz—or just possibly Holl—provided the original *Riss* that Alberthal executed as well as he then knew how for the Haunsheim church. But it is not necessary to assume that one or the other of them also proposed the novel plan and section of the large and grand Dillingen Studienkirche (Fig. 69) two years later. Heintz and Holl had been collaborating in Augsburg ever since the one designed and the other began to construct the east facade of the Zeughaus there in 1602. However, as was underlined earlier in noting Heintz's share of the responsibility for the design of the Stadtmetzg, he died in 1609. That was just before Alberthal was commissioned in 1610 to build the Studienkirche; Holl up to this time seems not to have been much involved in church design or construction except, probably, for the modest edifice of St. Georg at Lützelburg.[55]

Relevant to the probability of Alberthal's authorship of the Dillingen church is the fact that in 1603, in connection with his earlier work for the Jesuits there, he was called merely *murarius* (mason), while in 1610 he is referred to both as *architectus* and *Hofbaumeist-*

er (court-architect) of the bishop. He received equivalent professional recognition again in a document of 1618, the year after he completed the Studienkirche, and usually thereafter while employed later in life in Hungary.

There seems no real reason to suppose the Dillingen Jesuits asked the architect, whoever he may have been, to follow the model of their Munich church, for the section is quite different. A more likely model, here as at Neuburg, might have been their St. Paulus in Regensburg which is not far away. As that church is not extant, however, most authorities have ignored it beyond noting that its unknown architect was an Italian. The significant novelty in the Dillingen Studienkirche (Fig. 69) is the way the vaults are supported, not by the outer wall nor by freestanding members as at Neuburg, but by what amount to broad internal buttresses in a way that the handling of the piers in the interior at Haunsheim already timidly approached. This scheme differs from the two-storeyed interior structure of St. Michael but it does have some similarity to many German Gothic churches, most conspicuously the fifteenth century Frauenkirche in Munich. Variant late examples described earlier are those at Wittenberg and at Schneeberg (Fig. 14, Pl. 36) but these have tribunes—shallow though they are in both instances—which were omitted at Dillingen. That limited similarity hardly justifies, however, considering the system, later so commonly used in the Baroque period,[56] as *Nachgotik*. Certainly the Studienkirche does not at all resemble the rib-vaulted and pointed-arched churches of the Jesuits to the west, neither the earliest one in Münster (Pl. 261) of the 1590s nor those of this decade at Koblenz and Cologne (Pl. 452). It is equally unlike the considerably less remote pilgrimage church at Dettelbach, just east of Würzburg in Swabia (Pl. 448), which the prince-bishop of Würzburg, Julius Echter, began the same year the Dillingen church was commissioned. That, as well as the Rhineland churches, will shortly be described.

The Rococo investiture of the interior of the Studienkirche, carried out in 1750-1768, makes it difficult to see this church today as structurally of the early 17th century. The frescoes of C. T. Scheffler all but obliterate the barrel shape of both the main vault and the intersecting vaults over the wide bays at the sides.

---

[55] Neu-Otten, *Landkreis Augsburg*, pp. 208-209.

[56] Often incorrectly called the "Vorarlberg scheme" because of the many architects from the Austrian Vorarlberg who employed it in southern Germany even though they had not originated it and it was not even used in the Vorarlberg.

The high altar by the local wood-carver J. M. Fischer and the joiner Joseph Hartmuth entirely fills the segmental apse, while other elaborate altars rise high against the west sides of the piers in the nave and mask their tectonic character.[57] Not even the pairs of pilasters and the entablatures above on these structural piers, moreover, seem to be in quite their original form. Hauttmann noted, however, that in his day some fragments of the original decoration in stucco survived behind the high altar and on the upper gallery at the west end; these are not now visible. He also provided a view of St. Ignatius at Landshut, built by the Jesuit Johann Holl (†1648) from Berlin-Kölln, in which the original decoration of 1631-1641[58] is intact, to suggest what the Studienkirche may have looked like before 1750. In general, however, the Landshut church follows St. Michael in Munich rather than the Studienkirche, though not very closely in its mid-century stucco decoration.

The exterior of the Dillingen Studienkirche is doubtless as Alberthal built it. The membering of the pilaster order and the window-framing has something still of the clumsiness of the architectural elements on the Haunsheim church, though Alberthal's model here may well have been the Hofkirche at Neuburg (Pl. 437)—he will hardly have known St.-Martin far away at Montbéliard.

To underline the structural idiosyncrasy of the Swabian Studienkirche it should be considered as regards plan and interval elevation in relation to two other large and prominent Catholic churches in construction elsewhere in northern Europe in the same years. One of these lies to the west in the southern Netherlands, Coebergher's Basiliek at Scherpenheuvel, of which some description has already been given; the other is well to the southeast in Salzburg. Neither of them, it may be noted, was emulated in Germany in the years before the outbreak of the Thirty Years' War. The Salzburg church may be discussed first, for that was certainly better known to contemporaries—as it is still to posterity—even though it is slightly the later of the two in date.

The Romanesque cathedral of Salzburg burned in 1598 and the ruins were demolished in 1600. In 1606-1607 Archbishop Wolf Dietrich, the ruler of Salzburg, obtained from Vincenzo Scamozzi (1552-1616), who

was then the leading architect of Venice in succession to Palladio, plans for a vast new church.[59] In 1611 the construction of a reduced version of Scamozzi's design began, but it never rose above the foundations and the vaults of the crypt. That preparatory work was demolished, moreover, before erection of the only slightly more modest existing edifice started in 1614 at the command of Archbishop Markus Sittikus. Sittikus's architect, Santino Solari (1576-1646), came not from the Veneto or from Rome but from Lombardy where he was an older and less advanced contemporary of F. M. Ricchino in Milan. However, in the church he planned, Solari followed considerably more closely than the Paduan Morando at Zamošč the model of the Gesù (Fig. 70)—if, indeed, Morando

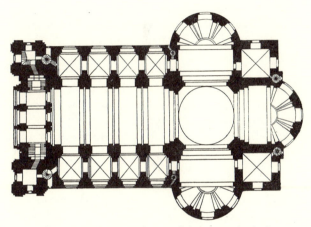

Fig. 70. Santino Solari: Salzburg, Cathedral, begun 1614, plan

had any such intention, which is not very likely. All the same, the tribunes here, missing altogether at Zamošč, are considerably taller than in the Roman church. Solari did not, however, open them to the nave through broad arches, as had already been done earlier in the Klagenfurt Münster (Pl. 255), to the south in Carinthia, or later at St. Michael in Bavaria (Pl. 256) and the Neuburg Hofkirche (Pl. 436) in the Upper Palatinate.

In the nave at Salzburg (Pl. 439), moreover, the pilasters of the giant order are coupled as on the piers at Dillingen (Fig. 69), not single as at Klagenfurt and Neuburg. No clerestorey windows were introduced over the entablature of the nave like the ones in the Gesù or at Zamošč, but light pours in at the east end through three rows of windows in the apse. As in the choir of St. Michael the topmost of these rise up into the ribbed vault in contrast to the unbroken half-dome that roofs the window-less apse of the Gesù. At the crossing—a feature lacking in all the comparable northern churches except the one in Munich as that was extended in the 1590s—even more light is provided by big windows in the tall drum of the dome as was true also of several Roman churches of the late sixteenth century. In addition there are windows at the ends on the sides of the transepts further to increase the illumination in the central area.

The Salzburg cathedral can be considered essentially an Italian Counter-Reformation church if not, considered as a whole, either a copy of the Gesù or specifically Lombard. Though the facade is flanked by two tall towers not unlike those Lorenzo Binago (1554-1628) intended for Sant'Alessandro in Milan, begun in 1602, Solari's work on the whole is more Academic than Early Baroque. It certainly has none of the pregnant originality of Ricchino's San Giuseppe in Milan as begun in 1607. Even the gable, with its concave quadrants and plain pediment, recalling a little that on the front of the Rathaus in Augsburg (Pl. 415), remains rather more remote than Holl's from those over the church facades then in construction in Rome and in Milan, or even in the north such as Trevano's in Poland and Coebergher's in Brabant. The models for all of them are still those provided long before by Serlio's and Vignola's plates it should be noted, not contemporary Roman or Milanese.

The Salzburg cathedral was effectively complete by 1628 when it was consecrated. However, the towers were carried to their full height only in 1652-1655, long after Alberthal's single tower of 1624-1627 (Pl. 437) on the front of the Neuburg Hofkirche. They resemble that tower, moreover, only in the octagonal plan of the top stage and the terminal *welsche Hauben* capped by tiny open lanterns. The richer membering of Alberthal's octagonal stage and its more plastic mass contrast, in a fashion that can be considered already at least faintly Baroque, with the Academic severity of the Doric pilaster order along the exterior walls of both of these churches. Moreover, the treatment of the attic of the central projection below the Neuburg tower, including a clock framed by a broken pediment—for which Alberthal was doubtless responsible in the 1620s rather than Heintz before his death in 1609—is also considerably more plastic than

the broad flat plane of the Salzburg facade set well back between the two towers.

Scherpenheuvel is in southern Brabant, some two-thirds of the way from Antwerp to Hasselt. As stated earlier, the pilgrimage church there was begun by Wencelas Coebergher in 1609 and completed in 1627.[60] After his return home to Antwerp from France and Italy in 1604 this Antwerp-born painter and architect was closely associated with Rubens when the latter also came back from Italy. Rubens, for example, supplied the altarpieces for Coebergher's Antwerp church of Sint-Augustinus, built 1615-1618, as has been noted.

The model for the Scherpenheuvel Basiliek is supposed to have been St. Peter's in Rome; certainly it owes nothing to the Protestant *Temples* Coebergher may have known in France, except just possibly its polygonal plan. With its alternation of six wide and six narrow bays and its two-storeyed internal elevation, including very large segmental-arched windows in the second storey—actually the drum of the dome—the resemblance to the reputed Roman model is certainly very slight; yet the generically "Late Renaissance" character of the interior can hardly be more specifically described either as Academic or proto-Baroque, much less Northern Mannerist.

The exterior of the Scherpenheuvel Basiliek is rather different and even less like that of St. Peter's. On the outside, the great scrolled buttresses at the corners, prefiguring Baldassare Longhena's on Santa Maria della Salute in Venice as begun more than a score of years later, are even more Baroque than the facade. That derives, like Trevano's at Kraków of these years, from the late sixteenth-century ones of Vignola and Giacomo della Porta in Rome rather than from Maderno's Santa Susanna there of 1598-1603 or Ricchino's San Giuseppe in Milan—which was, as has been noted, begun only two years before the Basiliek. This retardation is hardly surprising so early in the new century and so far from Milan and Rome, though Coebergher doubtless remained as much in touch with current Italian developments in the arts as did his friend Rubens.

Less advanced toward the full Baroque than these facades by Trevano and Coebergher is the grander three-storeyed composition fronting Huyssen's Sint-Carolus Borromeuskerk of 1614-1621 in Antwerp. But neither that sumptuous but rather confused frontispiece, on the decoration of which Rubens collaborated, nor the more modest and idiosyncratic facade of Coe-

---

[60] Baedekers *Benelux*, pp. 84-85.

bergher's own Sint-Augustinus there is relevant, except by contrast, to this account of the terminal decades of the German Renaissance. Their plans and sections, moreover—both are aisled basilicas without tribunes—are not very similar to the advanced schemes of the Neuburg Hofkirche and the Dillingen Studienkirche.

It should not be too much to claim, as already proposed, that those two big churches, the Protestant one at Neuburg and the Catholic one at Dillingen, led the way towards the later German Baroque rather more directly than the earlier and better known church in Munich whether or not that is credited to Sustris. Yet, ever since Hauttmann's day, greater significance has usually been assigned to St. Michael by scholars both German and foreign than to the works of Heintz or Alberthal. That Heintz—in any case a painter not an architect—had less familiarity than Sustris with Italian architectural design of the late sixteenth century or than Coebergher with that of around 1600, and little if any direct knowledge of work in Rome or Milan of the following decades may perhaps be presumed. Certainly that was true of Alberthal. This presumption makes their innovations in plan and section all the more notable historically. It was the current in German church-architecture of which these men were the effective initiators that led later to a German Baroque as autochthonous as its largely northern origins. Yet that German Baroque when it matured would be quite as different from the late Northern Mannerism of the great churches at Wolfenbüttel and Bückeburg (Pls. 431, 434) which were contemporary with the Neuburg Hofkirche as from the *Nachgotik* favoured in these early years of the seventeenth century by German Jesuits (Pls. 450, 452) and still in use much later.

The next steps along the road towards the German Baroque in church design, as in the case of secular architecture, were not taken until well after the outbreak of the Thirty Years' War that spread so far and lasted so long. The war began in Bohemia in 1618, it will be recalled, when the Emperor Ferdinand II set out to suppress the rebels who would, the next year, call the Elector Palatine Friedrich V, the builder of the Englischer Bau at Heidelberg, to be their king. Construction did not, however, cease at once everywhere in Germany.

Before discussing such signal and, in a sense, concluding works as the remodelling and extension of the pilgrimage church at Polling in Bavaria, begun only in 1621, and the construction of the Jesuits' con-

temporary St. Andreas at Düsseldorf, some further reference at least should be made to certain chapels in Schlösser. These include at one extreme the conservative one at Heidelberg of 1601-1607, which has already been partially described, and at the other the chapel of central plan of the next decade in the Carolath Zamek at Siedlisko in Silesia. Almost all are Protestant. A few notable Catholic churches, such as the pilgrimage church at Dettelbach of 1610-1613 and Mariä Himmelfahrt in Cologne of 1618-1627, both characterized already as *Nachgotik*, will also be discussed in some detail despite their stylistic retardation and their inferior quality.

As was said previously in discussing the chapel in the Friedrichsbau of the Heidelberg Schloss (Pl. 425), the interior of that seems at first sight almost as Gothic as the Torgau chapel (Pl. 125), of which it is a considerably enlarged late version. Though the chapel has little in common with the profuse carved decoration by Götz on the facades of the new wing (Pl. 366) where it occupies the ground storey, various details such as the Corinthianesque capitals of the half-columns that lead up to the vaulting ribs and the slim balusters of the parapets of the tribunes are of a belated Early Renaissance character.

The Frederiksborg *Slotkirke* (castle church) at Hillerød in Denmark (Fig. 71), carried out in much the same years probably by one of the younger van Steenwinckels, contrasts in several ways with the one at Heidelberg. The length at Heidelberg must be less than half; and the treatment of the interior elevations differs as much as does the Dano-Dutch Mannerism of the great U-shaped Slot, all of brick trimmed with

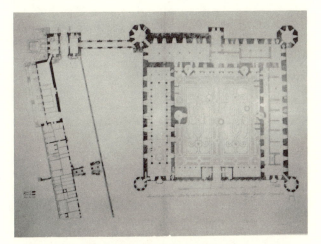

Fig. 71. Hillerød, Frederiksborg Slot, begun 1602, plan including chapel on left

stone, from Schoch's somewhat retardataire stone fa-cades at Heidelberg which echo belatedly the Otthein-richsbau there. But the elaboration of the Frederiks-borg church with its two storeys of molded arches and svelte colonnettes, not to speak of the decorative intri-cacy of the double-bayed rib-vaulting and the profu-sion of carved, painted and gilded ornament is unique in this period, though perhaps exaggerated in the nineteenth-century restoration. Except in Schloss Wil-helmsburg at Schmalkalden (Pl. 267), moreover, nothing so grand and so sumptuous as the interior at Hillerød was attempted in the chapel of a German Schloss. Only the new fittings in the old mediaeval chapel at Celle (Pl. 207), dating from the 1560s and 1570s, and those of this period in the one at Bücke-burg (Pl. 359) are more than comparable.

It is not surprising, therefore, that a church-fitting —if a ducal pew may be so-called when it is, in fact, an almost wholly independent room in a gallery above the altar—in the chapel of Schloss Gottorf in the borderline duchy of Schleswig, dated 1609-1613,[61] should be the nearest rival in richness of treatment to the chapel of the Frederiksborg Slot. Earlier, in 1523, Schleswig had provided Denmark with a king, Fred-erik I, duke of Schleswig in a former line, and Schles-wig has over the centuries been as often Danish as German in its political affiliation. Known as the *Bet-stübel der Herzogin* (prayer-closet of the duchess), this sumptuous Fürstenloge (Pl. 440) was carried out by the carvers Andres Salgen (†1612) and Jürgen Gower (†1642) for Duke Johann Adolf, who had built the chapel immediately upon his accession in 1590.

As with the ducal pew in the Celle Schlosskapelle (Pl. 207) of a generation and more before this, the Gottorf Betstübel is glazed on the side that looks into the church and the carving around the windows is polychromed and gilded like the Fürstenloge in Ernst von Schaumburg's contemporary Stadtkirche at Bückeburg (Pl. 434). Inside, however, the wainscoting is elaborated with intarsia in woods of various tones, a type of decoration that had long been in use for secular interiors in Germany. This recalls, for exam-ple, two masterpieces of the genre. One of them is the very exceptional Fredenhagsches Zimmer (Pl. 441) in Lübeck, with its alabaster inlay, the richest surviving sixteenth-century room other than some of the great halls in Schlösser. This was executed within the years

1572-1583[62] by Hans Dreger. Carried out not for a prince but for a rich merchant, Klaus von Berken, this has only been referred to earlier in Chapter VI. The other is the gorgeous ceiling of the relatively modest hall in the Schloss at Ortenburg (Pl. 352), of the opening years of the new century, which was de-scribed in Chapter VII. Comparison with contempo-rary Elizabethan or Jacobean woodwork reveals the greater technical virtuosity and delicacy of scale of the German—or, in the case of the Gottorf Betstübel, one might equally well say Danish—work. It is not clear whether the executants were native or, as is often sup-posed to have been the case in contemporary England, refugees from the southern Netherlands. The contri-bution made by artists from Italy at this point in Ger-many was very different. The sharp contrast between such final flourishes of Northern Mannerism in inte-riors and the new Academic work of the day is espe-cially striking, as has been noted earlier, in work for which Ernst von Schaumburg was the client.

The Stadthagen mausoleum that Ernst commis-sioned from G. M. Nosseni in 1608, the year before the Gottorf Betstübel was begun, is not a Schlosska-pelle like Johann Adolf's or the one Ernst had just finished furnishing so elaborately in his Schloss at Bückeburg (Pl. 359). Indeed, it is not attached to the older family seat at Stadthagen but to the rear of the parish church of St. Martin. There, it will be re-called, the tomb of Count Otto IV, whom Ernst had succeeded, and his wives occupies much of the east end beside the altar. Behind the altar a dark passage, usually locked on the church side, leads into the grand polygonal interior of the chapel. Construction of this began in 1609,[63] was then carried forward after 1613 under the direction of the painter Anton Boten, and only completed in 1625 after Ernst's death.

[61] E. Schlee, *Das Schloss Gottorf in Schleswig*, Flensburg [1965] pp. 28-36.

[62] Dehio, *Hamburg*, pp. 391-393. This extraordinary Lübeck interior, brought here from Berken's house at Schüsselbuden 16 in 1840, includes over a thousand small carved figures, mostly of oak and other woods but with some tiny reliefs in alabaster. The window wall is of 1840 and the righthand door of 1753 but with a middle panel of 1891. Chrono-logically, of course, this is a full generation earlier than the interiors with which it is here associated. In the degree of its elaboration, if not in kind, this is a unique survival of its own period and not, as pieced together and extended in its present location, a coherent or intelligible architectural entity. It has for that reason been introduced at this point rather than in one of the earlier chapters where it would belong chronologically; though the climax of mercantile lux-ury the room was certainly never a "great hall."

[63] Kreft-Soenke, *Weserrenaissance*, pp. 282-283; Reclams *Niedersachsen*, pp. 706-707.

Externally the Stadthagen mausoleum impresses thanks to its great size and scale in comparison with the awkwardly contiguous apse of the modest mediaeval church. It is, however, almost impossible to photograph satisfactorily so close does it lie to the latter. Arched windows open only high on the three western faces of the polygon and, except for the window frames, the architectural membering of the walls is restricted to bent pilasters at the angles and an entablature with an inscription in the frieze. Above an attic, however, there is a tent-like copper roof crowned by a lantern. The interior of Ernst's mausoleum (Pl. 442) is not only equally large in its scale but very dramatic as well, especially as one first enters from the obscure passage of which the entrance is totally masked by the altar in the church. Light pours down from the west windows above on to the principal monument, the work of Adriaen de Fries (†1626), in the center.

Adriaen who was, like the considerably older Frederik Sustris, a Netherlander born in The Hague—in his case around 1560[64]—had received a thorough Italian training as one of the most accomplished pupils of Giovanni da Bologna. First commissioned by the Emperor Rudolf II in Rome for a portrait bust in 1593, he later entered in Prague the service of Rudolf, who had been employing Joseph Heintz since 1591 as *Hofmaler*, and received a parallel appointment as *Kammerbildhauer* (court sculptor) a decade later in 1601.

Well before that, however, Adriaen de Fries was commissioned in 1596 to design two fountains in Augsburg: the Merkurbrunnen, executed by 1599, which was based on Giovanni da Bologna's Mercury now in the Bargello in Florence, and another with a Hercules, modelled after a drawing by Hans von Aachen, that was completed in 1602 when the statue was cast in bronze by Wolfgang II Neidhard. Adriaen may well have been responsible also, as was noted, for the marble holy water basin dated 1605-1607 in Sts. Ulrich and Afra in Augsburg. After Rudolf's death in 1612 he left Prague for good and Ernst von Schaumburg became his principal patron. Negotiations between them led to the production in 1613 of a model for the Stadthagen monument and the monument itself carries the dates 1618 and 1620.

This complex sculptural composition in the Stadthagen mausoleum, one of the masterpieces of the in-

ternational Late Renaissance,[65] occupies most of the interior, somewhat as the earlier cenotaph of Moritz of Saxony (Pl. 208) does the crossing of the Freiberg Münster and the Wiemken monument (Pl. 203) the choir of the church at Jever. Here, however, the setting is very different in its Academic severity from that Nosseni had created when remodelling the choir at Freiberg (Pl. 270) in the 1580s and 1590s.

At the angles of the interior of the Stadthagen mausoleum there are giant bent pilasters, much as on the exterior, but with fluted shafts here and simplified Corinthian capitals. In between, edicules with more conventional Corinthian columns are capped by plain pediments. In the edicules in the four eastern bays the *Epitaphien* of Ernst's principal relatives are carved on marble slabs set in arched panels. Above the pediments, marble putti stand as supporters of paired armorial shields that are framed, beneath broader arches, by rather plain C-scrolls. These scrolls provide the only architectural ornamentation in the whole interior other than the orders, their entablatures and the molded archivolts of the arches. All of this, however, including the two stages of the central monument, is carried out in pale marbles of rather cool tones to provide a contrasting background for Adriaen's group of very animated bronze figures. These lead up to a Resurrected Christ, also of bronze, rising high beneath the dome.

Above, on the inner surface of the dome of the Stadthagen mausoleum, stronger colors appear in the frescoes of music-making angels. These frescoes were most probably executed by Anton Boten, a German artist whom the prince had earlier sent to Augsburg to study with Hans I Rottenhammer. More certainly by Boten are the Raising of Lazarus and the Last Judgment, dated respectively 1626 and 1627—some years after Ernst's death in 1622—on the walls below the windows. Very likely, moreover, it was he who painted the framed portrait of the prince[66] on his death-bed that hangs from the pilaster in the southeast corner. That was evidently an afterthought, not part of the original scheme.

---

[65] The term begs the question whether the work of Giovanni da Bologna and his northern assistants and emulators should be considered Late Mannerist or very Early Baroque like Rubens's painting. In describing analogous works of architecture there has been an attempt in this book to make more precise—if inevitably rather personal—distinctions in the use of stylistic terms. See Note IX 1.

[66] Ernst assumed the title of *Fürst* (prince) in 1619, "quasi de motu proprio," Habich, *Residenz Bückeburg*, p. 7.

---

[64] L. O. Larsson, *Adrian de Vries*, Vienna-Munich, 1967. As Adriaen came from Leeuwarden in Friesland, I have preferred to give his name as Adriaen de Fries (the Frisian).

This unexpected late work of Nosseni, completed as regards Boten's contribution only after the former's death in 1620, is at once Academic in its architectural membering and yet more early Baroque in its total effect than the slightly older Capella Paolina that the pope Paul V had Flaminio Ponzio add to Santa Maria Maggiore in Rome in 1605-1611. Not least this is because of Adriaen de Fries's recognized distinction as a sculptor; for he ranks higher with posterity than the contemporary Italians working in the Capella Paolina: Stefano Maderno, Pietro Bernini and Camillo Mariani, if not the younger and abler Francesco Mochi.

A quite different and much more modest chapel, like the one of 1563 at Hämelschenburg not attached directly to a Schloss, is the Gutskapelle at Stellichte as remodelled and furnished with family tombs by the local land-owner Dietrich Behr (Pl. 443). His family had possessed the estate since 1471 and originally built the chapel in 1479[67] in this tiny agricultural settlement north of Walsroda, not far off the Hannover-Bremen Autobahn, where only a much later manor house now survives. Externally the plain mediaeval walls of red brick were little affected by the remodelling though round-arched windows were introduced.

Inside the Stellichte Gutskapelle, however, there are many elaborate fittings: a polygonal organ gallery at the west end; the pulpit, arch and parapet at the edge of the raised chancel; and the font. All of these are of wood most elaborately carved, polychromed and gilded. Thus they combine to offer a somewhat rustic version of such sumptuous interiors as the earlier Fredenhagsches Zimmer (Pl. 441) in Lübeck and the contemporary Betstubel der Herzogin (Pl. 440) in Schleswig. The date of this work is uncertain, but the wall-tomb of Behr and his wife, also of carved and polychromed wood, is inscribed 1615, probably some years after the refurnishing of the church began. Thus this very regional, almost vernacular, chapel may well be almost precisely contemporary inside with the execution of the Stadthagen Mausoleum. But Nosseni's and Adriaen de Fries's work there of 1609-1618 was as much at the forefront of international development, one may well claim, as anything that yet existed even in Italy except for Maderno's facade of Santa Susanna or Ricchino's of San Giuseppe.

Much fairer for comparison with the Stellichte Gutskapelle would be such Schlosskapellen of these years as the already mentioned Catholic one at Aschaf-fenburg or the Protestant one of the Siedlisko Zamek in Silesia (Pls. 444-446), the former completed by 1614, the latter the following year. Ridinger's chapel rises like Schoch's in the Heidelberg Friedrichsbau through two storeys, with a gallery above the altar at the east end, and is in effect an aisle-less version of the latter which was finished, it will be recalled, somewhat earlier, in 1607. Though flattened, almost to the degree of the one in the Freudenstadt church (Pl. 424), to a low segmental section, the vault at Aschaffenburg with its net of ribbing is distinctly *Nachgotik* in character.

As was indicated earlier, Junker's elaborately sculptured altar of marble and alabaster, filling the east end in front of the gallery in the Aschaffenburg chapel, and his equally overloaded pulpit, both in place by 1618, provide the principal interest. These offer neither the rustic appeal of the Stellichte fittings nor the international distinction of Adriaen's monumental tomb at Stadthagen. They have, however, sometimes been considered to be already early Baroque in style with more justice than the Schloss as a whole.

Far more interesting is the chapel at the Carolath Zamek in Siedlisko, just across the Oder from Neusalz (Nova Sól) in Silesia, though in sad need of repair as is the whole structure. The main portion of that—what Poles call the *pałac*—as erected gradually over the years 1597 to 1618[68] is preceded by a gatehouse built by Valentin von Saebisch in 1611-1614. That is in better condition today than the wings facing on the court. The current attempt of the Boy Scouts who occupy the property to begin a restoration is worthy, but pathetically modest.

The Siedlisko chapel must have been completed around 1615, the date on a chimneypiece inside, but it may have been begun as early as 1608. It is rather exceptional for the early seventeenth-century in northern Europe in being vaulted with a dome on pendentives. Thus it resembles the burial chapels in Poland that carried on through the sixteenth century and beyond the tradition of Berrecci's Zygmunt Chapel in Kraków[69] of 1519-1523 (Pl. 39). The plan is cruciform, however, not square as in the Polish chapels, with barrel vaults over the short arms and a half-dome covering the tall eastern apse. Triple arcades in two storeys set off aisles and tribunes on the north, south and west sides (Pls. 444, 446). The shafts of the sturdy

[67] Reclams *Niedersachsen*, p. 715.

[68] Łozinski-Miłobedzki, *Guide*, p. 214; Knox, *Poland*, p. 63; Grundmann, *Kirchenbau*, pp. 15-17, fig. 13.
[69] See Note I 26.

Tuscan columns of the lower arcades are ornamented with jewelled diapering below, and this treatment is varied on those above either with fluting or with strapwork, likewise jewelled. In contrast to that characteristic Northern Mannerist detailing, however, the parapets still have open-work Gothic tracery.

This unique late work of the German Renaissance —for the district was German, not Polish, in the sixteenth century—was built by the master-mason Melchior Deckhard reputedly with the assistance of the sculptor Caspar Berger from Liegnitz (Legnica), nearby on the road to Wrocław. The latter would have been particularly responsible for the pulpit. That is carried on an octagonal shaft beside the northeast pier at the entrance to the short choir, not set at the middle of one side of the nave as was usual in Lutheran churches of this period and earlier. Which, if either, of these men designed the chapel is not clear, but in any case it is unlikely that its rather Byzantine plan and section result from knowledge of Orthodox church architecture of the period. The short arms with their tribunes, which are similar to those in the slightly earlier Weikersheim chapel, are merely added on to a central area which is like that of earlier Polish chapels.

Except for that at Aschaffenburg, the chapels just discussed were all Protestant, as is also true of those described in the preceding chapter other than the one at Heiligenberg. The balance would shift later as the Catholic reaction gathered force in Germany. But there are no early seventeenth-century examples that can be considered premonitory of this shift in sponsorship unless one considers as such the large freestanding Hofkirche at Neuburg. That was, in any case, Protestant when it was begun. It is rather such large edifices as the Jesuits' Studienkirche at Dillingen and the other churches, to be described below, which the Order built shortly after the one in Koblenz—and, more notably, that in Cologne—which demonstrate the rising strength of the Counter Reformation in Germany at this point. Of a somewhat different order is the Catholic pilgrimage church at Dettelbach eastward of Würzburg. This was contemporary in construction with Alberthal's church in Dillingen though completed a bit earlier in 1613.

Since 1504 a small wooden *Vesperbild*, in this case a Late Gothic Pietà, housed in a modest Gothic church had drawn religious pilgrims to Dettelbach. A hundred years later that prolific builder, Julius Echter, prince-bishop of Würzburg, came to the support of the local cult by erecting a large new church in front of the choir of the earlier one. As has been noted concerning Regensburg such a project could have— and doubtless did here also—economic as much as religious motivation. For the work Julius employed Lazaro Augustino, an Italian-Swiss who came originally, like his contemporary Pietro Albertalli, Johann Alberthal's father, from Roveredo in the Swiss Grigioni.

Julius had lately employed Augustino to build the vaults of the nave and transepts of the Romanesque cathedral of Würzburg; in 1609[70] he was also responsible for the church of the Premonstratensians, just outside Würzburg at Unterzell, where the monastic community that had been dispersed during the *Bauern Krieg* (Peasants' War) in 1562 was revived in 1606. There he later added the new monastery in 1611-1613. The Unterzell church, now secularized, is without aisles, but there are six bays in the nave and two in a choir ending in a three-sided apse, the whole covered with ribbed net-vaulting. Thus it is distinctly *Nachgotik* in character despite Augustino's southern origin.

Except for the retention of the existing choir—similar in plan to the one at Unterzell in any case—Dettelbach as begun by Augustino in 1610[71] is an enlarged version of his earlier church. The great difference is the introduction, between the three rectangular bays of the nave and the single bay of the new choir, of a generous crossing (Pl. 447) that is nearly square. To north and south are square transeptal bays, though the one on the north was largely filled in 1659 with a deep gallery to carry the organ. The vaulting ribs form star rather than net patterns, with most of the members curved and some, over the crossing, even cusped. Since the windows are all tall and pointed, with Gothic tracery in their heads, the interior of the church is as *Nachgotik* in character as Unterzell, with no reflection of the Roman arch-orders that had been used by Georg Robin in the Würzburg Neubaukirche for the same client nearly thirty years before. Such sequences, among other things, justify considering German *Nachgotik* as much a revival as a survival, despite the early date of the principal examples.

The walls of the Dettelbach church were up within a year and then the two masons in charge, Jobst Pfaff from Würzburg and Adam Zwinger from Iphofen,

---

[70] Reclams *Bayern*, pp. 938, 968; Hauttmann, *Kirchliche Baukunst*, pp. 38, 39. Hauttmann also attributes the enlargement of the Catholic parish-church at Frickenhausen in Lower Franconia to Augustino; Reclams *Bayern*, p. 302, dates the work there 1605-1616 but does not mention Augustino.

[71] Reclams *Bayern*, pp. 209-211.

executed the vaulting in 1611-1612. The non-Gothic aspect of the *Juliusstil* is apparent on the exterior (Pl. 448) in the design of the three-stage gables and the altar-like west portal. Yet the oculi—one above the portal, two in the lowest stage of each gable, and a fourth in the middle stage—are all filled with Gothic tracery in contrast to the predominantly Northern Mannerist detailing of the gables. These have, however, plain pilaster-strips on their faces, though the scrollwork at their sides is quite lively with the further addition on the one at the front of spiky obelisks. Zwinger erected the north gable, while those on the south and west were carried out by Peter Meurer, a mason from Kitzingen, who had just rebuilt the parish church at Rothenfels on the Main, halfway between Schweinfurt and Aschaffenburg, for Julius Echter in 1610-1611.[72]

The Dettelbach portal,[73] carrying the date 1613 of the consecration of the church, is a very elaborate Northern Mannerist confection with no Gothic elements except the cusped circles in the small rose window. In the niche under that stands the Madonna flanked by two bishops. The next stage below has a deep-cut relief of the Adoration of the Kings, while the niches on either side of the entrance arch hold statues of Sts. Peter and Paul.

The treatment of the orders on the Dettelbach portal, both the columns in the lower and middle stage and their entablatures, shows none of the respect for "correctness," so to call it, of Robin's Roman arch orders in the Neubaukirche. There is, however, little either of the idiosyncratic originality and architectonic subtlety that distinguish the work of such Hameln architects of the later Weserrenaissance as Tönnis, Wilkening or Hundertossen, on the one hand, nor of the bold scale and the aggressive plasticity of the facade of the Stadtkirche in Bückeburg (Pl. 435) on the other.

Beside the eclectic exuberance of the contemporary Bremen Rathaus (Pl. 376), moreover, this portal at Dettelbach appears provincial and retardataire, reminding us that Julius Echter, though he had been building for nearly forty years, was now seventy. Yet it is interesting to compare the Northern Mannerist sort of fantasy of the early seventeenth century on the portal and the gables here, mild though that is, with the later German Rococo fantasy so brilliantly illus-

trated in the shrine housing the Vesperbild at the crossing (Pl. 447). The shrine was executed by Augustin Bossi as late as 1778-1779—by which time the Rococo elsewhere was largely over—in emulation of the famous *Gnadenaltar* (altar of Grace) of the 1760s at Vierzehnheiligen designed by J.J.M. Küchel.

Julius died only in 1617, the year the church was completed. When this latest work (Pl. 447) he undertook is compared with the Würzburg Neubaukirche of the 1580s it is easy to understand why a sort of premature Gothic Revival has been recognized in the Catholic church architecture of the early seventeenth century in Germany. Even Alberthal, in the parish church he began to erect at Dillingen in 1619,[74] shortly after the Neuburg Hofkirche was consecrated and the Dillingen Studienkirche completed, reverted to the hall-church model Francke had been following for a decade at Wolfenbüttel for his Protestant duke, though without repeating its pointed arches. But the Jesuits' churches of the second decade of the century are the most notable examples of this *Nachgotik* that is already a sort of *Neugotik*. Their modest church of 1613-1617 at Koblenz, St. Johannes der Taufer, has been mentioned, but the principal example before Mariä Himmelfahrt in Cologne is St. Georg at Molsheim in Alsace of 1614-1619.[75]

Of the Koblenz church little survived the last war except the modest west front, but the much larger church at Molsheim is in excellent condition. The archbishop of Strasbourg, who was then the Archduke Leopold, a son of the Emperor Ferdinand II, had settled the Jesuits in Molsheim (Bas Rhin), which lies to the west of Strasbourg on the road to St. Dié, to combat the influence of the many varieties of Protestants in the titular city of his See. That had long been a center in which Lutheran and other "heresies" flourished in the *Hochschulen* ("high schools") from which they were exported over much of northern Europe. Leopold provided the funds for the Molsheim church and its designer was his *Hofarchitekt*, Christoph Wamser from Aschaffenburg. The Jesuits there, though they had arrived in 1602, had yet to begin their church. The big Molsheim church has a long nave, with tribunes above the side-aisles, low transepts and

[72] *Ibid.*, p. 775.

[73] Jahn, *Deutsche Renaissance*, pl. 34, offers a fine photograph by Klaus Beyer of the Dettelbach portal.

[74] Dehio, *Östliches Schwaben*, p. 80. Like the Dillingen Studienkirche, this was redecorated in the eighteenth century.

[75] For Molsheim: M. Barth, *Die Pfarrkirche St.-Georg von Molsheim*, Strasbourg, 1963; Braun, *Jesuiten* I, pp. 49-54, pls. 3a and b, 4a and b, figs. 2 and 3 (plans). This is no longer a Jesuit church. For Koblenz: Braun, *op. cit.*, I, pp. 32-49, pls. 2c and d, 3a, b and c, fig. 1 (plan).

an apse-ended choir of median height (Pls. 449, 450). The arches throughout are pointed though the section of the main vault is half-round. The plain round piers of the nave arcade continue upward across the panelled parapets of the tribunes and are crowned with Doric capitals. These have an egg-and-dart molding carved on the echinus—the only really Classical detail and incorrectly employed at that. From the abacuses of the capitals vertical moldings rise without a break to become the ribs of the net-vaulting.

In 1618, the year the Molsheim church was consecrated by the bishop of Basel, Wamser's design was chosen[76] for the Jesuits' church in Cologne, a building project for which the Archbishop-Elector of Cologne Ferdinand von Bayern and his brother Maximilian, the duke of Bavaria, were providing a large part of the funds. That these two sponsors were sons of Wilhelm V, who had built St. Michael in Munich for the Jesuits more than thirty years before, suggests that Wamser's use of *Nachgotik* here was definitely a case of revival and not of survival, at least as regards the motivation of the two Wittelsbach princes. They insisted that an architect from southern Germany be employed but Maximilian did not offer the services of Hans Krumpper who had worked on St. Michael. Krumpper would have supplied, or so one might suppose, a design that was not Gothic but related to his work on St. Michael and at Polling.

Mariä Himmelfahrt, as carried out under the supervision of the Jesuit Heinrich Scheren, is very like Molsheim but still larger and also more ornate (Fig. 72; Pl. 452). Like Molsheim, the nave here has seven bays with tribunes above the aisles. These tribunes are linked by a transverse gallery in the westernmost bay as they would be later at Polling (Pl. 453). The transepts consist of square bays that are lower than those of the nave but not as low as in the Alsatian church. Beyond two rectangular bays the choir, with vaulting taller than in the transepts but not as tall as in the nave, ends in a three-sided apse. The vaulting ribs, which form star-patterns between each pair of bays, rise from carved bosses in the spandrels of the arches of the tribunes, not as at Molsheim from molded wall-

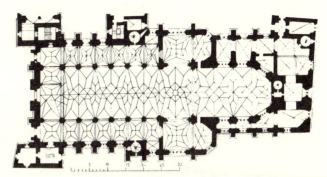

Fig. 72. Christoph Wamser: Cologne, Mariä Himmelfahrt, 1618-29, plan

strips. The pointed arches used throughout carry a great deal more applied ornament than those at Molsheim. In the spandrels of the nave arches, for example, there are carved angels and, on the capitals, semi-Gothic foliate decoration, while above the points of the arches of the tribunes there is further scrolled embellishment. All this was executed partly by Jeremias Geisselbrunn from Augsburg and partly under the direction of the Jesuit lay-brother Valentin Boltz, but probably only after the church Wamser planned was complete structurally.

The postwar restoration of Mariä Himmelfahrt has revived what was considered to have been the original coloring of the interior. The blue, grey, pink and white tones contrast with the plain ashlar masonry of the Molsheim interior and glitter everywhere with gilt. The high altar, designed by Geistselbrunn and executed by Johann Degler, was completely restored (not to say rebuilt) since the war. It dated from 1628 and was evidently modelled on the ones by Degler of 1604-1607 in Sts. Ulrich and Afra in Augsburg (Pl. 428). This altar is the only really up-to-date feature in this curious church; indeed some see the altar as already transitional to the Baroque. Others even consider that this interior as a whole approaches the Baroque, which is surely a gross misinterpretation. The west front (Pl. 451), however, may rather less inaccurately be considered to do so, despite the tall towers at either side which are more Neo-Romanesque than Neo-Gothic, much less Baroque.

These towers at the front of Mariä Himmelfahrt are balanced more or less by the single eastern tower at the other end of the church across from the main railway station of Cologne. Having now lost their double square *welsche Hauben*, the western towers seem even more alien to the rest of the facade than they must have originally. Happily, the "bonnets," one

[76] There were other designs and the prehistory of Mariä Himmelfahrt is more complicated than it seems necessary to recount in detail here: Braun, *Jesuiten* I, pp. 64-104, pls. 4c, d and e, 5, 6a, figs. 4-12 (alternative plans). Dehio, *Rheinland,* pp. 350-353, provides a more succinct account; Hipp's unpublished 1973 Tübingen dissertation emends Braun. Gerstenberg, *Sondergotik,* is also relevant here, *passim.*

above another, topping the terminal octagon of the eastern tower have been very plausibly rebuilt.

The other most conspicuous feature of the west front of Mariä Himmelfahrt, because of its great height the most impressive one of the period, is the tremendous pointed window. Though that is framed by a rectangular eared architrave, it is filled at the top with distinctly Gothic tracery and also flanked by tall pier-buttresses. Unlike the buttresses at Wolfenbüttel (Pl. 432), those on Mariä Himmelfahrt carry superposed orders of pilasters, Doric below and Ionic above, and are joined by continuous entablatures. These features clearly separate the nave from the aisles and two more mark off the aisles from the towers. However, the cornice of the lower order had to be mitered inward where it meets the sides of the west window at half-height. That may suggest the buttresses themselves were in part an afterthought, at least as regards their Classical membering, though originally required for statical reasons.

Above, vertical C-curves lead up from the ressauts of the upper order on the facade of Mariä Himmelfahrt to a plain pediment crowned with a cross. Only very modest obelisks further enliven the skyline. Thus the characteristic elaboration of German Renaissance gables was avoided here by Wamser to almost the degree of Holl on those of the Augsburg Rathaus (Pl. 415) which he was carrying out in these same years. Rather similarly, moreover, the increasing severity of treatment of the whole west front suggests there was some intention of emulating late sixteenth-century Roman church-facades, if hardly yet in the advanced spirit of Coebergher's and Trevano's facades then rising outside Germany to the west and to the east. Closest to the early Baroque here are the concave C-quadrants at either side above the front ends of the aisles. Such, however, are already to be seen on a Serlio project for a church facade in the *Quarto libro* dated 1537 of his *Architectura* and were also used several times by Vignola. Over-all, however, the effect is grand but stern in marked contrast both to the columniated complexity of the slightly earlier facade of the Order's Sint Carolus-Borromeus-Kerk in Antwerp and the Roman sophistication of that of the Jesuits' church in Kraków.

The disparity of the major features of the west front of Mariä Himmelfahrt—Romanesquoid, Gothic, proto-Baroque—is echoed in the minor ones. The small pointed windows at the ends of the aisles are set in eared architraves like the big west window but, like

that, these are headed with cusped tracery. On the other hand, the three round-arched portals are all flanked by Classical columns. Those by the central portal are paired, with statue-filled niches between them; above, an especially elaborate armorial achievement recalls the generosity of Maximilian, who had become an elector as well as duke of Bavaria in 1623, some years before the church was ready for use in 1629. The final consecration came only in 1678, long after Maximilian and his brother Ferdinand had died in the mid-century, and the northwest tower was not completed until 1689.

Mariä Himmelfahrt, as one sees it today, should not be accepted as being the church Wamser originally proposed in 1618 except in its main lines. As noted, the greater part of the decoration must belong, like the high altar, to the second quarter of the century and, in any case, has mostly been renewed in the postwar restoration completed in 1965. The reactionary features that make both the interior and the exterior something of an anachronism do not belong to the main line of German, much less international, stylistic mutation in these decades. Moreover, building in Germany was coming to a halt generally from the time the Thirty Years' War broke out, in the very year construction of Mariä Himmelfahrt started, so that the church had no immediate descendants in the Rhineland or elsewhere.

It would have been interesting to compare the Cologne church of the Jesuits with its contemporary, their Schutzengelkirche in Eichstätt as that was carried out originally in 1617-1620.[77] It was the work of Alberthal, whose Dillingen Studienkirche for the Jesuits is so much more premonitory of what was to come later than Wamser's. He may, however, have been following at Eichstätt, even if most probably not in Dillingen, a design provided by Matthias Kager. That artist was, in fact, employed by the Jesuits to provide the designs for the enlargement of a church at Innsbruck in the Tyrol in 1619, though a Jesuit lay-brother, Jakob Kurrer (1585-1647), supervised the job on the site, as was so often true of work done for the Order.[78] This church was renewed internally in 1661.

---

[77] Reclams *Bayern*, pp. 250-251; Braun, *Jesuiten*, II, pp. 141-156; pl. 4d, figs. 14, 15 (plan).

[78] The church collapsed in 1626 and was rebuilt 1627-1646 by P. Karl Fontaner: Hauttmann, *Kirchliche Baukunst*, pp. 36, 37; Dehio, *Tirol*, pp. 65-66. Kager also worked, at least as decorator, in the Benedictine abbey church at Zwiefalten in 1623: Dehio, *Westliches Schwaben*, p. 116. Kager's most important

With its *stucchi* by Francesco Gabrieli and frescoes by Johann Rosmer, both dated 1717, the Innsbruck Jesuit church preserves today even less of its original design than Alberthal's Studienkirche in Dillingen, but it certainly was never an example of *Nachgotik*.

The Catholic pilgrimage church at Violau, St. Michael, between Dillingen and Augsburg, was also begun in 1617[79] not by Alberthal but by David and Georg Höbel, with a tower of 1625 by Georg Meitinger. Echoing perhaps Alberthal's contemporary Dillingen Pfarrkirche, this was still a hall-church as was noted earlier. Like the Schutzengelkirche, however, it was so thoroughly redecorated and even partially remodelled in the 18th century by Simpert Kramer, with frescoes of 1751 by J. G. Dieffenbrunner and contemporary Rococo *stucchi*, that it offers today even less of an image of its original character than does the church in Eichstätt. However, an order of big Tuscan pilasters runs along the sides. Such an Academic exterior treatment seems first to have been proposed by Schickhardt in the earliest years of the century at Montbéliard on St.-Martin and then, it will be recalled, soon after used by Heintz not only on the Augsburg Siegel Haus, but also on the Neuburg Hofkirche and—if he did, indeed, design it—the Haunsheim parish church as well. The motif was evidently by now well-established in Swabia.

The Studienkirche of the Jesuits at Aschaffenburg of 1619-1621[80] was modelled on their Munich church as regards the side chapels and the tribunes, but reduced in length to a three-bay nave with rounded apse. The war damage has never been repaired and the church is still closed. It was in any case rather drastically restored in 1810, after being secularized in the eighteenth century in the manner of the period, and had a conspicuous array of Neo-Classic altars. On the other hand St. Michael at Aachen, as erected just before this in 1617-1628,[81] was of the *Nachgotik* character that the Order had preferred in their Rhineland

province ever since the Petrikirche was built at Münster in the 1590s. Very little of this but the original nave and tribune arches inside and the west front—of 1891—survived the war.

All these churches, it should be noted, were Catholic and most of them for the Jesuits, since by this second decade of the seventeenth century the Counter Reformation was a growing, if belated, force in Germany under the Order's leadership. Yet none of them, except Mariä Himmelfahrt in Cologne, rivalled in splendor—and only that in size—the contemporary Protestant churches in construction then at Wolfenbüttel and Bückeburg. The next major Protestant churches were built not in Germany but in Holland. There both de Keyser's Amsterdam Westerkerk and his Noorderkerk were begun in 1621, just before his death, as was mentioned earlier in this chapter.

Among minor German Protestant churches of the second decade of the century one of the most influential, especially in Hesse, was the Stadtkirche zum Heiligen Geist at Nidda,[82] on the Nidda river to the east of Bad Nauheim. Built by an architect from Mainz, probably Jakob Wustmann even though he was then in the employ of the Catholic elector-archbishop, this breaks with both the mediaeval and the Renaissance traditions of German church architecture more completely than any other considerable example up to this time that now survives. Through a sequence of exceptional Lutheran churches that seem to lead toward it a line may be traceable from Joachimstal in the 1530s (Fig. 15), through the Stuttgart Schlosskapelle (Pl. 159) of the sixties to several churches of the preceding decade of the new century.[83] That line is so discontinuous, however, one may well doubt its historical significance.

Externally the edifice at Nidda appears almost secular because of its gabled roof, double rows of windows and stair-towers at the sides. Only the "bonnet"-topped rear tower, rising above the original organ gallery, is at all church-like. Within, wooden galleries cross the west end and extend along the sides of the

---

work in Augsburg, the execution from Peter Candid's designs of the decorations in the Goldener Saal of the Rathaus, is dated 1620-1623 (Pl. 420) as noted earlier. His intervention at either Dillingen or Eichstätt is unsupported by contemporary evidence and not mentioned in Hauttmann, *Kirchliche Baukunst*.

[79] Completed 1619; consecrated 1620: Dehio, *Östliches Schwaben*, p. 36.

[80] Reclams *Bayern*, p. 69; Braun, *Jesuiten*, I, pp. 192-199, pl. 11a.

[81] Reclams *Rheinlande und Westfalen*, p. 16; Braun, *Jesuiten*, II, pp. 105-122, pl. 6b, c and d, fig. 14 (plan).

[82] Dehio, *Hessen*, p. 620.

[83] The latest before Nidda in this line of descent, although like that at Joachimsthal it is without galleries, would be the big Lutherkirche of 1610-1612 at Insterburg, southwest of Tilsit on the Pregel in East Prussia, which is now called Chemyskovsk by the Russians who occupy the district: C. Wünsch, *Ostpreussen* [Munich] 1960, p. 83, pl. 101. The tall, slim wooden piers of octagonal section in this church support a flat wooden ceiling painted in 1644-1653 by Michael Zeigermann and his assistant Hans Menio.

356

rectangular nave (Fig. 73, Pl. 456). They are thus much longer than the galleries in St.-Martin at Montbéliard and their rather plain wooden supports rise up here, as they do not there, to carry the flat ceiling. This ceiling is panelled between longitudinal beams and chiefly ornamented with simple geometrical patterns in stucco, though there is also some small-scale strapwork. In the center are displayed the arms of Landgrave Ludwig V of Hesse-Darmstadt and his wife, with the date 1616 of execution. The spandrels of the tall pointed chancel-arch, the one Gothic feature, have profuse strapwork decoration in stucco at the same delicate scale as that on the ceiling. The richly carved wooden pulpit resting on a stone base is dated 1616 too and the font, 1618. No early altar survives in the chancel.

The Nidda church clearly points in the direction that Protestant church architecture would henceforth be taking in much of Northern Europe and, soon, in the North American colonies as well. Quite as much as the long-lost Protestant *Temples* in France or St.-Martin at Montbéliard, and far more than de Keyser's grand structures in Amsterdam, this is a *Predigtkirche* or what is called by Americans not a "church" at all but a "meeting house." As has earlier been stressed, however, the galleries flanking the nave in earlier Protestant churches in Germany, beginning with the Torgau Schlosskapelle, had their source in such prominent Catholic edifices in Saxony as the

Wittenberg Schlosskirche of the 1490s, the Marienkirche at Pirna of 1502-1546 and the church at Schneeberg, where tribunes were added in 1536-1537. Squared ends[84] behind altars, moreover, had first been used in Catholic edifices as, for example, in the Fuggerkapelle at the west in St. Anna in Augsburg (Pl. 3) and in the Marktkirche in Halle (Pl. 37) at the east. Moreover, organs set high on an eastern gallery above the altar, rather than on a western one as today at Nidda, also appeared early in Catholic churches, beginning very likely with the one in the Fuggerkapelle—which, of course, is actually at the west. That dates from 1518, it will be recalled, but was not yet proposed in the project signed S.L., which is probably of 1509 or 1510 (Pl. 6).

At Nidda, however, these features, or at least several of them,[85] were more completely dominant than they had been hitherto and thus more premonitory of innumerable Protestant edifices in Germany of the late seventeenth and eighteenth centuries. To close this book with the account of the modest "meeting house" at Nidda, all the same, would necessarily be anticlimactic; it would also ignore the models for the decoration of later German Baroque interiors that were already offered in these years in certain large Catholic churches as had hardly been done earlier at St. Michael in Munich to the same degree.

As stated earlier in this chapter, two churches, one Protestant, at least when begun, though turned over to the Jesuits before completion, the other Catholic and built for the Jesuits, seem most particularly to have led the way toward the German Baroque well before the Nidda Predigtkirche was begun. Now around 1620, the chronological terminus of this book, the architects and the decorators of two other churches, that of the Augustinians at Polling, in Upper Bavaria, as extended, remodelled and newly decorated over the years 1621-1628, and another begun in 1622 for the Jesuits at Düsseldorf in the duchy of Berg on the Rhine, went rather further. The sponsor for the latter, St. Andreas, was Duke Wolfgang Wilhelm of Berg, the Catholic convert who had earlier turned over the Protestant Hofkirche at Neuburg in the Upper Palatinate, where he also ruled, to the Jesuits on his accession in 1614.

The Augustinian priory at Polling, just off the

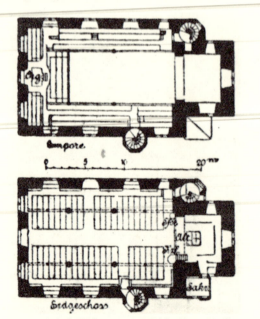

Fig. 73. Jakob Wustmann: Nidda, Zum Heiligen Geist, completed 1618, plan

[84] In England, of course, squared east ends were a very old tradition going back to Norman or even Saxon times.
[85] Squared off though it is, there is a deep chancel at Nidda, however, beyond the pointed eastern arch rather than an unbroken rectangle in plan as at Insterburg.

Olympiastrasse south of Weilheim, was first founded, according to legend, by Duke Tassilo III around 750; then refounded by the Emperor Heinrich II in 1010; and finally assigned to the Order by Pope Innocent II in 1036. After the thirteenth-century church burned in 1414 it was at once rebuilt in 1416-1420.[86] In 1605, at the behest of Duke Maximilian of Bavaria, later one of the sponsors of Mariä Himmelfahrt in Cologne, a great tower at the southwest corner of the church was begun by Hans Krumpper from nearby Weilheim. He was, it will be recalled, a son-in-law of Sustris and a principal member of the group of artists working on St. Michael and on the Residenz in Munich, first for Wilhelm V and then for Maximilian. The three storeys of the tower that Krumpper was able to complete (Pl. 454) before Maximilian recalled him to Munich in 1611 are decorated only with plain raised bands of stone. This treatment is somewhat like that of the upper portions of the facade of the Munich church (Pl. 258)—for the design of which he was at least partly responsible—but at much grander scale. The result has a superb dignity very rare in German Renaissance structures.[87] Though the idea for this simple sort of surface decoration goes back to Vignola, it is hardly to be considered Academic here but rather proto-Baroque.[88] The octagonal top-stage of the tower was added only in 1822.

In 1621, Prior Kilian Westenrieder decided to proceed with an extensive remodelling of the fifteenth-century nave and the addition of a deep choir at Polling. For this it is usually presumed that Krumpper provided the plans, despite the lack of relevant documentation and the marked difference between the austerity of his tower and the decorative richness of the interior. It was, however, Georg Schmuzer from nearby Wessobrunn who was chiefly responsible for the interior, he being both supervisor of the construction and stuccator.

Polling as decorated at this time is the more premonitory of the mature German Baroque and the Rococo just because this stuccator-builder contributed far more to the resulting *Gesamtkunstwerk* than

whoever provided the architectural design, Krumpper or some other. This was, indeed, what often happened in the later seventeenth and eighteenth centuries when the interiors of so many large and important mediaeval churches[89] in southern Germany were elaborately redecorated with *stucchi* and frescoes. It may even be no coincidence that a Schmuzer was responsible here, for in the later period a family of Schmuzers from nearby Wessobrunn, not improbably related to Georg, were among the most accomplished of the various groups of such craftsmen-designers many of the ablest of whom originated, like all the later Schmuzers, at Wessobrunn.

The work undertaken at Polling by Prior Westenrieder, as it proceeded through most of the 1620s, did not entail much structural modification, for the main body of the fifteenth-century hall-church was retained in the remodelling. That is almost square still because of the close spacing of the four original pillars on each side that divide the very broad nave from the relatively wide and equally tall aisles (Fig. 74). This nave

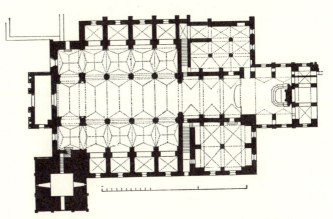

Fig. 74. Polling, Augustinian church as remodelled and extended 1621-28, plan

is further shortened in effect today, however, by the broad new gallery of the 1620s that extends into the second bay from the west (Pl. 453) somewhat as in Mariä Himmelfahrt. This gallery is connected by rounded corners with the much shallower ranges of tribunes running along the outer side of the aisles. The shape of the church as a whole is not now square, however, but a longitudinal oblong, for the eastern portion as extended for Prior Westenrieder is the same length as the nave, with three bays in the new choir and then, beyond a broad double rib, two more

[86] Dehio, *Oberbayern*, pp. 190-192; Hauttmann, *Kirchliche Baukunst*, pp. 34-35, 123 f.

[87] Compare, for example, Schickhardt's church tower of 1612-1613 at Cannstatt: Fleischhauer, *Württemberg*, fig. 140.

[88] Ammannati used it in the 1580s on the Collegio Romano and Bernini in the 1620s on the Propaganda Fide, to name conspicuous examples in Rome of earlier and of later date, the second manifestly Early Baroque and certainly not known to Krumpper.

[89] And some Renaissance ones: Violau is an example.

bays in the sanctuary. The original Gothic vaulting at Polling with its pointed arches was retained, but the vaults were completely masked with stucco in a system of panels that cover all the mediaeval ribs and severies. Framed by broad flat moldings which are most delicately detailed, these panels produce an overall linear pattern considerably freer than the Castellis' of a few years earlier in the Neuburg Hofkirche (Pl. 436). Centered in the larger fields, otherwise largely blank, are ornamental motifs in fairly high relief; while on the bevelled intradoses of the nave arches widely spaced medallions alternate with winged seraphim.

Though the octagonal section of the old piers was retained at Polling, their shafts were stuccoed and the tall slim panels on the cardinal sides were decorated with small-scale ornament in relief. Under wide square abacuses with similarly decorated edges the capitals are only loosely Corinthianesque—they have, for example, winged seraphim instead of volutes at the corners. However, the kinship to Francke's Northern Mannerist confections at Wolfenbüttel (Pl. 431) is not so close as to the more conventional capitals at Bückeburg (Pl. 434).

The richest surface treatment in the Polling interior is almost at eye-level. This is on the short piers carrying the segmental arches below the tribunes. It is also repeated on the continuations of these piers above the gallery parapet. The latter elements, acting as responds to the tall piers in the nave, also carry the deep wall-arches of the aisle vaulting. The shafts of the lower piers have pilaster-like panels with actual entasis and they are capped, below ressauts, with freely designed Ionic capitals; the upper ones are simpler in treatment. Other small but boldly shaped panels, with a distinct suggestion of jewelry in their bossy detailing, occupy the parapets of the tribunes. The Rococo screens of grillwork above were added in the eighteenth century.

At the east end of the nave of Polling the extrados of the transverse choir-arch is decorated with scrolls, garlands and even seraphim in a way that recalls a little the ornamentation above the nave arches in Mariä Himmelfahrt which is probably contemporary (Pl. 455). In the eastern arm the treatment of the choir side of the aisles, though much elaborated on the parapets, is largely repeated from the front portion of the church. Above, however, the tribunes of the choir run outward in barrel-vaulted cross-bays. These actually extend beyond the edge of the aisles that flank the nave all the way to the line of the walls confining

the outer chapels on each side. These chapels were additions—presumably made at this time, but possibly only in the eighteenth century—between the surviving mediaeval buttresses.

Overhead, in the choir of Polling, heavier garlands fill the triangular faces of the vaulting conoids on either side of panels which are quite similar to those on the nave vaults. Beyond the broad piers that carry the double rib at the eastern end of this section the decoration of the sanctuary is richer and more delicate in scale, with all the voids on the vaults occupied by garlands or other foliate elements.

The lower side walls of the sanctuary at Polling, all the same, are handled very much as are those of the aisles and the choir. Higher up, pairs of great windows on both sides flood the two-storeyed altar which fills the whole of the east end. This was projected in 1623 by Bartholomäus Steinle (†1628) and executed by the joiner Benedikt Meggas in association with Johann Degler from nearby Weilheim. Degler had executed earlier the altars of 1604 and 1607 in Sts. Ulrich and Afra in Augsburg and was, at about this time, executing the one in Mariä Himmelfahrt. Since it was considerably altered in the eighteenth century, the evident Baroque character of the high altar is only partially, if at all, due to Steinle's design or Degler's execution. Other eighteenth-century modifications are largely confined to the side chapels. These were stuccoed in 1761-1765 in a late Rococo vein by Tassilo Zöpf (1723-1807) and may, as has been noted, only have been added at that time.

Stucco decoration of Italianate design was first executed in quantity in Germany by the Mantuans who worked in the Stadtresidenz in Landshut eighty or ninety years before Georg Schmuzer was employed at Polling. Only in the late 1580s, at Schmalkalden, did Wilhelm Vernukken carry a more northern sort of stucco decoration over the entire interior of the chapel in Schloss Wilhelmsburg (Pl. 267). In the sixties and seventies it was Italian teams that produced the rich decoration in the vaulted interiors at Poznań and Augsburg (Pl. 215). As regards large churches however, it was, the Castellis—also Italians or, like Alberthal, from the Italian-Swiss Grigioni—who in 1616-1620 first covered a whole interior of the Neuburg Hofkirche with stucco decoration of a quite different sort. The original internal treatment of Alberthal's Dillingen church of 1610-1617 may well have been quite similar.

The Castellis' stucco-work in the Neuburg Hofkirche can more properly be considered Late Italian

Mannerist of a provincial sort than Northern Mannerist like Vernukken's. All the same, it resembles very little the more up-to-date and sophisticated sort of *stucchi* that Sustris and his team had introduced, directly from Italy, around 1570 at the Fuggerhäuser in Augsburg and that Hubert Gerhard, among others, continued to produce in some profusion for Wilhelm V in Munich in the eighties and nineties. Here at Polling, however, Georg Schmuzer can be credited with initiating the virtuoso sort of total stucco decoration in a great and complex interior that would eventually evolve, a hundred years and more later, into the German Rococo.[90]

In the eighteenth century some of the finest stuccoed interiors would again be created, as at Polling, within inherited mediaeval shells, beginning with the Asams' redecoration of Freising Cathedral in the early 1720s and culminating in J. B. Zimmermann's interior at Andechs as remodelled in the 1750s. But, from the 1680s for nearly a hundred years, great Baroque and Rococo churches would also be entirely new-built, especially in the south of Germany, as well as comparable secular interiors, these last carried out mostly for the Schönborns and the Wittelsbachs. The Wittelsbachs, moreover, though not yet the Schönborns—at Neuburg and at Landshut, at Heidelberg, and in Munich—were already important builders, as has recurrently been noted.

Maximilian, however, preoccupied with the considerable additions he was making to the Residenz in Munich, obstructed rather than advanced the earlier plans of 1605-1611 for building the tower at Polling;

whether he assisted financially or otherwise later in the twenties with the redecoration is uncertain. Maximilian's brother-in-law, Duke Wolfgang Wilhelm of Berg,[91] continued more effectively in his Rhineland capital, Düsseldorf, the notable patronage of post-mediaeval architecture characteristic of his own Pfalz-Neuburg line of Wittelsbachs. What he built, moreover, was as advanced for this period as the work of his maternal grandfather, Wilhelm V of Berg, at Jülich had been in the 1550s. At Cologne, as has been noted, Maximilian and his brother Ferdinand must have approved, if they did not dictate, the use of *Nachgotik* for the Jesuits' church; in Düsseldorf at St. Andreas Wolfgang Wilhelm gave his support to a further stylistic development beyond the Neuburg Hofkirche, begun by Heintz for his Protestant father Philipp Ludwig, which he had handed over to the Order on his accession in 1614, a few years before its completion.

The Jesuits had come to Düsseldorf in 1619 and St. Andreas was built a bit later[92] not only for their use but as the court church. It also provided eventually, in a mausoleum added behind the apse, a burial place for Wolfgang Wilhelm and his successors. The mausoleum is a plain hexagonal structure, flanked by low sacristies, that faintly recalls Ernst von Schaumburg's much grander one at Stadthagen (Pl. 442) but with no sculpture comparable to Adriaen de Fries's.

Before the imposing works initiated by Protestants in the years around 1610 at Wolfenbüttel, Bückeburg and Neuburg, few earlier German Renaissance churches had been of much interest from the outside and, of these three, only the last has any coherent architectural treatment. Bückeburg is as much an example of "facade-architecture" as the new church-fronts of the period in Italy, Poland and the southern Netherlands, while Wolfenbüttel lacks any completed

---

[90] Further east the decorations by the Italians Sebastiano Carlone and Teodoro Ghisi in the burial chapel of the Archduke Karl at Seckau in Styria of 1590-1600 and the somewhat later work of Vetrano for Zygmunt III in the Wawel Zamek at Kraków seem less relevant than Schmuzer's though both incorporate more painted areas: Baldass, *Österreich*, pls. 57, 58; Łozinski-Miłobedzki, *Guide*, p. 116.

The most sophisticated and up-to-date *stucchi* of around 1600 in the north incorporating painted areas were executed for Archbishop Wolf Dietrich von Reitenau of Salzburg in the Engelskapelle of the Franziskanerkirche there and in Dietrich's mausoleum in the Gabrielkapelle of 1577-1603. The latter, which is in the Sankt-Sebastians-Friedhof, is by Elia Castello (†1602): Dehio Handbuch, Die Kunstdenkmäler Österreichs, *Salzburg Land und Stadt*, 5th ed., Vienna [1963], p. 77; Baldass, *op. cit.*, pp. 34, 77, 88, pls. 59, 60. Castello was, like Santino Solari, a Lombard and is thought to have come from Como. Wholly exceptional is the decoration of the walls of the mausoleum by Castello with a checkered mosaic of white, green and yellow tesserae: Baldass, *op. cit.*, pl. XV (in colour).

[91] Wolfgang Wilhelm's father, Philipp Ludwig, thanks to his marriage to Anna, a daughter of Duke Wilhelm V of Jülich-Berg-Kleve, effectively succeeded Wilhelm's childless son Johann Wilhelm in 1609: See Note 29.

The rulers of the Rhineland duchies changed religion almost as often as their relatives the electors Palatine. Wilhelm returned to Catholicism in 1570. Philipp Ludwig, the husband of his daughter Anna, was Protestant but Wolfgang Wilhelm, who succeeded him in 1614, was Catholic. Under Philipp Wilhelm, his successor, there was sufficient tolerance to allow the Protestants to build the Neanderkirche in Düsseldorf in 1683-1687 as long as it was located in a court back from the street.

[92] Dehio, *Rheinland*, pp. 125-126; Braun, *Jesuiten*, II, pp. 199-220, pls. 11, b and c; 12, a and b.

west facade for all its impressive rear and the ranges of elaborate gables along the sides. Though simple and even severe like its prototype at Neuburg, St. Andreas[93] has considerable compositional variety, especially as seen from the northeast. There the two transeptal towers that take the place of the single front tower at Neuburg rise high above the polygonal mass of the burial chapel to the rear of the apse and the twin sacristies.

But it is in the interior (Pl. 457) of St. Andreas, looking down the five bays of the nave and the two of the crossing and the choir—the view barely interrupted by the thicker piers on the far side of the fifth bay—that one may truly feel the Renaissance is over and the early phase of the Baroque in Germany has begun. However, what one now sees, both outside and in, is by no means all of the 1620s. The towers flanking the crossing, features not originally intended, were completed only in 1637, and the mausoleum thirty years later. The heavily scaled stucco-work

[93] Dehio, *Rheinland, loc. cit.* The unrecorded architect was presumably a Jesuit.

within, including deeply fluted giant pilasters and massive entablature blocks, is of quite different order from the flatter, more delicate and much less conventional detail provided not long before this by the Castellis at Neuburg and by Schmuzer at Polling (Pls. 436, 453, 455).

Although the internal organization of St. Andreas in Düsseldorf, with tall tribunes rising over the aisles, is identical with that of the Neuburg Hofkirche, the grander scale and bolder membering seem already at least as Baroque as Maderno's nave of St. Peter's in Rome, completed by 1614, or that of Magenta's San Pietro in Bologna, executed largely after 1605 by others. The *stucchi* in St. Andreas, however, which are by Johann Kuhn from Strasbourg, were only executed in the years following 1632. Thus one may say, not exaggeratedly, that in this interior as in the Goldener Saal of the Augsburg Rathaus the German Renaissance has been left behind chronologically as well as stylistically. The story that began with the Fuggerkapelle around 1510 had come to an end little more than a hundred years later.

Pl. 1. Gerolamo Tedesco: Fontego dei Todeschi, Venice (1505-07), facade on the Grand Canal

Pl. 2. Hermann II Vischer: design for High Renaissance facade, c.1516

Pl. 3. S. L. (?Sebastian Loscher): Augsburg, St. Anna, Fuggerkapelle, 1510-12, interior as restored

Pl. 4. Antonio Gambello and Mauro Coducci: Venice, San
Zaccaria, begun 1485, interior looking east

Pl. 5. Esztergom, Cathedral, Bakócz Chapel,
begun 1506/07

Pl. 6. S. L. (?Sebastian Loscher): Drawing (? project) for Fuggerkapelle,
St. Anna, Augsburg, ?1509/10

Pl. 7. Hans Tirol: view of the Weinmarkt, Augsburg, in 1566

Pl. 8. Augsburg, Fuggerhäuser, Maximilianstrasse 36-38, 1512-15, east front as before 1944

Pl. 9. Bartolomeo Buon: Venice, Santa Maria dell'Orto, campanile, 1503

Pl. 10. Augsburg, Fuggerhäuser, Maximilianstrasse 36, 1512-15, Damenhof, capital in entrance hall

Pl. 11. Augsburg, Fuggerhäuser, Maximilianstrasse 36, 1512-15, Damenhof, court looking northeast

Pl. 12. Lauingen, St. Martin, begun 1513/15, exterior from east

Pl. 13. Lauingen, St. Martin, begun 1513/15, interior looking east

Pl. 14. Augsburg, St. Katherine, 1516-17, nave

Pl. 15. Daniel Hopfer: interior of St. Katherine, Augsburg, looking west

Pl. 16. Hans Schweiner: Heilbronn, St. Kilian, west tower with Oktagon, 1508-12, 1513-29

Pl. 17. Bastien and Martin François: Tours, Cathédrale Saint-Gatien, crown of north tower, 1505-07

Pl. 18. Augsburg, Fuggerei, 1516-23, Sparrenlech entrance

Pl. 19. Wroclav, Cathedral, sacristy doorway, 1517

Gedenket der vorigen Zeiten.

Pl. 20. ? Christoph Walther or Franz Maidburg: Annaberg, St. Anna, sacristy doorway, 1518

Pl. 21. Vienna, Salvatorkapelle, doorway, c.1525   Pl. 22. Wiener-Neustadt, Zeughaus, doorway, 1524

Pl. 23. Hans Hieber: model of
Perlachturm, 1519

Pl. 24. Munich, Frauenkirche, west towers,
as topped c.1525

Pl. 25. Hans Hieber: model of
project for Zur schönen Maria,
Regensburg, 1519-21, exterior
from west

Pl. 26. Hans Hieber: model of
project for Zur schönen Maria,
Regensburg, 1519-21, interior
of nave

Pl. 27. Hans Hieber: Regensburg, Neue
Pfarrkirche, sacristy, c.1520-24

Pl. 28. Hans Hieber: Regensburg,
Neue Pfarrkirche, begun c.1520,
exterior from east

Pl. 29. Hans Hieber: Regensburg, Neue Pfarrkirche,
begun c.1520, interior

Pl. 30. Stephan Rottaler: Freising, Bischofshof, court arcades, 1519

Pl. 31. ? Erhard or Ulrich Heydenreich: Regensburg, Dom, cloister windows, early 1520s, detail

Pl. 32. Albrecht Dürer: Triumphal Arch for the Emperor
Maximilian, woodcut, 1515-17

Pl. 33. Peter I Vischer and others:
Nürnberg, St. Sebald, Shrine of
St. Sebald, 1514-18

Pl. 34. Hermann II Vischer: project for
Shrine of St. Sebald, 1516

Pl. 35. Lübeck, Haus der Schiffergesellschaft, 1535

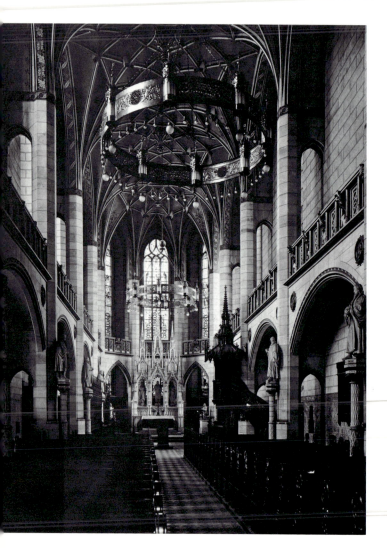

Pl. 36. Konrad Pflüger: Wittenberg, Schlosskirche, completed by 1509, interior to east as "restored" 1885-92

Pl. 37. Halle-a.-d.-Saale, Unsere liebe Frau (Marktkirche), begun 1529, galleries 1554-55, interior to east

Pl. 38. Konrad Pflüger and others: Annaberg, St. Anna, begun 1499, cons. 1519, interior to east

Pl. 39. Bartolomeo Berrecci: Kraków, Cathedral,
Sigismund Chapel, 1519-23, interior

Pl. 40. Hans Backoffen: Mainz, Dom, Tomb of Archbishop Uriel
von Gemmingen, †1514

Pl. 41. Rombout II Keldermans and Guyot de Beaugrand:
Mechelen, Palais de Savoie, 1517-26, exterior
from northwest

Pl. 42. Alessandro Pasqualini:
IJsselstein, church tower, lower
storeys completed 1535

Pl. 43. Alessandro Pasqualini:
Buren, Kasteel, scrolled gable
in court, 1539-44

Pl. 44. Jörg Unkair: Schloss Neuhaus,
Schloss, exterior from southwest,
begun c.1525

Pl. 45. Halle-a.-d.-Saale, Dom,
exterior from southeast, gables of c.1523

Pl. 46. Halle-a.-d.-Saale, Dom, western
gable, c.1523

Pl. 47. Halle-a.-d.-Saale, Dom, south
portal, 1525

Pl. 48. Jörg Unkair: Schelenburg, Schloss, main gable, c.1530

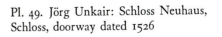

Pl. 49. Jörg Unkair: Schloss Neuhaus, Schloss, doorway dated 1526

Pl. 51. Jörg Unkair: Petershagen,
Schloss, stair-tower, 1546

Pl. 50. Franz Maidburg: Karl-Marx-Stadt (Chemnitz),
Schlosskirche, north portal, 1522-25

Pl. 53. Pössneck, Rathaus, outside stairs, 1530-31

Pl. 52. P. Lombardo and Mauro Coducci: Venice, Scuola di San Marco, 1488-c.1500

Pl. 54. Frankfurt-a.-d.-Oder, St. Nikolaikirche, gable, 1516-25

Pl. 55. Jakob Heilmann and Friedrich Schultheiss:
Zwickau, Gewandhaus, front, 1522-25

Pl. 56. Gifhorn, Schloss, gatehouse, c.1535

Pl. 57. Adolf and Hans Dauher: Annaberg, St. Anna, high altar, 1519-22

Pl. 58. Jan van Roome: Cologne, St. Maria-im-Kapitol,
Hackeney screen, 1523-24, detail

Pl. 59. Aschaffenburg, Stiftskirche, bronze baldacchin, 1536

Pl. 60. Lucas I Cranach and Peter II Vischer:
Wittenberg, Schlosskirche, tomb of Elector
Friedrich der Weise, 1527

Pl. 61. Wendel Rosskopf:
Lwówek Slazki, Rathaus, from
southeast, 1522-24 or later

Pl. 62. Görlitz, Neissestrasse 29, 1570

Pl. 63. Wendel Rosskopf: Görlitz, Schönhof, 1526, from northwest

Pl. 64. Görlitz, Untermarkt 23, 1536

Pl. 65. Wendel Rosskopf: Görlitz, Rathaus,
archive wing, 1534

Pl. 66. Wendel Rosskopf: Görlitz, Rathaus, oriel
in court, 1534

Pl. 67. Görlitz, Peterstrasse 8, 1528

Pl. 68. ? Wendel Rosskopf: Görlitz,
Brüderstrasse 11, 1547

Pl. 69. Wendel Rosskopf: Görlitz, Rathaus, portal, 1537

Pl. 70. Saalfeld, Rathaus, 1526-37

Pl. 71. Goslar, Brusttuch (1521), 1526   Pl. 72. Hildesheim, Knockenhaueramtshaus, 1529, before the war

Pl. 73. Hans Knotz: Neuburg-a.-d.-Donau, Schloss, entrance

Pl. 74. Hans Knotz: Neuburg-a.-d.-Donau, Schloss, court side of west wing, before 1534

Pl. 77. Binsfeld, Schloss, court arcade, 1533

Pl. 75. Hans Knotz: Neuburg-a.-d.-Donau, Schloss, gable on west wing, c.1532, watercolor by Vogel, c.1824

Pl. 76. Hans Knotz: Neuburg-a.-d.-Donau, Schloss, arcade on west wing, c.1540

Pl. 78. Konrad Krebs: Torgau, Schloss Hartenfels,
Johann-Friedrichs-Bau, court side, 1533-36

Pl. 79. ? Arnold von Westfalen; Konrad Krebs: Torgau, Schloss Hartenfels,
Albrechtsbau and Johann-Friedrichs-Bau, 1470; 1533-36

Pl. 80. Konrad Krebs: Torgau, Schloss Hartenfels, Johann-Friedrichs-Bau, 1533-36, stair-tower

Pl. 81. Arnold von Westfalen: Meissen, Albrechtsburg, begun 1471

Pl. 82. Konrad Krebs: Torgau, Schloss Hartenfels,
Johann-Friedrichs-Bau, 1533-36, detail of
balcony and watch-tower arcading

Pl. 85. Fratelli Rodari: Como, Cathedral
north portal, c.1490

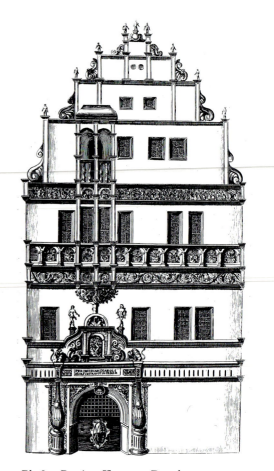

Pl. 83. Bastian Kramer: Dresden, Residenzschloss,
Georgenbau, c.1530-35, outer side

Pl. 84. Bastian Kramer: Dresden,
Residenzschloss, Georgenbau,
c.1530-35, court side

Pl. 86. Dresden, Residenzschloss,
Georgenbau, portal in court, c.1535

Pl. 87. Dresden, Residenzschloss,
Georgenbau, inner portal, 1535

Pl. 88. Dippoldiswalde, Schloss, court side, late 1530s

Pl. 89. Meissen, Dom, Georgenkapelle, inner portal, c.1534-39

Pl. 90. Hans Knotz: Neuburg-a.-d.-Donau, Schloss, north wing, 1534-38, west end with gable

Pl. 91. Hans Knotz: Neuburg-a.-d.-Donau, Schloss, north wing from southwest, 1534-38

Pl. 92. Jörg Unkair: Stadthagen, Schloss, c.1535-40,
south front

Pl. 93. ? Jörg Unkair: Stadthagen, Schloss, entrance
with oriel and arms of Otto IV, 1544

Pl. 94. Meppen, Rathaus,
remodelled 1601-05

Pl. 95. Alsfeld, Weinhaus, 1538

Pl. 96. ? Maerten de Vos: Celle, Schloss, altarpiece in chapel, side wing, c.1575, with view of Gifhorn Schloss

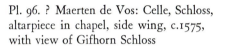

Pl. 97. ? Maerten de Vos: Celle, Schloss, altarpiece in chapel, side wing, c.1575, with view of Celle Schloss

Pl. 98. ? Frederic Soltesburg: Celle, Schloss,
east front, c.1535-60, after restoration

Pl. 99. Gifhorn, Kavalierhaus, 1540,
after restoration

Pl. 100. Caspar Theiss: Berlin, Schloss, Joachimsbau, begun 1538,
restored view from southeast

Pl. 101. Caspar Theiss: Berlin, Schloss, Joachimsbau, begun 1538,
restored view from court

Pl. 102. Celle, Hoppener Haus, 1532

Pl. 103. Brunswick, Langegasse 9, 1536

Pl. 104. Erfurt, Haus zur hohen Lilie, 1538

Pl. 105. ? Hans Knotz: Neuburg-a.-d.-Donau, Schloss, Rittersaal, 1534-37 and later

Pl. 106. Neuburg-am-Inn, Schloss, Rotmarmor Zimmer, c.1535

Pl. 107. Peter Flötner: Nürnberg, Hirschvogelsaal, 1534, now in Fembohaus

Pl. 108. Wittenberg, Melancthon Haus, study, 1536

Pl. 109. Schneeberg, Wolfgangskirche, 1515-40, interior with tribunes of 1536-37

Pl. 110. Cornelis Floris: title-page of *Libro segundo*, Antwerp, 1577, *Weeldeley niewe Inventien*

Pl. 111. Paolo della Stella; Bonifaz Wolmut: Prague, Belvedere, 1534-63

Pl. 112. Spittal-a.-d.-Drau,
Salamanca (Porcia) Schloss,
c.1535-60, court

Pl. 113. Spittal-a.-d.-Drau,
Salamanca (Porcia) Schloss,
c.1535-60, exterior from north

Pl. 114. Landshut, Stadtresidenz, 1536-43, loggia on west side of court
with frescoes by Ludwig Refinger

Pl. 115. Hans I Bocksberger and Hermann Postumus: Landshut, Stadtresidenz,
1536-43, Italienischer Saal, frescoes

Pl. 116. Hans I Bocksberger: Landshut, Stadtresidenz, 1536-43, Venuszimmer, frescoes

Pl. 117. Landshut, Stadtresidenz,
1536-43, court

Pl. 118. Landshut, Stadtresidenz,
1536-43, rear facade

Pl. 119. Landshut, Stadtresidenz, Festsaal in Deutscher Bau, ceiling, c.1540

Pl. 120. Landshut, Stadtresidenz, chapel, cons. 1542

Pl. 121. Neuburg-a.-d.-Donau, Schloss, chapel, c.1538-43, interior looking west

Pl. 122. Neuburg-a.-d.-Donau, Schloss, chapel, c.1538-43, interior looking east

Pl. 123. Neuburg-a.-d.-Donau, Schloss, stuccoed vault of entrance passage, 1545

Pl. 124. Hans Knotz: Grünau, Alter Bau, early 1530s (right rear); Neuer Bau, early 1550's (front left)

Pl. 125. Nickel Gromann: Torgau, Schloss Hartenfels, chapel, 1543-44, interior to east

Pl. 126. Stephan Hermsdorff: Torgau, Schloss Hartenfels, Schöner Erker, 1544

Pl. 127. Simon Schröter: Torgau, Schloss
Hartenfels, chapel, 1543-44, pulpit

Pl. 128. Simon Schröter: Torgau, Schloss
Hartenfels, chapel, 1543-44, entrance

Pl. 129. Gifhorn, Schloss, chapel, 1547

Pl. 130. ? Johann Maria and Hans II
Walther: Dresden, Residenzschloss, portal
of chapel, 1555

Pl. 131. Dresden, Residenzschloss, Moritzbau, court facade, c.1545-50

Pl. 132. Dresden, Residenzschloss, wooden model, c.1545-50

Pl. 133. Dresden, Residenzschloss, west side of court, c.1545-50

Pl. 134. ? Hans von Dehn-Rothfelser:
Moritzburg, Jagdschloss, 1542-46,
wooden model

Pl. 135. Brzég, Schloss, arcade
in court, c.1545-50

Pl. 136. Giacomo Parr: Brzég, Schloss, gatehouse, 1552-53

Pl. 137. Jörg Unkair and Cord Tönnis: Detmold,
Schloss, east front, 1548-57

Pl. 138. I. R.: Detmold, Schloss, gallery in court,
1557

Pl. 139. Heidelberg, Schloss, Gläserner Saalbau and
Ottheinrichsbau from east, c.1545-49; 1556-62

Pl. 140. ? Conrad Förster: Heidelberg, Schloss,
Gläserner Saalbau, arcades, completed 1549

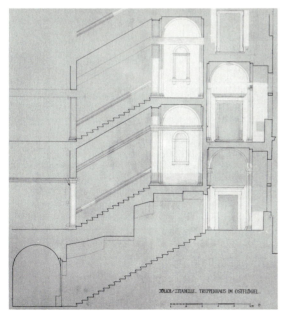

Pl. 141. Tomaso Vincidor: Breda, Kasteel, 1536-38, further side of court before remodelling

Pl. 142. Alessandro Pasqualini: Jülich, Zitadelle, 1548-58, staircase

Pl. 143. Alessandro Pasqualini: Jülich,
Zitadelle, chapel, 1552-53,
exterior from east

Pl. 144. Alessandro Pasqualini: Jülich,
Zitadelle, north portal, c.1555

Pl. 145. Alessandro Pasqualini: Jülich, Zitadelle
chapel, 1552-53, interior looking east

Pl. 146. ? Gabriel von Aken: Wismar, Fürstenhof, 1553-54, court front

Pl. 147. ? Valentin von Lyra: Wismar, Fürstenhof, 1553-54, exterior front

Pl. 148. Statius von Düren: Wismar,
Fürstenhof, 1553-54, court side, terra
cotta detail of doorway

Pl. 149. Freyenstein, Schloss, 1556

Pl. 150. Christoph Haubitz: Gadebusch, Schloss, 1570-71

Pl. 151. Lüneburg, Am Sande 1, 1548

Pl. 152. Lüneburg, Lünertorstrasse 5, c.1550

Pl. 153. Lübeck, Kohlmarkt 13, c.1555

Pl. 154. Ascheberg,
Herrenhaus Byink, 1558

Pl. 155. Wolbeck,
Drostenhof, 1554-57

Pl. 156. Münster, Krameramtshaus, 1588-89

Pl. 157. Alberlin Tretsch, Blasius
and Martin Berwart: Stuttgart, Altes
Schloss, 1553-62, exterior from west

Pl. 158. Alberlin Tretsch, Blasius
and Martin Berwart: Stuttgart, Altes
Schloss, 1553-62, court arcades
begun c.1560

Pl. 159. Alberlin Tretsch, Blasius and Martin Berwart:
Stuttgart, Altes Schloss, chapel, 1560-62;
remodelled 1864

Pl. 160. Plötzkau, Schloss, 1556-69

Pl. 161. ? Conrad Förster: Amberg, Kanzlei, 1544-46

Pl. 162. Plauen, Rathaus, 1508; gable, 1548

Pl. 163. Hieronymus Lotter *et al.*: Leipzig, Altes
Rathaus, 1556-64; arcade 1906-09; restored 1948-50

Pl. 164. Dettelbach, Rathaus,
interior, c.1550

Pl. 165. Dinkelsbühl, Ratstrinkstube,
c.1560

Pl. 166. Augsburg, Boeck von Boeckenstein Haus, now Maximilian Museum, 1544-46

Pl. 167. Lorch, Hilchenhaus, 1546; 1548-73

Pl. 168. Nickel Gromann:
Weimar, Cranach Haus, 1549

Pl. 169. Münster, Egidienstrasse
11, 1555

Pl. 170. Einbeck, Tiedexerstrasse, c.1540-60 and later

Pl. 171. Dinkelsbühl, Deutsches Haus, 1600

Pl. 172. Munich, Bayer. Nationalmuseum, "Stübchen"
from Fuggerhaus, Donauwörth, c.1555, portal

Pl. 173. Munich, Bayer. Nationalmuseum, "Stübchen"
from Fuggerhaus, Donauwörth, c.1555, ceiling

Pl. 174. Munich. Bayer. Nationalmuseum, "Stübchen" from Fuggerhaus,
Donauwörth, c. 1555, interior

Pl. 175. ? Cornelis Floris: Antwerp, Stadhuis, 1561-64

Pl. 176. Jan Vredeman de Fries: *Architectura*, 1563, plate 146

Pl. 177. Heidelberg, Schloss,
Ottheinrichsbau, court
facade, 1556-p.60

Pl. 178. Heidelberg, Schloss,
Ottheinrichsbau, window
detail, 1556-p.60

Pl. 179. Alexander Colin: Heidelberg,
Schloss, Ottheinrichsbau,
portal, 1558-59

Pl. 180. Arndt Johannssen: Horst,
Schloss, north side of
court, 1558-59

Pl. 181. ? Joist de la Cour: Horst, Schloss, east front, begun c.1526, elevation

Pl. 182. ? Arndt Johannssen: Horrem, Schloss Frens, northeast gable, ?c.1565

Pl. 183. Laurenz von Brachum or Arndt Johannssen:
Lippborg, Schloss Assen, court facade, begun 1564

Pl. 184. Arndt Johannssen *et al.*: Horst, Schloss,
north front; decoration by Wilhelm Vernukken
commissioned 1564

Pl. 185. Laurenz von Brachum: Hovestadt, Schloss, east front, begun 1563

Pl. 186. Franz Parr: Güstrow, Schloss, 1558-64, loggias in court

Pl. 187. Franz Parr: Güstrow, Schloss, 1558-64, southwest gable

Pl. 188. Franz Parr: Güstrow, Schloss, 1558-64, south side

Pl. 189. Franz Parr: Güstrow, Schloss, 1558-64, west front

Pl. 190. Nickel Gromann: Heldburg, Französischer Bau, 1560-62, court front

Pl. 191. Caspar Vischer and
Daniel Engelhardt:
Kulmbach, Plassenburg,
Schöner Hof looking
east, 1568-70

Pl. 192. Caspar Vischer and
Daniel Engelhardt:
Kulmbach, Plassenburg,
Schöner Hof looking
southwest, early 1550s,
1561-62, c.1565-67

Pl. 193. Daniel Engelhardt: Kulmbach, Plassenburg,
Schöner Hof, detail of carved arcading

Pl. 194. Uslar, Schloss, window-head, c.1559

Pl. 195. Hannoversch-
Münden, Schloss, north
wing, 1562-66

Pl. 196. Balthasar Wolff;
Heinrich Schickhardt:
Neuenstein, Schloss, from
east, c.1550; 1558; c.1600;
restored c.1870 and 1906

Pl. 197. Balthasar Wolff; Heinrich Schickhardt:
Neuenstein, Schloss, south side, 1558; c.1600;
restored c.1870 and 1906

Pl. 198. Rheydt, Schloss, left wing, 1567-69

Pl. 199. Rheydt, Schloss, court facade, 1580-81

Pl. 200. Hieronymus Lotter *et al*: Augustusburg, Schloss, 1567-73, exterior

Pl. 201. ? Erhard van der Meer *et al*.: Augustusburg,
Schloss, chapel, 1569-73, interior

Pl. 202. ? Erhard van der Meer *et al*.: Augustusburg, Schloss, 1567-73, exterior of chapel

Pl. 203. ? Hendrick Hagart: Jever, Parish church, tomb of Edo II von Wiemken, 1561-64

Pl. 204. Cornelis Floris: Antwerp,
Hanseaten Huis, c.1565

Pl. 205. ? Hendrick
Hagart: Jever, Schloss,
Audienzsaal, c.1560

Pl. 206. Elie Godefroy; Adam Liquir Beaumont: Kassel, St. Martin, tomb of Philip of Hessen-Kassel, 1567-72

Pl. 207. Celle, Schloss, chapel, interior looking east with pulpit dated 1565

Pl. 208. B. and G. de Thola, A. van Zerroen *et al.*: Freiberg, Münster, cenotaph of
the Elector Moritz, begun 1563

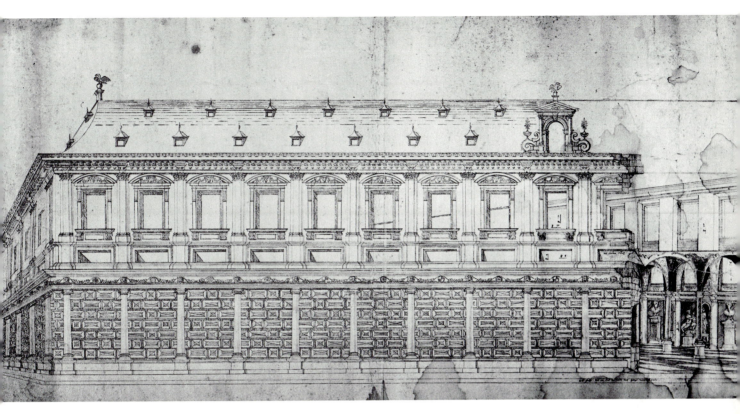

Pl. 209. Jacopo Strada: project for Antiquarium in Munich Residenz, exterior, c.1569

Pl. 210. Wilhelm Egckl: Munich, Münze, 1536-67, court

Pl. 211. Melchior Trost: Dresden, Residenzschloss,
Zeughaus, 1559-63

Pl. 212. ? Conrad Büttner: Offenbach, Schloss Isenburg, court facade, 1570-78

Pl. 213. Frederik Sustris: Landshut, Burg Trausnitz, court, 1573-78

Pl. 214. Frederik Sustris *et al.*: Landshut, Burg Trausnitz, interior

Pl. 215. Frederik Sustris, Antonio Ponzano and Carlo Pallago: Augsburg, Fuggerhäuser, Bibliothekzimmer, decorations, 1569-73

Pl. 216. Frederik Sustris, Antonio Ponzano and Carlo Pallago: Augsburg, Fuggerhäuser, Bibliothekzimmer, decorations, 1569-73

Pl. 217. Cord Tönnis: Rinteln, Archivhäuschen, 1565

Pl. 218. Batenhorst, Haus Aussel, 1580

Pl. 219. Cord Tönnis: Schwöbber, Herrenhaus, south wing, 1588; west wing, 1574-76; north wing, 1602-04

Pl. 220. Memmingen,
Siebendächerhaus, c.1560

Pl. 221. Höxter,
Dechanai, 1561

222. Münster, Herremannscher Hof, 1564

Pl. 223. Bückeburg,
Langestrasse 22, 1578

Pl. 224. Erfurt, Roter Ochse, 1562

Pl. 225. Lüneburg, Lünertorstrasse 14, 1574

Pl. 226. ? Hermann Wulff: Lemgo,
Hexenbürgermeisterhaus, 1568-71

Pl. 227. Cord Tönnis: Hameln, Johann Rike house, 1568-69

Pl. 228. Hameln, Jost Rike house, 1576

Pl. 229. Herford, Neuer Markt 2, 1560; gable, c.1577

Pl. 230. Frederic Soltesburg and Jakob Riess: Celle, Rathaus, east front, 1561-65

Pl. 231. Celle, Rathaus, north gable, 1577-79

232. Johann Buscheneer; Carsten Husmann; ? Luder von
[a]theim; Bremen, Schütting, 1536-38; left gable, 1565;
[cor]nice and balustrade, 1594

Pl. 233. Hans Meurer: Alsfeld, Hochzeitshaus,
1564-71

Pl. 234. Nickel Gromann: Altenburg, Rathaus, 1562-64

Pl. 235. C. F. (? Cornelis Floris): Project I for Doxal on Cologne Rathaus, 1557

Pl. 236. C. F. (? Cornelis Floris): Project II for Doxal on Cologne Rathaus, 1557

Pl. 237. Wilhelm Vernukken: Cologne, Rathaus, Doxal, 1567-71

Pl. 238. Hans Flemming and Herkules Midow: Lübeck, Rathaus, Laube, 1570-71

Pl. 239. Krempe, Rathaus, 1570

Pl. 240. Giacomo Parr and Bernardo Niuron:
Brzég, Rathaus, begun 1570

Pl. 241. G. B. di Quadro: Poznań, Rathaus,
arcaded front, 1553-60

Pl. 242. G. B. di Quadro: Poznań, Rathaus,
hall, 1553-60

Pl. 243. Leonard Weidmann;
Wolf Löscher and Hans
Helwig: Rothenburg-o.-d.-
Tauber, Rathaus, south front,
13th c.; eastward extension
begun 1570

Pl. 244. Nickel Hoffmann:
Schweinfurt, Rathaus, 1570-72

Pl. 245. Altdorf, College, 1571-75, court Pl. 246. Meissen, An der Frauenkirche 3, 1569-71

Pl. 247. Wittenberg, Rathaus, 1522-40; gables
and porch, 1570-73

Pl. 248. ? Nickel Gromann: Gera, Rathaus, 1573-76

Pl. 249. Hans Kessebrot: Marktbreit, Rathaus begun 1579; Maintor, 1600

Pl. 250. Hans Kessebrot: Marktbreit, Rathaus, begun 1579, interior

Pl. 251. Caspar Vischer;
Erasmus Braun and Pankraz
Wagner: Bamberg, Alte
Hofhaltung, 1570-77, Ratstube

Pl. 252. Caspar Vischer;
Erasmus Braun and Pankraz
Wagner: Bamberg, Alte
Hofhaltung, 1570-77, portal

Pl. 253. Antonis van Opbergen:
Helsingør, Kronborg Slot, chapel,
cons. 1582; restored in 1631 and 1838-43

Pl. 254. ? Frederik Sustris *et al.*:
Munich, St. Michael, interior looking
"east" before the war, 1583-97

Pl. 255. Klagenfurt, Münster, interior looking west, 1582-91, *stucchi* 1725-26

Pl. 256. ? Frederik Sustris: Munich, St. Michael, 1583-87, 1592-97, interior looking "east" after postwar restoration

257. ? Frederik Sustris: Munich, St. Michael, 1583-87, interior
king "west" after post-war restoration

Pl. 258. Hans Krumpper:
Munich, St. Michael, 1583-97,
"west" front before post-war
restoration

Pl. 259. Würzburg, Marienberg, 17th-century view with additions begun 1578

Pl. 260. Frederik Sustris: Munich, Jesuitenkolleg, 1585-97

Pl. 261. Johann Rosskott: Münster, Petrikirche, 1590-97, interior looking east after restoration

Pl. 262. Johann Rosskott: Münster, Petrikirche, 1590-97, exterior from south after restoration

Pl. 263. Wendelin Nufer *et al.*:
Hechingen, St. Luzen, 1586-89,
interior looking east

Pl. 264. Hans Ammann:
Hechingen, St. Luzen, pulpit,
1589

Pl. 265. ? Jörg Schwarzenberger: Heiligenberg, Schloss,
chapel, c.1590-96, interior looking east

Pl. 266. Hans Dürner: Heiligenberg, Schloss,
chapel, c.1590-96, organ gallery

Pl. 267. Christoph and Hans Müller; Wilhelm Vernukken and Hans Becher: Schmalkalden, Schloss Wilhelmsburg, chapel, 1586-90, interior looking "east"

Pl. 268. Christoph and Hans Müller: Schmalkalden, Schloss Wilhelmsburg, begun 1585, exterior from west

Pl. 269. Christoph and Hans Müller; Wilhelm Vernukken and Hans Becher: Schmalkaden, Schloss Wilhelmsburg, chapel, 1586-90, interior looking "west"

Pl. 270. G. M. Nosseni and Paul Irmisch: Freiberg, Münster, choir, remodelled 1585-c.95

Pl. 271. G. M. Nosseni *et al*.: Freiberg, Münster, choir vault, 1585–c.95

Pl. 272. G. M. Nosseni and Paul Irmisch: Freiberg, Münster, exterior of east end, c.1400; 1585-c.95

Pl. 273. Gideon Bacher: Ansbach, St. Gumbert, west towers, 1594-97

Pl. 274. Breese-im-Bruch,
Gutskapelle, begun 1592,
interior looking west

Pl. 275. Bristow, Gutskirche, altar,
etc., completed 1601

Pl. 276. Andreas Schilling: Geithain, St. Nikolaus, painted ceiling, 1594-95

Pl. 277. Ahrensburg, Woldenhorner Church, 1594-96, interior looking east

Pl. 278. Žórawina, Parish Church,
14th century; 1597-1602, interior

Pl. 279. Žórawina, Parish Church, 14th century;
1597-1602, exterior from east

Pl. 280. Jacopo Strada and Wilhelm Egckl; Frederik Sustris, Peter Candid, Il Padovano
and Hans Thomaner: Munich, Residenz, Antiquarium, 1569-71; 1586-1600,
interior looking east

Pl. 281. Georg Beer: Stuttgart, Lustspielhaus, 1580-93, surviving arcades

Pl. 282. Frederik Sustris: Munich, Residenz, Grottenhof, 1580-88,
view looking east

Pl. 283. Georg Beer: Stuttgart, Lustspielhaus, 1580-93, reconstruction
by K. F. Beisbarthof, exterior

Pl. 284. Georg Beer and Wendel Dietterlin: Stuttgart, Lustspielhaus,
1580-93, upper storey, from F. Brentel engraving, 1619

Pl. 285. G. M. Nosseni, Carlo di Cesare and Sebastian Walther: Dresden, Lusthaus, 1589-p.1617, reconstruction by F. Hagedorn, 1889, exterior

Pl. 286. Eberhard Wilkening: Barntrup, Schloss, 1584-88, south front

Pl. 287. Eberhard Wilkening: Barntrup, Schloss, 1584-88, east end

Pl. 288. Hermann Wulff:
Brake, Schloss, c.1585-92,
exterior from southwest

Pl. 289. Hermann Wulff:
Brake, Schloss, c.1585-92,
north side

Pl. 290. Hermann Wulff: Brake,
Schloss, c.1585-92, court front

Pl. 291. Wilhelm Vernukken and Hans Becher:
Schmalkalden, Schloss Wilhelmsburg, 1585-90,
Weisser Saal, stucco-work

Pl. 292. Paul Büchner, Hans Irmisch, and ? G. M. Nosseni: Dresden, Residenzschloss,
Langer Gang, 1586-91, from painting of c.1600 in the Historisches Museum, Dresden

Pl. 293. Paul Büchner and Hans Irmisch: Dresden, Residenzschloss, Kleiner
Schlosshof, 1592-93

Pl. 294. Georg Stegle and Wolfgang Beringer: Weikersheim, Schloss,
1586-1604, garden front

Pl. 295. ? Hermann Baumhauer: Schloss Neuhaus, Schloss, north and west wings, 1590

Pl. 296. Johann Bierbaum: Varenholz, Schloss, southeast front, 1591-1600

Pl. 297. Johann Bierbaum: Varenholz, Schloss, court with oriel, 1599

Pl. 298. ? Johann Edeler; Heinrich Rumpf: Wolfsburg, Schloss, c.1580-98

Pl. 299. Hämelschenburg, Schloss and Schlosskapelle, from east

Pl. 300. Hämelschenburg, Schloss, northeast gable, 1588-92

Pl. 301. Hämelschenburg, Schloss, north side of court, 1588-92

Pl. 302. Hämelschenburg, Schloss, from east, with entrance archway, 1588-92

Pl. 303. Hämelschenburg, Schloss, south front, 1592-97

Pl. 304. Hämelschenburg,
Schloss, south side of
court, 1592-97

Pl. 305. Hämelschenburg,
Schloss, Pilgerlaube, ? c.1600

Pl. 306. Steinbach, Schloss Fürstenau, entrance arch, 1588

Pl. 307. Ebert Baldewein: Giessen, Zeughaus,
1586-90

Pl. 308. Gideon Bacher: Ansbach, Kanzlei,
begun 1594, exterior

Pl. 309. Peter Sengelaub: Coburg, Kanzlei, begun 1597

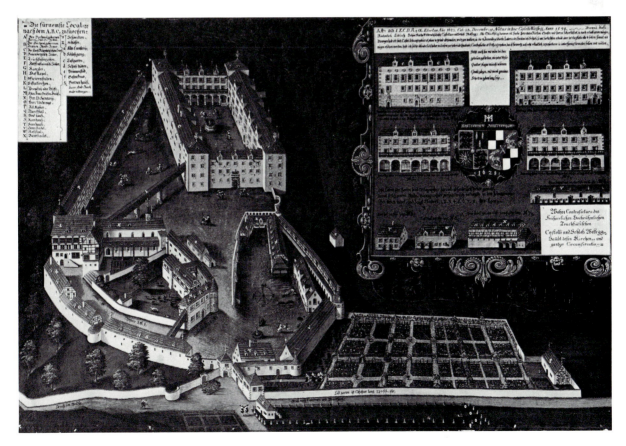

Pl. 310. Wolfegg, Schloss, 1580-83, from a painting dated 1628

Pl. 311. ? Leonard Greneisen:
Vohenstrauss, Schloss
Friedrichsburg, 1586-90

Pl. 312. Oldenswort,
Herrenhaus Hoyerswort,
1591-94

Pl. 313. Nickels Karies: Glücksburg, Schloss, 1582-87, exterior

Pl. 314. Ahrensburg, Schloss, 1594-98, exterior

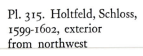

Pl. 315. Holtfeld, Schloss,
1599-1602, exterior
from northwest

Pl. 316. Holtfeld, Schloss,
1599-1602, south gable

Pl. 317. Sommersell, Haus
Thienhausen, gable, 1609

Pl. 318. Cord Tönnis: Hameln, Gerd
Leist house, 1585-89; Stiftsherrenhaus,
1556-58, to left

Pl. 319. Hildesheim, Kaiserhaus, 1586-89, before demolition

Pl. 320. Leonhardt Weidmann:
Rothenburg-o.-d.-Tauber,
Baumeister Haus, 1594

Pl. 321. Heidelberg, Haus zum Ritter, 1592

Pl. 322. ? Johann Robin: Minden, Haus
Hagemeyer am Scharn, completed 1592

Pl. 323. [Bad] Salzuflen, Johann von Barkhausen
house on left, c.1585; house
on right, c.1600

Pl. 324. Nürnberg, Fembohaus, c.1590-98

Pl. 327. Rinteln, Rathaus, 1583; extended to left, c.160c

Pl. 325. ? Hermann Baumhauer:
Paderborn, Heisingsches
Haus, c.1600

Pl. 326. [Bad] Salzuflen,
Rathaus, 1545; gable, c.1590

Pl. 328. Kronach, Rathaus, 1583; portal, c.1610

Pl. 329. Christoph Junghans: Arnstadt, Rathaus, 1581-83, right wing

Pl. 330. Georg Robin: Würzburg, Juliusuniversität, begun 1582, court with north side of Neubaukirche, 1583-91, on left

Pl. 331. Erhard Barg and Johann von Deundam: Würzburg, Juliusuniversität, main portal, c.1590

Pl. 332. ? Lüder von Bentheim: Bremen, Stadtwage, 1587-88

Pl. 333. Paul Francke: Helmstedt, Juleum, 1592-97, south front

Pl. 334. Paul Francke: Helmstedt, Juleum, 1592-97, interior of ground storey

Pl. 335. Heinrich Schickhardt: Esslingen, Rathaus, 1586, exterior

Pl. 336. Heinrich Schickhardt: Esslingen, Rathaus, 1586, interior of ground storey

Pl.. 337. Meister Wolfers: Brunswick, Gewandhaus, west front, 1589

Pl. 338. Hans Lampe *et al*.: Brunswick, Gewandhaus, east front, 1590-91

Pl. 339. Caspar Schmid and Matthäus Gaiser: Ulm, Kornhaus, 1594

Pl. 340. ? Robert Coppens: Lübeck, Rathaus, outside stair, 1594, as rebuilt 1893-94

Pl. 341. ? Cord Reineking and
Johann Robin: Stadthagen,
Rathaus, west front, 1595-96

Pl. 342. [Bad] Hersfeld,
Rathaus, remodelled
1597 and 1612

Pl. 343. Jakob Wastmann: Darmstadt, Rathaus, 1588-90

Pl. 344. Heinrich Overkatte: Gandersheim, Convent, 1599-1600

Pl. 345. Konstanz, Rathaus, court facade, c.1595-98

Pl. 346. Einbeck, Rathaus, enlarged 1593 and later

Pl. 347. Heinrich Teufel: Innsbruck, Schloss Ambras, court, frescoes before restoration, 1566-67

Pl. 348. Konrad Gottlieb and Anton Brack: Innsbruck, Schloss Ambras,
Spanischer Saal, 1570-71

Pl. 349. Benedikt and Hans II Oertlen; Jörg Schwartzenberger: Heiligenberg,
Schloss, Rittersaal, c.1580

Pl. 350. Wendel Dietrich, Hubert Gerhard nad Carlo Pallago: Kirchheim-a.-
d.-Mindel, Fuggerschloss, Cedernsaal, 1583-85

Pl. 351. Gerhard Schmidt, Elias Gunzenhäuser, Balthasar Katzenberger *et al.*:
Weikersheim, Schloss, Rittersaal, 1597-1605

Pl. 352. Ortenburg, Schloss, Festsaal, ceiling, c.1600

Pl. 353. Gerhard Schmidt: Weikersheim, Schloss,
Rittersaal, detail of stucco decoration, c.1605

Pl. 354. Wendel Dietterlin, design for portal, *Architectura*,
Strasbourg, 1594

Pl. 355. Wendel Dietterlin, design for chimneypiece,
Architectura, Nürnberg, 1598

Pl. 356. Jakob Kauffmann: Langenburg, Schloss, court, 1610-16

Pl. 357. Ebbert II and Jonas Wulff: Bückeburg, Schloss, Goldener Saal, portal, 1604-05

Pl. 358. ? Hans Wulff: Bückeburg, Schloss, Kanzlei, entrance gate, 1604-07; Kammerkasse, 1609-10

Pl. 359. Ebbert II Wulff *et al.*:
Bückeburg, Schloss, chapel,
interior to east, 1603-08

Pl. 360. ? Hans Wulff: Bückeburg,
Schloss, Kammerkasse, 1609-10

Pl. 361. ? Christoph Jelin or Hans Braun: Tübingen,
Schloss, outer gate, 1606

Pl. 362. Paul Francke: Wolfenbüttel, Zeughaus, 1613-19

Pl. 363. Würzburg, Marienberg,
outer gate, 1606

Pl. 364. ? Hans Krumpper and Hubert Gerhard:
Munich, Residenz, Brunnenhof, c.1610;
Wittelsbach Fountain, 1611-14

Pl. 365. ? Hans Krumpper; Hans II
Reiffenstuel and Heinrich I Schön:
Munich, Residenz, north and west
fronts, 1612-16, from M. Merian,
Topographia Bavariae

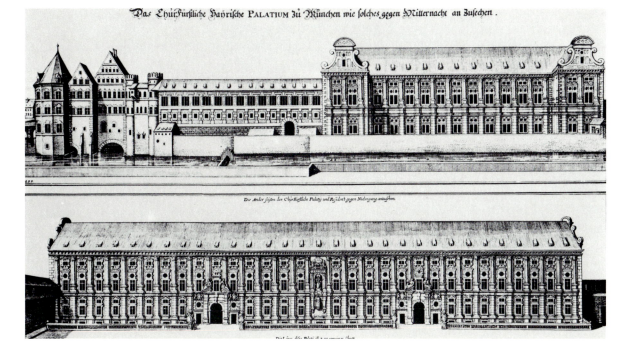

Pl. 366. Johannes Schoch: Heidelberg, Schloss, Friedrichsbau,
1601-07, court front

Pl. 367. Georg Ridinger: Aschaffenburg, Schloss Johannisburg,
1605-14, exterior from south

Pl. 368. Georg Ridinger: Aschaffenburg, Schloss Johannisburg, 1605-14, court

Pl. 369. Johann Hundertossen: Bevern, Schloss, 1603-12, exterior from southwest

Pl. 370. Johann Hundertossen: Bevern, Schloss, 1603-12, court

Pl. 371. ? Eberhard Wilkening: Haddenhausen, Schloss, 1613-16, entrance gate

Pl. 372. M.J.H. Sprenger and Joachim Rumpf: Hadamar, Schloss, begun 1566 but chiefly 1614-17

Pl. 373. Husum, Schloss, Torbau, 1612

Pl. 374. ? Peter Sengelaub: Coburg,
Casimirianeum, 1601-05

Pl. 375. Hans Marian: Gross Umstadt,
Rathaus, begun ? 1596
but chiefly 1604-06

Pl. 376. Lüder von Bentheim:
Bremen, Rathaus, 1551; 1595;
chiefly 1608-12

Pl. 377. Lüder von Bentheim
et al.: Bremen, Rathaus,
1608-12, great hall

Pl. 378. Lüder von Bentheim: Bremen, Rathaus, gable, 1612

Pl. 379. Johann Nacke and
Ernst Crossmann: Bremen,
Krameramtshaus, 1619-22

Pl. 380. Bocholt, Rathaus, begun
1618, front

Pl. 381. Johann von Bocholt:
Münster, Stadtweinhaus, 1615

Pl. 382. Nysa, Waga, 1604

Pl. 383. Georg Crossmann; Friedrich Weitmann;
Simon Hogel: Hannoversch-Munden,
Rathaus, 1603-19

Pl. 384. ? Eberhard Wilkening: Hameln,
Hochzeitshaus, 1610-17

Pl. 385. Hermann Baumhauer: Paderborn, Rathaus, 1612-18

Pl. 386. ? Eberhard Wilkening: Hameln, Hochzeitshaus, 1610-17, entrance

Pl. 387. ? Eberhard Wilkening: Hameln, Hochzeitshaus, 1610-17, wall detail

Pl. 388. Alfeld-a.-d.-Leine, Altes Seminar, 1610

Pl. 389. Hermann and Johann Roleff: Lemgo,
Rathaus, apothecary oriel, 1612

Pl. 390. Hameln, Rattenfängerhaus, 1602-03

Pl. 391. Hameln, Dempstersches Haus, 1607-08

Pl. 392. Rinteln, Bokelmann house, 1620

Pl. 393. Mosbach-a.-d.-Eltz, Palmhaus, 1610   Pl. 394. Gernsbach, Kast house, now Rathaus, 1617-18

Pl. 395. Jakob I Wolf: Nürnberg, Pellerhaus, 1602-05, facade before the war

Pl. 396. Jakob I Wolf: Nürnberg, Pellerhaus, court, 1607-08

Pl. 397. Erfurt, Haus zum Stockfisch, 1607

Pl. 398. Elias Holl: elevation of Augsburg Zeughaus, 1602

Pl. 399. Joseph Heintz and Elias Holl: Augsburg, Zeughaus, 1602-07

Pl. 400. Joseph Heintz and Elias Holl: Augsburg, Siegel Haus, 1605

Pl. 401. Wendel Dietterlin: Tuscan order from *Architectura*, Stuttgart, 1593

TVSCANA

Pl. 402. Elias Holl: Augsburg, Siegel Haus, elevation, 1605

Pl. 403. Elias Holl: Augsburg, Wertachbruckertor, 1605

Pl. 404. Elias Holl: Augsburg, project for Stadtmetzg, 1609, elevation

Pl. 405. ? Joseph Heintz and Elias Holl: Augsburg, Stadtmetzg, 1609

Pl. 406. Elias Holl and Johann Alberthal: Eichstätt, Schloss
Willibaldsburg, c.1609-19, view from west

Pl. 407. Elias Holl and Johann Alberthal: Eichstätt,
Schloss Willibaldsburg, c.1609-19, court

Pl. 408. Heinrich Schön: Schleissheim, Altes Schloss, begun 1616

Pl. 409. Elias Holl: Augsburg, Gymnasium St. Anna, 1613-15

Pl. 410. ? Inigo Jones and ? Salomon de Caus: Heidelberg, Englischer Bau, 1613-14, south side

Pl. 411. Salomon de Caus:
Heidelberg, Schloss,
Elisabethentor, completed 1615

Pl. 412. ? Elias Holl or
? Matthias Kager: model of
project for Augsburg
Rathaus, c.1610-15

Pl. 413. ? Matthias Kager; Elias Holl: Augsburg, Neuer Bau, 1614, after restoration

Pl. 414. ? Matthias Kaeger or Elias Holl: Augsburg, project for Neuer Bau, 1614

Pl. 415. Elias Holl: Augsburg, Rathaus, 1615-20, exterior from northwest

Pl. 416. Elias Holl: model of Augsburg Rathaus, 1615

Pl. 417. Elias Holl: Augsburg, Roter Tor, 1622

Pl. 418. Elias Holl: Augsburg, Rathaus, 1615-20, exterior from east

Pl. 419. Johann Alberthal: Dillingen, Klericalseminar, 1619-22

Pl. 420. Peter Candid and Matthias Kager: Augsburg, Rathaus,
Goldener Saal, 1620-23, before the war

Pl. 421. Jakob II Wolf: Nürnberg, Rathaus, from northwest, 1616-22

Pl. 422. Rene Mahieu and Jean d'Hollande: Hanau, Altstadt, parish church, 1600-08, exterior before the war

Pl. 423. Heinrich Schickhardt: Freudenstadt, Stadtkirche, 1601-09, exterior from northwest

Pl. 424. Heinrich Schickhardt: Freudenstadt, Stadtkirche, 1601-09, interior looking northwest

Pl. 425. Hans Schoch: Heidelberg,
Friedrichsbau, 1601-07, chapel,
interior looking west

Pl. 426. Alexander de Werda and Sebastiano Carlone; Teodoro Ghisi:
Seckau, Mausoleum of Karl II, 1587-1611

427. Jörg Zürn: Überlingen, St. Nikolaus, high altar, 1613-19

Pl. 428. ? Konrad Stoss; Johann Degler and
Elias I Greither: Augsburg, Sts. Ulrich
and Afra, choir vaulting completed,
1603; altars, 1604-07

Pl. 429. Joseph Heintz: project for Rathaus, Neuburg-a.-d.-Donau, c.1603

Pl. 430. Joseph Heintz: project for Hofkirche, Neuburg-a.-d.-Donau, c.1603-05, elevation

Pl. 431. Paul Francke *et al.*: Wolfenbüttel, Marienkirche, begun 1608, interior looking east

Pl. 432. Paul Francke *et al.*: Wolfenbüttel, Marienkirche, begun 1608, exterior from east

Pl. 433. Paul Francke *et al.*: Wolfenbüttel,
Marienkirche, begun 1608, exterior from north

Pl. 434. ? Hans Wulff: Bückeburg, Stadtkirche, 1610-15,
interior looking west

Pl. 435. ? Hans Wulff: Bückeburg, Stadtkirche, 1610-15, west front

Pl. 436. Joseph Heintz; Egidio Valentini and the Castellis: Neuburg-a.-d.-Donau, Hofkirche, 1607-18, interior to east

Pl. 437. Joseph Heintz, Egidio Valentini and Johann Alberthal: Neuburg-a.-d.-Donau, Hofkirche, 1607-18; tower, 1624-27, exterior from southeast

Pl. 438. Heinrich Schickhardt:
Montbéliard, St.-Martin, 1601-07,
exterior from south

Pl. 439. Santino Solari: Salzburg,
Cathedral, begun 1614, interior looking
east

Pl. 440. Andres Salgen and Jürgen Gower: Schleswig, Schloss Gottorf, chapel, Fürstenloge, 1609-13

Pl. 441. Hans Dreger: Lübeck, Haus der Kaufmannschaft, Fredenhagsches Zimmer, 1572-83

Pl. 442. G. M. Nosseni; Adriaen de Fries: Stadthagen, Mausoleum, interior, 1608-25; monument 1613-20

Pl. 443. Stellichte, Gutskapelle, interior, c.1610

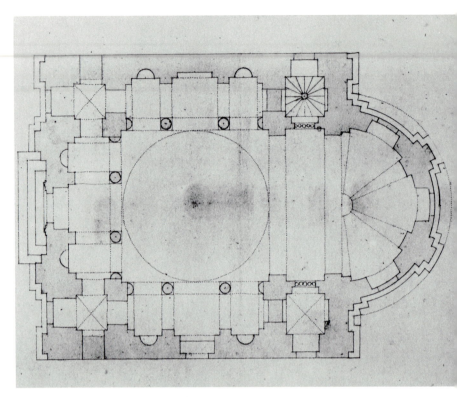

Pl. 445. Melchior Deckhard and Caspar Berger: Siedlisko, Zamek, chapel completed c.1615, plan

Pl. 444. Melchior Deckhard and Caspar Berger: Siedlisko, Zamek, chapel completed c.1615, interior to northwest

Pl. 446. Melchior Deckhard and Caspar Berger: Siedlisko, Zamek, chapel completed c.1615, section

Pl. 447. Lazaro Augustino; Jobst Pfaffer and Adam Zwinger: Dettelbach, pilgrimage church, 1610-13; shrine, 1778-79

Pl. 448. Lazaro Augustino; Adam Zwinger and Peter Meurer: Dettelbach, pilgrimage church, 1610-17, from southwest

Pl. 449. Christoph Wamser: Molsheim, former Jesuit church, 1614-18, exterior from northwest

Pl. 450. Christoph Wamser: Molsheim, former Jesuit church, 1614-18, interior looking east

Pl. 451. Christoph Wamser: Cologne, Mariä Himmelfahrt, 1618-29, west front

Pl. 452. Christoph Wamser; Jeremias Geisselbrunn: Cologne, Mariä Himmelfahrt, 1618-29, interior looking east

Pl. 453. ? Hans Krumpper; Georg Schmuzer: Polling,
Augustinian church, remodelled and decorated 1621-28,
interior looking west

Pl. 454. Hans Krumpper: Polling, Augustinian
church, southwest tower, 1605-11

Pl. 455. ? Hans Krumpper and Georg Schmuzer: Polling,
Augustinian church, remodelled and decorated 1621-28,
interior looking east

Pl. 456. Jakob Wustmann: Nidda, Zum Heiligen
Geist, completed 1618, interior looking west

Pl. 457. Düsseldorf, St. Andreas, 1622-29, interior to east; stucco-work, 1632-37